KNELL'S STATUTES

Employment Law

Third Edition

D G Cracknell
LLB, of the Middle Temple, Barrister

OLD BAILEY PRESS

OLD BAILEY PRESS
at Holborn College, Woolwich Road,
Charlton, London, SE7 8LN

First published 1998
Third edition 2006

ISBN 1 85836 587 2

British Library Cataloguing-in-Publication Data

A catalogue record for this book is available from the
British Library.

Printed and bound in Great Britain

CONTENTS

Contents

PREFACE

A vast array of statutory material now regulates the hiring and dismissal of employees, their rights at work, including equal pay and the prevention of discrimination, and provisions for their health and safety. The relationship between employers and trade unions has also become increasingly subject to legislative regulation. To this has been added the flow of directives from the European Union. The role of the courts has become largely confined to the interpretation and application of the enactments.

All this accounts for the size of this book, intended primarily for the use of students of Employment Law (sometimes termed Labour Law or Industrial Law) at degree and postgraduate level. Clearly some selection of the material has had to be made, but the aim has been to include provisions covering the generality of employment situations, with emphasis on the private sector, with which students need to be familiar.

This edition covers legislation in force on 1 October 2005. Additions include the Employment Relations Act 2004, the Disability Discrimination Act 2005 and the Disability Discrimination Act 1995 (Amendment) Regulations 2003. Whenever a statutory provision is here included, the text incorporates any amendments (repeals, insertions or substitutions) made on or before that date. A note at the end of the Act or Regulations indicates the source of any changes.

Exceptions to the 1 October 2005 cut-off date have been made in the case of the relatively few amendments made by the Licensing Act 2003, the Civil Partnership Act 2004 and the Disability Discrimination Act 2005 where, at 1 October, an early commencement date was known.

The few relevant provisions of the Employment Act 2002, and the provisions of the Constitutional Reform Act 2005 concerning employment tribunals, which were not in force on 1 October have been included in the Appendix and attention is drawn to them in the main text.

Suggestions as to additional areas of Employment Law which it would be helpful to cover in future editions would be gratefully received.

ALPHABETICAL TABLE OF STATUTES AND REGULATIONS

SEX DISQUALIFICATION (REMOVAL) ACT 1919

(9 & 10 Geo 5 c 71)

1 Removal of disqualification on grounds of sex

A person shall not be disqualified by sex or marriage from the exercise of any public function, or from being appointed to or holding any civil or judicial office or post, or from entering or assuming or carrying on any civil profession or vocation, or for admission to any incorporated society (whether incorporated by Royal Charter or otherwise).

As amended by the Courts Act 1971, ss35(7), 56, Schedule 11, Pt I; Criminal Justice Act 1972, s64(2), Schedule 6, Pt I; Statute Law (Repeals) Act 1989.

EQUAL PAY ACT 1970
(1970 c 41)

1   Requirement of equal treatment for men and women in same employment

(1) If the terms of a contract under which a woman is employed at an establishment in Great Britain do not include (directly or by reference to a collective agreement or otherwise) an equality clause they shall be deemed to include one.

(2) An equality clause is a provision which relates to terms (whether concerned with pay or not) of a contract under which a woman is employed (the 'woman's contract'), and has the effect that –

   (a) where the woman is employed on like work with a man in the same employment –

      (i) if (apart from the equality clause) any term of the woman's contract is or becomes less favourable to the woman than a term of a similar kind in the contract under which that man is employed, that term of the woman's contract shall be treated as so modified as not to be less favourable, and

      (ii) if (apart from the equality clause) at any time the woman's contract does not include a term corresponding to a term benefiting that man included in the contract under which he is employed, the woman's contract shall be treated as including such a term;

   (b) where the woman is employed on work rated as equivalent with that of a man in the same employment –

      (i) if (apart from the equality clause) any term of the woman's contract determined by the rating of the work is or becomes less favourable to the woman than a term of a similar kind in the contract under which that man is employed, that term of the woman's contract shall be treated as so modified as not to be less favourable, and

      (ii) if (apart from the equality clause) at any time the woman's contract does not include a term corresponding to a term benefiting that man included in the contract under which he is employed and determined by the rating of the work, the woman's contract shall be treated as including such a term.

   (c) where a woman is employed on work which, not being work in relation to which paragraph (a) or (b) above applies, is, in terms of the demands made on her (for instance under such headings as effort, skill and decision), of equal value to that of a man in the same employment –

(i) if (apart from the equality clause) any term of the woman's contract is or becomes less favourable to the woman than a term of a similar kind in the contract under which that man is employed, that term of the woman's contract shall be treated as so modified as not to be less favourable, and

(ii) if (apart from the equality clause) at any time the woman's contract does not include a term corresponding to a term benefiting that man included in the contract under which he is employed, the woman's contract shall be treated as including such a term.

(3) An equality clause shall not operate in relation to a variation between the woman's contract and the man's contract if the employer proves that the variation is genuinely due to a material factor which is not the difference of sex and that factor –

(a) in the case of an equality clause falling within subsection (2)(a) or (b) above, must be a material difference between the woman's case and the man's; and

(b) in the case of an equality clause falling within subsection (2)(c) above, may be such a material difference.

(4) A woman is to be regarded as employed on like work with men if, but only if, her work and theirs is of the same or a broadly similar nature, and the differences (if any) between the things she does and the things they do are not of practical importance in relation to terms and conditions of employment; and accordingly in comparing her work with theirs regard shall be had to the frequency or otherwise with which any such differences occur in practice as well as to the nature and extent of the differences.

(5) A woman is to be regarded as employed on work rated as equivalent with that of any men if, but only if, her job and their job have been given an equal value, in terms of the demand made on a worker under various headings (for instance effort, skill, decision), on a study undertaken with a view to evaluating in those terms the jobs to be done by all or any of the employees in an undertaking or group of undertakings, or would have been given an equal value but for the evaluation being made on a system setting different values for men and women on the same demand under any heading.

(6) Subject to the following subsections, for purposes of this section –

(a) 'employed' means employed under a contract of service or of apprenticeship or a contract personally to execute any work or labour, and related expressions shall be construed accordingly;

(c) two employers are to be treated as associated if one is a company of which the other (directly or indirectly) has control or if both are companies of which a third person (directly or indirectly) has control,

and men shall be treated as in the same employment with a woman if they are men employed by her employer or any associated employer at the same establishment or at establishments in Great Britain which include that one and at which common terms and conditions of employment are observed either generally or for employees of the relevant classes.

(8) This section shall apply to –

    (a) service for purposes of a Minister of the Crown or government department, other than service of a person holding a statutory office, or

    (b) service on behalf of the Crown for purposes of a person holding a statutory office or purposes of a statutory body,

as it applies to employment by a private person, and shall so apply as if references to a contract of employment included references to the terms of service.

(10) In this section 'statutory body' means a body set up by or in pursuance of an enactment (including an enactment comprised in, or in an instrument made under, an Act of the Scottish Parliament), and 'statutory office' means an office so set up; and service 'for purposes of' a Minister of the Crown or government department does not include service in any office in Schedule 2 (Ministerial offices) to the House of Commons Disqualification Act 1975 as for the time being in force. ...

(11) For the purposes of this Act it is immaterial whether the law which (apart from this subsection) is the law applicable to a contract is the law of any part of the United Kingdom or not.

(12) In this Act 'Great Britain' includes such of the territorial waters of the United Kingdom as are adjacent to Great Britain.

(13) Provisions of this section and sections 2 and 2A below framed with reference to women and their treatment relative to men are to be read as applying equally in a converse case to men and their treatment relative to women.

2   Disputes as to, and enforcement of, requirement of equal treatment

(1) Any claim in respect of the contravention of a term modified or included by virtue of an equality clause, including a claim for arrears of remuneration or damages in respect of the contravention may be presented by way of a complaint to an employment tribunal.

(1A) Where a dispute arises in relation to the effect of an equality clause the employer may apply to an employment tribunal for an order declaring the rights of the employer and the employee in relation to the matter in question.

(2) Where it appears to the Secretary of State that there may be a question whether the employer or any woman is or has been contravening a term modified or included by virtue of their equality clauses, but that it is not reasonable to expect them to take steps to have the question determined, the question may be referred to him as respects all or any of them to an employment tribunal and shall be dealt with as if the reference were of a claim by the women or woman against the employer.

(3) Where it appears to the court in which any proceedings are pending that a claim or counterclaim in respect of the operation of an equality clause could more conveniently be disposed of separately by an employment tribunal, the court may direct that the claim or counterclaim shall be struck out; and (without prejudice to the foregoing) where in proceedings before any court a question arises as to the

operation of an equality clause, the court may on the application of any party to the proceedings or otherwise refer that question, or direct it to be referred by a party to the proceedings, to an employment tribunal for determination by the tribunal, and may stay ... the proceedings in the meantime.

(4) No determination may be made by an employment tribunal in the following proceedings –

(a) on a complaint under subsection (1) above,

(b) on an application under subsection (1A) above, or

(c) on a reference under subsection (2) above,

unless the proceedings are instituted on or before the qualifying date (determined in accordance with section 2ZA below).

(5) A woman shall not be entitled, in proceedings brought in respect of a contravention of a term modified or included by virtue of an equality clause (including proceedings before an employment tribunal), to be awarded any payment by way of arrears of remuneration or damages –

(a) in proceedings in England and Wales, in respect of a time earlier than the arrears date (determined in accordance with section 2ZB below) ...

2ZA 'Qualifying date' under section 2(4)

(1) This section applies for the purpose of determining the qualifying date, in relation to proceedings in respect of a woman's employment, for the purposes of section 2(4) above.

(2) In this section –

'concealment case' means a case where –

(a) the employer deliberately concealed from the woman any fact (referred to in this section as a 'qualifying fact') –

(i) which is relevant to the contravention to which the proceedings relate, and

(ii) without knowledge of which the woman could not reasonably have been expected to institute the proceedings, and

(b) the woman did not discover the qualifying fact (or could not with reasonable diligence have discovered it) until after –

(i) the last day on which she was employed in the employment, or

(ii) the day on which the stable employment relationship between her and the employer ended,

(as the case may be);

'disability case' means a case where the woman was under a disability at any time during the six months after –

(a) the last day on which she was employed in the employment,

(b) the day on which the stable employment relationship between her and the employer ended, or

(c) the day on which she discovered (or could with reasonable diligence have discovered) the qualifying fact deliberately concealed from her by the employer (if that day falls after the day referred to in paragraph (a) or (b) above, as the case may be),

(as the case may be);

'stable employment case' means a case where the proceedings relate to a period during which a stable employment relationship subsists between the woman and the employer, notwithstanding that the period includes any time after the ending of a contract of employment when no further contract of employment is in force;

'standard case' means a case which is not –

(a) a stable employment case,

(b) a concealment case,

(c) a disability case, or

(d) both a concealment and a disability case.

(3) In a standard case, the qualifying date is the date falling six months after the last day on which the woman was employed in the employment.

(4) In a case which is a stable employment case (but not also a concealment or a disability case or both), the qualifying date is the date falling six months after the day on which the stable employment relationship ended.

(5) In a case which is a concealment case (but not also a disability case), the qualifying date is the date falling six months after the day on which the woman discovered the qualifying fact in question (or could with reasonable diligence have discovered it).

(6) In a case which is a disability case (but not also a concealment case), the qualifying date is the date falling six months after the day on which the woman ceased to be under a disability.

(7) In a case which is both a concealment and a disability case, the qualifying date is the later of the dates referred to in subsections (5) and (6) above.

2ZB 'Arrears date' in proceedings in England and Wales under section 2(5)

(1) This section applies for the purpose of determining the arrears date, in relation to an award of any payment by way of arrears of remuneration or damages in proceedings in England and Wales in respect of a woman's employment, for the purposes of section 2(5)(a) above.

(2) In this section –

'concealment case' means a case where –

(a) the employer deliberately concealed from the woman any fact –

(i) which is relevant to the contravention to which the proceedings relate, and

(ii) without knowledge of which the woman could not reasonably have been expected to institute the proceedings, and

(b) the woman instituted the proceedings within six years of the day on which she discovered the fact (or could with reasonable diligence have discovered it);

'disability case' means a case where –

(a) the woman was under a disability at the time of the contravention to which the proceedings relate, and

(b) the woman instituted the proceedings within six years of the day on which she ceased to be under a disability;

'standard case' means a case which is not –

(a) a concealment case,

(b) a disability case, or

(c) both.

(3) In a standard case, the arrears date is the date falling six years before the day on which the proceedings were instituted.

(4) In a case which is a concealment or a disability case or both, the arrears date is the date of the contravention.

2A   Procedure before tribunal in certain cases

(1) Where on a complaint or reference made to an employment tribunal under section 2 above, a dispute arises as to whether any work is of equal value as mentioned in section 1(2)(c) above the tribunal may either –

(a) proceed to determine that question; or

(b) require a member of the panel of independent experts to prepare a report with respect to that question.

(1A) Subsections (1B) and (1C) below apply in a case where the tribunal has required a member of the panel of independent experts to prepare a report under paragraph (b) of subsection (1) above.

(1B) The tribunal may –

(a) withdraw the requirement, and

(b) request the member of the panel of independent experts to provide it with any documentation specified by it or make any other request to him connected with the withdrawal of the requirement.

(1C) If the requirement has not been withdrawn under paragraph (a) of subsection (1B) above, the tribunal shall not make any determination under paragraph (a) of subsection (1) above unless it has received the report.

(2) Subsection (2A) below applies in a case where –

(a) a tribunal is required to determine whether any work is of equal value as mentioned in section 1(2)(c) above, and

(b) the work of the woman and that of the man in question have been given different values on a study such as is mentioned in section 1(5) above.

(2A) The tribunal shall determine that the work of the woman and that of the man are not of equal value unless the tribunal has reasonable grounds for suspecting that the evaluation contained in the study –

(a) was (within the meaning of subsection (3) below) made on a system which discriminates on grounds of sex, or

(b) is otherwise unsuitable to be relied upon.

(3) An evaluation contained in a study such as is mentioned in section 1(5) above is made on a system which discriminates on grounds of sex where a difference, or coincidence, between values set by that system on different demands under the same or different headings is not justifiable irrespective of the sex of the person on whom those demands are made.

(4) In this section a reference to a member of the panel of independent experts is a reference to a person who is for the time being designated by the Advisory, Conciliation and Arbitration Service for the purposes of that paragraph as such a member, being neither a member of the Council of that Service nor one of its officers or servants.

6   Exclusion from ss1 to 5 of pensions, etc

(1) An equality clause shall not operate in relation to terms –

(a) affected by compliance with the laws regulating the employment of women, or

(b) affording special treatment to women in connection with pregnancy or childbirth.

(1B) An equality clause shall not operate in relation to terms relating to a person's membership of, or rights under, an occupational pension scheme, being terms in relation to which, by reason only of any provision made by or under sections 62 to 64 of the Pensions Act 1995 (equal treatment), an equal treatment rule would not operate if the terms were included in the scheme.

(1C) In subsection (1B), 'occupational pension scheme' has the same meaning as in the Pensions Schemes Act 1993 and 'equal treatment rule' has the meaning given by section 62 of the Pensions Act 1995.

7B   Questioning of employer

(1) For the purposes of this section –

(a) a person who considers that she may have a claim under section 1 above is referred to as 'the complainant', and

(b) a person against whom the complainant may decide to make, or has made, a complaint under section 2(1) or 7A(3) above is referred to as "the respondent".

(2) With a view to helping a complainant to decide whether to institute proceedings and, if she does so, to formulate and present her case in the most effective manner, the Secretary of State shall by order prescribe –

(a) forms by which the complainant may question the respondent on any matter which is or may be relevant, and

(b) forms by which the respondent may if he so wishes reply to any questions.

(3) Where the complainant questions the respondent (whether in accordance with an order under subsection (2) above or not), the question and any reply by the respondent (whether in accordance with such an order or not) shall, subject to the following provisions of this section, be admissible as evidence in any proceedings under section 2(1) or 7A(3) above.

(4) If in any proceedings under section 2(1) or 7A(3) above it appears to the employment tribunal that the complainant has questioned the respondent (whether in accordance with an order under subsection (2) above or not) and that –

(a) the respondent deliberately and without reasonable excuse omitted to reply within such period as the Secretary of State may by order prescribe, or

(b) the respondent's reply is evasive or equivocal,

it may draw any inference which it considers it just and equitable to draw, including an inference that the respondent has contravened a term modified or included by virtue of the complainant's equality clause or corresponding term of service.

(5) Where the Secretary of State questions an employer in relation to whom he may decide to make, or has made, a reference under section 2(2) above, the question and any reply by the employer shall, subject to the following provisions of this section, be admissible as evidence in any proceedings under that provision.

(6) If in any proceedings on a reference under section 2(2) above it appears to the employment tribunal that the Secretary of State has questioned the employer to whom the reference relates and that –

(a) the employer deliberately and without reasonable excuse omitted to reply within such period as the Secretary of State may by order prescribe, or

(b) the employer's reply is evasive or equivocal,

it may draw any inference which it considers it just and equitable to draw, including an inference that the employer has contravened a term modified or included by virtue of the equality clause of the woman, or women, as respects whom the reference is made.

(7) The Secretary of State may by order –

(a) prescribe the period within which questions must be duly served in order to be admissible under subsection (3) or (5) above, and

(b) prescribe the manner in which a question, and any reply, may be duly served.

(8) This section is without prejudice to any other enactment or rule of law regulating interlocutory and preliminary matters in proceedings before an employment tribunal, and has effect subject to any enactment or rule of law regulating the admissibility of evidence in such proceedings.

(9) Power to make orders under this section is exercisable by statutory instrument subject to annulment in pursuance of a resolution of either House of Parliament.

(10) An order under this section may make different provision for different cases.

11 Short title, interpretation and extent ...

(2) in this Act the expressions 'man' and 'woman' shall be read as applying to persons of whatever age.

(2A) For the purposes of this Act a woman is under a disability –

(a) in the case of proceedings in England and Wales, if she is a minor or of unsound mind (which has the same meaning as in section 38(2) of the Limitation Act 1980 ...

As amended by the Sex Discrimination Act 1975, s8(1), Schedule 1, Pt I, paras 1–3; Employment Protection (Consolidation) Act 1978, s159(3), Schedule 17; Equal Pay (Amendment) Regulations 1983, regs 2, 3(1), (2); Sex Discrimination Act 1986, s9(1)(, (3); Contracts (Applicable Law) Act 1990, s5, Schedule 4, para 1; Pensions Act 1995, s66(1); Sex Discrimination and Equal Pay (Miscellaneous Amendments) Regulations 1996, reg 3; Armed Forces Act 1996, s24(1), 35(2), Schedule 7, Pt III; Employment Rights Act 1996, s240, Schedule 1, para 1; Employment Rights (Dispute Resolution) Act 1998, s1(2)(a); Scotland Act 1998 (Consequential Modifications) Order 2000, art 2, Schedule, Pt I, para 4; Employment Act 2002, s42; Equal Pay Act 1970 (Amendment) Regulations 2003, regs 3–5, 9; Equal Pay Act 1970 (Amendment) Regulations 2004, reg 2.

HEALTH AND SAFETY AT WORK ETC ACT 1974

(1974 c 37)

PART I

HEALTH, SAFETY AND WELFARE IN CONNECTION WITH WORK, AND CONTROL OF DANGEROUS SUBSTANCES AND CERTAIN EMISSIONS INTO THE ATMOSPHERE

1 Preliminary

(1) The provisions of this Part shall have effect with a view to –

(a) securing the health, safety and welfare of persons at work;

(b) protecting persons other than persons at work against risks to health or safety arising out of or in connection with the activities of persons at work;

(c) controlling the keeping and use of explosive or highly flammable or otherwise dangerous substances, and generally preventing the unlawful acquisition, possession and use of such substances.

(2) The provisions of this Part relating to the making of health and safety regulations and the preparation and approval of codes of practice shall in particular have effect with a view to enabling the enactments specified in the third column of Schedule 1 and the regulations, orders and other instruments in force under those enactments to be progressively replaced by a system of regulations and approved codes of practice operating in combination with the other provisions of this Part and designed to maintain or improve the standards of health, safety and welfare established by or under those enactments.

(3) For the purposes of this Part risks arising out of or in connection with the activities of persons at work shall be treated as including risks attributable to the manner of conducting an undertaking, the plant or substances used for the purposes of an undertaking and the condition of premises so used or any part of them.

(4) References in this Part to the general purposes of this Part are references to the purposes mentioned in subsection (1) above.

2   General duties of employers to their employees

(1) It shall be the duty of every employer to ensure, so far as is reasonably practicable, the health, safety and welfare at work of all his employees.

(2) Without prejudice to the generality of an employer's duty under the preceding subsection, the matters to which that duty extends include in particular –

(a) the provision and maintenance of plant and systems of work that are, so far as is reasonably practicable, safe and without risks to health;

(b) arrangements for ensuring, so far as is reasonably practicable, safety and absence of risks to health in connection with the use, handling, storage and transport of articles and substances;

(c) the provision of such information, instruction, training and supervision as is necessary to ensure, so far as is reasonably practicable, the health and safety at work of his employees;

(d) so far as is reasonably practicable as regards any place of work under the employer's control, the maintenance of it in a condition that is safe and without risks to health and the provision and maintenance of means of access to and egress from it that are safe and without such risks;

(e) the provision and maintenance of a working environment for his employees that is, so far as is reasonably practicable, safe, without risks to health, and adequate as regards facilities and arrangements for their welfare at work.

(3) Except in such cases as may be prescribed, it shall be the duty of every employer to prepare and as often as may be appropriate revise a written statement of his general policy with respect to the health and safety at work of his employees and the organisation and arrangements for the time being in force for carrying out that policy, and to bring the statement and any revision of it to the notice of all his employees.

(4) Regulations made by the Secretary of State may provide for the appointment in prescribed cases by recognised trade unions (within the meaning of the regulations) of safety representatives from amongst the employees, and those representatives shall represent the employees in consultations with the employers under subsection (6) below and shall have such other functions as may be prescribed.

(6) It shall be the duty of every employer to consult any such representatives with a view to the making and maintenance of arrangements which will enable him and his employees to co-operate effectively in promoting and developing measures to ensure the health and safety at work of the employees, and in checking the effectiveness of such measures.

(7) In such cases as may be prescribed it shall be the duty of every employer, if requested to do so by the safety representatives mentioned in subsection (4) above, to establish, in accordance with regulations made by the Secretary of State, a safety committee having the function of keeping under review the measures taken to ensure the health and safety at work of his employees and such other functions as may be prescribed.

3 General duties of employers and self-employed to persons other than their employees

(1) It shall be the duty of every employer to conduct his undertaking in such a way as to ensure, so far as is reasonably practicable, that persons not in his employment who may be affected thereby are not thereby exposed to risks to their health or safety.

(2) It shall be the duty of every self-employed person to conduct his undertaking in such a way as to ensure, so far as is reasonably practicable, that he and other persons (not being his employees) who may be affected thereby are not thereby exposed to risks to their health or safety.

(3) In such cases as may be prescribed, it shall be the duty of every employer and every self-employed person, in the prescribed circumstances and in the prescribed manner, to give to persons (not being his employees) who may be affected by the way in which he conducts his undertaking the prescribed information about such aspects of the way in which he conducts his undertaking as might affect their health or safety.

4 General duties of persons concerned with premises to persons other than their employees

(1) This section has effect for imposing on persons duties in relation to those who –

(a) are not their employees; but

(b) use non-domestic premises made available to them as a place of work or as a place where they may use plant or substances provided for their use there,

and applies to premises so made available and other non-domestic premises used in connection with them.

(2) It shall be the duty of each person who has, to any extent, control of premises to which this section applies or of the means of access thereto or egress therefrom or of any plant or substance in such premises to take such measures as it is reasonable for a person in his position to take to ensure, so far as is reasonably practicable, that the premises, all means of access thereto or egress therefrom available for use by persons using the premises, and any plant or substance in the premises or, as the case may be, provided for use there, is or are safe and without risks to health.

(3) Where a person has, by virtue of any contract or tenancy, an obligation of any extent in relation to –

(a) the maintenance or repair of any premises to which this section applies or any means of access thereto or egress therefrom; or

(b) the safety of or the absence of risks to health arising from plant or substances in any such premises;

that person shall be treated, for the purposes of subsection (2) above, as being a person who has control of the matters to which his obligation extents.

(4) Any reference in this section to a person having control of any premises or

matter is a reference to a person having control of the premises or matter in connection with the carrying on by him of a trade, business or other undertaking (whether for profit or not).

6 General duties of manufacturers, etc as regards articles and substances for use at work

(1) It shall be the duty of any person who designs, manufactures, imports or supplies any article for use at work or any article of fairground equipment –

(a) to ensure, so far as is reasonably practicable, that the article is so designed and constructed that it will be safe and without risks to health at all times when it is being set, used, cleaned or maintained by a person at work;

(b) to carry out or arrange for the carrying out of such testing and examination as may be necessary for the performance of the duty imposed on him by the preceding paragraph;

(c) to take such steps as are necessary to secure that persons supplied by that person with the article are provided with adequate information about the use for which the article is designed or has been tested and about any conditions necessary to ensure that it will be safe and without risks to health at all such times as are mentioned in paragraph (a) above and when it is being dismantled or disposed of; and

(d) to take such steps as are necessary to secure, so far as is reasonably practicable, that persons so supplied are provided with all such revisions of information provided to them by virtue of the preceding paragraph as are necessary by reason of its becoming known that anything gives rise to a serious risk to health or safety. ...

(2) It shall be the duty of any person who undertakes the design or manufacture of any article for use at work or of any article of fairground equipment to carry out or arrange for the carrying out of any necessary research with a view to the discovery and, so far as is reasonably practicable, the elimination or minimisation of any risks to health or safety to which the design or article may give rise.

(3) It shall be the duty of any person who erects or installs any article for use at work in any premises where that article is to be used by persons at work or who erects or installs any article of fairground equipment to ensure, so far as is reasonably practicable, that nothing about the way in which the article is erected or installed makes it unsafe or a risk to health at any such time as is mentioned in paragraph (a) of subsection (1) or, as the case may be, in paragraph (a) of subsection (1) or (1A) [fairground equipment] above.

(4) It shall be the duty of any person who manufactures, imports or supplies any substance –

(a) to ensure, so far as is reasonably practicable, that the substance will be safe and without risks to health at all times when it is being used, handled, processed, stored or transported by a person at work or in premises to which section 4 above applies;

(b) to carry out or arrange for the carrying out of such testing and examination as may be necessary for the performance of the duty imposed on him by the preceding paragraph;

(c) to take such steps as are necessary to secure that persons supplied by that person with the substance are provided with adequate information about any risks to health or safety to which the inherent properties of the substance may give rise, about the results of any relevant tests which have been carried out on or in connection with the substance and about any conditions necessary to ensure that the substance will be safe and without risk to health at all such times as are mentioned in paragraph (a) above and when the substance is being disposed of; and

(d) to take such steps as are necessary to secure, so far as is reasonably practicable, that persons so supplied are provided with all such revisions of information provided to them by virtue of the preceding paragraph as are necessary by reason of its becoming known that anything gives rise to a serious risk to health or safety.

(5) It shall be the duty of any person who undertakes the manufacture of any substance to carry out or arrange for the carrying out of any necessary research with a view to the discovery and, so far as is reasonably practicable, the elimination or minimisation of any risks to health or safety to which the substance may give rise to all such times as are mentioned in paragraph (a) of subsection (4) above.

(6) Nothing in the preceding provisions of this section shall be taken to require a person to repeat any testing, examination or research which has been carried out otherwise than by him or at his instance, in so far as it is reasonable for him to rely on the results thereof for the purposes of those provisions.

(7) Any duty imposed on any person by any of the preceding provisions of this section shall extent only to things done in the course of a trade, business or other undertaking carried on by him (whether for profit or not) and to matters within his control.

(8) Where a person designs, manufactures, imports or supplies an article for use at work or an article of fairground equipment and does so for or to another on the basis of a written undertaking by that other to take specified steps sufficient to ensure, so far as is reasonably practicable, that the article will be safe and without risks to health at all such times as are mentioned in paragraph (a) of subsection (1) or, as the case may be, in paragraph (a) of subsection (1) or (1A) above, the undertaking shall have the effect of relieving the first-mentioned person from the duty imposed by virtue of that paragraph to such extent as is reasonable having regard to the terms of the undertaking.

(8A) Nothing in subsection (7) or (8) above shall relieve any person who imports any article or substance from any duty in respect of anything which –

(a) in the case of an article designed outside the United Kingdom, was done by and in the course of any trade, profession or other undertaking carried on by, or was within the control of, the person who designed the article; or

(b) in the case of an article or substance manufactured outside the United Kingdom, was done by and in the course of any trade, profession or other undertaking carried on by, or was within the control of, the person who manufactured the article or substance.

(9) Where a person ('the ostensible supplier') supplies any article or substance to another ('the customer') under a hire-purchase agreement, conditional sale agreement or credit-sale agreement, and the ostensible supplier –

(a) carries on the business of financing the acquisition of goods by others by means of such agreements; and

(b) in the course of that business acquired his interest in the article or substance supplied to the customer as a means of financing its acquisition by the customer from a third person ('the effective supplier'),

the effective supplier and not the ostensible supplier shall be treated for the purposes of this section as supplying the article or substance to the customer, and any duty imposed by the preceding provisions of this section on suppliers shall accordingly fall on the effective supplier and not on the ostensible supplier.

(10) For the purposes of this section an absence of safety or a risk to health shall be disregarded in so far as the case in or in relation to which it would arise is shown to be one the occurrence of which could not reasonably be foreseen; and in determining whether any duty imposed by virtue of paragraph (a) of subsection (1), (1A) or (4) above has been performed regard shall be had to any relevant information or advice which has been provided to any person by the person by whom the article has been designed, manufactured, imported or supplied or, as the case may be, by the person by whom the substance has been manufactured, imported or supplied.

7 General duties of employees at work

It shall be the duty of every employee while at work –

(a) to take reasonable care for the health and safety of himself and of other persons who may be affected by his acts or omissions at work; and

(b) as regards any duty or requirement imposed on his employer or any other person by or under any of the relevant statutory provisions, to co-operate with him so far as is necessary to enable that duty or requirement to be performed or complied with.

8 Duty not to interfere with or misuse things provided pursuant to certain provisions

No person shall intentionally or recklessly interfere with or misuse anything provided in the interests of health, safety or welfare in pursuance of any of the relevant statutory provisions.

9 Duty not to charge employees for things done or provided pursuant to certain specific requirements

No employer shall levy or permit to be levied on any employee of his any charge in respect of anything done or provided in pursuance of any specific requirement of the relevant statutory provisions.

10 Establishment of the Commission and the Executive

(1) There shall be two bodies corporate to be called the Health and Safety Commission and the Health and Safety Executive which shall be constituted in accordance with the following provisions of this section.

(2) The Health and Safety Commission (hereafter in this Act referred to as 'the Commission') shall consist of a chairman appointed by the Secretary of State and not less than six nor more than nine other members appointed by the Secretary of State in accordance with subsection (3) below.

(3) Before appointing the members of the Commission (other than the chairman) the Secretary of State shall –

(a) as to three of them, consult such organisations representing employers as he considers appropriate;

(b) as to three others, consult such organisations representing employees as he considers appropriate; and

(c) as to any other members he may appoint, consult such organisations representing local authorities and such other organisations, including professional bodies, the activities of whose members are concerned with matters relating to any of the general purposes of this Part, as he considers appropriate.

(4) The Secretary of State may appoint one of the members to be deputy chairman of the Commission.

(5) The Health and Safety Executive (hereinafter in this Act referred to as 'the Executive') shall consist of three persons of whom one shall be appointed by the Commission with the approval of the Secretary of State to be the director of the Executive and the others shall be appointed by the Commission with the like approval after consultation with the said director. ...

11 General functions of the Commission and the Executive

(1) In addition to the other functions conferred on the Commission by virtue of this Act, but subject to subsection (3) below, it shall be the general duty of the Commission to do such things and make such arrangements as it considers appropriate for the general purposes of this Part.

(2) It shall be the duty of the Commission –

(a) to assist and encourage persons concerned with matters relevant to any of the general purposes of this Part to further those purposes;

(b) to make such arrangements as it considers appropriate for the carrying out of research, the publication of the results of research and the provision of training and information in connection with those purposes, and to encourage research and the provision of training and information in that connection by others;

(c) to make such arrangements as it considers appropriate for securing that government departments, employers, employees, organisations representing employers and employees respectively, and other persons concerned with matters relevant to any of those purposes are provided with an information and advisory service and are kept informed of, and adequately advised on, such matters;

(d) to submit from time to time to the authority having power to make regulations under any of the relevant statutory provisions such proposals as the Commission considers appropriate for the making of regulations under that power. ...

(4) In addition to any other functions conferred on the Executive by virtue of this Part, it shall be the duty of the Executive –

(a) to exercise on behalf of the Commission such of the Commission's functions as the Commission directs it to exercise; and

(b) to give effect to any directions given to it by the Commission otherwise than in pursuance of paragraph (a) above;

but, except for the purpose of giving effect to directions given to the Commission by the Secretary of State, the Commission shall not give to the Executive any directions as to the enforcement of any of the relevant statutory provisions in a particular case. ...

14 Power of the Commission to direct investigations and inquiries

(1) This section applies to the following matters, that is to say any accident, occurrence, situation or other matter whatsoever which the Commission thinks it necessary or expedient to investigate for any of the general purposes of this Part or with a view to the making of regulations for those purposes; and for the purposes of this subsection it is immaterial whether the Executive is or is not responsible for securing the enforcement of such (if any) of the relevant statutory provisions as relate to the matter in question.

(2) The Commission may at any time –

(a) direct the Executive or authorise any other person to investigate and make a special report on any matter to which this section applies; or

(b) with the consent of the Secretary of State direct an inquiry to be held into any such matter. ...

(5) In the case of a special report made by virtue of subsection (2)(a) above or a report made by the person holding an inquiry held by virtue of subsection (2)(b) above, the Commission may cause the report, or so much of it as the Commission thinks fit, to be made public at such time and in such manner as the Commission thinks fit. ...

15   Health and safety regulations

(1) Subject to the provisions of section 50, the Secretary of State shall have power to make regulations under this section for any of the general purposes of this Part (and regulations so made are in this Part referred to as 'health and safety regulations'). ...

16   Approval of codes of practice by the Commission

(1) For the purpose of providing practical guidance with respect to the requirements of any provision of sections 2 to 7 or of health and safety regulations or of any of the existing statutory provisions, the Commission may, subject to the following subsection –

(a) approve and issue such codes of practice (whether prepared by it or not) as in its opinion are suitable for that purpose;

(b) approve such codes of practice issued or proposed to be issued otherwise than by the Commission as in its opinion are suitable for that purpose.

(2) The Commission shall not approve a code of practice under subsection (1) about without the consent of the Secretary of State, and shall, before seeking his consent, consult –

(a) any government department or other body that appears to the Commission to be appropriate (and, in particular, in the case of a code relating to electro-magnetic radiations, the Health Protection Agency); and

(b) such government departments and other bodies, if any, as in relation to any matter dealt with in the code, the Commission is required to consult under this section by virtue of directions given to it by the Secretary of State. ...

17   Use of approved codes of practice in criminal proceedings

(1) A failure on the part of any person to observe any provision of an approved code of practice shall not of itself render him liable to any civil or criminal proceedings; but where in any criminal proceedings a party is alleged to have committed an offence by reason of a contravention of any requirement or prohibition imposed by or under any such provision as is mentioned in section 16(1) being a provision for which there was an approved code of practice at the time of the alleged contravention, the following subsection shall have effect with respect to that code in relation to those proceedings.

(2) Any provision of the code of practice which appears to the court to be relevant to the requirement or prohibition alleged to have been contravened shall be admissible in evidence in the proceedings; and if it is proved that there was at any material time a failure to observe any provision of the code which appears to the court to be relevant to any matter which it is necessary for the prosecution to prove in order to establish a contravention of that requirement or prohibition, that matter shall be taken as proved unless the court is satisfied that the requirement or prohibition was in respect of that matter complied with otherwise than by way of observance of that provision of the code. ...

18 Authorities responsible for enforcement of the relevant statutory provisions

(1) It shall be the duty of the Executive to make adequate arrangements for the enforcement of the relevant statutory provisions except to the extent that some other authority or class of authorities is by any of those provisions or by regulations [made by the Secretary of State] under subsection (2) below made responsible for their enforcement. ...

(4) It shall be the duty of every local authority –

(a) to make adequate arrangements for the enforcement within their area of the relevant statutory provisions to the extent that they are by any of those provisions or by regulations under subsection (2) above made responsible for their enforcement; and

(b) to perform the duty imposed on them by the preceding paragraph and any other functions conferred on them by any of the relevant statutory provisions in accordance with such guidance as the Commission may give them. ...

(7) In this Part –

(a) 'enforcing authority' means the Executive or any other authority which is by any of the relevant statutory provisions or by regulations under subsection (2) above made responsible for the enforcement of any of those provisions to any extent; and

(b) any reference to an enforcing authority's field of responsibility is a reference to the field over which that authority's responsibility for the enforcement of those provisions extends for the time being; ...

19 Appointment of inspectors

(1) Every enforcing authority may appoint as inspectors (under whatever title it may from time to time determine) such persons having suitable qualifications as it thinks necessary for carrying into effect the relevant statutory provisions within its field of responsibility, and may terminate any appointment made under this section. ...

20 Powers of inspectors

(1) Subject to the provisions of section 19 and this section, an inspector may, for the purpose of carrying into effect any of the relevant statutory provisions within the field of responsibility of the enforcing authority which appointed him, exercise the powers set out in subsection (2) below.

(2) The powers of an inspector referred to in the preceding subsection are the following, namely –

(a) at any reasonable time (or, in a situation which in his opinion is or may be dangerous, at any time) to enter any premises which he has reason to believe it is necessary for him to enter for the purpose mentioned in subsection (1) above;

(b) to take with him a constable if he has reasonable cause to apprehend any serious obstruction in the execution of his duty;

(c) without prejudice to the preceding paragraph, on entering any premises by virtue of paragraph (a) above to take with him –

(i) any other person duly authorised by his (the inspector's) enforcing authority; and

(ii) any equipment or materials required for any purpose for which the power of entry is being exercised;

(d) to make such examination and investigation as may in any circumstances be necessary for the purpose mentioned in subsection (1) above;

(e) as regards any premises which he has power to enter, to direct that those premises or any part of them, or anything therein, shall be left undisturbed (whether generally or in particular respects) for so long as is reasonably necessary for the purpose of any examination or investigation under paragraph (d) above;

(f) to take such measurements and photographs and make such recordings as he considers necessary for the purpose of any examination or investigation under paragraph (d) above;

(g) to take samples of any articles or substances found in any premises which he has power to enter, and of the atmosphere in or in the vicinity of any such premises;

(h) in the case of any article or substance found in any premises which he has power to enter, being an article or substance which appears to him to have caused or to be likely to cause danger to health or safety, to cause it to be dismantled or subjected to any process or test (but not so as to damage or destroy it unless this is in the circumstances necessary for the purpose mentioned in subsection (1) above);

(i) in the case of any such article or substance as is mentioned in the preceding paragraph, to take possession of it and detain it for so long as is necessary for all or any of the following purposes, namely –

(i) to examine it and do to it anything which he has power to do under that paragraph;

(ii) to ensure that it is not tampered with before his examination of it is completed;

(iii) to ensure that it is available for use as evidence in any proceedings for an offence under any of the relevant statutory provisions or any proceedings relating to a notice under section 21 or 22;

(j) to require any person whom he has reasonable cause to believe to be able to give any information relevant to any examination or investigation under paragraph (d) above to answer (in the absence of persons other than a person nominated by him to be present and any persons whom the inspector may allow to be present) such questions as the inspector thinks fit to ask and to sign a declaration of the truth of his answers;

(k) to require the production of, inspect, and take copies of or of any entry in –

(i) any books or documents which by virtue of any of the relevant statutory provisions are required to be kept; and

(ii) any other books or documents which it is necessary for him to see for the purposes of any examination or investigation under paragraph (d) above;

(l) to require any person to afford him such facilities and assistance with respect to any matters or things within that person's control or in relation to which that person has responsibilities as are necessary to enable the inspector to exercise any of the powers conferred on him by this section;

(m) any other power which is necessary for the purpose mentioned in subsection (1) above. ...

(7) No answer given by a person in pursuance of a requirement imposed under subsection (2)(j) above shall be admissible in evidence against that person or the spouse or civil partner of that person in any proceedings.

(8) Nothing in this section shall be taken to compel the production by any person of a document of which he would on grounds of legal professional privilege be entitled to withhold production on an order for discovery in an action in the High Court. ...

21   Improvement notices

If an inspector is of the opinion that a person –

(a) is contravening one or more of the relevant statutory provisions; or

(b) has contravened one or more of those provisions in circumstances that make it likely that the contravention will continue or be repeated,

he may serve on him a notice (in this Part referred to as 'an improvement notice') stating that he is of that opinion, specifying the provision or provisions as to which he is of that opinion, giving particulars of the reasons why he is of that opinion, and requiring that person to remedy the contravention or, as the case may be, the matters occasioning it within such period (ending not earlier than the period within which an appeal against the notice can be brought under section 24) as may be specified in the notice.

22   Prohibition notices

(1) This section applies to any activities which are being or are likely to be carried on by or under the control of any person, being activities to or in relation to which any of the relevant statutory provisions apply or will, if the activities are so carried on, apply.

(2) If as regards any activities to which this section applies an inspector is of the opinion that, as carried on or likely to be carried on by or under the control of the person in question, the activities involve or, as the case may be, will involve a risk of serious personal injury, the inspector may serve on that person a notice (in this Part referred to as 'a prohibition notice').

(3) A prohibition notice shall –

(a) state that the inspector is of the said opinion;

(b) specify the matters which in his opinion give or, as the case may be, will give rise to the said risk;

(c) where in his opinion any of those matters involves or, as the case may be, will involve a contravention of any of the relevant statutory provisions, state that he is of that opinion, specify the provision or provisions as to which he is of that opinion, and give particulars of the reasons why he is of that opinion; and

(d) direct that the activities to which the notice relates shall not be carried on by or under the control of the person on whom the notice is served unless the matters specified in the notice in pursuance of paragraph (b) above and any associated contraventions of provisions so specified in pursuance of paragraph (c) above have been remedied.

(4) A direction contained in a prohibition notice in pursuance of subsection (3)(d) above shall take effect –

(a) at the end of the period specified in the notice; or

(b) if the notice so declares, immediately.

24   Appeal against improvement or prohibition notice

(1) In this section 'a notice' means an improvement notice or a prohibition notice.

(2) A person on whom a notice is served may within such period from the date of its service as may be prescribed appeal to an employment tribunal; and on such an appeal the tribunal may either cancel or affirm the notice and, if it affirms it, may do so either in its original form or with such modifications as the tribunal may in the circumstances think fit.

(3) Where an appeal under this section is brought against a notice within the period allowed under the preceding subsection, then –

(a) in the case of an improvement notice, the bringing of the appeal shall have the effect of suspending the operation of the notice until the appeal is finally disposed of or, if the appeal is withdrawn, until the withdrawal of the appeal;

(b) in the case of a prohibition notice, the bringing of the appeal shall have the like effect if, but only if, on the application of the appellant the tribunal so directs (and then only for the giving of the direction).

(4) One or more assessors may be appointed for the purposes of any proceedings brought before an employment tribunal under this section.

25   Power to deal with cause of imminent danger

(1) Where, in the case of any article or substance found by him in any premises which he has power to enter, an inspector has reasonable cause to believe that, in the circumstances in which he finds it, the article or substance is a cause of

imminent danger of serious personal injury, he may seize it and cause it to be rendered harmless (whether by destruction or otherwise).

(2) Before there is rendered harmless under this section –

(a) any article that forms part of a batch of similar articles; or

(b) any substance,

the inspector shall, if it is practicable for him to do so, take a sample thereof and give to a responsible person at the premises where the article or substance was found by him a portion of the sample marked in a manner sufficient to identify it.

(3) As soon as may be after any article or substance has been seized and rendered harmless under this section, the inspector shall prepare and sign a written report giving particulars of the circumstances in which the article or substance was seized and so dealt with by him, and shall –

(a) give a signed copy of the report to a responsible person at the premises where the article or substance was found by him; and

(b) unless that person is the owner of the article or substance, also serve a signed copy of the report on the owner;

and if, where paragraph (b) above applies, the inspector cannot after reasonable enquiry ascertain the name or address of the owner, the copy may be served on him by giving it to the person to whom a copy was given under the preceding paragraph.

25A Power of customs officer to detain articles and substances

(1) A customs officer may, for the purpose of facilitating the exercise or performance by any enforcing authority or inspector of any of the powers or duties of the authority or inspector under any of the relevant statutory provisions, seize any imported article or imported substance and detain it for not more than two working days. ...

(3) In subsection (1) above the reference to two working days is a reference to a period of forty-eight hours calculated from the time when the goods in question are seized but disregarding so much of any period as falls on a Saturday or Sunday or on Christmas Day, Good Friday or a day which is a bank holiday under the Banking and Financial Dealings Act 1971 in the part of Great Britain where the goods are seized.

33 Offences

(1) It is an offence for a person –

(a) to fail to discharge a duty to which he is subject by virtue of sections 2 to 7;

(b) to contravene section 8 or 9;

(c) to contravene any health and safety regulations or any requirement or prohibition imposed under any such regulations (including any requirement or prohibition to which he is subject to virtue of the terms of or any condition or restriction attached to any licence, approval, exemption or other authority issued, given or granted under the regulations);

(d) to contravene any requirement imposed by or under regulations under section 14 or intentionally to obstruct any person in the exercise of his powers under that section;

(e) to contravene any requirement imposed by an inspector under section 20 or 25;

(f) to prevent or attempt to prevent any other person from appearing before an inspector or from answering any question to which an inspector may by virtue of section 20(2) require an answer;

(g) to contravene any requirement or prohibition imposed by an improvement notice or a prohibition notice (including any such notice as modified on appeal);

(h) intentionally to obstruct an inspector in the exercise or performance of his powers or duties or to obstruct a customs officer in the exercise of his powers under section 25A; ...

(k) to make a statement which he knows to be false or recklessly to make a statement which is false where the statement is made –

(i) in purported compliance with a requirement to furnish any information imposed by or under any of the relevant statutory provisions; or

(ii) for the purpose of obtaining the issue of a document under any of the relevant statutory provisions to himself or another person;

(l) intentionally to make a false entry in any register, book, notice or other document required by or under any of the relevant statutory provisions to be kept, served or given or, with intent to deceive, to make use of any such entry which he knows to be false;

(m) with intent to deceive, to use a document issued or authorised to be issued under any of the relevant statutory provisions or required for any purpose thereunder or to make or have in his possession a document so closely resembling any such document as to be calculated to deceive;

(n) falsely to pretend to be an inspector; ...

35 Venue

An offence under any of the relevant statutory provisions committed in connection with any plant or substance may, if necessary for the purpose of bringing the offence within the field of responsibility of any enforcing authority or conferring jurisdiction on any court to entertain proceedings for the offence, be treated as having been committed at the place where that plant or substance is for the time being.

36 Offences due to fault of other person

(1) Where the commission by any person of an offence under any of the relevant statutory provisions is due to the act or default of some other person, that other person shall be guilty of the offence, and a person may be charged with and

convicted of the offence by virtue of this subsection whether or not proceedings are taken against the first-mentioned person....

(3) The preceding provisions of this section are subject to any provision made by virtue of section 15(6) [health and safety regulations].

37   Offences by bodies corporate

(1) Where an offence under any of the relevant statutory provisions committed by a body corporate is proved to have been committed with the consent or connivance of, or to have been attributable to any neglect on the part of, any director, manager, secretary or other similar officer of the body corporate or a person who was purporting to act in any such capacity, he as well as the body corporate shall be guilty of that offence and shall be liable to be proceeded against and punished accordingly.

(2) Where the affairs of a body corporate are managed by its members, the preceding subsection shall apply in relation to the acts and defaults of a member in connection with his functions of management as if he were a director of the body corporate.

38   Restriction on institution of proceedings in England and Wales

Proceedings for an offence under any of the relevant statutory provisions shall not, in England and Wales, be instituted except by an inspector or the Environment Agency or by or with the consent of the Director of Public Prosecutions.

47   Civil liability

(1) Nothing in this Part shall be construed –

   (a) as conferring a right of action in any civil proceedings in respect of any failure to comply with any duty imposed by sections 2 to 7 or any contravention of section 8; or

   (b) as affecting the extent (if any) to which breach of a duty imposed by any of the existing statutory provisions is actionable; ...

(2) Breach of duty imposed by health and safety regulations shall, so far as it causes damage, be actionable except in so far as the regulations provide otherwise.

(3) No provision made by virtue of section 15(6)(b) [specified defence in proceedings for an offence] shall afford a defence in any civil proceedings, whether brought by virtue of subsection (2) above or not; but as regards any duty imposed as mentioned in subsection (2) above health and safety regulations may provide for any defence specified in the regulations to be available in any action for breach of that duty.

(4) Subsections (1)(a) and (2) above are without prejudice to any right of action which exists apart from the provisions of this Act, and subsection (3) above is without prejudice to any defence which may be available apart from the provisions of the regulations there mentioned.

(5) Any term of an agreement which purports to exclude or restrict the operation of subsection (2) above, or any liability arising by virtue of that subsection, shall be void, except in so far as health and safety regulations provide otherwise.

(6) In this section 'damage' includes the death of, or injury to, any person (including any disease and any impairment of a person's physical or mental condition).

50 Regulations under the relevant statutory provisions

(1) Where any power to make regulations under any of the relevant statutory provisions is exercisable by the Secretary of State. the Minister of Agriculture, Fisheries and Food or both of them acting jointly that power may be exercised either so as to give effect (without or without modifications) to proposals submitted by the Commission under section 11(2)(d) or independently of any such proposals; but the authority who is to exercise the power shall not exercise it independently of proposals from the Commission unless he has consulted the Commission and such other bodies as appear to him to be appropriate. ...

51 Exclusion of application to domestic employment

Nothing in this Part shall apply in relation to a person by reason only that he employs another, or is himself employed, as a domestic servant in a private household.

52 Meaning of work and at work

(1) For the purposes of this Part –

(a) 'work' means work as an employee or as a self-employed person;

(b) an employee is at work throughout the time when he is in the course of his employment, but not otherwise;

(bb) a person holding the office of a constable is at work throughout the time when he is on duty, but not otherwise; and

(c) a self-employed person is at work throughout such time as he devotes to work as a self-employed person;

and, subject to the following subsection, the expression 'work' and 'at work', in whatever context, shall be construed accordingly.

(2) Regulations made under this subsection may –

(a) extend the meaning of 'work' and 'at work' for the purposes of this Part; and

(b) in that connection provide for any of the relevant statutory provisions to have effect subject to such adaptations as may be specified in the regulations. ...

53 General interpretation of Part I

(1) In this Part, unless the context otherwise requires –

'article for use at work' means –

(a) any plant designed for use or operation (whether exclusively or not) by persons at work, and

(b) any article designed for use as a component in any such plant; ...

'code of practice' (without prejudice to section 16(8)) includes a standard, a specification and any other documentary form of practical guidance;

'the Commission' has the meaning assigned by section 10(2);

'conditional sale agreement' means an agreement for the sale of goods under which the purchase price or part of it is payable by instalments, and the property in the goods is to remain in the seller (notwithstanding that the buyer is to be in possession of the goods) until such conditions as to the payment of instalments or otherwise as may be specified in the agreement are fulfilled;

'contract of employment' means a contract of employment or appreciation (whether express or implied and, if express, whether oral or in writing);

'credit-sale agreement' means an agreement for the sale of goods, under which the purchase price or part of it is payable by instalments, but which is not a conditional sale agreement;

'customs officer' means an officer within the meaning of the Customs and Excise Management Act 1979;

'domestic premises' means premises occupied as a private dwelling (including any garden, yard, garage, outhouse or other appurtenance of such premises which is not used in common by the occupants of more than one such dwelling), and 'non-domestic premises' shall be construed accordingly.

'employee' means an individual who works under a contract of employment ... and related expressions shall be construed accordingly;

'enforcing authority' has the meaning assigned by section 18(7);

'the Executive' has the meaning assigned by section 10(5);

'the existing statutory provisions' means the following provisions while and to the extent that they remain in force, namely the provisions of the Acts mentioned in Schedule 1 which are specified in the third column of that Schedule and of the regulations, orders or other instruments of a legislative character made or having effect under any provision so specified;

'the general purposes of this Part' has the meaning assigned by section 1; ...

'health and safety regulations' has the meaning assigned by section 15(1);

'hire-purchase agreement' means an agreement other than a conditional sale agreement, under which –

(a) goods are bailed or (in Scotland) hired in return for periodical payments by the person to whom they are bailed or hired; and

(b) the property in the goods will pass to that person if the terms of the agreement are complied with and one or more of the following occurs:

(i) the exercise of an option to purchase by that person;

(ii) the doing of any other specified act by any party to the agreement;

(iii) the happening of any other event;

and 'hire-purchase' shall be construed accordingly;

'improvement notice' means a notice under section 21;

'inspector' means an inspector appointed under section 19;

'local authority' means –

(a) in relation to England, a county council, a district council, a London borough council, the Common Council of the City of London, the Sub-Treasurer of the Inner Temple or the Under-Treasurer of the Middle Temple;

(aa) in relation to Wales, a county council or a county borough council; ...

'personal injury' includes any disease and any impairment of a person's physical or mental condition;

'plant' includes any machinery, equipment or appliance;

'premises' includes any place and, in particular, includes –

(a) any vehicle, vessel, aircraft or hovercraft,

(b) any installation on land (including the foreshore and other land intermittently covered by water), any offshore installation, and any other installation (whether floating, or resting on the seabed or the subsoil thereof, or resting on other land covered with water or the subsoil thereof), and

(c) any tent or movable structure;

'prescribed' means prescribed by regulations made by the Secretary of State;

'prohibition notice' means a notice under section 22;

'the relevant statutory provisions' means –

(a) the provisions of this Part and of any health and safety regulations; and

(b) the existing statutory provisions;

'self-employed person' means an individual who works for gain or reward otherwise than under a contract of employment, whether or not he himself employs others;

'substance' means any natural or artificial substance (including micro-organisms), whether in solid or liquid form or in the form of a gas or vapour;

'supply', where the reference is to supplying articles or substances, means supplying them by way of sale, lease, hire or hire-purchase, whether as principal or agent for another.

82   General provisions as to interpretation and regulations

(1) In this Act – ...

(b) 'contravention' includes failure to comply, and 'contravene' has a corresponding meaning; ...

As amended by the Employment Protection Act 1975, ss116, 125(3), Schedule 15, paras 1, 2, 4, 5, 7, 11, 14, 16, 18, Schedule 18; Forgery and Counterfeiting Act 1981, s30, Schedule, Pt I; Local Government Act 1985, s102(2), Schedule 17; Consumer Protection Act 1987, ss36,

48(3), Schedule 3, paras 1, 2, 6, 7, Schedule 5; Environmental Protection Act 1990, s162(2), Schedule 16, Pt I; Local Government (Wales) Act 1994, ss22(3), 66(8), Schedule 9, para 9, Schedule 18; Environment Act 1995, s120(1), Schedule 22, para 30(1), (7); Police (Health and Safety) Act 1997, s2; Employment Rights (Dispute Resolution) Act 1998, s1(2); Ministry of Agriculture, Fisheries and Food (Dissolution) Order 2002, art 5(2), Schedule 2; Health Protection Agency Act 2004, s11(1), Schedule 3, para 5(1), (2); Civil Partnership Act 2004, s261(1), Schedule 27, para 49.

SEX DISCRIMINATION ACT 1975

(1975 c 65)

PART I

DISCRIMINATION TO WHICH ACT APPLIES

1   Direct and indirect discrimination against women

(1) In any circumstances relevant for the purposes of any provision of this Act, other than a provision to which subsection (2) applies, a person discriminates against a woman if –

(a) on the ground of her sex he treats her less favourably than he treats or would treat a man, or

(b) he applies to her a requirement or condition which he applies or would apply equally to a man but –

(i) which is such that the proportion of women who can comply with it is considerably smaller than the proportion of men who can comply with it, and

(ii) which he cannot show to be justifiable irrespective of the sex of the person to whom it is applied, and

(iii) which is to her detriment because she cannot comply with it.

(2) In any circumstances relevant for the purposes of a provision to which this subsection applies, a person discriminates against a woman if –

(a) on the ground of her sex, he treats her less favourably than he treats or would treat a man, or

(b) he applies to her a provision, criterion or practice which he applies or would apply equally to a man but –

(i) which is such that it would be to the detriment of a considerably larger proportion of women than of men, and

(ii) which he cannot show to be justifiable irrespective of the sex of the person to whom it is applied, and

(iii) which is to her detriment.

(3) Subsection (2) applies to –

(a) any provision of Part 2,

(b) sections 35A and 35B, and

(c) any other provision of Part 3, so far as it applies to vocational training.

2 Sex discrimination against men

(1) Section 1, and the provisions of Parts II and III relating to sex discrimination against women, are to be read as applying equally to the treatment of men, and for that purpose shall have effect with such modifications as are requisite.

(2) In the application of subsection (1) no account shall be taken of special treatment afforded to women in connection with pregnancy or childbirth.

2A Discrimination on the grounds of gender reassignment

(1) A person ('A') discriminates against another person ('B') in any circumstances relevant for the purposes of –

   (a) any provision of Part II.
   (b) section 35A or 35B, or
   (c) any other provision of Part III, so far as it applies to vocational training,

if he treats B less favourably than he treats or would treat other persons, and does so on the ground that B intends to undergo, is undergoing or has undergone gender reassignment.

(2) Subsection (3) applies to arrangements made by any person in relation to another's absence from work or from vocational training.

(3) For the purposes of subsection (1), B is treated less favourably than others under such arrangements if, in the application of the arrangements to any absence due to B undergoing gender reassignment –

   (a) he is treated less favourably than he would be if the absence was due to sickness or injury, or
   (b) he is treated less favourably than he would be if the absence was due to some other cause and, having regard to the circumstances of the case, it is reasonable for him to be treated no less favourably.

(4) In subsections (2) and (3) 'arrangements' includes terms, conditions or arrangements on which employment, a pupillage or tenancy or vocational training is offered.

(5) For the purposes of subsection (1), a provision mentioned in that subsection framed with reference to discrimination against women shall be treated as applying equally to the treatment of men with such modifications as are requisite.

3 Discrimination against married persons and civil partners in employment field

(1) In any circumstances relevant for the purposes of any provision of Part 2, a person discriminates against a person ('A') who fulfils the condition in subsection (2) if –

(a) on the ground of the fulfilment of the condition, he treats A less favourably than he treats or would treat a person who does not fulfil the condition, or

(b) he applies to A a provision, criterion or practice which he applies or would apply equally to a person who does not fulfil the condition, but –

(i) which puts or would put persons fulfilling the condition at a particular disadvantage when compared with persons not fulfilling the condition, and

(ii) which puts A at that disadvantage, and

(iii) which he cannot show to be a proportionate means of achieving a legitimate aim.

(2) The condition is that the person is –

(a) married, or

(b) a civil partner.

(3) For the purposes of subsection (1), a provision of Part 2 framed with reference to discrimination against women is to be treated as applying equally to the treatment of men, and for that purpose has effect with such modifications as are requisite.

4   Discrimination by way of victimisation

(1) A person ('the discriminator') discriminates against another person ('the person victimised') in any circumstances relevant for the purposes of any provision of this Act if he treats the person victimised less favourably than in those circumstances he treats or would treat other persons, and does so by reason that the person victimised has –

(a) brought proceedings against the discriminator or any other person under this Act or the Equal Pay Act 1970 or sections 62 to 65 of the Pensions Act 1995, or

(b) given evidence or information in connection with proceedings brought by any person against the discriminator or any other person under this Act or the Equal Pay Act 1970 or sections 62 to 65 of the Pensions Act 1995, or

(c) otherwise done anything under or by reference to this Act or the Equal Pay Act 1970 or sections 62 to 65 of the Pensions Act 1995 in relation to the discriminator or any other person, or

(d) alleged that the discriminator or any other person has committed an act which (whether or not the allegation so states) would amount to a contravention of this Act or give rise to a claim under the Equal Pay Act 1970 or under sections 62 to 65 of the Pensions Act 1995,

or by reason that the discriminator knows the person victimised intends to do any of those things, or suspects the person victimised has done, or intends to do, any of them.

(2) Subsection (1) does not apply to treatment of a person by reason of any allegation made by him if the allegation was false and not made in good faith.

(3) For the purposes of subsection (1), a provision of Part II or III framed with reference to discrimination against women shall be treated as applying equally to the treatment of men and for that purpose shall have effect with such modifications as are requisite.

5 Interpretation

(1) In this Act –

(a) references to discrimination refer to any discrimination falling within sections 1 to 4; and

(b) references to sex discrimination refer to any discrimination falling within section 1 or 2,

and related expressions shall be construed accordingly.

(2) In this Act –

'woman' includes a female of any age, and

'man' includes a male of any age.

(3) Each of the following comparisons, that is –

(a) a comparison of the cases of persons of different sex under section 1(1) or (2),

(b) a comparison of the cases of persons required for the purposes of section 2A, and

(c) a comparison of the cases of persons who do and who do not fulfil the condition in section 3(2),

must be such that the relevant circumstances in the one case are the same, or not materially different, in the other.

PART II

DISCRIMINATION IN THE EMPLOYMENT FIELD

6 Discrimination against applicants and employees

(1) It is unlawful for a person, in relation to employment by him at an establishment in Great Britain, to discriminate against a woman –

(a) in the arrangements he makes for the purpose of determining who should be offered that employment, or

(b) in the terms on which he offers her that employment, or

(c) by refusing or deliberately omitting to offer her that employment.

(2) It is unlawful for a person, in the case of a woman employed by him at an establishment in Great Britain, to discriminate against her –

(a) in the way he affords her access to opportunities for promotion, transfer or training, or to any other benefits, facilities or services, or by refusing or deliberately omitting to afford her access to them, or

(b) by dismissing her, or subjecting her to any other detriment.

(4) Subsections (1)(b) and (2) do not render it unlawful for a person to discriminate against a woman in relation to her membership of, or rights under, an occupational pension scheme in such a way that, were any term of the scheme to provide for discrimination in that way, then, by reason only of any provision made by or under sections 62 to 64 of the Pensions Act 1995 (equal treatment), an equal treatment rule would not operate in relation to that term.

(4A) In subsection (4), 'occupational pension scheme' has the same meaning as in the Pension Schemes Act 1993 and 'equal treatment rule' has the meaning given by section 62 of the Pensions Act 1995.

(5) Subject to section 8(3), subsection (1)(b) does not apply to any provision for the payment of money which, if the woman in question were given the employment, would be included (directly or otherwise) in the contract under which she was employed.

(6) Subsection (2) does not apply to benefits consisting of the payment of money when the provision of those benefits is regulated by the woman's contract of employment.

(7) Subsection (2) does not apply to benefits, facilities or services of any description if the employer is concerned with the provision (for payment or not) of benefits, facilities or services of that description to the public, or to a section of the public comprising the woman in question, unless –

(a) that provision differs in a material respect from the provision of the benefits, facilities or services by the employer to his employees, or

(b) the provision of the benefits, facilities or services to the woman in question is regulated by her contract of employment, or

(c) the benefits, facilities or services relate to training.

(8) In its application to any discrimination falling within section 2A, this section shall have effect with the omission of subsections (4) to (6).

7   Exception where sex is a genuine occupational qualification

(1) In relation to sex discrimination –

(a) section 6(1)(a) or (c) does not apply to any employment where being a man is a genuine occupational qualification for the job, and

(b) section 6(2)(a) does not apply to opportunities for promotion or transfer to, or training for, such employment.

(2) Being a man is a genuine occupational qualification for a job only where –

(a) the essential nature of the job calls for a man for reasons of physiology (excluding physical strength or stamina) or, in dramatic performances or other entertainment, for reasons of authenticity, so that the essential nature of the job would be materially different if carried out by a woman; or

(b) the job needs to be held by a man to preserve decency or privacy because –

(i) it is likely to involve physical contact with men in circumstances where they might reasonably object to its being carried out by a woman, or

(ii) the holder of the job is likely to do his work in circumstances where men might reasonably object to the presence of a woman because they are in a state of undress or are using sanitary facilities; or

(ba) the job is likely to involve the holder of the job doing his work, or living, in a private home and needs to be held by a man because objection might reasonably be taken to allowing to a woman –

(i) the degree of physical or social contact with a person living in the home, or

(ii) the knowledge of intimate details of such a person's life,

which is likely, because of the nature or circumstances of the job or of the home, to be allowed to, or available to, the holder of the job; or

(c) the nature or location of the establishment makes it impracticable for the holder of the job to live elsewhere than in premises provided by the employer, and –

(i) the only such premises which are available for persons holding that kind of job are lived in, or normally lived in, by men and are not equipped with separate sleeping accommodation for women and sanitary facilities which could be used by women in privacy from men, and

(ii) it is not reasonable to expect the employer either to equip those premises with such accommodation and facilities or to provide other premises for women; or

(d) the nature of the establishment, or of the part of it within which the work is done, requires the job to be held by a man because –

(i) it is, or is part of, a hospital, prison or other establishment for persons requiring special care, supervision or attention, and

(ii) those persons are all men (disregarding any woman whose presence is exceptional), and

(iii) it is reasonable, having regard to the essential character of the establishment or that part, that the job should not be held by a woman; or

(e) the holder of the job provides individuals with personal services promoting their welfare or education, or similar personal services, and those services can most effectively be provided by a man, or

(g) the job needs to be held by a man because it is likely to involve the performance of duties outside the United Kingdom in a country whose laws or customs are such that the duties could not, or could not effectively, be performed by a woman, or

(h) the job is one of two to be held by –

(i) by a married couple,

(ii) by a couple who are civil partners of each other, or

(iii) by a married couple or a couple who are civil partners of each other.

(3) Subsection (2) applies where some only of the duties of the job fall within paragraphs (a) to (g) as well as where all of them do.

(4) Paragraph (a), (b), (c), (d), (e) or (g) of subsection (2) does not apply in relation to the filling of a vacancy at a time when the employer already has male employees –

(a) who are capable of carrying out the duties falling within that paragraph, and

(b) whom it would be reasonable to employ on those duties, and

(c) whose numbers are sufficient to meet the employer's likely requirements in respect of those duties without undue inconvenience.

7A   Corresponding exception relating to gender reassignment

(1) In their application to discrimination falling within section 2A, subsections (1) and (2) of section 6 do not make unlawful an employer's treatment of another person if –

(a) in relation to the employment in question –

(i) being a man is a genuine occupational qualification for the job, or

(ii) being a woman is a genuine occupational qualification for the job, and

(b) the employer can show that the treatment is reasonable in view of the circumstances described in the relevant paragraph of section 7(2) and any other relevant circumstances.

(2) In subsection (1) the reference to the employment in question is a reference –

(a) in relation to any paragraph of section 6(1), to the employment mentioned in that paragraph;

(b) in relation to section 6(2) –

(i) in its application to opportunities for promotion or transfer to any employment or for training for any employment, to that employment;

(ii) otherwise, to the employment in which the person discriminated against is employed or from which that person is dismissed.

(3) In determining for the purposes of subsection (1) whether being a man or being a woman is a genuine occupational qualification for a job, section 7(4) applies in relation to dismissal from employment as it applies in relation to the filling of a vacancy.

(4) Subsection (1) does not apply in relation to discrimination against a person whose gender has become the acquired gender under the Gender Recognition Act 2004.

7B   Supplementary exceptions relating to gender reassignment

(1) In relation to discrimination falling within section 2A –

(a) section 6(1)(a) or (c) does not apply to any employment where there is a supplementary genuine occupational qualification for the job,

(b) section 6(2)(a) does not apply to a refusal or deliberate omission to afford access to opportunities for promotion or transfer to or training for such employment, and

(c) section 6(2)(b) does not apply to dismissing an employee from, or otherwise not allowing him to continue in, such employment.

(2) Subject to subsection (3), there is a supplementary genuine occupational qualification for a job only if –

(a) the job involves the holder of the job being liable to be called upon to perform intimate physical searches pursuant to statutory powers;

(b) the job is likely to involve the holder of the job doing his work, or living, in a private home and needs to be held otherwise than by a person who is undergoing or has undergone gender reassignment, because objection might reasonably be taken to allowing to such a person –

(i) the degree of physical or social contact with a person living in the home, or

(ii) the knowledge of intimate details of such a person's life,

which is likely, because of the nature or circumstances of the job or of the home, to be allowed to, or available to, the holder of the job;

(c) the nature or location of the establishment makes it impracticable for the holder of the job to live elsewhere than in premises provided by the employer, and –

(i) the only such premises which are available for persons holding that kind of job are such that reasonable objection could be taken, for the purpose of preserving decency and privacy, to the holder of the job sharing accommodation and facilities with either sex whilst undergoing gender reassignment, and

(ii) it is not reasonable to expect the employer either to equip those premises with suitable accommodation or to make alternative arrangements; or

(d) the holder of the job provides vulnerable individuals with personal services promoting their welfare, or similar personal services, and in the reasonable view of the employer those services cannot be effectively provided by a person whilst that person is undergoing gender reassignment.

(3) Subsection (2) does not apply in relation to discrimination against a person whose gender has become the acquired gender under the Gender Recognition Act 2004.

8   Equal Pay Act 1970 ...

(2) Section 1(1) of the Equal Pay Act 1970 ... does not apply in determining for the purposes of section 6(1)(b) of this Act the terms on which employment is offered.

(3) Where a person offers a woman employment on certain terms, and if she accepted the offer then, by virtue of an equality clause, any of those terms would fall to be modified, or any additional term would fall to be included, the offer shall be taken to contravene section 6(1)(b).

(4) Where a person offers a woman employment on certain terms, and subsection (3) would apply but for the fact that, on her acceptance of the offer, section 1(3) of the Equal Pay Act 1970 ... would prevent the equality clause from operating, the offer shall be taken not to contravene section 6(1)(b).

(5) An Act does not contravene section 6(2) if –

(a) it contravenes a term modified or included by virtue of an equality clause, or

(b) it would contravene such a term but for the fact that the equality clause is prevented from operating by section 1(3) of the Equal Pay Act 1970. ...

(7) In its application to any discrimination falling within section 2A, this section shall have effect with the omission of subsections (3), (4) and (5)(b).

10 Meaning of employment at establishment in Great Britain

(1) For the purposes of this Part and section 1 of the Equal Pay Act 1970 ('the relevant purposes'), employment is to be regarded as being at an establishment in Great Britain unless the employee does his work wholly outside Great Britain. ...

(4) Where work is not done at an establishment it shall be treated for the relevant purposes as done at the establishment from which it is done or (where it is not done from any establishment) at the establishment with which it has the closest connection. ...

11 Partnerships

(1) It is unlawful for a firm, in relation to a position as partner in the firm, to discriminate against a woman –

(a) in the arrangements they make for the purpose of determining who should be offered that position, or

(b) in the terms on which they offer her that position, or

(c) by refusing or deliberately omitting to offer her that position, or

(d) in a case where the woman already holds that position –

(i) in the way they afford her access to any benefits, facilities or services, or by refusing or deliberately omitting to afford her access to them, or

(ii) by expelling her from that position, or subjecting her to any other detriment.

(2) Subsection (1) shall apply in relation to persons proposing to form themselves into a partnership as it applies in relation to a firm.

(3) Subject to subsection (3A), subsection (1)(a) and (c) do not apply to a position as

partner where, if it were employment, being a man would be a genuine occupational qualification for the job.

(3A) Subsection (3) does not apply in relation to discrimination falling within section 2A.

(3B) In relation to discrimination falling within section 2A, subsection (1) does not make unlawful a firm's treatment of a person in relation to a position as partner where –

(a) if it were employment –

(i) being a man would be a genuine occupational qualification for the job, or

(ii) being a woman would be a genuine occupational qualification for the job, and

(b) the firm can show that the treatment is reasonable in view of the circumstances relevant for the purposes of paragraph (a) and any other relevant circumstances.

(3C) In relation to discrimination falling within section 2A, subsection (1)(a), (c) and, so far as it relates to expulsion, (d)(ii) do not apply to a position as partner where, if it were employment, there would be a supplementary genuine occupational qualification for the job.

(3D) Subsections (3B) and (3C) do not apply in relation to discrimination against a person whose gender has become the acquired gender under the Gender Recognition Act 2004.

(4) Subsection (1)(b) and (d) do not apply to provision made in relation to death or retirement except in so far as, in their application to provision made in relation to retirement, they render it unlawful for a firm to discriminate against a woman –

(a) in such of the terms on which they offer her a position as partner as provide for her expulsion from that position; or

(b) by expelling her from a position as partner or subjecting her to any detriment which results in her expulsion from such a position.

(5) In the case of a limited partnership references in subsection (1) to a partner shall be construed as references to a general partner as defined in section 3 of the Limited Partnerships Act 1907.

(6) This section applies to a limited liability partnership as it applies to a firm; and, in its application to a limited partnership, references to a partner in a firm are references to a member of the limited liability partnership.

12 Trade unions, etc

(1) This section applies to an organisation of workers, an organisation of employers, or any other organisation whose members carry on a particular profession or trade for the purposes of which the organisation exists.

(2) It is unlawful for an organisation to which this section applies, in the case of a woman who is not a member of the organisation, to discriminate against her –

(a) in the terms on which it is prepared to admit her to membership, or

(b) by refusing, or deliberately omitting to accept, her application for membership.

(3) It is unlawful for an organisation to which this section applies, in the case of a woman who is a member of the organisation, to discriminate against her –

(a) in the way it affords her access to any benefits, facilities or services, or by refusing or deliberately omitting to afford her access to them, or

(b) by depriving her of membership, or varying the terms on which she is a member, or

(c) by subjecting her to any other detriment.

(4) This section does not apply to provision made in relation to the death or retirement from work of a member.

13   Qualifying bodies

(1) It is unlawful for an authority or body which can confer an authorisation or qualification which is needed for, or facilitates, engagement in a particular profession or trade to discriminate against a woman –

(a) in the terms on which it is prepared to confer on her that authorisation or qualification, or

(b) by refusing or deliberately omitting to grant her application for it, or

(c) by withdrawing it from her or varying the terms on which she holds it.

(2) Where an authority or body is required by law to satisfy itself as to his good character before conferring on a person an authorisation or qualification which is needed for, or facilitates, his engagement in any profession or trade then, without prejudice to any other duty to which it is subject, that requirement shall be taken to impose on the authority or body a duty to have regard to any evidence tending to show that he, or any of his employees, or agents (whether past or present), has practised unlawful discrimination in, or in connection with, the carrying on of any profession or trade.

(3) In this section –

(a) 'authorisation or qualification' includes recognition, registration, enrolment, approval and certification,

(b) 'confer' includes renew or extend.

(4) Subsection (1) does not apply to discrimination which is rendered unlawful by section 22 or 23 [discrimination by bodies in charge of educational establishments and other discrimination by local education authorities respectively].

14   Persons concerned with provisions of vocational training

(1) It is unlawful, in the case of a woman seeking or undergoing training which would help fit her for any employment, for any person who provides, or makes arrangements for the provision of, facilities for such training to discriminate against her –

(a) in the terms on which that person affords her access to any training course or other facilities concerned with such training, or

(b) by refusing or deliberately omitting to afford her such access, or

(c) by terminating her training, or

(d) by subjecting her to any detriment during the course of her training.

(2) Subsection (1) does not apply to –

(a) discrimination which is rendered unlawful by section 6(1) or (2) or section 22 or 23, or

(b) discrimination which would be rendered unlawful by any of those provisions but for the operation of any other provision of this Act.

19   Ministers of religion, etc

(1) Nothing in this Part applies to employment for purposes of an organised religion where the employment is limited to one sex so as to comply with the doctrines of the religion or avoid offending the religious susceptibilities of a significant number of its followers.

(2) Nothing in section 13 applies to an authorisation or qualification (as defined in that section) for purposes of an organised religion where the authorisation or qualification is limited to one sex so as to comply with the doctrines of the religion or avoid offending the religious susceptibilities of a significant number of its followers.

(3) In relation to discrimination falling within section 2A, this Part does not apply to employment for purposes of an organised religion where the employment is limited to persons who are not undergoing and have not undergone gender reassignment, if the limitation is imposed to comply with the doctrines of the religion or avoid offending the religious susceptibilities of a significant number of its followers.

(4) In relation to discrimination falling within section 2A, section 13 does not apply to an authorisation or qualification (as defined in that section) for purposes of an organised religion where the authorisation or qualification is limited to persons who are not undergoing and have not undergone gender reassignment, if the limitation is imposed to comply with the doctrines of the religion or avoid offending the religious susceptibilities of a significant number of its followers.

20A Relationships which have come to an end

(1) This section applies where –

(a) there has been a relevant relationship between a woman and another person ('the relevant person'), and

(b) the relationship has come to an end (whether before or after the commencement of this section).

(2) In this section, a 'relevant relationship' is a relationship during the course of which an act of discrimination by one party to the relationship against the other party to it is unlawful under any preceding provision of this Part.

(3) It is unlawful for the relevant person to discriminate against the woman by subjecting her to a detriment where the discrimination arises out of and is closely connected to the relevant relationship.

PART III

DISCRIMINATION IN OTHER FIELDS

35A Discrimination by, or in relation to, barristers

(1) It is unlawful for a barrister or barrister's clerk, in relation to any offer of a pupillage or tenancy, to discriminate against a woman –

(a) in the arrangements which are made for the purpose of determining to whom it should be offered;

(b) in respect of any terms on which it is offered; or

(c) by refusing, or deliberately omitting, to offer it to her.

(2) It is unlawful for a barrister or barrister's clerk, in relation to a woman who is a pupil or tenant in the chambers in question, to discriminate against her –

(a) in respect of any terms applicable to her as a pupil or tenant;

(b) in the opportunities for training, or gaining experience, which are afforded or denied to her;

(c) in the benefits, facilities or services which are afforded or denied to her; or

(d) by terminating her pupillage or by subjecting her to any pressure to leave the chambers or other detriment.

(3) It is unlawful for any person, in relation to the giving, withholding or acceptance of instructions to a barrister, to discriminate against a woman.

(4) In this section –

'barrister's clerk' includes any person carrying out any of the functions of a barrister's clerk; and

'pupil', 'pupillage', 'tenancy' and 'tenant' have the meanings commonly associated with their use in the context of a set of barristers' chambers.

(5) Section 3 applies for the purposes of this section as it applies for the purposes of any provision of Part II. ...

35C Relationships which have come to an end

(1) This section applies where –

(a) there has been a relevant relationship between a woman and another person ('the relevant person'), and

(b) the relationship has come to an end (whether before or after the commencement of this section).

(2) In this section, a 'relevant relationship' is a relationship during the course of which an act of discrimination by one party to the relationship against the other party to it is unlawful under –

(a) section 35A ..., or

(b) any other provision of this Part, so far as the provision applies to vocational training.

(3) It is unlawful for the relevant person to discriminate against the woman by subjecting her to a detriment where the discrimination arises out of and is closely connected to the relevant relationship.

PART IV

OTHER UNLAWFUL ACTS

37 Discriminatory practices

(1) In this section 'discriminatory practice' means –

(a) the application of a provision, criterion or practice which results in an act of discrimination which is unlawful by virtue of any provision of Part 2 or 3 taken with section 1(2)(b) or 3(1)(b) or which would be likely to result in such an act of discrimination of the persons to whom it is applied were not all of one sex, or

(b) the application of a requirement or condition which results in an act of discrimination which is unlawful by virtue of any provision of Part 3 taken with section 1(1)(b) or which would be likely to result in such an act of discrimination if the persons to whom it is applied were not all of one sex.

(2) A person acts in contravention of this section if and so long as –

(a) he applies a discriminatory practice, or

(b) he operates practices or other arrangements which in any circumstances would call for the application by him of a discriminatory practice.

(3) Proceedings in respect of a contravention of this section shall be brought only by the Commission in accordance with sections 67 to 71.

38 Discriminatory advertisements

(1) It is unlawful to publish or cause to be published an advertisement which

indicates, or might reasonably be understood as indicating, an intention by a person to do any act which is or might be unlawful by virtue of Part II or III.

(2) Subsection (1) does not apply to an advertisement if the intended act would not in fact be unlawful.

(3) For the purposes of subsection (1), use of a job description with a sexual connotation (such as 'waiter', 'salesgirl', 'postman' or 'stewardess') shall be taken to indicate an intention to discriminate, unless the advertisement contains an indication to the contrary.

(4) The publisher of an advertisement made unlawful by subsection (1) shall not be subject to any liability under that subsection in respect of the publication of the advertisement if he proves –

(a) that the advertisement was published in reliance on a statement made to him by the person who caused it to be published to the effect that, by reason of the operation of subsection (2), the publication would not be unlawful, and

(b) that it was reasonable for him to rely on the statement.

(5) A person who knowingly or recklessly makes a statement such as is referred to in subsection (4) which in a material respect is false or misleading commits an offence, and shall be liable on summary conviction to a fine not exceeding level 5 on the standard scale.

39   Instructions to discriminate

It is unlawful for a person –

(a) who has authority over another person, or

(b) in accordance with whose wishes that other person is accustomed to act,

to instruct him to do any act which is unlawful by virtue of Part II or III, or procure or attempt to procure the doing by him of any such act.

40   Pressure to discriminate

(1) It is unlawful to induce, or attempt to induce, a person to do any act which contravenes Part II or III by –

(a) providing or offering to provide him with any benefit, or

(b) subjecting or threatening to subject him to any detriment.

(2) An offer or threat is not prevented from falling within subsection (1) because it is not made directly to the person in question, if it is made in such a way that he is likely to hear of it.

41   Liability of employers and principals

(1) Anything done by a person in the course of his employment shall be treated for the purposes of this Act as done by his employer as well as by him, whether or not it was done with the employer's knowledge or approval.

(2) Anything done by a person as agent for another person with the authority (whether express or implied, and whether precedent or subsequent) of that other person shall be treated for the purposes of this Act as done by that other person as well as by him.

(3) In proceedings brought under this Act against any person in respect of an act alleged to have been done by an employee of his it shall be a defence for that person to prove that he took such steps as were reasonably practicable to prevent the employee from doing that act, or from doing in the course of his employment acts of that description.

42 Aiding unlawful acts

(1) A person who knowingly aids another person to do an act made unlawful by this Act shall be treated for the purposes of this Act as himself doing an unlawful act of the like description.

(2) For the purposes of subsection (1) an employee or agent for whose act the employer or principal is liable under section 41 (or would be so liable but for section 41(3)) shall be deemed to aid the doing of the act by the employer or principal.

(3) A person does not under this section knowingly aid another to do an unlawful act if –

(a) he acts in reliance on a statement made to him by that other person that, by reason of any provision of this Act, the act which he aids would not be unlawful, and

(b) it is reasonable for him to rely on the statement.

(4) A person who knowingly or recklessly makes a statement such as is referred to in subsection (3)(a) which in a material respect is false or misleading commits an offence, and shall be liable on summary conviction to a fine not exceeding level 5 of the standard scale.

PART V

GENERAL EXCEPTIONS FROM PARTS II TO IV

47 Discriminatory training by certain bodies

(1) Nothing in Parts II to IV shall render unlawful any act done in relation to particular work by any person in, or in connection with –

(a) affording women only, or men only, access to facilities for training which would help to fit them for that work, or

(b) encouraging women only, or men only, to take advantage of opportunities for doing that work;

where it reasonably appears to that person that at any time within the 12 months immediately preceding the doing of the act there were no persons of the sex in question doing that work in Great Britain, or the number of person of that sex doing the work in Great Britain was comparatively small.

(2) Where in relation to particular work it reasonably appears to any person that although the condition for the operation of subsection (1) is not met for the whole of Great Britain it is met for an area within Great Britain, nothing in Parts II to IV shall render unlawful any act done by that person in, or in connection with –

(a) affording persons who are of the sex in question, and who appear likely to take up that work in that area, access to facilities for training which would help to fit them for that work, or

(b) encouraging persons of that sex to take advantage of opportunities in the area for doing that work.

(3) Nothing in Parts II to IV shall render unlawful any act done by any person in, or in connection with, affording persons access to facilities for training which would help to fit them for employment, where it reasonably appears to that person that those persons are in special need of training by reason of the period for which they have been discharging domestic or family responsibilities to the exclusion of regular full time employment.

The discrimination in relation to which this subsection applies may result from confining the training to persons who have been discharging domestic or family responsibilities, or from the way persons are selected for training, or both.

(4) The preceding provisions of this section shall not apply in relation to any discrimination which is rendered unlawful by section 6.

48 Other discriminatory training, etc

(1) Nothing in Parts II to IV shall render unlawful any act done by an employer in relation to particular work in his employment, being an act done in, or in connection with, –

(a) affording his female employees only, or his male employees only, access to facilities for training which would help to fit them for that work, or

(b) encouraging women only, or men only, to take advantage of opportunities for doing that work,

where at any time within the twelve months immediately preceding the doing of the act there were no persons of the sex in question among those doing that work or the number of persons of that sex doing the work was comparatively small.

(2) Nothing in section 12 shall render unlawful any act done by an organisation to which that section applies in, or in connection with, –

(a) affording female members of the organisation only, or male members of the organisation only, access to facilities for training which would help to fit them for holding a post of any kind in the organisation, or

(b) encouraging female members only, or male members only, to take advantage of opportunities for holding such posts in the organisation, where at any time within the twelve months immediately preceding the doing of the act there were no persons of the sex in question among persons holding such posts in the organisation or the number of persons of that sex holding such posts was comparatively small.

(3) Nothing in Parts II to IV shall render unlawful any act done by an organisation to which section 12 applies in, or in connection with, encouraging women only, or men only, to become members of the organisation where at any time within the twelve months immediately preceding the doing of the act there were no persons of the sex in question among those members or the number of persons of that sex among the members was comparatively small.

49   Trade unions, etc: elective bodies

(1) If an organisation to which section 12 applies comprises a body the membership of which is wholly or mainly elected, nothing in section 12 shall render unlawful provision which ensures that a minimum number of persons of one sex are members of the body –

  (a) by reserving seats on the body for persons of that sex, or

  (b) by making extra seats on the body available (by election or co-option or otherwise) for persons of that sex on occasions when the number of persons of that sex in the other seats is below the minimum,

where in the opinion of the organisation the provision is in the circumstances needed to secure a reasonable lower limit to the number of members of that sex serving on the body; and nothing in Parts II to IV shall render unlawful any act done in order to give effect to such a provision.

(2) This section shall not be taken as making lawful –

  (a) discrimination in the arrangements for determining the persons entitled to vote in an election of members of the body, or otherwise to choose the persons to serve on the body, or

  (b) discrimination in any arrangements concerning membership of the organisation itself.

50   Indirect access to benefits, etc

(1) References in this Act to the affording by any person of access to benefits, facilities or services are not limited to benefits, facilities or services provided by that person himself, but include any means by which it is in that person's power to facilitate access to benefits, facilities or services provided by any other person (the 'actual provider').

(2) Where by any provision of this Act the affording by any person of access to benefits, facilities or services in a discriminatory way is in certain circumstances prevented from being unlawful, the effect of the provision shall extend also to the liability under this Act of any actual provider.

51   Acts done for purposes of protection of women

(1) Nothing in the following provisions, namely –

(a) Part II,

(b) Part III so far as it applies to vocational training, or

(c) Part IV so far as it has effect in relation to the provisions mentioned in paragraphs (a) and (b),

shall render unlawful any act done by a person in relation to a woman if –

(i) it was necessary for that person to do it in order to comply with a requirement of an existing statutory provision concerning the protection of women, or

(ii) it was necessary for that person to do it in order to comply with a requirement of a relevant statutory provision (within the meaning of Part I of the Health and Safety at Work etc Act 1974) and it was done by that person for the purpose of the protection of the woman in question (or of any class of women that included that woman).

(2) In subsection (1) –

(a) the reference in paragraph (i) of that subsection to an existing statutory provision concerning the protection of women is a reference to any such provision having effect for the purpose of protecting women as regards –

(i) pregnancy or maternity, or

(ii) other circumstances giving rise to risks specifically affecting women,

whether the provision relates only to such protection or to the protection of any other class of persons as well; and

(b) the reference in paragraph (ii) of that subsection to the protection of a particular woman or class of women is a reference to the protection of that woman or those women as regards any circumstances falling within paragraph (a)(i) or (ii) above.

(3) In this section 'existing statutory provision' means (subject to subsection (4)) any provision of –

(a) an Act passed before this Act, or

(b) an instrument approved or made by or under such an Act (including one approved or made after the passing of this Act).

(4) Where an Act passed after this Act re-enacts (with or without modification) a provision of an Act passed before this Act, that provision as re-enacted shall be treated for the purposes of subsection (3) as if it continued to be contained in an Act passed before this Act.

51A Acts done under statutory authority to be exempt from certain provisions of Part III

(1) Nothing in –

(a) the relevant provisions of Part III, or

(b) Part IV so far as it has effect in relation to those provisions,

shall render unlawful any act done by a person if it was necessary for that person to do it in order to comply with a requirement of an existing statutory provision within the meaning of section 51.

(2) In subsection (1) 'the relevant provisions of Part III' means that provisions of that Part except so far as they apply to vocational training.

52 Acts safeguarding national security

(1) Nothing in Parts II to IV shall render unlawful an act done for the purpose of safeguarding national security. ...

52A Construction of references to vocational training

In the following provisions, namely –

(a) sections 51 and 51A, and

(b) the provisions of any Order in Council modifying the effect of section 52,

'vocational training' includes advanced vocational training and retraining; and any reference to vocational training in those provisions shall be construed as including a reference to vocational guidance.

PART VI

EQUAL OPPORTUNITIES COMMISSION

53 Establishment and duties of Commission

(1) There shall be a body of Commissioners named the Equal Opportunities Commission, consisting of at least eight but not more than fifteen individuals each appointed by the Secretary of State on a full-time or part-time basis, which shall have the following duties –

(a) to work towards the elimination of discrimination,

(b) to promote equality of opportunity between men and women generally,

(ba) to promote equality of opportunity, in the field of employment and of vocational training, for persons who intend to undergo, are undergoing or have undergone gender reassignment, and

(c) to keep under review the working of this Act and the Equal Pay Act 1970 and, when they are so required by the Secretary of State or otherwise think it necessary, draw up and submit to the Secretary of State proposals for amending them. ...

(2) The Secretary of State shall appoint –

(a) one of the Commissioners to be chairman of the Commission, and

(b) either one or two of the Commissioners (as the Secretary of State thinks fit) to be deputy chairman or deputy chairmen of the Commission. ...

55   Review of discriminatory provisions in health and safety legislation

(1) Without prejudice to the generality of section 53(1), the Commission, in pursuance of the duties imposed by paragraphs (a) and (b) of that subsection –

(a) shall keep under review the relevant statutory provisions in so far as they require men and women to be treated differently, and

(b) if so required by the Secretary of State, make to him a report on any matter specified by him which is connected with those duties and concerns the relevant statutory provisions.

Any such report shall be made within the time specified by the Secretary of State, and the Secretary of State shall cause the report to be published.

(2) Whenever the Commission think it necessary, they shall draw up and submit to the Secretary of State proposals for amending the relevant statutory provisions.

(3) The Commission shall carry out their duties in relation to the relevant statutory provisions in consultation with the Health and Safety Commission.

(4) In this section 'the relevant statutory provisions' has the meaning given by section 53 of the Health and Safety at Work etc Act 1974.

56A Codes of practice

(1) The Commission may issue codes of practice containing such practical guidance as the Commission think fit for one or more of the following purposes, namely –

(a) the elimination of discrimination in the field of employment;

(b) the promotion of equality of opportunity in that field between men and women;

(ba) the promotion of equality of opportunity in that field for persons who intend to undergo, are undergoing or have undergone gender reassignment. ...

PART VII

ENFORCEMENT

62   Restriction of proceedings for breach of Act

(1) Except as provided by this Act no proceedings, whether civil or criminal, shall lie against any person in respect of an act by reason that the act is unlawful by virtue of a provision of this Act.

(2) Subsection (1) does not preclude the making of an order of certiorari, mandamus or prohibition. ...

63   Jurisdiction of employment tribunals

(1) A complaint by any person ('the complainant') that another person ('the respondent') –

(a) has committed an act of discrimination against the complainant which is unlawful by virtue of Part II, or

(b) is by virtue of section 41 or 42 to be treated as having committed such an act of discrimination against the complainant,

may be presented to an employment tribunal.

(2) Subsection (1) does not apply to a complaint under section 13(1) of an act in respect of which an appeal, or proceedings in the nature of an appeal, may be brought under any enactment.

63A Burden of proof: employment tribunals

(1) This section applies to any complaint presented under section 63 to an employment tribunal.

(2) Where, on the hearing of the complaint, the complainant proves facts from which the tribunal could, apart from this section, conclude in the absence of an adequate explanation that the respondent –

(a) has committed an act of discrimination against the complainant which is unlawful by virtue of Part 2, or

(b) is by virtue of section 41 or 42 to be treated as having committed such an act of discrimination against the complainant,

the tribunal shall uphold the complaint unless the respondent proves that he did not commit, or, as the case may be, is not to be treated as having committed, that act.

65   Remedies on complaint under section 63

(1) Where an employment tribunal finds that a complaint presented to it under section 63 is well-founded the tribunal shall make such of the following as it considers just and equitable –

(a) an order declaring the rights of the complainant and the respondent in relation to the act to which the complaint relates;

(b) an order requiring the respondent to pay to the complainant compensation of an amount corresponding to any damages he could have been ordered by a county court or by a sheriff court to pay to the complainant if the complaint had fallen to be dealt with under section 66;

(c) a recommendation that the respondent take within a specified period action appearing to the tribunal to be practicable for the purpose of obviating or reducing the adverse effect on the complainant of any act of discrimination to which the complaint relates.

(1A) In applying section 66 for the purposes of subsection (1)(b), no account shall be taken of subsection (3) of that section.

(1B) As respects an unlawful act of discrimination falling within section 1(2)(b) or section 3(1)(b), if the respondent proves that the provision, criterion or practice in question was not applied with the intention of treating the complainant unfavourably on the ground of his sex or (as the case may be) fulfilment of the condition in section 3(2), an order may be made under subsection (1)(b) only if the employment tribunal –

(a) makes such order under subsection (1)(a) and such recommendation under subsection (1)(c) (if any) as it would have made if it had no power to make an order under subsection (1)(b); and

(b) (where it makes an order under subsection (1)(a) or a recommendation under subsection (1)(c) or both) considers that it is just and equitable to make an order under subsection (1)(b) as well.

(3) If without reasonable justification the respondent to a complaint fails to comply with a recommendation made by an employment tribunal under subsection (1)(c), then, if they think it just and equitable to do so –

(a) the tribunal may increase the amount of compensation required to be paid to the complainant in respect of the complaint by an order made under subsection (1)(b), or

(b) if an order under subsection (1)(b) was not made, the tribunal may make such an order.

66   Claims under Part III

(1) A claim by any person ('the claimant') that another person ('the respondent') –

(a) has committed an act of discrimination against the claimant which is unlawful by virtue of Part III, or

(b) is by virtue of section 41 or 42 to be treated as having committed such an act of discrimination against the claimant,

may be made the subject of civil proceedings in like manner as any other claim in tort …

(2) Proceedings under subsection (1) –

(a) shall be brought in England and Wales only in a county court …

but all such remedies shall be obtainable in such proceedings as, apart from this subsection and section 62(1), would be obtainable in the High Court …

(3) As respects an unlawful act of discrimination falling within section 1(1)(b) no award of damages shall be made if the respondent proves that the requirement or condition in question was not applied with the intention of treating the claimant unfavourably on the ground of his sex.

(3A) Subsection 3 does not affect the award of damages in respect of an unlawful act of discrimination falling within section 1(2)(b).

(4) For the avoidance of doubt it is hereby declared that damages in respect of an unlawful act of discrimination may include compensation for injury to feelings whether or not they include compensation under any other head. ...

66A Burden of proof: county ... courts

(1) This section applies to any claim brought under section 66(1) in a county court in England and Wales ...

(2) Where, on the hearing of the claim, the claimant proves facts from which the court could, apart from this section, conclude in the absence of an adequate explanation that the respondent –

    (a) has committed an act of discrimination against the claimant which is unlawful by virtue of –

        (i) section 35A or 35B, or

        (ii) any other provision of Part 3 so far as it applies to vocational training, or

    (b) is by virtue of section 41 or 42 to be treated as having committed such an act of discrimination against the claimant,

the court shall uphold the claim unless the respondent proves that he did not commit, or, as the case may be, is not be to be treated as having committed, that act.

67 Issue of non-discrimination notice

(1) This section applies to –

    (a) an unlawful discriminatory act, and

    (b) a contravention of section 37, and

    (c) a contravention of section 38, 39 or 40, and

    (d) an act in breach of a term modified or included by virtue of an equality clause,

and so applies whether or not proceedings have been brought in respect of the act.

(2) If in the course of a formal investigation the Commission becomes satisfied that a person is committing, or has committed, any such acts, the Commission may in the prescribed manner serve on him a notice in the prescribed form ('a non-discrimination notice') requiring him –

    (a) not to commit any such acts, and

    (b) where compliance with paragraph (a) involves changes in any of his practices or other arrangements –

        (i) to inform the Commission that he has effected those changes and what those changes are, and

        (ii) to take such steps as may be reasonably required by the notice for the purpose of affording that information to other persons concerned. ...

68 Appeal against non-discrimination notice

(1) Not later than six weeks after a non-discrimination notice is served on any person he may appeal against any requirement of the notice –

(a) to an employment tribunal, so far as the requirement relates to acts which are within the jurisdiction of the tribunal;

(b) to a county court ... so far as the requirement relates to acts which are within the jurisdiction of the court and are not within the jurisdiction of an employment tribunal.

(2) Where the court or tribunal considers a requirement in respect of which an appeal is brought under subsection (1) to be unreasonable because it is based on an incorrect finding of fact or for any other reason, the court or tribunal shall quash the requirement.

(3) On quashing a requirement under subsection (2) the court or tribunal may direct that the non-discrimination notice shall be treated as if, in place of the requirement quashed, it had contained a requirement in terms specified in the direction.

(4) Subsection (1) does not apply to a requirement treated as included in a non-discrimination notice by virtue of a direction under subsection (3).

71 Persistent discrimination

(1) If, during the period of five years beginning on the date on which either of the following became final in the case of any person, namely, –

(a) a non-discrimination notice served on him,

(b) a finding by a court or tribunal under section 63 or 66, or section 2 of the Equal Pay Act 1970, that he has done an unlawful discriminatory act or an act in breach of a term modified or included by virtue of an equality clause,

it appears to the Commission that unless restrained he is likely to do one or more acts falling within paragraph (b), or contravening section 37, the Commission may apply to a county court for an injunction ... restraining him from doing so; and the court, if satisfied that the application is well-founded, may grant the injunction or order in the terms applied for or in more limited terms.

(2) In proceedings under this section the Commission shall not allege that the person to whom the proceedings relate has done an act which is within the jurisdiction of an employment tribunal unless a finding by an employment tribunal that he did that act has become final.

72 Enforcement of ss38 to 40

(1) Proceedings in respect of a contravention of section 38, 39 or 40 shall be brought only by the Commission in accordance with the following provisions of this section.

(2) The proceedings shall be –

(a) an application for a decision whether the alleged contravention occurred, or

(b) an application under subsection (4) below,

or both.

(3) An application under subsection (2)(a) shall be made –

(a) in a case based on any provision of Part II, to an employment tribunal, and

(b) in any other case to a county court ...

(4) If it appears to the Commission –

(a) that a person has done an act which by virtue of section 38, 39 or 40 was unlawful, and

(b) that unless restrained he is likely to do further acts which by virtue of that section are unlawful,

the Commission may apply to a county court for an injunction ... restraining him from doing such acts; and the court, if satisfied that the application is well-founded, may grant the injunction ... in the terms applied for or more limited terms.

(5) In proceedings under subsection (4) the Commission shall not allege that the person to whom the proceedings relate has done an act which is unlawful under this Act and within the jurisdiction of an employment tribunal unless a finding by an employment tribunal that he did that act has become final.

73 Preliminary action in employment cases

(1) With a view to making an application under section 71(1) or 72(4) in relation to a person the Commission may present to an employment tribunal a complaint that he has done an act within the jurisdiction of an employment tribunal, and if the tribunal considers that the complaint is well-founded they shall make a finding to that effect and, if they think it just and equitable to do so in the case of an act contravening any provision of Part II may also (as if the complaint had been presented by the person discriminated against) make an order such as is referred to in section 65(1)(a), or a recommendation such as is referred to in section 65(1)(c), or both.

(2) Subsection (1) is without prejudice to the jurisdiction conferred by section 72(2).

(3) Any finding of an employment tribunal under –

(a) this Act, or

(b) the Equal Pay Act 1970,

in respect of any act shall, if it has become final, be treated as conclusive –

(i) by the county court ... on an application under section 71(1) or 72(4) or in proceedings on an equality clause,

(ii) by an employment tribunal on a complaint made by the person affected by the act under section 63 or in relation to an equality clause.

(4) In sections 71 and 72 and this section, the acts 'within the jurisdiction of an

employment tribunal' are those in respect of which such jurisdiction is conferred by sections 63 and 72 and by section 2 of the Equal Pay Act 1970.

76   Period within which proceedings to be brought

(1) An employment tribunal shall not consider a complaint under section 63 unless it is presented to the tribunal before the end of –

(a) the period of three months beginning when the act complained of was done; or

(b) in a case to which section 85(9A) [armed forces] applies, the period of six months so beginning.

(2) A county court ... shall not consider a claim under section 66 unless proceedings in respect of the claim are instituted before the end of –

(a) the period of six months beginning when the act complained of was done; or

(b) in a case to which section 66(5) [education] applies, the period of eight months so beginning. ...

(3) An employment tribunal [or] county court ... shall not consider an application under section 72(2)(a) unless it is made before the end of the period of six months beginning when the act to which it relates was done; and a county court ... shall not consider an application under section 72(4) unless it is made before the end of the period of five years so beginning.

(4) An employment tribunal shall not consider a complaint under section 73(1) unless it is presented to the tribunal before the end of the period of six months beginning when the act complained of was done.

(5) A court or tribunal may nevertheless consider any such complaint, claim or application which is out of time if, in all the circumstances of the case, it considers that it is just and equitable to do so.

(6) For the purposes of this section –

(a) where the inclusion of any term in a contract renders the making of the contract an unlawful act that act shall be treated as extending throughout the duration of the contract, and

(b) any act extending over a period shall be treated as done at the end of that period, and

(c) a deliberate omission shall be treated as done when the person in question decided upon it,

and in the absence of evidence establishing the contrary a person shall be taken for the purposes of this section to decide upon an omission when he does an act inconsistent with doing the omitted act or, if he has done no such inconsistent act, when the period expires within which he might reasonably have been expected to do the omitted act if it was to be done.

PART VIII

SUPPLEMENTAL

77 Validity and revision of contracts

(1) A term of a contract is void where –

(a) its inclusion renders the making of the contract unlawful by virtue of this Act, or

(b) it is included in furtherance of an act rendered unlawful by this Act, or

(c) it provides for the doing of an act which would be rendered unlawful by this Act.

(2) Subsection (1) does not apply to a term the inclusion of which constitutes, or is in furtherance of, or provides for, unlawful discrimination against a party to the contract, but the term shall be unenforceable against that party.

(3) A term in a contract which purports to exclude or limit any provision of this Act or the Equal Pay Act 1970 is unenforceable by any person in whose favour the term would operate apart from this subsection.

(4) Subsection (3) does not apply –

(a) to a contract settling a complaint to which section 63(1) of this Act or section 2 of the Equal Pay Act 1970 applies where the contract is made with the assistance of a conciliation officer;

(aa) to a contract settling a complaint to which section 63(1) of this Act or section 2 of the Equal Pay Act 1970 applies if the conditions regulating compromise contracts under this Act are satisfied in relation to the contract;

(b) to a contract settling a claim to which section 66 applies.

(4A) The conditions regulating compromise contracts under this Act are that –

(a) the contract must be in writing;

(b) the contract must relate to the particular complaint;

(c) the complainant must have received advice from a relevant independent adviser as to the terms and effect of the proposed contract and in particular its effect on his ability to pursue his complaint before an employment tribunal;

(d) there must be in force, when the adviser gives the advice, a contract of insurance, or an indemnity provided for members of a profession or professional body, covering the risk of a claim by the complainant in respect of loss arising in consequence of the advice;

(e) the contract must identify the adviser; and

(f) the contract must state that the conditions regulating compromise contracts under this Act are satisfied.

(4B) A person is a relevant independent adviser for the purposes of subsection (4A)(c) –

(a) if he is a qualified lawyer,

(b) if he is an officer, official, employee or member of an independent trade union who has been certified in writing by the trade union as competent to give advice and as authorised to do so on behalf of the trade union,

(c) if he works at an advice centre (whether as an employee or a volunteer) and has been certified in writing by the centre as competent to give advice and as authorised to do so on behalf of the centre, or

(d) if he is a person of a description specified in an order made by the Secretary of State.

(4BA) But a person is not a relevant independent adviser for the purposes of subsection (4A)(c) in relation to the complainant –

(a) if he is, is employed by or is acting in the matter for the other party or a person who is connected with the other party,

(b) in the case of a person within subsection (4B)(b) or (c), if the trade union or advice centre is the other party or a person who is connected with the other party,

(c) in the case of a person within subsection (4B)(c), if the complainant makes a payment for the advice received from him, or

(d) in the case of a person of a description specified in an order under subsection (4B)(d), if any condition specified in the order in relation to the giving of advice by persons of that description is not satisfied.

(4BB) In subsection (4B)(a) 'qualified lawyer' means –

(a) as respects England and Wales, a barrister (whether in practice as such or employed to give legal advice), a solicitor who holds a practising certificate, or a person other than a barrister or solicitor who is an authorised advocate or authorised litigator (within the meaning of the Courts and Legal Services Act 1990), ...

(4BC) In subsection (4B)(b) 'independent trade union' has the same meaning as in the Trade Union and Labour Relations (Consolidation) Act 1992.

(4C) For the purposes of subsection (4BA) any two persons are to be treated as connected –

(a) if one is a company of which the other (directly or indirectly) has control, or

(b) if both are companies of which a third person (directly or indirectly) has control.

(4D) An agreement under which the parties agree to submit a dispute to arbitration –

(a) shall be regarded for the purposes of subsection (4)(a) and (aa) as being a contract settling a complaint if –

(i) the dispute is covered by a scheme having effect by virtue of an order under section 212A of the Trade Union and Labour Relations (Consolidation) Act 1992, and

(ii) the agreement is to submit it to arbitration in accordance with the scheme, but

(b) shall be regarded for those purposes as neither being nor including such a contract in any other case.

(5) On the application of any person interested in a contract to which subsection (2) applies, a county court or sheriff court may make such order as it thinks just for removing or modifying any term made unenforceable by that subsection; but such an order shall not be made unless all persons affected have been given notice of the application (except where under rules of court notice may be dispensed with) and have been afforded an opportunity to make representation to the court.

(6) An order under subsection (5) may include provision as respects any period before the making of the order.

82 General interpretation provisions

(1) In this Act, unless the context otherwise requires –

'access' shall be construed in accordance with section 50;

'act' includes a deliberate omission;

'advertisement' includes every form of advertisement, whether to the public or not, and whether in a newspaper or other publication, by television or radio, by display of notices, signs, labels, showcards or goods, by distribution of samples, circulars, catalogues, price lists or other material, by exhibition of pictures, models or films, or in any other way, and references to the publishing of advertisements shall be construed accordingly;

'associated employer' shall be construed in accordance with subsection (2); ...

'the Commission' means the Equal Opportunities Commission; ...

'discrimination' and related terms shall be construed in accordance with section 5(1); ...

'employment' means employment under a contract of service or of apprenticeship or a contract personally to execute any work or labour, and related expressions shall be construed accordingly;

'employment agency' means a person who, for profit or not, provides services for the purpose of finding employment for workers or supplying employers with workers; ...

'equality clause' has the meaning given in section 1(2) of the Equal Pay Act 1970 (as [substituted by] section 8(1) of this Act); ...

'final' shall be construed in accordance with sub-section (4);

'firm' has the meaning given by section 4 of the Partnership Act 1890;

'formal investigation' means an investigation under section 57; ...

'gender reassignment' means a process which is undertaken under medical supervision for the purpose of reassigning a person's sex by changing physiological or other characteristics of sex, and includes any part of such a process;

'general notice', in relation to any person, means a notice published by him at a time and in a manner appearing to him suitable for securing that the notice is seen within a reasonable time by persons likely to be affected by it;

'genuine occupational qualification' shall be construed in accordance with section 7(2), except in the expression 'supplementary genuine occupational qualification', which shall be construed in accordance with section 7B(2);

'Great Britain' includes such of the territorial waters of the United Kingdom as are adjacent to Great Britain; ...

'man' includes a male of any age; ...

'non-discrimination notice' means a notice under section 67;

'notice' means a notice in writing;

'prescribed' means prescribed by regulations made by the Secretary of State by statutory instrument;

'profession' includes any vocation or occupation; ...

'provision, criterion or practice' includes 'requirement or condition';

'retirement' includes retirement (whether voluntary or not) on grounds of age, length of service or incapacity; ...

'trade' includes any business;

'training' includes any form of education or instruction; ...

'woman' includes a female of any age.

(1A) References in this Act to the dismissal of a person from employment or to the expulsion of a person from a position as partner includes references –

(a) to the termination of that person's employment or partnership by the expiration of any period (including a period expiring by references to an event or circumstance), not being a termination immediately after which the employment or partnership is renewed on the same terms; and

(b) to the termination of that person's employment or partnership by any act of his (including the giving of notice) in circumstances such that he is entitled to terminate it without notice by reason of the conduct of the employer or, as the case may be, the conduct of the other partners.

(2) For the purposes of this Act two employers are to be treated as associated if one is a company of which the other (directly or indirectly) has control or if both are companies of which a third person (directly or indirectly) has control. ...

(4) For the purposes of this Act a non-discrimination notice or a finding by a court or tribunal becomes final when an appeal against the notice or finding is dismissed, withdrawn or abandoned or when the time for appealing expires without an appeal having been brought; and for this purpose an appeal against a non-discrimination notice shall be taken to be dismissed if, notwithstanding that a requirement of the notice is quashed on appeal, a direction is given in respect of it under section 68(3).

(5) For the purposes of this Act a person is a near relative of another if that person is the wife or husband or civil partner, or parent or child, a grandparent or grandchild, or a brother or sister of the other (whether of full blood or half-blood or

by marriage or civil partnership), and 'child' includes an illegitimate child and the wife or husband or civil partner of an illegitimate child. ...

As amended by the Employment Protection Act 1975, s125(3), Schedule 18; Race Relations Act 1976, ss76, 79(4), Schedule 4, paras 1, 3, 5(1), 8; Criminal Justice Act 1982, ss38, 46; Industrial Training Act 1982, s20, Schedule 3, para 5(b), Schedule 4; Sex Discrimination Act 1986, ss1(1), (2), (3), 2(1)–(3), 4, 9(2), Schedule, Pt II; Employment Act 1989, ss3(1)–(4), 7(1), 29(4), Schedule 7, Pt II; Courts and Legal Services Act 1990, s64(1); Trade Union Reform and Employment Rights Act 1993, s39(2), Schedule 6, para 1; Sex Discrimination and Equal Pay (Remedies) Regulations 1993, regs 1(3), 2, Schedule, para 1; Pensions Act 1995, s66(2), (3); Sex Discrimination and Equal Pay (Miscellaneous Amendments) Regulations 1996, reg 2; Armed Forces Act 1996, s21(6); Employment Rights (Dispute Resolution) Act 1998, ss1(2), 8(1), 9(1), (2)(a), 10(1), (2)(a), 15, Schedule 1, para 2; Equal Opportunities (Employment Legislation) (Territorial Limits) Regulations 1999, reg 2(1), (3); Sex Discrimination (Gender Reassignment) Regulations 1999, regs 2(1)–(3), 3(1), (2), 4(1), (4)–(6), 5, 7(1), (2); Sex Discrimination (Indirect Discrimination and Burden of Proof) Regulations 2001, regs 3–7, 8(1)–(4); Limited Liability Partnerships Regulations 2001, reg 9, Schedule 5, para 6; Sex Discrimination Act 1975 (Amendment) Regulations 2003, regs 3, 4; Gender Recognition Act 2004, s14, Schedule 6, Pt 1, paras 1–3, 5; Civil Partnership Act 2004, ss251, 261(1), (4), Schedule 27, para 54, Schedule 30.

RACE RELATIONS ACT 1976
(1976 c 74)

PART I

DISCRIMINATION TO WHICH ACT APPLIES

1 Racial discrimination

(1) A person discriminates against another in any circumstances relevant for the purposes of any provision of this Act if –

(a) on racial grounds he treats that other less favourably than he treats or would treat other persons; or

(b) he applies to that other a requirement or condition which he applies or would apply equally to persons not of the same racial group as that other but –

(i) which is such that the proportion of persons of the same racial group as that other who can comply with it is considerably smaller than the proportion of persons not of that racial group who can comply with it; and

(ii) which he cannot show to be justifiable irrespective of the colour, race, nationality or ethnic or national origins of the person to whom it is applied; and

(iii) which is to the detriment of that other because he cannot comply with it.

(1A) A person also discriminates against another if, in any circumstances relevant for the purposes of any provision referred to in subsection (1B), he applies to that other a provision, criterion or practice which he applies or would apply equally to persons not of the same race or ethnic or national origins as that other, but –

(a) which puts or would put persons of the same race or ethnic or national origins as that other at a particular disadvantage when compared with other persons,

(b) which puts that other at that disadvantage, and

(c) which he cannot show to be a proportionate means of achieving a legitimate aim.

(1B) The provisions mentioned in subsection (1A) are –

(a) Part II;

(b) sections 17 to 18D;

(c) section 19B, so far as relating to –

(i) any form of social security;

(ii) health care;

(iii) any other form of social protection; and

(iv) any form of social advantage;

which does not fall within section 20;

(d) sections 20 to 24;

(e) sections 26A and 26B;

(f) sections 76 and 76ZA; and

(g) Part IV, in its application to the provisions referred to in paragraphs (a) to (f).

(1C) Where, by virtue of subsection (1A), a person discriminates against another, subsection (1)(b) does not apply to him.

(2) It is hereby declared that, for the purposes of this Act, segregating a person from other persons on racial grounds is treating him less favourably than they are treated.

2 Discrimination by way of victimisation

(1) A person ('the discriminator') discriminates against another person ('the person victimised') in any circumstances relevant for the purposes of any provision of this Act if he treats the person victimised less favourably than in those circumstances he treats or would treat other persons, and does so by reason that the person victimised has –

(a) brought proceedings against the discriminator or any other person under this Act; or

(b) given evidence or information in connection with proceedings brought by any person against the discriminator or any other person under this Act; or

(c) otherwise done anything under or by reference to this Act in relation to the discriminator or any other person; or

(d) alleged that the discriminator or any other person has committed an act which (whether or not the allegation so states) would amount to a contravention of this Act,

or by reason that the discriminator knows that the person victimised intends to do any of those things, or suspects that the person victimised has done, or intends to do, any of them.

(2) Subsection (1) does not apply to treatment of a person by reason of any allegation made by him if the allegation was false and not made in good faith.

3 Meaning of 'racial grounds', 'racial group', etc

(1) In this Act, unless the context otherwise requires –

'racial grounds' means any of the following grounds, namely colour, race, nationality or ethnic or national origins;

'racial group' means a group of persons defined by reference to colour, race, nationality or ethnic or national origins, and references to a person's racial group refer to any racial group into which he falls.

(2) The fact that a racial group comprises two or more distinct racial groups does not prevent it from constituting a particular racial group for the purposes of this Act.

(3) In this Act –

(a) references to discriminate refer to any discrimination falling within section 1 or 2; and

(b) references to racial discrimination refer to any discrimination falling within section 1,

and related expressions shall be construed accordingly.

(4) A comparison of the case of a person of a particular racial group with that of a person not of that group under section 1(1) or (1A) must be such that the relevant circumstances in the one case are the same, or not materially different, in the other.

3A   Harassment

(1) A person subjects another to harassment in any circumstances relevant for the purposes of any provision referred to in section 1(1B) where, on grounds of race or ethnic or national origins, he engages in unwanted conduct which has the purpose or effect of –

(a) violating that other person's dignity, or

(b) creating an intimidating, hostile, degrading, humiliating or offensive environment for him.

(2) Conduct shall be regarded as having the effect specified in paragraph (a) or (b) of subsection (1) only if, having regard to all the circumstances, including in particular the perception of that other person, it should reasonably be considered as having that effect.

PART II

DISCRIMINATION IN THE EMPLOYMENT FIELD

4   Applicants and employees

(1) It is unlawful for a person, in relation to employment by him at an establishment in Great Britain, to discriminate against another –

(a) in the arrangements he makes for the purpose of determining who should be offered that employment; or

(b) in the terms on which he offers him that employment; or

(c) by refusing or deliberately omitting to offer him that employment.

(2) It is unlawful for a person, in the case of a person employed by him at an establishment in Great Britain, to discriminate against that employee –

(a) in the terms of employment which he affords him; or

(b) in the way he affords him access to opportunities for promotion, transfer or training, or to any other benefits, facilities or services, or by refusing or deliberately omitting to afford him access to them; or

(c) by dismissing him, or subjecting him to any other detriment.

(2A) It is unlawful for an employer, in relation to employment by him at an establishment in Great Britain, to subject to harassment a person whom he employs or who has applied to him for employment.

(3) Except in relation to discrimination falling within section 2 or discrimination on grounds of race or ethnic or national origins, subsections (1) and (2) do not apply to employment for the purposes of a private household.

(4) Subsection (2) does not apply to benefits, facilities or services of any description if the employer is concerned with the provision (for payment or not) of benefits, facilities or services of that description to the public, or to a section of the public comprising the employee in question, unless –

(a) that provision differs in a material respect from the provision of the benefits, facilities or services by the employer to his employees; or

(b) the provision of the benefits, facilities or services to the employee in question is regulated by his contract of employment; or

(c) the benefits, facilities or services relate to training.

(4A) In subsection (2)(c) reference to the dismissal of a person from employment includes, where the discrimination is on grounds of race or ethnic or national origins, reference –

(a) to the termination of that person's employment by the expiration of any period (including a period expiring by reference to an event or circumstance), not being a termination immediately after which the employment is renewed on the same terms; and

(b) to the termination of that person's employment by any act of his (including the giving of notice) in circumstances such that he is entitled to terminate it without notice by reason of the conduct of the employer.

4A   Exception for genuine occupational requirement

(1) In relation to discrimination on grounds of race or ethnic or national origins –

(a) section 4(1)(a) or (c) does not apply to any employment; and

(b) section 4(2)(b) does not apply to promotion or transfer to, or training for, any employment; and

(c) section 4(2)(c) does not apply to dismissal from any employment;

where subsection (2) applies.

(2) This subsection applies where, having regard to the nature of the employment or the context in which it is carried out –

(a) being of a particular race or of particular ethnic or national origins is a genuine and determining occupational requirement;

(b) it is proportionate to apply that requirement in the particular case; and

(c) either –

(i) the person to whom that requirement is applied does not meet it, or

(ii) the employer is not satisfied, and in all the circumstances it is reasonable for him not to be satisfied, that that person meets it.

5 Exceptions for genuine occupational qualifications

(1) In relation to racial discrimination in cases where section 4A does not apply –

(a) section 4(1)(a) or (c) does not apply to any employment where being of a particular racial group is a genuine occupational qualification for the job; and

(b) section 4(2)(b) does not apply to opportunities for promotion or transfer to, or training for, such employment.

(2) Being of a particular racial group is a genuine occupational qualification for a job only where –

(a) the job involves participation in a dramatic performance or other entertainment in a capacity for which a person of that racial group is required for reasons of authenticity; or

(b) the job involves participation as an artist's or photographic model in the production of a work of art, visual image or sequence of visual images for which a person of that racial group is required for reasons of authenticity; or

(c) the job involves working in a place where food or drink is (for payment or not) provided to and consumed by members of the public or a section of the public in a particular setting for which, in that job, a person of that racial group is required for reasons of authenticity; or

(d) the holder of the job provides persons of that racial group with personal services promoting their welfare, and those services can most effectively be provided by a person of that racial group.

(3) Subsection (2) applies where some only of the duties of the job fall within paragraph (a), (b), (c) or (d) as well as where all of them do.

(4) Paragraph (a), (b), (c) or (d) of subsection (2) does not apply in relation to the filling of a vacancy at a time when the employer already has employees of the racial group in question –

(a) who are capable of carrying out the duties falling within that paragraph; and

(b) whom it would be reasonable to employ on those duties; and

(c) whose numbers are sufficient to meet the employer's likely requirements in respect of those duties without undue inconvenience.

6   Exception for employment intended to provide training in skills to be exercised outside Great Britain

Nothing in section 4 shall render unlawful any act done by an employer, on grounds other than those of race or ethnic or national origins, for the benefit of a person not ordinarily resident in Great Britain in or in connection with employing him at an establishment in Great Britain, where the purpose of that employment is to provide him with training in skills which he appears to the employer to intend to exercise wholly outside Great Britain.

8   Meaning of employment at establishment in Great Britain

(1) For the purposes of this Part ('the relevant purposes'), employment is to be regarded as being at an establishment in Great Britain if the employee –

    (a) does his work wholly or partly in Great Britain; or

    (b) does his work wholly outside Great Britain and subsection (1A) applies.

(1A) This subsection applies if, in a case involving discrimination on grounds of race or ethnic or national origins, or harassment –

    (a) the employer has a place of business at an establishment in Great Britain;

    (b) the work is for the purposes of the business carried on at that establishment; and

    (c) the employee is ordinarily resident in Great Britain –

        (i) at the time when he applies for or is offered the employment, or

        (ii) at any time during the course of the employment. ...

(4) Where work is not done at an establishment it shall be treated for the relevant purposes as done at the establishment for which it is done or (where it is not done from any establishment) at the establishment with which it has the closest connection. ...

10   Partnerships

(1) It is unlawful for a firm consisting of six or more partners, in relation to a position as partner in the firm, to discriminate against a person –

    (a) in the arrangements they make for the purpose of determining who should be offered that position; or

    (b) in the terms on which they offer him that position; or

    (c) by refusing or deliberately omitting to offer him that position; or

    (d) in a case where the person already holds that position –

        (i) in the way they afford him access to any benefits, facilities or services, or by refusing or deliberately omitting to afford him access to them; or

        (ii) by expelling him form that position, or subjecting him to any other detriment.

(1A) The limitation of subsection (1) to six or more partners does not apply in relation to discrimination on grounds of race or ethnic or national origins.

(1B) It is unlawful for a firm, in relation to a position as a partner in the firm, to subject to harassment a person who holds or has applied for that position.

(2) Subsections (1), (1A) and (1B) shall apply in relation to persons proposing to form themselves into a partnership as it applies in relation to a firm.

(3) Subsection (1)(a) and (c) do not apply to a position as partner where, if it were employment, section 4A or 5 would apply to such employment.

(4) In the case of a limited partnership references in this section to a partner shall be construed as references to a general partner as defined in section 3 of the Limited Partnerships Act 1907.

(5) This section applies to a limited liability partnership as it applies to a firm; and, in its application to a limited liability partnership, references to a partner in a firm are references to a member of the limited liability partnership.

(6) In subsection (1)(d)(ii) reference to the expulsion of a person from a position as partner includes, where the discrimination is on grounds of race or ethnic or national origins, reference –

(a) to the termination of that person's partnership by the expiration of any period (including a period expiring by reference to an event or circumstance), not being a termination immediately after which the partnership is renewed on the same terms; and

(b) to the termination of that person's partnership by any act of his (including the giving of notice) in circumstances such that he is entitled to terminate it without notice by reason of the conduct of the other partners.

11   Trade unions, etc

(1) This section applies to an organisation of workers, an organisation of employers, or any other organisation whose members carry on a particular profession or trade for the purposes of which the organisation exists.

(2) It is unlawful for an organisation to which this section applies, in the case of a person who is not a member of the organisation, to discriminate against him –

(a) in the terms on which it is prepared to admit him to membership; or

(b) by refusing, or deliberately omitting to accept, his application for membership.

(3) It is unlawful for an organisation to which this section applies, in the case of a person who is a member of the organisation, to discriminate against him –

(a) in the way it affords him access to any benefits, facilities or services, or by refusing or deliberately omitting to afford him access to them; or

(b) by depriving him of membership, or varying the terms on which he is a member; or

(c) by subjecting him to any other detriment.

(4) It is unlawful for an organisation to which this section applies, in relation to a person's membership or application for membership of that organisation, to subject him to harassment.

12   Qualifying bodies

(1) It is unlawful for an authority or body which can confer an authorisation or qualification which is needed for, or facilitates, engagement in a particular profession or trade to discriminate against a person –

(a) in the terms on which it is prepared to confer on him that authorisation or qualification; or

(b) by refusing, or deliberately omitting to grant, his application for it; or

(c) by withdrawing it from him or varying the terms on which he holds it.

(1A) It is unlawful for an authority or body to which subsection (1) applies, in relation to an authorisation or qualification conferred by it, to subject to harassment a person who holds or applies for such an authorisation or qualification.

(2) In this section –

(a) 'authorisation or qualification' includes recognition, registration, enrolment, approval and certification;

(b) 'confer' includes renew or extend.

(3) Subsections (1) and (1A) do not apply to discrimination or harassment which is rendered unlawful by section 17 or 18 [discrimination by bodies in charge of educational establishments and other discrimination by local education authorities respectively].

13   Persons concerned with provision of vocational training

(1) It is unlawful, in the case of an individual seeking or undergoing training which would help fit him for any employment, for any person who provides, or makes arrangements for the provision of, facilities for such training to discriminate against him –

(a) in the terms on which that person affords him access to any training course or other facilities concerned with such training; or

(b) by refusing or deliberately omitting to afford him such access; or

(c) by terminating his training; or

(d) by subjecting him to any detriment during the course of his training.

(2) Subsection (1) does not apply to –

(a) discrimination which is rendered unlawful by section 4(1) or (2) or section 17 or 18; or

(b) discrimination which would be rendered unlawful by any of those provisions but for the operation of any other provision of this Act.

(3) It is unlawful for any person who provides, or makes arrangements for the provision of, facilities for training to which subsection (1) applies, in relation to such facilities or training, to subject to harassment a person to whom he provides such training or who is seeking to undergo such training.

(4) Subsection (3) does not apply to harassment which is rendered unlawful by section 4(2A) or by section 17 or 18.

PART III

DISCRIMINATION IN OTHER FIELDS

26A Discrimination by, or in relation to, barristers

(1) It is unlawful for a barrister or barrister's clerk, in relation to any offer of a pupillage or tenancy, to discriminate against a person –

(a) in the arrangements which are made for the purpose of determining to whom it should be offered;

(b) in respect of any terms on which it is offered; or

(c) by refusing, or deliberately omitting, to offer it to him.

(2) It is unlawful for a barrister or barrister's clerk, in relation to a pupil or tenant in the chambers in question, to discriminate against him –

(a) in respect of any terms applicable to him as a pupil or tenant;

(b) in the opportunities for training, or gaining experience which are afforded or denied to him;

(c) in the benefits, facilities or services which are afforded or denied to him; or

(d) by terminating his pupillage or by subjecting him to any pressure to leave the chambers or other detriment.

(3) It is unlawful for any person, in relation to the giving, withholding or acceptance of instructions to a barrister, to discriminate against any person.

(4) In this section –

'barrister's clerk' includes any person carrying out any of the functions of a barrister's clerk; and

'pupil', 'pupillage', 'tenancy' and 'tenant' have the meanings commonly associated with their use in the context of a set of barrister's chambers. ...

PART IV

OTHER UNLAWFUL ACTS

28 Discriminatory practices

(1) In this section 'discriminatory practice' means the application of a requirement or condition which results in an act of discrimination which is unlawful by virtue

of any provision of Part II or III taken with section 1(1)(b), or which would be likely to result in such an act of discrimination if the persons to whom it is applied included persons of any particular racial group as regards which there has been no occasion for applying it.

(2) A person acts in contravention of this section if and so long as –

(a) he applies a discriminatory practice; or

(b) he operates practices or other arrangements which in any circumstances would call for the application by him of a discriminatory practice.

(3) Proceedings in respect of a contravention of this section shall be brought only by the Commission in accordance with sections 58 to 62.

29   Discriminatory advertisements

(1) It is unlawful to publish or to cause to be published an advertisement which indicates, or might reasonably be understood as indicating, an intention by a person to do an act of discrimination, whether the doing of that act by him would be lawful or, by virtue of Part II or III, unlawful.

(2) Subsection (1) does not apply to an advertisement –

(a) if the intended act would be lawful by virtue of any of sections 5, 6, 7(3) and (4), 10(3), 26, 34(2)(b), 35 to 39 and 41; or

(b) if the advertisement relates to the services of an employment agency (within the meaning of section 14(1)) and the intended act only concerns employment which the employer could by virtue of section 5, 6 or 7(3) or (4) lawfully refuse to offer to persons against whom the advertisement indicates an intention to discriminate.

(3) Subsection (1) does not apply to an advertisement which indicates that persons of any class defined otherwise than by reference to colour, race or ethnic or national origins are required for employment outside Great Britain.

(4) The publisher of an advertisement made unlawful by subsection (1) shall not be subject to any liability under that subsection in respect of the publication of the advertisement if he proves –

(a) that the advertisement was published in reliance on a statement made to him by the person who caused it to be published to the effect that, by reason of the operation of subsection (2) or (3), the publication would not be unlawful; and

(b) that it was reasonable for him to rely on the statement.

(5) A person who knowingly or recklessly makes a statement such as is mentioned in subsection (4)(a) which in a material respect is false or misleading commits an offence, and shall be liable on summary conviction to a fine not exceeding level 5 on the standard scale.

30 Instructions to discriminate

It is unlawful for a person –

(a) who has authority over another person; or

(b) in accordance with whose wishes that other person is accustomed to act,

to instruct him to do any act which is unlawful by virtue of Part II or III, or procure or attempt to procure the doing by him of any such act.

31 Pressure to discriminate

(1) It is unlawful to induce, or attempt to induce, a person to do any act which contravenes Part II or III.

(2) An attempted inducement is not prevented from falling within subsection (1) because it is not made directly to the person in question, if it is made in such a way that he is likely to hear of it.

32 Liability of employers and principals

(1) Anything done by a person in the course of his employment shall be treated for the purposes of this Act (except as regards offences thereunder) as done by his employer as well as by him, whether or not it was done with the employer's knowledge or approval.

(2) Anything done by a person as agent for another person with the authority (whether express or implied, and whether precedent or subsequent) of that other person shall be treated for the purposes of this Act (except as regards offences thereunder) as done by that other person as well as by him.

(3) In proceedings brought under this Act against any person in respect of an act alleged to have been done by an employee of his it shall be a defence for that person to prove that he took such steps as were reasonably practicable to prevent the employee from doing that act, or from doing in the course of his employment acts of that description.

33 Aiding unlawful acts

(1) A person who knowingly aids another person to do an act made unlawful by this Act shall be treated for the purposes of this Act as himself doing an unlawful act of the like description.

(2) For the purposes of subsection (1) an employee or agent for whose act the employer or principal is liable under section 32 (or would be so liable but for section 32(3)) shall be deemed to aid the doing of the act by the employer or principal.

(3) A person does not under this section knowingly aid another to do an unlawful act if –

(a) he acts in reliance on a statement made to him by that other person that, by reason of any provision of this Act, the act which he aids would not be unlawful; and

(b) it is reasonable for him to rely on the statement.

(4) A person who knowingly or recklessly makes a statement such as is mentioned in subsection (3)(a) which in a material respect is false or misleading commits an offence, and shall be liable on summary conviction to a fine not exceeding level 5 on the standard scale.

PART VI

GENERAL EXCEPTIONS FROM PARTS II TO IV

35 Special needs of racial groups in regard to education, training or welfare

Nothing in Parts II to IV shall render unlawful any act done in affording persons of a particular racial group access to facilities or services to meet the special needs of persons of that group in regard to their education, training or welfare, or any ancillary benefits.

36 Provision of education or training for persons not ordinarily resident in Great Britain

Nothing in Parts II to IV shall render unlawful any act done by a person for the benefit of persons not ordinarily resident in Great Britain in affording them access to facilities for education or training or any ancillary benefits, where it appears to him that the persons in question do not intend to remain in Great Britain after their period of education or training there.

37 Discriminatory training by certain bodies

(1) Nothing in Parts II to IV shall render unlawful any act done in relation to particular work by any person in or in connection with –

(a) affording only persons of a particular racial group access to facilities for training which would help to fit them for that work; or

(b) encouraging only persons of a particular racial group to take advantage of opportunities for doing that work,

where it reasonably appears to that person that at any time within the twelve months immediately preceding the doing of the act –

(i) there were no persons of that group among those doing that work in Great Britain; or

(ii) the proportion of persons of that group among those doing that work in Great Britain was small in comparison with the proportion of persons of that group among the population of Great Britain.

(2) Where in relation to particular work it reasonably appears to any person that

although the condition for the operation of subsection (1) is not met for the whole of Great Britain it is met for an area within Great Britain, nothing in Parts II to IV shall render unlawful any act done by that person in or in connection with –

(a) affording persons who are of the racial group in question, and who appear likely to take up that work in that area, access to facilities for training which would help to fit them for that work; or

(b) encouraging persons of that group to take advantage of opportunities in the area for doing that work.

(3) The preceding provisions of this section shall not apply to any discrimination which is rendered unlawful by section 4(1) or (2).

38 Other discriminatory training, etc

(1) Nothing in Parts II to IV shall render unlawful any act done by an employer in relation to particular work in his employment at a particular establishment in Great Britain, being an act done in or in connection with –

(a) affording only those of his employees working at that establishment who are of a particular racial group access to facilities for training which would help to fit them for that work; or

(b) encouraging only persons of a particular racial group to take advantage of opportunities for doing that work at that establishment,

where any of the conditions in subsection (2) was satisfied at any time within the twelve months immediately preceding the doing of the act.

(2) Those conditions are –

(a) that there are no persons of the racial group in question among those doing that work at that establishment; or

(b) that the proportion of persons of that group among those doing that work at that establishment is small in comparison with the proportion of persons of that group –

(i) among all those employed by that employer there; or

(ii) among the population of the area from which that employer normally recruits persons for work in his employment at that establishment.

(3) Nothing in section 11 shall render unlawful any act done by an organisation to which that section applies in or in connection with –

(a) affording only members of the organisation who are of a particular racial group access to facilities for training which would help to fit them for holding a post of any kind in the organisation; or

(b) encouraging only members of the organisation who are of a particular racial group to take advantage of opportunities for holding such posts in the organisation,

where either of the conditions in subsection (4) was satisfied at any time within the twelve months immediately preceding the doing of the act.

(4) Those conditions are –

(a) that there are no persons of the racial group in question among persons holding such posts in that organisation; or

(b) that the proportion of persons of that group among those holding such posts in that organisation is small in comparison with the proportion of persons of that group among the members of the organisation.

(5) Nothing in Parts II to IV shall render unlawful any act done by an organisation to which section 11 applies in or in connection with encouraging only persons of a particular racial group to become members of the organisation where at any time within the twelve months immediately preceding the doing of the act –

(a) no persons of that group were members of the organisation; or

(b) the proportion of persons of that group among members of the organisation was small in comparison with the proportion of persons of that group among those eligible for membership of the organisation.

(6) Section 8 (meaning of employment at establishment in Great Britain) shall apply for the purposes of this section as if this section were contained in Part II.

40 Indirect access to benefits, etc

(1) References in this Act to the affording by any person of access to benefits, facilities or services are not limited to benefits, facilities or services provided by that person himself, but include any means by which it is in that person's power to facilitate access to benefits, facilities or services provided by any other person (the 'actual provider').

(2) Where by any provision of this Act the affording by any person of access to benefits, facilities or services in a discriminatory way is in certain circumstances prevented from being unlawful, the effect of the provision shall extend also to the liability under this Act of any actual provider.

41 Acts done under statutory authority, etc

(1) Nothing in Parts II to IV shall render unlawful any act of discrimination done –

(a) in pursuance of any enactment or Order in Council; or

(b) in pursuance of any instrument made under any enactment by a Minister of the Crown; or

(c) in order to comply with any condition or requirement imposed by a Minister of the Crown (whether before or after the passing of this Act) by virtue of any enactment.

References in this subsection to an enactment, Order in Council or instrument include an enactment, Order in Council or instrument passed or made after the passing of this Act.

(2) Nothing in Parts II to IV shall render unlawful any act whereby a person

discriminates against another on the basis of that other's nationality or place of ordinary residence or the length of time for which he has been present or resident in or outside the United Kingdom or an area within the United Kingdom, if that act is done –

(a) in pursuance of any arrangements made (whether before or after the passing of this Act) by or with the approval of, or for the time being approved by, a Minister of the Crown; or

(b) in order to comply with any condition imposed (whether before or after the passing of this Act) by a Minister of the Crown.

42 Acts safeguarding national security

Nothing in Parts II to IV shall render unlawful an act done for the purpose of safeguarding national security.

PART VII

THE COMMISSION FOR RACIAL EQUALITY

43 Establishment and duties of Commission

(1) There shall be a body of Commissioners named the Commission for Racial Equality consisting of at least eight but not more than fifteen individuals each appointed by the Secretary of State on a full-time or part-time basis, which shall have the following duties –

(a) to work towards the elimination of discrimination;

(b) to promote equality of opportunities, and good relations, between persons of different racial groups generally; and

(c) to keep under review the working of this Act and, when they are so required by the Secretary of State or otherwise think it necessary, draw up and submit to the Secretary of State proposals for amending it. ...

(2) The Secretary of State shall appoint –

(a) one of the Commissioners to be chairman of the Commission; and

(b) either one or more of the Commissioners (as the Secretary of State thinks fit) to be deputy chairman or deputy chairman of the Commission. ...

47 Codes of practice

(1) The Commission may issue codes of practice containing such practical guidance as the Commission think fit for all or any of the following purposes, namely –

(a) the elimination of discrimination in the field of employment;

(b) the promotion of equality of opportunity in that field between persons of different racial groups; ...

PART VIII

ENFORCEMENT

53   Restriction of proceedings for breach of Act

(1) Except as provided by this Act or the Special Immigration Appeals Commission Act 1997 or Part IV of the Immigration and Asylum Act 1999 no proceedings, whether civil or criminal, shall lie against any person in respect of an act by reason that the act is unlawful by virtue of a provision of this Act.

(2) Subsection (1) does not preclude the making of an order of certiorari, mandamus or prohibition. ...

54   Jurisdiction of employment tribunals

(1) A complaint by any person ('the complainant') that another person ('the respondent') –

   (a) has committed an act of discrimination against the complainant which is unlawful by virtue of Part II; or

   (b) is by virtue of section 32 or 33 to be treated as having committed such an act of discrimination against the complainant,

may be presented to an employment tribunal.

(2) Subsection (1) does not apply to a complaint under section 12(1) of an act in respect of which an appeal, or proceedings in the nature of an appeal, may be brought under any enactment.

56   Remedies on complaint under s54

(1) Where an employment tribunal finds that a complaint presented to it under section 54 is well-founded, the tribunal shall make such of the following as it considers just and equitable –

   (a) an order declaring the rights of the complainant and the respondent in relation to the act to which the complaint relates;

   (b) an order requiring the respondent to pay to the complainant compensation of an amount corresponding to any damages he could have been ordered by a county court ... to pay to the complainant if the complaint had fallen to be dealt with under section 57;

   (c) a recommendation that the respondent take within a specified period action appearing to the tribunal to be practicable for the purpose of obviating or reducing the adverse effect on the complainant of any act of discrimination to which the complaint relates.

(4) If without reasonable justification the respondent to a complaint fails to comply with a recommendation made by an employment tribunal under subsection (1)(c), then, if it thinks it just and equitable to do so –

(a) the tribunal may increase the amount of compensation required to be paid to the complainant in respect of the complaint by an order made under subsection (1)(b); or

(b) if an order under subsection (1)(b) could have been made but was not, the tribunal may make such an order.

(5) The Secretary of State may by regulations make provision –

(a) for enabling a tribunal, where an amount of compensation falls to be awarded under subsection (1)(b), to include in the award interest on that amount; and

(b) specifying, for cases where a tribunal decides that an award is to include an amount in respect of interest, the manner in which and the periods and rate by reference to which the interest is to be determined;

and the regulations may contain such incidental and supplementary provisions as the Secretary of State considers appropriate.

(6) The Secretary of State may by regulations modify the operation of any order made under section 14 of the Employment Tribunals Act 1996 (power to make provision as to interest on sums payable in pursuance of employment tribunal decisions) to the extent that it relates to an award of compensation under subsection (1)(b).

57   Claims under Part III

(1) A claim by any person ('the claimant') that another person ('the respondent') –

(a) has committed an act of discrimination against the claimant which is unlawful by virtue of Part III; or

(b) is by virtue of section 32 or 33 to be treated as having committed such an act of discrimination against the claimant,

may be made the subject of civil proceedings in like manner as any other claim in tort …

(2) Proceedings under subsection (1) –

(a) shall, in England and Wales, be brought only in a designated county court;
…

but all such remedies shall be obtainable in such proceedings as, apart from this subsection and section 53(1), would be obtainable in the High Court …

(3) As respects an unlawful act of discrimination falling within section 1(1)(b), no award of damages shall be made if the respondent proves that the requirement or condition in question was not applied with the intention of treating the claimant unfavourable on racial grounds.

(4) For the avoidance of doubt it is hereby declared that damages in respect of an unlawful act of discrimination may include compensation for injury to feelings whether or not they include compensation under any other head. …

58   Issue of non-discrimination notice

(1) This section applies to –

(a) an unlawful discriminatory act; and

(b) an act contravening section 28; and

(c) an act contravening section 29, 30 or 31,

and so applies whether or not proceedings have been brought in respect of the act.

(2) If in the course of a formal investigation the Commission become satisfied that a person is committing, or has committed, any such acts, the Commission may in the prescribed manner serve on him a notice in the prescribed form ('a non-discrimination notice') requiring him –

(a) not to commit any such acts; and

(b) where compliance with paragraph (a) involves changes in any of his practices or other arrangements –

(i) to inform the Commission that he has effected those changes and what those changes are; and

(ii) to take such steps as may be reasonably required by the notice for the purpose of affording that information to other persons concerned. ...

59   Appeal against non-discrimination notice

(1) Not later than six weeks after a non-discrimination notice is served on any person he may appeal against any requirement of the notice –

(a) to an employment tribunal, so far as the requirement relates to acts which are within the jurisdiction of the tribunal;

(b) to a designated county court ... so far as the requirement relates to acts which are within the jurisdiction of the court (ignoring sections 57A [claims under section 19B in immigration cases]) and are not within the jurisdiction of an employment tribunal.

(2) Where the tribunal or court considers a requirement in respect of which an appeal is brought under subsection (1) to be unreasonable because it is based on an incorrect finding of fact or for any other reason, the tribunal or court shall quash the requirement.

(3) On quashing a requirement under subsection (2) the tribunal or court may direct that the non-discrimination notice shall be treated as if, in place of the requirement quashed, it had contained a requirement in terms specified in the direction.

(4) Subsection (1) does not apply to a requirement treated as included in a non-discrimination notice by virtue of a direction under subsection (3).

62   Persistent discrimination

(1) If, during the period of five years beginning on the date on which any of the following became final in the case of any person, namely –

(a) a non-discrimination notice served on him; or

(b) a finding by a tribunal or court under section 54 or 57; that he has done an unlawful discriminatory act; or

(ba) a finding under the Special Immigration Appeals Commission Act 1997 or Part IV of the Immigration and Asylum Act 1999 that he has done an act which was unlawful by virtue of section 19B; or ...

it appears to the Commission that unless restrained he is likely to do one or more acts falling within paragraph (b), or contravening section 28, the Commission may apply to a designated county court for an injunction, ... restraining him from doing so; and the court, if satisfied that the application is well-founded, may grant the injunction or order in the terms applied for or in more limited terms.

(2) In proceedings under this section the Commission shall not allege that the person to whom the proceedings relate has done an act falling within subsection (1)(b) or contravening section 28 which is within the jurisdiction of an employment tribunal unless a finding by an employment tribunal that he did that act has become final.

63   Enforcement of ss29 to 31

(1) Proceedings in respect of a contravention of section 29, 30 or 31 shall be brought only by the Commission in accordance with the following provisions of this section.

(2) The proceedings shall be –

(a) an application for a decision whether the alleged contravention occurred; or

(b) an application under subsection (4),

or both.

(3) An application under subsection (2)(a) shall be made –

(a) in a case based on any provision of Part II, to an employment tribunal; and

(b) in any other case, to a designated county court ...

(4) If it appears to the Commission –

(a) that a person has done an act which by virtue of section 29, 30 or 31 was unlawful; and

(b) that unless restrained he is likely to do further acts which by virtue of that section are unlawful,

the Commission may apply to a designated county court for an injunction ... restraining him from doing such acts; and the court, if satisfied that the application is well-founded, may grant the injunction ... in the terms applied for or more limited terms.

(5) In proceedings under subsection (4) the Commission shall not allege that the person to whom the proceedings relate has done an act which is unlawful under this Act and within the jurisdiction of an employment tribunal unless a finding by an employment tribunal that he did that act has become final.

64 Preliminary action in employment cases

(1) With a view to making an application under section 62(1) or 63(4) in relation to a person the Commission may present to an employment tribunal a complaint that he has done an act within the jurisdiction of an employment tribunal, and if the tribunal considers that the complaint is well-founded it shall make a finding to that effect and, if it thinks it just and equitable to do so in the case of an act contravening any provision of Part II may also (as if the complaint had been presented by the person discriminated against) make an order such as is referred to in section 56(1)(a), or a recommendation such as is referred to in section 56(1)(c), or both.

(2) Subsection (1) is without prejudice to the jurisdiction conferred by section 63(2).

(3) In sections 62 and 63 and this section, the acts 'within the jurisdiction of an employment tribunal' are those in respect of which such jurisdiction is conferred by sections 54 and 63.

67 ... designated county courts

(1) For the purposes of this Act a 'designated' county court is one designated for the time being for those purposes by an order made by the Lord Chancellor. ...

(4) In any proceedings under this Act in a designated county court ... the judge ... shall, unless with the consent of the parties he sits without assessors, be assisted by two assessors appointed from a list of persons prepared and maintained by the Secretary of State, being persons appearing to the Secretary of State to have special knowledge and experience of problems connected with relations between persons of different racial groups. ...

68 Period within which proceedings to be brought

(1) An employment tribunal shall not consider a complaint under section 54 unless it is presented to the tribunal before the end of –

  (a) the period of three months beginning when the act complained of was done; or

  (b) in a case to which section 75(8) [armed forces] applies, the period of six months so beginning.

(2) Subject to subsection (2A)a county court ... shall not consider a claim under section 57 unless proceedings in respect of the claim are instituted before the end of –

  (a) the period of six months beginning when the act complained of was done.

(2A) In relation to an immigration claim within the meaning of section 57A, the period of six months mentioned in subsection (2)(a) begins on the expiry of the period during which, by virtue of section 57A(1)(a), no proceedings may be brought under section 57(1) in respect of the claim.

(3) Where, in relation to proceedings or prospective proceedings by way of a claim under section 57, an application for assistance under section 66 is made to the Commission before the end of the period of six months mentioned in paragraph (a) of subsection (2), the period allowed by that paragraph for instituting proceedings in respect of the claim shall be extended by two months.

(4) An employment tribunal [or] county court ... shall not consider an application under section 63(2)(a) unless it is made before the end of the period of six months beginning when the act to which it relates was done; and a county court ... shall not consider an application under section 63(4) unless it is made before the end of the period of five years so beginning.

(5) An employment tribunal shall not consider a complaint under section 64(1) unless it is presented to the tribunal before the end of the period of six months beginning when the act complained of was done.

(6) A court or tribunal may nevertheless consider any such complaint, claim or application which is out of time if, in all the circumstances of the case, it considers that it is just and equitable to do so.

(7) For the purposes of this section –

(a) when the inclusion of any term in a contract renders the making of the contract an unlawful act, that act shall be treated as extending throughout the duration of the contract; and

(b) any act extending over a period shall be treated as done at the end of that period; and

(c) a deliberate omission shall be treated as done when the person in question decided upon it;

and in the absence of evidence establishing the contrary a person shall be taken for the purposes of this section to decide upon an omission when he does an act inconsistent with doing the omitted act or, if he has done no such inconsistent act, when the period expires within which he might reasonably have been expected to do the omitted act if it was to be done.

PART X

SUPPLEMENTAL

72 Validity and revision of contracts

(1) A term of a contract is void where –

(a) its inclusion renders the making of the contract unlawful by virtue of this Act; or

(b) it is included in furtherance of an act rendered unlawful by this Act; or

(c) it provides for the doing of an act which would be rendered unlawful by this Act.

(2) Subsection (1) does not apply to a term the inclusion of which constitutes, or is in furtherance of, or provides for, unlawful discrimination against a party to the contract, but the term shall be unenforceable against that party.

(3) A term in a contract which purports to exclude or limit any provision of this Act is unenforceable by any person in whose favour the term would operate apart from this subsection.

(4) Subsection (3) does not apply –

(a) to a contract settling a complaint to which section 54(1) applies where the contract is made with the assistance of a conciliation officer; or

(aa) to a contract settling a complaint to which section 54(1) applies if the conditions regulating compromise contracts under this Act are satisfied in relation to the contract;

(b) to a contract settling a claim to which section 57 applies.

(4A) The conditions regulating compromise contracts under this Act are that –

(a) the contract must be in writing;

(b) the contract must relate to the particular complaint;

(c) the complainant must have received advice from a relevant independent adviser as to the terms and effect of the proposed contract and in particular its effect on his ability to pursue his complaint before an employment tribunal;

(d) there must be in force, when the adviser gives the advice, a contract of insurance, or an indemnity provided for members of a profession or professional body, covering the risk of a claim by the complainant n respect of loss arising in consequence of the advice;

(e) the contract must identify the adviser; and

(f) the contract must state that the conditions regulating compromise contracts under this Act are satisfied.

(4B) A person is a relevant independent adviser for the purposes of subsection (4A)(c) –

(a) if he is a qualified lawyer,

(b) if he is an officer, official, employee or member of an independent trade union who has been certified in writing by the trade union as competent to give advice and as authorised to do so on behalf of the trade union,

(c) if he works at an advice centre (whether as an employee or a volunteer) and has been certified in writing by the centre as competent to give advice and as authorised to do so on behalf of the centre, or

(d) if he is a person of a description specified in an order made by the Secretary of State.

(4BA) But a person is not a relevant independent adviser for the purposes of subsection (4A)(c) in relation to the complainant –

(a) if he is, is employed by or is acting in the matter for the other party or a person who is connected with the other party,

(b) in the case of a person within subsection (4B)(b) or (c), if the trade union or advice centre is the other party or a person who is connected with the other party,

(c) in the case of a person within subsection (4B)(c), if the complainant makes a payment for the advice received from him, or

(d) in the case of a person of a description specified in an order under subsection (4B)(d), if any condition specified in the order in relation to the giving of advice by persons of that description is not satisfied.

(4BB) In subsections (4B)(a) 'qualified lawyer' means –

(a) as respects England and Wales, a barrister (whether in practice as such or employed to give legal advice), a solicitor who holds a practising certificate, or a person other than a barrister or solicitor who is an authorised advocate or authorised litigator (within the meaning of the Courts and Legal Services Act 1990), and

(b) as respects Scotland, an advocate (whether in practice as such or employed to give legal advice), or a solicitor who holds a practising certificate.

(4BC) In subsection (4B)(b) 'independent trade union' has the same meaning as in the Trade Union and Labour Relations (Consolidation) Act 1992.

(4C) For the purposes of subsection (4BA) any two persons are to be treated as connected –

(a) if one is a company of which the other (directly or indirectly) has control, or

(b) if both are companies of which a third person (directly or indirectly) has control.

(4D) An agreement under which the parties agree to submit a dispute to arbitration –

(a) shall be regarded for the purposes of subsection (4)(a) and (aa) as being a contract settling a complaint if –

(i) the dispute is covered by a scheme having effect by virtue of an aorder under section 212A of the Trade Union and Labour Relations (Consolidation) Act 1992, and

(ii) the agreement is to submit it to arbitration in accordance with the scheme, but

(b) shall be regarded for those purposes as neither being nor including such a contract in any other case.

(5) On the application of any person interested in a contract to which subsection (2) applies, a designated county court or a sheriff court may make such order as it thinks just for removing or modifying any term made unenforceable by that subsection; but such an order shall not be made unless all persons affected have been given notice of the application (except where under rules of court notice may

be dispensed with) and have been afforded an opportunity to make representations to the court.

(6) An order under subsection (5) may include provision as respects any period before the making of the order.

78   General interpretation provisions

(1) In this Act, unless the context otherwise requires – ...

'act' includes a deliberate omission;

'advertisement' includes every form of advertisement or notice, whether to the public or not, and whether in a newspaper or other publication, by television or radio, by display of notices, signs, labels, showcards or goods, by distribution of samples, circulars, catalogues, price lists or other material, by exhibition of pictures, models or films, or in any other way, and references to the publishing of advertisements shall be construed accordingly; ...

'the Commission' means the Commission for Racial Equality; ...

'designated county court' has the meaning given by section 67(1);

'discrimination' and related terms shall be construed in accordance with section 3(3); ...

'education' includes any form of training or instruction; ...

'employment' means employment under a contract of service or of apprenticeship or a contract personally to execute any work or labour, and related expressions shall be construed accordingly;

'employment agency' means a person who, for profit or not, provides services for the purpose of finding employment for workers or supplying employers with workers; ...

'final' shall be construed in accordance with subsection (4);

'firm' has the meaning given by section 4 of the Partnership Act 1890;

'formal investigation' means an investigation under section 48; ...

'general notice', in relation to any person, means a notice published by him at a time and in a manner appearing to him suitable for securing that the notice is seen within a reasonable time by persons likely to be affected by it;

'genuine occupational qualification' shall be construed in accordance with section 5;

'Great Britain' includes such of the territorial waters of the United Kingdom as are adjacent to Great Britain; ...

'non-discrimination notice' means a notice under section 58;

'notice' means a notice in writing;

'prescribed' means prescribed by regulations made by the Secretary of State;

'profession' includes any vocation or occupation; ...

'racial grounds' and 'racial group' have the meaning given by section 3(1); ...

'trade' includes any business;

'training' includes any form of education or instruction; ...

(4) For the purposes of this Act a non-discrimination notice or a finding by a court or tribunal becomes final when an appeal against the notice or finding is dismissed, withdrawn or abandoned or when the time for appealing expires without an appeal having been brought; and for this purpose an appeal against a non-discrimination notice shall be taken to be dismissed if, notwithstanding that a requirement of the notice is quashed on appeal, a direction is given in respect of it under section 59(3).
...

As amended by the Criminal Justice Act 1982, ss38, 46; Housing Act 1988, s137; Employment Act 1989, s7(2), (3); Courts and Legal Services Act 1990, s64(2); Trade Union Reform and Employment Rights Act 1993, s39(2), Schedule 6, para 2; Sex Discrimination and Equal Pay (Remedies) Regulations 1993, reg 1(3), Schedule, para 1; Race Relations (Remedies) Act 1994, ss1(1), 2(1), 3(2), Schedule; Armed Forces Act 1996, ss23(4), 35(2), Schedule 7, Pt III; Industrial Tribunals Act 1996, s43, Schedule 1, para 4(1), (2); Employment Rights (Dispute Resolution) Act 1998, ss1(2)(a), (b), 8(2), 9(1), (2)(b), 10(1), (2)(b), 15, Schedule 1, para 3; Equal Opportunities (Employment Legislation) (Territorial Limits) Regulations 1999, reg 3(1), (2); Race Relations (Amendment) Act 2000, s9(1), (2), Schedule 2, paras 4, 8, 9, 13, 14, Schedule 3; Limited Liability Partnerships Regulations 2001, reg 9, Schedule 5, para 7; Race Relations Act 1976 (Amendment) Regulations 2003, regs 3–9, 11–15.

PATENTS ACT 1977

(1977 c 37)

39 Right to employee's inventions

(1) Notwithstanding anything in any rule of law, an invention made by an employee shall, as between him and his employer, be taken to belong to his employer for the purposes of this Act and all other purposes if –

(a) it was made in the course of the normal duties of the employee or in the course of duties falling outside his normal duties, but specifically assigned to him, and the circumstances in either case were such that an invention might reasonably be expected to result from the carrying out of his duties; or

(b) the invention was made in the course of the duties of the employee and, at the time of making the invention, because of the nature of his duties and the particular responsibilities arising from the nature of his duties he had a special obligation to further the interests of the employer's undertaking.

(2) Any other invention made by an employee shall, as between him and his employer, be taken for those purposes to belong to the employee.

(3) Where by virtue of this section an invention belongs, as between him and his employer, to an employee, nothing done –

(a) by or on behalf of the employee or any person claiming under him for the purposes of pursuing an application for a patent, or

(b) by any person for the purpose of performing or working the invention,

shall be taken to infringe any copyright or design right to which, as between him and his employer, his employer is entitled in any model or document relating to the invention.

40 Compensation of employees for certain inventions

(1) Where it appears to the court or the comptroller on an application made by an employee within the prescribed period that –

(a) the employee has made an invention belonging to the employer for which a patent has been granted,

(b) having regard among other things to the size and nature of the employer's undertaking, the invention or the patent for it (or the combination of both) is of outstanding benefit to the employer, and

(c) by reason of those facts it is just that the employee should be awarded compensation to be paid by the employer,

the court or the comptroller may award him such compensation of an amount determined under section 41 below.

(2) Where it appears to the court or the comptroller on an application made by an employee within the prescribed period that –

(a) a patent has been granted for an invention made by and belonging to the employee;

(b) his rights in the invention, or in any patent or application for a patent for the invention, have since the appointed day been assigned to the employer or an exclusive licence under the patent or application has since the appointed day been granted to the employer;

(c) the benefit derived by the employee from the contract of assignment, assignation or grant or any ancillary contract ('the relevant contract') is inadequate in relation to the benefit derived by the employer from the invention or the patent for it (or both); and

(d) by reason of those facts it is just that the employee should be awarded compensation to be paid by the employer in addition to the benefit derived from the relevant contract;

the court or the comptroller may award him such compensation of an amount determined under section 41 below.

(3) Subsections (1) and (2) above shall not apply to the invention of an employee where a relevant collective agreement provides for the payment of compensation in respect of inventions of the same description as that invention to employees of the same description as that employee.

(4) Subsection (2) above shall have effect notwithstanding anything in the relevant contract or any agreement applicable to the invention (other than any such collective agreement).

(5) If it appears to the comptroller on an application under this section that the application involves matters which would more properly be determined by the court, he may decline to deal with it.

(6) In this section –

'the prescribed period', in relation to proceedings before the court, means the period prescribed by rules of court, and

'relevant collective agreement' means a collective agreement within the meaning of the Trade Union and Labour Relations (Consolidation) Act 1992, made by or on behalf of a trade union to which the employee belongs, and by the employer or an employers' association to which the employer belongs which is in force at the time of the making of the invention.

(7) References in this section to an invention belonging to an employer or employee are references to it so belonging as between the employer and the employee.

41   Amount of compensation

(1) An award of compensation to an employee under section 40(1) or (2) above shall be such as will secure for the employee a fair share (having regard to all the circumstances) of the benefit which the employer has derived, or may reasonably be expected to derive, from any of the following –

(a) the invention in question;

(b) the patent for the invention;

(c) the assignment, assignation or grant of –

(i) the property or any right in the invention, or

(ii) the property in, or any right in or under, an application for the patent,

to a person connected with the employer.

(2) For the purposes of subsection (1) above the amount of any benefit derived or expected to be derived by an employer from the assignment, assignation or grant of –

(a) the property in, or any right in or under, a patent for the invention or an application for such a patent; or

(b) the property or any right in the invention;

to a person connected with him shall be taken to be the amount which could reasonably be expected to be so derived by the employer if that person had not been connected with him. ...

(4) In determining the fair share of the benefit to be secured for an employee in respect of an invention which has always belonged to an employer, the court or the comptroller shall, among other things, take the following matters into account, that is to say –

(a) the nature of the employee's duties, his remuneration and the other advantages he derives or has derived from his employment or has derived in relation to the invention under this Act;

(b) the effort and skill which the employee has devoted to making the invention;

(c) the effort and skill which any other person has devoted to making the invention jointly with the employee concerned, and the advice and other assistance contributed by any other employee who is not a joint inventor of the invention; and

(d) the contribution made by the employer to the making, developing and working of the invention by the provision of advice, facilities and other assistance, by the provision of opportunities and by his managerial and commercial skills and activities.

(5) In determining the fair share of the benefit to be secured for an employee in respect of an invention which originally belonged to him, the court or the comptroller shall, among other things, take the following matters into account, that is to say –

(a) any conditions in a licence or licences granted under this Act or otherwise in respect of the invention or the patent for it;

(b) the extent to which the invention was made jointly by the employee with any other person; and

(c) the contribution made by the employer to the making, developing and working of the invention as mentioned in subsection (4)(d) above.

(6) Any order for the payment of compensation under section 40 above may be an order for the payment of a lump sum or for periodical payment, or both. ...

42   Enforceability of contracts relating to employees' inventions

(1) This section applies to any contract (whenever made) relating to inventions made by an employee, being a contract entering into by him –

(a) with the employer (alone or with another); or

(b) with some other person at the request of the employer or in pursuance of the employee's contract of employment.

(2) Any term in a contract to which this section applies which diminishes the employee's rights in inventions of any description made by him after the appointed day and the date of the contract, or in or under patents for those inventions or applications for such patents, shall be unenforceable against him to the extent that it diminishes his rights in an invention of that description so made, or in or under a patent for such an invention or an application for any such patent.

(3) Subsection (2) above shall not be construed as derogating from any duty of confidentiality owed to his employer by an employee by virtue of any rule of law or otherwise.

(4) This section applies to any arrangement made with a Crown employee by or on behalf of the Crown as his employer as it applies to any contract made between an employee and an employer other than the Crown, and for the purposes of this section 'Crown employee' means a person employed under or for the purposes of a government department or any officer or body exercising on behalf of the Crown functions conferred by any enactment or a person serving in the naval, military or air forces of the Crown.

43   Supplementary

(1) Sections 39 to 42 above shall not apply to an invention made before the appointed day.

(2) Sections 39 to 42 above shall not apply to an invention made by an employee unless at the time he made the invention one of the following conditions was satisfied in his case, that is to say –

(a) he was mainly employed in the United Kingdom; or

(b) he was not mainly employed anywhere or his place of employment could not be determined, but his employer had a place of business in the United

Kingdom to which the employee was attached, whether or not he was also attached elsewhere.

(3) In sections 39 to 42 above and this section, except so far as the context otherwise requires, references to the making of an invention by an employee are references to his making it alone or jointly with any other person, but do not include references to his merely contributing advice or other assistance in the making of an invention by another employee.

(4) Any references in sections 39 to 42 above to a patent and to a patent being granted are respectively references to a patent or other protection and to its being granted whether under the law of the United Kingdom or the la win force in any other country or under any treaty or international convention.

(5) For the purposes of sections 40 and 41 above the benefit derived or expected to be derived by an employer from an invention or patent shall, where he dies before any award is made under section 40 above in respect of it, include any benefit derived or expected to be derived from it by his personal representatives or by any person in whom it was vested by their assent.

(5A) For the purposes of section 40 and 41 above the benefit derived or expected to be derived by an employer from an invention shall not include any benefit derived or expected to be derived from the invention after the patent for it has expired or has been surrendered or revoked.

(6) Where an employee dies before an award is made under section 40 above in respect of a patented invention made by him, his personal representatives or their successors in title may exercise his right to make or proceed with an application for compensation under subsection (1) or (2) of that section.

(7) In sections 40 and 41 above and this section 'benefit' means benefit in money or money's worth.

(8) Section 533 of the Income and Corporation Taxes Act 1970 (definition of connected persons) shall apply for determining for the purposes of section 41(2) above whether one person is connected with another as it applies for determining that question for the purposes of the Tax Acts.

130 Interpretation

(1) In this Act, except so far as the context otherwise requires – ...

'appointed day', in any provision of this Act, means the day appointed under section 132 below for the coming into operation of that provision; ...

'comptroller' means the Comptroller-General of Patents, Designs and Trade Marks; ...

'court' means –

(a) as respects England and Wales, the High Court or any patents county court having jurisdiction by virtue of an order under section 287 of the Copyright, Designs and Patents Act 1988; ...

'employee' means a person who works or (where the employment has ceased) worked under a contract of employment or in employment under or for the purposes of a government department or a person who serves (or served) in the naval, military or air forces of the Crown;

'employer', in relation to an employee, means the person by whom the employee is or was employed; ...

'exclusive licence' means a licence from the proprietor of or applicant for a patent conferring on the licensee, or on him and persons authorised by him, to the exclusion of all other persons (including the proprietor or applicant), any right in respect of the invention to which the patent or application relates, and 'exclusive licensee' and 'non-exclusive licence' shall be construed accordingly; ...

'patent' means a patent under this Act; ...

'patented invention' means an invention for which a patent is granted and 'patented process' shall be construed accordingly; ...

'right', in relation to any patent or application, includes an interest in the patent or application and, without prejudice to the foregoing, any reference to a right in a patent includes a reference to a share in the patent; ...

(8) Part I of the Arbitration Act 1996 shall not apply to any proceedings before the comptroller under this Act. ...

NB Section 533 of the Income and Corporation Taxes Act 1970 was repealed by the Income and Corporation Taxes Act 1988. 'Connected persons' is defined in s839, as amended, of that Act.

As amended by the Armed Forces Act 1981, s22(1)–(3); Copyright, Designs and Patents Act 1988, s295, Schedule 5, paras 5, 11(1), (2); Trade Union and Labour Relations (Consolidation) Act 1992, s300(2), Schedule 2, para 9; Arbitration Act 1996, s107(1), Schedule 3, para 33; Patents Act 2004, s10(1)–(7).

SEX DISCRIMINATION ACT 1986

(1986 c 59)

6   Collective agreements and rules of undertakings

(1) Without prejudice to the generality of section 77 of the 1975 Act (which makes provision with respect to the validity and revision of contracts), that section shall apply, as it applies in relation to the term of a contract, to the following, namely –

(a) any term of a collective agreement, including an agreement which was not intended, or is presumed not to have been intended, to be a legally enforceable contract;

(b) any rule made by an employer for application to all or any of the persons who are employed by him or who apply to be, or are, considered by him for employment;

(c) any rule made by an organisation, authority or body to which subsection (2) below applies for application to all or any of its members or prospective members or to all or any of the persons on whom it has conferred authorisations or qualifications or who are seeking the authorisations or qualifications which it has power to confer;

and that section shall so apply whether the agreement was entered into, or the rule made, before or after the coming into force of this section.

(2) This subsection applies to –

(a) any organisation of workers;

(b) any organisation of employers;

(c) any organisation whose members carry on a particular profession or trade for the purposes of which the organisation exists;

(d) any authority or body which can confer an authorisation or qualification which is needed for, or facilitates, engagement in a particular profession or trade.

(3) For the purposes of the said section 77 a term or rule shall be deemed to provide for the doing of an act which would be rendered unlawful by the 1975 Act if –

(a) it provides for the inclusion in any contract of employment of any term which by virtue of an equality clause would fall either to be modified or to be supplemented by an additional term; and

(b) that clause would not be prevented from operating in relation to that contract by section 1(3) of the Equal Pay Act 1970 (material factors justifying discrimination).

(4) Nothing in the said section 77 shall affect the operation of any term or rule in so far as it provides for the doing of a particular act in circumstances where the doing of that act would not be, or be deemed by virtue of subsection (3) above to be, rendered unlawful by the 1975 Act.

(4A) A person to whom this subsection applies may present a complaint to an employment tribunal that a term or rule is void by virtue of subsection (1) of the said section 77 if he has reason to believe –

(a) that the term or rule may at some future time have effect in relation to him, and

(b) where he alleges that it is void by virtue of paragraph (c) of that subsection, that –

(i) an act for the doing of which it provides may at some such time be done in relation to him, and

(ii) the act would be, or be deemed by virtue of subsection (3) above to be, rendered unlawful by the 1975 Act if done in relation to him in present circumstances.

(4B) In the case of a complaint about –

(a) a term of a collective agreement made by or on behalf of –

(i) an employer,

(ii) an organisation of employers of which an employer is a member, or

(iii) an association of such organisations of one of which an employer is a member, or

(b) a rule made by an employer,

subsection (4A) applies to any person who is, or is genuinely and actively seeking to become, one of his employees.

(4C) In the case of a complaint about a rule made by an organisation, authority or body to which subsection (2) above applies, subsection (4A) applies to any person –

(a) who is, or is genuinely and actively seeking to become, a member of the organisation, authority or body,

(b) on whom the organisation, authority or body has conferred an authorisation or qualification, or

(c) who is genuinely and actively seeking an authorisation or qualification which the organisation, authority or body has power to confer.

(4D) When an employment tribunal finds that a complaint presented to it under subsection (4A) above is well-founded the tribunal shall make an order declaring that the term or rule is void.

(5) The avoidance by virtue of the said section 77 of any term or rule which provides

for any person to be discriminated against shall be without prejudice to the following rights except in so far as they enable any person to require another person to be treated less favourably than himself, namely –

(a) such of the rights of the person to be discriminated against; and

(b) such of the rights of any person who will be treated more favourably in direct or indirect consequence of the discrimination,

as are conferred by or in respect of a contract made or modified wholly or partly in pursuance of, or by reference to, that term or rule.

(6) In this section 'collective agreement' means any agreement relating to one or more of the matters mentioned in section 178(2) of the Trade Union and Labour Relations (Consolidation) Act 1992, being an agreement made by or on behalf of one or more employers or one or more organisations of employers or associations of such organisations with one or more organisations of workers or associations of such organisations.

(7) Any expression used in this section and in the 1975 Act has the same meaning in this section as in that Act, and this section shall have effect as if the terms of any service to which Parts II and IV of that Act apply by virtue of subsection (2) of section 85 of that Act (Crown application) were terms of a contract of employment and, in relation to the terms of any such service, as if service for the purposes of any person mentioned in that subsection were employment by that person.

As amended by the Trade Union and Labour Relations (Consolidation) Act 1992, s300(2), Schedule 2, para 36; Trade Union Reform and Employment Rights Act 1993, s32; Employment Rights (Dispute Resolution) Act 1998, s1(2)(a).

EMPLOYMENT ACT 1989

(1989 c 38)

1 Overriding of statutory requirements which conflict with certain provisions of 1975 Act

(1) Any provision of –

(a) an Act passed before the Sex Discrimination Act 1975, or

(b) an instrument approved or made by or under such an Act (including one approved or made after the passing of the 1975 Act),

shall be of no effect in so far as it imposes a requirement to do an act which would be rendered unlawful by any of the provisions of that Act referred to in subsection (2).

(2) Those provisions are –

(a) Part II (discrimination as respects employment);

(b) Part III (discrimination as respects education etc) so far as it applies to vocational training; and

(c) Part IV (other unlawful acts) so far as it has effect in relation to the provisions mentioned in paragraphs (a) and (b) above.

(3) Where in any legal proceedings (of whatever nature) there falls to be determined the question whether subsection (1) operates to negative the effect of any provisions in so far as it requires the application by any person of a provision, criterion or practice falling within section 1(2)(b)(i) or 3(1)(b)(i) of the 1975 Act (indirect discrimination on grounds of sex or marital status) –

(a) it shall be for any party to the proceedings who claims that subsection (1) does not so operate in relation to that provision to show the provision, criterion or practice in question to be justifiable as mentioned in section 1(2)(b)(ii) or 3(1)(b)(ii) of that section; and

(b) the said section 1(2)(b)(ii) or 3(1)(b)(ii) shall accordingly have effect in relation to the provision, criterion or practice as if the reference to the person applying it were a reference to any such party to the proceedings.

(4) Where an Act passed after the 1975 Act, whether before or after the passing of this Act, re-enacts (with or without modification) a provision of an Act passed before the 1975 Act, that provision as re-enacted shall be treated for the purposes of subsection (1) as if it continued to be contained in an Act passed before the 1975 Act.

4 Exemption for discrimination under certain provisions concerned with the protection of women at work

(1) Without prejudice to the operation of section 51 of the 1975 Act (as substituted by section 3(3) above), nothing in –

(a) Part II of that Act,

(b) Part III of that Act so far as it applies to vocational training, or

(c) Part IV of that Act so far as it has effect in relation to the provisions mentioned in paragraphs (a) and (b) above,

shall render unlawful any act done by a person in relation to a woman if it was necessary for that person to do that act in order to comply with any requirement of any of the provisions specified in Schedule 1 to this Act (which are concerned with the protection of women at work). ...

(3) In this section 'woman' means a female person of any age.

5 Exemption for discrimination in connection with certain educational appointments

(1) Nothing in Parts II to IV of the 1975 Act shall render unlawful any act done by a person in connection with the employment of another person as the head teacher or principal of any educational establishment if it was necessary for that person to do that act in order to comply with any requirement of any instrument relating to the establishment that its head teacher or principal should be a member of a particular religious order.

(2) Nothing in –

(a) Part II of the 1975 Act, or

(b) Part IV of that Act so far as it has effect in relation to Part II,

shall render unlawful any act done by a person in connection with the employment of another person as a professor in any university if the professorship in question is, in accordance with any Act or instrument relating to the university, either a canon professorship or one to which a canonry is annexed.

(3) Nothing in the provisions of the 1975 Act referred to in subsection (2)(a) or (b) shall render unlawful any act done by a person in connection with the employment of another person as the head, a fellow or any other member of the academic staff of any college, or institution in the nature of a college, in a university if it was necessary for that person to do that act in order to comply with any requirement of any instrument relating to the college or institution that the holder of the position in question should be a woman.

(4) Subsection (3) shall not apply in relation to instruments taking effect after the commencement of that subsection; and section 6(b) of the Interpretation Act 1978 (words importing the feminine gender to include the masculine) shall not apply to that subsection.

(5) The Secretary of State may by order provide that any provision of subsections (1) to (3) shall not have effect in relation to –

(a) any educational establishment or university specified in the order; or

(b) any class or description of education establishments so specified.

(6) In this section 'educational establishment' means –

(a) any school within the meaning of the Education Act 1944 ...

(b) any college, or institution in the nature of a college, in a university;

(ba) any institution designated by order under section 28 of the Further and Higher Education Act 1992;

(c) any institution designated by order made or having effect as if made under section 129 of the Education Reform Act 1988.

(7) Nothing in this section shall be construed as prejudicing the operation of section 19 of the 1975 Act (exemption for discrimination in relation to employment of ministers of religion).

6 Power of Secretary of State to exempt particular acts of discrimination required by or under statute

(1) The Secretary of State may by order make such provision as he considers appropriate –

(a) for disapplying subsection (1) of section 1 above in the case of any provision to which it appears to him that that subsection would otherwise apply;

(b) for rendering lawful under any of the provisions of the 1975 Act falling within section 1(2) above acts done in order to comply with any requirement –

(i) of a provision whose effect is preserved by virtue of paragraph (a) above, or

(ii) of an instrument approved or made by or under an Act passed after the 1975 Act but before this Act (including one approved or made after the passing of this Act).

(2) Where an Act passed after this Act re-enacts (with or without modification) a provision of an Act passed as mentioned in sub-paragraph (ii) of subsection (1)(b), that provision as re-enacted shall be treated for the purposes of that sub-paragraph as if it continued to be contained in an Act passed as mentioned in that sub-paragraph.

8 Power to exempt discrimination in favour of lone parents in connection with training

(1) The Secretary of State may by order provide with respect to –

(a) any specified arrangements made under section 2 of the Employment and Training Act 1973 (functions of the Secretary of State as respects employment and training) ... or

(b) any specified class or description of training for employment provided otherwise than in pursuance of [that section],

that this section shall apply to such special treatment afforded to or in respect of lone parents in connection with their participation of those arrangements, or in that training or scheme, as is specified or referred to in the order.

(2) Where this section applies to any treatment afforded to or in respect of lone parents, neither the treatment so afforded nor any act done in the implementation of any such treatment shall be regarded for the purposes of the 1975 Act as giving rise to any discrimination falling within section 3 of that Act (discrimination against married persons for purposes of Part II of that Act).

(3) An order under subsection (1) above may specify or refer to special treatment afforded as mentioned in that subsection –

(a) whether it is afforded by the making of any payment or by the fixing of special conditions for participation in the arrangements, training or scheme in question, or otherwise, and

(b) whether it is afforded by the Secretary of State or by some other person;

and, without prejudice to the generality of paragraph (b) of that subsection, any class or description of training for employment specified in such an order by virtue of that paragraph may be framed by reference to the person, or the class or description of persons, by whom the training is provided.

(4) In this section –

(a) 'employment' and 'training' have the same meaning as in the Employment and Training Act 1973; and

(b) 'lone parent' has the same meaning as it has for the purposes of any regulations made in pursuance of section 20(1)(a) of the Social Security Act 1986 (income support).

11 Exemption of Sikhs from requirement to wear safety helmets on construction sites

(1) Any requirement to wear a safety helmet which (apart from this section) would, by virtue of any statutory provisions or rule of law, be imposed on a Sikh who is on a construction site shall not apply to him at any time when he is wearing a turban.

(2) Accordingly, where –

(a) a Sikh who is on a construction site is for the time being wearing a turban, and

(b) (apart from this section) any associated requirement would, by virtue of any statutory provision or rule of law, be imposed –

(i) on the Sikh, or

(ii) on any other person,

in connection with the wearing by the Sikh of a safety helmet, that requirement shall not apply to the Sikh or (as the case may be) to that other person.

(3) In subsection (2) 'associated requirement' means any requirement (other than one falling within subsection (1)) which is related to or connected with the wearing, provision or maintenance of safety helmets.

(4) It is hereby declared that, where a person does not comply with any requirement, being a requirement which for the time being does not apply to him by virtue of subsection (1) or (2) –

(a) he shall not be liable in tort to any person in respect of any injury, loss or damage caused by his failure to comply with that requirement; ...

(5) If a Sikh who is on a construction site –

(a) does not comply with any requirement to wear a safety helmet, being a requirement which for the time being does not apply to him by virtue of subsection (1), and

(b) in consequence of any act or omission of some other person sustains any injury, loss or damage which is to any extent attributable to the fact that he is not wearing a safety helmet in compliance with the requirement,

that other person shall, if liable to the Sikh in tort ... be so liable only to the extent that injury, loss or damage would have been sustained by the Sikh even if he had been wearing a safety helmet in compliance with the requirement.

(6) Where –

(a) the act or omission referred to in subsection (5) causes the death of the Sikh, and

(b) the Sikh would have sustained some injury (other than loss of life) in consequence of the act or omission even if he had been wearing a safety helmet in compliance with the requirement in question,

the amount of any damages which, by virtue of that subsection, are recoverable in tort ... in respect of that injury shall not exceed the amount of any damages which would (apart from that subsection) be so recoverable in respect of the Sikh's death.

(7) In this section –

'building operations' and 'works of engineering construction' have the same meaning as in the Factories Act 1961;

'construction site' means any place where any building operations or works of engineering construction are being undertaken;

'injury' includes loss of life, any impairment of a person's physical or mental condition and any disease;

'safety helmet' means any form of protective headgear; and

'statutory provision' means a provision of an Act or of subordinate legislation.

(8) In this section –

(a) any reference to a Sikh is a reference to a follower of the Sikh religion; and

(b) any reference to a Sikh being on a construction site is a reference to his being there whether while at work or otherwise. ...

12 Protection of Sikhs from racial discrimination in connection with wearing of safety helmets

(1) Where –

(a) any person applies to a Sikh any requirement or condition relation go the wearing by him of a safety helmet while he is on a construction site, and

(b) at the time when he so applies the requirement or condition that person has no reasonable grounds for believing that the Sikh would not wear a turban at all times when on such a site,

then, for the purpose of determining whether the application of the requirement or condition to the Sikh constitutes an act of discrimination falling within section 1(1)(b) of the Race Relations Act 1976 (indirect racial discrimination), the requirement or condition shall be taken to be one which cannot be shown to be justifiable as mentioned in sub-paragraph (ii) of that provision.

(2) Any special treatment afforded to a Sikh in consequence of section 11(1) or (2) above shall not be regarded for the purposes of the Race Relations Act 1976 as giving rise, in relation to any other person, to any discrimination falling within section 1 of that Act.

(3) Subsections (7) to (10) of section 11 above [subsections (9) and (10) relate to construction sites within the territorial sea] shall apply for the purposes of this section as they apply for the purposes of that section.

29 Interpretation, minor and consequential amendments, repeals, etc

(1) In this Act –

'the 1975 Act' means the Sex Discrimination Act 1975;
'act' includes a deliberate omission;
'subordinate legislation' has the same meaning as in the Interpretation Act 1978;
'vocational training' includes advanced vocational training and retraining.

(2) Any reference in this Act to vocational training shall be construed as including a reference to vocational guidance. ...

SCHEDULE 1

PROVISIONS CONCERNED WITH PROTECTION OF
WOMEN AT WORK

Enactments ...

Section 205 of the Public Health Act 1936.

Sections 74, 128 and 131 of the Factories Act 1961.

Statutory instruments

Regulation 3 of the Regulations dated 21st January 1907 (Manufacture of paints and colours). ...

As amended by the Further and Higher Education Act 1992, s93(1), Schedule 8, Pt II, para 93; Employment Rights Act 1996, s242, Schedule 3, Pt I; Sex Discrimination (Indirect Discrimination and Burden of Proof) Regulations 2001, reg 9; Statute Law (Repeals) Act 2004, s1(1), Schedule 1, Pt 8.

SOCIAL SECURITY CONTRIBUTIONS AND BENEFITS ACT 1992

(1992 c 4)

PART XI

STATUTORY SICK PAY

151 Employer's liability

(1) Where an employee has a day of incapacity for work in relation to his contract of service with an employer, that employer shall, if the conditions set out in sections 152 to 154 below are satisfied, be liable to make him, in accordance with the following provisions of this Part of this Act, a payment (to be known as 'statutory sick pay') in respect of that day.

(2) Any agreement shall be void to the extent that it purports –

(a) to exclude, limit or otherwise modify any provision of this Part of this Act, or

(b) to require an employee to contribute (whether directly or indirectly) towards any costs incurred by his employer under this Part of this Act.

(3) For the avoidance of doubt, any agreement between an employer and an employee authorising any deductions from statutory sick pay which the employer is liable to pay to the employee in respect of any period shall not be void by virtue of subsection (2)(a) above if the employer –

(a) is authorised by that or another agreement to make the same deductions from any contractual remuneration which he is liable to pay in respect of the same period, or

(b) would be so authorised if he were liable to pay contractual remuneration in respect of that period.

(4) For the purposes of this Part of this Act a day of incapacity for work in relation to a contract of service means a day on which the employee concerned is, or is deemed in accordance with regulations to be, incapable by reason of some specific disease or bodily or mental disablement of doing work which he can reasonably be expected to do under that contract.

(5) In any case where an employee has more than one contract of service with the same employer the provisions of this Part of this Act shall, except in such cases as

may be prescribed and subject to the following provisions of this Part of this Act, have effect as if the employer were a different employer in relation to each contract of service.

(6) Circumstances may be prescribed in which, notwithstanding the provisions of subsections (1) to (5) above, the liability to make payments of statutory sick pay is to be a liability of the Commissioners for Her Majesty's Revenue and Customs. ...

152 Period of incapacity for work

(1) The first condition is that the day in question forms part of a period of incapacity for work.

(2) In this Part of this Act 'period of incapacity for work' means any period of four or more consecutive days, each of which is a day of incapacity for work in relation to the contract of service in question.

(3) Any two periods of incapacity for work which are separated by a period of not more than 8 weeks shall be treated as a single period of incapacity for work. ...

(5) No day of the week shall be disregarded in calculating any period of consecutive days for the purposes of this section.

(6) A day may be a day of incapacity for work in relation to a contract of service, and so form part of a period of incapacity for work, notwithstanding that –

(a) it falls before the making of the contract or after the contract expires or is brought to an end; or

(b) it is not a day on which the employee concerned would be required by that contract to be available for work.

153 Period of entitlement

(1) The second condition is that the day in question falls within a period which is, as between the employee and his employer, a period of entitlement.

(2) For the purposes of this Part of this Act a period of entitlement, as between an employee and his employer, is a period beginning with the commencement of a period of incapacity for work and ending with whichever of the following first occurs –

(a) the termination of that period of incapacity for work;

(b) the day on which the employee reaches, as against the employer concerned, his maximum entitlement to statutory sick pay (determined in accordance with section 155 below);

(c) the day on which the employee's contract of service with the employer concerned expires or is brought to an end;

(d) in the case of an employee who is, or has been, pregnant, the day immediately preceding the beginning of the disqualifying period.

(3) Schedule 11 to this Act has effect for the purpose of specifying circumstances in which a period of entitlement does not arise in relation to a particular period of incapacity for work.

(4) A period of entitlement as between an employee and an employer of his may also be, or form part of, a period of entitlement as between him and another employer of his.

(5) The Secretary of State may by regulations – ...

(7) In a case where the employee's contract of service first takes effect on a day which falls within a period of incapacity for work, the period of entitlement begins with that day.

(8) In a case where the employee's contract of service first takes effect between two periods of incapacity for work which by virtue of section 152(3) above are treated as one, the period of entitlement begins with the first day of the second of those periods.

(9) In any case where, otherwise than by virtue of section 6(1)(b) above, an employee's earnings under a contract of service in respect of the day on which the contract takes effect do not attract a liability to pay secondary Class 1 contributions, subsections (7) and (8) above shall have effect as if for any reference to the contract first taking effect there were substituted a reference to the first day in respect of which the employee's earnings attract such a liability.

(10) Regulations shall make provisions as to an employer's liability under this Part of this Act to pay statutory sick pay to an employee in any case where the employer's contract of service with that employee has been brought to an end by the employer solely, or mainly, for the purpose of avoiding liability for statutory sick pay.

(11) Subsection (2)(d) above does not apply in relation to an employee who has been pregnant if her pregnancy terminated, before the beginning of the disqualifying period, otherwise than by confinement.

(12) In this section –

'confinement' is to be construed in accordance with section 171(1) below;
'disqualifying period' means –

(a) in relation to a woman entitled to statutory maternity pay, the maternity pay period; and
(b) in relation to a woman entitled to maternity allowance, the maternity allowance period;

'maternity allowance period' has the meaning assigned to it by section 35(2) above, and
'maternity pay period' has the meaning assigned to it by section 165(1) below.

154 Qualifying days

(1) The third condition is that the day in question is a qualifying day.

(2) The days which are for the purposes of this Part of this Act to be qualifying days as between an employee and an employer of his (that is to say, those days of

the week on which he is required by his contract of service with that employer to be available for work or which are chosen to reflect the terms of that contract) shall be such day or days as may, subject to regulations, be agreed between the employee and his employer or, failing such agreement, determined in accordance with regulations.

(3) In any case where qualifying days are determined by agreement between an employee and his employer there shall, in each week (beginning with Sunday), be at least one qualifying day.

(4) A day which is a qualifying day as between an employee and an employer of his may also be a qualifying day as between him and another employer of his.

155 Limitations on entitlement

(1) Statutory sick pay shall not be payable for the first three qualifying days in any period of entitlement.

(2) An employee shall not be entitled, as against any one employer, to an aggregate amount of statutory sick pay in respect of any one period of entitlement which exceeds his maximum entitlement.

(3) The maximum entitlement as against any one employer is reached on the day on which the amount to which the employee has become entitled by way of statutory sick pay during the period of entitlement in question first reaches or passes the entitlement limit.

(4) The entitlement limit is an amount equal to 28 times the weekly rate applicable in accordance with section 157 below. ...

156 Notification of incapacity for work

(1) Regulations shall prescribe the manner in which, and the time within which, notice of any day of incapacity for work is to be given by or on behalf of an employee to his employer.

(2) An employer who would, apart from this section, be liable to pay an amount of statutory sick pay to an employee in respect of a qualifying day (the 'day in question') shall be entitled to withhold payment of that amount if –

  (a) the day in question is one in respect of which he has not been duly notified in accordance with regulations under subsection (1) above; or

  (b) he has not been so notified in respect of any of the first three qualifying days in a period of entitlement (a 'waiting day') and the day in question is the first qualifying day in that period of entitlement in respect of which the employer is not entitled to withhold payment –

    (i) by virtue of paragraph (a) above; or

    (ii) in respect of an earlier waiting day by virtue of this paragraph.

(3) Where an employer withholds any amount of statutory sick pay under this section –

(a) the period of entitlement in question shall not be affected; and

(b) for the purposes of calculating his maximum entitlement in accordance with section 155 above the employee shall not be taken to have become entitled to the amount so withheld.

157 Rates of payment

(1) Statutory sick pay shall be payable by an employer at the weekly rate of £68.20. ...

(3) The amount of statutory sick pay payable by any one employer in respect of any day shall be the weekly rate applicable on that day divided by the number of days which are, in the week (beginning with Sunday) in which that day falls, qualifying days as between that employer and the employee concerned.

159A Power to provide for recovery by employers of sums paid by way of statutory sick pay

(1) The Secretary of State may by order provide for the recovery by employers in accordance with the order, of the amount (if any) by which their payments of, or liability incurred for, statutory sick pay in any period exceeds the specified percentage of the amount of their liability for contributions payments in respect of the corresponding period. ...

(3) In this section –

'contributions payments' means payments which a person is required by or under any enactment to make in discharge of any liability of his as an employer in respect of primary or secondary Class 1 contributions; and

'specified' means specified in or determined in accordance with an order under subsection (1). ...

160 Relationship with benefits and other payments, etc

Schedule 12 to this Act has effect with respect to the relationship between statutory sick pay and certain benefits and payments.

163 Interpretation of Part XI and supplementary provisions

(1) In this Part of this Act –

'contract of service' (except in paragraph (a) of the definition below of 'employee) includes any arrangement providing for the terms of appointment of an employee;

'employee' means a person who is –

(a) gainfully employed in Great Britain either under a contract of service or in an office (including elective office) with general earnings (as defined by section 7 of the Income Tax (Earnings and Pensions) Act 2003; and

(b) over the age of 16;

but subject to regulations, which may provide for cases where any such person is not to be treated as an employee for the purposes of this Part of this Act and for cases where any person who would not otherwise be an employee for those purposes is to be treated as an employee for those purposes;

'employer', in relation to an employee and a contract of service of his, means a person who under section 6 above is, or but for the condition in subsection (1)(b) of that section would be, liable to pay secondary Class 1 contributions in relation to any earnings of the employee under the contract;

'period of entitlement' has the meaning given by section 153 above;

'period of incapacity for work' has the meaning given by section 152 above;

'prescribed' means prescribed by regulations;

'qualifying day' has the meaning given by section 154 above;

'week' means any period of 7 days.

(2) For the purposes of this Part of this Act an employee's normal weekly earnings shall, subject to subsection (4) below, be taken to be the average weekly earnings which in the relevant period have been paid to him or paid for his benefit under his contract of service with the employer in question.

(3) For the purposes of subsection (2) above, the expressions 'earning' and 'relevant period' shall have the meaning given to them by regulations.

(4) In such cases as may be prescribed an employee's normal weekly earnings shall be calculated in accordance with regulations. ...

PART XII

STATUTORY MATERNITY PAY

164 Statutory maternity pay – entitlement and liability to pay

(1) Where a woman who is or has been an employee satisfies the conditions set out in this section, she shall be entitled, in accordance with the following provisions of this Part of this Act, to payments to be known as 'statutory maternity pay'.

(2) The conditions mentioned in subsection (1) above are –

(a) that she has been in employed earner's employment with an employer for a continuous period of at least 26 weeks ending with the week immediately preceding the 14th week before the expected week of confinement but has ceased to work for him;

(b) that her normal weekly earnings for the period of 8 weeks ending with the week immediately preceding the 14th week before the expected week of confinement are not less than the lower earnings limit in force under section 5(1)(a) above immediately before the commencement of the 14th week before the expected week of confinement; and

(c) that she had become pregnant and has reached, or been confined before reaching, the commencement of the 11th week before the expected week of confinement.

(3) The liability to make payments of statutory maternity pay to a woman is a liability of any person of whom she has been an employee as mentioned in subsection (2)(a) above.

(4) A woman shall be entitled to payments of statutory maternity pay only if –

(a) she gives the person who will be liable to pay it notice of the date from which she expects his liability to pay her statutory maternity pay to begin; and

(b) the notice is given at least 28 days before that date or, if that is not reasonably practicable, as soon as is reasonably practicable.

(5) The notice shall be in writing if the person who is liable to pay the woman statutory maternity pay so requests.

(6) Any agreement shall be void to the extent that it purports –

(a) to exclude, limit or otherwise modify any provisions of this Part of this Act; or

(b) to require an employee or former employee to contribute (whether directly or indirectly) towards any costs incurred by her employer or former employer under this Part of this Act.

(7) For the avoidance of doubt, any agreement between an employer and an employee authorising any deductions from statutory maternity pay which the employer is liable to pay to the employee in respect of any period shall not be void by virtue of subsection (6)(a) above if the employer –

(a) is authorised by that or another agreement to make the same deductions from any contractual remuneration which he is liable to pay in respect of the same period, or

(b) would be so authorised if he were liable to pay contractual remuneration in respect of that period.

(8) Regulations shall make provision as to a former employer's liability to pay statutory maternity pay to a woman in any case where the former employer's contract of service with her has been brought to an end by the former employer solely, or mainly, for the purpose of avoiding liability for statutory maternity pay.

(9) The Secretary of State may by regulations – ...

165 The maternity pay period

(1) Statutory maternity pay shall be payable, subject to the provisions of this Part of this Act, in respect of each week during a prescribed period ('the maternity pay period') of a duration not exceeding 26 weeks.

(2) Subject to subsections (3) and (7) below, the first week of the maternity pay period shall be the 11th week before the expected week of confinement.

(3) Cases may be prescribed in which the first week of the period is to be a prescribed week later than the 11th week before the expected week of confinement,

but not later than the week immediately following the week in which she is confined.

(4) Statutory maternity pay shall not be payable to a woman by a person in respect of any week during any part of which she works under a contract of service with him.

(5) It is immaterial for the purposes of subsection (4) above whether the work referred to in that subsection is work under a contract of service which existed immediately before the maternity pay period or a contract of service which did not so exist.

(6) Except in such cases as may be prescribed, statutory maternity pay shall not be payable to a woman in respect of any week after she had been confined and during any part of which she works for any employer who is not liable to pay her statutory maternity pay.

(7) Regulations may provide that this section shall have effect subject to prescribed modifications ...

166 Rate of statutory maternity pay

(1) Statutory maternity pay shall be payable to a woman –

(a) at the earnings-related rate, in respect of the first 6 weeks in respect of which it is payable; and

(b) at whichever is the lower of the earnings-related rate and such weekly rate as may be prescribed, in respect of the remaining portion of the maternity pay period.

(2) The earnings-related rate is a weekly rate equivalent to 90 per cent of a woman's normal weekly earnings for the period of 8 weeks immediately preceding the 14th week before the expected week of confinement.

(3) The weekly rate prescribed under subsection (1)(b) above must not be less than the weekly rate of statutory sick pay for the time being specified in section 157(1) above or, if two or more such rates are for the time being so specified, the higher or highest of those rates.

167 Funding of employers' liabilities in respect of statutory maternity pay

(1) Regulations shall make provision for the payment by employers of statutory maternity pay to be funded by the Commissioners of Inland Revenue to such extent as may be prescribed.

(2) Regulations under subsection (1) shall –

(a) make provision for a person who has made a payment of statutory maternity pay to be entitled, except in prescribed circumstances, to recover an amount equal to the sum of –

(i) the aggregate of such of those payments as qualify for small employers' relief; and

(ii) an amount equal to 92 per cent of the aggregate of such of those payments as do not so qualify; and

(b) include provision for a person who has made a payment of statutory maternity pay qualifying for small employers' relief to be entitled, except in prescribed circumstances, to recover an additional amount, determined in such manner as may be prescribed –

(i) by reference to secondary Class 1 contributions paid in respect of statutory maternity pay;

(ii) by reference to secondary Class 1 contributions paid in respect of statutory sick pay; or

(iii) by reference to the aggregate of secondary Class 1 contributions paid in respect of statutory maternity pay and secondary Class 1 contributions paid in respect of statutory sick pay.

(3) For the purposes of this section a payment of statutory maternity pay which a person is liable to make to a woman qualifies for small employers' relief if, in relation to that woman's maternity pay period, the person liable to make the payment is a small employer.

(4) For the purposes of this section 'small employer', in relation to a woman's maternity pay period, shall have the meaning assigned to it by regulations, and, without prejudice to the generality of the foregoing, any such regulations –

(a) may define that expression by reference to the amount of a person's contributions payments for any prescribed period; and

(b) if they do so, may in that connection make provision for the amount of those payments for that prescribed period –

(i) to be determined without regard to any deductions that may be made from them under this section or under any other enactment or instrument; and

(ii) in prescribed circumstances, to be adjusted, estimated or otherwise attributed to him by reference to their amount in any other prescribed period.

(5) Regulations under subsection (1) may, in particular, make provision –

(a) for funding in advance as well as in arrear;

(b) for funding, or the recovery of amounts due under provision made by virtue of subsection (2)(b), by means of deductions from such amounts for which employers are accountable to the Commissioners of Inland Revenue as may be prescribed, or otherwise;

(c) for the recovery by the Commissioners of Inland Revenue of any sums overpaid to employers under the regulations.

(6) Where in accordance with any provision of regulations under subsection (1) an amount has been deducted from an employer's contributions payments, the amount

so deducted shall (except in such cases as may be prescribed) be treated for the purposes of any provision made by or under any enactment in relation to primary or secondary Class 1 contributions –

(a) as having been paid (on such date as may be determined in accordance with the regulations), and

(b) as having been received by the Commissioners of Inland Revenue,

towards discharging the employer's liability in respect of such contributions.

(7) Regulations under this section must be made with the concurrence of the Commissioners of Inland Revenue.

(8) In this section 'contributions payments', in relation to an employer, means any payments which the employer is required, by or under any enactment, to make in discharge of any liability in respect of primary or secondary Class 1 contributions.

171 Interpretation of Part XII and supplementary provisions

(1) In this Part of this Act –

'confinement' means –

(a) labour resulting in the issue of a living child, or

(b) labour after 24 weeks of pregnancy resulting in the issue of a child whether alive or dead,

and 'confined' shall be construed accordingly; and where a woman's labour begun on one day results in the issue of a child on another day she shall be taken to be confined on the day of the issue of the child or, if labour results in the issue of twins or a greater number of children, she shall be taken to be confined on the day of the issue of the last of them;

'dismissed' is to be construed in accordance with Part X of the Employment Rights Act 1996;

'employee' means a woman who is –

(a) gainfully employed in Great Britain either under a contract of service or in an office (including elective office) with general earnings (as defined by section 7 of the Income Tax (Earnings and Pensions) Act 2003); and

(b) over the age of 16;

but subject to regulations made with the concurrence of Her Majesty's Revenue and Customs which may provide for cases where any such woman is not to be treated as an employee for the purposes of this Part of this Act and for cases where a woman who would not otherwise be an employee for those purposes is to be treated as an employee for those purposes;

'employer', in relation to a woman who is an employee, means a person who under section 6 above is, or but for the condition in subsection (1)(b) of that section would be, liable to pay secondary Class 1 contributions in relation to any of her earnings;

'maternity pay period' has the meaning assigned to it by section 165(1) above;

'modifications' includes additions, omissions and amendments, and related expressions shall be construed accordingly;

'prescribed' means specified in or determined in accordance with regulations;

'week' means a period of 7 days beginning with Sunday or such other period as may be prescribed in relation to any particular case or class of cases. ...

(4) For the purposes of this Part of this Act a woman's normal weekly earnings shall, subject to subsection (6) below, be taken to be the average weekly earnings which in the relevant period have been paid to her or paid for her benefit under the contract of service with the employer in question.

(5) For the purposes of subsection (4) above 'earnings' and 'relevant period' shall have the meanings given to them by regulations.

(6) In such case as may be prescribed a woman's normal weekly earnings shall be calculated in accordance with regulations. ...

PART 12ZA

STATUTORY PATERNITY PAY

171ZA Entitlement: birth

(1) Where a person satisfies the conditions in subsection (2) below, he shall be entitled in accordance with the following provisions of this Part to payments to be known as "statutory paternity pay".

(2) The conditions are –

(a) that he satisfies prescribed conditions –

(i) as to relationship with a newborn child, and

(ii) as to relationship with the child's mother;

(b) that he has been in employed earner's employment with an employer for a continuous period of at least 26 weeks ending with the relevant week;

(c) that his normal weekly earnings for the period of 8 weeks ending with the relevant week are not less than the lower earnings limit in force under section 5(1)(a) above at the end of the relevant week; and

(d) that he has been in employed earner's employment with the employer by reference to whom the condition in paragraph (b) above is satisfied for a continuous period beginning with the end of the relevant week and ending with the day on which the child is born.

(3) The references in subsection (2) above to the relevant week are to the week immediately preceding the 14th week before the expected week of the child's birth.

(4) A person's entitlement to statutory paternity pay under this section shall not be affected by the birth, or expected birth, of more than one child as a result of the same pregnancy.

(5) In this section, 'newborn child' includes a child stillborn after twenty-four weeks of pregnancy.

171ZB Entitlement: adoption

(1) Where a person satisfies the conditions in subsection (2) below, he shall be entitled in accordance with the following provisions of this Part to payments to be known as 'statutory paternity pay'.

(2) The conditions are –

    (a) that he satisfies prescribed conditions –

        (i) as to relationship with a child who is placed for adoption under the law of any part of the United Kingdom, and

        (ii) as to relationship with a person with whom the child is so placed for adoption;

    (b) that he has been in employed earner's employment with an employer for a continuous period of at least 26 weeks ending with the relevant week;

    (c) that his normal weekly earnings for the period of 8 weeks ending with the relevant week are not less than the lower earnings limit in force under section 5(1)(a) at the end of the relevant week;

    (d) that he has been in employed earner's employment with the employer by reference to whom the condition in paragraph (b) above is satisfied for a continuous period beginning with the end of the relevant week and ending with the day on which the child is placed for adoption; and

    (e) where he is a person with whom the child is placed for adoption, that he has elected to receive statutory paternity pay.

(3) The references in subsection (2) to the relevant week are to the week in which the adopter is notified of being matched with the child for the purposes of adoption.

(4) A person may not elect to receive statutory paternity pay if he has elected in accordance with section 171ZL below to receive statutory adoption pay.

(5) Regulations may make provision about elections for the purposes of subsection (2)(e) above.

(6) A person's entitlement to statutory paternity pay under this section shall not be affected by the placement for adoption of more than one child as part of the same arrangement.

(7) In this section, 'adopter', in relation to a person who satisfies the condition under subsection (2)(a)(ii) above, means the person by reference to whom he satisfies that condition.

171ZC Entitlement: general

(1) A person shall be entitled to payments of statutory paternity pay in respect of any period only if –

(a) he gives the person who will be liable to pay it notice of the date from which he expects the liability to pay him statutory paternity pay to begin; and

(b) the notice is given at least 28 days before that date or, if that is not reasonably practicable, as soon as is reasonably practicable.

(2) The notice shall be in writing if the person who is liable to pay the statutory paternity pay so requests.

(3) The Secretary of State may by regulations – ...

171ZD Liability to make payments

(1) The liability to make payments of statutory paternity pay under section 171ZA or 171ZB above is a liability of any person of whom the person entitled to the payments has been an employee as mentioned in subsection (2)(b) and (d) of that section.

(2) Regulations shall make provision as to a former employer's liability to pay statutory paternity pay to a person in any case where the former employee's contract of service with him has been brought to an end by the former employer solely, or mainly, for the purpose of avoiding liability for statutory paternity pay.

(3) The Secretary of State may, with the concurrence of the Commissioners for Her Majesty's Revenue and Customs, by regulations specify circumstances in which, notwithstanding this section, liability to make payments of statutory paternity pay is to be a liability of the Commissioners.

171ZE Rate and period of pay

(1) Statutory paternity pay shall be payable at such fixed or earnings-related weekly rate as may be prescribed by regulations, which may prescribe different kinds of rate for different cases.

(2) Statutory paternity pay shall be payable in respect of –

(a) a period of two consecutive weeks within the qualifying period beginning on such date within that period as the person entitled may choose in accordance with regulations, or

(b) if regulations permit the person entitled to choose to receive statutory paternity pay in respect of –

(i) a period of a week, or

(ii) two non-consecutive periods of a week,

such week or weeks within the qualifying period as he may choose in accordance with regulations.

(3) For the purposes of subsection (2) above, the qualifying period shall be determined in accordance with regulations, which shall secure that it is a period of at least 56 days beginning –

(a) in the case of a person to whom the conditions in section 171ZA(2) above apply, with the date of the child's birth, and

(b) in the case of a person to whom the conditions in section 171ZB(2) above apply, with the date of the child's placement for adoption.

(4) Statutory paternity pay shall not be payable to a person in respect of a statutory pay week if it is not his purpose at the beginning of the week –

(a) to care for the child by reference to whom he satisfies the condition in sub-paragraph (i) of section 171ZA(2)(a) or 171ZB(2)(a) above, or

(b) to support the person by reference to whom he satisfies the condition in sub-paragraph (ii) of that provision.

(5) A person shall not be liable to pay statutory paternity pay to another in respect of a statutory pay week during any part of which the other works under a contract of service with him.

(6) It is immaterial for the purposes of subsection (5) above whether the work referred to in that subsection is work under a contract of service which existed immediately before the statutory pay week or a contract of service which did not so exist.

(7) Except in such cases as may be prescribed, statutory paternity pay shall not be payable to a person in respect of a statutory pay week during any part of which he works for any employer who is not liable to pay him statutory paternity pay.

(8) The Secretary of State may by regulations specify circumstances in which there is to be no liability to pay statutory paternity pay in respect of a statutory pay week.

(9) Where more than one child is born as a result of the same pregnancy, the reference in subsection (3)(a) to the date of the child's birth shall be read as a reference to the date of birth of the first child born as a result of the pregnancy.

(10) Where more than one child is placed for adoption as part of the same arrangement, the reference in subsection (3)(b) to the date of the child's placement shall be read as a reference to the date of placement of the first child to be placed as part of the arrangement.

(11) In this section –

'statutory pay week', in relation to a person entitled to statutory paternity pay, means a week chosen by him as a week in respect of which statutory paternity pay shall be payable;

'week' means any period of seven days.

171ZF Restrictions on contracting out

(1) Any agreement shall be void to the extent that it purports –

(a) to exclude, limit or otherwise modify any provision of this Part of this Act, or

(b) to require an employee or former employee to contribute (whether directly or indirectly) towards any costs incurred by his employer or former employer under this Part of this Act.

(2) For the avoidance of doubt, any agreement between an employer and an employee authorising any deductions from statutory paternity pay which the employer is liable to pay to the employee in respect of any period shall not be void by virtue of subsection (1)(a) above if the employer –

(a) is authorised by that or another agreement to make the same deductions from any contractual remuneration which he is liable to pay in respect of the same period, or

(b) would be so authorised if he were liable to pay contractual remuneration in respect of that period.

171ZG Relationship with contractual remuneration

(1) Subject to subsections (2) and (3) below, any entitlement to statutory paternity pay shall not affect any right of a person in relation to remuneration under any contract of service ('contractual remuneration').

(2) Subject to subsection (3) below –

(a) any contractual remuneration paid to a person by an employer of his in respect of any period shall go towards discharging any liability of that employer to pay statutory paternity pay to him in respect of that period; and

(b) any statutory paternity pay paid by an employer to a person who is an employee of his in respect of any period shall go towards discharging any liability of that employer to pay contractual remuneration to him in respect of that period.

(3) Regulations may make provision as to payments which are, and those which are not, to be treated as contractual remuneration for the purposes of subsections (1) and (2) above.

171ZH Crown employment-Part 12ZA

The provisions of this Part of this Act apply in relation to persons employed by or under the Crown as they apply in relation to persons employed otherwise than by or under the Crown. ...

171ZJ Part 12ZA: supplementary

(1) In this Part of this Act –

'employer', in relation to a person who is an employee, means a person who under section 6 above is, or but for the condition in subsection (1)(b) of that section would be, liable to pay secondary Class 1 contributions in relation to any of the earnings of the person who is an employee;

'modifications' includes additions, omissions and amendments, and related expressions are to be read accordingly;

'prescribed' means prescribed by regulations.

(2) In this Part of this Act, 'employee' means a person who is –

(a) gainfully employed in Great Britain either under a contract of service or in an office (including elective office) with general earnings (as defined by section 7 of the Income Tax (Earnings and Pensions) Act 2003); and

(b) over the age of 16.

(3) Regulations may provide –

(a) for cases where a person who falls within the definition in subsection (2) above is not to be treated as an employee for the purposes of this Part of this Act, and

(b) for cases where a person who would not otherwise be an employee for the purposes of this Part of this Act is to be treated as an employee for those purposes.

(4) Without prejudice to any other power to make regulations under this Part of this Act, regulations may specify cases in which, for the purposes of this Part of this Act or of such provisions of this Part of this Act as may be prescribed –

(a) two or more employers are to be treated as one;

(b) two or more contracts of service in respect of which the same person is an employee are to be treated as one.

(5) In this Part, except section 171ZE, 'week' means a period of 7 days beginning with Sunday or such other period as may be prescribed in relation to any particular case or class of cases.

(6) For the purposes of this Part of this Act, a person's normal weekly earnings shall, subject to subsection (8) below, be taken to be the average weekly earnings which in the relevant period have been paid to him or paid for his benefit under the contract of service with the employer in question.

(7) For the purposes of subsection (6) above, 'earnings' and 'relevant period' shall have the meanings given to them by regulations.

(8) In such cases as may be prescribed, a person's normal weekly earnings shall be calculated in accordance with regulations.

(9) Where –

(a) in consequence of the establishment of one or more National Health Service trusts under Part 1 of the National Health Service and Community Care Act 1990 (c 19) ..., a person's contract of employment is treated by a scheme under that Part or Act as divided so as to constitute two or more contracts, or

(b) an order under paragraph 23(1) of Schedule 5A to the National Health Service Act 1977 (c 49) provides that a person's contract of employment is so divided, regulations may make provision enabling the person to elect for all of those contracts to be treated as one contract for the purposes of this Part of this Act or such provisions of this Part of this Act as may be prescribed.

(10) Regulations under subsection (9) above may prescribe – ...

(11) The powers under subsections (9) and (10) are without prejudice to any other power to make regulations under this Part of this Act.

(12) Regulations under any of subsections (4) to (10) above must be made with the concurrence of the Board.

171ZK Power to apply Part 12ZA to adoption cases not involving placement

The Secretary of State may by regulations provide for this Part to have effect in relation to cases which involve adoption, but not the placement of a child for adoption under the law of any part of the United Kingdom, with such modifications as the regulations may prescribe.

PART 12ZB

STATUTORY ADOPTION PAY

171ZL Entitlement

(1) Where a person who is, or has been, an employee satisfies the conditions in subsection (2) below, he shall be entitled in accordance with the following provisions of this Part to payments to be known as 'statutory adoption pay'.

(2) The conditions are –

  (a) that he is a person with whom a child is, or is expected to be, placed for adoption under the law of any part of the United Kingdom;

  (b) that he has been in employed earner's employment with an employer for a continuous period of at least 26 weeks ending with the relevant week;

  (c) that he has ceased to work for the employer;

  (d) that his normal weekly earnings for the period of 8 weeks ending with the relevant week are not less than the lower earnings limit in force under section 5(1)(a) at the end of the relevant week; and

  (e) that he has elected to receive statutory adoption pay.

(3) The references in subsection (2)(b) and (d) above to the relevant week are to the week in which the person is notified that he has been matched with the child for the purposes of adoption.

(4) A person may not elect to receive statutory adoption pay if –

  (a) he has elected in accordance with section 171ZB above to receive statutory paternity pay, or

(b) where the child is, or is expected to be, placed for adoption with him as a member of a married couple or civil partnership and his spouse or civil partner is a person to whom the conditions in subsection (2) above apply, his spouse or civil partner has elected to receive statutory adoption pay.

(5) A person's entitlement to statutory adoption pay shall not be affected by the placement, or expected placement, for adoption of more than one child as part of the same arrangement.

(6) A person shall be entitled to payments of statutory adoption pay only if –

(a) he gives the person who will be liable to pay it notice of the date from which he expects the liability to pay him statutory adoption pay to begin; and

(b) the notice is given at least 28 days before that date or, if that is not reasonably practicable, as soon as is reasonably practicable.

(7) The notice shall be in writing if the person who is liable to pay the statutory adoption pay so requests.

(8) The Secretary of State may by regulations – ...

171ZM Liability to make payments

(1) The liability to make payments of statutory adoption pay is a liability of any person of whom the person entitled to the payments has been an employee as mentioned in section 171ZL(2)(b) above.

(2) Regulations shall make provision as to a former employer's liability to pay statutory adoption pay to a person in any case where the former employee's contract of service with him has been brought to an end by the former employer solely, or mainly, for the purpose of avoiding liability for statutory adoption pay.

(3) The Secretary of State may, with the concurrence of the Commissioners for Her Majesty's Revenue and Customs, by regulations specify circumstances in which, notwithstanding this section, liability to make payments of statutory adoption pay is to be a liability of the Commissioners.

171ZN Rate and period of pay

(1) Statutory adoption pay shall be payable at such fixed or earnings-related weekly rate as the Secretary of State may prescribe by regulations, which may prescribe different kinds of rate for different cases.

(2) Statutory adoption pay shall be payable, subject to the provisions of this Part of this Act, in respect of each week during a prescribed period ('the adoption pay period') of a duration not exceeding 26 weeks.

(3) A person shall not be liable to pay statutory adoption pay to another in respect of any week during any part of which the other works under a contract of service with him.

(4) It is immaterial for the purposes of subsection (3) above whether the work

referred to in that subsection is work under a contract of service which existed immediately before the adoption pay period or a contract of service which did not so exist.

(5) Except in such cases as may be prescribed, statutory adoption pay shall not be payable to a person in respect of any week during any part of which he works for any employer who is not liable to pay him statutory adoption pay.

(6) The Secretary of State may by regulations specify circumstances in which there is to be no liability to pay statutory adoption pay in respect of a week.

(7) In subsection (2) above, 'week' means any period of seven days.

(8) In subsections (3), (5) and (6) above, 'week' means a period of seven days beginning with the day of the week on which the adoption pay period begins.

171ZO Restrictions on contracting out

(1) Any agreement shall be void to the extent that it purports –

(a) to exclude, limit or otherwise modify any provision of this Part of this Act, or

(b) to require an employee or former employee to contribute (whether directly or indirectly) towards any costs incurred by his employer or former employer under this Part of this Act.

(2) For the avoidance of doubt, any agreement between an employer and an employee authorising any deductions from statutory adoption pay which the employer is liable to pay to the employee in respect of any period shall not be void by virtue of subsection (1)(a) above if the employer –

(a) is authorised by that or another agreement to make the same deductions from any contractual remuneration which he is liable to pay in respect of the same period, or

(b) would be so authorised if he were liable to pay contractual remuneration in respect of that period.

171ZP Relationship with benefits and other payments etc

(1) Except as may be prescribed, a day which falls within the adoption pay period shall not be treated as a day of incapacity for work for the purposes of determining, for this Act, whether it forms part of a period of incapacity for work for the purposes of incapacity benefit.

(2) Regulations may provide that in prescribed circumstances a day which falls within the adoption pay period shall be treated as a day of incapacity for work for the purposes of determining entitlement to the higher rate of short-term incapacity benefit or to long-term incapacity benefit.

(3) Regulations may provide that an amount equal to a person's statutory adoption pay for a period shall be deducted from any such benefit in respect of the same

period and a person shall be entitled to such benefit only if there is a balance after the deduction and, if there is such a balance, at a weekly rate equal to it.

(4) Subject to subsections (5) and (6) below, any entitlement to statutory adoption pay shall not affect any right of a person in relation to remuneration under any contract of service ('contractual remuneration').

(5) Subject to subsection (6) below –

(a) any contractual remuneration paid to a person by an employer of his in respect of a week in the adoption pay period shall go towards discharging any liability of that employer to pay statutory adoption pay to him in respect of that week; and

(b) any statutory adoption pay paid by an employer to a person who is an employee of his in respect of a week in the adoption pay period shall go towards discharging any liability of that employer to pay contractual remuneration to him in respect of that week.

(6) Regulations may make provision as to payments which are, and those which are not, to be treated as contractual remuneration for the purposes of subsections (4) and (5) above.

(7) In subsection (5) above, 'week' means a period of seven days beginning with the day of the week on which the adoption pay period begins.

171ZQ Crown employment-Part 12ZB

The provisions of this Part of this Act apply in relation to persons employed by or under the Crown as they apply in relation to persons employed otherwise than by or under the Crown.

171ZR Special classes of person

(1) The Secretary of State may with the concurrence of the Treasury make regulations modifying any provision of this Part of this Act in such manner as he thinks proper in its application to any person who is, has been or is to be –

(a) employed on board any ship, vessel, hovercraft or aircraft;

(b) outside Great Britain at any prescribed time or in any prescribed circumstances; or

(c) in prescribed employment in connection with continental shelf operations, as defined in section 120(2) above.

(2) Regulations under subsection (1) above may, in particular, provide – ...

171ZS Part 12ZB: supplementary

(1) In this Part of this Act –

'adoption pay period' has the meaning given by section 171ZN(2) above;

'employer', in relation to a person who is an employee, means a person who under section 6 above is, or but for the condition in subsection (1)(b) of that section would be, liable to pay secondary Class 1 contributions in relation to any of the earnings of the person who is an employee;

'modifications' includes additions, omissions and amendments, and related expressions are to be read accordingly;

'prescribed' means prescribed by regulations.

(2) In this Part of this Act, 'employee' means a person who is –

(a) gainfully employed in Great Britain either under a contract of service or in an office (including elective office) with general earnings (as defined by section 7 of the Income Tax (Earnings and Pensions) Act 2003); and

(b) over the age of 16.

(3) Regulations may provide –

(a) for cases where a person who falls within the definition in subsection (2) above is not to be treated as an employee for the purposes of this Part of this Act, and

(b) for cases where a person who would not otherwise be an employee for the purposes of this Part of this Act is to be treated as an employee for those purposes.

(4) Without prejudice to any other power to make regulations under this Part of this Act, regulations may specify cases in which, for the purposes of this Part of this Act or of such provisions of this Part of this Act as may be prescribed –

(a) two or more employers are to be treated as one;

(b) two or more contracts of service in respect of which the same person is an employee are to be treated as one.

(5) In this Part, except sections 171ZN and 171ZP, 'week' means a period of 7 days beginning with Sunday or such other period as may be prescribed in relation to any particular case or class of cases.

(6) For the purposes of this Part of this Act, a person's normal weekly earnings shall, subject to subsection (8) below, be taken to be the average weekly earnings which in the relevant period have been paid to him or paid for his benefit under the contract of service with the employer in question.

(7) For the purposes of subsection (6) above, 'earnings' and 'relevant period' shall have the meanings given to them by regulations.

(8) In such cases as may be prescribed, a person's normal weekly earnings shall be calculated in accordance with regulations.

(9) Where –

(a) in consequence of the establishment of one or more National Health Service trusts under Part 1 of the National Health Service and Community Care Act 1990 (c 19) ..., a person's contract of employment is treated by a scheme under that Part or Act as divided so as to constitute two or more contracts, or

(b) an order under paragraph 23(1) of Schedule 5A to the National Health Service Act 1977 (c 49) provides that a person's contract of employment is so divided,

regulations may make provision enabling the person to elect for all of those contracts to be treated as one contract for the purposes of this Part of this Act or such provisions of this Part of this Act as may be prescribed.

(10) Regulations under subsection (9) above may prescribe – ...

(11) The powers under subsections (9) and (10) are without prejudice to any other power to make regulations under this Part of this Act.

(12) Regulations under any of subsections (4) to (10) above must be made with the concurrence of the Board.

171ZT Power to apply Part 12ZB to adoption cases not involving placement

The Secretary of State may by regulations provide for this Part to have effect in relation to cases which involve adoption, but not the placement of a child for adoption under the law of any part of the United Kingdom, with such modifications as the regulations may prescribe.

SCHEDULE 11

CIRCUMSTANCES IN WHICH PERIODS OF ENTITLEMENT TO STATUTORY SICK PAY DO NOT ARISE

1. A period of entitlement does not arise in relation to a particular period of incapacity for work in any of the circumstances set out in paragraph 2 below or in such other circumstances as may be prescribed. ...

2. The circumstances are that –

(a) at the relevant date the employee is over the age of 65;

(c) at the relevant date the employee's normal weekly earnings are less than the lower earnings limit then in force under section 5(1)(a) above;

(d) in the period of 57 days ending immediately before the relevant date the employee had at least one day on which –

(i) he was entitled to incapacity benefit (or would have been so entitled had he satisfied the contribution conditions mentioned in section 30A(2)(a) above);

(f) the employee has done no work for his employer under his contract of service;

(g) on the relevant date there is a stoppage of work due to a trade dispute at the employee's place of employment;

(h) the employee is, or has been, pregnant and the relevant date falls within the disqualifying period (within the meaning of section 153(12) above).

3. In this Schedule 'relevant date' means the date on which a period of entitlement

would begin in accordance with section 153 above if this Schedule did not prevent it arising. ...

SCHEDULE 12

RELATIONSHIP OF STATUTORY SICK PAY WITH BENEFITS AND OTHER PAYMENTS, ETC

1. Any day which –

(a) is a day of incapacity for work in relation to any contract of service; and

(b) falls within a period of entitlement (whether or not it is also a qualifying day),

shall not be treated for the purposes of this Act as a day of incapacity for work for the purposes of determining whether a period is a period of incapacity for work for the purposes of incapacity benefit.

2. – (1) Subject to sub-paragraphs (2) and (3) below, any entitlement to statutory sick pay shall not affect any right of an employee in relation to remuneration under any contract of service ('contractual remuneration').

(2) Subject to sub-paragraph (3) below –

(a) any contractual remuneration paid to an employee by an employer of his in respect of a day of incapacity for work shall go towards discharging any liability of that employer to pay statutory sick pay to that employee in respect of that day; and

(b) any statutory sick pay paid by an employer to an employee of his in respect of a day of incapacity for work shall go towards discharging any liability of that employer to pay contractual remuneration to that employee in respect of that day.

(3) Regulations may make provision as to payments which are, and those which are not, to be treated as contractual remuneration for the purposes of sub-paragraph (1) or (2) above. ...

As amended by the Still-Birth (Definition) Act 1992, ss2(1), 4(2); Maternity Allowance and Statutory Maternity Pay Regulations 1994, regs 1(2), (3), 4, 5(1)–(3); Social Security (Incapacity for Work) Act 1994, ss8(4), 11(1), Schedule 1, Pt I, paras 34, 43, 44, Schedule 2; Statutory Sick Pay Act 1994, ss1(2), 3(1); Jobseekers Act 1995, s41(5), Schedule 3; Employment Rights Act 1996, s240, Schedule 1, para 51(1), (5); Social Security Act 1998, ss73, 86(1), (2), Schedule 7, paras 74, 75, Schedule 8; Social Security Contributions (Transfer of Functions, etc) Act 1999, s1(1), Schedule 1(1), paras 9, 13(1)–(3), 15(1), (2); Welfare Reform and Pensions Act 1999, s88, Schedule 13, Pt IV; Social Security Benefits Up-rating Order 2002, art 9; Fixed-term Employees (Prevention of Less Favourable Treatment) Regulations 2002, reg 11, Schedule 2, Pt I, para 1(a); Employment Act 2002, ss2, 4, 18–20, 21(1), 54, Schedule 8(1); Income Tax (Earnings and Pensions) Act 2003, s722, Schedule 6, Pt 2, paras 169, 181, 183, 184; Civil Partnership Act 2004, s254(1), Schedule 24, Pt 3, para 50; Commissioners for Revenue and Customs Act 2005, s50(6), Schedule 4, para 43; Social Security Benefits Up-rating Order 2005, art 9.

SOCIAL SECURITY ADMINISTRATION ACT 1992

(1992 c 5)

14 Duties of employees, etc in relation to statutory sick pay

(1) Any employee who claims to be entitled to statutory sick pay from his employer shall, if so required by his employer, provide such information as may reasonably be required for the purpose of determining the duration of the period of entitlement in question or whether a period of entitlement exists as between them. ...

(3) Where an employee asks an employer of his to provide him with a written statement, in respect of a period before the request is made, of one or more of the following –

   (a) the days within that period which the employer regards as days in respect of which he is liable to pay statutory sick pay to that employee;

   (b) the reasons why the employer does not so regard the other days in that period;

   (c) the employer's opinion as to the amount of statutory sick pay to which the employee is entitled in respect of each of those days,

the employer shall, to the extent to which the request was reasonable, comply with it within a reasonable time.

15 Duties of women, etc in relation to statutory maternity pay

(1) A woman shall provide the person who is liable to pay her statutory maternity pay –

   (a) with evidence as to her pregnancy and the expected date of confinement in such form and at such time as may be prescribed; and

   (b) where she commences work after her confinement but within the maternity pay period, with such additional information as may be prescribed. ...

(2) Where a woman asks an employer or former employer of hers to provide her with a written statement, in respect of a period before the request is made, of one or more of the following –

   (a) the weeks within that period which he regards as weeks in respect of which he is liable to pay statutory maternity pay to the woman;

   (b) the reasons why he does not so regard the other weeks in this period; and

(c) his opinion as to the amount of statutory maternity pay to which the woman is entitled in respect of each of the weeks in respect of which he regards himself as liable to make a payment,

the employer or former employer shall, to the extent to which the request was reasonable, comply with it within a reasonable time.

129 Disclosure by Secretary of State for purpose of determination of period of entitlement to statutory sick pay

Where the Secretary of State considers that it is reasonable for information held by him to be disclosed to an employer, for the purpose of enabling that employer to determine the duration of a period of entitlement under Part XI of the Contributions and Benefits Act [ie, the Social Security Contributions and Benefits Act 1992] in respect of an employee, or whether such a period exists, he may disclose the information to that employer.

130 Duties of employers – statutory sick pay and claims for other benefits

(1) Regulations may make provisions requiring an employer, in a case falling within subsection (3) below to furnish information in connection with the making, by a person who is, or has been, an employee of that employer, of a claim for – ...

(b) a maternity allowance; ...

(3) The cases are –

(a) where, by virtue of paragraph 2 of Schedule 11 to the Contributions and Benefits Act or of regulations made under paragraph 1 of that Schedule, a period of entitlement does not arise in relation to a period of incapacity for work;

(b) where a period of entitlement has come to an end but the period of incapacity for work which was running immediately before the period of entitlement came to an end continues; and

(c) where a period of entitlement has not come to an end but, on the assumption that –

(i) the period of incapacity for work in question continues to run for a prescribed period; and

(ii) there is no material change in circumstances,

the period of entitlement will have ended on or before the end of the prescribed period. ...

131 Disclosure by Secretary of State for purpose of determination of period of entitlement to statutory maternity pay

Where the Secretary of State considers that it is reasonable for information held by him to be disclosed to a person liable to make payments of statutory maternity pay for the purpose of enabling that person to determine –

(a) whether a maternity pay period exists in relation to a woman who is or has been an employee of his; and

(b) if it does, the date of its commencement and the weeks in it in respect of which he may be liable to pay statutory maternity pay,

he may disclose the information to that person.

132 Duties of employers – statutory maternity pay and claims for other benefits

(1) Regulations may make provision requiring an employer in prescribed circumstances to furnish information in connection with the making of a claim by a woman who is or has been his employee for –

(a) a maternity allowance; ...

192 Short title, commencement and extent ...

(2) This Act is to be read, where appropriate, with the Contributions and Benefits Act [1992] ...

TRADE UNION AND LABOUR RELATIONS (CONSOLIDATION) ACT 1992

(1992 c 52)

PART I

TRADE UNIONS

CHAPTER I

INTRODUCTORY

1 Meaning of 'trade union'

In this Act a 'trade union' means an organisation (whether temporary or permanent) –

(a) which consists wholly or mainly of workers of one or more descriptions and whose principal purposes include the regulations of relations between workers of that description or those descriptions and employers or employers' associations; or

(b) which consists wholly or mainly of –

(i) constituent or affiliated organisations which fulfil the conditions in paragraph (a) (or themselves consist wholly or mainly of constituent or affiliated organisations which fulfil those conditions), or

(ii) representatives of such constituent or affiliated organisations,

and whose principal purposes include the regulation of relations between workers and employers or between workers and employers' associations, or the regulations of relations between its constituent or affiliated organisations.

2 The list of trade unions

(1) The Certification Officer shall keep a list of trade unions containing the names of –

(a) the organisations whose names were, immediately before the commencement of this Act, duly entered in the list of trade unions kept by him under section 8 of the Trade Union and Labour Relations Act 1974, and

(b) the names of the organisations entitled to have their names entered in the list in accordance with this Part.

(2) The Certification Officer shall keep copies of the list of trade unions, as for the time being in force, available for public inspection at all reasonable hours free of charge.

(3) A copy of the list shall be included in his annual report.

(4) The fact that the name of an organisation is included in the list of trade unions is evidence ... that the organisation is a trade union.

(5) On the application of an organisation whose name is included in the list, the Certification Officer shall issue it with a certificate to that effect.

(6) A document purporting to be such a certificate is evidence ... that the name of the organisation is entered in the list.

3   Application to have name entered in the list

(1) An organisation of workers, whenever formed, whose name is not entered in the list of trade unions may apply to the Certification Officer to have its name entered in the list.

(2) The application shall be made in such form and manner as the Certification Officer may require and shall be accompanied by –

    (a) a copy of the rules of the organisation,
    (b) a list of its officers,
    (c) the address of its head or main office, and
    (d) the name under which it is or is to be known,

and by the prescribed fee.

(3) If the Certification Officer is satisfied –

    (a) that the organisation is a trade union,
    (b) that subsection (2) has been complied with, and
    (c) that entry of the name in the list is not prohibited by subsection (4),

he shall enter the name of the organisation in the list of trade unions.

(4) The Certification Officer shall not enter the name of an organisation in the list of trade unions if the name is the same as that under which another organisation –

    (a) was on 30th September 1971 registered as a trade union under the Trade Union Acts 1871 to 1964,
    (b) was at any time registered as a trade union or employers' association under the Industrial Relations Act 1971, or
    (c) is for the time being entered in the list of trade unions or in the list of employers' associations kept under Part II of this Act,

or if the name is one so nearly resembling any such name as to be likely to deceive the public.

4   Removal of name from the list

(1) If it appears to the Certification Officer, on application made to him or otherwise, that an organisation whose name is entered in the list of trade unions is not a trade union, he may remove its name from the list.

(2) He shall not do so without giving the organisation notice of his intention and considering any representations made to him by the organisation within such period (of not less than 28 days beginning with the date of the notice) as may be specified in the notice.

(3) The Certification Officer shall remove the name of an organisation from the list of trade unions if –

(a) he is requested by the organisation to do so, or

(b) he is satisfied that the organisation has ceased to exist.

5   Meaning of 'independent trade union'

In this Act an 'independent trade union' means a trade union which –

(a) is not under the domination or control of an employer or group of employers or of one or more employers' associations, and

(b) is not liable to interference by an employer or any such group or association (arising out of the provision of financial or material support or by any other means whatsoever) tending towards such control;

and references to 'independence', in relation to a trade union, shall be construed accordingly.

6   Application for certificate of independence

(1) A trade union whose name is entered on the list of trade unions may apply to the Certification Officer for a certificate that is independent. The application shall be made in such form and manner as the Certification Officer may require and shall be accompanied by the prescribed fee.

(2) The Certification Officer shall maintain a record showing details of all applications made to him under this section and shall keep it available for public inspection (free of charge) at all reasonable hours.

(3) If an application is made by a trade union whose name is not entered on the list of trade unions, the Certification Officer shall refuse a certificate of independence and shall enter that refusal on the record.

(4) In any other case, he shall not come to a decision on the application before the end of the period of one month after it has been entered on the record; and before coming to his decision he shall make such enquiries as he thinks fit and shall take into account any relevant information submitted to him by any person.

(5) He shall then decide whether the applicant trade union is independent and shall enter his decision and the date of his decision on the record.

(6) If he decides that the trade union is independent he shall issue a certificate accordingly; and if he decides that it is not, he shall give reasons for his decision.

7 Withdrawal or cancellation of certificate

(1) The Certification Officer may withdraw a trade union's certificate of independence if he is of the opinion that the union is no longer independent.

(2) Where he proposes to do so he shall notify the trade union and enter notice of the proposal in the record.

(3) He shall not come to a decision on the proposal before the end of the period of one month after notice of it was entered on the record; and before coming to his decision he shall make such enquiries as he thinks fit and shall take into account any relevant information submitted to him by any person.

(4) He shall then decide whether the trade union is independent and shall enter his decision and the date of his decision on the record.

(5) He shall confirm or withdraw the certificate accordingly; and if he decides to withdraw it, he shall give reasons for his decision.

(6) Where the name of an organisation is removed from the list of trade unions, the Certification Officer shall cancel any certificate of independence in force in respect of that organisation by entering on the record the fact that the organisation's name has been removed from that list and that the certificate is accordingly cancelled.

8 Conclusive effect of Certification Officer's decision

(1) A certificate of independence which is in force is conclusive evidence for all purposes that a trade union is independent; and a refusal, withdrawal or cancellation of a certificate of independence, entered on the record, is conclusive evidence for all purposes that a trade union is not independent.

(2) A document purporting to be a certificate of independence and to be signed by the Certification Officer, or by a person authorised to act on his behalf, shall be taken to be such a certificate unless the contrary is proved.

(3) A document purporting to be a certified copy of an entry on the record and to be signed by the Certification Officer, or by a person authorised to ac ton his behalf, shall be taken to be a true copy of such an entry unless the contrary is proved.

(4) If in any proceedings before a court, the Employment Appeal Tribunal, the Central Arbitration Committee, ACAS or an employment tribunal a question arises whether a trade union is independent and there is no certificate of independence in force and no refusal, withdrawal or cancellation of a certificate recorded in relation to that trade union –

    (a) that question shall not be decided in those proceedings, and

    (b) the proceedings shall instead be stayed ... until a certificate of independence has been issued or refused by the Certification Officer.

(5) The body before whom the proceedings are stayed … may refer the question of the independence of the trade union to the Certificate Officer who shall proceed in accordance with section 6 as on an application by that trade union.

9   Appeal against decision of Certification Officer

(1) An organisation aggrieved by the refusal of the Certification Officer to enter its name in the list of trade unions, or by a decision of his to remove its name from the list, may appeal to the Employment Appeal Tribunal on any appealable question.

(2) A trade union aggrieved by the refusal of the Certification Officer to issue it with a certificate of independence, or by a decision of his to withdraw its certificate, may appeal to the Employment Appeal Tribunal on any appealable question.

(4) For the purposes of this section, an appealable question is any question of law arising in the proceedings before, or arising from the decision of, the Certification Officer.

CHAPTER II

STATUS AND PROPERTY OF TRADE UNIONS

10   Quasi-corporate status of trade unions

(1) A trade union is not a body corporate but –

   (a) it is capable of making contracts;

   (b) it is capable of suing and being sued in its own name, whether in proceedings relating to property or founded on contract or tort or any other cause of action; and

   (c) proceedings for an offence alleged to have been committed by it or on its behalf may be brought against it in its own name.

(2) A trade union shall not be treated as if it were a body corporate except to the extent authorised by the provisions of this Part.

(3) A trade union shall not be registered –

   (a) as a company under the Companies Act 1985, or

   (b) under the Friendly Societies Act 1974 or the Industrial and Provident Societies Act 1965;

and any such registration of a trade union (whenever effected) is void.

11   Exclusion of common law rules as to restraint of trade

(1) The purposes of a trade union are not, by reason only that they are in restraint of trade, unlawful so as –

   (a) to make any member of the trade union liable to criminal proceedings for conspiracy or otherwise, or

(b) to make any agreement or trust void or voidable.

(2) No rule of a trade union is unlawful or unenforceable by reason only that it is in restraint of trade.

12 Property to be vested in trustees

(1) All property belonging to a trade union shall be vested in trustees in trust for it.

(2) A judgment, order or award made in proceedings of any description brought against a trade union is enforceable, by way of execution, diligence, punishment for contempt or otherwise, against any property held in trust for it to the same extent that in the same manner as if it were a body corporate.

(3) Subsection (2) has effect subject to section 23 (restriction on enforcement of awards against certain property).

15 Prohibition on use of funds to indemnify unlawful conduct

(1) It is unlawful for property of a trade union to be applied in or towards –

(a) the payment for an individual of a penalty which has been or may be imposed on him for an offence or for contempt of court,

(b) the securing of any such payment, or

(c) the provision of anything for indemnifying an individual in respect of such a penalty.

(2) Where any property of a trade union is so applied for the benefit of an individual on whom a penalty has been or may be imposed, then –

(a) in the case of a payment, an amount equal to the payment is recoverable by the union from him, and

(b) in any other case, he is liable to account to the union for the value of the property applied.

(3) If a trade union fails to bring or continue proceedings which it is entitled to bring by virtue of subsection (2), a member of the union who claims that the failure is unreasonable may apply to the court on that ground for an order authorising him to bring or continue the proceedings on the union's behalf and at the union's expense.

(4) In this section 'penalty', in relation to an offence, includes an order to pay compensation and an order for the forfeiture of any property; and references to the imposition of a penalty for an offence shall be construed accordingly.

(5) The Secretary of State may by order designate offences in relation to which the provisions of this section do not apply. ...

(6) This section does not affect –

(a) any other enactment, any rule of law or any provision of the rules of a trade union which makes it unlawful for the property of a trade union to be applied in a particular way; or

(b) any other remedy available to a trade union, the trustees of its property or any of its members in respect of an unlawful application of the union's property.

(7) In this section 'member', in relation to a trade union consisting wholly or partly of, or of representatives of, constituent or affiliated organisations, includes a member of any of the constituent or affiliated organisations.

16 Remedy against trustees for unlawful use of union property

(1) A member of a trade union who claims that the trustees of the union's property –

(a) have so carried out their functions, or are proposing so to carry out their functions, as to cause or permit an unlawful application of the union's property, or

(b) have complied, or are proposing to comply, with an unlawful direction which has been or may be given, or purportedly given, to them under the rules of the union,

may apply to the court for an order under this section.

(2) In a case relating to property which has already been unlawfully applied, or to an unlawful direction that has already been complied with, an application under this section may be made only by a person who was a member of the union at the time when the property was applied or, as the case may be, the direction complied with.

(3) Where the court is satisfied that the claim is well-founded, it shall make such order as it considers appropriate.

The court may in particular –

(a) require the trustees (if necessary, on behalf of the union) to take all such steps as may be specified in the order for protecting or recovering the property of the union;

(b) appoint a receiver ... the property of the union;

(c) remove one or more of the trustees.

(4) Where the court makes an order under this section in a case in which –

(a) property of the union has been applied in contravention of an order of any court, or in compliance with a direction given in contravention of such an order, or

(b) the trustees were proposing to apply property in contravention of such an order or to comply with any such direction,

the court shall by its order remove all the trustees except any trustee who satisfies the court that there is a good reason for allowing him to remain a trustee.

(5) Without prejudice to any other power of the court, the court may on an application for an order under this section grant such interlocutory relief ... as it considers appropriate.

(6) This section does not affect any other remedy available in respect of a breach of trust by the trustees of a trade union's property.

(7) In this section 'member', in relation to a trade union consisting wholly or partly of, or of representatives of, constituent or affiliated organisations, includes a member of any of the constituent or affiliated organisations.

20 Liability of trade union in certain proceedings in tort

(1) Where proceedings in tort are brought against a trade union –

(a) on the ground that an act –

(i) induces another person to break a contract or interferes or induces another person to interfere with its performance, or

(ii) consists in threatening that a contract (whether one to which the union is a party or not) will be broken or its performance interfered with, or that the union will induce another person to break a contract or interfere with its performance, or

(b) in respect of an agreement or combination by two or more persons to do or to procure the doing of an act which, if it were done without any such agreement or combination, would be actionable in tort on such a ground,

then, for the purpose of determining in those proceedings whether the union is liable in respect of the act in question, that act shall be taken to have been done by the union if, but only if, it is to be taken to have been authorised or endorsed by the trade union in accordance with the following provisions.

(2) An act shall be taken to have been authorised or endorsed by a trade union if it was done, or was authorised or endorsed –

(a) by any person empowered by the rules to do, authorise or endorse acts of the kind in question, or

(b) by the principal executive committee or the president or general secretary, or

(c) by any other committee of the union or any other official of the union (whether employed by it or not).

(3) For the purposes of paragraph (c) of subsection (2) –

(a) any group of persons constituted in accordance with the rules of the union is a committee of the union; and

(b) an act shall be taken to have been done, authorised or endorsed by an official if it was done, authorised or endorsed by, or by any member of, any group of persons of which he was at the material time a member, the purposes of which included organising or co-ordinating industrial action.

(4) The provisions of paragraphs (b) and (c) of subsection (2) apply notwithstanding anything in the rules of the union, or in any contract or rule of law, but subject to the provisions of section 21 (repudiation by union of certain acts).

(5) Where for the purposes of any proceedings an act is by virtue of this section taken to have been one by a trade union, nothing in this section shall affect the liability of another person, in those or any other proceedings, in respect of that act.

(6) In proceedings arising out of an act which is by virtue of this section taken to have been done by a trade union, the power of the court to grant an injunction ... includes power to require the union to take such steps as the court considers appropriate for ensuring –

(a) that there is no, or no further, inducement of persons to take part or to continue to take part in industrial action, and

(b) that no person engages in any conduct after the granting of the injunction or interdict by virtue of having been induced before it was granted to take part or to continue to take part in industrial action.

The provisions of subsections (2) to (4) above apply in relation to proceedings for failure to comply with any such injunction or interdict as they apply in relation to the original proceedings.

(7) In this section 'rules', in relation to a trade union, means the written rules of the union and any other written provision forming part of the contract between a member and the other members.

21 Repudiation by union of certain acts

(1) An act shall not be taken to have been authorised or endorsed by a trade union by virtue only of paragraph (c) of section 20(2) if it was repudiated by the executive, president or general secretary as soon as reasonably practicable after coming to the knowledge of any of them.

(2) Where an act is repudiated –

(a) written notice of the repudiation must be given to the committee or official in question, without delay, and

(b) the union must do its best to give individual written notice of the fact and date of repudiation, without delay –

(i) to every member of the union who the union has reason to believe is taking part, or might otherwise take part, in industrial action as a result of the act, and

(ii) to the employer of every such member.

(3) The notice given to members in accordance with paragraph (b)(i) of subsection (2) must contain the following statement –

'Your union has repudiated the call (or calls) for industrial action to which this notice relates and will give no support to unofficial industrial action taken in response to it (or them). If you are dismissed while taking unofficial industrial action, you will have no right to complain of unfair dismissal.'

(4) If subsection (2) or (3) is not complied with, the repudiation shall be treated as ineffective.

(5) An act shall not be treated as repudiated if at any time after the union concerned purported to repudiate it the executive, president or general secretary has behaved in a manner which is inconsistent with the purported repudiation.

(6) The executive, president or general secretary shall be treated as so behaving if, on a request made to any of them within three months of the purported repudiation by a person who –

(a) is a party to a commercial contract whose performance has been or may be interfered with as a result of the act in question, and

(b) has not been given written notice by the union of the repudiation,

it is not forthwith confirmed in writing that the act has been repudiated.

(7) In this section 'commercial contract' means any contract other than –

(a) a contract of employment, or

(b) any other contract under which a person agrees personally to do work or perform services for another.

22 Limit on damages awarded against trade unions in actions in tort

(1) This section applies to any proceedings in tort brought against a trade union, except –

(a) proceedings for personal injury as a result of negligence, nuisance or breach of duty;

(b) proceedings for breach of duty in connection with the ownership, occupation, possession, control or use of property;

(c) proceedings brought by virtue of Part I of the Consumer Protection Act 1987 (product liability)

(2) In any proceedings in tort to which this section applies the amount which may be awarded against the union by way of damages shall not exceed the following limit –

Number of members of union	Maximum award of damages
Less than 5,000	£10,000
5,000 or more but less than 25,000	£50,000
25,000 or more but less than 100,000	£125,000
100,000 or more	£250,000

(3) The Secretary of State may by order amend subsection (2) so as to vary any of the sums specified; and the order may make such transitional provision as the Secretary of State considers appropriate. ...

(5) In this section –

'breach of duty' means breach of a duty imposed by any rule of law or by or under any enactment;

'personal injury' includes any disease and any impairment of a person's physical or mental condition; and

'property' means any property, whether real or personal ...

23 Restriction on enforcement of awards against certain property

(1) Where in any proceedings an amount is awarded by way of damages, costs or expenses –

(a) against a trade union,

(b) against trustees in whom property is vested in trust for a trade union, in their capacity as such (and otherwise than in respect of a breach of trust on their part), or

(c) against members or officials of a trade union on behalf of themselves and all of the members of the union,

no part of that amount is recoverable by enforcement against any protected property.

(2) The following is protected property –

(a) property belonging to the trustees otherwise than in their capacity as such;

(b) property belonging to any member of the union otherwise than jointly or in common with the other members;

(c) property belonging to an official of the union who is neither a member nor a trustee;

(d) property comprised in the union's political fund where that fund –

(i) is subject to rules of the union which prevent property which is or has been comprised in the fund from being used for financing strikes or other industrial action, and

(ii) was so subject at the time when the act in respect of which the proceedings are brought was done;

(e) property comprised in a separate fund maintained in accordance with the rules of the union for the purpose only of providing provident benefits.

(3) For this purpose 'provident benefits' includes –

(a) any payment expressly authorised by the rules of the union which is made –

(i) to a member during sickness or incapacity from personal injury or while out of work, or

(ii) to an aged member by way of superannuation, or

(iii) to a member who has met with an accident or has lost his tools by fire or theft;

(b) a payment in discharge or aid of funeral expenses on the death of a member or the spouse or civil partner of a member or as provision for the children of a deceased member.

CHAPTER IV

ELECTIONS FOR CERTAIN POSITIONS

46   Duty to hold elections for certain positions

(1) A trade union shall secure –

(a) that every person who holds a position in the union to which this Chapter applies does so by virtue of having been elected to it at an election satisfying the requirements of this Chapter, and

(b) that no person continues to hold such a position for more than five years without being re-elected at such an election.

(2) The position to which this Chapter applies (subject as mentioned below) are –

(a) member of the executive,

(b) any position by virtue of which a person is a member of the executive,

(c) president, and

(d) general secretary.

(3) In this Chapter 'member of the executive' includes any person who, under the rules or practice of the union, may attend and speak at some or all of the meetings of the executive, otherwise than for the purpose of providing the committee with factual information or with technical or professional advice with respect to matters taken into account by the executive in carrying out its functions.

(4) This Chapter does not apply to the position of president or general secretary if the holder of that position –

(a) is not, in respect of that position, either a voting member of the executive or an employee of the union,

(b) holds that position for a period which under the rules of the union cannot end more than 13 months after he took it up, and

(c) has not held either position at any time in the period of twelve months ending with the day before he took up that position.

(4A) This Chapter also does not apply to the position of president if –

(a) the holder of that position was elected or appointed to it in accordance with the rules of the union,

(b) at the time of his election or appointment as president he held a position mentioned in paragraph (a), (b) or (d) of subsection (2) by virtue of having been elected to it at a qualifying election,

(c) it is no more than five years since –

(i) he was elected, or re-elected, to the position mentioned in paragraph (b) which he held at the time of his election or appointment as president, or

(ii) he was elected to another position of a kind mentioned in that paragraph at a qualifying election held after his election or appointment as president of the union, and

(d) he has, at all times since his election or appointment as president, held a position mentioned in paragraph (a), (b) or (d) of subsection (2) by virtue of having been elected to it at a qualifying election.

(5) In subsection (4) a 'voting member of the executive' means a person entitled in his own right to attend meetings of the executive and to vote on matters on which votes are taken by the executive (whether or not he is entitled to attend all such meetings or to vote on all such matters or in all circumstances).

(5A) In subsection (4A) 'qualifying election' means an election satisfying the requirements of this Chapter.

(5B) The 'requirements of this Chapter' referred to in subsections (1) and (5A) are those set out in sections 47 to 52 below.

(6) The provisions of this Chapter apply notwithstanding anything in the rules or practice of the union; and the terms and conditions on which a person is employed by the union shall be disregarded in so far as they would prevent the union from complying with the provisions of this Chapter.

47   Candidates

(1) No member of the trade union shall be unreasonably excluded from standing as a candidate.

(2) No candidate shall be required, directly or indirectly, to be a member of a political party.

(3) A member of a trade union shall not be taken to be unreasonably excluded from standing as a candidate if he is excluded on the ground that he belongs to a class of which all the members are excluded by the rules of the union. But a rule which provides for such a class to be determined by reference to whom the union chooses to exclude shall be disregarded.

48   Election addresses

(1) The trade union shall –

(a) provide every candidate with an opportunity of preparing an election address in his own words and of submitting it to the union to be distributed to the persons accorded entitlement to vote in the election; and

(b) secure that, so far as reasonably practicable, copies of every election address submitted to it in time are distributed to each of those persons by post along with the voting papers for the election.

(2) The trade union may determine the time by which an election address must be submitted to it for distribution; but the time so determined must not be earlier than the latest time at which a person my become a candidate in the election. ...

(8) No-one other than the candidate himself shall incur any civil or criminal liability in respect of the publication of a candidate's election address or of any copy required to be made for the purposes of this section.

49 Appointment of independent scrutineer

(1) The trade union shall, before the election is held, appoint a qualified independent person ('the scrutineer') to carry out –

(a) the functions in relation to the election which are required under this section to be contained in his appointment; and

(b) such additional functions in relation to the election as may be specified in his appointment. ...

50 Entitlement to vote

(1) Subject to the provisions of this section, entitlement to vote shall be accorded equally to all members of the trade union.

(2) The rules of the union may exclude entitlement to vote in the case of all members belonging to one of the following classes, or to a class falling within one of the following –

(a) members who are not in employment;

(b) members who are in arrears in respect of any subscription or contribution due to the union;

(c) members who are apprentices, trainees or students or new members of the union. ...

51 Voting

(1) The method of voting must be by the marking of a voting paper by the person voting. ...

(4) So far as is reasonably practicable, every person who is entitled to vote at the election must –

(a) have sent to him by post, at his home address or another address which he has requested the trade union in writing to treat as his postal address, a voting paper which either lists the candidates at the election or is accompanied by a separate list of those candidates; and

(b) be given a convenient opportunity to vote by post.

(5) The ballot shall be conducted so as to secure that –

(a) so far as is reasonably practicable, those voting do so in secret, and

(b) the votes given at the election are fairly and accurately counted. ...

51A Counting of votes, etc by independent person

(1) The trade union shall ensure that –

(a) the storage and distribution of the voting papers for the purposes of the election, and

(b) the counting of the votes cast in the election,

are undertaken by one or more independent persons appointed by the union. ...

52   Scrutineer's report

(1) The scrutineer's report on the election shall state –

(a) the number of voting papers distributed for the purposes of the election,

(b) the number of voting papers returned to the scrutineer,

(c) the number of valid votes cast in the election for each candidate,

(d) the number of spoiled or otherwise invalid voting papers returned, and

(e) the name of the person (or of each of the persons) appointed under section 51A or, if no person were so appointed, that fact. ...

53   Uncontested elections

Nothing in this Chapter shall be taken to require a ballot to be held at an uncontested election.

54   Remedy for failure to comply with requirements: general

(1) The remedy for a failure on the part of a trade union to comply with the requirements of this Chapter is by way of application under section 55 (to the Certification Officer) or section 56 (to the court).

(2) An application under those sections may be made –

(a) by a person who is a member of the trade union (provided, where the election has been held, he was also a member at the time when it was held), or

(b) by a person who is or was a candidate at the election;

and the references in those sections to a person having a sufficient interest are to such a person.

(3) Where an election has been held, no application under those sections with respect to that election may be made after the end of the period of one year beginning with the day on which the union announced the result of the election.

59   Period for giving effect to election

Where a person holds a position to which this Chapter applies immediately before an election at which he is not re-elected to that position, nothing in this Chapter shall be taken to require the union to prevent him from continuing to hold that position for such period (not exceeding six months) as may reasonably be required for effect to be given to the result of the election.

61   Other supplementary provisions

(1) For the purposes of this Chapter the date on which a contested election is held shall be taken, in the case of an election in which votes may be cast on more than one day, to be the last of those days.

(2) Nothing in this Chapter affects the validity of anything done by a person holding a position to which this Chapter applies.

CHAPTER V

RIGHTS OF TRADE UNION MEMBERS

62 Right to a ballot before industrial action

(1) A member of a trade union who claims that members of the union, including himself, are likely to be or have been induced by the union to take part or to continue to take part in industrial action which does not have the support of a ballot may apply to the court for an order under this section. In this section 'the relevant time' means the time when the application is made.

(2) For this purpose industrial action shall be regarded as having the support of a ballot only if –

(a) the union has held a ballot in respect of the action –

(i) in relation to which the requirements of section 226B so far as applicable before and during the holding of the ballot were satisfied,

(ii) in relation to which the requirements of sections 227 to 231 were satisfied, and

(iii) in which the majority voting in the ballot answered 'Yes' to the question applicable in accordance with section 229(2) to industrial action of the kind which the applicant has been or is likely to be induced to take part in;

(b) such of the requirements of the following sections as have fallen to be satisfied at the relevant time have been satisfied, namely –

(i) section 226B so far as applicable after the holding of the ballot, and

(ii) section 231B;

(bb) section 232A does not prevent the industrial action from being regarded as having the support of the ballot; and

(c) the requirements of section 233 (calling of industrial action with support of ballot) are satisfied.

Any reference in this subsection to a requirement of a provision which is disapplied or modified by section 232 has effect subject to that section.

(3) Where on an application under this section the court is satisfied that the claim is well-founded, it shall make such order as it considers appropriate for requiring the union to take steps for ensuring –

(a) that there is no, or no further, inducement of members of the union to take part or to continue to take part in the industrial action to which the application relates, and

(b) that no member engaged in conduct after the making of the order by virtue of having been induced before the making of the order to take part or continue to take part in the action.

(4) Without prejudiced to any other power of the court, the court may on an

application under this section grant such interlocutory relief (in Scotland, such interim order) as it considers appropriate.

(5) For the purposes of this section an act shall be taken to be done by a trade union if it is authorised or endorsed by the union; and the provisions of section 20(2) to (4) apply for the purpose of determining whether an act is to be taken to be so authorised or endorsed.

Those provisions also apply in relation to proceedings for failure to comply with an order under this section as they apply in relation to the original proceedings.

(6) In this section –

'inducement' includes an inducement which is or would be ineffective, whether because of the member's unwillingness to be influenced by it or for any other reason; and

'industrial action' means a strike or other industrial action by persons employed under contracts of employment.

(7) Where a person holds any office or employment under the Crown on terms which do not constitute a contract of employment between that person and the Crown, those terms shall nevertheless be deemed to constitute such a contract for the purposes of this section.

(8) References in this section to a contract of employment include any contract under which one person personally does work or performs services for another; and related expressions shall be construed accordingly.

(9) Nothing in this section shall be construed as requiring a trade union to hold separate ballots for the purposes of this section and sections 226 to 234 (requirement of ballot before action by trade union).

63 Right not to be denied access to the courts

(1) This section applies where a matter is under the rules of a trade union required or allowed to be submitted for determination or conciliation in accordance with the rules of the union, but a provision of the rules purporting to provide for that to be a person's only remedy has no effect (or would have no effect if there were one).

(2) Notwithstanding anything in the rules of the union or in the practice of any court, if a member or former member of the union begins proceedings in a court with respect to a matter to which this section applies, then if –

(a) he has previously made a valid application to the union for the matter to be submitted for determination or conciliation in accordance with the union's rules, and

(b) the court proceedings are begun after the end of the period of six months beginning with the day on which the union received the application,

the rules requiring or allowing the matter to be so submitted, and the fact that any relevant steps remain to be taken under the rules, shall be regarded for all purposes as irrelevant to any question whether the court proceedings should be dismissed, stayed … or adjourned.

(3) An application shall be deemed to be valid for the purposes of subsection (2)(a) unless the union informed the applicant, before the end of the period of 28 days beginning with the date on which the union received the application, of the respects in which the application contravened the requirements of the rules.

(4) If the court is satisfied that any delay in the taking of relevant steps under the rules is attributable to unreasonable conduct of the person who commenced the proceedings, it may treat the period specified in subsection (2)(b) as extended by such further period as it considers appropriate.

(5) In this section –

(a) references to the rules of a trade union include any arbitration or other agreement entered into in pursuance of a requirement imposed by or under the rules; and

(b) references to the relevant steps under the rules, in relation to any matter, include any steps falling to be taken in accordance with the rules for the purposes of or in connection with the determination or conciliation of the matter, or any appeal, review or reconsideration of any determination or award.

(6) This section does not affect any enactment or rule of law by virtue of which a court would apart from this section disregard any such rules of a trade union or any such fact as is mentioned in subsection (2).

64   Right not to be unjustifiably disciplined

(1) An individual who is or has been a member of a trade union has the right not to be unjustifiably disciplined by the union.

(2) For this purpose an individual is 'disciplined' by a trade union if a determination is made, or purportedly made, under the rules of the union or by an official of the union or a number of persons including an official that –

(a) he should be expelled from the union or a branch or section of the union,

(b) he should pay a sum to the union, to a branch or section of the union or to any other person,

(c) sums tendered by him in respect of an obligation to pay subscriptions or other sums to the union, or to a branch or section of the union, should be treated as unpaid or paid for a different purpose,

(d) he should be deprived to any extent of, or of access to, any benefits, services or facilities which would otherwise be provided or made available to him by virtue of his membership of the union, or a branch or section of the union,

(e) another trade union, or a branch or section of it, should be encouraged or advised not to accept him as a member, or

(f) he should be subjected to some other detriment;

and whether an individual is 'unjustifiably disciplined' shall be determined in accordance with section 65.

(3) Where a determination made in infringement of an individual's right under this section requires the payment of a sum or the performance of an obligation, no person is entitled in any proceedings to rely on that determination for the purpose of recovering the sum or enforcing the obligation.

(4) Subject to that, the remedies for infringement of the right conferred by this section are as provided by sections 66 and 67, and not otherwise.

(5) The right not to be unjustifiably disciplined is in addition to (and not in substitution for) any right which exists apart from this section; and, subject to section 66(4), nothing in this section or sections 65 to 67 affects any remedy for infringement of any such right.

65   Meaning of 'unjustifiably disciplined'

(1) An individual is unjustifiably disciplined by a trade union if the actual or supposed conduct which constitutes the reason, or one of the reasons, for disciplining him is –

(a) conduct to which this section applies, or

(b) something which is believed by the union to amount to such conduct;

but subject to subsection (6) (cases of bad faith in relation to assertion of wrongdoing).

(2) This section applies to conduct which consists in –

(a) failing to participate in or support a strike or other industrial action (whether by members of the union or by others), or indicating opposition to or a lack of support for such action;

(b) failing to contravene, for a purpose connected with such a strike or other industrial action, a requirement imposed on him by or under a contract of employment;

(c) asserting (whether by bringing proceedings or otherwise) that the union, any official or representative of it or a trustee of its property has contravened, or is proposing to contravene, a requirement which is, or is thought to be, imposed by or under the rules of the union or any other agreement or by or under any enactment (whenever passed) or any rule of law;

(d) encouraging or assisting a person –

(i) to perform an obligation imposed on him by a contract of employment, or

(ii) to make or attempt to vindicate any such assertion as is mentioned in paragraph (c);

(e) contravening a requirement imposed by or in consequence of a determination which infringes the individual's or another individual's right not to be unjustifiably disciplined;

(f) failing to agree, or withdrawing agreements, to the making from his wages (in accordance with arrangements between his employer and the union) of deductions representing payments to the union in respect of his membership;

(g) resigning or proposing to resign from the union or from another union, becoming or proposing to become a member of another union, refusing to become a member of another union, or being a member of another union;

(h) working with, or proposing to work with, individuals who are not members of the union or who are or are not members of another union,

(i) working for, or proposing to work for, an employer who employs or who has employed individuals who are not members of the union or who are or are not members of another union; or

(j) requiring the union to do an act which the union is, by any provision of this Act, required to do on the requisition of a member.

(3) This section applies to conduct which involves the Certification Officer being consulted or asked to provide advice or assistance with respect to any matter whatever, or which involves any person being consulted or asked to provide advice or assistance with respect to a matter which forms, or might form, the subject-matter of any such assertion as is mentioned in subsection (2)(c) above.

(4) This section also applies to conduct which consists in proposing to engage in, or doing anything preparatory or incidental to, conduct falling within subsection (2) or (3).

(5) This section does not apply to an act, omission or statement comprised in conduct falling within subsection (2), (3) or (4) above if it is shown that the act, omission or statement is one in respect of which individuals would be disciplined by the union irrespective of whether their acts, omissions or statements were in connection with conduct within subsection (2) or (3) above.

(6) An individual is not unjustifiably disciplined if it is shown –

(a) that the reason for disciplining him, or one of them, is that he made such an assertion as is mentioned in subsection (2)(c), or encouraged or assisted another person to make or attempt to vindicate such an assertion,

(b) that the assertion was false, and

(c) that he made the assertion, or encouraged or assisted another person to make or attempt to vindicate it, in the belief that it was false or otherwise in bad faith,

and that there was no other reason for disciplining him or that the only other reasons were reasons in respect of which he does not fall to be treated as unjustifiably disciplined.

(7) In this section –

'conduct' includes statements, acts and omissions;

'contract of employment', in relation to an individual, includes any agreement between that individual and a person for whom he works or normally works, 'employer' includes such a person and related expressions shall be construed accordingly;

'representative', in relation to a union, means a person acting or purporting to act –

(a) in his capacity as a member of the union, or

(b) on the instructions or advice of a person acting or purporting to act in that capacity or in the capacity of an official of the union;

'require' (on the part of an individual) includes request or apply for, and 'requisition' shall be construed accordingly; and

'wages' shall be construed in accordance with the definitions of 'contract of employment', 'employer' and related expressions.

(8) Where a person holds any office or employment under the Crown on terms which do not constitute a contract of employment between him and the Crown, those terms shall nevertheless be deemed to constitute such a contract for the purposes of this section.

66 Complaint of infringement of right

(1) An individual who claims that he has been unjustifiably disciplined by a trade union may present a complaint against the union to an employment tribunal.

(2) The tribunal shall not entertain such a complaint unless it is presented –

(a) before the end of the period of three months beginning with the date of the making of the determination claimed to infringe the right, or

(b) where the tribunal is satisfied –

(i) that it was not reasonably practicable for the complaint to be presented before the end of that period, or

(ii) that any delay in making the complaint is wholly or partly attributable to a reasonable attempt to appeal against the determination or to have it reconsidered or reviewed,

within such further period as the tribunal considers reasonable.

(3) Where the tribunal finds the complaint well-founded, it shall make a declaration to that effect.

(4) Where a complaint relating to an expulsion which is presented under this section is declared to be well-founded, no complaint in respect of the expulsion shall be presented or proceeded with under section 174 (right not to be excluded or expelled from trade union).

67 Further remedies for infringement of right

(1) An individual whose complaint under section 66 has been declared to be well-founded may make an application to an employment tribunal for one or both of the following –

(a) an award of compensation to be paid to him by the union;

(b) an order that the union pay him an amount equal to any sum which he has paid in pursuance of any such determination as is mentioned in section 64(2)(b).

(3) An application under this section shall not be entertained if made before the end of the period of four weeks beginning with the date of the declaration or after the end of the period of six months beginning with that date.

(5) The amount of compensation awarded shall, subject to the following provisions, be such as the employment tribunal considers just and equitable in all the circumstances.

(6) In determining the amount of compensation to be awarded, the same rule shall be applied concerning the duty of a person to mitigate his loss as applies to damages recoverable under the common law in England and Wales …

(7) Where the employment tribunal finds that the infringement complained of was to any extent caused or contributed to by the action of the applicant, it shall reduce the amount of the compensation by such proportion as it considers just and equitable having regard to that finding.

(8) The amount of compensation calculated in accordance with subsections (5) to (7) shall not exceed the aggregate of –

(a) an amount equal to 30 times the limit for the time being imposed by section 227(1)(a) of the Employment Rights Act 1996 (maximum amount of a week's pay for basic award in unfair dismissal cases), and

(b) an amount equal to the limit for the time being imposed by section 124(1) of that Act (maximum compensatory award in such cases).

(8A) If on the date on which the application was made –

(a) the determination infringing the applicant's right not to be unjustifiably disciplined has not been revoked, or

(b) the union has failed to take all the steps necessary for securing the reversal of anything done for the purpose of giving effect to the determination,

the amount of compensation shall be not less than the amount for the time being specified in section 176(6A).

68   Right not to suffer deduction of unauthorised subscriptions

(1) Where arrangements ('subscription deduction arrangements') exist between the employer of a worker and a trade union relating to the making from workers' wages of deductions representing payments to the union in respect of the workers' membership of the union ('subscription deductions'), the employer shall ensure that no subscription deduction is made from wages payable to the worker on any day unless –

(a) the worker has authorised in writing the making from his wages of subscription deductions; and

(b) the worker has not withdrawn the authorisation.

(2) A worker withdraws an authorisation given for the purposes of subsection (1), in relation to a subscription deduction which falls to be made from wages payable to him on any day, if a written notice withdrawing the authorisation has been received by the employer in time for it to be reasonably practicable for the employer to secure that no such deduction is made.

(3) A worker's authorisation of the making of subscription deductions from his wages shall not give rise to any obligation on the part of the employer to the worker to maintain or continue to maintain subscription deduction arrangements.

(4) In this section and section 68A, 'employer', 'wages' and 'worker' have the same meanings as in the Employment Rights Act 1996.

68A Complaint of infringement of rights

(1) A worker may present a complaint to an employment tribunal that his employer has made a deduction from his wages in contravention of section 68 –

(a) within the period of three months beginning with the date of the payment of the wages from which the deduction, or (if the complaint relates to more than one deduction) the last of the deductions, was made, or

(b) where the tribunal is satisfied that it was not reasonably practicable for the complaint to be presented within that period, within such further period as the tribunal considers reasonable.

(2) Where a tribunal finds that a complaint under this section is well-founded, it shall make a declaration to that effect and shall order the employer to pay to the worker the whole amount of the deduction, less any such part of the amount as has already been paid to the worker by the employer. ...

69 Right to terminate membership of union

In every contract of membership of a trade union, whether made before or after the passing of this Act, a term conferring a right on the member, on giving reasonable notice and complying with any reasonable conditions, to terminate his membership of the union shall be implied.

CHAPTER VA

COLLECTIVE BARGAINING: RECOGNITION

70A Recognition of trade unions

Schedule A1 shall have effect.

70B Training

(1) This section applies where –

(a) a trade union is recognised, in accordance with Schedule A1, as entitled to conduct collective bargaining on behalf of a bargaining unit (within the meaning of Part I of that Schedule), and

(b) a method for the conduct of collective bargaining is specified by the Central Arbitration Committee under paragraph 31(3) of that Schedule (and is not the subject of an agreement under paragraph 31(5)(a) or (b)).

(2) The employer must from time to time invite the trade union to send representatives to a meeting for the purpose of –

(a) consulting about the employer's policy on training for workers within the bargaining unit,

(b) consulting about his plans for training for those workers during the period of six months starting with the day of the meeting, and

(c) reporting about training provided for those workers since the previous meeting.

(3) The date set for a meeting under subsection (2) must not be later than –

(a) in the case of a first meeting, the end of the period of six months starting with the day on which this section first applies in relation to a bargaining unit, and

(b) in the case of each subsequent meeting, the end of the period of six months starting with the day of the previous meeting.

(4) The employer shall, before the period of two weeks ending with the date of a meeting, provide to the trade union any information –

(a) without which the union's representatives would be to a material extent impeded in participating in the meeting, and

(b) which it would be in accordance with good industrial relations practice to disclose for the purposes of the meeting.

(5) Section 182(1) shall apply in relation to the provision of information under subsection (4) as it applies in relation to the disclosure of information under section 181.

(6) The employer shall take account of any written representations about matters raised at a meeting which he receives from the trade union within the period of four weeks starting with the date of the meeting.

(7) Where more than one trade union is recognised as entitled to conduct collective bargaining on behalf of a bargaining unit, a reference in this section to 'the trade union' is a reference to each trade union.

(8) Where at a meeting under this section (Meeting 1) an employer indicates his intention to convene a subsequent meeting (Meeting 2) before the expiry of the period of six months beginning with the date of Meeting 1, for the reference to a period of six months in subsection (2)(b) there shall be substituted a reference to the expected period between Meeting 1 and Meeting 2. ...

70C Section 70B: complaint to employment tribunal

(1) A trade union may present a complaint to an employment tribunal that an employer has failed to comply with his obligations under section 70B in relation to a bargaining unit.

(2) An employment tribunal shall not consider a complaint under this section unless it is presented –

(a) before the end of the period of three months beginning with the date of the alleged failure, or

(b) within such further period as the tribunal considers reasonable in a case where it is satisfied that it was not reasonably practicable for the complaint to be presented before the end of that period of three months.

(3) Where an employment tribunal finds a complaint under this section well-founded it –

(a) shall make a declaration to that effect, and

(b) may make an award of compensation to be paid by the employer to each person who was, at the time when the failure occurred, a member of the bargaining unit.

(4) The amount of the award shall not, in relation to each person, exceed two weeks' pay.

(5) For the purpose of subsection (4) a week's pay –

(a) shall be calculated in accordance with Chapter II of Part XIV of the Employment Rights Act 1996 (taking the date of the employer's failure as the calculation date), and

(b) shall be subject to the limit in section 227(1) of that Act.

(6) Proceedings for enforcement of an award of compensation under this section –

(a) may, in relation to each person to whom compensation is payable, be commenced by that person, and

(b) may not be commenced by a trade union.

CHAPTER VI

APPLICATION OF FUNDS FOR POLITICAL OBJECTS

71 Restriction on use of funds for political objects

(1) The funds of a trade union shall not be applied in the furtherance of the political objects to which this Chapter applies unless –

(a) there is in force in accordance with this Chapter a resolution (a 'political resolution') approving the furtherance of those objects as an object of the union (see sections 73 to 81), and

(b) there are in force rules of the union as to –

(i) the making of payments in furtherance of those objects out of a separate fund, and

(ii) the exemption of any member of the union objecting to contribute to that fund,

which comply with this Chapter (see sections 82, 84 and 85) and have been approved by the Certification Officer.

(2) This applies whether the funds are so applied directly, or in conjunction with another trade union, association or body, or otherwise indirectly.

72   Political objects to which restriction applies

(1) The political objects to which this Chapter applies are the expenditure of money –

(a) on any contribution to the funds of, or on the payment of expenses incurred directly or indirectly by, a political party;

(b) on the provision of any service or property for use by or on behalf of any political party;

(c) in connection with the registration of electors, the candidature of any person, the selection of any candidate or the holding of any ballot by the union in connection with any election to a political office;

(d) on the maintenance of any holder of a political office;

(e) on the holding of any conference or meeting by or on behalf of a political party or of any other meeting the main purpose of which is the transaction of business in connection with a political party.

(f) on the production, publication or distribution of any literature, document, film, sound recording or advertisement the main purpose of which is to persuade people to vote for a political party or candidate or to persuade them not to vote for a political party or candidate.

(2) Where a person attends a conference or meeting as a delegate or otherwise as a participator in the proceedings, any expenditure incurred in connection with his attendance as such shall, for the purposes of subsection (1)(e), be taken to be expenditure incurred on the holding of the conference or meeting.

(3) In determining for the purposes of subsection (1) whether a trade union has incurred expenditure of a kind mentioned in that subsection, no account shall be taken of the ordinary administrative expenses of the union.

(4) In this section –

'candidate' means a candidate for election to a political office and includes a prospective candidate;

'contribution', in relation to the funds of a political party, includes any fee payable for affiliation to, or membership of, the party and any loan made to the party;

'electors' means electors at an election to a political office;

'film' includes any record, however made, of a sequence of visual images, which is capable of being used as a means of showing that sequence as a moving picture;

'local authority' means a local authority within the meaning of section 270 of the Local Government Act 1972 or section 235 of the Local Government (Scotland) Act 1973; and

'political office' means the office of member of Parliament, member of the European Parliament or member of a local authority or any position within a political party.

72A Application of funds in breach of section 71

(1) A person who is a member of a trade union and who claims that it has applied its funds in breach of section 71 may apply to the Certification Officer for a declaration that it has done so.

(2) On an application under this section the Certification Officer –

(a) shall make such enquiries as he thinks fit,

(b) shall give the applicant and the union an opportunity to be heard,

(c) shall ensure that, so far as is reasonably practicable, the application is determined within six months of being made,

(d) may make or refuse the declaration asked for,

(e) shall, whether he makes or refuses the declaration, give reasons for his decision in writing, and

(f) may make written observations on any matter arising from, or connected with, the proceedings.

(3) If he makes a declaration he shall specify in it –

(a) the provisions of section 71 breached, and

(b) the amount of the funds applied in breach.

(4) If he makes a declaration and is satisfied that the union has taken or agreed to take steps with a view to –

(a) remedying the declared breach, or

(b) securing that a breach of the same or any similar kind does not occur in future,

he shall specify those steps in making the declaration.

(5) If he makes a declaration he may make such order for remedying the breach as he thinks just under the circumstances.

(6) Where the Certification Officer requests a person to furnish information to him in connection with enquiries made by him under this section, he shall specify the date by which that information is to be furnished and, unless he considers that it would be inappropriate to do so, shall proceed with his determination of the

application notwithstanding that the information has not been furnished to him by the specified date.

(7) A declaration made by the Certification Officer under this section may be relied on as if it were a declaration made by the court.

(8) Where an order has been made under this section, any person who is a member of the union and was a member at the time it was made is entitled to enforce obedience to the order as if he had made the application on which the order was made.

(9) An order made by the Certification Officer under this section may be enforced in the same way as an order of the court. ...

73 Passing and effect of political resolution

(1) A political resolution must be passed by a majority of those voting on a ballot of the members of the trade union held in accordance with this Chapter.

(2) A political resolution so passed shall take effect as if it were a rule of the union and may be rescinded in the same manner and subject to the same provision as such a rule. ...

74 Approval of political ballot rules

(1) A ballot on a political resolution must be held in accordance with rules of the trade union (its 'political ballot rules') approved by the Certification Officer. ...

75 Appointment of independent scrutineer

(1) The trade union shall, before the ballot is held, appoint a qualified independent person ('the scrutineer') to carry out –

   (a) the functions in relation to the ballot which are required under this section to be contained in his appointment; and

   (b) such additional functions in relation to the ballot as may be specified in his appointment. ...

76 Entitlement to vote

Entitlement to vote in the ballot shall be accorded equally to all members of the trade union.

77 Voting

(1) The method of voting must be by the marking of a voting paper by the person voting. ...

(4) So far as is reasonably practicable, every person who is entitled to vote in the ballot must –

(a) have a voting paper sent to him by post at his home address or another address which he has requested the trade union in writing to treat as his postal address, and

(b) be given a convenient opportunity to vote by post.

(5) The ballot shall be conducted so as to secure that –

(a) so far as is reasonably practicable, those voting do so in secret, and

(b) the votes given in the ballot are fairly and accurately counted.

For the purposes of paragraph (b) an inaccuracy in counting shall be disregarded if it is accidental and on a scale which could not affect the result of the ballot.

77A Counting of votes, etc by independent person

(1) The trade union shall ensure that –

(a) the storage and distribution of the voting papers for the purposes of the ballot, and

(b) the counting of the votes cast in the ballot,

are undertaken by one or more independent persons appointed by the union. ...

78   Scrutineer's report

(1) The scrutineer's report on the ballot shall state –

(a) the number of voting papers distributed for the purposes of the ballot,

(b) the number of voting papers returned to the scrutineer,

(c) the number of valid votes cast in the ballot for and against the resolution,

(d) the number of spoiled or otherwise invalid voting papers returned, and

(e) the name of the person (or of each of the persons) appointed under section 77A or, if no person was so appointed, that fact. ...

79   Remedy for failure to comply with ballot rules: general

(1) The remedy for –

(a) the taking by a trade union of a ballot on a political resolution otherwise than in accordance with political ballot rules approved by the Certification Officer, or

(b) the failure of a trade union, in relation to a proposed ballot on a political resolution, to comply with the political ballot rules so approved,

is by way of application under section 80 (to the Certification Officer) or 81 (to the court).

(2) An application under those sections may be made only by a person who is a member of the trade union and, where the ballot has been held, was a member at the time when it was held. References in those sections to a person having a sufficient interest are to such a person.

(3) No such application may be made after the end of the period of one year beginning with the day on which the union announced the result of the ballot.

82 Rules as to political fund

(1) The trade union's rules must provide –

(a) that payments in the furtherance of the political objects to which this Chapter applies shall be made out of a separate fund (the 'political fund' of the union);

(b) that a member of the union who gives notice in accordance with section 84 that he objects to contributing to the political fund shall be exempt from any obligation to contribute to it;

(c) that a member shall not by reason of being so exempt –

(i) be excluded from any benefits of the union, or

(ii) be placed in any respect either directly or indirectly under a disability or at a disadvantage as compared with other members of the union (except in relation to the control or management of the political fund); and

(d) that contribution to the political fund shall not be made a condition for admission to the union.

(2) A member of a trade union who claims that he is aggrieved by a breach of any rule made in pursuance of this section may complaint to the Certification Officer.

(2A) On a complaint being made to him the Certification Officer shall make such enquiries as he thinks fit.

(3) Where, after giving the member and a representative of the union an opportunity of being heard, the Certification Officer considers that a breach has been committed, he may make such order for remedying the breach as he thinks just under the circumstances.

(3A) Where the Certification Officer requests a person to furnish information to him in connection with enquiries made by him under this section, he shall specify the date by which that information is to be furnished and, unless he considers that it would be inappropriate to do so, shall proceed with his determination of the application notwithstanding that the information has not been furnished to him by the specified date.

(4A) Where an order has been made under this section, any person who is a member of the union and was a member at the time it was made is entitled to enforce obedience to the order as if he had made the complaint on which it was made.

(4B) An order made by the Certification Officer under this section may be enforced –

(a) in England and Wales, in the same way as an order of the county court …

83 Assets and liabilities of political fund

(1) There may be added to a union's political fund only –

(a) sums representing contributions made to the fund by members of the union or by any person other than the union itself, and

(b) property which accrues to the fund in the course of administering the assets of the fund.

(2) The rules of the union shall not be taken to require any member to contribute to the political fund at a time when there is no political resolution in force in relation to the union.

(3) No liability of a union's political fund shall be discharged out of any other fund of the union. This subsection applies notwithstanding any term or condition on which the liability was incurred or that an asset of the other fund has been charged in connection with the liability.

84   Notice of objection to contributing to political fund

(1) A member of a trade union may give notice in the following form, or in a form to the like effect, that he objects to contribute to the political fund:–

Name of Trade Union

POLITICAL FUND (EXEMPTION NOTICE)

I give notice that I object to contributing to the Political Fund of the Union, and am in consequence exempt, in manner provided by Chapter VI of Part I of the Trade Union and Labour Relations (Consolidation) Act 1992, from contributing to that fund.

A.B.

Address

day of   19

(2) On the adoption of a political resolution, notice shall be given to members of the union acquainting them –

(a) that each member has a right to be exempted from contributing to the union's political fund, and

(b) that a form of exemption notice can be obtained by or on behalf of a member either by application at or by post from –

(i) the head office or any branch office of the union, or

(ii) the office of the Certification Officer.

(3) The notice to members shall be given in accordance with rules of the union approved for the purpose by the Certification Officer, who shall have regard in each case to the existing practice and character of the union.

(4) On giving an exemption notice in accordance with this section, a member shall be exempt from contributing to the union's political fund –

(a) where the notice is given within one month of the giving of notice to members under subsection (2) following the passing of a political resolution on a ballot held at a time when no such resolution is in force, as from the date on which the exemption notice is given;

(b) in any other case, as from the 1st January next after the exemption notice is given.

(5) An exemption notice continues to have effect until it is withdrawn.

85 Manner of giving effect to exemptions

(1) Effect may be given to the exemption of members from contributing to the political fund of a union either –

(a) by a separate levy of contributions to that fund from the members who are not exempt, or

(b) by relieving members who are exempt from the payment of the whole or part of any periodical contribution required from members towards the expenses of the union. ...

86 Certificate of exemption or objection to contributing to political fund

(1) If a member of a trade union which has a political fund certifies in writing to his employer that, or to the effect that –

(a) he is exempt from the obligation to contribute to the fund, or

(b) he has, in accordance with section 84, notified the union in writing of his objection to contributing to the fund,

the employer shall ensure that no amount representing a contribution to the political fund is deducted by him from emoluments payable to the member. ...

87 Complaint in respect of employer's failure

(1) A person who claims his employer has failed to comply with section 86 in deducting or refusing to deduct any amount from emoluments payable to him may present a complaint to an employment tribunal.

(2) A tribunal shall not consider a complaint under subsection (1) unless it is presented –

(a) within the period of three months beginning with the date of the payment of the emoluments or (if the complaint relates to more than one payment) the last of the payments, or

(b) where the tribunal is satisfied that it was not reasonably practicable for the complaint to be presented within that period, within such further period as the tribunal considers reasonable.

(3) Where on a complaint under subsection (1) arising out of subsection (3) (refusal to deduct union dues) of section 86 the question arises whether the employer's

refusal to deduct an amount was attributable to the giving of the certificate or was otherwise connected with the duty imposed by subsection (1) of that section, it is for the employer to satisfy the tribunal that it was not.

(4) Where a tribunal finds that a complaint under subsection (1) is well-founded –

(a) it shall make a declaration to that effect and, where the complaint arises out of subsection (1) of section 86, order the employer to pay to the complainant the amount deducted in contravention of that subsection less any part of that amount already paid to him by the employer, and

(b) it may, if it considers it appropriate to do so in order to prevent a repetition of the failure, make an order requiring the employer to take, within a specified time, the steps specified in the order in relation to emoluments payable by him to the complainant. ...

92   Manner of making union rules

If the Certification Officer is satisfied, and certifies, that rules of a trade union made for any of the purposes of this Chapter and requiring approval by him have been approved –

(a) by a majority of the members of the union voting for the purpose, or

(b) by a majority of delegates of the union at a meeting called for the purpose,

the rules shall have effect as rules of the union notwithstanding that the rules of the union as to the alteration of rules or the making of new rules have not been complied with.

95   Appeals from Certification Officer

An appeal lies to the Employment Appeal Tribunal on any question of law arising in proceedings before or arising from any decision of the Certification Officer under this Chapter.

96   Meaning of 'date of the ballot'

In this Chapter the 'date of the ballot' means, in the case of a ballot in which votes may be cast on more than one day, the last of those days.

CHAPTER VIIA

BREACH OF RULES

108A   Right to apply to Certification Officer

(1) A person who claims that there has been a breach or threatened breach of the rules of a trade union relating to any of the matters mentioned in subsection (2) may apply to the Certification Officer for a declaration to that effect, subject to subsections (3) to (7).

(2) The matters are –

(a) the appointment or election of a person to, or the removal of a person from, any office;

(b) disciplinary proceedings by the union (including expulsion);

(c) the balloting of members on any issue other than industrial action;

(d) the constitution or proceedings of any executive committee or of any decision-making meeting;

(e) such other matters as may be specified in an order made by the Secretary of State.

(3) The applicant must be a member of the union, or have been one at the time of the alleged breach or threatened breach.

(4) A person may not apply under subsection (1) in relation to a claim if he is entitled to apply under section 80 [ballot on a political resolution] in relation to the claim.

(5) No application may be made regarding-

(a) the dismissal of an employee of the union;

(b) disciplinary proceedings against an employee of the union.

(6) An application must be made-

(a) within the period of six months starting with the day on which the breach or threatened breach is alleged to have taken place, or

(b) if within that period any internal complaints procedure of the union is invoked to resolve the claim, within the period of six months starting with the earlier of the days specified in subsection (7).

(7) Those days are –

(a) the day on which the procedure is concluded, and

(b) the last day of the period of one year beginning with the day on which the procedure is invoked.

(8) The reference in subsection (1) to the rules of a union includes references to the rules of any branch or section of the union.

(9) In subsection (2)(c) 'industrial action' means a strike or other industrial action by persons employed under contracts of employment. ...

(14) If a person applies to the Certification Officer under this section in relation to an alleged breach or threatened breach he may not apply to the court in relation to the breach or threatened breach; but nothing in this subsection shall prevent such a person from exercising any right to appeal against or challenge the Certification Officer's decision on the application to him.

(15) If –

(a) a person applies to the court in relation to an alleged breach or threatened breach, and

(b) the breach or threatened breach is one in relation to which he could have made an application to the Certification Officer under this section,

he may not apply to the Certification Officer under this section in relation to the breach or threatened breach.

108B   Declarations and orders

(1) The Certification Officer may refuse to accept an application under section 108A unless he is satisfied that the applicant has taken all reasonable steps to resolve the claim by the use of any internal complaints procedure of the union.

(2) If he accepts an application under section 108A the Certification Officer –

(a) shall make such enquiries as he thinks fit,

(b) shall give the applicant and the union an opportunity to be heard,

(c) shall ensure that, so far as is reasonably practicable, the application is determined within six months of being made,

(d) may make or refuse the declaration asked for, and

(e) shall, whether he makes or refuses the declaration, give reasons for his decision in writing.

(3) Where the Certification Officer makes a declaration he shall also, unless he considers that to do so would be inappropriate, make an enforcement order, that is, an order imposing on the union one or both of the following requirements –

(a) to take such steps to remedy the breach, or withdraw the threat of a breach, as may be specified in the order;

(b) to abstain from such acts as may be so specified with a view to securing that a breach or threat of the same or a similar kind does not occur in future.

(4) The Certification Officer shall in an order imposing any such requirement as is mentioned in subsection (3)(a) specify the period within which the union is to comply with the requirement. ...

(6) A declaration made by the Certification Officer under this section may be relied on as if it were a declaration made by the court.

(7) Where an enforcement order has been made, any person who is a member of the union and was a member at the time it was made is entitled to enforce obedience to the order as if he had made the application on which the order was made.

(8) An enforcement order made by the Certification Officer under this section may be enforced in the same way as an order of the court.

108C   Appeals from Certification Officer

An appeal lies to the Employment Appeal Tribunal on any question of law arising in proceedings before or arising from any decision of the Certification Officer under this Chapter

CHAPTER IX

MISCELLANEOUS AND GENERAL PROVISIONS

119 Expressions relating to trade unions

In this Act, in relation to a trade union –

'agent' means a banker or solicitor of, or any person employed as an auditor by, the union or any branch or section of the union;

'branch or section', except where the context otherwise requires, includes a branch or section which is itself a trade union;

'executive' means the principal committee of the union exercising executive functions, by whatever name it is called.

'financial affairs' means affairs of the union relating to any fund which is applicable for the purposes of the union (including any fund of a branch or section of the union which is so applicable);

'general secretary' means the official of the union who holds the office of general secretary or, where there is no such office, holds an office which is equivalent, or (except in section 14(4)) the nearest equivalent, to that of general secretary;

'officer' includes –

(a) any member of the governing body of the union, and

(b) any trustee of any fund applicable for the purposes of the union;

'official' means –

(a) an officer of the union or of a branch or section of the union, or

(b) a person elected or appointed in accordance with the rules of the union to be a representative of its members or of some of them,

and includes a person so elected or appointed who is an employee of the same employer as the members or one or more of the members whom he is to represent;

'president' means the official of the union who holds the office of president or, where there is no such office, who holds an office which is equivalent, or (except in section 14(4) or Chapter IV) the nearest equivalent, to that of president; ...

121 Meaning of 'the court'

In this Part 'the court' (except where the reference is expressed to be in the county court ...) means the High Court ...

PART II

EMPLOYERS' ASSOCIATIONS

122 Meaning of 'employers' association'

(1) In this Act an 'employers' association' means an organisation (whether temporary or permanent) –

(a) which consists wholly or mainly of employers or individual owners of undertakings of one or more descriptions and whose principal purposes include the regulation of relations between employers of that description or those descriptions and workers or trade unions; or

(b) which consists wholly or mainly of –

(i) constituent or affiliated organisations which fulfil the conditions in paragraph (a) (or themselves consist wholly or mainly of constituent or affiliated organisations which fulfil those conditions), or

(ii) representatives of such constituent or affiliated organisations,

and whose principal purposes include the regulations of relations between employers and workers or between employees and trade unions, or the regulation of relations between its constituent or affiliated organisations.

(2) References in this Act to employers' associations include combinations of employers and employers' associations.

123 The list of employers' associations

(1) The Certification Officer shall keep a list of employers' associations containing the names of –

(a) the organisations whose names were, immediately before the commencement of this Act, duly entered in the list of employers' associations kept by him under section 8 of the Trade Union and Labour Relations Act 1974, and

(b) the names of the organisations entitled to have their names entered in the list in accordance with this Part. ...

127 Corporate or quasi-corporate status of employers' associations

(1) An employers' association may be either a body corporate or an unincorporated association.

(2) Where an employers' association is unincorporated –

(a) it is capable of making contracts;

(b) it is capable of suing and being sued in its own name, whether in proceedings relating to property or founded on contract or tort or any other cause of action; and

(c) proceedings for an offence alleged to have been committed by it or on its behalf may be brought against it in its own name.

128 Exclusion of common law rules as to restraint of trade

(1) The purposes of an unincorporated employers' association and, so far as they relate to the regulation of relations between employers and workers or trade unions, the purposes of an employers' association which is a body corporate are not, by reason only that they are in restraint of trade, unlawful so as –

(a) to make any member of the association liable to criminal proceedings for conspiracy or otherwise, or

(b) to make any agreement or trust void or voidable.

(2) No rule of an unincorporated employers' association or, so far as it relates to the regulation of relations between employers and workers or trade unions, of an employers' association which is a body corporate, is unlawful or unenforceable by reason only that it is in restraint of trade.

130 Restriction on enforcement of awards against certain property

(1) Where in any proceedings an amount is awarded by way of damages, costs or expenses –

(a) against an employers' association,

(b) against trustees in whom property is vested n trust for an employers' association, in their capacity as such (and otherwise than in respect of a breach of trust on their part), or

(c) against members or officials of an employers' association on behalf of themselves and all of the members of the association,

no part of that amount is recoverable by enforcement against any protected property.

(2) The following is protected property –

(a) property belonging to the trustees otherwise than in their capacity as such;

(b) property belonging to any member of the association otherwise than jointly or in common with the other members;

(c) property belonging to an official of the association who is neither a member nor a trustee.

132 Application of funds for political objects

(1) Subject to subsections (2) to (5), the provisions of Chapter VI of Part I of this Act (application of funds for political objects) apply to an unincorporated employers' association as in relation to a trade union.

(2) Subsection (1) does not apply to these provisions –

(a) Section 72A; ...

(3) In its application to an unincorporated employers' association, section 79 shall have effect as if at the end of subsection (1) there were inserted –

'The making of an application to the Certification Officer does not prevent the applicant, or any other person, from making an application to the court in respect of the same matter.' ...

PART III

RIGHTS IN RELATION TO UNION MEMBERSHIP AND ACTIVITIES

137 Refusal of employment on grounds related to union membership

(1) It is unlawful to refuse a person employment –

(a) because he is, or is not, a member of a trade union, or

(b) because he is unwilling to accept a requirement –

(i) to take steps to become or cease to be, or to remain or not to become, a member of a trade union, or

(ii) to make payments or suffer deductions in the event of his not being a member of a trade union.

(2) A person who is thus unlawfully refused employment has a right of complaint to an employment tribunal.

(3) Where an advertisement is published which indicates, or might reasonably be understood as indicating –

(a) that employment to which the advertisement relates is open only to a person who is, or is not, a member of a trade union, or

(b) that any such requirement as is mentioned in subsection (1)(b) will be imposed in relation to employment to which the advertisement relates,

a person who does not satisfy that condition or, as the case may be, is unwilling to accept that requirement, and who seeks and is refused employment to which the advertisement relates, shall be conclusively presumed to have been refused employment for that reason.

(4) Where there is an arrangement or practice under which employment is offered only to persons put forward or approved by a trade union, and the trade union puts forward or approves only persons who are members of the union, a person who is not a member of the union and who is refused employment in pursuance of the arrangement or practice shall be taken to have been refused employment because he is not a member of the trade union.

(5) A person shall be taken to be refused employment if he seeks employment of any description with a person and that person –

(a) refuses or deliberately omits to entertain and process his application or enquiry, or

(b) causes him to withdraw or cease to pursue his application or enquiry, or

(c) refuses or deliberately omits to offer him employment of that description, or

(d) makes him an offer of such employment the terms of which are such as no reasonable employer who wishes to fill the post would offer and which is not accepted, or

(e) makes him an offer of such employment but withdraws it or causes him not to accept it.

(6) Where a person is offered employment on terms which include a requirement that he is, or is not, a member of a trade union, or any such requirement as is mentioned in subsection (1)(b), and he does not accept the offer because he does not satisfy or, as the case may be, is unwilling to accept that requirement, he shall be treated as having been refused employment for that reason.

(7) Where a person may not be considered for appointment or election to an office in a trade union unless he is a member of the union, or of a particular branch or section of the union or of one of a number of particular branches or sections of the union, nothing in this section applies to anything done for the purpose of securing compliance with that condition although as holder of the office he would be employed by the union.

For this purpose an 'office' means any position –

(a) by virtue of which the holder is an official of the union, or

(b) to which Chapter IV of Part I applies (duty to hold elections).

(8) The provisions of this section apply in relation to an employment agency acting, or purporting to act, on behalf of an employer as in relation to an employer.

138 Refusal of service of employment agency on grounds related to union membership

(1) It is unlawful for an employment agency to refuse a person any of its services –

(a) because he is, or is not, a member of a trade union, or

(b) because he is unwilling to accept a requirement to take steps to become or cease to be, or to remain or not to become, a member of a trade union.

(2) A person who is thus unlawfully refused any service of an employment agency has a right of complaint to an employment tribunal.

(3) Where an advertisement is published which indicates, or might reasonably be understood as indicating –

(a) that any service of an employment agency is available only to a person who is, or is not, a member of a trade union, or

(b) that any such requirement as is mentioned in subsection (1)(b) will be imposed in relation to a service to which the advertisement relates,

a person who does not satisfy that condition or, as the case may be, is unwilling to accept that requirement, and who seeks to avail himself of and is refused that service, shall be conclusively presumed to have been refused it for that reason.

(4) A person shall be taken to be refused a service if he seeks to avail himself of it and the agency –

(a) refuses or deliberately omits to make the service available to him, or

(b) causes him not to avail himself of the service or to cease to avail himself of it, or

(c) does not provide the same service, on the same terms, as is provided to others.

(5) Where a person is offered a service on terms which include a requirement that he is, or is not, a member of a trade union, or any such requirement as is mentioned in subsection (1)(b), and he does not accept the offer because he does not satisfy or, as the case may be, is unwilling to accept that requirement, he shall be treated as having been refused the service for that reason.

139 Time limit for proceedings

(1) An employment tribunal shall not consider a complaint under section 137 or 138 unless it is presented to the tribunal –

(a) before the end of the period of three months beginning with the date of the conduct to which the complaint relates, or

(b) where the tribunal is satisfied that it was not reasonably practicable for the complaint to be presented before the end of that period, within such further period as the tribunal considers reasonable. ...

140 Remedies

(1) Where the employment tribunal finds that a complaint under section 137 or 138 is well-founded, it shall make a declaration to that effect and may make such of the following as it considers just and equitable –

(a) an order requiring the respondent to pay compensation to the complainant of such amount as the tribunal may determine;

(b) a recommendation that the respondent take within a specified period action appearing to the tribunal to be practicable for the purpose of obviating or reducing the adverse effect on the complainant of any conduct to which the complaint relates.

(2) Compensation shall be assessed on the same basis as damages for breach of statutory duty and may include compensation for injury to feelings.

(3) If the respondent fails without reasonable justification to comply with a recommendation to take action, the tribunal may increase its award of compensation or, if it has not made such an award, make one.

(4) The total amount of compensation shall not exceed the limit for the time being imposed by section 124(1) of the Employment Rights Act 1996 (limit on compensation for unfair dismissal).

141 Complaint against employer and employment agency

(1) Where a person has a right of complaint against a prospective employer and against an employment agency arising out of the same facts, he may present a complaint against either of them or against them jointly. ...

142 Awards against third parties

(1) If in proceedings on a complaint under section 137 or 138 either the complainant or the respondent claims that the respondent was induced to act in the manner complained of by pressure which a trade union or other person exercised on him by calling, organising, procuring or financing a strike or other industrial action, or by threatening to do so, the complainant or the respondent may request the employment tribunal to direct that the person who he claims exercised the pressure be joined... as a party to the proceedings. ...

(4) Where by virtue of section 141 (complaint against employer and employment agency) there is more than one respondent, the above provisions apply to either or both of them.

143 Interpretation and other supplementary provisions

(1) In sections 137 to 143 –

'advertisement' includes every form of advertisement or notice, whether to the public or not, and references to publishing an advertisement shall be construed accordingly;

'employment' means employment under a contract of employment, and related expressions shall be construed accordingly; and

'employment agency' means a person who, for profit or not, provides services for the purpose of finding employment for workers or supplying employers with workers, but subject to subsection (2) below.

(2) For the purposes of sections 137 to 143 as they apply to employment agencies –

(a) services other than those mentioned in the definition of 'employment agency' above shall be disregarded, and

(b) a trade union shall not be regarded as an employment agency by reason of services provided by it only for, or in relation to, its members.

(3) References in sections 137 to 143 to being or not being a member of a trade union are to being or not being a member of any trade union, of a particular trade union or of one of a number of particular trade unions. Any such reference includes a reference to being or not being a member of a particular branch or section of a trade union or of one of a number of particular branches or sections of a trade union.

(4) The remedy of a person for conduct which is unlawful by virtue of section 137 or 138 is by way of a complaint to an employment tribunal in accordance with his Part, and not otherwise. No other legal liability arises by reason that conduct is unlawful by virtue of either of those sections.

144 Union membership requirement in contract for goods or services void

A term or condition of a contract for the supply of goods or services is void in so far as it purports to require that the whole, or some part, of the work done for the purposes of the contract is done only by persons who are, or are not, members of trade unions or of a particular trade union.

145 Refusal to deal on union membership grounds prohibited

(1) A person shall not refuse to deal with a supplier or prospective supplier of goods or services on union membership grounds. 'Refuse to deal' and 'union membership grounds' shall be construed as follows.

(2) A person refuses to deal with a person if, where he maintains (in whatever form) a list of approved suppliers of goods or services, or of persons from whom tenders for the supply of goods or services may be invited, he fails to include the name of that person in that list. He does so on union membership grounds if the ground, or one of the grounds, for failing to include his name is that if that person were to enter into a contract with him for the supply of goods or services, work to be done for the purposes of the contract would, or would be likely to, be done by persons who were, or who were not, members of trade unions or of a particular trade union.

(3) A person refuses to deal with a person if, in relation to a proposed contract for the supply of goods or services –

(a) he excludes that person from the group of persons from whom tenders for the supply of the goods or services are invited, or

(b) he fails to permit that person to submit such a tender, or

(c) he otherwise determines not to enter into a contract with that person for the supply of the goods or services.

He does so on union membership grounds if the ground, or one of the grounds, on which he does so is that if the proposed contract were entered into with that person, work to be done for the purposes of the contract would, or would be likely to, be done by persons who were, or who were not, members of trade unions or of a particular trade union.

(4) A person refuses to deal with a person if he terminates a contract with him for the supply of goods or services. He does so on union membership grounds if the ground, or one of the grounds, on which he does so is that work done, or to be done, for the purposes of the contract has been, or is likely to be, done by persons who are or are not members of trade unions or of a particular trade union.

(5) The obligation to comply with this section is a duty owed to the person with whom there is a refusal to deal and to any other person who may be adversely affected by its contravention; and a breach of the duty is actionable accordingly (subject to the defences and other incidents applying to actions for breach of statutory duty).

145A Inducements relating to union membership or activities

(1) A worker has the right not to have an offer made to him by his employer for the sole or main purpose of inducing the worker –

(a) not to be or seek to become a member of an independent trade union,

(b) not to take part, at an appropriate time, in the activities of an independent trade union,

(c) not to make use, at an appropriate time, of trade union services, or

(d) to be or become a member of any trade union or of a particular trade union or of one of a number of particular trade unions.

(2) In subsection (1) 'an appropriate time' means –

(a) a time outside the worker's working hours, or

(b) a time within his working hours at which, in accordance with arrangements agreed with or consent given by his employer, it is permissible for him to take part in the activities of a trade union or (as the case may be) make use of trade union services.

(3) In subsection (2) 'working hours', in relation to a worker, means any time when, in accordance with his contract of employment (or other contract personally to do work or perform services), he is required to be at work.

(4) In subsections (1) and (2) –

(a) 'trade union services' means services made available to the worker by an independent trade union by virtue of his membership of the union, and

(b) references to a worker's 'making use' of trade union services include his consenting to the raising of a matter on his behalf by an independent trade union of which he is a member.

(5) A worker or former worker may present a complaint to an employment tribunal on the ground that his employer has made him an offer in contravention of this section.

145B Inducements relating to collective bargaining

(1) A worker who is a member of an independent trade union which is recognised, or seeking to be recognised, by his employer has the right not to have an offer made to him by his employer if –

(a) acceptance of the offer, together with other workers' acceptance of offers which the employer also makes to them, would have the prohibited result, and

(b) the employer's sole or main purpose in making the offers is to achieve that result.

(2) The prohibited result is that the workers' terms of employment, or any of those terms, will not (or will no longer) be determined by collective agreement negotiated by or on behalf of the union.

(3) It is immaterial for the purposes of subsection (1) whether the offers are made to the workers simultaneously.

(4) Having terms of employment determined by collective agreement shall not be regarded for the purposes of section 145A (or section 146 or 152) as making use of a trade union service.

(5) A worker or former worker may present a complaint to an employment tribunal on the ground that his employer has made him an offer in contravention of this section.

145C   Time limit for proceedings

An employment tribunal shall not consider a complaint under section 145A or 145B unless it is presented –

    (a) before the end of the period of three months beginning with the date when the offer was made or, where the offer is part of a series of similar offers to the complainant, the date when the last of them was made, or

    (b) where the tribunal is satisfied that it was not reasonably practicable for the complaint to be presented before the end of that period, within such further period as it considers reasonable.

145D   Consideration of complaint

(1) On a complaint under section 145A it shall be for the employer to show what was his sole or main purpose in making the offer.

(2) On a complaint under section 145B it shall be for the employer to show what was his sole or main purpose in making the offers.

(3) On a complaint under section 145A or 145B, in determining any question whether the employer made the offer (or offers) or the purpose for which he did so, no account shall be taken of any pressure which was exercised on him by calling, organising, procuring or financing a strike or other industrial action, or by threatening to do so; and that question shall be determined as if no such pressure had been exercised.

(4) In determining whether an employer's sole or main purpose in making offers was the purpose mentioned in section 145B(1), the matters taken into account must include any evidence –

    (a) that when the offers were made the employer had recently changed or sought to change, or did not wish to use, arrangements agreed with the union for collective bargaining,

    (b) that when the offers were made the employer did not wish to enter into arrangements proposed by the union for collective bargaining, or

    (c) that the offers were made only to particular workers, and were made with the sole or main purpose of rewarding those particular workers for their high level of performance or of retaining them because of their special value to the employer.

145E   Remedies

(1) Subsections (2) and (3) apply where the employment tribunal finds that a complaint under section 145A or 145B is well-founded.

(2) The tribunal –

(a) shall make a declaration to that effect, and

(b) shall make an award to be paid by the employer to the complainant in respect of the offer complained of.

(3) The amount of the award shall be £2,500 (subject to any adjustment of the award that may fall to be made under Part 3 of the Employment Act 2002).

(4) Where an offer made in contravention of section 145A or 145B is accepted –

(a) if the acceptance results in the worker's agreeing to vary his terms of employment, the employer cannot enforce the agreement to vary, or recover any sum paid or other asset transferred by him under the agreement to vary;

(b) if as a result of the acceptance the worker's terms of employment are varied, nothing in section 145A or 145B makes the variation unenforceable by either party.

(5) Nothing in this section or sections 145A and 145B prejudices any right conferred by section 146 or 149.

(6) In ascertaining any amount of compensation under section 149, no reduction shall be made on the ground –

(a) that the complainant caused or contributed to his loss, or to the act or failure complained of, by accepting or not accepting an offer made in contravention of section 145A or 145B, or

(b) that the complainant has received or is entitled to an award under this section.

145F   Interpretation and other supplementary provisions

(1) References in sections 145A to 145E to being or becoming a member of a trade union include references –

(a) to being or becoming a member of a particular branch or section of that union, and

(b) to being or becoming a member of one of a number of particular branches or sections of that union.

(2) References in those sections –

(a) to taking part in the activities of a trade union, and

(b) to services made available by a trade union by virtue of membership of the union,

shall be construed in accordance with subsection (1).

(3) In sections 145A to 145E –

'worker' means an individual who works, or normally works, as mentioned in paragraphs (a) to (c) of section 296(1), and

'employer' means –

(a) in relation to a worker, the person for whom he works;

(b) in relation to a former worker, the person for whom he worked.

(4) The remedy of a person for infringement of the right conferred on him by section 145A or 145B is by way of a complaint to an employment tribunal in accordance with this Part, and not otherwise.

146 Detriment on grounds related to union membership or activities

(1) A worker has the right not to be subjected to any detriment as an individual by any act, or any deliberate failure to act, by his employer if the act or failure takes place for the sole or main purpose of –

(a) preventing or deterring him from being or seeking to become a member of an independent trade union, or penalising him for doing so,

(b) preventing or deterring him from taking part in the activities of an independent trade union at an appropriate time, or penalising him for doing so,

(ba) preventing or deterring him from making use of trade union services at an appropriate time, or penalising him for doing so, or

(c) compelling him to be or become a member of any trade union or of a particular trade union or of one of a number of particular trade unions.

(2) In subsection (1) 'an appropriate time' means –

(a) a time outside the worker's working hours, or

(b) a time within his working hours at which, in accordance with arrangements agreed with or consent given by his employer, it is permissible for him to take part in the activities of a trade union or (as the case may be) make use of trade union services;

and for this purpose 'working hours', in relation to a worker, means any time when, in accordance with his contract of employment (or other contract personally to do work or perform services), he is required to be at work.

(2A) In this section –

(a) 'trade union services' means services made available to the worker by an independent trade union by virtue of his membership of the union, and

(b) references to a worker's 'making use' of trade union services include his consenting to the raising of a matter on his behalf by an independent trade union of which he is a member.

(2B) If an independent trade union of which a worker is a member raises a matter on his behalf (with or without his consent), penalising the worker for that is to be treated as penalising him as mentioned in subsection (1)(ba).

(2C) A worker also has the right not to be subjected to any detriment as an individual by any act, or any deliberate failure to act, by his employer if the act or failure takes place because of the worker's failure to accept an offer made in contravention of section 145A or 145B.

(2D) For the purposes of subsection (2C), not conferring a benefit that, if the offer had been accepted by the worker, would have been conferred on him under the resulting agreement shall be taken to be subjecting him to a detriment as an individual (and to be a deliberate failure to act).

(3) A worker also has the right not to be subjected to any detriment as an individual by any act, or any deliberate failure to act, by his employer if the act or failure takes place for the purpose of enforcing a requirement (whether or not imposed by a contract of employment or in writing) that, in the event of his not being a member of any trade union or of a particular trade union or of one of a number of particular trade unions, he must make one or more payments.

(4) For the purposes of subsection (3) any deduction made by an employer from the remuneration payable to a worker in respect of his employment shall, if it is attributable to his not being a member of any trade union or of a particular trade union or of one of a number of particular trade unions, be treated as a detriment to which he has been subjected as an individual by an act of his employer taking place for the sole or main purpose of enforcing a requirement of a kind mentioned in that subsection.

(5) A worker or former worker may present a complaint to an employment tribunal on the ground that he has been subjected to a detriment by his employer in contravention of this section.

(5A) This section does not apply where –

(a) the worker is an employee; and

(b) the detriment in question amounts to dismissal.

147 Time limit for proceedings

(1) An employment tribunal shall not consider a complaint under section 146 unless it is presented –

(a) before the end of the period of three months beginning with the date of the act or failure to which the complaint relates or, where that act or failure is part of a series of similar acts or failures (or both) the last of them, or

(b) where the tribunal is satisfied that it was not reasonably practicable for the complaint to be presented before the end of that period, within such further period as it considers reasonable.

(2) For the purposes of subsection (1) –

(a) where an act extends over a period, the reference to the date of the act is a reference to the last day of that period;

(b) a failure to act shall be treated as done when it was decided on.

(3) For the purposes of subsection (2), in the absence of evidence establishing the contrary an employer shall be taken to decide on a failure to act –

(a) when he does an act inconsistent with doing the failed act, or

(b) if he has done no such inconsistent act, when the period expires within which he might reasonably have been expected to do the failed act if it was to be done.

148 Consideration of complaint

(1) On a complaint under section 146 it shall be for the employer to show what was the sole or main purpose for which he acted or failed to act.

(2) In determining any question whether the employer acted or failed to act, or the purpose for which he did so, no account shall be taken of any pressure which was exercised on him by calling, organising, procuring or financing a strike or other industrial action, or by threatening to do so; and that question shall be determined as if no such pressure had been exercised.

149 Remedies

(1) Where the employment tribunal finds that a complaint under section 146 is well-founded, it shall make a declaration to that effect and may make an award of compensation to be paid by the employer to the complainant in respect of the act or failure complained of.

(2) The amount of the compensation awarded shall be such as the tribunal considers just and equitable in all the circumstances having regard to the infringement complained of and to any loss sustained by the complainant which is attributable to the act or failure which infringed his right.

(3) The loss shall be taken to include –

(a) any expenses reasonably incurred by the complainant in consequence of the act or failure complained of, and

(b) loss of any benefit which he might reasonably be expected to have had but for that act or failure.

(4) In ascertaining the loss, the tribunal shall apply the same rule concerning the duty of a person to mitigate his loss as applies to damages recoverable under the common law of England and Wales ...

(5) In determining the amount of compensation to be awarded no account shall be taken of any pressure which was exercised on the employer by calling, organising, procuring or financing a strike or other industrial action, or by threatening to do so; and that question shall be determined as if no such pressure had been exercised.

(6) Where the tribunal finds that the act or failure complained of was to any extent caused or contributed to by action of the complainant, it shall reduce the amount of the compensation by such proportion as it considers just and equitable having regard to that finding.

150 Awards against third parties

(1) If in proceedings on a complaint under section 146 –

(a) the complaint is made on the ground that the complainant has been subjected to detriment by an act or failure by his employer taking place for the sole or main purpose of compelling him to be or become a member of any trade union or of a particular trade union or of one of a number of particular trade unions, and

(b) either the complainant or the employer claims in proceedings before the tribunal that the employer was induced to act or fail to act in the way complained of by pressure which a trade union or other person exercised on him by calling, organising, procuring or financing a strike or other industrial action, or by threatening to do so,

the complainant or the employer may request the tribunal to direct that the person who he claims exercised the pressure be joined … as a party to the proceedings.

(2) The request shall be granted if it is made before the hearing of the complaint begins, but may be refused if it is made after the time; and no such request may be made after the tribunal has made a declaration that the complaint is well-founded.

(3) Where a person has been so joined … as a party to proceedings and the tribunal –

(a) makes an award of compensation, and

(b) finds that the claim mentioned in subsection (1)(b) is well-founded,

it may order that the compensation shall be paid by the person joined instead of by the employer, or partly by that person and partly by the employer, as the tribunal may consider just and equitable in the circumstances.

151 Interpretation and other supplementary provisions

(1) References in sections 146 to 150 to being, becoming or ceasing to remain a member of a trade union include references to being, becoming or ceasing to remain a member of a particular branch or section of that union and to being, becoming or ceasing to remain a member of one of a number of particular branches or sections of that union.

(1A) References in those sections –

(a) to taking part in the activities of a trade union, and

(b) to services made available by a trade union by virtue of membership of the union,

shall be construed in accordance with subsection (1).

(1B) In sections 146 to 150 –

'worker' means an individual who works, or normally works, as mentioned in paragraphs (a) to (c) of section 296(1), and

'employer' means –

(a) in relation to a worker, the person for whom he works;

(b) in relation to a former worker, the person for whom he worked.

(2) The remedy of a person for infringement of the right conferred on him by section 146 is by way of a complaint to an employment tribunal in accordance with this Part, and not otherwise.

152 Dismissal of employee on grounds related to union membership or activities

(1) For purposes of Part X of the Employment Rights Act 1996 (unfair dismissal) the dismissal of an employee shall be regarded as unfair if the reason for it (or, if more than one, the principal reason) was that the employee –

(a) was, or proposed to become, a member of an independent trade union,

(b) had taken part, or proposed to take part, in the activities of an independent trade union at an appropriate time,

(ba) had made use, or proposed to make use, of trade union services at an appropriate time,

(bb) had failed to accept an offer made in contravention of section 145A or 145B, or

(c) was not a member of any trade union, or of a particular trade union, or of one of a number of particular trade unions, or had refused, or proposed to refuse, to become or remain a member.

(2) In subsection (1) 'an appropriate time' means –

(a) a time outside the employee's working hours, or

(b) a time within his working hours at which, in accordance with arrangements agreed with or consent given by his employer, it is permissible for him to take part in the activities of a trade union or (as the case may be) make use of trade union services;

and for this purpose 'working hours', in relation to an employee, means any time when, in accordance with his contract of employment, he is required to be at work.

(2A) In this section –

(a) 'trade union services' means services made available to the worker by an independent trade union by virtue of his membership of the union, and

(b) references to a worker's 'making use' of trade union services include his consenting to the raising of a matter on his behalf by an independent trade union of which he is a member.

(2B) If an independent trade union of which a worker is a member raises a matter on his behalf (with or without his consent), penalising the worker for that is to be treated as penalising him as mentioned in subsection (1)(ba).

(3) Where the reason, or one of the reasons, for the dismissal was –

(a) the employee's refusal, or proposed refusal, to comply with a requirement (whether or not imposed by his contract of employment or in writing) that, in the event of his not being a member of a trade union, or of a particular trade union, or of one of a number of particular trade unions, he must make one or more payments, or

(b) his objection, or proposed objection (however expressed) to the operation of a provision (whether or not forming part of his contract of employment or in writing) under which, in the event mentioned in paragraph (a), his employer is entitled to deduct one or more sums from the remuneration payable to him in respect of his employment,

the reason shall be treated as falling within subsection (1)(c).

(4) References in this section to being, becoming or ceasing to remain a member of a trade union include references to being, becoming or ceasing to remain a member of a particular branch or section of that union or of one of a number of particular branches or sections of that trade union.

(5) References in this section –

(a) to taking part in the activities of a trade union, and

(b) to services made available by a trade union by virtue of membership of the union,

shall be construed in accordance with subsection (4).

153 Selection for redundancy on grounds related to union membership or activities

Where the reason or principal reason for the dismissal of an employee was that he was redundant, but it is shown –

(a) that the circumstances constituting the redundancy applied equally to one or more other employees in the same undertaking who held positions similar to that held by him and who have not been dismissed by the employer, and

(b) that the reason (or, if more than one, the principal reason) why he was selected for dismissal was one of those specified in section 152(1),

the dismissal shall be regarded as unfair for the purposes of Part X of the Employment Rights Act 1996 (unfair dismissal).

154 Disapplication of qualifying period and upper age limit for unfair dismissal

Sections 108(1) and 109(1) of the Employment Rights Act 1996 (qualifying period and upper age limit for unfair dismissal protection) do not apply to a dismissal which by virtue of section 152 or 153 is regarded as unfair for the purposes of Part 10 of that Act.

155 Matters to be disregarded in assessing contributory fault

(1) Where an employment tribunal makes an award of compensation for unfair dismissal in a case where the dismissal is unfair by virtue of section 152 or 153, the tribunal shall disregard, in considering whether it would be just and equitable to reduce, or further reduce, the amount of any part of the award, any such conduct or action of the complainant as is specified below.

(2) Conduct or action of the complainant shall be disregarded in so far as it constitutes a breach or proposed breach of a requirement –

(a) to be or become a member of any trade union or of a particular trade union or of one of a number of particular trade unions,

(b) to cease to be, or refrain from becoming, a member of any trade union or of a particular trade union or of one of a number of particular trade unions,

(c) not to take part in the activities of any trade union or of a particular trade union or of one of a number of particular trade unions, or

(d) not to make use of services made available by any trade union or by a particular trade union or by one of a number of particular trade unions.

For the purposes of this subsection requirement means a requirement imposed on the complainant by or under an arrangement or contract of employment or other agreement.

(2A) Conduct or action of the complainant shall be disregarded in so far as it constitutes acceptance of or failure to accept an offer made in contravention of section 145A or 145B.

(3) Conduct or action of the complainant shall be disregarded in so far as it constitutes a refusal, or proposed refusal, to comply with a requirement of a kind mentioned in section 152(3)(a) (payments in lieu of membership) or an objection, or proposed, objection (however expressed) to the operation of a provision of a kind mentioned in section 152(3)(b) (deductions in lieu of membership).

156 Minimum basic award

(1) Where a dismissal is unfair by virtue of section 152(1) or 153, the amount of the basic award of compensation, before any reduction is made under section 122 of the Employment Rights Act 1996, shall be not less than £3,800.

(2) But where the dismissal is unfair by virtue of section 153, subsection (2) of that section (reduction for contributory fault) applies in relation to so much of the basic award as is payable because of subsection (1) above.

160 Awards against third parties

(1) If in proceedings before an employment tribunal on a complaint of unfair dismissal either the employer or the complainant claims –

(a) that the employer was induced to dismiss the complainant by pressure which a trade union or other person exercised on the employer by calling, organising, procuring or financing a strike or other industrial action, or by threatening to do so, and

(b) that the pressure was exercised because the complainant was not a member of any trade union or of a particular trade union or of one of a number of particular trade unions,

the employer or the complainant may request the tribunal to direct that the person who he claims exercised the pressure be joined … as a party to the proceedings.

(2) The request shall be granted if it is made before the hearing of the complaint begins, but may be refused after that time; and no such request may be made after the tribunal has made an award of compensation for unfair dismissal or an order for reinstatement or re-engagement.

(3) Where a person has been so joined … as a party to the proceedings and the tribunal –

(a) makes an award of compensation for unfair dismissal, and

(b) finds that the claim mentioned in subsection (1) is well-founded,

the tribunal may order that the compensation shall be paid by that person instead of the employer, or partly by that person and partly by the employer, as the tribunal may consider just and equitable.

161 Application for interim relief

(1) An employee who presents a complaint of unfair dismissal alleging that the dismissal is unfair by virtue of section 152 may apply to the tribunal for interim relief.

(2) The tribunal shall not entertain an application for interim relief unless it is presented to the tribunal before the end of the period of seven days immediately following the effective date of termination (whether before, on or after that date).

(3) In a case where the employee relies on section 152(1)(a), (b) or (ba), or on section 152(1)(bb) otherwise than in relation to an offer made in contravention of section 145A(1)(d), the tribunal shall not entertain an application for interim relief unless before the end of that period there is also so presented a certificate in writing signed by an authorised official of the independent trade union of which the employee was or proposed to become a member stating –

(a) that on the date of the dismissal the employee was or proposed to become a member of the union, and

(b) that there appear to be reasonable grounds for supposing that the reason for his dismissal (or, if more than one, the principal reason) was one alleged in the complaint.

(4) An 'authorised official' means an official of the trade union authorised by it to act for the purposes of this section.

(5) A document purporting to be an authorisation of an official by a trade union to act for the purposes of this section and to be signed on behalf of the union shall be

taken to be such an authorisation unless the contrary is proved; and a document purporting to be a certificate signed by such an official shall be taken to be signed by him unless the contrary is proved.

(6) For the purposes of subsection (3) the date of dismissal shall be taken to be –

(a) where the employee's contract of employment was terminated by notice (whether given by his employer or by him), the date on which the employer's notice was given, and

(b) in any other case, the effective date of termination.

162 Application to be promptly determined

(1) An employment tribunal shall determine an application for interim relief as soon as practicable after receiving the application and, where appropriate, the requisite certificate.

(2) The tribunal shall give to the employer, not later than seven days before the hearing, a copy of the application and of any certificate, together with notice of the date, time and place of the hearing.

(3) If a request under section 160 (awards against third parties) is made three days or more before the date of the hearing, the tribunal shall also give to the person to whom the request relates, as soon as reasonably practicable, a copy of the application and of any certificate, together with notice of the date, time and place of the hearing.

(4) The tribunal shall not exercise any power it has of postponing the hearing of an application for interim relief except where it is satisfied that special circumstances exist which justify it in doing so.

163 Procedure on hearing of application and making of order

(1) If on hearing an application for interim relief it appears to the tribunal that it is likely that on determining the complaint to which the application relates that it will find that, by virtue of section 152, the complainant has been unfairly dismissed, the following provisions apply.

(2) The tribunal shall announce its findings and explain to both parties (if present) what powers the tribunal may exercise on the application and in what circumstances it will exercise them, and shall ask the employer (if present) whether he is willing, pending the determination or settlement of the complaint –

(a) to reinstate the employee, that is to say, to treat him in all respects as if he had not been dismissed, or

(b) if not, to re-engage him in another job on terms and conditions not less favourable than those which would have been applicable to him if he had not been dismissed.

(3) For this purpose 'terms and conditions not less favourable than those which would have been applicable to him if he had not been dismissed' means as regards

seniority, pension rights and other similar rights that the period prior to the dismissal shall be regarded as continuous with his employment following the dismissal.

(4) If the employer states that he is willing to reinstate the employee, the tribunal shall make an order to that effect.

(5) If the employer states that he is willing to re-engage the employee in another job, and specifies the terms and conditions on which he is willing to do so, the tribunal shall ask the employee whether he is willing to accept the job on those terms and conditions; and –

(a) if the employee is willing to accept the job on those terms and conditions, the tribunal shall make an order to that effect, and

(b) if he is not, then, if the tribunal is of the opinion that the refusal is reasonable, the tribunal shall make an order for the continuation of his contract of employment, and otherwise the tribunal shall make no order.

(6) If on the hearing of an application for interim relief the employer fails to attend before the tribunal, or states that he is unwilling either to reinstate the employee or re-engage him as mentioned in subsection (2), the tribunal shall make an order for the continuation of the employee's contract of employment.

164 Order for continuation of contract of employment

(1) An order under section 163 for the continuation of a contract of employment is an order that the contract of employment continue in force –

(a) for the purposes of pay or any other benefit derived from the employment, seniority, pension rights and other similar matters, and

(b) for the purpose of determining for any purpose the period for which the employee has been continuously employed,

from the date of its termination (whether before or after the making of the order) until the determination or settlement of the complaint.

(2) Where the tribunal makes such an order it shall specify in the order the amount which is to be paid by the employer to the employee by way of pay in respect of each normal pay period, or part of any such period, falling between the date of dismissal and the determination or settlement of the complaint.

(3) Subject as follows, the amount so specified shall be that which the employee could reasonably have been expected to earn during that period, or part, and shall be paid –

(a) in the case of payment for any such period falling wholly or partly after the making of the order, on the normal pay day for that period, and

(b) in the case of a payment for any past period, within such time as may be specified in the order.

(4) If an amount is payable in respect only of part of a normal pay period, the

amount shall be calculated by reference to the whole period and reduced proportionately.

(5) Any payment made to an employee by an employer under his contract of employment, or by way of damages for breach of that contract, in respect of a normal pay period or part of any such period shall go towards discharging the employer's liability in respect of that period under subsection (2); and conversely any payment under that subsection in respect of a period shall go towards discharging any liability of the employer under, or in respect of the breach of, the contract of employment in respect of that period.

(6) If an employee, on or after being dismissed by his employer, receives a lump sum which, or part of which, is in lieu of wages but is not referable to any normal pay period, the tribunal shall take the payment into account in determining the amount of pay to be payable in pursuance of any such order.

(7) For the purposes of this section the amount which an employee could reasonably have been expected to earn, his normal pay period and the normal pay day for each such period shall be determined as if he had not been dismissed.

165 Application for variation or revocation of order

(1) At any time between the making of an order under section 163 and the determination or settlement of the complaint, the employer or the employment may apply to an employment tribunal for the revocation or variation of the order on the ground of a relevant change of circumstances since the making of the order.

(2) Sections 161 to 163 apply in relation to such an application as in relation to an original application for interim relief, except that –

(a) no certificate need be presented to the tribunal under section 161(3), and

(b) in the case of an application by the employer, section 162(2) (service of copy of application and notice of hearing) has effect with the substitution of a reference to the employee for the reference to the employer.

166 Consequences of failure to comply with order

(1) If on the application of an employee an employment tribunal is satisfied that the employer has not complied with the terms of an order for the reinstatement or re-engagement of the employee under section 163(4) or (5), the tribunal shall –

(a) make an order for the continuation of the employee's contract of employment, and

(b) order the employer to pay the employee such compensation as the tribunal considers just and equitable in all the circumstances having regard –

(i) to the infringement of the employee's right to be reinstated or re-engaged in pursuance of the order, and

(ii) to any loss suffered by the employee in consequence of the non-compliance.

(2) Section 164 applies to an order under subsection (1)(a) as in relation to an order under section 163.

(3) If on the application of an employee an employment tribunal is satisfied that the employer has not complied with the terms of an order for the continuation of a contract of employment, the following provisions apply.

(4) If the non-compliance consists of a failure to pay an amount by way of pay specified in the order, the tribunal shall determine the amount owed by the employer on the date of the determination. If on that date the tribunal also determines the employee's complaint that he has been unfairly dismissed, it shall specify that amount separately from any other sum awarded to the employee.

(5) In any other case, the tribunal shall order the employer to pay the employee such compensation as the tribunal considers just and equitable in all the circumstances having regard to any loss suffered by the employee in consequence of the non-compliance.

167 Interpretation and other supplementary provisions

(1) Part X of the Employment Rights Act 1996 (unfair dismissal) has effect subject to the provisions of sections 152 to 166 above.

(2) Those sections shall be construed as one with that Part; and in those sections –

'complaint of unfair dismissal' means a complaint under section 111 of the Employment Rights Act 1996;

'award of compensation for unfair dismissal' means an award of compensation for unfair dismissal under section 112(4) or 117(3)(a) of that Act; and

'order for reinstatement or re-engagement' means an order for reinstatement or re-engagement under section 113 of that Act.

(3) Nothing in those sections shall be construed as conferring a right to complain of unfair dismissal from employment of a description to which Part does not otherwise apply.

168 Time off for carrying out trade union duties

(1) An employer shall permit an employee of his who is an official of an independent trade union recognised by the employer to take time off during his working hours for the purpose of carrying out any duties of his, as such an official, concerned with –

(a) negotiations with the employer related to or connected with matters falling within section 178(2) (collective bargaining) in relation to which the trade union is recognised by the employer, or

(b) the performance on behalf of employees of the employer of functions related to or connected with matters falling within that provision which the employer has agreed may be so performed by the trade union, or

(c) receipt of information from the employer and consultation by the employer under section 188 (redundancies) or under the Transfer of Undertakings (Protection of Employment) Regulations 1981.

(2) He shall also permit such an employee to take time off during his working hours for the purpose of undergoing training in aspects of industrial relations –

(a) relevant to the carrying out of such duties as are mentioned in subsection (1), and

(b) approved by the Trades Union Congress or by the independent trade union of which he is an official.

(3) The amount of time off which an employee is to be permitted to take under this section and the purposes for which, the occasions on which and any conditions subject to which time off may be so taken are those that are reasonable in all the circumstances having regard to any relevant provisions of a Code of Practice issued by ACAS.

(4) An employee may present a complaint to an employment tribunal that his employer has failed to permit him to take time off as required by this section.

168A   Time off for union learning representatives

(1) An employer shall permit an employee of his who is –

(a) a member of an independent trade union recognised by the employer, and

(b) a learning representative of the trade union,

to take time off during his working hours for any of the following purposes.

(2) The purposes are –

(a) carrying on any of the following activities in relation to qualifying members of the trade union –

(i) analysing learning or training needs,

(ii) providing information and advice about learning or training matters,

(iii) arranging learning or training, and

(iv) promoting the value of learning or training,

(b) consulting the employer about carrying on any such activities in relation to such members of the trade union,

(c) preparing for any of the things mentioned in paragraphs (a) and (b).

(3) Subsection (1) only applies if –

(a) the trade union has given the employer notice in writing that the employee is a learning representative of the trade union, and

(b) the training condition is met in relation to him.

(4) The training condition is met if –

(a) the employee has undergone sufficient training to enable him to carry on the activities mentioned in subsection (2), and the trade union has given the employer notice in writing of that fact,

(b) the trade union has in the last six months given the employer notice in writing that the employee will be undergoing such training, or

(c) within six months of the trade union giving the employer notice in writing that the employee will be undergoing such training, the employee has done so, and the trade union has given the employer notice of that fact.

(5) Only one notice under subsection (4)(b) may be given in respect of any one employee.

(6) References in subsection (4) to sufficient training to carry out the activities mentioned in subsection (2) are to training that is sufficient for those purposes having regard to any relevant provision of a Code of Practice issued by ACAS or the Secretary of State.

(7) If an employer is required to permit an employee to take time off under subsection (1), he shall also permit the employee to take time off during his working hours for the following purposes –

(a) undergoing training which is relevant to his functions as a learning representative, and

(b) where the trade union has in the last six months given the employer notice under subsection (4)(b) in relation to the employee, undergoing such training as is mentioned in subsection (4)(a).

(8) The amount of time off which an employee is to be permitted to take under this section and the purposes for which, the occasions on which and any conditions subject to which time off may be so taken are those that are reasonable in all the circumstances having regard to any relevant provision of a Code of Practice issued by ACAS or the Secretary of State.

(9) An employee may present a complaint to an employment tribunal that his employer has failed to permit him to take time off as required by this section.

(10) In subsection (2)(a), the reference to qualifying members of the trade union is to members of the trade union –

(a) who are employees of the employer of a description in respect of which the union is recognised by the employer, and

(b) in relation to whom it is the function of the union learning representative to act as such.

(11) For the purposes of this section, a person is a learning representative of a trade union if he is appointed or elected as such in accordance with its rules.

169 Payment for time off under section 168

(1) An employer who permits and employee to take time off under section 168 or 168A shall pay him for the time taken off pursuant to the permission.

(2) Where the employee's remuneration for the work he would ordinarily have been doing during that time does not vary with the amount of work done, he shall be paid as if he had worked at that work for the whole of that time.

(3) Where the employee's remuneration for the work he would ordinarily have been

doing during that time varies with the amount of work done, he shall be paid an amount calculated by reference to the average hourly earnings for that work. The average hourly earnings shall be those of the employee concerned or, if no fair estimate can be made of those earnings, the average hourly earnings for work of that description of persons in comparable employment with the same employer or, if there are no such persons, a figure of average hourly earnings which is reasonable in the circumstances.

(4) A right to be paid an amount under this section does not affect any right of an employee in relation to remuneration under his contract of employment, but –

(a) any contractual remuneration paid to an employee in respect of a period of time off to which this section applies shall go towards discharging any liability of the employer under this section in respect of that period, and

(b) any payment under this section in respect of a period shall go towards discharging any liability of the employer to pay contractual remuneration in respect of that period.

(5) An employee may present a complaint to an employment tribunal that his employer has failed to pay him in accordance with this section.

170 Time off for trade union activities

(1) An employer shall permit an employee of his who is a member of an independent trade union recognised by the employer in respect of that description of employee to take time off during his working hours for the purpose of taking part in –

(a) any activities of the union, and

(b) any activities in relation to which the employee is acting as a representative of the union.

(2) The right conferred by subsection (1) does not extend to activities which themselves consist of industrial action, whether or not in contemplation or furtherance of a trade dispute.

(2A) The right conferred by subsection (1) does not extend to time off for the purpose of acting as, or having access to services provided by, a learning representative of a trade union.

(2B) An employer shall permit an employee of his who is a member of an independent trade union recognised by the employer in respect of that description of employee to take time off during his working hours for the purpose of having access to services provided by a person in his capacity as a learning representative of the trade union.

(2C) Subsection (2B) only applies if the learning representative would be entitled to time off under subsection (1) of section 168A for the purpose of carrying on in relation to the employee activities of the kind mentioned in subsection (2) of that section.

(3) The amount of time off which an employee is to be permitted to take under this

section and the purposes for which, the occasions on which and any conditions subject to which time off may be so taken are those that are reasonable in all the circumstances having regard to any relevant provisions of a Code of Practice issued by ACAS.

(4) An employee may present a complaint to an employment tribunal that his employer has failed to permit him to take time off as required by this section.

(5) For the purposes of this section –

(a) a person is a learning representative of a trade union if he is appointed or elected as such in accordance with its rules, and

(b) a person who is a learning representative of a trade union acts as such if he carries on the activities mentioned in section 168A(2) in that capacity.

171 Time limit for proceedings

An employment tribunal shall not consider a complaint under section 168, 168A, 169 or 170 unless it is presented to the tribunal –

(a) within three months of the date when the failure occurred, or

(b) where the tribunal is satisfied that it was not reasonably practicable for the complaint to be presented within that period, within such further period as the tribunal considers reasonable.

172 Remedies

(1) Where the tribunal finds a complaint under section 168, 168A or 170 is well-founded, it shall make a declaration to that effect and may make an award of compensation to be paid by the employer to the employee.

(2) The amount of the compensation shall be such as the tribunal considers just and equitable in all the circumstances having regard to the employer's default in failing to permit time off to be taken by the employee and to any loss sustained by the employee which is attributable to the matters complained of.

(3) Where on a complaint under section 169 the tribunal finds that the employer has failed to pay the employee in accordance with that section, it shall order him to pay the amount which it finds to be due.

173 Interpretation and other supplementary provisions

(1) For the purposes of sections 168, 168A and 170 the working hours of an employee shall be taken to be any time when in accordance with his contract of employment he is required to be at work.

(2) The remedy of an employee for infringement of the rights conferred on him by section 168, 169 or 170 is by way of complaint to an employment tribunal in accordance with this Part, and not otherwise.

(3) The Secretary of State may by order made by statutory instrument amend

section 168A for the purpose of changing the purposes for which an employee may take time off under that section.

(4) No order may be made under subsection (3) unless a draft of the order has been laid before and approved by resolution of each House of Parliament.'

174 Right not to be excluded or expelled from union

(1) An individual shall not be excluded or expelled from a trade union unless the exclusion or expulsion is permitted by this section.

(2) The exclusion or expulsion of an individual from a trade union is permitted by this section if (and only if) –

(a) he does not satisfy, or no longer satisfies, an enforceable membership requirement contained in the rules of the union,

(b) he does not qualify, or no longer qualifies, for membership of the union by reason of the union operating only in a particular part or particular parts of Great Britain,

(c) in the case of a union whose purpose is the regulation of relations between its members and one particular employer or a number of particular employers who are associated, he is not, or is no longer employed by that employer or one of those employers, or

(d) the exclusion or expulsion is entirely attributable to conduct of his (other than excluded conduct) and the conduct to which it is wholly or mainly attributable is not protected conduct.

(3) A requirement in relation to a membership of a union is 'enforceable' for the purposes of subsection (2)(a) if it restricts membership solely by reference to one or more of the following criteria –

(a) employment in a specified trade, industry or profession,

(b) occupational description (including grade, level or category of appointment), and

(c) possession of specified trade, industrial or professional qualifications or work experience.

(4) For the purposes of subsection (2)(d) 'excluded conduct', in relation to an individual, means –

(a) conduct which consists in his being or ceasing to be, or having been or ceased to be, a member of another trade union,

(b) conduct which consists in his being or ceasing to be, or having been or ceased to be, employed by a particular employer or at a particular place, or

(c) conduct to which section 65 (conduct for which an individual may not be disciplined by a union) applies or would apply if the references in that section to the trade union which is relevant for the purposes of that section were references to any trade union.

(4A) For the purposes of subsection (2)(d) 'protected conduct' is conduct which consists in the individual's being or ceasing to be, or having been or ceased to be, a member of a political party.

(4B) Conduct which consists of activities undertaken by an individual as a member of a political party is not conduct falling within subsection (4A).

(5) An individual who claims that he has been excluded or expelled from a trade union in contravention of this section may present a complaint to an employment tribunal.

175 Time limit for proceedings

An employment tribunal shall not entertain a complaint under section 174 unless it is presented –

(a) before the end of the period of six months beginning with the date of the exclusion or expulsion, or

(b) where the tribunal is satisfied that it was not reasonably practicable for the complaint to be presented before the end of that period, within such further period as the tribunal considers reasonable.

176 Remedies

(1) Where the employment tribunal finds a complaint under section 174 is well-founded, it shall make a declaration to that effect.

(1A) If a tribunal makes a declaration under subsection (1) and it appears to the tribunal that the exclusion or expulsion was mainly attributable to conduct falling within section 174(4A) it shall make a declaration to that effect.

(1B) If a tribunal makes a declaration under subsection (1A) and it appears to the tribunal that the other conduct to which the exclusion or expulsion was attributable consisted wholly or mainly of conduct of the complainant which was contrary to –

(a) a rule of the union, or

(b) an objective of the union,

it shall make a declaration to that effect.

(1C) For the purposes of subsection (1B), it is immaterial whether the complainant was a member of the union at the time of the conduct contrary to the rule or objective.

(1D) A declaration by virtue of subsection (1B)(b) shall not be made unless the union shows that, at the time of the conduct of the complainant which was contrary to the objective in question, it was reasonably practicable for that objective to be ascertained –

(a) if the complainant was not at that time a member of the union, by a member of the general public, and

(b) if he was at that time a member of the union, by a member of the union.

(2) An individual whose complaint has been declared to be well-founded may make an application to an employment tribunal for an award of compensation to be paid to him by the union.

(3) The application shall not be entertained if made –

(a) before the end of the period of four weeks beginning with the date of the declaration under subsection (1), or

(b) after the end of the period of six months beginning with that date.

(4) The amount of compensation awarded shall, subject to the following provisions, be such as the employment tribunal or the Employment Appeal Tribunal considers just and equitable in all the circumstances.

(5) Where the employment tribunal finds that the exclusion or expulsion complained of was to any extent caused or contributed to by the action of the applicant, it shall reduce the amount of the compensation by such proportion as it considers just and equitable having regard to that finding.

(6) The amount of compensation calculated in accordance with subsections (4) and (5) shall not exceed the aggregate of –

(a) an amount equal to thirty times the limit for the time being imposed by section 227(1)(a) of the Employment Rights Act 1996 (maximum amount of a week's pay for basic award in unfair dismissal cases), and

(b) an amount equal to the limit for the time being imposed by section 124(1) of that Act (maximum compensatory award in such cases).

(6A) If on the date on which the application was made the applicant had not been admitted or re-admitted to the union, the award shall not be less than £5,900.

(6B) Subsection (6A) does not apply in a case where the tribunal which made the declaration under subsection (1) also made declarations under subsections (1A) and (1B).

177 Interpretation and other supplementary provisions

(1) For the purposes of section 174 –

(a) 'trade union' does not include an organisation falling within paragraph (b) of section 1,

(b) 'conduct' includes statements, acts and omissions, and

(c) 'employment' includes any relationship whereby an individual personally does work or performs services for another person (related expressions being construed accordingly).

(2) For the purposes of sections 174 to 176 –

(a) if an individual's application for membership of a trade union is neither granted nor rejected before the date of the period within which it might reasonably have been expected to be granted if it was to be granted, he shall be treated as having been excluded from the union on the last day of that period, and

(b) an individual who under the rules of a trade union ceases to be a member of the union on the happening of an event specified in the rules shall be treated as having been expelled from the union.

(3) The remedy of an individual for infringement of the rights conferred by section 174 is by way of a complaint to an employment tribunal in accordance with that section, sections 175 and 176 and this section, and not otherwise.

(4) Where a complaint relating to an expulsion which is presented under section 174 is declared to be well-founded, no complaint in respect of the expulsion shall be presented or proceeded with under section 66 (complaint of infringement of right not to be unjustifiably disciplined).

(5) The rights conferred by section 174 are in addition to, and not in substitution for, any right which exists apart from that section; and, subject to subsection (4), nothing in that section, section 175 or 176 or this section affects any remedy for infringement of any such right.

PART IV

INDUSTRIAL RELATIONS

CHAPTER I

COLLECTIVE BARGAINING

178 Collective agreements and collective bargaining

(1) In this Act 'collective agreement' means any agreement or arrangement made by or on behalf of one or more trade unions and one or more employers or employers' associations and relating to one or more of the matters specified below; and 'collective bargaining' means negotiations relating to or connected with one or more of those matters.

(2) The matters referred to above are –

(a) terms and conditions of employment, or the physical conditions in which any workers are required to work;

(b) engagement or non-engagement, or termination or suspension of employment or the duties of employment, of one or more workers;

(c) allocation of work or the duties of employment between workers or groups of workers;

(d) matters of discipline;

(e) a worker's membership or non-membership of a trade union;

(f) facilities for officials of trade unions; and

(g) machinery for negotiation or consultation, and other procedures, relating to any of the above matters, including the recognition by employers or employers' associations of the right of a trade union to represent workers in such negotiation or consultation or in the carrying out of such procedures.

(3) In this Act 'recognition', in relation to a trade union, means the recognition of the union by an employer, or two or more associated employers, to any extent, for the purpose of collective bargaining; and 'recognised' and other related expressions shall be construed accordingly.

179 Whether agreement intended to be a legally enforceable contract

(1) A collective agreement shall be conclusively presumed not to have been intended by the parties to be a legally enforceable contract unless the agreement –

(a) is in writing, and

(b) contains a provision which (however expressed) states that the parties intend that the agreement shall be a legally enforceable contract.

(2) A collective agreement which does satisfy those conditions shall be conclusively presumed to have been intended by the parties to be a legally enforceable contract.

(3) If a collective agreement is in writing and contains a provision which (however expressed) states that the parties intend that one or more parts of the agreement specified in that provision, but not the whole of the agreement, shall be a legally enforceable contract, then –

(a) the specified part or parts shall be conclusively presumed to have been intended by the parties to be a legally enforceable contract, and

(b) the remainder of the agreement shall be conclusively presumed not to have been intended by the parties to be such a contract.

(4) A part of a collective agreement which by virtue of subsection (3)(b) is not a legally enforceable contract may be referred to for the purpose of interpreting a party of the agreement which is such a contract.

180 Effect of provisions restricting right to take industrial action

(1) Any terms of a collective agreement which prohibit or restrict the right of workers to engage in a strike or other industrial action, or have the effect of prohibiting or restricting that right, shall not form part of any contract between a worker and the person for whom he works unless the following conditions are met.

(2) The conditions are that the collective agreement –

(a) is in writing,

(b) contains a provision expressly stating that those terms shall or may be incorporated in such a contract,

(c) is reasonably accessible at his place of work to the worker to whom it applies and is available for him to consult during working hours, and

(d) is one where each trade union which is a party to the agreement is an independent trade union;

and that the contract with the worker expressly or impliedly incorporates those terms in the contract.

(3) The above provisions have effect notwithstanding anything in section 179 and notwithstanding any provision to the contrary in any agreement (including a collective agreement or a contract with any worker).

181 General duty of employers to disclose information

(1) An employer who recognises an independent trade union shall, for the purposes of al stages of collective bargaining about matters and in relation to descriptions of workers, in respect of which the union is recognised by him, disclose to representatives of the union, on request, the information required by this section. In this section and sections 182 to 185 'representative', in relation to a trade union, means an official or other person authorised by the union to carry on such collective bargaining.

(2) The information to be disclosed is all information relating to the employer's undertaking which is in his possession, or that of an associated employer, and is information –

  (a) without which the trade union representatives would be to a material extent impeded in carrying on collective bargaining with him, and

  (b) which it would be in accordance with good industrial relations practice that he should disclose to them for the purposes of collective bargaining.

(3) A request by trade union representatives for information under this section shall, if the employer so requests, be in writing or be confirmed in writing.

(4) In determining what would be in accordance with good industrial relations practice, regard shall be had to the relevant provisions of any Code of Practice issued by ACAS, but not so as to exclude any other evidence of what that practice is.

(5) Information which an employer is required by virtue of this section to disclose to trade union representatives shall, if they so request, be disclosed or confirmed in writing.

182 Restrictions on general duty

(1) An employer is not required by section 181 to disclose information –

  (a) the disclosure of which would be against the interests of national security, or

  (b) which he could not disclose without contravening a prohibition imposed by or under an enactment, or

  (c) which has been communicated to him in confidence, or which he has otherwise obtained in consequence of the confidence reposed in him by another person, or

  (d) which relates specifically to an individual (unless that individual has consented to its being disclosed), or

  (e) the disclosure of which would cause substantial injury to his undertaking for reasons other than its effect on collective bargaining, or

  (f) obtained by him for the purpose of bringing, prosecuting or defending any legal proceedings.

In formulating the provisions of any Code of Practice relating to the disclosure of information, ACAS shall have regard to the provisions of this subsection.

(2) In the performance of his duty under section 181 an employer is not required –

(a) to produce, or allow inspection of, any document (other than a document prepared for the purpose of conveying or confirming the information) or to make a copy of or extracts from any document, or

(b) to compile or assemble any information where the compilation or assembly would involve an amount of work or expenditure out of reasonable proportion to the value of the information in the conduct of collective bargaining.

183 Complaint of failure to disclose information

(1) A trade union may present a complaint to the Central Arbitration Committee that an employer has failed –

(a) to disclose to representatives of the union information which he was required to disclose to them by section 181, or

(b) to confirm such information in writing in accordance with that section.

The complaint must be in writing and in such form as the Committee may require.

(2) If on receipt of a complaint the Committee is of the opinion that it is reasonably likely to be settled by conciliation, it shall refer the complaint to ACAS and shall notify the trade union and employer accordingly, whereupon ACAS shall seek to promote a settlement of the matter. If a complaint so referred is not settled or withdrawn and ACAS is of the opinion that further attempts at conciliation are unlikely to result in a settlement, it shall inform the Committee of its opinion.

(3) If the complaint is not referred to ACAS or, if it is so referred, on ACAS informing the Committee of its opinion that further attempts at conciliation are unlikely to result in a settlement, the Committee shall proceed to hear and determine the complaint and shall make a declaration stating whether it finds the complaint well-founded, wholly or in part, and stating the reasons for its findings.

(4) On the hearing of a complaint any person who the Committee considers has a proper interest in the complaint is entitled to be heard by the Committee, but a failure to accord a hearing to a person other than a trade union and employer directly concerned does not affect the validity of any decision of the Committee in those proceedings.

(5) If the Committee finds the complaint wholly or partly well-founded, the declaration shall specify –

(a) the information in respect of which the Committee finds that the complaint is well founded,

(b) the date (or, if more than one, the earliest date) on which the employer refused or failed to disclose or, as the case may be, to confirm in writing, any of the information in question, and

(c) a period (not being less than one week from the date of the declaration) within which the employer ought to disclose that information, or, as the case may be, to confirm it in writing.

(6) On a hearing of a complaint under this section a certificate signed by or on behalf of a Minister of the Crown and certifying that a particular request for information could not be complied with except by disclosing information the disclosure of which would have been against the interests of national security shall be conclusive evidence of that fact. A document which purports to be such a certificate shall be taken to be such a certificate unless the contrary is proved.

184 Further complaint of failure to comply with declaration

(1) After the expiration of the period specified in a declaration under section 183(5)(c) the trade union may present a further complaint to the Central Arbitration Committee that the employer has failed to disclose or, as the case may be, to confirm in writing to representatives of the union information specified in the declaration. The complaint must be in writing and in such form as the Committee may require.

(2) On receipt of a further complaint the Committee shall proceed to hear and determine the complaint and shall make a declaration stating whether they find the complaint well-founded, wholly or in part, and stating the reasons for their finding.

(3) On the hearing of a further complaint any person who the Committee consider has a proper interest in that complaint shall be entitled to be heard by the Committee, but a failure to accord a hearing to a person other than the trade union and employer directly concerned shall not affect the validity of any decision of the Committee in those proceedings.

(4) If the Committee find the further complaint wholly or partly well-founded the declaration shall specify the information in respect of which the Committee find that that complaint is well-founded.

185 Determination of claim and award

(1) On or after presenting a further complaint under section 184 the trade union may present to the Central Arbitration Committee a claim, in writing, in respect of one or more descriptions of employees (but not workers who are not employees) specified in the claim that their contracts should include the terms and conditions specified in the claim.

(2) The right to present a claim expires if the employer discloses or, as the case may be, confirms in writing, to representatives of the trade union the information specified in the declaration under section 183(5) or 184(4); and a claim presented shall be treated as withdrawn if the employer does so before the Committee make an award on the claim.

(3) If the Committee find, or have found, the further complaint wholly or partly well-founded, they may, after hearing the parties, make an award that in respect of any description of employees specified in the claim the employer shall, from a specified date, observe either –

(a) the terms and conditions specified in the claim; or

(b) other terms and conditions which the Committee consider appropriate.

The date specified may be earlier than that on which the award is made but not earlier than the date specified in accordance with section 183(5)(b) in the declaration made by the Committee on the original complaint.

(4) An award shall be made only in respect of a description of employees, and shall compromise only terms and conditions relating to matters in respect of which the trade union making the claim is recognised by the employer.

(5) Terms and conditions which by an award under this section an employer is required to observe in respect of an employee have effect as part of the employee's contract of employment as from the date specified in the award, except in so far as they are superseded or varied –

(a) by a subsequent award under this section,

(b) by a collective agreement between the employer and the union for the time being representing that employee, or

(c) by express or implied agreement between the employee and the employer so far as that agreement effects an improvement in terms and conditions having effect by virtue of the award.

(6) Where –

(a) by virtue of any enactment, other than one contained in this section, providing for minimum remuneration or terms and conditions, a contract of employment is to have effect as modified by an award, order or other instrument under that enactment, and

(b) by virtue of an award under this section any terms and conditions are to have effect as part of that contract,

that contract shall have effect in accordance with that award, order or other instrument or in accordance with the award under this section, whichever is the more favourable, in respect of any terms and conditions of that contract, to the employee.

(7) No award may be made under this section in respect of terms and conditions of employment which are fixed by virtue of any enactment.

186 Recognition requirement in contract for goods or services void

A term or condition of a contract for the supply of goods or services is void in so far as it purports to require a party to the contract –

(a) to recognise one or more trade unions (whether or not named in the contract) for the purpose of negotiating on behalf of workers, or any class of workers, employed by him, or

(b) to negotiate or consult with, or with an official of, one or more trade unions (whether or not so named).

187 Refusal to deal on grounds of union exclusion prohibited

(1) A person shall not refuse to deal with a supplier or prospective supplier of goods or services if the ground or one of the grounds for his action is that the person against whom it is taken does not, or is not likely to –

(a) recognise one or more trade unions for the purpose of negotiating on behalf of workers, or any class of worker, employed by him, or

(b) negotiate or consult with, or with an official of, one or more trade unions.

(2) A person refuses to deal with a person if –

(a) where he maintains (in whatever form) a list of approved suppliers of goods or services, or of persons from whom tenders for the supply of goods or services may be invited, he fails to include the name of that person in that list; or

(b) in relation to a proposed contract for the supply of goods or services –

(i) he excludes that person from the group of persons from whom tenders for the supply of the goods or services are invited, or

(ii) he fails to permit that person to submit such a tender, or

(iii) he otherwise determines not to enter into a contract with that person for the supply of the goods or services; or

(c) he terminates a contract with that person for the supply of goods or services.

(3) The obligation to comply with this section is a duty owed to the person with whom there is a refusal to deal and to any other person who may be adversely affected by its contravention; and a breach of the duty is actionable accordingly (subject to the defences and other incidents applying to actions for breach of statutory duty).

CHAPTER II

PROCEDURE FOR HANDLING REDUNDANCIES

188 Duty of employer to consult representatives

(1) Where an employer is proposing to dismiss as redundant 20 or more employees at one establishment within a period of 90 days or less, the employer shall consult about the dismissals all the persons who are appropriate representatives of any of the employees who may be affected by the proposed dismissals or may be affected by measures taken in connection with those dismissals.

(1A) The consultation shall begin in good time and in any event –

(a) where the employer is proposing to dismiss 100 or more employees as mentioned in subsection (1), at least 90 days, and

(b) otherwise, at least 30 days,

before the first of the dismissals takes effect.

(1B) For the purposes of this section the appropriate representatives of any affected employees are –

(a) if the employees are of a description in respect of which an independent trade union is recognised by their employer, representatives of the trade union, or

(b) in any other case, whichever of the following employee representatives the employer chooses –

(i) employee representatives appointed or elected by the affected employees otherwise than for the purposes of this section, who (having regard to the purposes for and the method by which they were appointed or elected) have authority from those employees to receive information and to be consulted about the proposed dismissals on their behalf;

(ii) employee representatives elected by the affected employees, for the purposes of this section, in an election satisfying the requirements of section 188A(1).

(2) The consultation shall include consultation about ways of –

(a) avoiding the dismissals,

(b) reducing the numbers of employees to be dismissed, and

(c) mitigating the consequences of the dismissals,

and shall be undertaken by the employer with a view to reaching agreement with the appropriate representatives.

(3) In determining how many employees an employer is proposing to dismiss as redundant no account shall be taken of employees in respect of whose proposed dismissals consultation has already begun.

(4) For the purposes of the consultation the employer shall disclose in writing to the appropriate representatives –

(a) the reasons for his proposals,

(b) the numbers and descriptions of employees whom it is proposed to dismiss as redundant,

(c) the total number of employees of any such description employed by the employer at the establishment in question,

(d) the proposed method of selecting the employees who may be dismissed,

(e) the proposed method of carrying out the dismissals, with due regard to any agreed procedure, including the period over which the dismissals are to take effect, and

(f) the proposed method of calculating the amount of any redundancy payments to be made (otherwise than in compliance with an obligation imposed by or by virtue of any enactment) to employees who may be dismissed.

(5) That information shall be given to each of the appropriate representatives by being delivered to them, or sent by post to an address notified by them to the employer, or (in the case of representatives of a trade union) sent by post to the union at the address of its head or main office.

(5A) The employer shall allow the appropriate representatives access to the affected employees and shall afford to those representatives such accommodation and other facilities as may be appropriate.

(7) If in any case there are special circumstances which render it not reasonably practicable for the employer to comply with a requirement of subsection (1A), (2) or (4), the employer shall take all such steps towards compliance with that requirement as are reasonably practicable in those circumstances. Where the decision leading to the proposed dismissals is that of a person controlling the employer (directly or indirectly), a failure on the part of that person to provide information to the employer shall not constitute special circumstances rendering it not reasonably practicable for the employer to comply with such a requirement.

(7A) Where –

(a) the employer has invited any of the affected employees to elect employee representatives, and

(b) the invitation was issued long enough before the time when the consultation is required by subsection (1A)(a) or (b) to begin to allow them to elect representatives by that time,

the employer shall be treated as complying with the requirements of this section in relation to those employees if he complies with those requirements as soon as is reasonably practicable after the election of the representatives.

(7B) If, after the employer has invited affected employees to elect representatives, the affected employees fail to do so within a reasonable time, he shall give to each affected employee the information set out in subsection (4).

(8) This section does not confer any rights on a trade union, a representative or an employee except as provided by sections 189 to 192 below.

188A [Election of employee representatives]

(1) The requirements for the election of employee representatives under section 188(1B)(b)(ii) are that –

(a) the employer shall make such arrangements as are reasonably practical to ensure that the election is fair;

(b) the employer shall determine the number of representatives to be elected so that there are sufficient representatives to represent the interests of all the affected employees having regard to the number and classes of those employees;

(c) the employer shall determine whether the affected employees should be represented either by representatives of all the affected employees or by representatives of particular classes of those employees;

(d) before the election the employee shall determine the term of office as employee representatives so that it is of sufficient length to enable information to be given and consultations under section 188 to be completed;

(e) the candidates for election as employee representatives are affected employees on the date of the election;

(f) no affected employee is unreasonably excluded from standing for election;

(g) all affected employees on the date of the election are entitled to vote for employee representatives;

(h) the employees entitled to vote may vote for as many candidates as there are representatives to be elected to represent them or, if there are to be representatives for particular classes of employees, may vote for as many candidates as there are representatives to be elected to represent their particular class of employee;

(i) the election is conducted so as to secure that –

(i) so far as is reasonably practicable, those voting do so in secret, and

(ii) the votes given at the election are accurately counted.

(2) Where, after an election of employee representatives satisying the requirements of subsection (1) has been held, one of those elected ceases to act as an employee representative and any of those employees are no longer represented, they shall elect another representative by an election satisfying the requirements of subsection (1)(a), (e), (f) and (i).

189 Complaint and protective award

(1) Where an employer has failed to comply with a requirement of section 188 or section 188A, a complaint may be presented to an employment tribunal on that ground –

(a) in the case of a failure relating to the election of employee representatives, by any of the affected employees or by any of the employees who have been dismissed as redundant;

(b) in the case of any other failure relating to employee representatives, by any of the employee representatives to whom the failure related,

(c) in the case of a failure relating to representatives of a trade union, by the trade union, and

(d) in any other case, by any of the affected employees or by any of the employees who have been dismissed as redundant.

(1A) If on a complaint under subsection (1) a question arises as to whethr or not any employee representative was an appropriate representative for the purposes of section 188, it shall be for the employer to show that the employee representative had the authority to represent the affected employees.

(1B) On a complaint under subsection (1)(a) it shall be for the employer to show that the requirements in section 188A have been satisfied.

(2) If the tribunal finds the complaint well-founded it shall make a declaration to that effect and may also make a protective award.

(3) A protective award is an award in respect of one or more descriptions of employees –

(a) who have been dismissed as redundant, or whom it is proposed to dismiss as redundant, and

(b) in respect of whose dismissal or proposed dismissal the employer has failed to comply with a requirement of section 188,

ordering the employer to pay remuneration for the protected period.

(4) The protected period –

(a) begins with the date on which the first of the dismissals to which the complaint relates takes effect, or the date of the award, whichever is the earlier, and

(b) is of such length as the tribunal determines to be just and equitable in all the circumstances having regard to the seriousness of the employer's default in complying with any requirement of section 188;

but shall not exceed 90 days.

(5) An employment tribunal shall not consider a complaint under this section unless it is presented to the tribunal –

(a) before the date on which the last of the dismissals to which the complaint relates takes effect, or

(b) during the period of three months beginning with that date, or

(c) where the tribunal is satisfied that it was not reasonably practicable for the complaint to be presented during the period of three months, within such further period as it considers reasonable.

(6) If on a complaint under this section a question arises –

(a) whether there were special circumstances which rendered it not reasonably practicable for the employer to comply with any requirement of section 188, or

(b) whether he took all such steps towards compliance with that requirement as were reasonably practicable in those circumstances,

it is for the employer to show that there were and that he did.

190 Entitlement under protective award

(1) Where an employment tribunal has made a protective award, every employee of a description to which the award relates is entitled, subject to the following provisions and to section 191, to be paid remuneration by his employer for the protected period.

(2) The rate of remuneration payable is a week's pay for each week of the period; and remuneration in respect of a period less than one week shall be calculated by reducing proportionately the amount of a week's pay.

(4) An employee is not entitled to remuneration under a protective award in respect of a period during which he is employed by the employer unless he would be entitled to be paid by the employer in respect of that period –

(a) by virtue of his contract of employment, or

(b) by virtue of sections 87 to 91 of the Employment Rights Act 1996 (rights of employee in period of notice),

if that period fell within the period of notice required to be given by section 86(1) of that Act.

(5) Chapter II of Part XIV of the Employment Rights Act 1996 applies with respect to the calculation of a week's pay for the purposes of this section. The calculation date for the purposes of that Chapter is the date on which the protective award was made or, in the case of an employee who was dismissed before the date on which the protective award was made, the date which by virtue of section 226(5) is the calculation date for the purpose of computing the amount of a redundancy payment in relation to that dismissal (whether or not the employee concerned is entitled to any such payment).

(6) If an employee of a description to which a protective award relates dies during the protected period, the award has effect in his case as if the protected period ended on his death.

191 Termination of employment during protected period

(1) Where the employee is employed by the employer during the protected period and –

(a) he is fairly dismissed by his employer otherwise than as redundant, or

(b) he unreasonably terminates the contract of employment,

then, subject to the following provisions, he is not entitled to remuneration under the protective award in respect of any period during which but for that dismissal or termination he would have been employed.

(2) If an employer makes an employee an offer (whether in writing or not and whether before or after the ending of his employment under the previous contract) to renew his contract of employment, or to re-engage him under a new contract, so that the renewal or re-engagement would take effect before or during the protected period, and either –

(a) the provisions of the contract as renewed, or of the new contract, as to the capacity and place in which he would be employed, and as to the other terms and conditions of his employment, would not differ from the corresponding provisions of the previous contract, or

(b) the offer constitutes an offer of suitable employment in relation to the employee,

the following subsections have effect.

(3) If the employee unreasonably refuses the offer, he is not entitled to remuneration under the protective award in respect of a period during which but for that refusal he would have been employed.

(4) If the employee's contract of employment is renewed, or he is re-engaged under

a new contract of employment, in pursuance of such an offer as is referred to in subsection (2)(b), there shall be a trial period in relation tot he contract as renewed, or the new contract (whether or not there has been a previous trial period under this section).

(5) The trial period begins with the ending of his employment under the previous contract and ends with the expiration of the period of four weeks beginning with the date on which he starts work under the contract as renewed, or the new contract, or such longer period as may be agreed in accordance with subsection (6) for the purpose of retraining the employee for employment under that contract.

(6) Any such agreement –

(a) shall be made between the employer and the employee or his representative before the employee starts work under the contract as renewed or, as the case may be, the new contract,

(b) shall be in writing,

(c) shall specify the date of the end of the trial period, and

(d) shall specify the terms and conditions of employment which will apply in the employee's case after the end of that period.

(7) If during the trial period –

(a) the employee, for whatever reason, terminates the contract, or gives notice to terminate it and the contract is thereafter, in consequence, terminated, or

(b) the employer, for a reason connected with or arising out of the change to the renewed, or new, employment, terminates the contract, or gives notice to terminate it and the contract is thereafter, in consequence, terminated,

the employee remains entitled under the protective award unless, in a case falling within paragraph (a), he acted unreasonably in terminating or giving notice to terminate the contract.

192 Complaint by employee to employment tribunal

(1) An employee may present a complaint to an employment tribunal on the ground that he is a an employee of a description to which a protective award relates and that his employer has failed, wholly or in part, to pay him remuneration under the award.

(2) An employment tribunal shall not entertain a complaint under this section unless it is presented to the tribunal –

(a) before the end of the period of three months beginning with the day (or, if the complaint relates to more than one day, the last of the days) in respect of which the complaint is made of failure to pay remuneration, or

(b) where the tribunal is satisfied that it was not reasonably practicable for the complaint to be presented within the period of three months, within such further period as it may consider reasonable.

(3) Where the tribunal finds a complaint under this section well-founded it shall

order the employer to pay the complainant the amount of remuneration which it finds is due to him.

(4) The remedy of an employee for infringement of his right to remuneration under a protective award is by way of complaint under this section, and not otherwise.

193 Duty of employer to notify Secretary of State of certain redundancies

(1) An employer proposing to dismiss as redundant 100 or more employees at one establishment within a period of 90 days or less shall notify the Secretary of State, in writing, of his proposal at least 90 days before the first of those dismissals takes effect.

(2) An employer proposing to dismiss as redundant 20 or more employees at one establishment within such a period shall notify the Secretary of State, in writing, of his proposal at least 30 days before the first of those dismissals takes effect.

(3) In determining how many employees an employer is proposing to dismiss as redundant within the period mentioned in subsection (1) or (2), no account shall be taken of employees in respect of whose proposed dismissal notice has already been given to the Secretary of State.

(4) A notice under this section shall –

(a) be given to the Secretary of State by delivery to him or by sending it by post to him, at such address as the Secretary of State may direct in relation to the establishment where the employees proposed to be dismissed are employed,

(b) where there are representatives to be consulted under section 188, identify them and state the date when consultation with them under that section began, and

(c) be in such form and contain such particulars, in addition to those required by paragraph (b), as the Secretary of State may direct.

(5) After receiving a notice under this section from an employer the Secretary of State may be written notice require the employer to give him such further information as may be specified in the notice.

(6) Where there are representatives to be consulted under section 188, the employer shall give to each of them a copy of any notice given under subsections (1) or (2). The copy shall be delivered to them or sent by post to an address notified by them to the employer, or (in the case of representatives of a trade union) sent by post to the union at the address of its head or main office.

(7) If in any case there are special circumstances rendering it not reasonably practicable for the employer to comply with any of the requirements of subsections (1) to (6), he shall take all such steps towards compliance with that requirement as are reasonably practicable in the circumstances. Where the decision leading to the proposed dismissals is that of a person controlling the employer (directly or indirectly), a failure on the part of that person to provide information to the

employer shall not constitute special circumstances rendering it not reasonably practicable for the employer to comply with such a requirement.

194 Offence of failure to notify

(1) An employer who fails to give notice to the Secretary of State in accordance with section 193 commits an offence and is liable on summary conviction to a fine not exceeding level 5 on the standard scale. ...

195 Construction of references to dismissal as redundant, etc

(1) In this Chapter references to dismissal as redundant are references to dismissal for a reason not related to the individual concerned or for a number of reasons all of which are not so related.

(2) For the purposes of any proceedings under this Chapter, where an employee is or is proposed to be dismissed it shall be presumed, unless the contrary is proved, that he is or is proposed to be dismissed as redundant.

196 Construction of references to representatives

(1) For the purposes of this Chapter persons are employee representatives if –

(a) they have been elected by employees for the specific purpose of being consulted by their employer about dismissals proposed by him, or

(b) having been elected or appointed by employees (whether before or after dismissals have been proposed by their employer) otherwise than for that specific purpose, it is appropriate (having regard to the purposes for which they were elected) for the employer to consult them about dismissals proposed by him,

and (in either case) they are employed by the employer at the time when they are elected or appointed.

(2) References in this Chapter to representatives of a trade union, in relation to an employer, are to officials or other persons authorised by the trade union to carry on collective bargaining with the employer.

(3) References in this Chapter to affected employees are to employees who may be affected by the proposed dismissals or who may be affected by measures taken in connection with such dismissals.

CHAPTER III

CODES OF PRACTICE

199 Issue of Codes of Practice by ACAS

(1) ACAS may issue Codes of Practice containing such practical guidance as it thinks fit for the purpose of promoting the improvement of industrial relations or for purposes connected with trade union learning representatives.

(2) In particular, ACAS shall in one or more Codes of Practice provide practical guidance on the following matters –

(a) the time off to be permitted by an employer to a trade union official in accordance with section 168 (time off for carrying out trade union duties);

(b) the time off to be permitted by an employer to a trade union member in accordance with section 170 (time off for trade union activities); and

(c) the information to be disclosed by employers to trade union representatives in accordance with sections 181 and 182 (disclosure of information for purposes of collective bargaining). ...

200 Procedure for issue of Code by ACAS

(1) Where ACAS proposes to issue a Code of Practice, or a revised Code, it shall prepare and publish a draft of the Code, shall consider any representations made to it about the draft and may modify the draft accordingly. ...

203 Issue of Codes of Practice by the Secretary of State

(1) The Secretary of State may issue Codes of Practice containing such practical guidance as he thinks fit for the purpose –

(a) of promoting the improvement of industrial relations, or

(b) of promoting what appear to him to be to be desirable practices in relation to the conduct by trade unions of ballots and elections or for purposes connected with trade union learning representatives. ...

207 Effect of failure to comply with Code

(1) A failure on the part of any person to observe any provision of a Code of Practice issued under this Chapter shall not of itself render him liable to any proceedings.

(2) In any proceedings before an employment tribunal or the Central Arbitration Committee any Code of Practice issued under this Chapter by ACAS shall be admissible in evidence, and any provision of the Code which appears to the tribunal or Committee to be relevant to any question arising in the proceedings shall be taken into account in determining that question.

(3) In any proceedings before a court or employment tribunal or the Central Arbitration Committee any Code of Practice issued under this Chapter by the Secretary of State shall be admissible in evidence, and any provision of the Code which appears to the court, tribunal or Committee to be relevant to any question arising in the proceedings shall be taken into account in determining that question.

CHAPTER IV

GENERAL

209 General duty to promote improvement of industrial relations

It is the general duty of ACAS to promote the improvement of industrial relations.

210 Conciliation

(1) Where a trade dispute exists or is apprehended ACAS may, at the request of one or more parties to the dispute or otherwise, offer the parties to the dispute its assistance with a view to bringing about a settlement.

(2) The assistance may be by way of conciliation or by other means, and may include the appointment of a person other than an officer or servant of ACAS to offer assistance to the parties to the dispute with a view to bringing about a settlement.

(3) In exercising its functions under this section ACAS shall have regard to the desirability of encouraging the parties to a dispute to use any appropriate agreed procedures for negotiation or the settlement of disputes.

210A Information required by ACAS for purposes of settling recognition disputes

(1) This section applies where ACAS is exercising its functions under section 210 with a view to bringing about a settlement of a recognition dispute.

(2) The parties to the recognition dispute may jointly request ACAS or a person nominated by ACAS to do either or both of the following –

(a) hold a ballot of the workers involved in the dispute;

(b) ascertain the union membership of the workers involved in the dispute.

(3) In the following provisions of this section references to ACAS include references to a person nominated by ACAS; and anything done by such a person under this section shall be regarded as done in the exercise of the functions of ACAS mentioned in subsection (1).

(4) At any time after ACAS has received a request under subsection (2), it may require any party to the recognition dispute –

(a) to supply ACAS with specified information concerning the workers involved in the dispute, and

(b) to do so within such period as it may specify.

(5) ACAS may impose a requirement under subsection (4) only if it considers that it is necessary to do so –

(a) for the exercise of the functions mentioned in subsection (1); and

(b) in order to enable or assist it to comply with the request.

(6) The recipient of a requirement under this section must, within the specified

period, supply ACAS with such of the specified information as is in the recipient's possession.

(7) A request under subsection (2) may be withdrawn by any party to the recognition dispute at any time and, if it is withdrawn, ACAS shall take no further steps to hold the ballot or to ascertain the union membership of the workers involved in the dispute.

(8) If a party to a recognition dispute fails to comply with subsection (6), ACAS shall take no further steps to hold the ballot or to ascertain the union membership of the workers involved in the dispute.

(9) Nothing in this section requires ACAS to comply with a request under subsection (2).

(10) In this section –

'party', in relation to a recognition dispute, means each of the employers, employers' associations and trade unions involved in the dispute;

'a recognition dispute' means a trade dispute between employers and workers which is connected wholly or partly with the recognition by employers or employers' associations of the right of a trade union to represent workers in negotiations, consultations or other procedures relating to any of the matters mentioned in paragraphs (a) to (f) of section 218(1);

'specified' means specified in a requirement under this section; and

'workers' has the meaning given in section 218(5).

211 Conciliation officers

(1) ACAS shall designate some of its officers to perform the functions of conciliation officers under any enactment (whenever passed) relating to matters which are or could be the subject of proceedings before an employment tribunal.

(2) References in any such enactment to a conciliation officer are to an officer designated under this section.

212 Arbitration

(1) Where a trade dispute exists or is apprehended ACAS may, at the request of one or more of the parties to the dispute and with the consent of all the parties to the dispute, refer all or any of the matters to which the dispute relates for settlement to the arbitration of –

(a) one or more persons appointed by ACAS for that purpose (not being officers or employees of ACAS), or

(b) the Central Arbitration Committee.

(2) In exercising its functions under this section ACAS shall consider the likelihood of the dispute being settled by conciliation.

(3) Where there exist appropriate agreed procedures for negotiation or the

settlement of disputes, ACAS shall not refer a matter for settlement to arbitration under this section unless –

(a) those procedures have been used and have failed to result in a settlement, or

(b) there is, in ACAS's opinion, a special reason which justifies arbitration under this section as an alternative to those procedures.

(4) Where a matter is referred to arbitration under subsection (1)(a) –

(a) if more than one arbitrator or arbiter is appointed, ACAS shall appoint one of them to act as chairman; and

(b) the award may be published if ACAS so decides and all the parties consent.

(5) Part I of the Arbitration Act 1996 (general provisions as to arbitration) does not apply to an arbitration under this section.

212A   Arbitration scheme for unfair dismissal cases, etc

(1) ACAS may prepare a scheme providing for arbitration in the case of disputes involving proceedings, or claims which could be the subject of proceedings, before an employment tribunal under, or arising out of a contravention or alleged contravention of –

(za) section 80G(1) or 80H(1)(b) of the Employment Rights Act 1996 (flexible working),

(a) Part X of that Act (unfair dismissal), or

(b) any enactment specified in an order made by the Secretary of State.

(2) When ACAS has prepared such a scheme it shall submit a draft of the scheme to the Secretary of State who, if he approves it, shall make an order-

(a) setting out the scheme, and

(b) making provision for it to come into effect.

(3) ACAS may from time to time prepare a revised version of such a scheme and, when it has done so, shall submit a draft of the revised scheme to the Secretary of State who, if he approves it, shall make an order-

(a) setting out the revised scheme, and

(b) making provision for it to come into effect.

(4) ACAS may take any steps appropriate for promoting awareness of a scheme prepared under this section.

(5) Where the parties to any dispute within subsection (1) agree in writing to submit the dispute to arbitration in accordance with a scheme having effect by virtue of an order under this section, ACAS shall refer the dispute to the arbitration of a person appointed by ACAS for the purpose (not being an officer or employee of ACAS).

(6) Nothing in the Arbitration Act 1996 shall apply to an arbitration conducted in accordance with a scheme having effect by virtue of an order under this section

except to the extent that the order provides for any provision of Part I of that Act so to apply; and the order may provide for any such provision so to apply subject to modifications. ...

(8) Where a scheme set out in an order under this section includes provision for the making of re-employment orders in arbitrations conducted in accordance with the scheme, the order setting out the scheme may require employment tribunals to enforce such orders-

(a) in accordance with section 117 of the Employment Rights Act 1996 (enforcement by award of compensation), or

(b) in accordance with that section as modified by the order.

For this purpose 're-employment orders' means orders requiring that persons found to have been unfairly dismissed be reinstated, re-engaged or otherwise re-employed.

(9) An order under this section setting out a scheme may provide that, in the case of disputes within subsection (1)(a), such part of an award made in accordance with the scheme as is specified by the order shall be treated as a basic award of compensation for unfair dismissal for the purposes of section 184(1)(d) of the Employment Rights Act 1996 (which specifies such an award as a debt which the Secretary of State must satisfy if the employer has become insolvent).

(10) An order under this section shall be made by statutory instrument. ...

213 Advice

(1) ACAS may, on request or otherwise, give employers, employers' associations, workers and trade unions such advice as it thinks appropriate on matters concerning with or affecting or likely to affect industrial relations.

(2) ACAS may also publish general advice on matters concerned with or affecting or likely to affect industrial relations.

214 Inquiry

(1) ACAS may, if it thinks fit, inquire into any question relating to industrial relations generally or to industrial relations in any particular industry or in any particular undertaking or part of an undertaking.

(2) The findings of an inquiry under this section, together with any advice given by ACAS in connection with those findings, may be published by ACAS if –

(a) it appears to ACAS that publication is desirable for the improvement of industrial relations, either generally or in relation to the specific question inquired into, and

(b) after sending a draft of the findings to all parties appearing to be concerned and taking account of their views, it thinks fit.

215 Inquiry and report by court of inquiry

(1) Where a trade dispute exists or is apprehended, the Secretary of State may inquire into the causes and circumstances of the dispute and, if he thinks fit, appoint a court of inquiry and refer to it any matters appearing to him to be connected with or relevant to the dispute.

(2) The court shall inquire into the matters referred to it and report on them to the Secretary of State; and it may make interim reports if it thinks fit.

(3) Any report of the court, and any minority report, shall be laid before both Houses of Parliament as soon as possible.

(4) The Secretary of State may, before or after the report has been laid before Parliament, publish or cause to be published from time to time, in such manner as he thinks fit, any information obtained or conclusions arrived at by the court as the result or in the course of its inquiry.

(5) No report or publication made or authorised by the court or the Secretary of State shall include any information obtained by the court of inquiry in the course of its inquiry –

    (a) as to any trade union, or

    (b) as to any individual business (whether carried on by a person, firm, or company),

which is not available otherwise than through evidence given at the inquiry, except with the consent of the secretary of the trade union or of the person, firm or company in question.

Nor shall any individual member of the court or any person concerned in the inquiry disclose such information without such consent. ...

216 Constitution and proceedings of court of inquiry

(1) A court of inquiry shall consist of –

    (a) a chairman and such other persons as the Secretary of State thinks fit to appoint, or

    (b) one person appointed by the Secretary of State,

as the Secretary of State thinks fit. ...

(3) A court may conduct its inquiry in public or in private, at its discretion. ...

218 Meaning of 'trade dispute' in Part IV

(1) In this Part 'trade dispute' means a dispute between employers and workers, or between workers and workers, which is connected with one or more of the following matters –

    (a) terms and conditions of employment, or the physical conditions in which any workers are required to work;

(b) engagement or non-engagement, or termination or suspension of employment or the duties of employment, of one or more workers;

(c) allocation of work or the duties of employment as between workers or groups of workers;

(d) matters of discipline;

(e) the membership or non-membership of a trade union on the part of a worker;

(f) facilities for officials of trade unions; and

(g) machinery for negotiation or consultation, and other procedures, relating to any of the foregoing matters, including the recognition by employers or employers' associations of the right of a trade union to represent workers in any such negotiation or consultation or in the carrying out of such procedures.

(2) A dispute between a Minister of the Crown and any workers shall notwithstanding that he is not the employer of those workers, be treated for the purposes of this Part as a dispute between an employer and those workers if the dispute relates –

(a) to matters which have been referred for consideration by a joint body on which, by virtue of any provision made by or under any enactment, that Minister is represented, or

(b) to matters which cannot be settled without that Minister exercising a power conferred on him by or under an enactment.

(3) There is a trade dispute for the purpose of this Part even though it relates to matters occurring outside Great Britain.

(4) A dispute to which a trade union or employer's association is a party shall be treated for the purposes of this Part as a dispute to which workers or, as the case may be, employers are parties.

(5) In this section –

'employment' includes any relationship whereby one person personally does work or performs services for another; and

'worker', in relation to a dispute to which an employer is a party, includes any worker even if not employed by that employer.

PART V

INDUSTRIAL ACTION

219 Protection from certain tort liabilities

(1) An act done by a person in contemplation or furtherance of a trade dispute is not actionable in tort on the ground only –

(a) that it induces another person to break a contract or interferes or induces another person to interfere with its performance, or

(b) that it consists in his threatening that a contract (whether one to which he is a party or not) will be broken or its performance interfered with, or that he will induce another person to break a contract or interfere with its performance.

(2) An agreement or combination by two or more persons to do or procure the doing of an act in contemplation or furtherance of a trade dispute is not actionable in tort if the act is one which if done without any such agreement or combination would not be actionable in tort.

(3) Nothing in subsections (1) and (2) prevents an act done in the course of picketing from being actionable in tort unless it is done in the course of attendance declared lawful by section 220 (peaceful picketing).

(4) Subsections (1) and (2) have effect subject to sections 222 to 225 (action excluded from protection) and to sections 226 (requirement of ballot before action by trade union) and 234A (requirement of notice to employer of industrial action); and in those sections 'not protected' means excluded from the protection afforded by this section or, where the expression is used with reference to a particular person, excluded from that protection as respects that person.

220 Peaceful picketing

(1) It is lawful for a person in contemplation or furtherance of a trade dispute to attend –

(a) at or near his own place of work, or

(b) if he is an official of a trade union, at or near the place of work of a member of the union whom he is accompanying and whom he represents,

for the purpose only of peacefully obtaining or communicating information, or peacefully persuading any person to work or abstain from working.

(2) If a person works or normally works –

(a) otherwise than at any one place, or

(b) at a place the location of which is such that attendance there for a purpose mentioned in subsection (1) is impracticable,

his place of work for the purposes of that subsection shall be any premises of his employer from which he works or from which his work is administered.

(3) In the case of a worker not in employment where –

(a) his last employment was terminated in connection with a trade dispute, or

(b) the termination of his employment was one of the circumstances giving rise to a trade dispute,

in relation to that dispute his former place of work shall be treated for the purposes of subsection (1) as being his place of work.

(4) A person who is an official of a trade union by virtue only of having been elected or appointed to be a representative of some of the members of the union shall be regarded for the purposes of subsection (1) as representing only those members; but

otherwise an official of a union shall be regarded for those purposes as representing all its members.

221 Restrictions on grant of injunctions ...

(1) Where –

(a) an application for an injunction ... is made to a court inn the absence of the party against whom it is sought or any representative of his, and

(b) he claims, or in the opinion of the court would be likely to claim, that he acted in contemplation or furtherance of a trade dispute,

the court shall not grant the injunction ... unless satisfied that all steps which in the circumstances were reasonable have been taken with a view to securing that notice of the application and an opportunity of being heard with respect to the application have been given to him.

(2) Where –

(a) an application for an interlocutory injunction is made to a court pending the trial of an action, and

(b) the party against whom it is sought claims that he acted in contemplation or furtherance of a trade dispute,

the court shall, in exercising its discretion whether or not to grant the injunction, have regard to the likelihood of that party's succeeding at the trial of the action in establishing any matter which would afford a defence to the action under section 219 (protection from certain tort liabilities) or section 220 (peaceful picketing). ...

222 Action to enforce trade union membership

(1) An act is not protected if the reason, or one of the reasons, for which it is done is the fact or belief that a particular employer –

(a) is employing, has employed or might employ a person who is not a member of a trade union, or

(b) is failing, has failed or might fail to discriminate against such a person.

(2) For the purposes of subsection (1)(b) an employer discriminates against a person if, but only if, he ensures that his conduct in relation to –

(a) persons, or persons of any description, employed by him, or who apply to be, or are, considered by him for employment, or

(b) the provision of employment for such persons,

is different, in some or all cases, according to whether or not they are members of a trade union, and is more favourable to those who are.

(3) An act is not protected if it constitutes, or is one of a number of acts which together constitute, an inducement or attempted inducement of a person –

(a) to incorporate in a contract to which that person is a party, or a proposed contract to which he intends to be a party, a term or condition which is or would be void by virtue of section 144 (union membership requirement in contract for goods or services), or

(b) to contravene section 145 (refusal to deal with person on grounds relating to union membership).

(4) References in this section to an employer employing a person are to a person acting in the capacity of the person for whom a worker works or normally works.

(5) References in this section to not being a member of a trade union are to not being a member of any trade union, of a particular trade union or of one of a number of particular trade unions. Any such reference includes a reference to not being a member of a particular branch or section of a trade union or of one of a number of particular branches or sections of a trade union.

223 Action taken because of dismissal for taking unofficial action

An act is not protected if the reason, or one of the reasons, for doing it is the fact or belief that an employer has dismissed one or more employees in circumstances such that by virtue of section 237 (dismissal in connection with unofficial action) they have no right to complain of unfair dismissal.

224 Secondary action

An act is not protected if one of the facts relied on for the purpose of establishing liability is that there has been secondary action which is not lawful picketing.

(2) There is secondary action in relation to a trade dispute when, and only when, a person –

(a) induces another to break a contract of employment or interferes or induces another to interfere with its performance, or

(b) threatened that a contract of employment under which he or another is employed will be broken or its performance interfered with, or that he will induce another to break a contract of employment or to interfere with its performance.

and the employer under the contract of employment is not the employer party to the dispute.

(3) Lawful picketing means acts done in the course of such attendance as is declared lawful by section 220 (peaceful picketing) –

(a) by a worker employed (or, in the case of a worker not in employment, last employed) by the employer party to the dispute, or

(b) by a trade union official whose attendance is lawful by virtue of subsection (1)(b) of that section.

(4) For the purposes of this section an employer shall not be treated as party to a dispute between another employer and workers of that employer; and where more than one employer is in dispute with his workers, the dispute between each

employer and his workers shall be treated as a separate dispute. In this subsection 'worker' has the same meaning as in section 244 (meaning of 'trade dispute').

(5) An act in contemplation or furtherance of a trade dispute which is primary action in relation to that dispute may not be relied on as secondary action in relation to another trade dispute. Primary action means such action as is mentioned in paragraph (a) or (b) of subsection (2) where the employer under the contract of employment is the employer party to the dispute.

(6) In this section 'contract of employment' includes any contract under which one person personally does work or perform services for another, and related expressions shall be construed accordingly.

225 Pressure to impose union recognition requirement

(1) An act is not protected if it constitutes, or is one of a number of acts which together constitute, an inducement or attempted inducement of a person –

(a) to incorporate in a contract to which that person is a party, or a proposed contract to which he intends to be a party, a term or condition which is or would be void by virtue of section 186 (recognition requirement in contract for goods or services), or

(b) to contravene section 187 (refusal to deal with person on grounds of union exclusion).

(2) An act is not protected if –

(a) it interferes with the supply (whether or not under a contract) of goods or services, or can reasonably be expected to have that effect, and

(b) one of the facts relied upon for the purpose of establishing liability is that a person has –

(i) induced another to break a contract of employment or interfered or induced another to interfere with its performance, or

(ii) threatened that a contract of employment under which he or another is employed will be broken or its performance interfered with, or that he will induce another to break a contract of employment or to interfere with its performance, and

(c) the reason, or one of the reasons, for doing the act is the fact or belief that the supplier (not being the employer under the contract of employment mentioned in paragraph (b)) does not, or might not –

(i) recognise one or more trade unions for the purpose of negotiating on behalf of workers, or any class of worker, employed by him, or

(ii) negotiate or consult with, or with an official of, one or more trade unions.

226 Requirement of ballot before action by trade union

(1) An act done by a trade union to induce a person to take part, or continue to take part, in industrial action –

(a) is not protected unless the industrial action has the support of a ballot, and

(b) where section 226A falls to be complied with in relation to the person's employer, is not protected as respects the employer unless the trade union has complied with section 226A in relation to him.

In this section 'the relevant time', in relation to an act by a trade union to induce a person to take part, or continue to take part, in industrial action, means the time at which proceedings are commenced in respect of the act.

(2) Industrial action shall be regarded as having the support of a ballot only if –

(a) the union has held a ballot in respect of the action –

(i) in relation to which the requirements of section 226B so far as applicable before and during the holding of the ballot were satisfied,

(ii) in relation to which the requirements of sections 227 to 231 were satisfied, and

(iii) in which the majority voting in the ballot answered 'Yes' to the question applicable in accordance with section 229(2) to industrial action of the kind to which the act of inducement relates;

(b) such of the requirements of the following sections as have fallen to be satisfied at the relevant time have been satisfied, namely –

(i) section 226B so far as applicable after the holding of the ballot, and

(ii) section 231B;

(bb) section 232A does not prevent the industrial action from being regarded as having the support of the ballot; and

(c) the requirements of section 233 (calling of industrial action with support of ballot) are satisfied.

Any reference in this subsection to a requirement of a provision which is disapplied or modified by section 232 has effect subject to that section.

(3) Where separate workplace ballots are held by virtue of section 228(1)–

(a) industrial action shall be regarded as having the support of a ballot if the conditions specified in subsection (2) are satisfied, and

(b) the trade union shall be taken to have complied with the requirements relating to a ballot imposed by section 226A if those requirements are complied with,

in relation to the ballot for the place of work of the person induced to take part, or continue to take part, in the industrial action.

(3A) If the requirements of section 231A fall to be satisfied in relation to an employer, as respects that employer industrial action shall not be regarded as having the support of a ballot unless those requirements are satisfied in relation to that employer.

(4) For the purposes of this section an inducement, in relation to a person, includes

an inducement which is or would be ineffective, whether because of his unwillingness to be influenced by it or for any other reason.

226A   Notice of ballot and sample voting paper for employers

(1) The trade union must take such steps as are reasonably necessary to ensure that –

(a) not later than the seventh day before the opening day of the ballot, the notice specified in subsection (2), and

(b) not later than the third day before the opening day of the ballot, the sample voting paper specified in subsection (2F),

is received by every person who it is reasonable for the union to believe (at the latest time when steps could be taken to comply with paragraph (a)) will be the employer of persons who will be entitled to vote in the ballot.

(2) The notice referred to in paragraph (a) of subsection (1) is a notice in writing –

(a) stating that the union intends to hold the ballot,

(b) specifying the date which the union reasonably believes will be the opening day of the ballot, and

(c) containing –

(i) the lists mentioned in subsection (2A) and the figures mentioned in subsection (2B), together with an explanation of how those figures were arrived at, or

(ii) where some or all of the employees concerned are employees from whose wages the employer makes deductions representing payments to the union, either those lists and figures and that explanation or the information mentioned in subsection (2C).

(2A) The lists are –

(a) a list of the categories of employee to which the employees concerned belong, and

(b) a list of the workplaces at which the employees concerned work.

(2B) The figures are –

(a) the total number of employees concerned,

(b) the number of the employees concerned in each of the categories in the list mentioned in subsection (2A)(a), and

(c) the number of the employees concerned who work at each workplace in the list mentioned in subsection (2A)(b).

(2C) The information referred to in subsection (2)(c)(ii) is such information as will enable the employer readily to deduce –

(a) the total number of employees concerned,

(b) the categories of employee to which the employees concerned belong and the number of the employees concerned in each of those categories, and

(c) the workplaces at which the employees concerned work and the number of them who work at each of those workplaces.

(2D) The lists and figures supplied under this section, or the information mentioned in subsection (2C) that is so supplied, must be as accurate as is reasonably practicable in the light of the information in the possession of the union at the time when it complies with subsection (1)(a).

(2E) For the purposes of subsection (2D) information is in the possession of the union if it is held, for union purposes –

(a) in a document, whether in electronic form or any other form, and

(b) in the possession or under the control of an officer or employee of the union.

(2F) The sample voting paper referred to in paragraph (b) of subsection (1) is –

(a) a sample of the form of voting paper which is to be sent to the employees concerned, or

(b) where the employees concerned are not all to be sent the same form of voting paper, a sample of each form of voting paper which is to be sent to any of them.

(2G) Nothing in this section requires a union to supply an employer with the names of the employees concerned.

(2H) In this section references to the 'employees concerned' are references to those employees of the employer in question who the union reasonably believes will be entitled to vote in the ballot.

(2I) For the purposes of this section, the workplace at which an employee works is –

(a) in relation to an employee who works at or from a single set of premises, those premises, and

(b) in relation to any other employee, the premises with which his employment has the closest connection.

(4) In this section references to the opening day of the ballot are references to the first day when a voting paper is sent to any person entitled to vote in the ballot. ...

226B Appointment of scrutineer

(1) The trade union shall, before the ballot in respect of the industrial action is held, appoint a qualified person ('the scrutineer') whose terms of appointment shall require him to carry out in relation to the ballot the functions of –

(a) taking such steps as appear to him to be appropriate for the purpose of enabling him to make a report to the trade union (see section 231B); and

(b) making the report as soon as reasonably practicable after the date of the ballot and, in any event, not later than the end of the period of four weeks beginning with that date. ...

226C   Exclusion for small ballots

Nothing in section 226B, section 229(1A)(a) or section 231B shall impose a requirement on a trade union unless –

(a) the number of members entitled to vote in the ballot, or

(b) where separate workplace ballots are held in accordance with section 228(1), the aggregate of the number of members entitled to vote in each of them,

exceeds 50.

227   Entitlement to vote in ballot

(1) Entitlement to vote in the ballot must be accorded equally to all the members of the trade union who it is reasonable at the time of the ballot for the union to believe will be induced by the union to take part or, as the case may be, to continue to take part in the industrial action in question, and to no others.

228   Separate workplace ballots

(1) Subject to subsection (2), this section applies if the members entitled to vote in a ballot by virtue of section 227 do not all have the same workplace.

(2) This section does not apply if the union reasonably believes that all those members have the same workplace.

(3) Subject to section 228A, a separate ballot shall be held for each workplace; and entitlement to vote in each ballot shall be accorded equally to, and restricted to, members of the union who –

(a) are entitled to vote by virtue of section 227, and

(b) have that workplace.

(4) In this section and section 228A 'workplace' in relation to a person who is employed means –

(a) if the person works at or from a single set of premises, those premises, and

(b) in any other case, the premises with which the person's employment has the closest connection.

228A   Separate workplaces: single and aggregate ballots

(1) Where section 228(3) would require separate ballots to be held for each workplace, a ballot may be held in place of some or all of the separate ballots if one of subsections (2) to (4) is satisfied in relation to it.

(2) This subsection is satisfied in relation to a ballot if the workplace of each member entitled to vote in the ballot is the workplace of at least one member of the union who is affected by the dispute.

(3) This subsection is satisfied in relation to a ballot if entitlement to vote is accorded to, and limited to, all the members of the union who –

(a) according to the union's reasonable belief have an occupation of a particular kind or have any of a number of particular kinds of occupation, and

(b) are employed by a particular employer, or by any of a number of particular employers, with whom the union is in dispute.

(4) This subsection is satisfied in relation to a ballot if entitlement to vote is accorded to, and limited to, all the members of the union who are employed by a particular employer, or by any of a number of particular employers, with whom the union is in dispute.

(5) For the purposes of subsection (2) the following are members of the union affected by a dispute –

(a) if the dispute relates (wholly or partly) to a decision which the union reasonably believes the employer has made or will make concerning a matter specified in subsection (1)(a), (b) or (c) of section 244 (meaning of 'trade dispute'), members whom the decision directly affects,

(b) if the dispute relates (wholly or partly) to a matter specified in subsection (1)(d) of that section, members whom the matter directly affects,

(c) if the dispute relates (wholly or partly) to a matter specified in subsection (1)(e) of that section, persons whose membership or non-membership is in dispute,

(d) if the dispute relates (wholly or partly) to a matter specified in subsection (1)(f) of that section, officials of the union who have used or would use the facilities concerned in the dispute.

229 Voting paper

(1) The method of voting in a ballot must be by the marking of a voting paper by the person voting.

(1A) Each voting paper must –

(a) state the name of the independent scrutineer,

(b) clearly specify the address to which, and the date by which, it is to be returned,

(c) be given one of a series of consecutive whole numbers every one of which is used in giving a different number in that series to each voting paper printed or otherwise produced for the purposes of the ballot, and

(d) be marked with its number. ...

(2) The voting paper must contain at least one of the following questions –

(a) a question (however framed) which requires the person answering it to say, by answering 'Yes' or 'No', whether he is prepared to take part or, as the case may be, to continue to take part in a strike;

(b) a question (however framed) which requires the person answering it to say, by answering 'Yes' or 'No', ,whether he is prepared to take part or, as the case may be, to continue to take part in industrial action short of a strike.

(2A) For the purposes of subsectiom (2) an overtime ban and a call-out ban constitute industrial action short of a strike.

(3) The voting paper must specify who, in the event of a vote in favour of industrial action, is authorised for the purposes of section 233 to call upon members to take part or continue to take part in the industrial action. The person or description of persons so specified need not be authorised under the rules of the union but must be within section 20(2) (persons for whose acts the union is taken to be responsible).

(4) The following statement must (without being qualified or commented upon by anything else on the voting paper) appear on every voting paper –

'If you take part in a strike or other industrial action, you may be in breach of your contract of employment. However, if you are dismissed for taking part in a strike or other industrial action which is called officially and is otherwise lawful, the dismissal will be unfair if it takes place fewer than twelve weeks after you started taking part in the action, and depending on the circumstances may be unfair if it takes place later.'

230 Conduct of ballot

(1) Every person who is entitled to vote in the ballot must –

(a) be allowed to vote without interference from, or constraint imposed by, the union or any of its members, officials or employees, and

(b) so far as is reasonably practicable, be enabled to do so without incurring any direct cost to himself.

(2) Except as regards persons falling within subsection (2A) [merchant seamen], so far as is reasonably practicable, every person who is entitled to vote in the ballot must –

(a) have a voting paper sent to him by post at his home address or any other address which he has requested the trade union in writing to treat as his postal address; and

(b) be given a convenient opportunity to vote by post. ...

(4) A ballot shall be conducted so as to secure that –

(a) so far as is reasonably practicable, those voting do so in secret, and

(b) the votes given in the ballot are fairly and accurately counted.

For the purposes of paragraph (b) an inaccuracy in counting shall be disregarded if it is accidental and on a scale which could not affect the result of the ballot.

231 Information as to result of ballot

As soon as is reasonably practicable after the holding of the ballot, the trade union shall take such steps as are reasonably necessary to ensure that all persons entitled to vote in the ballot are informed of the number of –

(a) votes cast in the ballot,

(b) individuals answering 'Yes' to the question, or as the case may be, to each question,

(c) individuals answering 'No' to the question, or, as the case may be, to each question, and

(d) spoiled voting papers.

231A Employers to be informed of ballot result

(1) As soon as reasonably practicable after the holding of the ballot, the trade union shall take such steps as are reasonably necessary to ensure that every relevant employer is informed of the matters mentioned in section 231.

(2) In subsection (1) 'relevant employer' means a person who it is reasonable for the trade union to believe (at the time when the steps are taken) was at the time of the ballot the employer of any persons entitled to vote.

231B Scrutineer's report

(1) The scrutineer's report on the ballot shall state whether the scrutineer is satisfied –

(a) that there are no reasonable grounds for believing that there was any contravention of a requirement imposed by or under any enactment in relation to the ballot,

(b) that the arrangements made with respect to the production, storage, distribution, return or other handling of the voting papers used in the ballot, and the arrangements for the counting of the votes, included all such security arrangements as were reasonably practicable for the purpose of minimising the risk that any unfairness or malpractice might occur, and

(c) that he has been able to carry out the functions conferred on him under section 226B(1) without any interference from the trade union or any of its members, officials or employees;

and if he is not satisfied as to any of those matters, the report shall give particulars of his reason for not being satisfied as to that matter. ...

232A Inducement of member denied entitlement to vote

Industrial action shall not be regarded as having the support of a ballot if the following conditions apply in the case of any person –

(a) he was a member of the trade union at the time when the ballot was held,

(b) it was reasonable at that time for the trade union to believe he would be induced to take part or, as the case may be, to continue to take part in the industrial action,

(c) he was not accorded entitlement to vote in the ballot, and

(d) he was induced by the trade union to take part or, as the case may be, to continue to take part in the industrial action.

232B   Small accidental failures to be disregarded

(1) If –

(a) in relation to a ballot there is a failure (or there are failures) to comply with a provision mentioned in subsection (2) or with more than one of those provisions, and

(b) the failure is accidental and on a scale which is unlikely to affect the result of the ballot or, as the case may be, the failures are accidental and taken together are on a scale which is unlikely to affect the result of the ballot,

the failure (or failures) shall be disregarded for all purposes (including, in particular, those of section 232A(c)).

(2) The provisions are section 227(1), section 230(2) and section 230(2B).

233   Calling of industrial action with support of ballot

(1) Industrial action shall not be regarded as having the support of a ballot unless it is called by a specified person and the conditions specified below are satisfied.

(2) A 'specified person' means a person specified or of a description specified in the voting paper for the ballot in accordance with section 229(3).

(3) The conditions are that –

(a) there must have been no call by the trade union to take part or continue to take part in industrial action to which the ballot relates, or any authorisation or endorsement by the union of any such industrial action, before the date of the ballot;

(b) there must be a call for industrial action by a specified person, and industrial action to which it relates must begin, before the ballot ceases to be effective in accordance with section 234.

(4) For the purposes of this section a call shall be taken to have been made by a trade union if it was authorised or endorsed by the union; and the provisions of section 20(2) to (4) apply for the purpose of determining whether a call, or industrial action, is to be taken to have been so authorised or endorsed.

234   Period after which ballot ceases to be effective

(1) Subject to the following provisions, a ballot ceases to be effective for the purposes of section 233(3)(b) in relation to industrial action by members of a trade union at the end of the period, beginning with the date of the ballot –

(a) of four weeks, or

(b) of such longer duration not exceeding eight weeks as is agreed between the union and the members' employer.

(2) Where for the whole or part of that period the calling or organising of industrial action is prohibited –

(a) by virtue of a court order which subsequently lapses or is discharged, recalled or set aside, or

(b) by virtue of an undertaking given to a court by any person from which he is subsequently released or by which he ceases to be bound,

the trade union may apply to the court for an order that the period during which the prohibition had effect shall not count towards the period referred to in subsection (1).

(3) The application must be made forthwith upon the prohibition ceasing to have effect –

(a) to the court by virtue of whose decision it ceases to have effect, or

(b) where an order lapses or an undertaking ceases to bind without any such decision, to the court by which the order was made or to which the undertaking was given;

and no application may be made after the end of the period of eight weeks beginning with the date of the ballot.

(4) The court shall not make an order if it appears to the court –

(a) that the result of the ballot no longer represents the views of the union members concerned, or

(b) that an event is likely to occur as a result of which those members would vote against industrial action if another ballot were to be held.

(5) No appeal lies from the decision of the court to make or refuse an order under this section.

(6) The period between the making of an application under this section and its determination does not count towards the period referred to in subsection (1). But a ballot shall not by virtue of this subsection (together with any order of the court) be regarded as effective for the purposes of section 233(3)(b) after the end of the period of twelve weeks beginning with the date of the ballot.

234A   Notice to employers of industrial action

(1) An act done by a trade union to induce a person to take part, or continue to take part, in industrial action is not protected as respects his employer unless the union has taken or takes such steps as are reasonably necessary to ensure that the employer receives within the appropriate period a relevant notice covering the act.

(2) Subsection (1) imposes a requirement in the case of an employer only if it is reasonable for the union to believe, at the latest time when steps could be taken to ensure that he receives such a notice, that he is the employer of persons who will be or have been induced to take part, or continue to take part, in the industrial action.

(3) For the purposes of this section a relevant notice is a notice in writing which –

(a) contains –

(i) the lists mentioned in subsection (3A) and the figures mentioned in subsection (3B), together with an explanation of how those figures were arrived at, or

(ii) where some or all of the affected employees are employees from whose wages the employer makes deductions representing payments to the union, either those lists and figures and that explanation or the information mentioned in subsection (3C), and

(b) states whether industrial action is intended to be continuous or discontinuous and specifies –

(i) where it is to be continuous, the intended date for any of the affected employees to begin to take part in the action,

(ii) where it is to be discontinuous, the intended dates for any of the affected employees to take part in the action.

(3A) The lists referred to in subsection (3)(a) are –

(a) a list of the categories of employee to which the affected employees belong, and

(b) a list of the workplaces at which the affected employees work.

(3B) The figures referred to in subsection (3)(a) are –

(a) the total number of the affected employees,

(b) the number of the affected employees in each of the categories in the list mentioned in subsection (3A)(a), and

(c) the number of the affected employees who work at each workplace in the list mentioned in subsection (3A)(b).

(3C) The information referred to in subsection (3)(a)(ii) is such information as will enable the employer readily to deduce –

(a) the total number of the affected employees,

(b) the categories of employee to which the affected employees belong and the number of the affected employees in each of those categories, and

(c) the workplaces at which the affected employees work and the number of them who work at each of those workplaces.

(3D) The lists and figures supplied under this section, or the information mentioned in subsection (3C) that is so supplied, must be as accurate as is reasonably practicable in the light of the information in the possession of the union at the time when it complies with subsection (1).

(3E) For the purposes of subsection (3D) information is in the possession of the union if it is held, for union purposes –

(a) in a document, whether in electronic form or any other form, and

(b) in the possession or under the control of an officer or employee of the union.

(3F) Nothing in this section requires a union to supply an employer with the names of the affected employees.

(4) For the purposes of subsection (1) the appropriate period is the period –

(a) beginning with the day when the union satisfies the requirement of section 231A in relation to the ballot in respect of the industrial action, and

(b) ending with the seventh day before the day, or before the first of the days, specified in the relevant notice.

(5) For the purposes of subsection (1) a relevant notice covers an act done by the union if the person induced falls within a notified category of employee and the workplace at which he works is a notified workplace and –

(a) where he is induced to take part or continue to take part in industrial action which the union intends to be continuous, if –

(i) the notice states that the union intends the industrial action to be continuous, and

(ii) there is no participation by him in the industrial action before the date specified in the notice in consequence of any inducement by the union not covered by a relevant notice; and

(b) where he is induced to take part or continue to take part in industrial action which the union intends to be discontinuous, if there is no participation by him in the industrial action on a day not so specified in consequence of any inducement by the union not covered by a relevant notice.

(5B) In subsection (5) –

(a) a 'notified category of employee' means –

(i) a category of employee that is listed in the notice, or

(ii) where the notice contains the information mentioned in subsection (3C), a category of employee that the employer (at the time he receives the notice) can readily deduce from the notice is a category of employee to which some or all of the affected employees belong, and

(b) a 'notified workplace' means –

(i) a workplace that is listed in the notice, or

(ii) where the notice contains the information mentioned in subsection (3C), a workplace that the employer (at the time he receives the notice) can readily deduce from the notice is the workplace at which some or all of the affected employees work.

(5C) In this section references to the 'affected employees' are references to those employees of the employer who the union reasonably believes will be induced by the union, or have been so induced, to take part or continue to take part in the industrial action.

(5D) For the purposes of this section, the workplace at which an employee works is –

(a) in relation to an employee who works at or from a single set of premises, those premises, and

(b) in relation to any other employee, the premises with which his employment has the closest connection.

(6) For the purposes of this section –

(a) a union intends industrial action to be discontinuous if it intends it to take place only on some days on which there is an opportunity to take the action, and

(b) a union intends industrial action to be continuous if it intends it to be not so restricted.

(7) Subject to subsections (7A) and (7B), where –

(a) continuous industrial action which has been authorised or endorsed by a union ceased to be so authorised or endorsed, and

(b) the industrial action has at a later date again been authorised or endorsed by the union (whether as continuous or discontinuous action),

no relevant notice covering acts done to induce persons to take part in the earlier action shall operate to cover acts done to induce persons to take part in the action authorised or endorsed at the later date and this section shall apply in relation to an act to induce a person to take part, or continue to take part, in the industrial action after that date as if the references in subsection (3)(b)(i) to the industrial action were to the industrial action taking place after that date.

(7A) Subsection (7) shall not apply where industrial action ceases to be authorised or endorsed in order to enable the union to comply with a court order or an undertaking given to a court.

(7B) Subsection (7) shall not apply where –

(a) a union agrees with an employer, before industrial action ceases to be authorised or endorsed, that it will cease to be authorised or endorsed with effect from a date specified in the agreement ('the suspension date') and that it may again be authorised or endorsed with effect from a date not earlier than a date specified in the agreement ('the resumption date'),

(b) the action ceases to be authorised or endorsed with effect from the suspension date, and

(c) the action is again authorised or endorsed with effect from a date which is not earlier than the resumption date or such later date as may be agreed between the union and the employer.

(8) The requirement imposed on a trade union by subsection (1) shall be treated as having been complied with if the steps were taken by other relevant persons or committees whose acts were authorised or endorsed by the union and references to the belief or intention of the union in subsection (2) or, as the case may be, subsections (3), (5), (5C) and (6) shall be construed as references to the belief or the intention of the person or committee taking the steps.

(9) The provisions of section 20(2) to (4) apply for the purpose of determining for the purposes of subsection (1) who are relevant persons or committees and whether the trade union is to be taken to have authorised or endorsed the steps the person

or committee took and for the purposes of subsection (7) to (7B) whether the trade union is to be taken to have authorised or endorsed the industrial action.

235 Construction of references to contract of employment

In section 226 to 234A (requirement of ballot before action by trade union) references to a contract of employment include any contract under which one person personally does work or perform services for another; and related expressions shall be construed accordingly.

235A Industrial action affecting supply of goods or services to an individual

(1) Where an individual claims that –

(a) any trade union or other person has done, or is likely to do, an unlawful act to induce any person to take part, or to continue to take part, in industrial action, and

(b) an effect, or a likely effect, of the industrial action is or will be to –

(i) prevent or delay the supply of goods or services, or

(ii) reduce the quality of goods or services supplied,

to the individual making the claim,

he may apply to the High Court ... for an order under this section.

(2) For the purposes of this section an act to induce any person to take part, or to continue to take part, in industrial action is unlawful –

(a) if it is actionable in tort by any one or more persons, or

(b) (where it is or would be the act of a trade union) if it could form the basis of an application by a member under section 62.

(3) In determining whether an individual may make an application under this section it is immaterial whether or not the individual is entitled to be supplied with the goods or services in question.

(4) Where on an application under this section the court is satisfied that the claim is well-founded, it shall make such order as it considers appropriate for requiring the person by whom the act of inducement has been, or is likely to be, done to take steps for ensuring –

(a) that no, or no further, act is done by him to induce any persons to take part or to continue to take part in the industrial action, and

(b) that no person engages in conduct after the making of the order by virtue of having been induced by him before the making of the order to take part or continue to take part in the industrial action.

(5) Without prejudice to any other power of the court, the court may on an application under this section grant such interlocutory relief ... as it considers appropriate.

(6) For the purposes of this section an act of inducement shall be taken to be done by a trade union if it is authorised or endorsed by the union; and the provisions of section 20(2) to (4) apply for the purposes of determining whether such an act is to be taken to be so authorised or endorsed. Those provisions also apply in relation to proceedings for failure to comply with an order under this section as they apply in relation to the original proceedings.

236 No compulsion to work

No court shall, whether by way of –

(a) an order for specific performance ... of a contract of employment, or

(b) an injunction ... restraining a breach or threatened breach of such a contract,

compel an employee to do any work or attend at any place for the doing of any work.

237 Dismissal of those taking part in unofficial industrial action

(1) An employee has no right to complain of unfair dismissal if at the time of dismissal he was taking part in an unofficial strike or other unofficial industrial action.

(1A) Subsection (1) does not apply to the dismissal of the employee if it is shown that the reason (or, if more than one, the principal reason) for the dismissal or, in a redundancy case, for selecting the employee for dismissal was one of those specified in or under –

(a) section 98B, 99, 100, 101A(d), 103, 103A or 104C of the Employment Rights Act 1996 (dismissal in jury service, family, health and safety, working time, employee representative, protected disclosure and flexible working cases),

(b) section 104 of that Act in its application in relation to time off under section 57A of that Act (dependants);

In this subsection 'redundancy case' has the meaning given in section 105(9) of that Act; and a reference to a specified reason for dismissal includes a reference to specified circumstances of dismissal.

(2) A strike or other industrial action is unofficial in relation to an employee unless –

(a) he is a member of a trade union and the action is authorised or endorsed by that union, or

(b) he is not a member of a trade union but there are among those taking part in the industrial action members of a trade union by which the action has been authorised or endorsed.

Provided that, a strike or other industrial action shall not be regarded as unofficial if none of those taking part in it are members of a trade union.

(3) The provisions of section 20(2) apply for the purpose of determining whether

industrial action is to be taken to have been authorised or endorsed by a trade union.

(4) The question whether industrial action is to be so taken in any case shall be determined by reference to the facts as at the time of dismissal. Provided that, where an act is repudiated as mentioned in section 21, industrial action shall not thereby be treated as unofficial before the end of the next working day after the day on which the repudiation takes place.

(5) In this section the 'time of dismissal' means –

(a) where the employee's contract of employment is terminated by notice, when the notice is given,

(b) where the employee's contract of employment is terminated without notice, when the termination takes effect, and

(c) where the employee is employed under a contract for a fixed term which expires without being renewed under the same contract, when that term expires;

and a 'working day' means any day which is not a Saturday or Sunday, Christmas Day, Good Friday or a bank holiday under the Banking and Financial Dealings Act 1971.

(6) For the purpose of this section membership of a trade union for purposes unconnected with the employment in question shall be disregarded; but an employee who was a member of a trade union when he began to take part in industrial action shall continue to be treated as a member for the purpose of determining whether that actin is unofficial in relation to him or another notwithstanding that he may in fact have ceased to be a member.

238 Dismissals in connection with other industrial action

(1) This section applies in relation to an employee who has a right to complain of unfair dismissal (the 'complainant') and who claims to have been unfairly dismissed, where at the date of the dismissal –

(a) the employer was conducting or instituting a lock-out, or

(b) the complainant was taking part in a strike or other industrial action.

(2) In such a case an employment tribunal shall not determine whether the dismissal was fair or unfair unless it is shown –

(a) that one or more relevant employees of the same employer have not been dismissed, or

(b) that a relevant employee has before the expiry of the period of three months beginning with the date of his dismissal been offered re-engagement and that the complainant has not been offered re-engagement.

(2A) Subsection (2) does not apply to the dismissal of the employee if it is shown that the reason (or, if more than one, the principal reason) for the dismissal or, in a redundancy case, for selecting the employee for dismissal was one of those specified in or under –

(a) section 98B, 99, 100, 101A(d), 103 or 104C of the Employment Rights Act 1996 (dismissal in jury service, family, health and safety, working time, employee representative and flexible working cases),

(b) section 104 of that Act in its application in relation to time off under section 57A of that Act (dependants);

In this subsection 'redundancy case' has the meaning given in section 105(9) of that Act; and a reference to a specified reason for dismissal includes a reference to specified circumstances of dismissal.

(2B) Subsection (2) does not apply in relation to an employee who is regarded as unfairly dismissed by virtue of section 238A below.

(3) For this purpose 'relevant employees' means –

(a) in relation to a lock-out, employees who were directly interested in the dispute in contemplation or furtherance of which the lock-out occurred, and

(b) in relation to a strike or other industrial action, those employees at the establishment of the employer at or from which the complainant works who at the date of his dismissal were taking part in the action.

Nothing in section 237 (dismissal of those taking part in unofficial industrial action) affects the question who are relevant employees for the purposes of this section.

(4) An offer of re-engagement means an offer (made either by the original employer or by a successor of that employer or an associated employer) to re-engage an employee, either in the job which he held immediately before the date of dismissal or in a different job which would be reasonably suitable in his case.

(5) In this section 'date of dismissal' means –

(a) where the employee's contract of employment was terminated by notice, the date on which the employer's notice was given, and

(b) in any other case, the effective date of termination.

238A Participation in official industrial action

(1) For the purposes of this section an employee takes protected industrial action if he commits an act which, or a series of acts each of which, he is induced to commit by an act which by virtue of section 219 is not actionable in tort.

(2) An employee who is dismissed shall be regarded for the purposes of Part X of the Employment Rights Act 1996 (unfair dismissal) as unfairly dismissed if –

(a) the reason (or, if more than one, the principal reason) for the dismissal is that the employee took protected industrial action, and

(b) subsection (3), (4) or (5) applies to the dismissal.

(3) This subsection applies to a dismissal if the date of dismissal is within the protected period.

(4) This subsection applies to a dismissal if –

(a) the date of dismssal is after the end of that period, and

(b) the employee had stopped taking protected industrial action before the end of that period.

(5) This subsection applies to a dismissal if –

(a) the date of dismissal is after the end of that period,

(b) the employee had not stopped taking protected industrial action before the end of that period, and

(c) the employer had not taken such procedural steps as would have been reasonable for the purposes of resolving the dispute to which the protected industrial action relates.

(6) In determining whether an employer has taken those steps regard shall be had, in particular, to –

(a) whether the employer or a union had complied with procedures established by any applicable collective or other agreement;

(b) whether the employer or a union offered or agreed to commence or resume negotiations after the start of the protected industrial action;

(c) whether the employer or a union unreasonably refused, after the start of the protected industrial action, a request that conciliation services be used;

(d) whether the employer or a union unreasonably refused, after the start of the protected industrial action, a request that mediation services be used in relation to procedures to be adopted for the purposes of resolving the dispute;

(e) where there was agreement to use either of the services mentioned in paragraphs (c) and (d), the matters specified in section 238B.

(7) In determining whether an employer has taken those steps no regard shall be had to the merits of the dispute.

(7A) For the purposes of this section 'the protected period', in relation to the dismissal of an employee, is the sum of the basic period and any extension period in relation to that employee.

(7B) The basic period is twelve weeks beginning with the first day of protected industrial action.

(7C) An extension period in relation to an employee is a period equal to the number of days falling on or after the first day of protected industrial action (but before the protected period ends) during the whole or any part of which the employee is locked out by his employer.

(7D) In subsections (7B) and (7C), the 'first day of protected industrial action' means the day on which the employee starts to take protected industrial action (even if on that day he is locked out by his employer).

(8) For the purposes of this section no account shall be taken of the repudiation of any act by a trade union as mentioned in section 21 in relation to anything which

occurs before the end of the next working day (within the meaning of section 237) after the day on which the repudiation takes place.

(9) In this section 'date of dismissal' has the meaning given by section 238(5).

238B   Conciliation and mediation: supplementary provisions

(1) The matters referred to in subsection (6)(e) of section 238A are those specified in subsections (2) to (5); and references in this section to 'the service provider' are to any person who provided a service mentioned in subsection (6)(c) or (d) of that section.

(2) The first matter is: whether, at meetings arranged by the service provider, the employer or, as the case may be, a union was represented by an appropriate person.

(3) The second matter is: whether the employer or a union, so far as requested to do so, co-operated in the making of arrangements for meetings to be held with the service provider.

(4) The third matter is: whether the employer or a union fulfilled any commitment given by it during the provision of the service to take particular action.

(5) The fourth matter is: whether, at meetings arranged by the service provider between the parties making use of the service, the representatives of the employer or a union answered any reasonable question put to them concerning the matter subject to conciliation or mediation.

(6) For the purposes of subsection (2) an 'appropriate person' is –

(a) in relation to the employer –

(i) a person with the authority to settle the matter subject to conciliation or mediation on behalf of the employer, or

(ii) a person authorised by a person of that type to make recommendations to him with regard to the settlement of that matter, and

(b) in relation to a union, a person who is responsible for handling on the union's behalf the matter subject to conciliation or mediation.

(7) For the purposes of subsection (4) regard may be had to any timetable which was agreed for the taking of the action in question or, if no timetable was agreed, to how long it was before the action was taken.

(8) In any proceedings in which regard must be had to the matters referred to in section 238A(6)(e) –

(a) notes taken by or on behalf of the service provider shall not be admissible in evidence;

(b) the service provider must refuse to give evidence as to anything communicated to him in connection with the performance of his functions as a conciliator or mediator if, in his opinion, to give the evidence would involve his making a damaging disclosure; and

(c) the service provider may refuse to give evidence as to whether, for the purposes of subsection (5), a particular question was or was not a reasonable one.

(9) For the purposes of subsection (8)(b) a 'damaging disclosure' is –

(a) a disclosure of information which is commercially sensitive, or

(b) a disclosure of information that has not previously been disclosed which relates to a position taken by a party using the conciliation or mediation service on the settlement of the matter subject to conciliation or mediation,

to which the person who communicated the information to the service provider has not consented.

239 Supplementary provisions relating to unfair dismissal

(1) Sections 237 to 238A (loss of unfair dismissal protection in connection with industrial action) shall be construed as one with Part X of the Employment Rights Act 1996 (unfair dismissal); but sections 108 and 109 of that Act (qualifying period and age limit) shall not apply in relation to section 238A of this Act.

(2) In relation to a complaint to which section 238 or 238A applies, section 111(2) of that Act (time limit for complaint) does not apply, but an employment tribunal shall not consider the complaint unless it is presented to the tribunal –

(a) before the end of the period of six months beginning with the date of the complainant's dismissal (as defined by section 238(5)), or

(b) where the tribunal is satisfied that it was not reasonably practicable for the complaint to be presented before the end of that period, within such further period as the tribunal considers reasonable.

(3) Where it is shown that the condition referred to in section 238(2)(b) is fulfilled (discriminatory re-engagement), the references in –

(a) sections 98 to 106 of the Employment Rights Act 1996, and

(b) sections 152 and 153 of this Act,

to the reason or principal reason for which the complainant was dismissed shall be read as references to the reason or principal reason he has not been offered re-engagement.

(4) In relation to a complaint under section 111 of the 1996 Act (unfair dismissal: complaint to employment tribunal) that a dismissal was unfair by virtue of section 238A of this Act –

(a) no order shall be made under section 113 of the 1996 Act (reinstatement or re-engagement) until after the conclusion of protected industrial action by any employee in relation to the relevant dispute,

(b) regulations under section 7 of the Employment Tribunals Act 1996 may make provision about the adjournment and renewal of applications (including provision requiring adjournment in specified circumstances), and

(c) regulations under section 9 of that Act may require a pre-hearing review to be carrried out in specified circumstances.

240 Breach of contract involving injury to persons or property

(1) A person commits an offence who wilfully and maliciously breaks a contract of service or hiring, knowing or having reasonable cause to believe that the probable consequences of his so doing, either alone or in combination with others, will be –

(a) to endanger human life or cause serious bodily injury, or

(b) to expose valuable property, whether real or personal, to destruction or serious injury.

(2) Subsection (1) applies equally whether the offence is committed from malice conceived against the person endangered or injured or, as the case may be, the owner of the property destroyed or injured, or otherwise.

(3) A person guilty of an offence under this section is liable on summary conviction to imprisonment for a term not exceeding three months or to a fine not exceeding level 2 on the standard scale or both. ...

241 Intimidation or annoyance by violence or otherwise

(1) A person commits an offence who, with a view to compelling another person to abstain from doing or to do any act which that person has a legal right to do or abstain from doing, wrongfully and without legal authority –

(a) uses violence to or intimidates that person or his spouse or civil partner or children, or injures his property,

(b) persistently follows that person about from place to place,

(c) hides any tools, clothes or other property owned or used by that person, or deprives him of or hinders him in the use thereof,

(d) watches or besets the house or other place where that person resides, works, carries on business or happens to be, or the approach to any such house or place, or

(e) follows that person with two or more other persons in a disorderly manner in or through any street or road.

(2) A person guilty of an offence under this section is liable on summary conviction to imprisonment for a term not exceeding six months or a fine not exceeding level 5 on the standard scale, or both. ...

242 Restriction of offence of conspiracy: England and Wales

(1) Where in pursuance of any such agreement as is mentioned in section 1(1) of the Criminal Law Act 1977 (which provides for the offence of conspiracy) the acts in question in relation to an offence are to be done in contemplation or furtherance of a trade dispute, the offence shall be disregarded for the purposes of that subsection if it is a summary offence which is not punishable with imprisonment. ...

244 Meaning of 'trade dispute' in Part V

(1) In this Part of 'trade dispute' means a dispute between workers and their employer which relates wholly or mainly to one or more of the following –

(a) terms and conditions of employment, or the physical conditions in which any workers are required to work;

(b) engagement or non-engagement, or termination or suspension of employment or the duties of employment, of one or more workers;

(c) allocation of work or the duties of employment between workers or groups of workers;

(d) matters of discipline;

(e) a worker's membership or non-membership of a trade union;

(f) facilities for officials of trade unions; and

(g) machinery for negotiation or consultation, and other procedures, relating to any of the above matters, including the recognition by employers or employers' associations of the right of a trade union to represent workers in such negotiation or consultation or in the carrying out of such procedures.

(2) A dispute between a Minister of the Crown and any workers shall, notwithstanding that he is not the employer of those workers, be treated as a dispute between those workers and their employer if the dispute relates to matters which –

(a) have been referred for consideration by a joint body on which, by virtue of provision made by or under any enactment, he is represented, or

(b) cannot be settled without him exercising a power conferred on him by or under an enactment.

(3) There is a trade dispute even though it relates to matters occurring outside the United Kingdom, so long as the person or persons whose actions in the United Kingdom are said to be in contemplation or furtherance of a trade dispute relating to matters occurring outside the United Kingdom are likely to be affected in respect of one or more of the matters specified in subsection (1) by the outcome of the dispute.

(4) An act, threat or demand done or made by one person or organisation against another which, if resisted, would have led to a trade dispute with that other, shall be treated as being done or made in contemplation of a trade dispute with that other, notwithstanding that because that other submits to the act or threat or accedes to the demand no dispute arises.

(5) In this section –

'employment' includes any relationship whereby one person personally does work or performs services for another; and

'worker', in relation to a dispute with an employer, means –

(a) a worker employed by that employer; or

(b) a person who has ceased to be so employed if his employment was terminated in connection with the dispute or if the termination of his employment was one of the circumstances giving rise to the dispute.

246 Minor definitions

In this Part –

'date of the ballot' means, in the case of a ballot in which votes may be cast on more than one day, the last of those days;

'strike' means (except for the purposes of section 229(2)) any concerted stoppage of work;

'working hours', in relation to a person, means any time when under his contract of employment, or other contract personally to do work or perform services, he is required to be at work.

PART VI

ADMINISTRATIVE PROVISIONS

247 ACAS

(1) There shall continue to be a body called the Advisory, Conciliation and Arbitration Service (referred to in this Act as 'ACAS').

(2) ACAS is a body corporate of which the corporators are the members of its Council.

(3) Its functions, and those of its officers and servants, shall be performed on behalf of the Crown, but not so as to make it subject to directions of any kind from any Minister of the Crown as to the manner in which it is to exercise its functions under any enactment.

(4) For the purposes of civil proceedings arising out of those functions the Crown Proceedings Act 1947 applies to ACAS as if it were a government department ...

(6) ACAS shall maintain offices in such of the major centres of employment in Great Britain as it thinks fit for the purposes of discharging its functions under any enactment.

248 The Council of ACAS

(1) ACAS shall be directed by a Council which, subject to the following provisions, shall consist of a chairman and nine ordinary members appointed by the Secretary of State.

(2) Before appointing those ordinary members of the Council, the Secretary of State shall –

(a) as to three of them, consult such organisations representing employers as he considers appropriate, and

(b) as to three of them, consult such organisations representing workers as he considers appropriate.

(3) The Secretary of State may, if he thinks fit, appoint a further two ordinary members of the Council (who shall be appointed so as to take office at the same time); and before making those appointments he shall –

(a) as to one of them, consult such organisations representing employers as he considers appropriate, and

(b) as to one of them, consult such organisations representing workers as he considers appropriate. ...

249 Terms of appointment of members of Council

(1) The members of the Council shall hold and vacate office in accordance with their terms of appointment, subject to the following provisions.

(2) Appointment as chairman or as deputy chairman, or as an ordinary member of the Council, may be a full-time or part-time appointment; and the Secretary of State may, with the consent of the member concerned, vary the terms of his appointment as to whether his appointment is full-time or part-time.

(3) A person shall not be appointed to the Council for a term exceeding five years, but previous membership does not affect eligibility for re-appointment. ...

251A   Fees for exercise of functions by ACAS

(1) ACAS may, in any case in which it thinks it appropriate to do so, but subject to any directions under subsection (2) below, charge a fee for exercising a function in relation to any person.

(2) The Secretary of State may direct ACAS to charge fees, in accordance with the direction, for exercising any function specified in the direction, but the Secretary of State shall not give a direction under this subsection without consulting ACAS.

(3) A direction under subsection (2) above may require ACAS to charge fees in respect of the exercise of a function only in specified descriptions of case.

(4) A direction under subsection (2) above shall specify whether fees are to be charged in respect of the exercise of any specified function –

(a) at the full economic cost level, or

(b) at a level less than the full economic cost but not less than a specified proportion or percentage of the full economic cost. ...

(7) No liability to pay a fee charged under this section shall arise on the part of any person unless ACAS has notified that person that a fee may or will be charged. ...

254 The Certification Officer

(1) There shall continue to be an officer called the Certification Officer.

(2) The Certification Officer shall be appointed by the Secretary of State after consultation with ACAS. ...

(5) ACAS shall provide for the Certification Officer the requisite staff (from among the officers and servants of ACAS) and the requisite accommodation, equipment and other facilities. ...

256 Procedure before the Certification Officer

(1) Except in relation to matters as to which express provision is made by or under an enactment, the Certification Officer may regulate the procedure to be followed –

(a) on any application or complaint made to him, or

(b) where his approval is sought with respect to any matter.

(2) He shall in particular make provision about the disclosure, and restriction of the disclosure, of the identity of an individual who has made or is proposing to make any such application or complaint.

(2A) Provision under subsection (2) shall be such that if the application or complaint relates to a trade union –

(a) the individual's identity is disclosed to the union unless the Certification Officer thinks the circumstances are such that it should not be so disclosed;

(b) the individual's identity is disclosed to such other persons (if any) as the Certification Officer thinks fit. ...

256ZA Striking out

(1) At any stage of proceedings on an application or complaint made to the Certification Officer, he may –

(a) order the application or complaint, or any response, to be struck out on the grounds that it is scandalous, vexatious, has no reasonable prospect of success or is otherwise misconceived,

(b) order anything in the application or complaint, or in any response, to be amended or struck out on those grounds, or

(c) order the application or complaint, or any response, to be struck out on the grounds that the manner in which the proceedings have been conducted by or on behalf of the applicant or complainant or (as the case may be) respondent has been scandalous, vexatious, or unreasonable.

(2) The Certification Officer may order an application or complaint made to him to be struck out for excessive delay in proceeding with it.

(3) An order under this section may be made on the Certification Officer's own initiative and may also be made –

(a) if the order sought is to strike out an application or complaint, or to amend or strike out anything in an application or complaint, on an application by the respondent, or

(b) if the order sought is to strike out any response, or to amend or strike out anything in any response, on an application by the person who made the application or complaint mentioned in subsection (1).

(4) Before making an order under this section, the Certification Officer shall send notice to the party against whom it is proposed that the order should be made giving him an opportunity to show cause why the order should not be made.

(5) Subsection (4) shall not be taken to require the Certification Officer to send a notice under that subsection if the party against whom it is proposed that the order under this section should be made has been given an opportunity to show cause orally why the order should not be made.

(6) Nothing in this section prevents the Certification Officer from making further provision under section 256(1) about the striking out of proceedings on any application or complaint made to him.

(7) An appeal lies to the Employment Appeal Tribunal on any question of law arising from a decision of the Certification Officer under this section.

(8) In this section –

'response' means any response made by a trade union or other body in the exercise of a right to be heard, or to make representations, in response to the application or complaint;
'respondent' means any trade union, or other body, that has such a right.

256A Vexatious litigants

(1) The Certification Officer may refuse to entertain any application or complaint made to him under a provision of Chapters III to VIIA of Part I by a vexatious litigant.

(2) The Certification Officer must give reasons for such a refusal.

(3) Subsection (1) does not apply to a complaint under section 37E(1)(b) [accounts] or to an application under section 41 [superannuation scheme exemption].

(4) For the purposes of subsection (1) a vexatious litigant is a person who is the subject of –

(b) a civil proceedings order or an all proceedings order which is made under section 42(1) of the Supreme Court Act 1981 and which remains in force. ...

259 The Central Arbitration Committee

(1) There shall continue to be a body called the Central Arbitration Committee.

(2) The functions of the Committee shall be performed on behalf of the Crown, but not so as to make it subject to directions of any kind from any Minister of the Crown as to the manner in which it is to exercise its functions.

(3) ACAS shall provide for the Committee the requisite staff (from among the

officers and servants of ACAS) and the requisite accommodation, equipment and other facilities.

260 The members of the Committee

(1) The Central Arbitration Committee shall consist of members appointed by the Secretary of State.

(2) The Secretary of State shall appoint a member as chairman, and may appoint a member as deputy chairman or members as deputy chairmen.

(3) The Secretary of State may appoint as members only persons experienced in industrial relations, and they shall include some persons whose experience is as representatives of employers and some whose experience is as representatives of workers.

(3A) Before making an appointment under subsection (1) or (2) the Secretary of State shall consult ACAS and may consult other persons. ...

261 Terms of appointment of members of Committee

(1) The members of the Central Arbitration Committee shall hold and vacate office in accordance with their terms of appointment, subject to the following provisions.

(2) A person shall not be appointed to the Committee for a term exceeding five years, but previous membership does not affect eligibility for re-appointment. ...

PART VII

MISCELLANEOUS AND GENERAL

273 Crown employment

(1) The provisions of this Act have effect (except as mentioned below) in relation to Crown employment and persons in Crown employment as in relation to other employment and other workers or employees.

(2) The following provisions are excepted from subsection (1) –

section 87(4)(b) (power of tribunal to make order in respect of employer's failure to comply with duties as to union contributions);
sections 184 and 185 (remedy for failure to comply with declaration as to disclosure of information);
Chapter II of Part IV (procedure for handling redundancies).

(3) In this section 'Crown employment' means employment under or for the purposes of a government department or any officer or body exercising on behalf of the Crown functions conferred by an enactment.

(4) For the purposes of the provisions of this Act as they apply in relation to Crown employment or persons in Crown employment – ...

(d) the reference in 182(1)(e) (disclosure of information for collective bargaining: restrictions on general duty) to the employer's undertaking shall be construed as a reference to the national interest; and

(e) any other reference to an undertaking shall be construed, in relation to a Minister of the Crown, as a reference to his functions or (as the context may require) to the department of which he is in charge, and in relation to a government department, officer or body shall be construed as a reference to the functions of the department, officer or body or (as the context may require) to the department, officer or body. ...

282 Short-term employment

(1) The provisions of Chapter II of Part IV (procedure for handling redundancies) do not apply to employment –

(a) under a contract for a fixed term of three months or less, or

(b) under a contract made in contemplation of the performance of a specific task which is not expected to last for more than three months,

where the employee has not been continuously employed for a period of more than three months.

(2) Chapter I of Part XIV of the Employment Rights Act 1996 (computation of period of continuous employment), and any provision modifying or supplementing that Chapter for the purposes of that Act, apply for the purposes of this section.

288 Restriction on contracting out

(1) Any provision in an agreement (whether a contract of employment or not) is void in so far as it purports –

(a) to exclude or limit the operation of any provision of this Act, or

(b) to preclude a person from bringing –

(i) proceedings before an employment tribunal or the Central Arbitration Committee under any provision of this Act.

(2) Subsection (1) does not apply to an agreement to refrain from instituting or continuing proceedings where a conciliation officer has taken action under section 18 of the Employment Tribunals Act 1996 (conciliation).

(2A) Subsection (1) does not apply to an agreement to refrain from instituting or continuing any proceedings, other than excepted proceedings, specified in subsection (1)(b) of that section before an employment tribunal if the conditions regulating compromise agreements under this Act are satisfied in relation to the agreement.

(2B) The conditions regulating compromise agreements under this Act are that –

(a) the agreement must be in writing;

(b) the agreement must relate to the particular proceedings;

(c) the complainant must have received advice from a relevant independent adviser as to the terms and effect of the proposed agreement and in particular its effect on his ability to pursue his rights before an employment tribunal;

(d) there must be in force, when the adviser gives the advice, a contract of insurance, or an indemnity provided for members of a profession or professional body, covering the risk of a claim by the complainant in respect of loss arising in consequence of the advice;

(e) the agreement must identify the adviser; and

(f) the agreement must state that the conditions regulating compromise agreements under this Act are satisfied.

(2C) The proceedings excepted from subsection (2A) are proceedings on a complaint of non-compliance with section 188.

(3) Subsection (1) does not apply –

(a) to such an agreement as is referred to in section 185(5)(b) or (c) to the extent that it varies or supersedes an award under that section;

(b) to any provision in a collective agreement excluding rights under Chapter II of Part IV (procedure for handling redundancies), if an order under section 198 [power to adapt provisions in case of collective agreement] is in force in respect of it.

(4) A person is a relevant independent adviser for the purposes of subsection (2B)(c) –

(a) if he is a qualified lawyer,

(b) if he is an officer, official, employee or member of an independent trade union who has been certified in writing by the trade union as competent to give advice and as authorised to do so on behalf of the trade union,

(c) if he works at an advice centre (whether as an employee or a volunteer) and has been certified in writing by the centre as competent to give advice and as authorised to do so on behalf of the centre, or

(d) if he is a person of a description specified in an order made by the Secretary of State.

(4A) But a person is not a relevant independent adviser for the purposes of subsection (2B)(c) in relation to the complainant –

(a) if he is, is employed by or is acting in the matter for the other party or a person who is connected with the other party,

(b) in the case of a person within subsection (4)(b) or (c), if the trade union or advice centre is the other party or a person who is connected with the other party,

(c) in the case of a person within subsection (4)(c), if the complainant makes a payment for the advice received from him, or

(d) in the case of a person of a description specified in an order under subsection (4)(d), if any condition specified in the order in relation to the giving of advice by persons of that description is not satisfied.

(4B) In subsection (4)(a) 'qualified lawyer' means –

(a) as respects England and Wales, a barrister (whether in practice as such or employed to give legal advice), a solicitor who holds a practising certificate, or a person other than a barrister or solicitor who is an authorised advocate or authorised litigator (within the meaning of the Courts and Legal Services Act 1990) ...

(4C) An order under subsection (4)(d) shall be made by statutory instrument which shall be subject to annulment in pursuance of a resolution of either House of Parliament.

(5) For the purposes of subsection (4A) any two persons are to be treated as connected –

(a) if one is a company of which the other (directly or indirectly) has control, or

(b) if both are companies of which a third person (directly or indirectly) has control.

(6) An agreement under which the parties agree to submit a dispute to arbitration –

(a) shall be regarded for the purposes of subsections (2) and (2A) as being an agreement to refrain from instituting or continuing proceedings if –

(i) the dispute is covered by a scheme having effect by virtue of an order under section 212A, and

(ii) the agreement is to submit it to arbitration in accordance with the scheme, but

(b) shall be regarded for those purposes as neither being nor including such an agreement in any other case.

289 Employment governed by foreign law

For the purposes of this Act it is immaterial whether the law which (apart from this Act) governs any person's employment is the law of the United Kingdom, or of a part of the United Kingdom, or not.

292 Death of employee or employer

(1) This section has effect in relation to the following provisions so far as they confer rights on employees or make provisions in connection therewith –

(b) sections 168 to 173 (time off for trade union duties and activities);

(c) sections 188 to 198 (procedure for handling redundancies).

(1A) This section also has effect in relation to sections 145A to 151 so far as those sections confer rights on workers or make provision in connection therewith.

(2) Where the employee or worker or employer dies, tribunal proceedings may be instituted or continued by a personal representative of the deceased employee or worker or, as the case may be, defended by a personal representative of the deceased employer.

(3) If there is no personal representative of a deceased employee or worker, tribunal proceedings or proceedings to enforce a tribunal award may be instituted or continued on behalf of his estate by such other person as the employment tribunal may appoint, being either –

(a) a person authorised by the employee or worker to act in connection with the proceedings before his death, or

(b) the widower, widow, surviving civil partner, child, father, mother, brother or sister of the employee or worker.

In such a case any award made by the employment tribunal shall be in such terms and shall be enforceable in such manner as may be prescribed.

(4) Any right arising under any of the provisions mentioned in subsection (1) or (1A) which by virtue of this section accrues after the death of the employee or worker in question shall devolve as if it had accrued before his death.

(5) Any liability arising under any of those provisions which by virtue of this section accrues after the death of the employer in question shall be treated for all purposes as if it had accrued immediately before his death.

295 Meaning of 'employee' and related expressions

(1) In this Act –

'contract of employment' means a contract of service or of apprenticeship,

'employee' means an individual who has entered into or works under (or, where the employment has ceased, worked under) a contract of employment, and

'employer', in relation to an employee, means the person by whom the employee is (or, where the employment has ceased, was) employed.

(2) Subsection (1) has effect subject to section 235 and other provisions conferring a wider meaning on 'contract of employment' or related expressions.

296 Meaning of 'worker' and related expressions

(1) In this Act 'worker' means an individual who works, or normally works or seeks to work

(a) under a contract of employment, or

(b) under any other contract whereby he undertakes to do or perform personally any work or services for another party to the contract who is not a professional client of his, or

(c) in employment under or for the purposes of a government department (otherwise than as a member of the naval, military or air forces of the Crown) in so far as such employment does not fall within paragraph (a) or (b) above.

(2) In this Act 'employer', in relation to a worker, means a person for whom one or more workers work, or have worked or normally work or seek to work.

(3) This section has effect subject to sections 68(4), 145F(3) and 151(1B).

297 Associated employers

For the purposes of this Act any two employers shall be treated as associated if –

(a) one is a company of which the other (directly or indirectly) has control, or

(b) both are companies of which a third person (directly or indirectly) has control;

and 'associated employer' shall be construed accordingly.

298 Minor definitions: general

In this Act, unless the context otherwise requires –

'act' and 'action' each includes omission, and references to doing an act or taking action shall be construed accordingly;

'certificate of independence' means a certificate issued under –

(a) section 6(6), or

(b) section 101A(4);

'contravention' includes a failure to comply, and cognate expressions shall be construed accordingly;

'dismiss', 'dismissal' and 'effective date of termination', in relation to an employee, shall be construed in accordance with Part X of the Employment Rights Act 1996.

SCHEDULE A1

COLLECTIVE BARGAINING: RECOGNITION

PART I

RECOGNITION

1. A trade union (or trade unions) seeking recognition to be entitled to conduct collective bargaining on behalf of a group or groups of workers may make a request in accordance with this Part of this Schedule.

2. – (1) This paragraph applies for the purposes of this Part of this Schedule.

(2) References to the bargaining unit are to the group of workers concerned (or the groups taken together).

(3) References to the proposed bargaining unit are to the bargaining unit proposed in the request for recognition. …

(4) References to the employer are to the employer of the workers constituting the bargaining unit concerned.

(5) References to the parties are to the union (or unions) and the employer.

3. – (1) This paragraph applies for the purposes of this Part of this Schedule.

(2) The meaning of collective bargaining given by section 178(1) shall not apply.

(3) References to collective bargaining are to negotiations relating to pay, hours and holidays; but this has effect subject to sub-paragraph (4).

(4) If the parties agree matters as the subject of collective bargaining, references to collective bargaining are to negotiations relating to the agreed matters; and this is the case whether the agreement is made before or after the time when the CAC issues a declaration, or the parties agree, that the union is (or unions are) entitled to conduct collective bargaining on behalf of a bargaining unit. ...

4. – (1) The union or unions seeking recognition must make a request for recognition to the employer.

(2) Paragraphs 5 to 9 apply to the request.

5. The request is not valid unless it is received by the employer.

6. The request is not valid unless the union (or each of the unions) has a certificate of independence.

7. – (1) The request is not valid unless the employer, taken with any associated employer or employers, employs –

    (a) at least 21 workers on the day the employer receives the request, or

    (b) an average of at least 21 workers in the 13 weeks ending with that day.

(2) To find the average under sub-paragraph (1)(b) –

    (a) take the number of workers employed in each of the 13 weeks (including workers not employed for the whole of the week);

    (b) aggregate the 13 numbers;

    (c) divide the aggregate by 13. ...

10. – (1) If before the end of the first period the parties agree a bargaining unit and that the union is (or unions are) to be recognised as entitled to conduct collective bargaining on behalf of the unit, no further steps are to be taken under this Part of this Schedule.

(2) If before the end of the first period the employer informs the union (or unions) that the employer does not accept the request but is willing to negotiate, sub-paragraph (3) applies.

(3) The parties may conduct negotiations with a view to agreeing a bargaining unit and that the union is (or unions are) to be recognised as entitled to conduct collective bargaining on behalf of the unit.

(4) If such an agreement is made before the end of the second period no further steps are to be taken under this Part of this Schedule.

(5) The employer and the union (or unions) may request ACAS to assist in conducting the negotiations.

(6) The first period is the period of 10 working days starting with the day after that on which the employer receives the request for recognition.

(7) The second period is –

(a) the period of 20 working days starting with the day after that on which the first period ends, or

(b) such longer period (so starting) as the parties may from time to time agree.

11. – (1) This paragraph applies if –

(a) before the end of the first period the employer fails to respond to the request, or

(b) before the end of the first period the employer informs the union (or unions) that the employer does not accept the request (without indicating a willingness to negotiate).

(2) The union (or unions) may apply to the CAC to decide both these questions –

(a) whether the proposed bargaining unit is appropriate;

(b) whether the union has (or unions have) the support of a majority of the workers constituting the appropriate bargaining unit.

12. – (1) Sub-paragraph (2) applies if –

(a) the employer informs the union (or unions) under paragraph 10(2), and

(b) no agreement is made before the end of the second period.

(2) The union (or unions) may apply to the CAC to decide both these questions –

(a) whether the proposed bargaining unit is appropriate;

(b) whether the union has (or unions have) the support of a majority of the workers constituting the appropriate bargaining unit.

(3) Sub-paragraph (4) applies if –

(a) the employer informs the union (or unions) under paragraph 10(2), and

(b) before the end of the second period the parties agree a bargaining unit but not that the union is (or unions are) to be recognised as entitled to conduct collective bargaining on behalf of the unit.

(4) The union (or unions) may apply to the CAC to decide the question whether the union has (or unions have) the support of a majority of the workers constituting the bargaining unit.

(5) But no application may be made under this paragraph if within the period of 10 working days starting with the day after that on which the employer informs the union (or unions) under paragraph 10(2) the employer proposes that ACAS be requested to assist in conducting the negotiations and –

(a) the union rejects (or unions reject) the proposal, or

(b) the union fails (or unions fail) to accept the proposal within the period of 10 working days starting with the day after that on which the employer makes the proposal. ...

18. – (1) If the CAC accepts an application under paragraph 11(2) or 12(2) it must

try to help the parties to reach within the appropriate period an agreement as to what the appropriate bargaining unit is. ...

30. – (1) This paragraph applies if the CAC issues a declaration under this Part of this Schedule that the union is (or unions are) recognised as entitled to conduct collective bargaining on behalf of a bargaining unit.

(2) The parties may in the negotiation period conduct negotiations with a view to agreeing a method by which they will conduct collective bargaining.

(3) If no agreement is made in the negotiation period the employer or the union (or unions) may apply to the CAC for assistance.

(4) The negotiation period is –

(a) the period of 30 working days starting with the start day, or

(b) such longer period (so starting) as the parties may from time to time agree.

(5) The start day is the day after that on which the parties are notified of the declaration. ...

As amended by the Trade Union Reform and Employment Rights Act 1993, ss2(1), (2), 3, 13–17, 18(1), (2), 19, 20(1)–(4), 21, 22, 34(1), (3)–(5), 39(2), 43(1)–(3), 44, 49(1), (2), 51, Schedule 1, paras 3, 4, Schedule 6, para 4, Schedule 7, paras 1, 17, 21–26, Schedule 8, paras 47–51, 58, 59, 63, 68–70, 72, 73, 75–77, 79, 80, 88, 89, Schedule 10; Collective Redundancies and Transfer of Undertakings (Protection of Employment) (Amendment) Regulations 1995, regs 3–7; Employment Rights Act 1996, s240, Schedule 1, para 56(1)–(3), (5)–(16), (18), (19); Employment Tribunals Act 1996, s43, Schedule 1, para 8; Arbitration Act 1996, s107(1), Schedule 3, para 56; Employment Rights (Dispute Resolutiuon) Act 1998, ss1(2)(a), (c), 6, 7, 8(3), 9(1), (2)(c), 10(1), (2)(c), 15, Schedule 1, paras 8, 9; Deregulation (Deduction from Pay of Union Subscriptions) Order 1998, art 2(1), (2); Employment Relations Act 1999, ss1, 2, 4, 5, 9, 16, 24, 26, 29, 36(1)(b), 44, Schedule 1, Schedule 2, paras 1–6, Schedule 3, paras 1–6, 8–11, Schedule 4, Pt III, paras 1–3, Schedule 5, paras 1–4, Schedule 6, paras 1, 9, 13, 14, 17, 19, 20, 22, 23, Schedule 9(5)–(7), (10); Collective Redundancies and Transfer of Undertakings (Protection of Employment) (Amendment) Regulations 1999, regs 2(2), 3–6, 14; Employment Rights (Increase of Limits) Order 2002, art 3, Schedule; Regulatory Reform (Removal of 20 Member Limit in Partnerships etc) Order 2002, art 4; Employment Act 2002, ss43(1)–(7), 53, Schedule 7, paras 18–22; Employment Relations Act 2004, ss1, 21–30, 31(1)–(7), 32–35, 40(8), (9), 41(1), (2), 48, 49(1), (9), 50–52, 57, Schedule 1, paras 5, 6, 8–14, 19–21, Schedule 2; Civil Partnership Act 2004, s261(1), Schedule 27, paras 144–146; Employment Rights (Increase of Limits) Order 2004, art 3, Schedule.

PENSIONS ACT 1995

(1995 c 26)

62   The equal treatment rule

(1) An occupational pension scheme which does not contain an equal treatment rule shall be treated as including one.

(2) An equal treatment rule is a rule which relates to the terms on which –

(a) persons become members of the scheme, and

(b) members of the scheme are treated.

(3) Subject to subsection (6), an equal treatment rule has the effect that where –

(a) a woman is employed on like work with a man in the same employment,

(b) a woman is employed on work rated as equivalent with that of a man in the same employment, or

(c) a woman is employed on work which, not being work in relation to which paragraph (a) or (b) applies, is, in terms of the demands made on her (for instance under such headings as effort, skill and decision) of equal value to that of a man in the same employment,

but (apart from the rule) any of the terms referred to in subsection (2) is or becomes less favourable to the woman than it is to the man, the term shall be treated as so modified as not to be less favourable.

(4) An equal treatment rule does not operate in relation to any difference as between a woman and a man in the operation of any of the terms referred to in subsection (2) if the trustees or managers of the scheme prove that the difference is genuinely due to a material factor which –

(a) is not the difference of sex, but

(b) is a material difference between the woman's case and the man's case.

(5) References in subsection (4) and sections 63 to 65 to the terms referred to in subsection (2), or the effect of any of those terms, include –

(a) a term which confers on the trustees or managers of an occupational pension scheme, or any other person, a discretion which, in a case within any of paragraphs (a) to (c) of subsection (3) –

(i) may be exercised so as to affect the way in which persons become members of the scheme, or members of the scheme are treated, and

(ii) may (apart from the equal treatment rule) be so exercised in a way less favourable to the woman than to the man, and

(b) the effect of any exercise of such a discretion;

and references to the terms on which members of the scheme are treated are to be read accordingly.

(6) In the case of a term within subsection (5)(a) the effect of an equal treatment rule is that the term shall be treated as so modified as not to permit the discretion to be exercised in a way less favourable to the woman than to the man.

63 Equal treatment rule: supplementary

(1) The reference in section 62(2) to the terms on which members of a scheme are treated includes those terms as they have effect for the benefit of dependants of members, and the reference in section 62(5) to the way in which members of a scheme are treated includes the way they are treated as it has effect for the benefit of dependants of members.

(2) Where the effect of any of the terms referred to in section 62(2) on persons of the same sex differs accordingly to their family or marital status, the effect of the term is to be compared for the purposes of section 62 with its effect on persons of the other sex who have the same status.

(3) An equal treatment rule has effect subject to paragraphs 5 and 6 of Schedule 5 to the Social Security Act 1989 (employment-related benefit schemes: maternity and family leave provisions).

(4) Section 62 shall be construed as one with section 1 of the Equal Pay Act 1970 (requirement of equal treatment for men and women in the same employment); and sections 2 and 2A of that Act (disputes and enforcement) shall have effect for the purposes of section 62 as if –

(a) references to an equality clause were to an equal treatment rule,

(b) references to employers and employees were to the trustees or managers of the scheme (on the one hand) and the members, or prospective members, of the scheme (on the other),

(c) for section 2(4) there were substituted –

'(4) No claim in respect of the operation of an equal treatment rule in respect of an occupational pension scheme shall be referred to an employment tribunal otherwise than by virtue of subsection (3) above unless the woman concerned has been employed in a description or category of employment to which the scheme relates within the six months preceding the date of the reference', and

(d) references to section 1(2)(c) of the Equal Pay Act 1970 were to section 62(3)(c) of this Act.

(5) Regulations may make provision for the Equal Pay Act 1970 to have effect, in relation to an equal treatment rule, with prescribed modifications; and subsection

(4) shall have effect subject to any regulations made by virtue of this subsection.

(6) Section 62, so far as it relates to the terms on which members of a scheme are treated, is to be treated as having had effect in relation to any pensionable service on or after 17th May 1990.

64   Equal treatment rule: exceptions

(1) An equal treatment rule does not operate in relation to any variation as between a woman and a man in the effect of any of the terms referred to in section 62(2) if the variation is permitted by or under any of the provisions of this section.

(2) Where a man and a woman are eligible, in prescribed circumstances, to receive different amounts by way of pension, the variation is permitted by this subsection if, in prescribed circumstances, the differences are attributable only to differences between men and women in the benefits under sections 43 to 55 of the Social Security Contributions and Benefits Act 1992 (State retirement pensions) to which, in prescribed circumstances, they are or would be entitled.

(3) A variation is permitted by this subsection if –

(a) the variation consists of the application of actuarial factors which differ for men and women to the calculation of contributions to a scheme by employers, being factors which fall within a prescribed class or description, or

(b) the variation consists of the application of actuarial factors which differ for men and women to the determination of benefits falling within a prescribed class or description;

and in this subsection 'benefits' include any payment or other benefit made to or in respect of a person as a member of the scheme.

(4) Regulations may –

(a) permit further variations, or

(b) amend or repeal subsection (2) or (3);

and regulations made by virtue of this subsection may have effect in relation to pensionable service on or after 17th May 1990 and before the date on which the regulations are made.

65   Equal treatment rule: consequential alteration of schemes

(1) The trustees or managers of an occupational pension scheme may, if –

(a) they do not (apart from this section) have power to make such alterations to the scheme as may be required to secure conformity with an equal treatment rule, or

(b) they have such power but the procedure for doing so –

(i) is liable to be unduly complex or protracted, or

(ii) involves the obtaining of consents which cannot be obtained, or can only be obtained with undue delay or difficulty,

by resolution make such alterations to the scheme.

(2) The alterations may have effect in relation to a period before the alterations are made.

66 Equal treatment rule: effect on terms of employment, etc ...

(4) Regulations may make provision –

(a) for the Equal Pay Act 1970 to have effect, in relation to terms of employment relating to membership of, or rights under, an occupational pension scheme with prescribed modifications, and

(b) for imposing requirements on employers as to the payment of contributions and otherwise in case of their failing or having failed to comply with any such terms.

(5) References in subsection (4) to terms of employment include (where the context permits) –

(a) any collective agreement or pay structure ...

As amended by the Employment Rights (Dispute Resolution) Act 1998, s1(2)(a).

DISABILITY DISCRIMINATION ACT 1995
(1995 c 50)

PART 1

DISABILITY

1 Meaning of 'disability' and 'disabled person'

(1) Subject to the provisions of Schedule 1, a person has a disability for the purposes of this Act if he has a physical or mental impairment which has a substantial and long-term adverse effect on his ability to carry out normal day-to-day activities.

(2) In this Act 'disabled person' means a person who has a disability.

2 Past disabilities

(1) The provisions of this Part and Parts 2 to 4 and 5A apply in relation to a person who has had a disability as they apply in relation to a person who has that disability.

(2) Those provisions are subject to the modifications made by Schedule 2.

(3) Any regulations or order made under this Act by the Secretary of State, the Scottish Ministers or the National Assembly for Wales may include provision with respect to persons who have had a disability.

(4) In any proceedings under Part 2, 3, 4 or 5A of this Act, the question whether a person had a disability at a particular time ('the relevant time') shall be determined, for the purposes of this section, as if the provisions of, or made under, this Act in force when the act complained of was done had been in force at the relevant time.

(5) The relevant time may be a time before the passing of this Act.

3 Guidance

(A1) The Secretary of State may issued guidance about matters to be taken into account in determining whether a person is a disabled person.

(1) Without prejudice to the generality of subsection (A1), the Secretary of State may, in particular, issue guidance about the matters to be taken into account in determining –

(a) whether an impairment has a substantial adverse effect on a person's ability to carry out normal day-to-day activities; or

(b) whether such an impairment has a long-term effect.

(2) Without prejudice to the generality of subsection (A1), guidance about the matters mentioned in subsection (1) may, among other things, give examples of –

(a) effects which it would be reasonable, in relation to particular activities, to regard for purposes of this Act as substantial adverse effects;

(b) effects which it would not be reasonable, in relation to particular activities, to regard for such purposes as substantial adverse effects;

(c) substantial adverse effects which it would be reasonable to regard, for such purposes, as long-term;

(d) substantial adverse effects which it would not be reasonable to regard, for such purposes, as long-term.

(3) An adjudicating body determining, for any purpose of this Act, whether a person is a disabled person, shall take into account any guidance which appears to it to be relevant.

(3A) 'Adjudicating body' means –

(a) a court;

(b) a tribunal; and

(c) any other person who, or body which, may decide a claim under Part 4.

(4) In preparing a draft of any guidance, the Secretary of State shall consult such persons as he considers appropriate.

(5) Where the Secretary of State proposes to issue any guidance, he shall publish a draft of it, consider any representations that are made to him about the draft and, if he thinks it appropriate, modify his proposals in the light of any of those representations. ...

(12) In this section – ...

'guidance' means guidance issued by the Secretary of State under this section and includes guidance which has been revised and re-issued.

PART 2

THE EMPLOYMENT FIELD AND MEMBERS OF
LOCALLY-ELECTABLE AUTHORITIES

3A   Meaning of 'discrimination'

(1) For the purposes of this Part, a person discriminates against a disabled person if –

(a) for a reason which relates to the disabled person's disability, he treats him less favourably than he treats or would treat others to whom that reason does not or would not apply, and

(b) he cannot show that the treatment in question is justified.

(2) For the purposes of this Part, a person also discriminates against a disabled person if he fails to comply with a duty to make reasonable adjustments imposed on him in relation to the disabled person.

(3) Treatment is justified for the purposes of subsection (1)(b) if, but only if, the reason for it is both material to the circumstances of the particular case and substantial.

(4) But treatment of a disabled person cannot be justified under subsection (3) if it amounts to direct discrimination falling within subsection (5).

(5) A person directly discriminates against a disabled person if, on the ground of the disabled person's disability, he treats the disabled person less favourably than he treats or would treat a person not having that particular disability whose relevant circumstances, including his abilities, are the same as, or not materially different from, those of the disabled person.

(6) If, in a case falling within subsection (1), a person is under a duty to make reasonable adjustments in relation to a disabled person but fails to comply with that duty, his treatment of that person cannot be justified under subsection (3) unless it would have been justified even if he had complied with that duty.

3B   Meaning of 'harassment'

(1) For the purposes of this Part, a person subjects a disabled person to harassment where, for a reason which relates to the disabled person's disability, he engages in unwanted conduct which has the purpose or effect of –

(a) violating the disabled person's dignity, or

(b) creating an intimidating, hostile, degrading, humiliating or offensive environment for him.

(2) Conduct shall be regarded as having the effect referred to in paragraph (a) or (b) of subsection (1) only if, having regard to all the circumstances, including in particular the perception of the disabled person, it should reasonably be considered as having that effect.'.

4   Employers: discrimination and harassment

(1) It is unlawful for an employer to discriminate against a disabled person –

(a) in the arrangements which he makes for the purpose of determining to whom he should offer employment;

(b) in the terms on which he offers that person employment; or

(c) by refusing to offer, or deliberately not offering, him employment.

(2) It is unlawful for an employer to discriminate against a disabled person whom he employs –

(a) in the terms of employment which he affords him;

(b) in the opportunities which he affords him for promotion, a transfer, training or receiving any other benefit;

(c) by refusing to afford him, or deliberately not affording him, any such opportunity; or

(d) by dismissing him, or subjecting him to any other detriment.

(3) It is also unlawful for an employer, in relation to employment by him, to subject to harassment –

(a) a disabled person whom he employs; or

(b) a disabled person who has applied to him for employment.

(4) Subsection (2) does not apply to benefits of any description if the employer is concerned with the provision (whether or not for payment) of benefits of that description to the public, or to a section of the public which includes the employee in question, unless –

(a) that provision differs in a material respect from the provision of the benefits by the employer to his employees;

(b) the provision of the benefits to the employee in question is regulated by his contract of employment; or

(c) the benefits relate to training.

(5) The reference in subsection (2)(d) to the dismissal of a person includes a reference –

(a) to the termination of that person's employment by the expiration of any period (including a period expiring by reference to an event or circumstance), not being a termination immediately after which the employment is renewed on the same terms; and

(b) to the termination of that person's employment by any act of his (including the giving of notice) in circumstances such that he is entitled to terminate it without notice by reason of the conduct of the employer.

(6) This section applies only in relation to employment at an establishment in Great Britain.

4A Employers: duty to make adjustments

(1) Where –

(a) a provision, criterion or practice applied by or on behalf of an employer, or

(b) any physical feature of premises occupied by the employer,

places the disabled person concerned at a substantial disadvantage in comparison with persons who are not disabled, it is the duty of the employer to take such steps as it is reasonable, in all the circumstances of the case, for him to have to take in order to prevent the provision, criterion or practice, or feature, having that effect.

(2) In subsection (1), 'the disabled person concerned' means –

(a) in the case of a provision, criterion or practice for determining to whom employment should be offered, any disabled person who is, or has notified the employer that he may be, an applicant for that employment;

(b) in any other case, a disabled person who is –

(i) an applicant for the employment concerned, or

(ii) an employee of the employer concerned.

(3) Nothing in this section imposes any duty on an employer in relation to a disabled person if the employer does not know, and could not reasonably be expected to know –

(a) in the case of an applicant or potential applicant, that the disabled person concerned is, or may be, an applicant for the employment; or

(b) in any case, that that person has a disability and is likely to be affected in the way mentioned in subsection (1).

4G   Occupational pension schemes: non-discrimination rule

(1) Every occupational pension scheme shall be taken to include a provision ('the non- discrimination rule') containing the following requirements –

(a) a requirement that the trustees or managers of the scheme refrain from discriminating against a relevant disabled person in carrying out any of their functions in relation to the scheme (including in particular their functions relating to the admission of members to the scheme and the treatment of members of the scheme);

(b) a requirement that the trustees or managers of the scheme do not subject a relevant disabled person to harassment in relation to the scheme.

(2) The other provisions of the scheme are to have effect subject to the non-discrimination rule.

(3) It is unlawful for the trustees or managers of an occupational pension scheme –

(a) to discriminate against a relevant disabled person contrary to requirement (a) of the non-discrimination rule; or

(b) to subject a relevant disabled person to harassment contrary to requirement (b) of the non-discrimination rule.

(4) The non-discrimination rule does not apply in relation to rights accrued, or benefits payable, in respect of periods of service prior to the coming into force of this section (but it does apply to communications with members or prospective members of the scheme in relation to such rights or benefits).

(5) The trustees or managers of an occupational pension scheme may, if –

(a) they do not (apart from this subsection) have power to make such alterations to the scheme as may be required to secure conformity with the non-discrimination rule, or

(b) they have such power but the procedure for doing so –

(i) is liable to be unduly complex or protracted, or

(ii) involves the obtaining of consents which cannot be obtained, or can only be obtained with undue delay or difficulty,

by resolution make such alterations to the scheme.

(6) The alterations referred to in subsection (5) may have effect in relation to a period before the alterations are made (but may not have effect in relation to a period before the coming into force of this section).

4H   Occupational pension schemes: duty to make adjustments

(1) Where –

(a) a provision, criterion or practice (including a scheme rule) applied by or onbehalf of the trustees or managers of an occupational pension scheme, or

(b) any physical feature of premises occupied by the trustees or managers,

places a relevant disabled person at a substantial disadvantage in comparison with persons who are not disabled, it is the duty of the trustees or managers to take such steps as it is reasonable, in all the circumstances of the case, for them to have to take in order to prevent the provision, criterion or practice, or feature, having that effect.

(2) The making of alterations to scheme rules is (in addition to the examples set out in section 18B(2)) an example of a step which trustees or managers may have to take in order to comply with the duty set out in subsection (1).

(3) Nothing in subsection (1) imposes any duty on trustees or managers in relation to a disabled person if they do not know, and could not reasonably be expected to know –

(a) that the disabled person is a relevant disabled person; or

(b) that that person has a disability and is likely to be affected in the way mentioned in subsection (1).

4I   Occupational pension schemes: procedure

(1) Where under section 17A a relevant disabled person presents a complaint to an employment tribunal that the trustees or managers of an occupational pension scheme have acted in relation to him in a way which is unlawful under this Part, the employer in relation to that scheme shall, for the purposes of the rules governing procedure, be treated as a party and be entitled to appear and be heard in accordance with those rules.

(2) In this section, 'employer', in relation to an occupational pension scheme, has the meaning given by section 124(1) of the Pensions Act 1995 as at the date of coming into force of this section.

4J   Occupational pension schemes: remedies

(1) This section applies where –

(a) under section 17A a relevant disabled person presents to an employment tribunal a complaint that –

(i) the trustees or managers of an occupational pension scheme have acted in relation to him in a way which is unlawful under this Part; or

(ii) an employer has so acted in relation to him;

(b) the complaint relates to –

(i) the terms on which persons become members of an occupational pension scheme, or

(ii) the terms on which members of the scheme are treated;

(c) the disabled person is not a pensioner member of the scheme; and

(d) the tribunal finds that the complaint is well-founded.

(2) The tribunal may, without prejudice to the generality of its power under section 17A(2)(a), make a declaration that the complainant has a right –

(a) (where subsection (1)(b)(i) applies) to be admitted to the scheme in question; or

(b) (where subsection (1)(b)(ii) applies) to membership of the scheme without discrimination.

(3) A declaration under subsection (2) –

(a) may be made in respect of such period as the declaration may specify (but may not be made in respect of any period before the coming into force of this section);

(b) may make such provision as the tribunal considers appropriate as to the terms upon which, or the capacity in which, the disabled person is to enjoy such admission or membership.

(4) The tribunal may not award the disabled person any compensation under section 17A(2)(b) (whether in relation to arrears of benefits or otherwise) other than –

(a) compensation for injury to feelings;

(b) compensation pursuant to section 17A(5).

4K Occupational pension schemes: supplementary

(1) In their application to communications, sections 4G to 4J apply in relation to a disabled person who is –

(a) entitled to the present payment of dependants' or survivors' benefits under an occupational pension scheme; or

(b) a pension credit member of such a scheme,

as they apply in relation to a disabled person who is a pensioner member of the scheme.

(2) In sections 4G to 4J and in this section –

'active member', 'deferred member', 'managers', 'pension credit member', 'pensioner member' and 'trustees or managers' have the meanings given by section 124(1) of the Pensions Act 1995 as at the date of coming into force of this section;

'communications' includes –

(i) the provision of information, and

(ii) the operation of a dispute resolution procedure;

'member', in relation to an occupational pension scheme, means any active, deferred or pensioner member;

'non-discrimination rule' means the rule in section 4G(1);

'relevant disabled person', in relation to an occupational pension scheme, means a disabled person who is a member or prospective member of the scheme; and

'prospective member' means any person who, under the terms of his contract of employment or the scheme rules or both –

(i) is able, at his own option, to become a member of the scheme,

(ii) will become so able if he continues in the same employment for a sufficiently long period,

(iii) will be admitted to it automatically unless he makes an election not to become a member, or

(iv) may be admitted to it subject to the consent of his employer.

7A   Barristers: discrimination and harassment

(1) It is unlawful for a barrister or a barrister's clerk, in relation to any offer of a pupillage or tenancy, to discriminate against a disabled person –

(a) in the arrangements which are made for the purpose of determining to whom it should be offered;

(b) in respect of any terms on which it is offered; or

(c) by refusing, or deliberately omitting, to offer it to him.

(2) It is unlawful for a barrister or a barrister's clerk, in relation to a disabled pupil or tenant in the set of chambers in question, to discriminate against him –

(a) in respect of any terms applicable to him as a pupil or tenant;

(b) in the opportunities for training, or gaining experience, which are afforded or denied to him;

(c) in the benefits which are afforded or denied to him;

(d) by terminating his pupillage or by subjecting him to any pressure to leave the chambers; or

(e) by subjecting him to any other detriment.

(3) It is unlawful for a barrister or barrister's clerk, in relation to a pupillage or tenancy, to subject to harassment a disabled person who is, or has applied to be, a pupil or tenant in the set of chambers in question.

(4) It is also unlawful for any person, in relation to the giving, withholding or acceptance of instructions to a barrister, to discriminate against a disabled person or to subject him to harassment.

(5) In this section and in section 7B –

'barrister's clerk' includes any person carrying out any of the functions of a barrister's clerk;

'pupil', 'pupillage' and 'set of chambers' have the meanings commonly associated with their use in the context of barristers practising in independent practice; and

'tenancy' and 'tenant' have the meanings commonly associated with their use in the context of barristers practising in independent practice, but they also include reference to any barrister permitted to practise from a set of chambers.

7B   Barristers: duty to make adjustments

(1) Where –

(a) a provision, criterion or practice applied by or on behalf of a barrister or barrister's clerk, or

(b) any physical feature of premises occupied by a barrister or a barrister's clerk,

places the disabled person concerned at a substantial disadvantage in comparison with persons who are not disabled, it is the duty of the barrister or barrister's clerk to take such steps as it is reasonable, in all the circumstances of the case, for him to have to take in order to prevent the provision, criterion or practice, or feature, having that effect.

(2) In a case where subsection (1) applies in relation to two or more barristers in a set of chambers, the duty in that subsection is a duty on each of them to take such steps as it is reasonable, in all of the circumstances of the case, for him to have to take.

(3) In this section, 'the disabled person concerned' means –

(a) in the case of a provision, criterion or practice for determining to whom a pupillage or tenancy should be offered, any disabled person who is, or has notified the barrister or the barrister's clerk concerned that he may be, an applicant for a pupillage or tenancy;

(b) in any other case, a disabled person who is –

(i) a tenant;

(ii) a pupil; or

(iii) an applicant for a pupillage or tenancy.

(4) Nothing in this section imposes any duty on a barrister or a barrister's clerk in relation to a disabled person if he does not know, and could not reasonably be expected to know –

(a) in the case of an applicant or potential applicant, that the disabled person concerned is, or may be, an applicant for a pupillage or tenancy; or

(b) in any case, that that person has a disability and is likely to be affected in the way mentioned in subsection (1).

13   Trade organisations: discrimination and harassment

(1) It is unlawful for a trade organisation to discriminate against a disabled person –

(a) in the arrangements which it makes for the purpose of determining who should be offered membership of the organisation;

(b) in the terms on which it is prepared to admit him to membership of the organisation; or

(c) by refusing to accept, or deliberately not accepting, his application for membership.

(2) It is unlawful for a trade organisation, in the case of a disabled person who is a member of the organisation, to discriminate against him –

(a) in the way it affords him access to any benefits or by refusing or deliberately omitting to afford him access to them;

(b) by depriving him of membership, or varying the terms on which he is a member; or

(c) by subjecting him to any other detriment.

(3) It is also unlawful for a trade organisation, in relation to membership of that organisation, to subject to harassment a disabled person who –

(a) is a member of the organisation; or

(b) has applied for membership of the organisation.

(4) In this section and section 14 'trade organisation' means –

(a) an organisation of workers;

(b) an organisation of employers; or

(c) any other organisation whose members carry on a particular profession or trade for the purposes of which the organisation exists.

14   Trade organisations: duty to make adjustments

(1) Where –

(a) a provision, criterion or practice applied by or on behalf of a trade organisation, or

(b) any physical feature of premises occupied by the organisation,

places the disabled person concerned at a substantial disadvantage in comparison with persons who are not disabled, it is the duty of the organisation to take such steps as it is reasonable, in all the circumstances of the case, for it to have to take in order to prevent the provision, criterion or practice, or feature, having that effect.

(2) In this section 'the disabled person concerned' means –

(a) in the case of a provision, criterion or practice for determining to whom membership should be offered, any disabled person who is, or has notified the organisation that he may be, an applicant for membership;

(b) in any other case, a disabled person who is –

(i) a member of the organisation, or

(ii) an applicant for membership of the organisation.

(3) Nothing in this section imposes any duty on an organisation in relation to a disabled person if the organisation does not know, and could not reasonably be expected to know –

(a) in the case of an applicant or potential applicant, that the disabled person concerned is, or may be, an applicant for membership of the organisation; or

(b) in any case, that that person has a disability and is likely to be affected in the way mentioned in subsection (1).

14C Practical work experience: discrimination and harassment

(1) It is unlawful, in the case of a disabled person seeking or undertaking a work placement, for a placement provider to discriminate against him –

(a) in the arrangements which he makes for the purpose of determining who should be offered a work placement;

(b) in the terms on which he affords him access to any work placement or any facilities concerned with such a placement;

(c) by refusing or deliberately omitting to afford him such access;

(d) by terminating the placement; or

(e) by subjecting him to any other detriment in relation to the placement.

(2) It is also unlawful for a placement provider, in relation to a work placement, to subject to harassment –

(a) a disabled person to whom he is providing a placement; or

(b) a disabled person who has applied to him for a placement.

(3) This section and section 14D do not apply –

(a) to anything which is unlawful under any provision of section 4, sections 19 to 21A, sections 21F to 21J or Part 4; or

(b) to anything which would be unlawful under any such provision but for the operation of any provision in or made under this Act.

(4) In this section and section 14D –

'work placement' means practical work experience undertaken for a limited period for the purposes of a person's vocational training;

'placement provider' means any person who provides a work placement to a person whom he does not employ.

(5) This section and section 14D do not apply to a work placement undertaken in any of the naval, military and air forces of the Crown.

14D Practical work experience: duty to make adjustments

(1) Where –

(a) a provision, criterion or practice applied by or on behalf of a placement provider, or

(b) any physical feature of premises occupied by the placement provider,

places the disabled person concerned at a substantial disadvantage in comparison with persons who are not disabled, it is the duty of the placement provider to take such steps as it is reasonable, in all the circumstances of the case, for him to have to take in order to prevent the provision, criterion or practice, or feature, having that effect.

(2) In this section, 'the disabled person concerned' means –

(a) in the case of a provision, criterion or practice for determining to whom a work placement should be offered, any disabled person who is, or has notified the placement provider that he may be, an applicant for that work placement;

(b) in any other case, a disabled person who is –

(i) an applicant for the work placement concerned, or

(ii) undertaking a work placement with the placement provider.

(3) Nothing in this section imposes any duty on a placement provider in relation to the disabled person concerned if he does not know, and could not reasonably be expected to know –

(a) in the case of an applicant or potential applicant, that the disabled person concerned is, or may be, an applicant for the work placement; or

(b) in any case, that that person has a disability and is likely to be affected in the way mentioned in subsection (1).

16A Relationships which have come to an end

(1) This section applies where –

(a) there has been a relevant relationship between a disabled person and another person ('the relevant person'), and

(b) the relationship has come to an end.

(2) In this section a 'relevant relationship' is –

(a) a relationship during the course of which an act of discrimination against, or harassment of, one party to the relationship by the other party to it is unlawful under any preceding provision of this Part, other than sections 15B and 15C; or

(b) a relationship between a person providing employment services and a person receiving such services.

(3) It is unlawful for the relevant person –

(a) to discriminate against the disabled person by subjecting him to a detriment, or

(b) to subject the disabled person to harassment,

where the discrimination or harassment arises out of and is closely connected to the relevant relationship.

(4) This subsection applies where –

(a) a provision, criterion or practice applied by the relevant person to the disabled person in relation to any matter arising out of the relevant relationship, or

(b) a physical feature of premises which are occupied by the relevant person,

places the disabled person at a substantial disadvantage in comparison with persons who are not disabled, but are in the same position as the disabled person in relation to the relevant person.

(5) Where subsection (4) applies, it is the duty of the relevant person to take such steps as it is reasonable, in all the circumstances of the case, for him to have to take in order to prevent the provision, practice or criterion, or feature, having that effect.

(6) Nothing in subsection (5) imposes any duty on the relevant person if he does not know, and could not reasonably be expected to know, that the disabled person has a disability and is likely to be affected in the way mentioned in that subsection.

(7) In subsection (2), reference to an act of discrimination or harassment which is unlawful includes, in the case of a relationship which has come to an end before the commencement of this section, reference to such an act which would, after the commencement of this section, be unlawful.

16B Discriminatory advertisements

(1) It is unlawful for a person to publish or cause to be published an advertisement which–

(a) invites applications for a relevant appointment or benefit; and

(b) indicates, or might reasonably be understood to indicate, that an application will or may be determined to any extent by reference to–

(i) the applicant not having any disability, or any particular disability,

(ii) the applicant not having had any disability, or any particular disability, or

(iii) any reluctance of the person determining the application to comply with a duty to make reasonable adjustments or (in relation to employment services) with the duty imposed by section 21(1) as modified by section 21A(6).

(2) Subsection (1) does not apply where it would not in fact be unlawful under this Part or, to the extent that it relates to the provision of employment services, Part

3 for an application to be determined in the manner indicated (or understood to be indicated) in the advertisement.

(2A) A person who publishes an advertisement of the kind described in subsection (1) shall not be subject to any liability under subsection (1) in respect of the publication of the advertisement if he proves–

(a) that the advertisement was published in reliance on a statement made to him by the person who caused it to be published to the effect that, by reason of the operation of subsection (2), the publication would not be unlawful; and

(b) that it was reasonable for him to rely on the statement.

(2B) A person who knowingly or recklessly makes a statement such as is mentioned in subsection (2A)(a) which in a material respect is false or misleading commits an offence, and shall be liable on summary conviction to a fine not exceeding level 5 on the standard scale.

(2C) Subsection (1) does not apply in relation to an advertisement so far as it invites persons to apply, in their capacity as members of an authority to which sections 15B and 15C apply, for a relevant appointment or benefit which the authority is intending to make or confer.

(3) In this section, 'relevant appointment or benefit' means –

(a) any employment, promotion or transfer of employment;

(b) membership of, or a benefit under, an occupational pension scheme;

(c) an appointment to any office or post to which section 4D applies;

(d) any partnership in a firm (within the meaning of section 6A);

(e) any tenancy or pupillage (within the meaning of section 7A or 7C);

(f) any membership of a trade organisation (within the meaning of section 13);

(g) any professional or trade qualification (within the meaning of section 14A);

(h) any work placement (within the meaning of section 14C);

(i) any employment services (within the meaning of Part 3).

(4) In this section, 'advertisement' includes every form of advertisement or notice, whether to the public or not.

16C Instructions and pressure to discriminate

(1) It is unlawful for a person –

(a) who has authority over another person, or

(b) in accordance with whose wishes that other person is accustomed to act,

to instruct him to do any act which is unlawful under this Part or, to the extent that it relates to the provision of employment services, Part 3, or to procure or attempt to procure the doing by him of any such act.

(2) It is also unlawful to induce, or attempt to induce, a person to do any act which

contravenes this Part or, to the extent that it relates to the provision of employment services, Part 3 by –

(a) providing or offering to provide him with any benefit, or

(b) subjecting or threatening to subject him to any detriment.

(3) An attempted inducement is not prevented from falling within subsection (2) because it is not made directly to the person in question, if it is made in such a way that he is likely to hear of it.

17A Enforcement, remedies and procedure

(1) A complaint by any person that another person –

(a) has discriminated against him, or subjected him to harassment, in a way which is unlawful under this Part, or

(b) is, by virtue of section 57 or 58, to be treated as having done so,

may be presented to an employment tribunal.

(1A) Subsection (1) does not apply to a complaint under section 14A(1) or (2) of an act in respect of which an appeal, or proceedings in the nature of an appeal, may be brought under any enactment.

(1C) Where, on the hearing of a complaint under subsection (1), the complainant proves facts from which the tribunal could, apart from this subsection, conclude in the absence of an adequate explanation that the respondent has acted in a way which is unlawful under this Part, the tribunal shall uphold the complaint unless the respondent proves that he did not so act.

(2) Where an employment tribunal finds that a complaint presented to it under this section is well-founded, it shall take such of the following steps as it considers just and equitable –

(a) making a declaration as to the rights of the complainant and the respondent in relation to the matters to which the complaint relates;

(b) ordering the respondent to pay compensation to the complainant;

(c) recommending that the respondent take, within a specified period, action appearing to the tribunal to be reasonable, in all the circumstances of the case, for the purpose of obviating or reducing the adverse effect on the complainant of any matter to which the complaint relates.

(3) Where a tribunal orders compensation under subsection (2)(b), the amount of the compensation shall be calculated by applying the principles applicable to the calculation of damages in claims in tort ...

(4) For the avoidance of doubt it is hereby declared that compensation in respect of discrimination in a way which is unlawful under this Part may include compensation for injury to feelings whether or not it includes compensation under any other head.

(5) If the respondent to a complaint fails, without reasonable justification, to comply

with a recommendation made by an employment tribunal under subsection (2)(c) the tribunal may, if it thinks it just and equitable to do so –

(a) increase the amount of compensation required to be paid to the complainant in respect of the complaint, where an order was made under subsection (2)(b); or

(b) make an order under subsection (2)(b).

(6) Regulations may make provision –

(a) for enabling a tribunal, where an amount of compensation falls to be awarded under subsection (2)(b), to include in the award interest on that amount; and

(b) specifying, for cases where a tribunal decides that an award is to include an amount in respect of interest, the manner in which and the periods and rate by reference to which the interest is to be determined.

(7) Regulations may modify the operation of any order made under section 14 of the Employment Tribunals Act 1996 (power to make provision as to interest on sums payable in pursuance of employment tribunal decisions) to the extent that it relates to an award of compensation under subsection (2)(b).

(8) Part I of Schedule 3 makes further provision about the enforcement of this Part and about procedure.

17B Enforcement of sections 16B(1) and 16C

(1) Only the Disability Rights Commission may bring proceedings in respect of a contravention of section 16B(1) (discriminatory advertisements) or section 16C (instructions and pressure to discriminate).

(2) The Commission shall bring any such proceedings in accordance with subsection (3) or (4).

(3) The Commission may present to an employment tribunal a complaint that a person has done an act which is unlawful under section 16B(1) or 16C; and if the tribunal finds that the complaint is well-founded it shall make a declaration to that effect.

(4) Where –

(a) a tribunal has made a finding pursuant to subsection (3) that a person has done an act which is unlawful under section 16B(1) or 16C,

(b) that finding has become final, and

(c) it appears to the Commission that, unless restrained, he is likely to do a further act which is unlawful under section 16B(1) or (as the case may be) section 16C,

the Commission may apply to a county court for an injunction ... restraining him from doing such an act; and the court, if satisfied that the application is well-founded, may grant the injunction or interdict in the terms applied for or in more limited terms.

(5) A finding of a tribunal under subsection (3) in respect of any act shall, if it has become final, be treated as conclusive by a county court ... upon an application under subsection (4).

(6) A finding of a tribunal becomes final for the purposes of this section when an appeal against it is dismissed, withdrawn or abandoned or when the time for appealing expires without an appeal having been brought.

(7) An employment tribunal shall not consider a complaint under subsection (3) unless it is presented before the end of the period of six months beginning when the act to which it relates was done; and a county court ... shall not consider an application under subsection (4) unless it is made before the end of the period of five years so beginning.

(8) A court or tribunal may consider any such complaint or application which is out of time if, in all the circumstances of the case, it considers that it is just and equitable to do so.

(9) The provisions of paragraph 3(3) and (4) of Schedule 3 apply for the purposes of subsection (7) as they apply for the purposes of paragraph 3(1) of that Schedule.

17C Validity of contracts, collective agreements and rules of undertakings

Schedule 3A shall have effect.

18A Alterations premises occupied under leases

(1) This section applies where –

(a) a person to whom a duty to make reasonable adjustments applies ('the occupier') occupies premises under a lease;

(b) but for this section, the occupier would not be entitled to make a particular alteration to the premises; and

(c) the alteration is one which the occupier proposes to make in order to comply with that duty.

(2) Except to the extent to which it expressly so provides, the lease shall have effect by virtue of this subsection as if it provided –

(a) for the occupier to be entitled to make the alteration with the written consent of the lessor;

(b) for the occupier to have to make a written application to the lessor for consent if he wishes to make the alteration;

(c) if such an application is made, for the lessor not to withhold his consent unreasonably; and

(d) for the lessor to be entitled to make his consent subject to reasonable conditions.

(3) In this section –

'lease' includes a tenancy, sub-lease or sub-tenancy and an agreement for a lease, tenancy, sub-lease or sub-tenancy; and

'sub-lease' and 'sub-tenancy' have such meaning as may be prescribed.

(4) If the terms and conditions of a lease –

(a) impose conditions which are to apply if the occupier alters the premises, or

(b) entitle the lessor to impose conditions when consenting to the occupier's altering the premises,

the occupier is to be treated for the purposes of subsection (1) as not being entitled to make the alteration.

(5) Part I of Schedule 4 supplements the provisions of this section.

18C Charities and support for particular groups of persons

(1) Nothing in this Part –

(a) affects any charitable instrument which provides for conferring benefits on one or more categories of person determined by reference to any physical or mental capacity; or

(b) makes unlawful any act done by a charity ... in pursuance of any of its charitable purposes, so far as those purposes are connected with persons so determined.

(2) Nothing in this Part prevents –

(a) a person who provides supported employment from treating members of a particular group of disabled persons more favourably than other persons in providing such employment; or

(b) the Secretary of State from agreeing to arrangements for the provision of supported employment which will, or may, have that effect.

(3) In this section –

'charitable instrument' means an enactment or other instrument (whenever taking effect) so far as it relates to charitable purposes;

'charity' has the same meaning as in the Charities Act 1993; ...

'supported employment' means facilities provided, or in respect of which payments are made, under section 15 of the Disabled Persons (Employment) Act 1944 [provision for registered persons who are seriously disabled of employment, or work on their own account, under special conditions].

(4) In the application of this section to England and Wales, 'charitable purposes' means purposes which are exclusively charitable according to the law of England and Wales. ...

18D Interpretation of Part 2

(1) Subject to any duty to make reasonable adjustments, nothing in this Part is to be taken to require a person to treat a disabled person more favourably than he treats or would treat others.

(2) In this Part –

'benefits' includes facilities and services;

'detriment', except in section 16C(2)(b), does not include conduct of the nature referred to in section 3B (harassment);

'discriminate', 'discrimination' and other related expressions are to be construed in accordance with section 3A;

'duty to make reasonable adjustments' means a duty imposed by or under section 4A, 4B(5) or (6), 4E, 6B, 7B, 7D, 14, 14B, 14D, 15C or 16A(5);

'employer' includes a person who has no employees but is seeking to employ another person;

'harassment' is to be construed in accordance with section 3B;

'physical feature', in relation to any premises, includes (subject to any provision under section 15C(4)(e)) any of the following (whether permanent or temporary) –

(a) any feature arising from the design or construction of a building on the premises,

(b) any feature on the premises of any approach to, exit from or access to such a building,

(c) any fixtures, fittings, furnishings, furniture, equipment or material in or on the premises,

(d) any other physical element or quality of any land comprised in the premises;

'provision, criterion or practice' includes any arrangements.'.

18E Premises provided otherwise than in course of a Part 2 relationship

(1) This Part does not apply in relation to the provision, otherwise than in the course of a Part 2 relationship, of premises by the regulated party to the other party.

(2) For the purposes of subsection (1) –

(a) 'Part 2 relationship' means a relationship during the course of which an act of discrimination against, or harassment of, one party to the relationship by the other party to it is unlawful under sections 4 to 15C; and

(b) in relation to a Part 2 relationship, 'regulated party' means the party whose acts of discrimination, or harassment, are made unlawful by sections 4 to 15C.

PART 7

SUPPLEMENTAL

53A Codes of practice

(1) The Disability Rights Commission may prepare and issue codes of practice giving practical guidance on how to avoid acts which are unlawful under Part 2, 3 or 4, or on any other matter relating to the operation of any provision of those Parts –

(a) employers;

(b) service providers;

(ba) public authorities within the meaning given by section 21B;

(bb) associations to which section 21F applies;

(c) bodies which are responsible bodies for the purposes of Chapter 1 or 2 of Part 4; or

(d) other persons to whom the provisions of Parts 2 or 3 or Chapter 2 or 2A of Part 4 apply.

(1A) The Commission may also prepare and issue codes of practice giving practical guidance to any persons on any other matter with a view to –

(a) promoting the equalisation of opportunities for disabled persons and persons who have had a disability; or

(b) encouraging good practice in the way such persons are treated,

in any field of activity regulated by any provision of Part 2, 3 or 4. ...

55 Victimisation

(1) For the purposes of Part 2 or Part 4, or Part 3 other than sections 24A to 24L, a person ('A') discriminates against another person ('B') if –

(a) he treats B less favourably than he treats or would treat other persons whose circumstances are the same as B's; and

(b) he does so for a reason mentioned in subsection (2).

(2) The reasons are that –

(a) B has –

(i) brought proceedings against A or any other person under this Act; or

(ii) given evidence or information in connection with such proceedings brought by any person; or

(iii) otherwise done anything under, or by reference to, this Act in relation to A or any other person; or

(iv) alleged that A or any other person has (whether or not the allegation so states) contravened this Act; or

(b) A believes or suspects that B has done or intends to do any of those things.

—— 278 ——

(3) Where B is a disabled person, or a person who has had a disability, the disability in question shall be disregarded in comparing his circumstances with those of any other person for the purposes of subsection (1)(a).

(3A) For the purposes of Chapter 1 of Part 4 –

(a) references in subsection (2) to B include references to –

(i) a person who is, for the purposes of that Chapter, B's parent; and

(ii) a sibling of B; and

(b) references in that subsection to this Act are, as respects a person mentioned in sub-paragraph (i) or (ii) of paragraph (a), restricted to that Chapter.

(4) Subsection (1) does not apply to treatment of a person because of an allegation made by him if the allegation was false and not made in good faith.

(5) In the case of an act which constitutes discrimination by virtue of this section, sections 4, 4B, 4D, 4G, 6A, 7A, 7C, 13, 14A, 14C, 15B and 16A also apply to discrimination against a person who is not disabled.

56 Help for aggrieved persons in obtaining information, etc

(1) For the purposes of this section –

(a) a person who considers that he may have been –

(i) discriminated against in contravention of Part 2 or 3, or

(ii) subjected to harassment in contravention of Part 2 or section 21A(2),

is referred to as 'the person aggrieved'; and

(b) a person against whom the person aggrieved may decide to institute, or has instituted, proceedings in respect of such discrimination or harassment is referred to as 'the respondent'.

(2) With a view to helping the person aggrieved decide whether to institute proceedings and, if he does so, to formulate and present his case in the most effective manner, the Secretary of State shall by order prescribe –

(a) forms by which the person aggrieved may question the respondent on his reasons for doing any relevant act, or on any other matter which is or may be relevant; and

(b) forms by which the respondent may if he so wishes reply to any questions.

(3) Where the person aggrieved questions the respondent in accordance with forms prescribed by an order under subsection (2) –

(a) the question, and any reply by the respondent (whether in accordance with such an order or not), shall be admissible as evidence in any proceedings under Part 2 or 3;

(b) if it appears to the court or tribunal in any such proceedings –

(i) that the respondent deliberately, and without reasonable excuse, omitted to reply within the period of eight weeks beginning with the day on which the question was served on him, or

(ii) that the respondent's reply is evasive or equivocal,

it may draw any inference which it considers it just and equitable to draw, including an inference that the respondent committed an unlawful act.

(4) The Secretary of State may by order –

(a) prescribe the period within which questions must be duly served in order to be admissible under subsection (3)(a); and

(b) prescribe the manner in which a question, and any reply by the respondent, may be duly served.

(5) Rules of court may enable a court entertaining a claim under section 25 to determine, before the date fixed for the hearing of the claim, whether a question or reply is admissible under this section or not.

(6) In proceedings in respect of a section 21B claim, subsection (3)(b) does not apply in relation to a failure to reply, or a particular reply, if the following conditions are met –

(a) that, at the time of doing any relevant act, the respondent was carrying out public investigator functions or was a public prosecutor; and

(b) that the respondent reasonably believes that a reply or (as the case may be) a different reply would be likely to prejudice any criminal investigation, any decision to institute criminal proceedings or any criminal proceedings or would reveal the reasons behind a decision not to institute, or a decision not to continue, criminal proceedings.

(7) Regulations may provide for this section not to have effect, or to have effect with prescribed modifications, in relation to section 21B claims of a prescribed description.

(8) This section is without prejudice to any other enactment or rule of law regulating interlocutory and preliminary matters in proceedings before a county court, the sheriff or an employment tribunal, and has effect subject to any enactment or rule of law regulating the admissibility of evidence in such proceedings.

(9) In this section 'section 21B claim' means a claim under section 25 by virtue of section 21B.

57 Aiding unlawful acts

(1) A person who knowingly aids another person to do an unlawful act is to be treated for the purposes of this Act as himself doing the same kind of unlawful act.

(2) For the purposes of subsection (1), an employee or agent for whose act the employer or principal is liable under section 58 (or would be so liable but for section 58(5)) shall be taken to have aided the employer or principal to do the act.

(3) For the purposes of this section, a person does not knowingly aid another to do an unlawful act if –

(a) he acts in reliance on a statement made to him by that other person that, because of any provision of this Act, the act would not be unlawful; and

(b) it is reasonable for him to rely on the statement.

(4) A person who knowingly or recklessly makes such a statement which is false or misleading in a material respect is guilty of an offence.

(5) Any person guilty of an offence under subsection (4) shall be liable on summary conviction to a fine not exceeding level 5 on the standard scale.

(6) 'Unlawful act' means an act made unlawful by any provision of this Act other than a provision contained in Chapter 1 of Part 4 [schools].

58   Liability of employers and principals

(1) Anything done by a person in the course of his employment shall be treated for the purposes of this Act as also done by his employer, whether or not it was done with the employer's knowledge or approval.

(2) Anything done by a person as agent for another person with the authority of that other person shall be treated for the purposes of this Act as also done by that other person.

(3) Subsection (2) applies whether the authority was –

(a) express or implied; or

(b) given before or after the act in question was done.

(4) Subsections (1) and (2) do not apply in relation to an offence under section 57(4).

(5) In proceedings under this Act against any person in respect of an act alleged to have been done by an employee of his, it shall be a defence for that person to prove that he took such steps as were reasonably practicable to prevent the employee from –

(a) doing that act; or

(b) doing, in the course of his employment, acts of that description.

59   Statutory authority and national security, etc

(1) Nothing in this Act makes unlawful any act done –

(a) in pursuance of any enactment; or

(b) in pursuance of any instrument made under any enactment by –

(i) a Minister of the Crown,

(ii) a member of the Scottish Executive, or

(iii) the National Assembly for Wales; or

(c) to comply with any condition or requirement –

(i) imposed by a Minister of the Crown (whether before or after the passing of this Act) by virtue of any enactment,

(ii) imposed by a member of the Scottish Executive (whether before or after the coming into force of this sub-paragraph) by virtue of any enactment, or

(iii) imposed by the National Assembly for Wales (whether before or after the coming into force of this sub-paragraph) by virtue of any enactment.

(2) In subsection (1) 'enactment' includes one passed or made after the date on which this Act is passed and 'instrument' includes one made after that date.

(2A) Nothing in –

(a) Part 2 of this Act, or

(b) Part 3 of this Act to the extent that it relates to the provision of employment services,

makes unlawful any act done for the purpose of safeguarding national security if the doing of the act was justified by that purpose.

(3) Nothing in any other provision of this Act makes unlawful any act done for the purpose of safeguarding national security.

PART VIII

MISCELLANEOUS

60   Appointment by Secretary of State of advisers

(1) The Secretary of State may appoint such persons as he thinks fit to advise or assist him in connection with matters relating to the employment of disabled persons and persons who have had a disability.

(2) Persons may be appointed by the Secretary of State to act generally or in relation to a particular area or locality. ...

68   Interpretation

(1) In this Act – ...

'act' includes a deliberate omission; ...

'conciliation officer' means a person designated under section 211 of the Trade Union and Labour Relations (Consolidation) Act 1992;

'employment' means, subject to any prescribed provision, employment under a contract of service or of apprenticeship or a contract personally to do any work, and related expressions are to be construed accordingly;

'employment at an establishment in Great Britain' is to be construed in accordance with subsections (2) to (4A);

'enactment' includes subordinate legislation and any Order in Council;

'Great Britain' includes such of the territorial waters of the United Kingdom as are adjacent to Great Britain; ...

'mental impairment' does not have the same meaning as in the Mental Health Act 1983 but the fact that an impairment would be a mental impairment for the purposes of that Act does not prevent it from being a mental impairment for the purposes of this Act;

'Minister of the Crown' includes the Treasury and the Defence Council;

'occupational pension scheme' has the same meaning as in the Pension Schemes Act 1993;

'premises' includes land of any description;

'prescribed' means prescribed by regulations, except in section 28D (where it has the meaning given by section 28D(17));

'profession' includes any vocation or occupation; ...

'regulations' means regulations made by the Secretary of State, except in sections 2(3), 28D, 28L(6), 28Q(7), 33, 49D to 49F and 67 (provisions where the meaning of 'regulations' is apparent); ...

'subordinate legislation' has the same meaning as in section 21 of the Interpretation Act 1978; ...

'trade' includes any business;

'trade organisation' has the meaning given in section 13; ...

(4) Employment of a prescribed kind, or in prescribed circumstances, is to be regarded as not being employment at an establishment in Great Britain. ...

SCHEDULE 1

PROVISIONS SUPPLEMENTING SECTION 1

2. – (1) The effect of an impairment is a long-term effect if –

(a) it has lasted at least 12 months;

(b) the period for which it lasts is likely to be at least 12 months; or

(c) it is likely to last for the rest of the life of the person affected.

(2) Where an impairment ceases to have a substantial adverse effect on a person's ability to carry out normal day –to –day activities, it is to be treated as continuing to have that effect if that effect is likely to recur. ...

3. – (1) An impairment which consists of a severe disfigurement is to be treated as having a substantial adverse effect on the ability of the person concerned to carry out normal day-to-day activities. ...

4. – (1) An impairment is to be taken to affect the ability of the person concerned to carry out normal day-to-day activities only if it affects one of the following –

(a) mobility;

(b) manual dexterity;

(c) physical co-ordination;

(d) continence;

(e) ability to lift, carry or otherwise move everyday objects;

(f) speech, hearing or eyesight;

(g) memory or ability to concentrate, learn or understand; or

(h) perception of the risk of physical danger. ...

6. – (1) An impairment which would be likely to have a substantial adverse effect on the ability of the person concerned to carry out normal day-to-day activities, but for the fact that measures are being taken to treat or correct it, is to be treated as having that effect.

(2) In sub-paragraph (1) 'measures' includes, in particular, medical treatment and the use of a prosthesis or other aid.

(3) Sub-paragraph (1) does not apply –

(a) in relation to the impairment of a person's sight, to the extent that the impairment is, in his case, correctable by spectacles or contact lenses or in such other ways as may be prescribed; ...

6A. – (1) Subject to sub-paragraph (2), a person who has cancer, HIV infection or multiple sclerosis is to be deemed to have a disability, and hence to be a disabled person.

(2) Regulations may provide for sub-paragraph (1) not to apply in the case of a person who has cancer if he has cancer of a prescribed description.

(3) A description of cancer prescribed under sub-paragraph (2) may (in particular) be framed by reference to consequences for a person of his having it.

7. – (1) Sub-paragraph (2) applies to any person whose name is, both on 12th January 1995 and on the date when this paragraph comes into force, in the register of disabled persons maintained under section 6 of the Disabled Persons (Employment) Act 1944.

(2) That person is to be deemed –

(a) during the initial period, to have a disability, and hence to be a disabled person; and

(b) afterwards, to have had a disability and hence to have been a disabled person during that period. ...

(7) In this paragraph – ...

'initial period' means the period of three years beginning with the date on which this paragraph comes into force.

8. – (1) Where –

(a) a person has a progressive condition (such as cancer, multiple sclerosis or muscular dystrophy or HIV infection),

(b) as a result of that condition, he has an impairment which has (or had) an effect on his ability to carry out normal day-to-day activities, but

(c) that effect is not (or was not) a substantial adverse effect, he shall be taken to have an impairment which has such a substantial adverse effect if the condition is likely to result in his having such an impairment. ...

9. In this Schedule 'HIV infection' means infection by a virus capable of causing the Acquired Immune Deficiency Syndrome.

SCHEDULE 2

PAST DISABILITIES

1. The modifications referred to in section 2 are as follows.

2. References in Parts II to 4 and 5A to a disabled person are to be read as references to a person who has had a disability. ...

2C. In section 3A(5), after 'not having that particular disability' insert 'and who has not had that particular disability'.

3. In sections 4A(1), 4B(4), 4E(1), 4H(1), 6B(1), 7B(1), 7D(1), 14(1), 14B(1), 14D(1) and 16A(4), section 21A(4)(a) (in the words to be read as section 19(1)(aa)) and section 21A(6)(a) (in the words to be substituted in section 21(1)), after 'not disabled' (in each place it occurs) insert 'and who have not had a disability'.

4. In sections 4A(3)(b), 4E(3)(b), 4H(3)(b), 6B(3)(b), 7B(4)(b), 7D(3)(b), 14(3)(b), 14B(3)(b), 14D(3)(b) and 16A(6), for 'has' (in each place it occurs) substitute 'has had'. ...

5. For paragraph 2(1) to [2] of Schedule 1, substitute –

'(1) The effect of an impairment is a long-term effect if it has lasted for at least 12 months.

(2) Where an impairment ceases to have a substantial adverse effect on a person's ability to carry out normal day-to-day activities, it is to be treated as continuing to have that effect if that effect recurs. ...'

SCHEDULE 3

ENFORCEMENT AND PROCEDURE

PART I

EMPLOYMENT

2. – (1) Except as provided by Part 2, no civil or criminal proceedings may be brought against any person in respect of an act merely because the act is unlawful under that Part.

(2) Sub-paragraph (1) does not prevent the making of an application for judicial review or the investigation or determination of any matter in accordance with Part 10 (investigations) of the Pension Schemes Act 1993 by the Pensions Ombudsman.

(3) Sub-paragraph (1) does not prevent the bringing of proceedings in respect of an offence under section 16B(2B).

3. – (1) An employment tribunal shall not consider a complaint under section 17A or 25(8) unless it is presented before the end of the period of three months beginning when the act complained of was done.

(2) A tribunal may consider any such complaint which is out of time if, in all the circumstances of the case, it considers that it is just and equitable to do so.

(3) For the purposes of sub-paragraph (1) –

(a) where an unlawful act of discrimination is attributable to a term in a contract, that act is to be treated as extending throughout the duration of the contract;

(b) any act extending over a period shall be treated as done at the end of that period; and

(c) a deliberate omission shall be treated as done when the person in question decided upon it.

(4) In the absence of evidence establishing the contrary, a person shall be taken for the purposes of this paragraph to decide upon an omission –

(a) when he does an act inconsistent with doing the omitted act; or

(b) if he has done no such inconsistent act, when the period expires within which he might reasonably have been expected to do the omitted act if it was to be done.

4. – (1) In any proceedings under section 17A or 25(8), a certificate signed by or on behalf of a Minister of the Crown and certifying –

(a) that any conditions or requirements specified in the certificate were imposed by a Minister of the Crown and were in operation at a time or throughout a time so specified,

shall be conclusive evidence of the matters certified. ...

(1B) In any proceedings under section 17A or 25(8), a certificate signed by or on behalf of the National Assembly for Wales and certifying that any conditions or requirements specified in the certificate –

(a) were imposed by the Assembly, and

(b) were in operation at a time or throughout a time so specified,

shall be conclusive evidence of the matters certified. ...

SCHEDULE 3A

VALIDITY OF CONTRACTS, COLLECTIVE AGREEMENTS AND RULES OF UNDERTAKINGS

PART 1

VALIDITY AND REVISION OF CONTRACTS

1. – (1) A term of a contract is void where –

(a) the making of the contract is, by reason of the inclusion of the term, unlawful by virtue of this Part of this Act;

(b) it is included in furtherance of an act which is unlawful by virtue of this Part of this Act; or

(c) it provides for the doing of an act which is unlawful by virtue of this Part of this Act.

(2) Sub-paragraph (1) does not apply to a term the inclusion of which constitutes, or is in furtherance of, or provides for, unlawful discrimination against, or harassment of, a party to the contract, but the term shall be unenforceable against that party.

(3) A term in a contract which purports to exclude or limit any provision of this Part of this Act is unenforceable by any person in whose favour the term would operate apart from this paragraph.

(4) Sub-paragraphs (1), (2) and (3) apply whether the contract was entered into before or after the date on which this Schedule comes into force; but in the case of a contract made before that date, those sub-paragraphs do not apply in relation to any period before that date.

2. – (1) Paragraph 1(3) does not apply –

(a) to a contract settling a complaint to which section 17A(1) or 25(8) applies where the contract is made with the assistance of a conciliation officer (within the meaning of the Trade Union and Labour Relations (Consolidation) Act 1992[42]); or

(b) to a contract settling a complaint to which section 17A(1) or 25(8) applies if the conditions regulating compromise contracts under this Schedule are satisfied in relation to the contract.

(2) The conditions regulating compromise contracts under this Schedule are that –

(a) the contract must be in writing;

(b) the contract must relate to the particular complaint;

(c) the complainant must have received advice from a relevant independent adviser as to the terms and effect of the proposed contract and in particular its effect on his ability to pursue a complaint before an employment tribunal;

(d) there must be in force, when the adviser gives the advice, a contract of insurance, or an indemnity provided for members of a profession or professional body, covering the risk of a claim by the complainant in respect of loss arising in consequence of the advice;

(e) the contract must identify the adviser; and

(f) the contract must state that the conditions regulating compromise contracts under this Schedule are satisfied. ...

(8) An agreement under which the parties agree to submit a dispute to arbitration –

(a) shall be regarded for the purposes of sub-paragraph (1)(a) and (b) as being a contract settling a complaint if –

(i) the dispute is covered by a scheme having effect by virtue of an order under section 212A of the Trade Union and Labour Relations (Consolidation) Act 1992, and

(ii) the agreement is to submit it to arbitration in accordance with the scheme; but

(b) shall be regarded as neither being nor including such a contract in any other case.

3. – (1) On the application of a disabled person interested in a contract to which paragraph 1(1) or (2) applies, a county court ... may make such order as it thinks fit for –

(a) removing or modifying any term rendered void by paragraph 1(1), or

(b) removing or modifying any term made unenforceable by paragraph 1(2);

but such an order shall not be made unless all persons affected have been given notice in writing of the application (except where under rules of court notice may be dispensed with) and have been afforded an opportunity to make representations to the court.

(2) An order under sub-paragraph (1) may include provision as respects any period before the making of the order (but after the coming into force of this Schedule). ...

SCHEDULE 4

PREMISES OCCUPIED UNDER LEASES

PART I

OCCUPATION BY EMPLOYER, ETC

1. If any question arises as to whether the occupier has failed to comply with any duty to make reasonable adjustments, by failing to make a particular alteration to the premises, any constraint attributable to the fact that he occupies the premises under a lease is to be ignored unless he has applied to the lessor in writing for consent to the making of the alteration.

2. – (1) In any proceedings on a complaint under section 17A, in a case to which

section 18A applies, the complainant or the occupier may ask the tribunal hearing the complaint to direct that the lessor be joined ... as a party to the proceedings. ...

(5) Where a lessor has been so joined ... as a party to the proceedings, the tribunal may determine –

(a) whether the lessor has –

(i) refused consent to the alteration, or

(ii) consented subject to one or more conditions, and

(b) if so, whether the refusal or any of the conditions was unreasonable.

(6) If, under sub-paragraph (5), the tribunal determines that the refusal or any of the conditions was unreasonable it may take one or more of the following steps –

(a) make such declaration as it considers appropriate;

(b) make an order authorising the occupier to make the alteration specified in the order;

(c) order the lessor to pay compensation to the complainant.

(7) An order under sub-paragraph (6)(b) may require the occupier to comply with conditions specified in the order.

(8) Any step taken by the tribunal under sub-paragraph (6) may be in substitution for, or in addition to, any step taken by the tribunal under section 17A(2).

(9) If the tribunal orders the lessor to pay compensation it may not make an order under section 17A(2) ordering the occupier to do so. ...

As amended by the Industrial Tribunals Act 1996, s43, Schedule 1, para 12(1)–(3); Employment Rights Act 1996, s240, Schedule 1, para 69(1), (2); Employment Rights (Dispute Resolution) Act 1998, ss1(2)(a), (c), 8(4), 9(1), (2)(d), 10(1), (2)(d), 15, Schedule 1, para 11; Disability Discrimination (Exemption for Small Employers) Order 1998, art 2; Disability Rights Commission Act 1999, ss9, 11; Employment Relations Act 1999, s41, 44, Schedule 8, para 7, Schedule 9, Pt 12; Equal Opportunities (Employment Legislation) (Territorial Limits) Regulations 1999, reg 4; Special Educational Needs and Disability Act 2001, ss36(1),(2), 38(1)–(4), (7)–(11); Disability Discrimination Act 1995 (Amendment) Regulations 2003, regs 3, 13, 14, 15(1), 16(2), 18, 20(a), 21, 23, 27, 29, Schedule; Disability Discrimination Act 1995 (Pensions) Regulations 2003, regs 2, 3, 4(3)–(5); Disability Discrimination Act 2005, ss10, 18, 19, Schedule 1, Pt 1, paras 1–4, 6–12, 28(1), (2), 29, 30, 34(1), (3)–(6), 36, 37(1), (2), 38(1)–(3), 40(1), (2), Schedule 2.

EMPLOYMENT TRIBUNALS ACT 1996
(1996 c 17)

PART I

EMPLOYMENT TRIBUNALS

1   Employment tribunals

(1) The Secretary of State may by regulations make provision for the establishment of tribunals to be known as employment tribunals.

(2) Regulations made wholly or partly under section 128(1) of the Employment Protection (Consolidation) Act 1978 and in force immediately before this Act comes into force shall, so far as made under that provision, continue to have effect (until revoked) as if made under subsection (1).

2   Enactments conferring jurisdiction on employment tribunals

Employment tribunals shall exercise the jurisdiction conferred on them by or by virtue of this Act or any other Act, whether passed before or after this Act.

3   Power to confer further jurisdiction on employment tribunals

(1) The appropriate Minister may by order provide that proceedings in respect of –

    (a) any claim to which this section applies, or

    (b) any claim to which this section applies and which is of a description specified in the order,

may, subject to such exceptions (if any) as may be so specified, be brought before an employment tribunal.

(2) Subject to subsection (3), this section applies to –

    (a) a claim for damages for breach of a contract of employment or other contract connected with employment,

    (b) a claim for a sum due under such a contract, and

    (c) a claim for the recovery of a sum in pursuance of any enactment relating to the terms or performance of such a contract,

if the claim is such that a court in England and Wales ... would under the law for the time being in force have jurisdiction to hear and determine an action in respect of the claim.

(3) This section does not apply to a claim for damages, or for a sum due, in respect of personal injuries.

(4) Any jurisdiction conferred on an employment tribunal by virtue of this section in respect of any claim is exercisable concurrently with any court in England and Wales… which has jurisdiction to hear and determine an action in respect of the claim.

(5) In this section –

'appropriate Minister', as respects a claim in respect of which an action could be heard and determined by a court in England and Wales, means the Lord Chancellor … and

'personal injuries' includes any disease and any impairment of a person's physical or mental condition.

(6) In this section a reference to breach of a contract includes a reference to breach of –

(a) a term implied in a contract by or under any enactment or otherwise,

(b) a term of a contract as modified by or under any enactment or otherwise, and

(c) a term which, although not contained in a contract, is incorporated in the contract by another term of the contract.

4   Composition of a tribunal

(1) Subject to the following provisions of this section and to section 7(3A), proceedings before an employment tribunal shall be heard by –

(a) the person who, in accordance with regulations made under section 1(1), is the chairman, and

(b) two other members, or (with the consent of the parties) one other member, selected as the other members (or member) in accordance with regulations so made.

(2) Subject to subsection (5), the proceedings specified in subsection (3) shall be heard by the person mentioned in subsection (1)(a) alone.

(3) The proceedings referred to in subsection (2) are –

(a) proceedings on a complaint under section 68A, 87 or 192 of the Trade Union and Labour Relations (Consolidation) Act 1992 or on an application under section 161, 165 or 166 of that Act;

(b) proceedings on a complaint under section 126 of the Pension Schemes Act 1993;

(c) proceedings on a reference under section 11, 163 or 170 of the Employment Rights Act 1996, on a complaint under section 23, 34 or 188 of that Act, on a complaint under section 70(1) of that Act relating to section 64 of that Act, on an application under section 128, 131 or 132 of that Act or for an appointment under section 206(4) of that Act;

(ca) proceedings on a complaint under regulation 11(5) of the Transfer of Undertakings (Protection of Employment) Regulations 1981;

(cc) proceedings on a complaint under section 11 of the National Minimum Wage Act 1998;

(cd) proceedings on an appeal under section 19 or 22 of the National Minimum Wage Act 1998;

(d) proceedings in respect of which an employment tribunal has jurisdiction by virtue of section 3 of this Act;

(e) proceedings in which the parties have given their written consent to the proceedings being heard in accordance with subsection (2) (whether or not they have subsequently withdrawn it); and

(g) proceedings in which the person (or, where more than one, each of the persons) against whom the proceedings are brought does not, or has ceased to, contest the case.

(4) The Secretary of State may by order amend the provisions of subsection (3).

(5) Proceedings specified in subsection (3) shall be heard in accordance with subsection (1) if a person who, in accordance with regulations made under section 1(1), may be the chairman of an employment tribunal, having regard to –

(a) whether there is a likelihood of a dispute arising on the facts which makes it desirable for the proceedings to be heard in accordance with subsection (1),

(b) whether there is a likelihood of an issue of law arising which would make it desirable for the proceedings to be heard in accordance with subsection (2),

(c) any views of any of the parties as to whether or not the proceedings ought to be heard in accordance with either of those subsections, and

(d) whether there are other proceedings which might be heard concurrently but which are not proceedings specified in subsection (3),

decides at any stage of the proceedings that the proceedings are to be heard in accordance with subsection (1).

(6) Where (in accordance with the following provisions of this Part) the Secretary of State makes employment tribunal procedure regulations, the regulations may provide that, any act which is required or authorised by the regulations to be done by an employment tribunal and is of a description specified by the regulations for the purposes of this subsection may be done by the person mentioned in subsection (1)(a) alone.

(6A) Subsection (6) in particular enables employment tribunal procedure regulations to provide that –

(a) the determination of proceedings in accordance with regulations under section 7(3A), (3B) or (3C)(a),

(b) the carrying-out of pre-hearing reviews in accordance with regulations under subsection (1) of section 9 (including the exercise of powers in connection with such reviews in accordance with regulations under paragraph (b) of that subsection), or

(c) the hearing and determination of a primary issue in accordance with regulations under section 9(4) (where it involves hearing witnesses other than the parties or their representatives as well as where, in accordance with regulations under section 7(3C)(b), it does not),

may be done by the person mentioned in subsection (1)(a) alone.

(6B) Employment tribunal procedure regulations may (subject to subsection (6C)) also provide that any act which –

(a) by virtue of subsection (6) may be done by the person mentioned in subsection (1)(a) alone, and

(b) is of a description specified by the regulations for the purposes of this subsection,

may be done by a person appointed as a legal officer in accordance with regulations under section 1(1); and any act so done shall be treated as done by an employment tribunal.

(6C) But regulations under subsection (6B) may not specify –

(a) the determination of any proceedings, other than proceedings in which the parties have agreed the terms of the determination or in which the person bringing the proceedings has given notice of the withdrawal of the case, or

(b) the carrying-out of pre-hearing reviews in accordance with regulations under section 9(1).

6 Conduct of hearings

(1) A person may appear before an employment tribunal in person or be represented by –

(a) counsel or a solicitor,

(b) a representative of a trade union or an employers' association, or

(c) any other person whom he desires to represent him.

(2) Part I of the Arbitration Act 1996 does not apply to any proceedings before an employment tribunal.

7 Employment tribunal procedure regulations

(1) The Secretary of State may by regulations ('employment tribunal procedure regulations') make such provision as appears to him to be necessary or expedient with respect to proceedings before employment tribunals.

(2) Proceedings before employment tribunals shall be instituted in accordance with employment tribunal procedure regulations. ...

7A Practice directions

(1) Employment tribunal procedure regulations may include provision –

(a) enabling the President to make directions about the procedure of employment tribunals, including directions about the exercise by tribunals of powers under such regulations,

(b) for securing compliance with such directions, and

(c) about the publication of such directions.

(2) Employment tribunal procedure regulations may, instead of providing for any matter, refer to provision made or to be made about that matter by directions made by the President.

(3) In this section, references to the President are to a person appointed in accordance with regulations under section 1(1) as –

(a) President of the Employment Tribunals (England and Wales), ...

8 Procedure in contract cases

(1) Where in proceedings brought by virtue of section 3 an employment tribunal finds that the whole or part of a sum claimed in the proceedings is due, the tribunal shall order the respondent to the proceedings to pay the amount which it finds due.

(2) An order under section 3 may provide that an employment tribunal shall not in proceedings in respect of a claim, or a number of claims relating to the same contract, order the payment of an amount exceeding such sum as may be specified in the order as the maximum amount which an employment tribunal may order to be paid in relation to a claim or in relation to a contract.

(3) An order under section 3 may include provisions –

(a) as to the manner in which and time within which proceedings are to be brought by virtue of that section, and

(b) modifying any other enactment.

(4) An order under that section may make different provision in relation to proceedings in respect of different descriptions of claims.

9 Pre-hearing reviews and preliminary matters

(1) Employment tribunal procedure regulations may include provision –

(a) for authorising the carrying-out by an employment tribunal of a preliminary consideration of any proceedings before it (a 'pre-hearing review'), and

(b) for enabling such powers to be exercised in connection with a pre-hearing review as may be prescribed by the regulations. ...

(2A) Regulations under subsection (1)(b), so far as relating to striking out, may not provide for striking out on a ground which does not apply outside a pre-hearing review. ...

[*See Appendix, Employment Act 2002, s28.*]

10   National security

(1) If on a complaint under –

(a) section 145A, 145B or 146 of the Trade Union and Labour Relations (Consolidation) Act 1992 (inducements and detriments in respect of trade union membership, etc), or

(b) section 111 of the Employment Rights Act 1996 (unfair dismissal),

it is shown that the action complained of was taken for the purpose of safeguarding national security, the employment tribunal shall dismiss the complaint.

(2) Employment tribunal procedure regulations may make provision about the composition of the tribunal (including provision disapplying or modifying section 4) for the purposes of proceedings in relation to which –

(a) a direction is given under subsection (3), or

(b) an order is made under subsection (4).

(3) A direction may be given under this subsection by a Minister of the Crown if –

(a) it relates to particular Crown employment proceedings, and

(b) the Minister considers it expedient in the interests of national security.

(4) An order may be made under this subsection by the President [of the Employment Tribunals] or a Regional Chairman in relation to particular proceedings if he considers it expedient in the interests of national security.

(5) Employment tribunal procedure regulations may make provision enabling a Minister of the Crown, if he considers it expedient in the interests of national security –

(a) to direct a tribunal to sit in private for all or part of particular Crown employment proceedings;

(b) to direct a tribunal to exclude the applicant from all or part of particular Crown employment proceedings;

(c) to direct a tribunal to exclude the applicant's representatives from all or part of particular Crown employment proceedings;

(d) to direct a tribunal to take steps to conceal the identity of a particular witness in particular Crown employment proceedings;

(e) to direct a tribunal to take steps to keep secret all or part of the reasons for its decision in particular Crown employment proceedings.

(6) Employment tribunal procedure regulations may enable a tribunal, if it considers it expedient in the interests of national security, to do in relation to particular proceedings before it anything of a kind which, by virtue of subsection (5), employment tribunal procedure regulations may enable a Minister of the Crown to direct a tribunal to do in relation to particular Crown employment proceedings. ...

(8) Proceedings are Crown employment proceedings for the purposes of this section if the employment to which the complaint relates –

(a) is Crown employment, or

(b) is connected with the performance of functions on behalf of the Crown. ...

10A Confidential information

(1) Employment tribunal procedure regulations may enable an employment tribunal to sit in private for the purpose of hearing evidence from any person which in the opinion of the tribunal is likely to consist of –

(a) information which he could not disclose without contravening a prohibition imposed by or by virtue of any enactment,

(b) information which has been communicated to him in confidence or which he has otherwise obtained in consequence of the confidence reposed in him by another person, or

(c) information the disclosure of which would, for reasons other than its effect on negotiations with respect to any of the matters mentioned in section 178(2) of the Trade Union and Labour Relations (Consolidation) Act 1992, cause substantial injury to any undertaking of his or in which he works.

(2) The reference in subsection (1)(c) to any undertaking of a person or in which he works shall be construed –

(a) in relation to a person in Crown employment, as a reference to the national interest ...

10B Restriction of publicity in cases involving national security

(1) This section applies where a tribunal has been directed under section 10(5) or has determined under section 10(6) –

(a) to take steps to conceal the identity of a particular witness, or

(b) to take steps to keep secret all or part of the reasons for its decision.

(2) It is an offence to publish –

(a) anything likely to lead to the identification of the witness, or

(b) the reasons for the tribunal's decision or the part of its reasons which it is directed or has determined to keep secret.

(3) A person guilty of an offence under this section is liable on summary conviction to a fine not exceeding level 5 on the standard scale.

(4) Where a person is charged with an offence under this section it is a defence to prove that at the time of the alleged offence he was not aware, and neither suspected nor had reason to suspect, that the publication in question was of, or included, the matter in question.

(5) Where an offence under this section committed by a body corporate is proved to have been committed with the consent or connivance of, or to be attributable to any neglect on the part of –

(a) a director, manager, secretary or other similar officer of the body corporate, or

(b) a person purporting to act in any such capacity,

he as well as the body corporate is guilty of the offence and liable to be proceeded against and punished accordingly.

(6) A reference in this section to publication includes a reference to inclusion in a programme which is included in a programme service, within the meaning of the Broadcasting Act 1990.

11   Restriction of publicity in cases involving sexual misconduct

(1) Employment tribunal procedure regulations may include provision –

(a) for cases involving allegations of the commission of sexual offences, for securing that the registration or other making available of documents or decisions shall be so effected as to prevent the identification of any person affected by or making the allegation, and

(b) for cases involving allegations of sexual misconduct, enabling an industrial tribunal, on the application of any party to proceedings before it or of its own motion, to make a restricted reporting order having effect (if not revoked earlier) until the promulgation of the decision of the tribunal. ...

(6) In this section – ...

'restricted reporting order' means an order –

(a) made in exercise of a power conferred by regulations made by virtue of this section, and

(b) prohibiting the publication in Great Britain of identifying matter in a written publication available to the public or its inclusion in a relevant programme for reception in Great Britain,

'sexual misconduct' means the commission of a sexual offence, sexual harassment or other adverse conduct (of whatever nature) related to sex, and conduct is related to sex whether the relationship with sex lies in the character of the conduct or in its having reference to the sex or sexual orientation of the person at whom the conduct is directed,

'sexual offence' means any offence to which section 4 of the Sexual Offences (Amendment) Act 1976 [or] the Sexual Offences (Amendment) Act 1992 applies (offences under the Sexual Offences Act 1956 ... and certain other enactments), ...

12   Restriction of publicity in disability cases

(1) This section applies to proceedings on a complaint under section 17A or 25(8) of the Disability Discrimination Act 1995 in which evidence of a personal nature is likely to be heard by the employment tribunal hearing the complaint.

(2) Industrial tribunal procedure regulations may include provision in relation to proceedings to which this section applies for –

(a) enabling an employment tribunal, on the application of the complainant or of its own motion, to make a restricted reporting order having effect (if not revoked earlier) until the promulgation of the decision of the tribunal, and

(b) where a restricted reporting order is made in relation to a complaint which is being dealt with by the tribunal together with any other proceedings, enabling the tribunal to direct that the order is to apply also in relation to those other proceedings or such part of them as the tribunal may direct. ...

(7) In this section –

'evidence of a personal nature' means any evidence of a medical, or other intimate, nature which might reasonably be assumed to be likely to cause significant embarrassment to the complainant if reported, ...

'restricted reporting order' means an order –

(a) made in exercise of a power conferred by regulations made by virtue of this section, and

(b) prohibiting the publication in Great Britain of identifying matter in a written publication available to the public or its inclusion in a relevant programme for reception in Great Britain ...

13   Costs and expenses

(1) Employment tribunal procedure regulations may include provision –

(a) for the award of costs or expenses;

(b) for the award of any allowances payable under section 5(2)(c) or (3).

(1A) Regulations under subsection (1) may include provision authorising an employment tribunal to have regard to a person's ability to pay when considering the making of an award against him under such regulations.

(1B) Employment tribunal procedure regulations may include provision for authorising an employment tribunal –

(a) to disallow all or part of the costs or expenses of a representative of a party to proceedings before it by reason of that representative's conduct of the proceedings;

(b) to order a representative of a party to proceedings before it to meet all or part of the costs or expenses incurred by a party by reason of the representative's conduct of the proceedings;

(c) to order a representative of a party to proceedings before it to meet all or part of any allowances payable by the Secretary of State under section 5(2)(c) or (3) by reason of the representative's conduct of the proceedings.

(1C) Employment tribunal procedure regulations may also include provision for taxing or otherwise settling the costs or expenses referred to in subsection (1)(a) or (1B)(b) (and, in particular in England and Wales, for enabling the amount of such costs to be assessed by way of detailed assessment in a county court).

(2) In relation to proceedings under section 111 of the Employment Rights Act 1996 –

(a) where the employee has expressed a wish to be reinstated or re-engaged which has been communicated to the employer at least seven days before the hearing of the complaint,

employment tribunal procedure regulations shall include provision for requiring the employer to pay the costs or expenses of any postponement or adjournment of the hearing caused by his failure, without a special reason, to adduce reasonable evidence as to the availability of the job from which the complainant was dismissed, or of comparable or suitable employment.

13A Payments in respect of preparation time

(1) Employment tribunal procedure regulations may include provision for authorising an employment tribunal to order a party to proceedings before it to make a payment to any other party in respect of time spent in preparing that other party's case.

(2) Regulations under subsection (1) may include provision authorising an employment tribunal to have regard to a person's ability to pay when considering the making of an order against him under such regulations.

(3) If employment tribunal procedure regulations include –

(a) provision of the kind mentioned in subsection (1), and
(b) provision of the kind mentioned in section 13(1)(a),

they shall also include provision to prevent an employment tribunal exercising its powers under both kinds of provision in favour of the same person in the same proceedings.

14 Interest

(1) The Secretary of State may by order made with the approval of the Treasury provide that sums payable in pursuance of decisions of employment tribunals shall carry interest at such rate and between such times as may be prescribed by the order.

(2) Any interest due by virtue of such an order shall be recoverable as a sum payable in pursuance of the decision. ...

15 Enforcement

(1) Any sum payable in pursuance of a decision of an employment tribunal in England and Wales which has been registered in accordance with employment tribunal procedure regulations shall, if a county court so orders, be recoverable by execution issued from the county court or otherwise as if it were payable under an order of that court. ...

(3) In this section a reference to a decision or order of an employment tribunal –

(a) does not include a decision or order which, on being reviewed, has been revoked by the tribunal, and

(b) in relation to a decision or order which on being reviewed, has been varied by the tribunal, shall be construed as a reference to the decision or order as so varied.

16 Power to provide for recoupment of benefits

(1) This section applies to payments which for recoupment are the subject of proceedings before employment tribunals and which are –

(a) payments of wages or compensation for loss of wages,

(b) payments by employers to employees under sections 146 to 151, sections 168 to 173 or section 192 of the Trade Union and Labour Relations (Consolidation) Act 1992,

(c) payments by employers to employees under –

(i) Part III, V, VI or VII,

(ii) section 93, or

(iii) Part X,

of the Employment Rights Act 1996, or

(d) payments by employers to employees of a nature similar to, or for a purpose corresponding to the purpose of, payments within paragraph (b) or (c),

and to payments of remuneration under a protective award under section 189 of the Trade Union and Labour Relations (Consolidation) Act 1992.

(2) The Secretary of State may by regulations make with respect to payments to which this section applies provision for any or all of the purposes specified in subsection (3).

(3) The purposes referred to in subsection (2) are –

(a) enabling the Secretary of State to recover from an employer, by way of total or partial recoupment of jobseeker's allowance or income support –

(i) a sum not exceeding the amount of the prescribed element of the monetary award, or

(ii) in the case of a protective award, the amount of the remuneration,

(b) requiring or authorising an employment tribunal to order the payment of such a sum, by way of total or partial recoupment of either benefit, to the Secretary of State instead of to an employee, and

(c) requiring an employment tribunal to order the payment to an employee of only the excess of the prescribed element of the monetary award over the amount of any jobseeker's allowance or income support shown to the tribunal to have been paid to the employee and enabling the Secretary of State to recover from the employer, by way of total or partial recoupment of the benefit, a sum not exceeding that amount.

(4) Regulations under this section may be framed –

(a) so as to apply to all payments to which this section applies or to one or more classes of those payments, and

(b) so as to apply to both jobseeker's allowance and income support, or to only jobseeker's allowance or income support.

(5) Regulations under this section may –

(a) confer powers and impose duties on employment tribunals or other persons,

(b) impose on an employer to whom a monetary award or protective award relates a duty –

(i) to furnish particulars connected with the award, and

(ii) to suspend payments in pursuance of the award during any period prescribed by the regulations,

(c) provide for an employer who pays a sum to the Secretary of State in pursuance of this section to be relieved from any liability to pay the sum to another person,

(cc) provide for the determination by the Secretary of State of any issue arising as to the total or partial recoupment in pursuance of the regulations of a jobseeker's allowance, unemployment benefit or income support,

(d) confer on an employee a right of appeal to an appeal tribunal constituted under Chapter I of Part I of the Social Security Act 1998 against any decision of the Secretary of State on any such issue, and

(e) provide for the proof in proceedings before employment tribunals (whether by certificate or in any other manner) of any amount of jobseeker's allowance or income support paid to an employee.

(6) Regulations under this section may make different provision for different cases.

17 Recoupment: further provisions

(1) Where in pursuance of any regulations further under section 16 a sum has been recovered by or paid to the Secretary of State by way of total or partial recoupment of jobseeker's allowance or income support –

(a) no sum shall be recoverable under Part III [Overpayments and adjustments of benefit] or V [Income support and the duty to maintain] of the Social Security Administration Act 1992, and

(b) no abatement, payment or reduction shall be made by reference to the jobseeker's allowance or income support recouped.

(2) Any amount found to have been duly recovered by or paid to the Secretary of State in pursuance of regulations under section 16 by way of total or partial recoupment of jobseeker's allowance shall be paid into the National Insurance Fund.

(3) In section 16 –

'monetary award' means the amount which is awarded, or ordered to be paid, to the employee by the tribunal or would be so awarded or ordered apart from any provision of regulations under that section, and

'the prescribed element', in relation to any monetary award, means so much of that award as is attributable to such matters as may be prescribed by regulations under that section.

(4) In section 16 'income-based jobseeker's allowance' has the same meaning as in the Jobseekers Act 1995.

18 Conciliation

(1) This section applies in the case of employment tribunal proceedings and claims which could be the subject of employment tribunal proceedings –

(a) under –

(i) section 2(1) of the Equal Pay Act 1970,

(ii) section 63 of the Sex Discrimination Act 1975, or

(iii) section 54 of the Race Relations Act 1976,

(b) arising out of a contravention, or alleged contravention, of section 64, 68, 86, 137, 138, 145A, 145B, 146, 168, 168A, 169, 170, 174, 188 or 190 of the Trade Union and Labour Relations (Consolidation) Act 1992,

(c) under section 17A or 25(8) of the Disability Discrimination Act 1995,

(d) under or arising out of a contravention, or alleged contravention, of section 8, 13, 15, 18(1), 21(1), 28, 80G(1), 80H(1)(b), 92 or 135, or of Part V, VI, VII or X, of the Employment Rights Act 1996,

(dd) under or by virtue of section 11, 18, 20(1)(a) or 24 of the National Minimum Wage Act 1998,

(e) which are proceedings in respect of which an employment tribunal has jurisdiction by virtue of section 3 of this Act,

(f) under or arising out of a contravention, or alleged contravention, of a provision specified by an order under subsection (8)(b) as a provision to which this paragraph applies,

(ff) under regulation 30 of the Working Time Regulations 1998,

(g) under regulation 27 or 32 of the Transnational Information and Consultation of Employees Regulations 1999,

(h) arising out of a contravention, or alleged contravention of regulation 5(1) or 7(2) of the Part-time Workers (Prevention of Less Favourable Treatment) Regulations 2000,

(i) arising out of a contravention, or alleged contravention of regulation 3 or 6(2) of the Fixed-term Employees (Prevention of Less Favourable Treatment) Regulations 2002,

(j) under regulation 9 of those Regulations,

(k) under regulation 28 of the Employment Equality (Sexual Orientation) Regulations 2003,

(l) under regulation 28 of the Employment Equality (Religion or Belief) Regulations 2003,

(m) under regulation 18 of the Merchant Shipping (Working Time: Inland Waterways) Regulations 2003,

(n) under regulation 41 or 45 of the European Public Limited-Liability Company Regulations 2004,

(o) under regulation 19 of the Fishing Vessels (Working Time: Sea-fishermen) Regulations 2004, or

(p) under regulation 29 or 33 of the Information and Consultation of Employees Regulations 2004.

(2) Where an application has been presented to an employment tribunal, and a copy of it has been sent to a conciliation officer, it is the duty of the conciliation officer –

(a) if he is requested to do so by the person by whom and the person against whom the proceedings are brought, or

(b) if, in the absence of any such request, the conciliation officer considers that he could act under this subsection with a reasonable prospect of success,

to endeavour to promote a settlement of the proceedings without their being determined by an employment tribunal.

(2A) Where employment tribunal procedure regulations includ provisions postponing the fixing of a time and place for a hearing for the purpose of giving an opportunity for the proceedings to be settled by way of conciliation and withdrawn, subsection (2) shall have effect from the end of the postponement to confer a power on the conciliation officer, instead of imposing a duty.

(3) Where at any time –

(a) a person claims that action has been taken in respect of which proceedings could be brought by him before an employment tribunal, but

(b) before any application relating to that action has been presented by him a request is made to a conciliation officer (whether by that person or by the person against whom the proceedings could be instituted) to make his services available to them,

the conciliation officer shall act in accordance with subsection (2) as if an application had been presented to an employment tribunal.

(4) Where a person who has presented a complaint to an employment tribunal under section 111 of the Employment Rights Act 1996 has ceased to be employed by the employer against whom the complaint was made, the conciliation officer shall (for the purpose of promoting a settlement of the complaint in accordance with subsection (2)) in particular –

(a) seek to promote the reinstatement or re-engagement of the complainant by the employer, or by a successor of the employer or by an associated employer, on terms appearing to the conciliation officer to be equitable, or

(b) where the complainant does not wish to be reinstated or re-engaged, or where reinstatement or re-engagement is not practicable, and the parties desire the conciliation officer to act, seek to promote agreement between them as to a sum by way of compensation to be paid by the employer to the complainant.

(5) Where at any time –

(a) a person claims that action has been taken in respect of which a complaint could be presented by him to an employment tribunal under section 111 of the Employment Rights Act 1996, but

(b) before any complaint relating to that action has been presented by him a request is made to a conciliation officer (whether by that person or by the employer) to make his services available to them,

the conciliation officer shall act in accordance with subsection (4) as if a complaint had been presented to an employment tribunal under section 111.

(6) In proceeding under this section a conciliation officer shall, where appropriate, have regard to the desirability of encouraging the use of other procedures available for the settlement of grievances.

(7) Anything communicated to a conciliation officer in connection with the performance of his functions under this section shall not be admissible in evidence in any proceedings before an employment tribunal, except with the consent of the person who communicated it to that officer.

(8) The Secretary of State may by order –

(a) direct that further provisions of the Employment Rights Act 1996 be added to the list in subsection (1)(d), or

(b) specify a provision of any other Act as a provision to which subsection (1)(f) applies.

19 Conciliation procedure

(1) Employment tribunal procedure regulations shall include in relation to employment tribunal proceedings in the case of which any enactment makes provision for conciliation –

(a) provisions requiring a copy of the application by which the proceedings are instituted, and a copy of any notice relating to it which is lodged by or on behalf of the person against whom the proceedings are brought, to be sent to a conciliation officer, and

(b) provisions securing that the applicant and the person against whom the proceedings are brought are notified that the services of a conciliation officer are available to them.

(2) If employment tribunal procedure regulations include provision postponing the fixing of a time and place for a hearing for the purpose of giving an opportunity for the proceedings to be settled by way of conciliation and withdrawn, they shall also include provision for the parties to proceedings to which the provision for

postponement applies to be notified that the services of a conciliation officer may no longer be available to them after the end of the postponement.

PART II

THE EMPLOYMENT APPEAL TRIBUNAL

20   The Appeal Tribunal

(1) The Employment Appeal Tribunal ('the Appeal Tribunal') shall continue in existence.

(2) The Appeal Tribunal shall have a central office in London but may sit at any time and in any place in Great Britain.

(3) The Appeal Tribunal shall be a superior court of record and shall have an official seal which shall be judicially noticed.

(4) Subsection (2) is subject to regulation 34 of the Transnational Information and Consultation of Employees Regulations 1999 and regulation 46(1) of the European Public Limited-Liability Company Regulations 2004.

21   Jurisdiction of Appeal Tribunal

(1) An appeal lies to the Appeal Tribunal on any question of law arising from any decision of, or arising in any proceedings before, an employment tribunal under or by virtue of –

    (a) the Equal Pay Act 1970,

    (b) the Sex Discrimination Act 1975,

    (c) the Race Relations Act 1976,

    (d) the Trade Union and Labour Relations (Consolidation) Act 1992,

    (e) the Disability Discrimination Act 1995,

    (f) the Employment Rights Act 1996,

    (g) this Act,

    (ga) the National Minimum Wage Act 1998,

    (gb) the Employment Relations Act 1999,

    (h) the Working Time Regulations 1998,

    (i) the Transnational Information and Consultation of Employees Regulations 1999,

    (j) the Part-time Workers (Prevention of Less Favourable Treatment) Regulations 2000,

    (k) the Fixed-term Employees (Prevention of Less Favourable Treatment) Regulations 2002,

    (l) the Employment Equality (Sexual Orientation) Regulations 2003,

    (m) the Employment Equality (Religion or Belief) Regulations 2003,

(n) the Merchant Shipping (Working Time: Inland Waterways) Regulations 2003,

(o) the European Public Limited-Liability Company Regulations 2004,

(p) the Fishing Vessels (Working Time: Sea-fishermen) Regulations 2004, or

(q) the Information and Consultation of Employees Regulations 2004.

(2) No appeal shall lie except to the Appeal Tribunal from any decision of an employment tribunal under or by virtue of the Acts listed or the Regulations referred to in subsection (1).

(3) Subsection (1) does not affect any provision contained in, or made under, any Act which provides for an appeal to lie to the Appeal Tribunal (whether from an employment tribunal, the Certification Officer or any other person or body) otherwise than on a question to which that subsection applies.

(4) The Appeal Tribunal also has any jurisdiction in respect of matters other than appeals which is conferred on it by or under –

(a) the Trade Union and Labour Relations (Consolidation) Act 1992,

(b) this Act, or

(c) any other Act.

22   Membership of Appeal Tribunal

(1) The Appeal Tribunal shall consist of –

(a) such number of judges as may be nominated from time to time by the Lord Chancellor from the judges (other than the Lord Chancellor) of the High Court and the Court of Appeal,

(b) at least one judge of the Court of Session nominated from time to time by the Lord President of the Court of Session, and

(c) such number of other members as may be appointed from time to time by Her Majesty on the joint recommendation of the Lord Chancellor and the Secretary of State ('appointed members').

(2) The appointed members shall be persons who appear to the Lord Chancellor and the Secretary of State to have special knowledge or experience of industrial relations either –

(a) as representatives of employers, or

(b) as representatives of workers (within the meaning of the Trade Union and Labour Relations (Consolidation) Act 1992).

(3) The Lord Chancellor shall, after consultation with the Lord President of the Court of Session, appoint one of the judges nominated under subsection (1) to be the President of the Appeal Tribunal.

(4) No judge shall be nominated a member of the Appeal Tribunal except with his consent.

[*See Appendix, Constitutional Reform Act 2005, Schedule 4, Pt 1, paras 245, 246, Schedule 18, Pt 2.*]

23 Temporary membership

(1) At any time when –

(a) the office of President of the Appeal Tribunal is vacant, or

(b) the person holding that office is temporarily absent or otherwise unable to act as the President of the Appeal Tribunal,

the Lord Chancellor may nominate another judge nominated under section 22(1)(a) to act temporarily in his place.

(2) At any time when a judge of the Appeal Tribunal nominated under paragraph (a) or (b) of subsection (1) of section 22 is temporarily absent or otherwise unable to act as a member of the Appeal Tribunal –

(a) in the case of a judge nominated under paragraph (a) of that subsection, the Lord Chancellor may nominate another judge who is qualified to be nominated under that paragraph to act temporarily in his place, and

(b) in the case of a judge nominated under paragraph (b) of that subsection, the Lord President of the Court of Session may nominate another judge who is qualified to be nominated under that paragraph to act temporarily in his place.

(3) At any time when an appointed member of the Appeal Tribunal is temporarily absent or otherwise unable to act as a member of the Appeal Tribunal, the Lord Chancellor and the Secretary of State may jointly appoint a person appearing to them to have the qualifications for appointment as an appointed member to act temporarily in his place.

(4) A person nominated or appointed to act temporarily in place of the President or any other member of the Appeal Tribunal, when so acting, has all the functions of the person in whose place he acts.

(5) No judge shall be nominated to act temporarily as a member of the Appeal Tribunal except with his consent.

[*See Appendix, Constitutional Reform Act 2005, Schedule 4, Pt 1, paras 245, 247.*]

24 Temporary additional judicial membership

(1) At any time when it appears to the Lord Chancellor that it is expedient to do so in order to facilitate in England and Wales the. disposal of business in the Appeal Tribunal, he may appoint a qualified person to be a temporary additional judge of the Appeal Tribunal during such period or on such occasions as the Lord Chancellor thinks fit.

(2) In subsection (1) 'qualified person' means a person who –

(a) is qualified for appointment as a judge of the High Court under section 10 of the Supreme Court Act 1981, or

(b) has held office as a judge of the High Court or the Court of Appeal.

(3) A person appointed to be a temporary additional judge of the Appeal Tribunal has all the functions of a judge nominated under section 22(1)(a).

[*See Appendix, Constitutional Reform Act 2005, Schedule 4, Pt 1, paras 245, 248, Schedule 11, Pt 1, para 1(2).*]

25   Tenure of appointed members

(1) Subject to subsections (2) to (4), an appointed member shall hold and vacate office in accordance with the terms of his appointment.

(2) An appointed member –

(a) may at any time resign his membership by notice in writing addressed to the Lord Chancellor and the Secretary of State, and

(b) shall vacate his office on the day on which he attains the age of seventy.

(3) Subsection (2)(b) is subject to section 26(4) to (6) of the Judicial Pensions and Retirement Act 1993 (Lord Chancellor's power to authorise continuance of office up to the age of seventy-five).

(4) If the Lord Chancellor, after consultation with the Secretary of State, is satisfied that an appointed member –

(a) has been absent from sittings of the Appeal Tribunal for a period longer than six consecutive months without the permission of the President of the Appeal Tribunal,

(b) has become bankrupt or made an arrangement with his creditors, or has had his estate sequestrated or made a trust deed for behoof of his creditors or a composition contract,

(c) is incapacitated by physical or mental illness, or

(d) is otherwise unable or unfit to discharge the functions of a member,

the Lord Chancellor may declare his office as a member to be vacant and shall notify the declaration in such manner as the Lord Chancellor thinks fit; and when the Lord Chancellor does so, the office becomes vacant.

[*See Appendix, Constitutional Reform Act 2005, Schedule 4, Pt 1, paras 245, 249.*]

28   Composition of Appeal Tribunal

(1) The Appeal Tribunal may sit, in accordance with directions given by the President of the Appeal Tribunal, either as a single tribunal or in two or more divisions concurrently.

(2) Subject to subsections (3) to (5), proceedings before the Appeal Tribunal shall be heard by a judge and either two or four appointed members, so that in either case there is an equal number –

(a) of persons whose knowledge or experience of industrial relations is as representatives of employers, and

(b) of persons whose knowledge or experience of industrial relations is as representatives of workers.

(3) With the consent of the parties, proceedings before the Appeal Tribunal may be

heard by a judge and one appointed member or by a judge and three appointed members.

(4) Proceedings on an appeal on a question arising from any decision of, or arising in any proceedings before, an employment tribunal consisting of the person mentioned in section 4(1)(a) alone shall be heard by a judge alone unless a judge directs that the proceedings shall be heard in accordance with subsections (2) and (3).

29   Conduct of hearings

(1) A person may appear before the Appeal Tribunal in person or be represented by –

(a) counsel or a solicitor,

(b) a representative of a trade union or an employers' association, or

(c) any other person whom he desires to represent him.

(2) The Appeal Tribunal has in relation to –

(a) the attendance and examination of witnesses,

(b) the production and inspection of documents, and

(c) all other matters incidental to its jurisdiction,

the same powers, rights, privileges and authority (in England and Wales) as the High Court and (in Scotland) as the Court of Session.

30   Appeal Tribunal procedure rules

(1) The Lord Chancellor, after. consultation with the Lord President of the Court of Session, shall make rules ('Appeal Tribunal procedure rules') with respect to proceedings before the Appeal Tribunal. ...

(3) Subject to Appeal Tribunal procedure rules, the Appeal Tribunal has power to regulate its own procedure.

31   Restriction of publicity in cases involving sexual misconduct

(1) Appeal Tribunal procedure rules may, as respects proceedings to which this section applies, include provision –

(a) for cases involving allegations of the commission of sexual offences, for securing that the registration or other making available of documents or decisions shall be so effected as to prevent the identification of any person affected by or making the allegation, and

(b) for cases involving allegations of sexual misconduct, enabling the Appeal Tribunal, on the application of any party to the proceedings before it or of its own motion, to make a restricted reporting order having effect (if not revoked earlier) until the promulgation of the decision of the Appeal Tribunal.

(2) This section applies to –

(a) proceedings on an appeal against a decision of an employment tribunal to make, or not to make, a restricted reporting order, and

(b) proceedings on an appeal against any interlocutory decision of an employment tribunal in proceedings in which the employment tribunal has made a restricted reporting order which it has not revoked. ...

(7) 'Restricted reporting order' means –

(a) in subsections (1) and (3) [contravention], an order –

(i) made in exercise of a power conferred by rules made by virtue of this section, and

(ii) prohibiting the publication in Great Britain of identifying matter in a written publication available to the public or its inclusion in a relevant programme for reception in Great Britain, and

(b) in subsection (2), an order which is a restricted reporting order for the purposes of section 11.

(8) In this section – ...

'sexual misconduct' means the commission of a sexual offence, sexual harassment or other adverse conduct (of whatever nature) related to sex, and conduct is related to sex whether the relationship with sex lies in the character of the conduct or in its having reference to the sex or sexual orientation of the person at whom the conduct is directed,

'sexual offence' means any offence to which section 4 of the Sexual Offences (Amendment) Act 1976 [or] the Sexual Offences (Amendment) Act 1992 ... applies (offences under the Sexual Offences Act 1956 ... and certain other enactments), ...

32 Restriction of publicity in disability cases

(1) This section applies to proceedings –

(a) on an appeal against a decision of an employment tribunal to make, or not to make, a restricted reporting order, or

(b) on an appeal against any interlocutory decision of an employment tribunal in proceedings in which the employment tribunal has made a restricted reporting order which it has not revoked.

(2) Appeal Tribunal procedure rules may, as respects proceedings to which this section applies, include provision for –

(a) enabling the Appeal Tribunal, on the application of the complainant or of its own motion, to make a restricted reporting order having effect (if not revoked earlier) until the promulgation of the decision of the Appeal Tribunal, and

(b) where a restricted reporting order is made in relation to an appeal which is being dealt with by the Appeal Tribunal together with any other proceedings, enabling the Appeal Tribunal to direct that the order is to apply also in relation to those other proceedings or such part of them as the Appeal Tribunal may direct. ...

(7) 'Restricted reporting order' means –

(a) in subsection (1), an order which is a restricted reporting order for the purposes of section 12, and

(b) in subsections (2) and (3) [contravention], an order –

(i) made in exercise of a power conferred by rules made by virtue of this section, and

(ii) prohibiting the publication in Great Britain of identifying matter in a written publication available to the public or its inclusion in a relevant programme for reception in Great Britain.

(8) In this section – ...

'complainant' means the person who made the complaint to which the proceedings before the Appeal Tribunal relate, ...

33   Restriction of vexatious proceedings

(1) If, on an application made by the Attorney General or the Lord Advocate under this section, the Appeal Tribunal is satisfied that a person has habitually and persistently and without any reasonable ground –

(a) instituted vexatious proceedings, whether before the Certification Officer, in an employment tribunal or before the Appeal Tribunal, and whether against the same person or against different persons, or

(b) made vexatious applications in any proceedings, whether before the Certification Officer in an employment tribunal or before the Appeal Tribunal,

the Appeal Tribunal may, after hearing the person or giving him an opportunity of being heard, make a restriction of proceedings order.

(2) A 'restriction of proceedings order' is an order that –

(a) no proceedings shall without the leave of the Appeal Tribunal be instituted before the Certification Officer, in any employment tribunal or before the Appeal Tribunal by the person against whom the order is made,

(b) any proceedings instituted by him before the Certification Officer, in any employment tribunal or before the Appeal Tribunal before the making of the order shall not be continued by him without the leave of the Appeal Tribunal, and

(c) no application (other than one for leave under this section) is to be made by him in any proceedings before the Certification Officer, in any employment tribunal or before the Appeal Tribunal without the leave of the Appeal Tribunal.

(3) A restriction of proceedings order may provide that it is to cease to have effect at the end of a specified period, but otherwise it remains in force indefinitely.

(4) Leave for the institution or continuance of, or for the making of an application in, any proceedings in an employment tribunal or before the Appeal Tribunal by a person who is the subject of a restriction of proceedings order shall not be given unless the Appeal Tribunal is satisfied –

(a) that the proceedings or application are not an abuse of the process of the tribunal in question, and

(b) that there are reasonable grounds for the proceedings or application.

(5) A copy of a restriction of proceedings order shall be published in the London Gazette and the Edinburgh Gazette.

34 Costs and expenses

(1) Appeal Tribunal procedure rules may include provision for the award of costs or expenses.

(2) Rules under subsection (1) may include provision authorising the Appeal Tribunal to have regard to a person's ability to pay when considering the making of an award against him under such rules.

(3) Appeal Tribunal procedure rules may include provision for authorising the Appeal Tribunal –

(a) to disallow all or part of the costs or expenses of a representative of a party to proceedings before it by reason of that representative's conduct of the proceedings;

(b) to order a representative of a party to proceedings before it to meet all or part of the costs or expenses incurred by a party by reason of the representative's conduct of the proceedings.

(4) Appeal Tribunal procedure rules may also include provision for taxing or otherwise settling the costs or expenses referred to in subsection (1) or (3)(b) (and, in particular in England and Wales, for enabling the amount of such costs to be assessed by way of detailed assessment in the High Court).

35 Powers of Appeal Tribunal

(1) For the purpose of disposing of an appeal, the Appeal Tribunal may –

(a) exercise any of the powers of the body or officer from whom the appeal was brought, or

(b) remit the case to that body or officer.

(2) Any decision or award of the Appeal Tribunal on an appeal has the same effect, and may be enforced in the same manner, as a decision or award of the body or officer from whom the appeal was brought.

36   Enforcement of decisions, etc

(4) No person shall be punished for contempt of the Appeal Tribunal except by, or with the consent of, a judge.

(5) A magistrates' court shall not remit the whole or part of a fine imposed by the Appeal Tribunal unless it has the consent of a judge who is a member of the Appeal Tribunal.

37   Appeals from Appeal Tribunal

(1) Subject to subsection (3), an appeal on any question of law lies from any decision or order of the Appeal Tribunal to the relevant appeal court with the leave of the Appeal Tribunal or of the relevant appeal court.

(2) In subsection (1) the 'relevant appeal court' means –

(a) in the case of proceedings in England and Wales, the Court of Appeal, ...

(3) No appeal lies from a decision of the Appeal Tribunal refusing leave for the institution or continuance of, or for the making of an application in, proceedings by a person who is the subject of a restriction of proceedings order made under section 33.

(4) This section is without prejudice to section 13 of the Administration of Justice Act 1960 (appeal in case of contempt of court).

PART III

SUPPLEMENTARY

38   Crown employment

(1) This Act has effect in relation to Crown employment and persons in Crown employment as it has effect in relation to other employment and other employees.

(2) In this Act 'Crown employment' means employment under or for the purposes of a government department or any officer or body exercising on behalf of the Crown functions conferred by a statutory provision.

(3) For the purposes of the application of this Act in relation to Crown employment in accordance with subsection (1) –

(a) references to an employee shall be construed as references to a person in Crown employment, and

(b) references to a contract of employment shall be construed as references to the terms of employment of a person in Crown employment.

(4) Subsection (1) applies to –

(a) service as a member of the naval, military or air forces of the Crown, and

(b) employment by an association established for the purposes of Part XI of the Reserve Forces Act 1996;

but Her Majesty may by Order in Council make any provision of this Act apply to service as a member of the naval, military or air forces of the Crown subject to such exceptions and modifications as may be specified in the Order in Council.

40   Power to amend Act

(1) The Secretary of State may by order –

(a) provide that any provision of this Act to which this section applies and which is specified in the order shall not apply to persons, or to employments, of such classes as may be prescribed in the order, or

(b) provide that any provision of this Act to which this section applies shall apply to persons or employments of such classes as may be prescribed in the order subject to such exceptions and modifications as may be so prescribed.

(2) This section applies to sections 3, 8, 16 and 17 and to section 18 so far as deriving from section 133 of the Employment Protection (Consolidation) Act 1978.

41   Orders, regulations and rules

(1) Any power conferred by this Act on a Minister of the Crown to make an order, and any power conferred by this Act to make regulations or rules, is exercisable by statutory instrument. ...

(4) Any power conferred by this Act which is exercisable by statutory instrument includes power to make such incidental, supplementary or transitional provision as appears to the Minister exercising the power to be necessary or expedient.

42   Interpretation

(1) In this Act –

'the Appeal Tribunal' means the Employment Appeal Tribunal,

'Appeal Tribunal procedure rules' shall be construed in accordance with section 30(1),

'appointed member' shall be construed in accordance with section 22(1)(c),

'Certification Officer' shall be construed in accordance with section 254 of the Trade Union and Labour Relations (Consolidation) Act 1992,

'conciliation officer' means an officer designated by the Advisory, Conciliation and Arbitration Service under section 211 of the Trade Union and Labour Relations (Consolidation) Act 1992,

'contract of employment' means a contract of service or apprenticeship, whether express or implied, and (if it is express) whether oral or in writing,

'employee' means an individual who has entered into or works under (or, where the employment has ceased, worked under) a contract of employment,

'employer', in relation to an employee, means the person by whom the employee is (or, where the employment has ceased, was) employed, 'employers' association' has the same meaning as in the Trade Union and Labour Relations (Consolidation) Act 1992,

'employment' means employment under a contract of employment and 'employed' shall be construed accordingly,

'employment tribunal procedure regulations' shall be construed in accordance with section 7(1),

'statutory provision' means a provision, whether of a general or a special nature, contained in, or in any document made or issued under, any Act, whether of a general or special nature,

'successor', in relation to the employer of an employee, means (subject to subsection (2)) a person who in consequence of a change occurring (whether by virtue of a sale or other disposition or by operation of law) in the ownership of the undertaking, or of the part of the undertaking, for the purposes of which the employee was employed, has become the owner of the undertaking or part, and

'trade union' has the meaning given by section 1 of the Trade Union and Labour Relations (Consolidation) Act 1992.

(2) The definition of 'successor' in subsection (1) has effect (subject to the necessary modifications) in relation to a case where –

(a) the person by whom an undertaking or part of an undertaking is owned immediately before a change is one of the persons by whom (whether as partners, trustees or otherwise) it is owned immediately after the change, or

(b) the persons by whom an undertaking or part of an undertaking is owned immediately before a change (whether as partners, trustees or otherwise) include the persons by whom, or include one or more of the persons by whom, it is owned immediately after the change,

as it has effect where the previous owner and the new owner are wholly different persons.

(3) For the purposes of this Act any two employers shall be treated as associated if –

(a) one is a company of which the other (directly or indirectly) has control, or

(b) both are companies of which a third person (directly or indirectly) has control;

and 'associated employer' shall be construed accordingly.

As amended by the Arbitration Act 1996, s107(1), Schedule 3, para 62; Employment Rights (Dispute) Resolution Act 1998, ss1(2)(a), (b), (d), (e), 3, 5, 11(1), 15, 17(3), Schedule 1, paras 12, 16, 17, Schedule 2; National Minimum Wage Act 1998, ss27(1), 29, 30(1), 53, Schedule 3; Social Security Act 1998, s86, Schedule 7, para 147, Schedule 8; Employment Relations Act 1999, ss9, 41, 44, Schedule 4, Pt III, para 4, Schedule 8, paras 2–4, Schedule 9(2), (12); Tax Credits Act 1999, ss7, 19(4), Schedule 3, para 5, Schedule 6; Tax Credits Act 2002, s60, Schedule 6; Employment Act 2002, ss22, 24, 53, 54, Schedule 7, para 23, Schedule 8(1); Disability Discrimination Act 1995 (Amendment) Regulations 2003, regs 3(2), 31(2); Employment Relations Act 2004, ss23, 36, 38, 49(1)–(8), 57(1), Schedule 1, para 24, 25, 27, Schedule 2; regulations identified in the text.

EMPLOYMENT RIGHTS ACT 1996
(1996 c 18)

PART I

EMPLOYMENT PARTICULARS

1   Statement of initial employment particulars

(1) Where an employee begins employment with an employer, the employer shall give to the employee a written statement of particulars of employment.

(2) The statement may (subject to section 2(4)) be given in instalments and (whether or not given in instalments) shall be given not later than two months after the beginning of the employment.

(3) The statement shall contain particulars of –

(a) the names of the employer and employee,

(b) the date when the employment began, and

(c) the date on which the employee's period of continuous employment began (taking into account any employment with a previous employer which counts towards that period).

(4) The statement shall also contain particulars, as at a specified date not more than seven days before the statement (or the instalment containing them) is given, of –

(a) the scale or rate of remuneration or the method of calculating remuneration,

(b) the intervals at which remuneration is paid (that is, weekly, monthly or other specified intervals),

(c) any terms and conditions relating to hours of work (including any terms and conditions relating to normal working hours),

(d) any terms and conditions relating to any of the following –

(i) entitlement to holidays, including public holidays, and holiday pay (the particulars given being sufficient to enable the employee's entitlement, including any entitlement to accrued holiday pay on the termination of employment, to be precisely calculated),

(ii) incapacity for work due to sickness or injury, including any provision for sick pay, and

(iii) pensions and pension schemes,

(e) the length of notice which the employee is obliged to give and entitled to receive to terminate his contract of employment,

(f) the title of the job which the employee is employed to do or a brief description of the work for which he is employed,

(g) where the employment is not intended to be permanent, the period for which it is expected to continue or, if it is for a fixed term, the date when it is to end,

(h) either the place of work or, where the employee is required or permitted to work at various places, an indication of that and of the address of the employer,

(j) any collective agreements which directly affect the terms and conditions of the employment including, where the employer is not a party, the persons by whom they were made, and

(k) where the employee is required to work outside the United Kingdom for a period of more than one month –

(i) the period for which he is to work outside the United Kingdom,

(ii) the currency in which remuneration is to be paid while he is working outside the United Kingdom,

(iii) any additional remuneration payable to him, and any benefits to be provided to or in respect of him, by reason of his being required to work outside the United Kingdom, and

(iv) any terms and conditions relating to his return to the United Kingdom.

(5) Subsection (4)(d)(iii) does not apply to an employee of a body or authority if –

(a) the employee's pension rights depend on the terms of a pension scheme established under any provision contained in or having effect under any Act, and

(b) any such provision requires the body or authority to give to a new employee information concerning the employee's pension rights or the determination of questions affecting those rights.

2   Statement of initial particulars: supplementary

(1) If, in the case of a statement under section 1, there are no particulars to be entered under any of the heads of paragraph (d) or (k) of subsection (4) of that section, or under any of the other paragraphs of subsection (3) or (4) of that section, that fact shall be stated.

(2) A statement under section 1 may refer the employee for particulars of any of the matters specified in subsection (4)(d)(ii) and (iii) of that section to the provisions of some other document which is reasonably accessible to the employee.

(3) A statement under section 1 may refer the employee for particulars of either of the matters specified in subsection (4)(e) of that section to the law or to the provisions of any collective agreement directly affecting the terms and conditions of the employment which is reasonably accessible to the employee.

(4) The particulars required by section 1(3) and (4)(a) to (c), (d)(i), (f) and (h) shall be included in a single document.

(5) Where before the end of the period of two months after the beginning of an employee's employment the employee is to begin to work outside the United Kingdom for a period of more than one month, the statement under section 1 shall be given to him not later than the time when he leaves the United Kingdom in order to begin so to work.

(6) A statement shall be given to a person under section 1 even if his employment ends before the end of the period within which the statement is required to be given.

3   Note about disciplinary procedures and pensions

(1) A statement under section 1 shall include a note –

(a) specifying any disciplinary rules applicable to the employee or referring the employee to the provisions of a document specifying such rules which is reasonably accessible to the employee,

(aa) specifying any procedure applicable to the taking of disciplinary decisions relating to the employee, or to a decision to dismiss the employee, or referring the employee to the provisions of a document specifying such a procedure which is reasonably accessible to the employee,

(b) specifying (by description or otherwise) –

(i) a person to whom the employee can apply if dissatisfied with any disciplinary decision relating to him or any decision to dismiss him, and

(ii) a person to whom the employee can apply for the purpose of seeking redress of any grievance relating to his employment,

and the manner in which any such application should be made, and

(c) where there are further steps consequent on any such application, explaining those steps or referring to the provisions of a document explaining them which is reasonably accessible to the employee.

(2) Subsection (1) does not apply to rules, disciplinary decisions, decisions to dismiss, grievances or procedures relating to health or safety at work.

(5) The note shall also state whether there is in force a contracting-out certificate (issued in accordance with Chapter I of Part III of the Pension Schemes Act 1993) stating that the employment is contracted-out employment (for the purposes of that Part of that Act).

4   Statement of changes

(1) If, after the material date, there. is a change in any of the matters particulars of which are required by sections 1 to 3 to be included or referred to in a statement under section 1, the employer shall give to the employee a written statement containing particulars of the change.

(2) For the purposes of subsection (1) –

(a) in relation to a matter particulars of which are included or referred to in a statement given under section 1 otherwise than in instalments, the material date is the date to which the statement relates,

(b) in relation to a matter particulars of which –

(i) are included or referred to in an instalment of a statement given under section 1, or

(ii) are required by section 2(4) to be included in a single document but are not included in an instalment of a statement given under section 1 which does include other particulars to which that provision applies,

the material date is the date to which the instalment relates, and

(c) in relation to any other matter, the material date is the date by which a statement under section 1 is required to be given.

(3) A statement under subsection (1) shall be given at the earliest opportunity and, in any event, not later than –

(a) one month after the change in question, or

(b) where that change results from the employee being required to work outside the United Kingdom for a period of more than one month, the time when he leaves the United Kingdom in order to begin so to work, if that is earlier.

(4) A statement under subsection (1) may refer the employee to the provisions of some other document which is reasonably accessible to the employee for a change in any of the matters specified in sections 1(4)(d)(ii) and (iii) and 3(1)(a) and (c).

(5) A statement under subsection (1) may refer the employee for a change in either of the matters specified in section 1(4)(e) to the law or to the provisions of any collective agreement directly affecting the terms and conditions of the employment which is reasonably accessible to the employee.

(6) Where, after an employer has given to an employee a statement under section 1, either –

(a) the name of the employer (whether an individual or a body corporate or partnership) is changed without any change in the identity of the employer, or

(b) the identity of the employer is changed in circumstances in which the continuity of the employee's period of employment is not broken,

and subsection (7) applies in relation to the change, the person who is the employer immediately after the change is not required to give to the employee a statement under section 1; but the change shall be treated as a change falling within subsection (1) of this section.

(7) This subsection applies in relation to a change if it does not involve any change in any of the matters (other than the names of the parties) particulars of which are required by sections 1 to 3 to be included or referred to in the statement under section 1.

(8) A statement under subsection (1) which informs an employee of a change such as

is referred to in subsection (6)(b) shall specify the date on which the employee's period of continuous employment began.

5 Exclusion from rights to statements

(1) Sections 1 to 4 apply to an employee who at any time comes or ceases to come within the exceptions from those sections provided by section 199, and under section 209, as if his employment with his employer terminated or began at that time.

(2) The fact that section 1 is directed by subsection (1) to apply to an employee as if his employment began on his ceasing to come within the exceptions referred to in that subsection does not affect the obligation under section 1(3)(b) to specify the date on which his employment actually began.

6 Reasonably accessible document or collective agreement

In sections 2 to 4 references to a document or collective agreement which is reasonably accessible to an employee are references to a document or collective agreement which –

(a) the employee has reasonable opportunities of reading in the course of his employment, or

(b) is made reasonably accessible to the employee in some other way.

7 Power to require particulars of further matters

The Secretary of State may by order provide that section 1 shall have effect as if particulars of such further matters as may be specified in the order were included in the particulars required by that section; and, for that purpose, the order may include such provisions amending that section as appear to the Secretary of State to be expedient.

7A Use of alternative documents to give particulars

(1) Subsections (2) and (3) apply where –

(a) an employer gives an employee a document in writing in the form of a contract of employment or letter of engagement,

(b) the document contains information which, were the document in the form of a statement under section 1, would meet the employer's obligation under that section in relation to the matters mentioned in subsections (3) and (4)(a) to (c), (d)(i), (f) and (h) of that section, and

(c) the document is given after the beginning of the employment and before the end of the period for giving a statement under that section.

(2) The employer's duty under section 1 in relation to any matter shall be treated as met if the document given to the employee contains information which, were the

document in the form of a statement under that section, would meet the employer's obligation under that section in relation to that matter.

(3) The employer's duty under section 3 shall be treated as met if the document given to the employee contains information which, were the document in the form of a statement under section 1 and the information included in the form of a note, would meet the employer's obligation under section 3.

(4) For the purposes of this section a document to which subsection (1)(a) applies shall be treated, in relation to information in respect of any of the matters mentioned in section 1(4), as specifying the date on which the document is given to the employee as the date as at which the information applies.

(5) Where subsection (2) applies in relation to any matter, the date on which the document by virtue of which that subsection applies is given to the employee shall be the material date in relation to that matter for the purposes of section 4(1).

(6) Where subsection (3) applies, the date on which the document by virtue of which that subsection applies is given to the employee shall be the material date for the purposes of section 4(1) in relation to the matters of which particulars are required to be given under section 3.

(7) The reference in section 4(6) to an employer having given a statement under section 1 shall be treated as including his having given a document by virtue of which his duty to give such a statement is treated as met.

7B   Giving of alternative documents before start of employment

A document in the form of a contract of employment or letter of engagement given by an employer to an employee before the beginning of the employee's employment with the employer shall, when the employment begins, be treated for the purposes of section 7A as having been given at that time.

8   Itemised pay statement

(1) An employee has the right to be given by his employer, at or before the time at which any payment of wages or salary is made to him, a written itemised pay statement.

(2) The statement shall contain particulars of –

(a) the gross amount of the wages or salary,

(b) the amounts of any variable, and (subject to section 9) any fixed, deductions from that gross amount and the purposes for which they are made,

(c) the net amount of wages or salary payable, and

(d) where different parts of the net amount are paid in different ways, the amount and method of payment of each part-payment.

9   Standing statement of fixed deductions

(1) A pay statement given in accordance with section 8 need not contain separate particulars of a fixed deduction if –

(a) it contains instead an aggregate amount of fixed deductions, including that deduction, and

(b) the employer has given to the employee, at or before the time at which the pay statement is given, a standing statement of fixed deductions which satisfies subsection (2).

(2) A standing statement of fixed deductions satisfies this subsection if –

(a) it is in writing,

(b) it contains, in relation to each deduction comprised in the aggregate amount of deductions, particulars of –

(i) the amount of the deduction,

(ii) the intervals at which the deduction is to be made, and

(iii) the purpose for which it is made, and

(c) it is (in accordance with subsection (5)) effective at the date on which the pay statement is given.

(3) A standing statement of fixed deductions may be amended, whether by –

(a) addition of a new deduction,

(b) a change in the particulars, or

(c) cancellation of an existing deduction,

by notice in writing, containing particulars of the amendment, given by the employer to the employee.

(4) An employer who has given to an employee a standing statement of fixed deductions shall –

(a) within the period of twelve months beginning with the date on which the first standing statement was given, and

(b) at intervals of not more than twelve months afterwards,

re-issue it in a consolidated form incorporating any amendments notified in accordance with subsection (3).

(5) For the purposes of subsection (2)(c) a standing statement of fixed deductions –

(a) becomes effective on the date on which it is given to the employee, and

(b) ceases to be effective at the end of the period of twelve months beginning with that date or, where it is re-issued in accordance with subsection (4), with the end of the period of twelve months beginning with the date of the last re-issue.

10   Power to amend provisions about pay and standing statements

The Secretary of State may by order –

(a) vary the provisions of sections 8 and 9 as to the particulars which must be included in a pay statement or a standing statement of fixed deductions by adding items to, or removing items from, the particulars listed in those sections or by amending any such particulars, and

(b) vary the provisions of subsections (4) and (5) of section 9 so as to shorten or extend the periods of twelve months referred to in those subsections, or those periods as varied from time to time under this section.

11   References to employment tribunals

(1) Where an employer does not give an employee a statement as required by section 1, 4 or 8 (either because he gives him no statement or because the statement he gives does not comply with what is required), the employee may require a reference to be made to an employment tribunal to determine what particulars ought to have been included or referred to in a statement so as to comply with the requirements of the section concerned.

(2) Where –

(a) a statement purporting to be a statement under section 1 or 4, or a pay statement or a standing statement of fixed deductions purporting to comply with section 8 or 9, has been given to an employee, and

(b) a question arises as to the particulars which ought to have been included or referred to in the statement so as to comply with the requirements of this Part,

either the employer or the employee may require the question to be referred to and determined by an employment tribunal.

(3) For the purposes of this section –

(a) a question as to the particulars which ought to have been included in the note required by section 3 to be included in the statement under section 1 does not include any question whether the employment is, has been or will be contracted-out employment (for the purposes of Part III of the Pension Schemes Act 1993), and

(b) a question as to the particulars which ought to have been included in a pay statement or standing statement of fixed deductions does not include a question solely as to the accuracy of an amount stated in any such particulars.

(4) An employment tribunal shall not consider a reference under this section in a case where the employment to which the reference relates has ceased unless an application requiring the reference to be made was made –

(a) before the end of the period of three months beginning with the date on which the employment ceased, or

(b) within such further period as the tribunal considers reasonable in a case where it is satisfied that it was not reasonably practicable for the application to be made before the end of that period of three months.

12   Determination of references

(1) Where, on a reference under section 11(1), an employment tribunal determines particulars as being those which ought to have been included or referred to in a statement given under section 1 or 4, the employer shall be deemed to have given to the employee a statement in which those particulars were included, or referred to, as specified in the decision of the tribunal.

(2) On determining a reference under section 11(2) relating to a statement purporting to be a statement under section 1 or 4, an employment tribunal may –

(a) confirm the particulars as included or referred to in the statement given by the employer,

(b) amend those particulars, or

(c) substitute other particulars for them,

as the tribunal may determine to be appropriate; and the statement shall be deemed to have been given by the employer to the employee in accordance with the decision of the tribunal.

(3) Where on a reference under section 11 an employment tribunal finds –

(a) that an employer has failed to give an employee any pay statement in accordance with section 8, or

(b) that a pay statement or standing statement of fixed deductions does not, in relation to a deduction, contain the particulars required to be included in that statement by that section or section 9,

the tribunal shall make a declaration to that effect.

(4) Where on a reference in the case of which subsection (3) applies the tribunal further finds that any unnotified deductions have been made from the pay of the employee during the period of thirteen weeks immediately preceding the date of the application for the reference (whether or not the deductions were made in breach of the contract of employment), the tribunal may order the employer to pay the employee a sum not exceeding the aggregate of the unnotified deductions so made.

(5) For the purposes of subsection (4) a deduction is an unnotified deduction if it is made without the employer giving the employee, in any pay statement or standing statement of fixed deductions, the particulars of the deduction required by section 8 or 9.

PART II

PROTECTION OF WAGES

13   Right not to suffer unauthorised deductions

(1) An employer shall not make a deduction from wages of a worker employed by him unless –

(a) the deduction is required or authorised to be made by virtue of a statutory provision or a relevant provision of the worker's contract, or

(b) the worker has previously signified in writing his agreement or consent to the making of the deduction.

(2) In this section 'relevant provision', in relation to a worker's contract, means a provision of the contract comprised –

(a) in one or more written terms of the contract of which the employer has given the worker a copy on an occasion prior to the employer making the deduction in question, or

(b) in one or more terms of the contract (whether express or implied and, if express, whether oral or in writing) the existence and effect, or combined effect, of which in relation to the worker the employer has notified to the worker in writing on such an occasion.

(3) Where the total amount of wages paid on any occasion by an employer to a worker employed by him is less than the total amount of the wages properly payable by him to the worker on that occasion (after deductions), the amount of the deficiency shall be treated for the purposes of this Part as a deduction made by the employer from the worker's wages on that occasion.

(4) Subsection (3) does not apply in so far as the deficiency is attributable to an error of any description on the part of the employer affecting the computation by him of the gross amount of the wages properly payable by him to the worker on that occasion.

(5) For the purposes of this section a relevant provision of a worker's contract having effect by virtue of a variation of the contract does not operate to authorise the making of a deduction on account of any conduct of the worker, or any other event occurring, before the variation took effect.

(6) For the purposes of this section an agreement or consent signified by a worker does not operate to authorise the making of a deduction on account of any conduct of the worker, or any other event occurring, before the agreement or consent was signified.

(7) This section does not affect any other statutory provision by virtue of which a sum payable to a worker by his employer but not constituting 'wages' within the meaning of this Part is not to be subject to a deduction at the instance of the employer.

14   Excepted deductions

(1) Section 13 does not apply to a deduction from a worker's wages made by his employer where the purpose of the deduction is the reimbursement of the employer in respect of –

(a) an overpayment of wages, or

(b) an overpayment in respect of expenses incurred by the worker in carrying out his employment,

made (for any reason) by the employer to the worker.

(2) Section 13 does not apply to a deduction from a worker's wages made by his employer in consequence of any disciplinary proceedings if those proceedings were held by virtue of a statutory provision.

(3) Section 13 does not apply to a deduction from a worker's wages made by his employer in pursuance of a requirement imposed on the employer by a statutory provision to deduct and pay over to a public authority amounts determined by that authority as being due to it from the worker if the deduction is made in accordance with the relevant determination of that authority.

(4) Section 13 does not apply to a deduction from a worker's wages made by his employer in pursuance of any arrangements which have been established –

(a) in accordance with a relevant provision of his contract to the inclusion of which in the contract the worker has signified his agreement or consent in writing, or

(b) otherwise with the prior agreement or consent of the worker signified in writing,

and under which the employer is to deduct and pay over to a third person amounts notified to the employer by that person as being due to him from the worker, if the deduction is made in accordance with the relevant notification by that person.

(5) Section 13 does not apply to a deduction from a worker's wages made by his employer where the worker has taken part in a strike or other industrial action and the deduction is made by the employer on account of the worker's having taken part in that strike or other action.

(6) Section 13 does not apply to a deduction from a worker's wages made by his employer with his prior agreement or consent signified in writing where the purpose of the deduction is the satisfaction (whether wholly or in part) of an order of a court or tribunal requiring the payment of an amount by the worker to the employer.

15   Right not to have to make payments to employer

(1) An employer shall not receive a payment from a worker employed by him unless –

(a) the payment is required or authorised to be made by virtue of a statutory provision or a relevant provision of the worker's contract, or

(b) the worker has previously signified in writing his agreement or consent to the making of the payment.

(2) In this section 'relevant provision', in relation to a worker's contract, means a provision of the contract comprised –

(a) in one or more written terms of the contract of which the employer has given the worker a copy on an occasion prior to the employer receiving the payment in question, or

(b) in one or more terms of the contract (whether express or implied and, if express, whether oral or in writing) the existence and effect, or combined effect, of which in relation to the worker the employer has notified to the worker in writing on such an occasion.

(3) For the purposes of this section a relevant provision of a worker's contract having effect by virtue of a variation of the contract does not operate to authorise the receipt of a payment on account of any conduct of the worker, or any other event occurring, before the variation took effect.

(4) For the purposes of this section an agreement or consent signified by a worker does not operate to authorise the receipt of a payment on account of any conduct of the worker, or any other event occurring, before the agreement or consent was signified.

(5) Any reference in this Part to an employer receiving a payment from a worker employed by him is a reference to his receiving such a payment in his capacity as the worker's employer.

16   Excepted payments

(1) Section 15 does not apply to a payment received from a worker by his employer where the purpose of the payment is the reimbursement of the employer in respect of –

(a) an overpayment of wages, or

(b) an overpayment in respect of expenses incurred by the worker in carrying out his employment,

made (for any reason) by the employer to the worker.

(2) Section 15 does not apply to a payment received from a worker by his employer in consequence of any disciplinary proceedings if those proceedings were held by virtue of a statutory provision.

(3) Section 15 does not apply to a payment received from a worker by his employer where the worker has taken part in a strike or other industrial action and the payment has been required by the employer on account of the worker's having taken part in that strike or other action.

(4) Section 15 does not apply to a payment received from a worker by his employer where the purpose of the payment is the satisfaction (whether wholly or in part) of

an order of a court or tribunal requiring the payment of an amount by the worker to the employer.

17 Introductory

(1) In the following provisions of this Part –

'cash shortage' means a deficit arising in relation to amounts received in connection with retail transactions, and

'stock deficiency' means a stock deficiency arising in the course of retail transactions.

(2) In the following provisions of this Part 'retail employment', in relation to a worker, means employment involving (whether or not on a regular basis) –

(a) the carrying out by the worker of retail transactions directly with members of the public or with fellow workers or other individuals in their personal capacities, or

(b) the collection by the worker of amounts payable in connection with retail transactions carried out by other persons directly with members of the public or with fellow workers or other individuals in their personal capacities.

(3) References in this section to a 'retail transaction' are to the sale or supply of goods or the supply of services (including financial services).

(4) References in the following provisions of this Part to a deduction made from wages of a worker in retail employment, or to a payment received from such a worker by his employer, on account of a cash shortage or stock deficiency include references to a deduction or payment so made or received on account of –

(a) any dishonesty or other conduct on the part of the worker which resulted in any such shortage or deficiency, or

(b) any other event in respect of which he (whether or not together with any other workers) has any contractual liability and which so resulted,

in each case whether or not the amount of the deduction or payment is designed to reflect the exact amount of the shortage or deficiency.

(5) References in the following provisions of this Part to the recovery from a worker of an amount in respect of a cash shortage or stock deficiency accordingly include references to the recovery from him of an amount in respect of any such conduct or event as is mentioned in subsection (4)(a) or (b).

(6) In the following provisions of this Part 'pay day', in relation to a worker, means a day on which wages are payable to the worker.

18 Limits on amount and time of deductions

(1) Where (in accordance with section 13) the employer of a worker in retail employment makes, on account of one or more cash shortages or stock deficiencies, a deduction or deductions from wages payable to the worker on a pay day, the

amount or aggregate amount of the deduction or deductions shall not exceed one-tenth of the gross amount of the wages payable to the worker on that day.

(2) Where the employer of a worker in retail employment makes a deduction from the worker's wages on account of a cash shortage or stock deficiency, the employer shall not be treated as making the deduction in accordance with section 13 unless (in addition to the requirements of that section being satisfied with respect to the deduction) –

(a) the deduction is made, or

(b) in the case of a deduction which is one of a series of deductions relating to the shortage or deficiency, the first deduction in the series was made,

not later than the end of the relevant period.

(3) In subsection (2) 'the relevant period' means the period of twelve months beginning with the date when the employer established the existence of the shortage or deficiency or (if earlier) the date when he ought reasonably to have done so.

19   Wages determined by reference to shortages, etc

(1) This section applies where –

(a) by virtue of an agreement between a worker in retail employment and his employer, the amount of the worker's wages or any part of them is or may be determined by reference to the incidence of cash shortages or stock deficiencies, and

(b) the gross amount of the wages payable to the worker on any pay day is, on account of any such shortages or deficiencies, less than the gross amount of the wages that would have been payable to him on that day if there had been no such shortages or deficiencies.

(2) The amount representing the difference between the two amounts referred to in subsection (1)(b) shall be treated for the purposes of this Part as a deduction from the wages payable to the worker on that day made by the employer on account of the cash shortages or stock deficiencies in question.

(3) The second of the amounts referred to in subsection (1)(b) shall be treated for the purposes of this Part (except subsection (1)) as the gross amount of the wages payable to him on that day.

(4) Accordingly –

(a) section 13, and

(b) if the requirements of section 13 and subsection (2) of section 18 are satisfied, subsection (1) of section 18,

have effect in relation to the amount referred to in subsection (2) of this section.

20 Limits on method and timing of payments

(1) Where the employer of a worker in retail employment receives from the worker a payment on account of a cash shortage or stock deficiency, the employer shall not be treated as receiving the payment in accordance with section 15 unless (in addition to the requirements of that section being satisfied with respect to the payment) he has previously –

(a) notified the worker in writing of the worker's total liability to him in respect of that shortage or deficiency, and

(b) required the worker to make the payment by means of a demand for payment made in accordance with the following provisions of this section.

(2) A demand for payment made by the employer of a worker in retail employment in respect of a cash shortage or stock deficiency –

(a) shall be made in writing, and

(b) shall be made on one of the worker's pay days.

(3) A demand for payment in respect of a particular cash shortage or stock deficiency, or (in the case of a series of such demands) the first such demand, shall not be made –

(a) earlier than the first pay day of the worker following the date when he is notified of his total liability in respect of the shortage or deficiency in pursuance of subsection (1)(a) or, where he is so notified on a pay day, earlier than that day, or

(b) later than the end of the period of twelve months beginning with the date when the employer established the existence of the shortage or deficiency or (if earlier) the date when he ought reasonably to have done so.

(4) For the purposes of this Part a demand for payment shall be treated as made by the employer on one of a worker's pay days if it is given to the worker or posted to, or left at, his last known address –

(a) on that pay day, or

(b) in the case of a pay day which is not a working day of the employer's business, on the first such working day following that pay day.

(5) Legal proceedings by the employer of a worker in retail employment for the recovery from the worker of an amount in respect of a cash shortage or stock deficiency shall not be instituted by the employer after the end of the period referred to in subsection (3)(b) unless the employer has within that period made a demand for payment in respect of that amount in accordance with this section.

21 Limit on amount of payments

(1) Where the employer of a worker in retail employment makes on any pay day one or more demands for payment in accordance with section 20, the amount or

aggregate amount required to be paid by the worker in pursuance of the demand or demands shall not exceed –

(a) one-tenth of the gross amount of the wages payable to the worker on that day, or

(b) where one or more deductions falling within section 18(1) are made by the employer from those wages, such amount as represents the balance of that one-tenth after subtracting the amount or aggregate amount of the deduction or deductions.

(2) Once an amount has been required to be paid by means of a demand for payment made in accordance with section 20 on any pay day, that amount shall not be taken into account under subsection (1) as it applies to any subsequent pay day, even though the employer is obliged to make further requests for it to be paid.

(3) Where in any legal proceedings the court finds that the employer of a worker in retail employment is (in accordance with section 15 as it applies apart from section 20(1)) entitled to recover an amount from the worker in respect of a cash shortage or stock deficiency, the court shall, in ordering the payment by the worker to the employer of that amount, make such provision as appears to the court to be necessary to ensure that it is paid by the worker at a rate not exceeding that at which it could be recovered from him by the employer in accordance with this section.

22   Final instalments of wages

(1) In this section 'final instalment of wages', in relation to a worker, means –

(a) the amount of wages payable to the worker which consists of or includes an amount payable by way of contractual remuneration in respect of the last of the periods for which he is employed under his contract prior to its termination for any reason (but excluding any wages referable to any earlier such period), or

(b) where an amount in lieu of notice is paid to the worker later than the amount referred to in paragraph (a), the amount so paid,

in each case whether the amount in question is paid before or after the termination of the worker's contract.

(2) Section 18(1) does not operate to restrict the amount of any deductions which may (in accordance with section 13(1)) be made by the employer of a worker in retail employment from the worker's final instalment of wages.

(3) Nothing in section 20 or 21 applies to a payment falling within section 20(1) which is made on or after the day on which any such worker's final instalment of wages is paid; but (even if the requirements of section 15 would otherwise be satisfied with respect to it) his employer shall not be treated as receiving any such payment in accordance with that section if the payment was first required to be made after the end of the period referred to in section 20(3)(b).

(4) Section 21(3) does not apply to an amount which is to be paid by a worker on or after the day on which his final instalment of wages is paid.

23 Complaints to employment tribunals

(1) A worker may present a complaint to an employment tribunal –

(a) that his employer has made a deduction from his wages in contravention of section 13 (including a deduction made in contravention of that section as it applies by virtue of section 18(2)),

(b) that his employer has received from him a payment in contravention of section 15 (including a payment received in contravention of that section as it applies by virtue of section 20(1)),

(c) that his employer has recovered from his wages by means of one or more deductions falling within section 18(1) an amount or aggregate amount exceeding the limit applying to the deduction or deductions under that provision, or

(d) that his employer has received from him in pursuance of one or more demands for payment made (in accordance with section 20) on a particular pay day, a payment or payments of an amount or aggregate amount exceeding the limit applying to the demand or demands under section 21(1).

(2) Subject to subsection (4), an employment tribunal shall not consider a complaint under this section unless it is presented before the end of the period of three months beginning with –

(a) in the case of a complaint relating to a deduction by the employer, the date of payment of the wages from which the deduction was made, or

(b) in the case of a complaint relating to a payment received by the employer, the date when the payment was received.

(3) Where a complaint is brought under this section in respect of –

(a) a series of deductions or payments, or

(b) a number of payments falling within subsection (1)(d) and made in pursuance of demands for payment subject to the same limit under section 21(1) but received by the employer on different dates,

the references in subsection (2) to the deduction or payment are to the last deduction or payment in the series or to the last of the payments so received.

(4) Where the employment tribunal is satisfied that it was not reasonably practicable for a complaint under this section to be presented before the end of the relevant period of three months, the tribunal may consider the complaint if it is presented within such further period as the tribunal considers reasonable.

(5) No complaint shall be presented under this section in respect of any deduction made in contravention of section 86 of the Trade Union and Labour Relations (Consolidation) Act 1992 (deduction of political fund contribution where certificate of exemption or objection has been given).

24　Determination of complaints

Where a tribunal finds a complaint under section 23 well-founded, it shall make a declaration to that effect and shall order the employer –

(a) in the case of a complaint under section 23(1)(a), to pay to the worker the amount of any deduction made in contravention of section 13,

(b) in the case of a complaint under section 23(1)(b), to repay to the worker the amount of any payment received in contravention of section 15,

(c) in the case of a complaint under section 23(1)(c), to pay to the worker any amount recovered from him in excess of the limit mentioned in that provision, and

(d) in the case of a complaint under section 23(1)(d), to repay to the worker any amount received from him in excess of the limit mentioned in that provision.

25　Determinations: supplementary

(1) Where, in the case of any complaint under section 23(1)(a), a tribunal finds that, although neither of the conditions set out in section 13(1)(a) and (b) was satisfied with respect to the whole amount of the deduction, one of those conditions was satisfied with respect to any lesser amount, the amount of the deduction shall for the purposes of section 24(a) be treated as reduced by the amount with respect to which that condition was satisfied.

(2) Where, in the case of any complaint under section 23(1)(b), a tribunal finds that, although neither of the conditions set out in section 15(1)(a) and (b) was satisfied with respect to the whole amount of the payment, one of those conditions was satisfied with respect to any lesser amount, the amount of the payment shall for the purposes of section 24(b) be treated as reduced by the amount with respect to which that condition was satisfied.

(3) An employer shall not under section 24 be ordered by a tribunal to pay or repay to a worker any amount in respect of a deduction or payment, or in respect of any combination of deductions or payments, in so far as it appears to the tribunal that he has already paid or repaid any such amount to the worker.

(4) Where a tribunal has under section 24 ordered an employer to pay or repay to a worker any amount in respect of a particular deduction or payment falling within section 23(1)(a) to (d), the amount which the employer is entitled to recover (by whatever means) in respect of the matter in relation to which the deduction or payment was originally made or received shall be treated as reduced by that amount.

(5) Where a tribunal has under section 24 ordered an employer to pay or repay to a worker any amount in respect of any combination of deductions or payments falling within section 23(1)(c) or (d), the aggregate amount which the employer is entitled to recover (by whatever means) in respect of the cash shortages or stock deficiencies in relation to which the deductions or payments were originally made or required to be made shall be treated as reduced by that amount.

26 Complaints and other remedies

Section 23 does not affect the jurisdiction of an employment tribunal to consider a reference under section 11 in relation to any deduction from the wages of a worker; but the aggregate of any amounts ordered by an employment tribunal to be paid under section 12(4) and under section 24 (whether on the same or different occasions) in respect of a particular deduction shall not exceed the amount of the deduction.

27 Meaning of 'wages', etc

(1) In this Part 'wages', in relation to a worker, means any sums payable to the worker in connection with his employment, including –

(a) any fee, bonus, commission, holiday pay or other emolument referable to his employment, whether payable under his contract or otherwise,

(b) statutory sick pay under Part XI of the Social Security Contributions and Benefits Act 1992,

(c) statutory maternity pay under Part XII of that Act,

(ca) statutory paternity pay under Part 12ZA of that Act,

(cb) statutory adoption pay under Part 12ZB of that Act,

(d) a guarantee payment (under section 28 of this Act),

(e) any payment for time off under Part VI of this Act or section 169 of the Trade Union and Labour Relations (Consolidation) Act 1992 (payment for time off for carrying out trade union duties etc),

(f) remuneration on suspension on medical grounds under section 64 of this Act and remuneration on suspension on maternity grounds under section 68 of this Act,

(g) any sum payable in pursuance of an order for reinstatement or re-engagement under section 113 of this Act,

(h) any sum payable in pursuance of an order for the continuation of a contract of employment under section 130 of this Act or section 164 of the Trade Union and Labour Relations (Consolidation) Act 1992, and

(j) remuneration under a protective award under section 189 of that Act,

but excluding any payments within subsection (2).

(2) Those payments are –

(a) any payment by way of an advance under an agreement for a loan or by way of an advance of wages (but without prejudice to the application of section 13 to any deduction made from the worker's wages in respect of any such advance),

(b) any payment in respect of expenses incurred by the worker in carrying out his employment,

(c) any payment by way of a pension, allowance or gratuity in connection with the worker's retirement or as compensation for loss of office,

(d) any payment referable to the worker's redundancy, and

(e) any payment to the worker otherwise than in his capacity as a worker.

(3) Where any payment in the nature of a non-contractual bonus is (for any reason) made to a worker by his employer, the amount of the payment shall for the purposes of this Part –

(a) be treated as wages of the worker, and

(b) be treated as payable to him as such on the day on which the payment is made.

(4) In this Part 'gross amount', in relation to any wages payable to a worker, means the total amount of those wages before deductions of whatever nature.

(5) For the purposes of this Part any monetary value attaching to any payment or benefit in kind furnished to a worker by his employer shall not be treated as wages of the worker except in the case of any voucher, stamp or similar document which is –

(a) of a fixed value expressed in monetary terms, and

(b) capable of being exchanged (whether on its own or together with other vouchers, stamps or documents, and whether immediately or only after a time) for money, goods or services (or for any combination of two or more of those things).

PART III

GUARANTEE PAYMENTS

28 Right to guarantee payment

(1) Where throughout a day during any part of which an employee would normally be required to work in accordance with his contract of employment the employee is not provided with work by his employer by reason of –

(a) a diminution in the requirements of the employer's business for work of the kind which the employee is employed to do, or

(b) any other occurrence affecting the normal working of the employer's business in relation to work of the kind which the employee is employed to do,

the employee is entitled to be paid by his employer an amount in respect of that day.

(2) In this Act a payment to which an employee is entitled under subsection (1) is referred to as a guarantee payment.

(3) In this Part –

(a) a day falling within subsection (1) is referred to as a 'workless day', and

(b) 'workless period' has a corresponding meaning.

(4) In this Part 'day' means the period of twenty-four hours from midnight to midnight.

(5) Where a period of employment begun on any day extends, or would normally extend, over midnight into the following day –

(a) if the employment before midnight is, or would normally be, of longer duration than that after midnight, the period of employment shall be treated as falling wholly on the first day, and

(b) in any other case, the period of employment shall be treated as falling wholly on the second day.

29   Exclusions from right to guarantee payment

(1) An employee is not entitled to a guarantee payment unless he has been continuously employed for a period of not less than one month ending with the day before that in respect of which the guarantee payment is claimed.

(3) An employee is not entitled to a guarantee payment in respect of a workless day if the failure to provide him with work for that day occurs in consequence of a strike, lock-out or other industrial action involving any employee of his employer or of an associated employer.

(4) An employee is not entitled to a guarantee payment in respect of a workless day if –

(a) his employer has offered to provide alternative work for that day which is suitable in all the circumstances (whether or not it is work which the employee is under his contract employed to perform), and

(b) the employee has unreasonably refused that offer.

(5) An employee is not entitled to a guarantee payment if he does not comply with reasonable requirements imposed by his employer with a view to ensuring that his services are available.

30   Calculation of guarantee payment

(1) Subject to section 31, the amount of a guarantee payment payable to an employee in respect of any day is the sum produced by multiplying the number of normal working hours on the day by the guaranteed hourly rate; and, accordingly, no guarantee payment is payable to an employee in whose case there are no normal working hours on the day in question.

(2) The guaranteed hourly rate, in relation to an employee, is the amount of one week's pay divided by the number of normal working hours in a week for that employee when employed under the contract of employment in force on the day in respect of which the guarantee payment is payable.

(3) But where the number of normal working hours differs from week to week or over a longer period, the amount of one week's pay shall be divided instead by –

(a) the average number of normal working hours calculated by dividing by twelve the total number of the employee's normal working hours during the period of twelve weeks ending with the last complete week before the day in respect of which the guarantee payment is payable, or

(b) where the employee has not been employed for a sufficient period to enable the calculation to be made under paragraph (a), a number which fairly represents the number of normal working hours in a week having regard to such of the considerations specified in subsection (4) as are appropriate in the circumstances.

(4) The considerations referred to in subsection (3)(b) are –

(a) the average number of normal working hours in a week which the employee could expect in accordance with the terms of his contract, and

(b) the average number of normal working hours of other employees engaged in relevant comparable employment with the same employer.

(5) If in any case an employee's contract has been varied, or a new contract has been entered into, in connection with a period of short-time working, subsections (2) and (3) have effect as if for the references to the day in respect of which the guarantee payment is payable there were substituted references to the last day on which the original contract was in force.

31   Limits on amount of and entitlement to guarantee payment

(1) The amount of a guarantee payment payable to an employee in respect of any day shall not exceed £18.40.

(2) An employee is not entitled to guarantee payments in respect of more than the specified number of days in any period of three months.

(3) The specified number of days for the purposes of subsection (2) is the number of days, not exceeding five, on which the employee normally works in a week under the contract of employment in force on the day in respect of which the guarantee payment is claimed.

(4) But where that number of days varies from week to week or over a longer period, the specified number of days is instead –

(a) the average number of such days, not exceeding five, calculated by dividing by twelve the total number of such days during the period of twelve weeks ending with the last complete week before the day in respect of which the guarantee payment is claimed, and rounding up the resulting figure to the next whole number, or

(b) where the employee has not been employed for a sufficient period to enable the calculation to be made under paragraph (a), a number which fairly represents the number of the employee's normal working days in a week, not exceeding five, having regard to such of the considerations specified in subsection (5) as are appropriate in the circumstances.

(5) The considerations referred to in subsection (4)(b) are –

(a) the average number of normal working days in a week which the employee could expect in accordance with the terms of his contract, and

(b) the average number of such days of other employees engaged in relevant comparable employment with the same employer.

(6) If in any case an employee's contract has been varied, or a new contract has been entered into, in connection with a period of short-time working, subsections (3) and (4) have effect as if for the references to the day in respect of which the guarantee payment is claimed there were substituted references to the last day on which the original contract was in force.

(7) The Secretary of State may by order vary –

(a) the length of the period specified in subsection (2);

(b) the limit specified in subsection (3) or (4).

32 Contractual remuneration

(1) A right to a guarantee payment does not affect any right of an employee in relation to remuneration under his contract of employment ('contractual remuneration').

(2) Any contractual remuneration paid to an employee in respect of a workless day goes towards discharging any liability of the employer to pay a guarantee payment in respect of that day; and, conversely, any guarantee payment paid in respect of a day goes towards discharging any liability of the employer to pay contractual remuneration in respect of that day.

(3) For the purposes of subsection (2), contractual remuneration shall be treated as paid in respect of a workless day –

(a) where it is expressed to be calculated or payable by reference to that day or any part of that day, to the extent that it is so expressed, and

(b) in any other case, to the extent that it represents guaranteed remuneration, rather than remuneration for work actually done, and is referable to that day when apportioned rateably between that day and any other workless period falling within the period in respect of which the remuneration is paid.

33 Power to modify provisions about guarantee payments

The Secretary of State may by order provide that in relation to any description of employees the provisions of –

(a) sections 28(4) and (5), 30, 31(3) to (5) (as originally enacted or as varied under section 31(7)) and 32, and

(b) so far as they apply for the purposes of those provisions, Chapter II of Part XIV and section 234,

shall have effect subject to such modifications and adaptations as may be prescribed by the order.

34   Complaints to employment tribunals

(1) An employee may present a complaint to an employment tribunal that his employer has failed to pay the whole or any part of a guarantee payment to which the employee is entitled.

(2) An employment tribunal shall not consider a complaint relating to a guarantee payment in respect of any day unless the complaint is presented to the tribunal –

(a) before the end of the period of three months beginning with that day, or

(b) within such further period as the tribunal considers reasonable in a case where it is satisfied that it was not reasonably practicable for the complaint to be presented before the end of that period of three months.

(3) Where an employment tribunal finds a complaint under this section well-founded, the tribunal shall order the employer to pay to the employee the amount of guarantee payment which it finds is due to him.

35   Exemption orders

(1) Where –

(a) at any time there is in force a collective agreement, or an agricultural wages order, under which employees to whom the agreement or order relates have a right to guaranteed remuneration, and

(b) on the application of all the parties to the agreement, or of the Board making the order, the appropriate Minister (having regard to the provisions of the agreement or order) is satisfied that section 28 should not apply to those employees,

he may make an order under this section excluding those employees from the operation of that section.

(2) In subsection (1) 'agricultural wages order' means an order made under-

(a) section 3 of the Agricultural Wages Act 1948 ...

(3) In subsection (1) 'the appropriate Minister' means –

(a) in relation to a collective agreement or to an order such as is referred to in subsection (2)(b), the Secretary of State, and

(b) in relation to an order such as is referred to in subsection (2)(a), the Secretary of State.

(4) The Secretary of State shall not make an order under this section in respect of an agreement unless –

(a) the agreement provides for procedures to be followed (whether by arbitration or otherwise) in cases where an employee claims that his employer has failed to pay the whole or any part of any guaranteed remuneration to which the employee is entitled under the agreement and those procedures include a right to arbitration or adjudication by an independent referee or body in cases where (by reason of an equality of votes or otherwise) a decision cannot otherwise be reached, or

(b) the agreement indicates that an employee to whom the agreement relates may present a complaint to an employment tribunal that his employer has failed to pay the whole or any part of any guaranteed remuneration to which the employee is entitled under the agreement.

(5) Where an order under this section is in force in respect of an agreement indicating as described in paragraph (b) of subsection (4) an employment tribunal shall have jurisdiction over a complaint such as is mentioned in that paragraph as if it were a complaint falling within section 34.

(6) An order varying or revoking an earlier order under this section may be made in pursuance of an application by all or any of the parties to the agreement in question, or the Board which made the order in question, or in the absence of such an application.

PART IV

SUNDAY WORKING FOR SHOP AND BETTING WORKERS

36 Protected shop workers and betting workers

(1) Subject to subsection (5), a shop worker or betting worker is to be regarded as 'protected' for the purposes of any provision of this Act if (and only if) subsection (2) or (3) applies to him.

(2) This subsection applies to a shop worker or betting worker if –

(a) on the day before the relevant commencement date he was employed as a shop worker or a betting worker but not to work only on Sunday,

(b) he has been continuously employed during the period beginning with that day and ending with the day which, in relation to the provision concerned, is the appropriate date, and

(c) throughout that period, or throughout every part of it during which his relations with his employer were governed by a contract of employment, he was a shop worker or a betting worker.

(3) This subsection applies to any shop worker or betting worker whose contract of employment is such that under it he –

(a) is not, and may not be, required to work on Sunday, and

(b) could not be so required even if the provisions of this Part were disregarded.

(4) Where on the day before the relevant commencement date an employee's relations with his employer had ceased to be governed by a contract of employment, he shall be regarded as satisfying subsection (2)(a) if –

(a) that day fell in a week which counts as a period of employment with that employer under section 212(2) or (3) or under regulations under section 219, and

(b) on the last day before the relevant commencement date on which his relations with his employer were governed by a contract of employment, the employee was employed as a shop worker or a betting worker but not to work only on Sunday.

(5) A shop worker is not a protected shop worker, and a betting worker is not a protected betting worker, if –

(a) he has given his employer an opting-in notice on or after the relevant commencement date, and

(b) after giving the notice, he has expressly agreed with his employer to do shop work, or betting work, on Sunday or on a particular Sunday.

(6) In this Act 'opting-in notice', in relation to a shop worker or a betting worker, means written notice, signed and dated by the shop worker or betting worker, in which the shop worker or betting worker expressly states that he wishes to work on Sunday or that he does not object to Sunday working.

(7) … in this Act 'the relevant commencement date' means –

(a) in relation to a shop worker, 26th August 1994, and

(b) in relation to a betting worker, 3rd January 1995. …

37 Contractual requirements relating to Sunday work

(1) Any contract of employment under which a shop worker or betting worker who satisfies section 36(2)(a) was employed on the day before the relevant commencement date is unenforceable to the extent that it –

(a) requires the shop worker to do shop work, or the betting worker to do betting work, on Sunday on or after that date, or

(b) requires the employer to provide the shop worker with shop work, or the betting worker with betting work, on Sunday on or after that date.

(2) Subject to subsection (3), any agreement entered into after the relevant commencement date between a protected shop worker, or a protected betting worker, and his employer is unenforceable to the extent that it –

(a) requires the shop worker to do shop work, or the betting worker to do betting work, on Sunday, or

(b) requires the employer to provide the shop worker with shop work, or the betting worker with betting work, on Sunday.

(3) Where, after giving an opting-in notice, a protected shop worker or a protected betting worker expressly agrees with his employer to do shop work or betting work on Sunday or on a particular Sunday (and so ceases to be protected), his contract of employment shall be taken to be varied to the extent necessary to give effect to the terms of the agreement.

(5) For the purposes of section 36(2)(b), the appropriate date –

(a) in relation to subsections (2) and (3) of this section, is the day on which the agreement is entered into.

38   Contracts with guaranteed hours

(1) This section applies where –

(a) under the contract of employment under which a shop worker or betting worker who satisfies section 36(2)(a) was employed on the day before the relevant commencement date, the employer is, or may be, required to provide him with shop work, or betting work, for a specified number of hours each week,

(b) under the contract the shop worker or betting worker was, or might have been, required to work on Sunday before that date, and

(c) the shop worker has done shop work, or the betting worker betting work, on Sunday in that employment (whether or not before that day) but has, on or after that date, ceased to do so.

(2) So long as the shop worker remains a protected shop worker, or the betting worker remains a protected betting worker, the contract shall not be regarded as requiring the employer to provide him with shop work, or betting work, on weekdays in excess of the hours normally worked by the shop worker or betting worker on weekdays before he ceased to do shop work, or betting work, on Sunday.

(3) For the purposes of section 36(2)(b), the appropriate date in relation to this section is any time in relation to which the contract is to be enforced.

39   Reduction of pay, etc

(1) This section applies where –

(a) under the contract of employment under which a shop worker or betting worker who satisfies section 36(2)(a) was employed on the day before the relevant commencement date, the shop worker or betting worker was, or might have been, required to work on Sunday before the relevant commencement date,

(b) the shop worker has done shop work, or the betting worker has done betting work, on Sunday in that employment (whether or not before that date) but has, on or after that date, ceased to do so, and

(c) it is not apparent from the contract what part of the remuneration payable, or of any other benefit accruing, to the shop worker or betting worker was intended to be attributable to shop work, or betting work, on Sunday.

(2) So long as the shop worker remains a protected shop worker, or the betting worker remains a protected betting worker, the contract shall be regarded as enabling the employer to reduce the amount of remuneration paid, or the extent of the other benefit provided, to the shop worker or betting worker in respect of any period by the relevant proportion.

(3) In subsection (2) 'the relevant proportion' means the proportion which the hours of shop work, or betting work, which (apart from this Part) the shop worker, or betting worker, could have been required to do on Sunday in the period ('the

contractual Sunday hours') bears to the aggregate of those hours and the hours of work actually done by the shop worker, or betting worker, in the period.

(4) Where, under the contract of employment, the hours of work actually done on weekdays in any period would be taken into account in determining the contractual Sunday hours, they shall be taken into account in determining the contractual Sunday hours for the purposes of subsection (3).

(5) For the purposes of section 36(2)(b), the appropriate date in relation to this section is the end of the period in respect of which the remuneration is paid or the benefit accrues.

40   Notice of objection to Sunday working

(1) A shop worker or betting worker to whom this section applies may at any time give his employer written notice, signed and dated by the shop worker or betting worker, to the effect that he objects to Sunday working.

(2) In this Act 'opting-out notice' means a notice given under subsection (1) by a shop worker or betting worker to whom this section applies.

(3) This section applies to any shop worker or betting worker who under his contract of employment –

  (a) is or may be required to work on Sunday (whether or not as a result of previously giving an opting-in notice), but

  (b) is not employed to work only on Sunday.

41   Opted-out shop workers and betting workers

(1) Subject to subsection (2), a shop worker or betting worker is to be regarded as 'opted-out' for the purposes of any provision of this Act if (and only if) –

  (a) he has given his employer an opting-out notice,

  (b) he has been continuously employed during the period beginning with the day on which the notice was given and ending with the day which, in relation to the provision concerned, is the appropriate date, and

  (c) throughout that period, or throughout every part of it during which his relations with his employer were governed by a contract of employment, he was a shop worker or a betting worker.

(2) A shop worker is not an opted-out shop worker, and a betting worker is not an opted-out betting worker, if –

  (a) after giving the opting-out notice concerned, he has given his employer an opting-in notice, and

  (b) after giving the opting-in notice, he has expressly agreed with his employer to do shop work, or betting work, on Sunday or on a particular Sunday.

(3) In this Act 'notice period', in relation to an opted-out shop worker or an opted-out betting worker, means, subject to section 42(2), the period of three months beginning with the day on which the opting-out notice concerned was given.

42   Explanatory statement

(1) Where a person becomes a shop worker or betting worker to whom section 40 applies, his employer shall, before the end of the period of two months beginning with the day on which that person becomes such a worker, give him a written statement in the prescribed form.

(2) If –

(a) an employer fails to comply with subsection (1) in relation to any shop worker or betting worker, and

(b) the shop worker or betting worker, on giving the employer an opting-out notice, becomes an opted-out shop worker or an opted-out betting worker,

section 41(3) has effect in relation to the shop worker or betting worker with the substitution for 'three months' of 'one month'.

(3) An employer shall not be regarded as failing to comply with subsection (1) in any case where, before the end of the period referred to in that subsection, the shop worker or betting worker has given him an opting-out notice.

(4) Subject to subsection (6), the prescribed form in the case of a shop worker is as follows –

'STATUTORY RIGHTS IN RELATION TO SUNDAY SHOP WORK

You have become employed as a shop worker and are or can be required under your contract of employment to do the Sunday work your contract provides for.

However, if you wish, you can give a notice, as described in the next paragraph, to your employer and you will then have the right not to work in or about a shop on any Sunday on which the shop is open once three months have passed from the date on which you gave the notice.

Your notice must –

be in writing;

be signed and dated by you;

say that you object to Sunday working.

For three months after you give the notice, your employer can still require you to do all the Sunday work your contract provides for. After the three month period has ended, you have the right to complain to an employment tribunal if, because of your refusal to work on Sundays on which the shop is open, your employer –

dismisses you, or

does something else detrimental to you, for example, failing to promote you.

Once you have the rights described, you can surrender them only by giving your employer a further notice, signed and dated by you, saying that you wish to work on Sunday or that you do not object to Sunday working and then agreeing with your employer to work on Sundays or on a particular Sunday.'

(5) Subject to subsection (6), the prescribed form in the case of a betting worker is as follows –

'STATUTORY RIGHTS IN RELATION TO SUNDAY BETTING WORK

You have become employed under a contract of employment under which you are or can be required to do Sunday betting work, that is to say, work –

at a track on a Sunday on which your employer is taking bets at the track, or

in a licensed betting office on a Sunday on which it is open for business.

However, if you wish, you can give a notice, as described in the next paragraph, to your employer and you will then have the right not to do Sunday betting work once three months have passed from the date on which you gave the notice.

Your notice must –

be in writing;

be signed and dated by you;

say that you object to doing Sunday betting work.

For three months after you give the notice, your employer can still require you to do all the Sunday betting work your contract provides for. After the three month period has ended, you have the right to complain to an employment tribunal if, because of your refusal to do Sunday betting work, your employer –

dismisses you, or

does something else detrimental to you, for example, failing to promote you.

Once you have the rights described, you can surrender them only by giving your employer a further notice, signed and dated by you, saying that you wish to do Sunday betting work or that you do not object to doing Sunday betting work and then agreeing with your employer to do such work on Sundays or on a particular Sunday.'

(6) The Secretary of State may by order amend the prescribed forms set out in subsections (4) and (5).

43   Contractual requirements relating to Sunday work

(1) Where a shop worker or betting worker gives his employer an opting-out notice, the contract of employment under which he was employed immediately before he gave that notice becomes unenforceable to the extent that it –

(a) requires the shop worker to do shop work, or the betting worker to do betting work, on Sunday after the end of the notice period, or

(b) requires the employer to provide the shop worker with shop work, or the betting worker with betting work, on Sunday after the end of that period.

(2) Subject to subsection (3), any agreement entered into between an opted-out shop worker, or an opted-out betting worker, and his employer is unenforceable to the extent that it –

(a) requires the shop worker to do shop work, or the betting worker to do betting work, on Sunday after the end of the notice period, or

(b) requires the employer to provide the shop worker with shop work, or the betting worker with betting work, on Sunday after the end of that period.

(3) Where, after giving an opting-in notice, an opted-out shop worker or an opted-out betting worker expressly agrees with his employer to do shop work or betting work on Sunday or on a particular Sunday (and so ceases to be opted-out), his contract of employment shall be taken to be varied to the extent necessary to give effect to the terms of the agreement.

(5) For the purposes of section 41(1)(b), the appropriate date –

(a) in relation to subsections (2) and (3) of this section, is the day on which the agreement is entered into.

PART IVA

PROTECTED DISCLOSURES

43A Meaning of 'protected disclosure'

In this Act a 'protected disclosure' means a qualifying disclosure (as defined by section 43B) which is made by a worker in accordance with any of sections 43C to 43H.

43B Disclosures qualifying for protection

(1) In this Part a 'qualifying disclosure' means any disclosure of information which, in the reasonable belief of the worker making the disclosure, tends to show one or more of the following –

(a) that a criminal offence has been committed, is being committed or is likely to be committed,

(b) that a person has failed, is failing or is likely to fail to comply with any legal obligation to which he is subject,

(c) that a miscarriage of justice has occurred, is occurring or is likely to occur,

(d) that the health or safety of any individual has been, is being or is likely to be endangered,

(e) that the environment has been, is being or is likely to be damaged, or

(f) that information tending to show any matter falling within any one of the preceding paragraphs has been, is being or is likely to be deliberately concealed.

(2) For the purposes of subsection (1), it is immaterial whether the relevant failure occurred, occurs or would occur in the United Kingdom or elsewhere, and whether the law applying to it is that of the United Kingdom or of any other country or territory.

(3) A disclosure of information is not a qualifying disclosure if the person making the disclosure commits an offence by making it.

(4) A disclosure of information in respect of which a claim to legal professional privilege (or, in Scotland, to confidentiality as between client and professional legal adviser) could be maintained in legal proceedings is not a qualifying disclosure if it is made by a person to whom the information had been disclosed in the course of obtaining legal advice.

(5) In this Part 'the relevant failure', in relation to a qualifying disclosure, means the matter falling within paragraphs (a) to (f) of subsection (1).

43C Disclosure to employer or other responsible person

(1) A qualifying disclosure is made in accordance with this section if the worker makes the disclosure in good faith –

(a) to his employer, or

(b) where the worker reasonably believes that the relevant failure relates solely or mainly to –

(i) the conduct of a person other than his employer, or

(ii) any other matter for which a person other than his employer has legal responsibility,

to that other person.

(2) A worker who, in accordance with a procedure whose use by him is authorised by his employer, makes a qualifying disclosure to a person other than his employer, is to be treated for the purposes of this Part as making the qualifying disclosure to his employer.

43D Disclosure to legal adviser

A qualifying disclosure is made in accordance with this section if it is made in the course of obtaining legal advice.

43E Disclosure to Minister of the Crown

A qualifying disclosure is made in accordance with this section if –

(a) the worker's employer is –

(i) an individual appointed under any enactment (including any enactment comprised in, or in an instrument made under, an Act of the Scottish Parliament) by a Minister of the Crown or a member of the Scottish Executive, or

(ii) a body any of whose members are so appointed, and

(b) the disclosure is made in good faith to a Minister of the Crown or a member of the Scottish Executive.

43F Disclosure to prescribed person

(1) A qualifying disclosure is made in accordance with this section if the worker –

(a) makes the disclosure in good faith to a person prescribed by an order made by the Secretary of State for the purposes of this section, and

(b) reasonably believes –

(i) that the relevant failure falls within any description of matters in respect of which that person is so prescribed, and

(ii) that the information disclosed, and any allegation contained in it, are substantially true.

(2) An order prescribing persons for the purposes of this section may specify persons or descriptions of persons, and shall specify the descriptions of matters in respect of which each person, or persons of each description, is or are prescribed.

43G Disclosure in other cases

(1) A qualifying disclosure is made in accordance with this section if –

(a) the worker makes the disclosure in good faith,

(b) he reasonably believes that the information disclosed, and any allegation contained in it, are substantially true,

(c) he does not make the disclosure for purposes of personal gain,

(d) any of the conditions in subsection (2) is met, and

(e) in all the circumstances of the case, it is reasonable for him to make the disclosure.

(2) The conditions referred to in subsection (1)(d) are –

(a) that, at the time he makes the disclosure, the worker reasonably believes that he will be subjected to a detriment by his employer if he makes a disclosure to his employer or in accordance with section 43F,

(b) that, in a case where no person is prescribed for the purposes of section 43F in relation to the relevant failure, the worker reasonably believes that it is likely that evidence relating to the relevant failure will be concealed or destroyed if he makes a disclosure to his employer, or

(c) that the worker has previously made a disclosure of substantially the same information –

(i) to his employer, or

(ii) in accordance with section 43F.

(3) In determining for the purposes of subsection (1)(e) whether it is reasonable for the worker to make the disclosure, regard shall be had, in particular, to –

(a) the identity of the person to whom the disclosure is made,

(b) the seriousness of the relevant failure,

(c) whether the relevant failure is continuing or is likely to occur in the future,

(d) whether the disclosure is made in breach of a duty of confidentiality owed by the employer to any other person,

(e) in a case falling within subsection (2)(c)(i) or (ii), any action which the employer or the person to whom the previous disclosure in accordance with section 43F was made has taken or might reasonably be expected to have taken as a result of the previous disclosure, and

(f) in a case falling within subsection (2)(c)(i), whether in making the disclosure to the employer the worker complied with any procedure whose use by him was authorised by the employer.

(4) For the purposes of this section a subsequent disclosure may be regarded as a disclosure of substantially the same information as that disclosed by a previous disclosure as mentioned in subsection (2)(c) even though the subsequent disclosure extends to information about action taken or not taken by any person as a result of the previous disclosure.

43H   Disclosure of exceptionally serious failure

(1) A qualifying disclosure is made in accordance with this section if –

(a) the worker makes the disclosure in good faith,

(b) he reasonably believes that the information disclosed, and any allegation contained in it, are substantially true,

(c) he does not make the disclosure for purposes of personal gain,

(d) the relevant failure is of an exceptionally serious nature, and

(e) in all the circumstances of the case, it is reasonable for him to make the disclosure.

(2) In determining for the purposes of subsection (1)(e) whether it is reasonable for the worker to make the disclosure, regard shall be had, in particular, to the identity of the person to whom the disclosure is made.

43J   Contractual duties of confidentiality

(1) Any provision in an agreement to which this section applies is void in so far as it purports to preclude the worker from making a protected disclosure.

(2) This section applies to any agreement between a worker and his employer (whether a worker's contract or not), including an agreement to refrain from instituting or continuing any proceedings under this Act or any proceedings for breach of contract.

43K   Extension of meaning of 'worker' etc for Part IVA

(1) For the purposes of this Part 'worker' includes an individual who is not a worker as defined by section 230(3) but who –

(a) works or worked for a person in circumstances in which –

(i) he is or was introduced or supplied to do that work by a third person, and

(ii) the terms on which he is or was engaged to do the work are or were in practice substantially determined not by him but by the person for whom he works or worked, by the third person or by both of them,

(b) contracts or contracted with a person, for the purposes of that person's business, for the execution of work to be done in a place not under the control or management of that person and would fall within section 230(3)(b) if for 'personally' in that provision there were substituted '(whether personally or otherwise)',

(ba) works or worked as a person performing services under a contract entered into by him with a Primary Care Trust or Local Health Board under section 28K or 28Q of the National Health Service Act 1977, ...

(c) works or worked as a person providing general dental services, general ophthalmic services or pharmaceutical services in accordance with arrangements made-

(i) by a Primary Care Trust or Health Authority under section 38 or 41 of the National Health Service Act 1977, or ...

(d) is or was provided with work experience provided pursuant to a training course or programme or with training for employment (or with both) otherwise than –

(i) under a contract of employment, or

(ii) by an educational establishment on a course run by that establishment;

and any reference to a worker's contract, to employment or to a worker being 'employed' shall be construed accordingly.

(2) For the purposes of this Part 'employer' includes –

(a) in relation to a worker falling within paragraph (a) of subsection (1), the person who substantially determines or determined the terms on which he is or was engaged,

(aa) in relation to a worker falling within paragraph (ba) of that subsection, the Primary Care Trust or Local Health Board referred to in that paragraph, ...

(b) in relation to a worker falling within paragraph (c) of that subsection, the authority or board referred to in that paragraph, and

(c) in relation to a worker falling within paragraph (d) of that subsection, the person providing the work experience or training.

(3) In this section 'educational establishment' includes any university, college, school or other educational establishment.

43L   Other interpretative provisions

(1) In this Part –

'qualifying disclosure' has the meaning given by section 43B;

'the relevant failure', in relation to a qualifying disclosure, has the meaning given by section 43B(5).

(2) In determining for the purposes of this Part whether a person makes a disclosure for purposes of personal gain, there shall be disregarded any reward payable by or under any enactment.

(3) Any reference in this Part to the disclosure of information shall have effect, in relation to any case where the person receiving the information is already aware of it, as a reference to bringing the information to his attention.

PART V

PROTECTION FROM SUFFERING DETRIMENT IN EMPLOYMENT

43M   Jury service

(1) An employee has the right not to be subjected to any detriment by any act, or any deliberate failure to act, by his employer on the ground that the employee –

(a) has been summoned under the Juries Act 1974, the Coroners Act 1988 ... to attend for service as a juror, or

(b) has been absent from work because he attended at any place in pursuance of being so summoned.

(2) This section does not apply where the detriment in question amounts to dismissal within the meaning of Part 10.

(3) For the purposes of this section, an employee is not to be regarded as having been subjected to a detriment by a failure to pay remuneration in respect of a relevant period unless under his contract of employment he is entitled to be paid that remuneration.

(4) In subsection (3) 'a relevant period' means any period during which the employee is absent from work because of his attendance at any place in pursuance of being summoned as mentioned in subsection (1)(a).

44   Health and safety cases

(1) An employee has the right not to be subjected to any detriment by any act, or any deliberate failure to act, by his employer done on the ground that –

(a) having been designated by the employer to carry out activities in connection with preventing or reducing risks to health and safety at work, the employee carried out (or proposed to carry out) any such activities,

(b) being a representative of workers on matters of health and safety at work or member of a safety committee –

(i) in accordance with arrangements established under or by virtue of any enactment, or

(ii) by reason of being acknowledged as such by the employer,

the employee performed (or proposed to perform) any functions as such a representative or a member of such a committee,

(ba) the employee took part (or proposed to take part) in consultation with the employer pursuant to the Health and Safety (Consultation with Employees) Regulations 1996 or in an election of representatives of employee safety within the meaning of those Regulations (whether as a candidate or otherwise),

(c) being an employee at a place where –

(i) there was no such representative or safety committee, or

(ii) there was such a representative or safety committee but it was not reasonably practicable for the employee to raise the matter by those means,

he brought to his employer's attention, by reasonable means, circumstances connected with his work which he reasonably believed were harmful or potentially harmful to health or safety,

(d) in circumstances of danger which the employee reasonably believed to be serious and imminent and which he could not reasonably have been expected to avert, he left (or proposed to leave) or (while the danger persisted) refused to return to his place of work or any dangerous part of his place of work, or

(e) in circumstances of danger which the employee reasonably believed to be serious and imminent, he took (or proposed to take) appropriate steps to protect himself or other persons from the danger.

(2) For the purposes of subsection (1)(e) whether steps which an employee took (or proposed to take) were appropriate is to be judged by reference to all the circumstances including, in particular, his knowledge and the facilities and advice available to him at the time.

(3) An employee is not to be regarded as having been subjected to any detriment on the ground specified in subsection (1)(e) if the employer shows that it was (or would have been) so negligent for the employee to take the steps which he took (or proposed to take) that a reasonable employer might have treated him as the employer did.

(4) This section does not apply where the detriment in question amounts to dismissal (within the meaning of Part X).

45   Sunday working for shop and betting workers

(1) An employee who is –

(a) a protected shop worker or an opted-out shop worker, or

(b) a protected betting worker or an opted-out betting worker,

has the right not to be subjected to any detriment by any act, or any deliberate failure to act, by his employer done on the ground that the employee refused (or proposed to refuse) to do shop work, or betting work, on Sunday or on a particular Sunday.

(2) Subsection (1) does not apply to anything done in relation to an opted-out shop worker or an opted-out betting worker on the ground that he refused (or proposed to refuse) to do shop work, or betting work, on any Sunday or Sundays falling before the end of the notice period.

(3) An employee who is a shop worker or a betting worker has the right not to be subjected to any detriment by any act, or any deliberate failure to act, by his employer done on the ground that the employee gave (or proposed to give) an opting-out notice to his employer.

(4) Subsections (1) and (3) do not apply where the detriment in question amounts to dismissal (within the meaning of Part X). ...

(5) For the purposes of this section a shop worker or betting worker who does not work on Sunday or on a particular Sunday is not to be regarded as having been subjected to any detriment by –

(a) a failure to pay remuneration in respect of shop work, or betting work, on a Sunday which he has not done,

(b) a failure to provide him with any other benefit, where that failure results from the application (in relation to a Sunday on which the employee has not done shop work, or betting work) of a contractual term under which the extent of that benefit varies according to the number of hours worked by the employee or the remuneration of the employee, or

(c) a failure to provide him with any work, remuneration or other benefit which by virtue of section 38 or 39 the employer is not obliged to provide.

(6) Where an employer offers to pay a sum specified in the offer to any one or more employees –

(a) who are protected shop workers or opted-out shop workers or protected betting workers or opted-out betting workers, or

(b) who under their contracts of employment are not obliged to do shop work, or betting work, on Sunday,

if they agree to do shop work, or betting work, on Sunday or on a particular Sunday subsections (7) and (8) apply.

(7) An employee to whom the offer is not made is not to be regarded for the purposes of this section as having been subjected to any detriment by any failure to make the offer to him or to pay him the sum specified in the offer.

(8) An employee who does not accept the offer is not to be regarded for the purposes of this section as having been subjected to any detriment by any failure to pay him the sum specified in the offer.

(9) For the purposes of section 36(2)(b) or 41(1)(b), the appropriate date in relation to this section is the date of the act or failure to act.

(10) For the purposes of subsection (9) –

(a) where an act extends over a period, the 'date of the act' means the first day of that period, and

(b) a deliberate failure to act shall be treated as done when it was decided on;

and, in the absence of evidence establishing the contrary, an employer shall be taken to decide on a failure to act when he does an act inconsistent with doing the failed act or, if he has done no such inconsistent act, when the period expires within which he might reasonably have been expected to do the failed act if it was to be done.

45A Working time cases

(1) A worker has the right not to be subjected to any detriment by any act, or any deliberate failure to act, by his employer done on the ground that the worker –

(a) refused (or proposed to refuse) to comply with a requirement which the employer imposed (or proposed to impose) in contravention of the Working Time Regulations 1998,

(b) refused (or proposed to refuse) to forgo a right conferred on him by those Regulations,

(c) failed to sign a workforce agreement for the purposes of those Regulations, or to enter into, or agree to vary or extend, any other agreement with his employer which is provided for in those Regulations,

(d) being –

(i) a representative of members of the workforce for the purposes of Schedule 1 to those Regulations, or

(ii) a candidate in an election in which any person elected will, on being elected, be such a representative,

performed (or proposed to perform) any functions or activities as such a representative or candidate,

(e) brought proceedings against the employer to enforce a right conferred on him by those Regulations, or

(f) alleged that the employer had infringed such a right.

(2) It is immaterial for the purposes of subsection (1)(e) or (f) –

(a) whether or not the worker has the right, or

(b) whether or not the right has been infringed,

but, for those provisions to apply, the claim to the right and that it has been infringed must be made in good faith.

(3) It is sufficient for subsection (1)(f) to apply that the worker, without specifying the right, made it reasonably clear to the employer what the right claimed to have been infringed was.

(4) This section does not apply where a worker is an employee and the detriment in question amounts to dismissal within the meaning of Part X. ...

46 Trustees of occupational pension schemes

(1) An employee has the right not to be subjected to any detriment by any act, or any deliberate failure to act, by his employer done on the ground that, being a trustee of a relevant occupational pension scheme which relates to his employment, the employee performed (or proposed to perform) any functions as such a trustee.

(2) This section does not apply where the detriment in question amounts to dismissal (within the meaning of Part X).

(2A) This section applies to an employee who is a director of a company which is a trustee of a relevant occupational pension scheme as it applies to an employee who is a trustee of such a scheme (references to such a trustee being read for this purpose as references to such a director).

(3) In this section 'relevant occupational pension scheme' means an occupational pension scheme (as defined in section 1 of the Pension Schemes Act 1993) established under a trust.

47 Employee representatives

(1) An employee has the right not to be subjected to any detriment by any act, or any deliberate failure to act, by his employer done on the ground that, being –

(a) an employee representative for the purposes of Chapter II of Part IV of the Trade Union and Labour Relations (Consolidation) Act 1992 (redundancies) or Regulations 10 and 11 of the Transfer of Undertakings (Protection of Employment) Regulations 1981, or

(b) a candidate in an election in which any person elected will, on being elected, be such an employee representative,

he performed (or proposed to perform) any functions or activities as such an employee representative or candidate.

(1A) An employee has the right not to be subject to any detriment by any act, or by any deliberate failure to act, by his employer done on the ground of his participation in an election of employee representatives for the purposes of Chapter II of Part IV of the Trade Union and Labour Relations (Consolidation) Act 1992 (redundancies) or Regulations 10 and 11 of the Transfer of Undertakings (Protection of Employment) Regulations 1981.

(2) This section does not apply where the detriment in question amounts to a dismissal (within the meaning of Part X).

47A Employees exercising the right to time off work for study or training

(1) An employee has the right not to be subjected to any detriment by any act, or any deliberate failure to act, by his employer or the principal (within the meaning of section 63A(3)) done on the ground that, being a person entitled to –

(a) time off under section 63A(1) or (3), and

(b) remuneration under section 63B(1) in respect of that time taken off,

the employee exercised (or proposed to exercise) that right or received (or sought to receive) such remuneration.

(2) This section does not apply where the detriment in question amounts to dismissal (within the meaning of Part X).

47B   Protected disclosures

(1) A worker has the right not to be subjected to any detriment by any act, or any deliberate failure to act, by his employer done on the ground that the worker has made a protected disclosure.

(2) This section does not apply where –

(a) the worker is an employee, and

(b) the detriment in question amounts to dismissal (within the meaning of Part X).

(3) For the purposes of this section, and of sections 48 and 49 so far as relating to this section, 'worker', 'worker's contract', 'employment' and 'employer' have the extended meaning given by section 43K.

47C   Leave for family and domestic reasons

(1) An employee has the right not to be subjected to any detriment by any act, or any deliberate failure to act, by his employer done for a prescribed reason.

(2) A prescribed reason is one which is prescribed by regulations made by the Secretary of State and which relates to –

(a) pregnancy, childbirth or maternity,

(b) ordinary, compulsory or additional maternity leave,

(ba) ordinary or additional adoption leave,

(c) parental leave,

(ca) paternity leave, or

(d) time off under section 57A.

(3) A reason prescribed under this section in relation to parental leave may relate to action which an employee takes, agrees to take or refuses to take under or in respect of a collective or workforce agreement.

(4) Regulations under this section may make different provision for different cases or circumstances.

47D   Tax credits

(1) An employee has the right not to be subjected to any detriment by any act, or any deliberate failure to act, by his employer, done on the ground that –

(a) any action was taken, or was proposed to be taken, by or on behalf of the employee with a view to enforcing, or otherwise securing the benefit of, a right conferred on the employee by regulations under section 25 of the Tax Credits Act 2002,

(b) a penalty was imposed on the employer, or proceedings for a penalty were brought against him, under that Act, as a result of action taken by or on behalf of the employee for the purpose of enforcing, or otherwise securing the benefit of, such a right, or

(c) the employee is entitled, or will or may be entitled, to working tax credit.

(2) It is immaterial for the purposes of subsection (1)(a) or (b) –

(a) whether or not the employee has the right, or

(b) whether or not the right has been infringed,

but, for those provisions to apply, the claim to the right and (if applicable) the claim that it has been infringed must be made in good faith.

(3) Subsections (1) and (2) apply to a person who is not an employee within the meaning of this Act but who is an employee within the meaning of section 25 of the Tax Credits Act 2002, with references to his employer in those subsections (and sections 48(2) and (4) and 49(1)) being construed in accordance with that section.

(4) Subsections (1) and (2) do not apply to an employee if the detriment in question amounts to dismissal (within the meaning of Part 10).

47E Flexible working

(1) An employee has the right not to be subjected to any detriment by any act, or any deliberate failure to act, by his employer done on the ground that the employee –

(a) made (or proposed to make) an application under section 80F,

(b) exercised (or proposed to exercise) a right conferred on him under section 80G,

(c) brought proceedings against the employer under section 80H, or

(d) alleged the existence of any circumstance which would constitute a ground for bringing such proceedings.

(2) This section does not apply where the detriment in question amounts to dismissal within the meaning of Part 10.

48 Complaints to employment tribunals

(1) An employee may present a complaint to an employment tribunal that he has been subjected to a detriment in contravention of section 43M, 44, 45, 46, 47, 47A, 47C or 47E.

(1ZA) A worker may present a complaint to an employment tribunal that he has been subjected to a detriment in contravention of section 45A.

(1A) A worker may present a complaint to an employment tribunal that he has been subjected to a detriment in contravention of section 47B.

(1B) A person may present a complaint to an employment tribunal that he has been subjected to a detriment in contravention of section 47D.

(2) On such a complaint it is for the employer to show the ground on which any act, or deliberate failure to act, was done.

(3) An employment tribunal shall not consider a complaint under this section unless it is presented –

(a) before the end of the period of three months beginning with the date of the act or failure to act to which the complaint relates or, where that act or failure is part of a series of similar acts or failures, the last of them, or

(b) within such further period as the tribunal considers reasonable in a case where it is satisfied that it was not reasonably practicable for the complaint to be presented before the end of that period of three months.

(4) For the purposes of subsection (3) –

(a) where an act extends over a period, the 'date of the act' means the last day of that period, and

(b) a deliberate failure to act shall be treated as done when it was decided on;

and, in the absence of evidence establishing the contrary, an employer shall be taken to decide on a failure to act when he does an act inconsistent with doing the failed act or, if he has done no such inconsistent act, when the period expires within which he might reasonably have been expected to do the failed act if it was to be done.

(5) In this section and section 49 any reference to the employer includes, where a person complains that he has been subjected to a detriment in contravention of section 47A, the principal (within the meaning of section 63A(3)).

49 Remedies

(1) Where an employment tribunal finds a complaint under section 48 well-founded, the tribunal –

(a) shall make a declaration to that effect, and

(b) may make an award of compensation to be paid by the employer to the complainant in respect of the act or failure to act to which the complaint relates.

(2) Subject to subsections (5A) and (6), the amount of the compensation awarded shall be such as the tribunal considers just and equitable in all the circumstances having regard to –

(a) the infringement to which the complaint relates, and

(b) any loss which is attributable to the act, or failure to act, which infringed the complainant's right.

(3) The loss shall be taken to include –

(a) any expenses reasonably incurred by the complainant in consequence of the act, or failure to act, to which the complaint relates, and

(b) loss of any benefit which he might reasonably be expected to have had but for that act or failure to act.

(4) In ascertaining the loss the tribunal shall apply the same rule concerning the duty of a person to mitigate his loss as applies to damages recoverable under the common law of England and Wales ...

(5) Where the tribunal finds that the act, or failure to act, to which the complaint relates was to any extent caused or contributed to by action of the complainant, it shall reduce the amount of the compensation by such proportion as it considers just and equitable having regard to that finding.

(5A) Where –

(a) the complaint is made under section 48(1ZA),

(b) the detriment to which the worker is subjected is the termination of his worker's contract, and

(c) that contract is not a contract of employment,

any compensation must not exceed the compensation that would be payable under Chapter II of Part X if the worker had been an employee and had been dismissed for the reason specified in section 101A.

(6) Where –

(a) the complaint is made under section 48(1A),

(b) the detriment to which the worker is subjected is the termination of his worker's contract, and

(c) that contract is not a contract of employment,

any compensation must not exceed the compensation that would be payable under Chapter II of Part X if the worker had been an employee and had been dismissed for the reason specified in section 103A.

(7) Where –

(a) the complaint is made under section 48(1B) by a person who is not an employee, and

(b) the detriment to which he is subjected is the termination of his contract with the person who is his employer for the purposes of section 25 of the Tax Credits Act 2002,

any compensation must not exceed the compensation that would be payable under Chapter 2 of Part 10 if the complainant had been an employee and had been dismissed for the reason specified in section 104B.

PART VI

TIME OFF WORK

50   Right to time off for public duties

(1) An employer shall permit an employee of his who is a justice of the peace to take time off during the employee's working hours for the purpose of performing any of the duties of his office.

(2) An employer shall permit an employee of his who is a member of –

(a) a local authority,

(b) a statutory tribunal,

(c) a police authority, ...

(d) a board of prison visitors ...

(e) a relevant health body,

(f) a relevant education body,

(g) the Environment Agency ...

to take time off during the employee's working hours for the purposes specified in subsection (3).

(3) The purposes referred to in subsection (2) are –

(a) attendance at a meeting of the body or any of its committees or sub-committees, and

(b) the doing of any other thing approved by the body, or anything of a class so approved, for the purpose of the discharge of the functions of the body or of any of its committees or sub-committees, and

(c) in the case of a local authority which are operating executive arrangements –

(i) attendance at a meeting of the executive of that local authority or committee of that executive; and

(ii) the doing of any other thing, by an individual member of that executive, for the purposes of the discharge of any function which is to any extent the responsibility of that executive.

(4) The amount of time off which an employee is to be permitted to take under this section, and the occasions on which and any conditions subject to which time off may be so taken, are those that are reasonable in all the circumstances having regard, in particular, to –

(a) how much time off is required for the performance of the duties of the office or as a member of the body in question, and how much time off is required for the performance of the particular duty,

(b) how much time off the employee has already been permitted under this section or sections 168 and 170 of the Trade Union and Labour Relations (Consolidation) Act 1992 (time off for trade union duties and activities), and

(c) the circumstances of the employer's business and the effect of the employee's absence on the running of that business.

(5) In subsection (2)(a) 'a local authority' means –

(a) a local authority within the meaning of the Local Government Act 1972 ...

(c) the Common Council of the City of London,

(d) a National Park authority, or

(e) the Broads Authority.

(6) The reference in subsection (2) to a member of a police authority is to a person appointed as such a member under Schedule 2 to the Police Act 1996.

(7) In subsection (2)(d) –

(a) 'a board of prison visitors' means a board of visitors appointed under section 6(2) of the Prison Act 1952 ...

(8) In subsection (2)(e) 'a relevant health body' means –

(a) a National Health Service trust established under Part I of the National Health Service and Community Care Act 1990 ...

(ab) an NHS foundation trust,

(b) a Strategic Health Authority or Health Authority established under section 8 of the National Health Service Act 1977, a Special Health Authority established under section 11 of that Act or a Primary Care Trust established under section 16A of that Act ...

(9) In subsection (2)(f) 'a relevant education body' means –

(a) a managing or governing body of an educational establishment maintained by a local education authority,

(b) a governing body of a further education corporation or higher education corporation ...

(9A) In subsection (3)(c) of this section 'executive' and 'executive arrangements' have the same meaning as in Part II of the Local Government Act 2000.

(10) The Secretary of State may by order –

(a) modify the provisions of subsections (1) and (2) and (5) to (9) by adding any office or body, removing any office or body or altering the description of any office or body, or

(b) modify the provisions of subsection (3).

(11) For the purposes of this section the working hours of an employee shall be taken to be any time when, in accordance with his contract of employment, the employee is required to be at work.

51 Complaints to employment tribunals

(1) An employee may present a complaint to an employment tribunal that his employer has failed to permit him to take time off as required by section 50.

(2) An employment tribunal shall not consider a complaint under this section that an employer has failed to permit an employee to take time off unless it is presented –

(a) before the end of the period of three months beginning with the date on which the failure occurred, or

(b) within such further period as the tribunal considers reasonable in a case where it is satisfied that it was not reasonably practicable for the complaint to be presented before the end of that period of three months.

(3) Where an employment tribunal finds a complaint under this section well-founded, the tribunal –

(a) shall make a declaration to that effect, and

(b) may make an award of compensation to be paid by the employer to the employee.

(4) The amount of the compensation shall be such as the tribunal considers just and equitable in all the circumstances having regard to –

(a) the employer's default in failing to permit time off to be taken by the employee, and

(b) any loss sustained by the employee which is attributable to the matters to which the complaint relates.

52   Right to time off to look for work or arrange training

(1) An employee who is given notice of dismissal by reason of redundancy is entitled to be permitted by his employer to take reasonable time off during the employee's working hours before the end of his notice in order to –

(a) look for new employment, or

(b) make arrangements for training for future employment.

(2) An employee is not entitled to take time off under this section unless, on whichever is the later of –

(a) the date on which the notice is due to expire, and

(b) the date on which it would expire were it the notice required to be given by section 86(1),

he will have been (or would have been) continuously employed for a period of two years or more.

(3) For the purposes of this section the working hours of an employee shall be taken to be any time when, in accordance with his contract of employment, the employee is required to be at work.

53   Right to remuneration for time off under section 52

(1) An employee who is permitted to take time off under section 52 is entitled to be

paid remuneration by his employer for the period of absence at the appropriate hourly rate.

(2) The appropriate hourly rate, in relation to an employee, is the amount of one week's pay divided by the number of normal working hours in a week for that employee when employed under the contract of employment in force on the day when the notice of dismissal was given.

(3) But where the number of normal working hours differs from week to week or over a longer period, the amount of one week's pay shall be divided instead by the average number of normal working hours calculated by dividing by twelve the total number of the employee's normal working hours during the period of twelve weeks ending with the last complete week before the day on which the notice was given.

(4) If an employer unreasonably refuses to permit an employee to take time off from work as required by section 52, the employee is entitled to be paid an amount equal to the remuneration to which he would have been entitled under subsection (1) if he had been permitted to take the time off.

(5) The amount of an employer's liability to pay remuneration under subsection (1) shall not exceed, in respect of the notice period of any employee, forty per cent of a week's pay of that employee.

(6) A right to any amount under subsection (1) or (4) does not affect any right of an employee in relation to remuneration under his contract of employment ('contractual remuneration').

(7) Any contractual remuneration paid to an employee in respect of a period of time off under section 52 goes towards discharging any liability of the employer to pay remuneration under subsection (1) in respect of that period; and, conversely, any payment of remuneration under subsection (1) in respect of a period goes towards discharging any liability of the employer to pay contractual remuneration in respect of that period.

54　Complaints to employment tribunals

(1) An employee may present a complaint to an employment tribunal that his employer –

(a) has unreasonably refused to permit him to take time off as required by section 52, or

(b) has failed to pay the whole or any part of any amount to which the employee is entitled under section 53(1) or (4).

(2) An employment tribunal shall not consider a complaint under this section unless it is presented –

(a) before the end of the period of three months beginning with the date on which it is alleged that the time off should have been permitted, or

(b) within such further period as the tribunal considers reasonable in a case where it is satisfied that it was not reasonably practicable for the complaint to be presented before the end of that period of three months.

(3) Where an employment tribunal finds a complaint under this section well-founded, the tribunal shall –

(a) make a declaration to that effect, and

(b) order the employer to pay to the employee the amount which it finds due to him.

(4) The amount which may be ordered by a tribunal to be paid by an employer under subsection (3) (or, where the employer is liable to pay remuneration under section 53, the aggregate of that amount and the amount of that liability) shall not exceed, in respect of the notice period of any employee, forty per cent. of a week's pay of that employee.

55 Right to time off for ante-natal care

(1) An employee who –

(a) is pregnant, and

(b) has, on the advice of a registered medical practitioner, registered midwife or registered nurse, made an appointment to attend at any place for the purpose of receiving ante-natal care,

is entitled to be permitted by her employer to take time off during the employee's working hours in order to enable her to keep the appointment.

(2) An employee is not entitled to take time off under this section to keep an appointment unless, if her employer requests her to do so, she produces for his inspection –

(a) a certificate from a registered medical practitioner, registered midwife or registered nurse stating that the employee is pregnant, and

(b) an appointment card or some other document showing that the appointment has been made.

(3) Subsection (2) does not apply where the employee's appointment is the first appointment during her pregnancy for which she seeks permission to take time off in accordance with subsection (1).

(4) For the purposes of this section the working hours of an employee shall be taken to be any time when, in accordance with her contract of employment, the employee is required to be at work.

(5) References in this section to a registered nurse are to such a nurse –

(a) who is also registered in the Specialist Community Public Health Nurses' Part of the register maintained under article 5 of the Nursing and Midwifery Order 2001, and

(b) whose entry in that Part of the register is annotated to show that he holds a qualification in health visiting.

56 Right to remuneration for time off under section 55

(1) An employee who is permitted to take time off under section 55 is entitled to be paid remuneration by her employer for the period of absence at the appropriate hourly rate.

(2) The appropriate hourly rate, in relation to an employee, is the amount of one week's pay divided by the number of normal working hours in a week for that employee when employed under the contract of employment in force on the day when the time off is taken.

(3) But where the number of normal working hours differs from week to week or over a longer period, the amount of one week's pay shall be divided instead by –

(a) the average number of normal working hours calculated by dividing by twelve the total number of the employee's normal working hours during the period of twelve weeks ending with the last complete week before the day on which the time off is taken, or

(b) where the employee has not been employed for a sufficient period to enable the calculation to be made under paragraph (a), a number which fairly represents the number of normal working hours in a week having regard to such of the considerations specified in subsection (4) as are appropriate in the circumstances.

(4) The considerations referred to in subsection (3)(b) are –

(a) the average number of normal working hours in a week which the employee could expect in accordance with the terms of her contract, and

(b) the average number of normal working hours of other employees engaged in relevant comparable employment with the same employer.

(5) A right to any amount under subsection (1) does not affect any right of an employee in relation to remuneration under her contract of employment ('contractual remuneration').

(6) Any contractual remuneration paid to an employee in respect of a period of time off under section 55 goes towards discharging any liability of the employer to pay remuneration under subsection (1) in respect of that period; and, conversely, any payment of remuneration under subsection (1) in respect of a period goes towards discharging any liability of the employer to pay contractual remuneration in respect of that period.

57 Complaints to employment tribunals

(1) An employee may present a complaint to an employment tribunal that her employer –

(a) has unreasonably refused to permit her to take time off as required by section 55, or

(b) has failed to pay the whole or any part of any amount to which the employee is entitled under section 56.

(2) An employment tribunal shall not consider a complaint under this section unless it is presented –

(a) before the end of the period of three months beginning with the date of the appointment concerned, or

(b) within such further period as the tribunal considers reasonable in a case where it is satisfied that it was not reasonably practicable for the complaint to be presented before the end of that period of three months.

(3) Where an employment tribunal finds a complaint under this section well-founded, the tribunal shall make a declaration to that effect.

(4) If the complaint is that the employer has unreasonably refused to permit the employee to take time off, the tribunal shall also order the employer to pay to the employee an amount equal to the remuneration to which she would have been entitled under section 56 if the employer had not refused.

(5) If the complaint is that the employer has failed to pay the employee the whole or part of any amount to which she is entitled under section 56, the tribunal shall also order the employer to pay to the employee the amount which it finds due to her.

57A Time off for dependants

(1) An employee is entitled to be permitted by his employer to take a reasonable amount of time off during the employee's working hours in order to take action which is necessary –

(a) to provide assistance on an occasion when a dependant falls ill, gives birth or is injured or assaulted,

(b) to make arrangements for the provision of care for a dependant who is ill or injured,

(c) in consequence of the death of a dependant,

(d) because of the unexpected disruption or termination of arrangements for the care of a dependant, or

(e) to deal with an incident which involves a child of the employee and which occurs unexpectedly in a period during which an educational establishment which the child attends is responsible for him.

(2) Subsection (1) does not apply unless the employee –

(a) tells his employer the reason for his absence as soon as reasonably practicable, and

(b) except where paragraph (a) cannot be complied with until after the employee has returned to work, tells his employer for how long he expects to be absent.

(3) Subject to subsections (4) and (5), for the purposes of this section 'dependant' means, in relation to an employee –

(a) a spouse,

(b) a child,

(c) a parent,

(d) a person who lives in the same household as the employee, otherwise than by reason of being his employee, tenant, lodger or boarder.

(4) For the purposes of subsection (1)(a) or (b) 'dependant' includes, in addition to the persons mentioned in subsection (3), any person who reasonably relies on the employee –

(a) for assistance on an occasion when the person falls ill or is injured or assaulted, or

(b) to make arrangements for the provision of care in the event of illness or injury.

(5) For the purposes of subsection (1)(d) 'dependant' includes, in addition to the persons mentioned in subsection (3), any person who reasonably relies on the employee to make arrangements for the provision of care.

(6) A reference in this section to illness or injury includes a reference to mental illness or injury.

57B Complaint to employment tribunal

(1) An employee may present a complaint to an employment tribunal that his employer has unreasonably refused to permit him to take time off as required by section 57A.

(2) An employment tribunal shall not consider a complaint under this section unless it is presented –

(a) before the end of the period of three months beginning with the date when the refusal occurred, or

(b) within such further period as the tribunal considers reasonable in a case where it is satisfied that it was not reasonably practicable for the complaint to be presented before the end of that period of three months.

(3) Where an employment tribunal finds a complaint under subsection (1) well-founded, it –

(a) shall make a declaration to that effect, and

(b) may make an award of compensation to be paid by the employer to the employee.

(4) The amount of compensation shall be such as the tribunal considers just and equitable in all the circumstances having regard to –

(a) the employer's default in refusing to permit time off to be taken by the employee, and

(b) any loss sustained by the employee which is attributable to the matters complained of.

58   Right to time off for pension scheme trustees

(1) The employer in relation to a relevant occupational pension scheme shall permit an employee of his who is a trustee of the scheme to take time off during the employee's working hours for the purpose of –

(a) performing any of his duties as such a trustee, or

(b) undergoing training relevant to the performance of those duties.

(2) The amount of time off which an employee is to be permitted to take under this section and the purposes for which, the occasions on which and any conditions subject to which time off may be so taken are those that are reasonable in all the circumstances having regard, in particular, to –

(a) how much time off is required for the performance of the duties of a trustee of the scheme and the undergoing of relevant training, and how much time off is required for performing the particular duty or for undergoing the particular training, and

(b) the circumstances of the employer's business and the effect of the employee's absence on the running of that business.

(2A) This section applies to an employee who is a director of a company which is a trustee of a relevant occupational pension scheme as it applies to an employee who is a trustee of such a scheme (references to such a trustee being read for this purpose as references to such a director).

(3) In this section –

(a) 'relevant occupational pension scheme' means an occupational pension scheme (as defined in section 1 of the Pension Schemes Act 1993) established under a trust, and

(b) references to the employer, in relation to such a scheme, are to an employer of persons in the description or category of employment to which the scheme relates, and

(c) references to training are to training on the employer's premises or elsewhere,

(4) For the purposes of this section the working hours of an employee shall be taken to be any time when, in accordance with his contract of employment, the employee is required to be at work.

59   Right to payment for time off under section 58

(1) An employer who permits an employee to take time off under section 58 shall pay him for the time taken off pursuant to the permission.

(2) Where the employee's remuneration for the work he would ordinarily have been doing during that time does not vary with the amount of work done, he must be paid as if he had worked at that work for the whole of that time.

(3) Where the employee's remuneration for the work he would ordinarily have been

doing during that time varies with the amount of work done, he must be paid an amount calculated by reference to the average hourly earnings for that work.

(4) The average hourly earnings mentioned in subsection (3) are –

(a) those of the employee concerned, or

(b) if no fair estimate can be made of those earnings, the average hourly earnings for work of that description of persons in comparable employment with the same employer or, if there are no such persons, a figure of average hourly earnings which is reasonable in the circumstances.

(5) A right to be paid an amount under subsection (1) does not affect any right of an employee in relation to remuneration under his contract of employment ('contractual remuneration').

(6) Any contractual remuneration paid to an employee in respect of a period of time off under section 58 goes towards discharging any liability of the employer under subsection (1) in respect of that period; and, conversely, any payment under subsection (1) in respect of a period goes towards discharging any liability of the employer to pay contractual remuneration in respect of that period.

60   Complaints to employment tribunals

(1) An employee may present a complaint to an employment tribunal that his employer –

(a) has failed to permit him to take time off as required by section 58, or

(b) has failed to pay him in accordance with section 59.

(2) An employment tribunal shall not consider a complaint under this section unless it is presented –

(a) before the end of the period of three months beginning with the date when the failure occurred, or

(b) within such further period as the tribunal considers reasonable in a case where it is satisfied that it was not reasonably practicable for the complaint to be presented before the end of that period of three months.

(3) Where an employment tribunal finds a complaint under subsection (1)(a) well-founded, the tribunal –

(a) shall make a declaration to that effect, and

(b) may make an award of compensation to be paid by the employer to the employee.

(4) The amount of the compensation shall be such as the tribunal considers just and equitable in all the circumstances having regard to –

(a) the employer's default in failing to permit time off to be taken by the employee, and

(b) any loss sustained by the employee which is attributable to the matters complained of.

(5) Where on a complaint under subsection (1)(b) an employment tribunal finds that an employer has failed to pay an employee in accordance with section 59, it shall order the employer to pay the amount which it finds to be due.

61   Right to time off for employee representatives

(1) An employee who is –

(a) an employee representative for the purposes of Chapter II of Part IV of the Trade Union and Labour Relations (Consolidation) Act 1992 (redundancies) or Regulations 10 and 11 of the Transfer of Undertakings (Protection of Employment) Regulations 1981, or

(b) a candidate in an election in which any person elected will, on being elected, be such an employee representative,

is entitled to be permitted by his employer to take reasonable time off during the employee's working hours in order to perform his functions as such an employee representative or candidate or in order to undergo training to perform such functions.

(2) For the purposes of this section the working hours of an employee shall be taken to be any time when, in accordance with his contract of employment, the employee is required to be at work.

62   Right to remuneration for time off under section 61

(1) An employee who is permitted to take time off under section 61 is entitled to be paid remuneration by his employer for the time taken off at the appropriate hourly rate.

(2) The appropriate hourly rate, in relation to an employee, is the amount of one week's pay divided by the number of normal working hours in a week for that employee when employed under the contract of employment in force on the day when the time off is taken.

(3) But where the number of normal working hours differs from week to week or over a longer period, the amount of one week's pay shall be divided instead by –

(a) the average number of normal working hours calculated by dividing by twelve the total number of the employee's normal working hours during the period of twelve weeks ending with the last complete week before the day on which the time off is taken, or

(b) where the employee has not been employed for a sufficient period to enable the calculation to be made under paragraph (a), a number which fairly represents the number of normal working hours in a week having regard to such of the considerations specified in subsection (4) as are appropriate in the circumstances.

(4) The considerations referred to in subsection (3)(b) are –

(a) the average number of normal working hours in a week which the employee could expect in accordance with the terms of his contract, and

(b) the average number of normal working hours of other employees engaged in relevant comparable employment with the same employer.

(5) A right to any amount under subsection (1) does not affect any right of an employee in relation to remuneration under his contract of employment ('contractual remuneration').

(6) Any contractual remuneration paid to an employee in respect of a period of time off under section 61 goes towards discharging any liability of the employer to pay remuneration under subsection (1) in respect of that period; and, conversely, any payment of remuneration under subsection (1) in respect of a period goes towards discharging any liability of the employer to pay contractual remuneration in respect of that period.

63 Complaints to employment tribunals

(1) An employee may present a complaint to an employment tribunal that his employer –

(a) has unreasonably refused to permit him to take time off as required by section 61, or

(b) has failed to pay the whole or any part of any amount to which the employee is entitled under section 62.

(2) An employment tribunal shall not consider a complaint under this section unless it is presented –

(a) before the end of the period of three months beginning with the day on which the time off was taken or on which it is alleged the time off should have been permitted, or

(b) within such further period as the tribunal considers reasonable in a case where it is satisfied that it was not reasonably practicable for the complaint to be presented before the end of that period of three months.

(3) Where an employment tribunal finds a complaint under this section well-founded, the tribunal shall make a declaration to that effect.

(4) If the complaint is that the employer has unreasonably refused to permit the employee to take time off, the tribunal shall also order the employer to pay to the employee an amount equal to the remuneration to which he would have been entitled under section 62 if the employer had not refused.

(5) If the complaint is that the employer has failed to pay the employee the whole or part of any amount to which he is entitled under section 62, the tribunal shall also order the employer to pay to the employee the amount which it finds due to him.

63A   Right to time off for young person for study or training

(1) An employee who –

(a) is aged 16 or 17,

(b) is not receiving full-time secondary or further education, and

(c) has not attained such standard of achievement as is prescribed by regulations made by the Secretary of State,

is entitled to be permitted by his employer to take time off during the employee's working hours in order to undertake study or training leading to a relevant qualification.

(2) In this section –

(a) 'secondary education' –

(i) in relation to England and Wales, has the same meaning as in the Education Act 1996, and ...

(b) 'further education' –

(i) in relation to England and Wales, has the same meaning as in the Education Act 1996, and ...

(c) 'relevant qualification' means an external qualification the attainment of which –

(i) would contribute to the attainment of the standard prescribed for the purposes of subsection (1)(c), and

(ii) would be likely to enhance the employee's employment prospects (whether with his employer or otherwise);

and for the purposes of paragraph (c) 'external qualification' means an academic or vocational qualification awarded or authenticated by such person or body as may be specified in or under regulations made by the Secretary of State.

(3) An employee who –

(a) satisfies the requirements of paragraphs (a) to (c) of subsection (1), and

(b) is for the time being supplied by his employer to another person ('the principal') to perform work in accordance with a contract made between the employer and the principal,

is entitled to be permitted by the principal to take time off during the employee's working hours in order to undertake study or training leading to a relevant qualification.

(4) Where an employee –

(a) is aged 18,

(b) is undertaking study or training leading to a relevant qualification, and

(c) began such study or training before attaining that age,

subsections (1) and (3) shall apply to the employee, in relation to that study or training, as if 'or 18' were inserted at the end of subsection (1)(a).

(5) The amount of time off which an employee is to be permitted to take under this section, and the occasions on which and any conditions subject to which time off may be so taken, are those that are reasonable in all the circumstances having regard, in particular, to –

(a) the requirements of the employee's study or training, and

(b) the circumstances of the business of the employer or the principal and the effect of the employee's time off on the running of that business.

(6) Regulations made for the purposes of subsections (1)(c) and (2) may make different provision for different cases, and in particular may make different provision in relation to England, Wales and Scotland respectively.

(7) References in this section to study or training are references to study or training on the premises of the employer or (as the case may be) principal or elsewhere.

(8) For the purposes of this section the working hours of an employee shall be taken to be any time when, in accordance with his contract of employment, the employee is required to be at work.

63B Right to remuneration for time off under section 63A

(1) An employee who is permitted to take time off under section 63A is entitled to be paid remuneration by his employer for the time taken off at the appropriate hourly rate.

(2) The appropriate hourly rate, in relation to an employee, is the amount of one week's pay divided by the number of normal working hours in a week for that employee when employed under the contract of employment in force on the day when the time off is taken.

(3) But where the number of normal working hours differs from week to week or over a longer period, the amount of one week's pay shall be divided instead by –

(a) the average number of normal working hours calculated by dividing by twelve the total number of the employee's working hours during the period of twelve weeks ending with the last complete week before the day on which the time off is taken, or

(b) where the employee has not been employed for a sufficient period to enable the calculation to be made under paragraph (a), a number which fairly represents the number of normal working hours in a week having regard to such of the considerations specified in subsection (4) as are appropriate in the circumstances.

(4) The considerations referred to in subsection (3)(b) are –

(a) the average number of normal working hours in a week which the employee could expect in accordance with the terms of his contract, and

(b) the average number of normal working hours of other employees engaged in relevant comparable employment with the same employer.

(5) A right to any amount under subsection (1) does not affect any right of an employee in relation to remuneration under his contract of employment ('contractual remuneration').

(6) Any contractual remuneration paid to an employee in respect of a period of time off under section 63A goes towards discharging any liability of the employer to pay remuneration under subsection (1) in respect of that period; and, conversely, any payment of remuneration under subsection (1) in respect of a period goes towards discharging any liability of the employer to pay contractual remuneration in respect of that period.

63C   Complaints to employment tribunals

(1) An employee may present a complaint to an employment tribunal that –

(a) his employer, or the principal referred to in subsection (3) of section 63A, has unreasonably refused to permit him to take time off as required by that section, or

(b) his employer has failed to pay the whole or any part of any amount to which the employee is entitled under section 63B.

(2) An employment tribunal shall not consider a complaint under this section unless it is presented –

(a) before the end of the period of three months beginning with the day on which the time off was taken or on which it is alleged the time off should have been permitted, or

(b) within such further period as the tribunal considers reasonable in a case where it is satisfied that it was not reasonably practicable for the complaint to be presented before the end of that period of three months.

(3) Where an employment tribunal finds a complaint under this section well-founded, the tribunal shall make a declaration to that effect.

(4) If the complaint is that the employer or the principal has unreasonably refused to permit the employee to take time off, the tribunal shall also order the employer or the principal, as the case may be, to pay to the employee an amount equal to the remuneration to which he would have been entitled under section 63B if the employer or the principal had not refused.

(5) If the complaint is that the employer has failed to pay the employee the whole or part of any amount to which he is entitled under section 63B, the tribunal shall also order the employer to pay to the employee the amount which it finds due to him.

PART VII

SUSPENSION FROM WORK

64 Right to remuneration on suspension on medical grounds

(1) An employee who is suspended from work by his employer on medical grounds is entitled to be paid by his employer remuneration while he is so suspended for a period not exceeding twenty-six weeks.

(2) For the purposes of this Part an employee is suspended from work on medical grounds if he is suspended from work in consequence of –

(a) a requirement imposed by or under a provision of an enactment or of an instrument made under an enactment, or

(b) a recommendation in a provision of a code of practice issued or approved under section 16 of the Health and Safety at Work etc. Act 1974,

and the provision is for the time being specified in subsection (3).

(3) The provisions referred to in subsection (2) are –

Regulation 16 of the Control of Lead at Work Regulations 1980,

Regulation 24 of the Ionising Radiations Regulations 1999, and

Regulation 11 of the Control of Substances Hazardous to Health Regulations 1988.

(4) The Secretary of State may by order add provisions to or remove provisions from the list of provisions specified in subsection (3).

(5) For the purposes of this Part an employee shall be regarded as suspended from work on medical grounds only if and for so long as he –

(a) continues to be employed by his employer, but

(b) is not provided with work or does not perform the work he normally performed before the suspension.

65 Exclusions from right to remuneration

(1) An employee is not entitled to remuneration under section 64 unless he has been continuously employed for a period of not less than one month ending with the day before that on which the suspension begins.

(3) An employee is not entitled to remuneration under section 64 in respect of any period during which he is incapable of work by reason of disease or bodily or mental disablement.

(4) An employee is not entitled to remuneration under section 64 in respect of any period if –

(a) his employer has offered to provide him with suitable alternative work during the period (whether or not it is work which the employee is under his contract, or was under the contract in force before the suspension, employed to perform) and the employee has unreasonably refused to perform that work, or

(b) he does not comply with reasonable requirements imposed by his employer with a view to ensuring that his services are available.

66   Meaning of suspension on maternity grounds

(1) For the purposes of this Part an employee is suspended from work on maternity grounds if, in consequence of any relevant requirement or relevant recommendation, she is suspended from work by her employer on the ground that she is pregnant, has recently given birth or is breastfeeding a child.

(2) In subsection (1) –

'relevant requirement' means a requirement imposed by or under a specified provision of an enactment or of an instrument made under an enactment, and

'relevant recommendation' means a recommendation in a specified provision of a code of practice issued or approved under section 16 of the Health and Safety at Work etc Act 1974;

and in this subsection 'specified provision' means a provision for the time being specified in an order made by the Secretary of State under this subsection.

(3) For the purposes of this Part an employee shall be regarded as suspended from work on maternity grounds only if and for so long as she –

(a) continues to be employed by her employer, but

(b) is not provided with work or (disregarding alternative work for the purposes of section 67) does not perform the work she normally performed before the suspension.

67   Right to offer of alternative work

(1) Where an employer has available suitable alternative work for an employee, the employee has a right to be offered to be provided with the alternative work before being suspended from work on maternity grounds.

(2) For alternative work to be suitable for an employee for the purposes of this section –

(a) the work must be of a kind which is both suitable in relation to her and appropriate for her to do in the circumstances, and

(b) the terms and conditions applicable to her for performing the work, if they differ from the corresponding terms and conditions applicable to her for performing the work she normally performs under her contract of employment, must not be substantially less favourable to her than those corresponding terms and conditions.

68   Right to remuneration

(1) An employee who is suspended from work on maternity grounds is entitled to be paid remuneration by her employer while she is so suspended.

(2) An employee is not entitled to remuneration under this section in respect of any period if –

(a) her employer has offered to provide her during the period with work which is suitable alternative work for her for the purposes of section 67, and

(b) the employee has unreasonably refused to perform that work.

69 Calculation of remuneration

(1) The amount of remuneration payable by an employer to an employee under section 64 or 68 is a week's pay in respect of each week of the period of suspension; and if in any week remuneration is payable in respect of only part of that week the amount of a week's pay shall be reduced proportionately.

(2) A right to remuneration under section 64 or 68 does not affect any right of an employee in relation to remuneration under the employee's contract of employment ('contractual remuneration').

(3) Any contractual remuneration paid by an employer to an employee in respect of any period goes towards discharging the employer's liability under section 64 or 68 in respect of that period; and, conversely, any payment of remuneration in discharge of an employer's liability under section 64 or 68 in respect of any period goes towards discharging any obligation of the employer to pay contractual remuneration in respect of that period.

70 Complaints to employment tribunals

(1) An employee may present a complaint to an employment tribunal that his or her employer has failed to pay the whole or any part of remuneration to which the employee is entitled under section 64 or 68.

(2) An employment tribunal shall not consider a complaint under subsection (1) relating to remuneration in respect of any day unless it is presented –

(a) before the end of the period of three months beginning with that day, or

(b) within such further period as the tribunal considers reasonable in a case where it is satisfied that it was not reasonably practicable for the complaint to be presented within that period of three months.

(3) Where an employment tribunal finds a complaint under subsection (1) well-founded, the tribunal shall order the employer to pay the employee the amount of remuneration which it finds is due to him or her.

(4) An employee may present a complaint to an employment tribunal that in contravention of section 67 her employer has failed to offer to provide her with work.

(5) An employment tribunal shall not consider a complaint under subsection (4) unless it is presented –

(a) before the end of the period of three months beginning with the first day of the suspension, or

(b) within such further period as the tribunal considers reasonable in a case where it is satisfied that it was not reasonably practicable for the complaint to be presented within that period of three months.

(6) Where an employment tribunal finds a complaint under subsection (4) well-founded, the tribunal may make an award of compensation to be paid by the employer to the employee.

(7) The amount of the compensation shall be such as the tribunal considers just and equitable in all the circumstances having regard to –

(a) the infringement of the employee's right under section 67 by the failure on the part of the employer to which the complaint relates, and

(b) any loss sustained by the employee which is attributable to that failure.

PART VIII

CHAPTER I

MATERNITY LEAVE

71 Ordinary maternity leave

(1) An employee may, provided that she satisfies any conditions which may be prescribed, be absent from work at any time during an ordinary maternity leave period.

(2) An ordinary maternity leave period is a period calculated in accordance with regulations made by the Secretary of State.

(3) Regulations under subsection (2) –

(a) shall secure that no ordinary maternity leave period is less than 18 weeks;

(b) may allow an employee to choose, subject to any prescribed restrictions, the date on which an ordinary maternity leave period starts.

(4) Subject to section 74, an employee who exercises her right under subsection (1) –

(a) is entitled, for such purposes and to such extent as may be prescribed, to the benefit of the terms and conditions of employment which would have applied if she had not been absent,

(b) is bound, for such purposes and to such extent as may be prescribed, by any obligations arising under those terms and conditions (except in so far as they are inconsistent with subsection (1)), and

(c) is entitled to return from leave to a job of a prescribed kind.

(5) In subsection (4)(a) 'terms and conditions of employment' –

(a) includes matters connected with an employee's employment whether or not they arise under her contract of employment, but

(b) does not include terms and conditions about remuneration.

(6) The Secretary of State may make regulations specifying matters which are, or are not, to be treated as remuneration for the purposes of this section.

(7) The Secretary of State may make regulations making provision, in relation to the right to return under subsection (4)(c) above, about –

(a) seniority, pension rights and similar rights;

(b) terms and conditions of employment on return.

72 Compulsory maternity leave

(1) An employer shall not permit an employee who satisfies prescribed conditions to work during a compulsory maternity leave period.

(2) A compulsory maternity leave period is a period calculated in accordance with regulations made by the Secretary of State.

(3) Regulations under subsection (2) shall secure –

(a) that no compulsory leave period is less than two weeks, and

(b) that every compulsory maternity leave period falls within an ordinary maternity leave period.

(4) Subject to subsection (5), any provision of or made under the Health and Safety at Work etc Act 1974 shall apply in relation to the prohibition under subsection (1) as if it were imposed by regulations under section 15 of that Act.

(5) Section 33(1)(c) of the 1974 Act shall not apply in relation to the prohibition under subsection (1); and an employer who contravenes that subsection shall be –

(a) guilty of an offence, and

(b) liable on summary conviction to a fine not exceeding level 2 on the standard scale.

73 Additional maternity leave

(1) An employee who satisfies prescribed conditions may be absent from work at any time during an additional maternity leave period.

(2) An additional maternity leave period is a period calculated in accordance with regulations made by the Secretary of State.

(3) Regulations under subsection (2) may allow an employee to choose, subject to prescribed restrictions, the date on which an additional maternity leave period ends.

(4) Subject to section 74, an employee who exercises her right under subsection (1) –

(a) is entitled, for such purposes and to such extent as may be prescribed, to the benefit of the terms and conditions of employment which would have applied if she had not been absent,

(b) is bound, for such purposes and to such extent as may be prescribed, by obligations arising under those terms and conditions (except in so far as they are inconsistent with subsection (1)), and

(c) is entitled to return from leave to a job of a prescribed kind.

(5) In subsection (4)(a) 'terms and conditions of employment' –

(a) includes matters connected with an employee's employment whether or not they arise under her contract of employment, but

(b) does not include terms and conditions about remuneration.

(5A) In subsection (4)(c), the reference to return from leave includes, where appropriate, a reference to a continuous period of absence attributable partly to additional maternity leave and partly to ordinary maternity leave.

(6) The Secretary of State may make regulations specifying matters which are, or are not, to be treated as remuneration for the purposes of this section.

(7) The Secretary of State may make regulations making provision, in relation to the right to return under subsection (4)(c), about –

(a) seniority, pension rights and similar rights;

(b) terms and conditions of employment on return.

74   Redundancy and dismissal

(1) Regulations under section 71 or 73 may make provision about redundancy during an ordinary or additional maternity leave period.

(2) Regulations under section 71 or 73 may make provision about dismissal (other than by reason of redundancy) during an ordinary or additional maternity leave period.

(3) Regulations made by virtue of subsection (1) or (2) may include –

(a) provision requiring an employer to offer alternative employment;

(b) provision for the consequences of failure to comply with the regulations (which may include provision for a dismissal to be treated as unfair for the purposes of Part X).

(4) Regulations under section 71 or 73 may make provision –

(a) for section 71(4)(c) or 73(4)(c) not to apply in specified cases, and

(b) about dismissal at the conclusion of an ordinary or additional maternity leave period.

75   Sections 71 to 73: supplemental

(1) Regulations under section 71, 72 or 73 may –

(a) make provision about notices to be given, evidence to be produced and other procedures to be followed by employees and employers;

(b) make provision for the consequences of failure to give notices, to produce evidence or to comply with other procedural requirements;

(c) make provision for the consequences of failure to act in accordance with a notice given by virtue of paragraph (a);

(d) make special provision for cases where an employee has a right which corresponds to a right under this Chapter and which arises under her contract of employment or otherwise;

(e) make provision modifying the effect of Chapter II of Part XIV (calculation of a week's pay) in relation to an employee who is or has been absent from work on ordinary or additional maternity leave;

(f) make provision applying, modifying or excluding an enactment, in such circumstances as may be specified and subject to any conditions specified, in relation to a person entitled to ordinary, compulsory or additional maternity leave;

(g) make different provision for different cases or circumstances.

(2) In sections 71 to 73 'prescribed' means prescribed by regulations made by the Secretary of State.

CHAPTER 1A

ADOPTION LEAVE

75A Ordinary adoption leave

(1) An employee who satisfies prescribed conditions may be absent from work at any time during an ordinary adoption leave period.

(2) An ordinary adoption leave period is a period calculated in accordance with regulations made by the Secretary of State.

(3) Subject to section 75C, an employee who exercises his right under subsection (1) –

(a) is entitled, for such purposes and to such extent as may be prescribed, to the benefit of the terms and conditions of employment which would have applied if he had not been absent,

(b) is bound, for such purposes and to such extent as may be prescribed, by any obligations arising under those terms and conditions (except in so far as they are inconsistent with subsection (1)), and

(c) is entitled to return from leave to a job of a prescribed kind.

(4) In subsection (3)(a) 'terms and conditions of employment' –

(a) includes matters connected with an employee's employment whether or not they arise under his contract of employment, but

(b) does not include terms and conditions about remuneration.

(5) In subsection (3)(c), the reference to return from leave includes, where appropriate, a reference to a continuous period of absence attributable partly to ordinary adoption leave and partly to maternity leave.

(6) The Secretary of State may make regulations specifying matters which are, or are not, to be treated as remuneration for the purposes of this section.

(7) The Secretary of State may make regulations making provision, in relation to the right to return under subsection (3)(c), about –

(a) seniority, pension rights and similar rights;

(b) terms and conditions of employment on return.

75B Additional adoption leave

(1) An employee who satisfies prescribed conditions may be absent from work at any time during an additional adoption leave period.

(2) An additional adoption leave period is a period calculated in accordance with regulations made by the Secretary of State.

(3) Regulations under subsection (2) may allow an employee to choose, subject to prescribed restrictions, the date on which an additional adoption leave period ends.

(4) Subject to section 75C, an employee who exercises his right under subsection (1) –

(a) is entitled, for such purposes and to such extent as may be prescribed, to the benefit of the terms and conditions of employment which would have applied if he had not been absent,

(b) is bound, for such purposes and to such extent as may be prescribed, by obligations arising under those terms and conditions (except in so far as they are inconsistent with subsection (1)), and

(c) is entitled to return from leave to a job of a prescribed kind.

(5) In subsection (4)(a) "terms and conditions of employment" –

(a) includes matters connected with an employee's employment whether or not they arise under his contract of employment, but

(b) does not include terms and conditions about remuneration.

(6) In subsection (4)(c), the reference to return from leave includes, where appropriate, a reference to a continuous period of absence attributable partly to additional adoption leave and partly to –

(a) maternity leave, or

(b) ordinary adoption leave,

or to both.

(7) The Secretary of State may make regulations specifying matters which are, or are not, to be treated as remuneration for the purposes of this section.

(8) The Secretary of State may make regulations making provision, in relation to the right to return under subsection (4)(c), about –

(a) seniority, pension rights and similar rights;

(b) terms and conditions of employment on return.

75C   Redundancy and dismissal

(1) Regulations under section 75A or 75B may make provision about –

    (a) redundancy, or

    (b) dismissal (other than by reason of redundancy).

during an ordinary or additional adoption leave period. …

75D   Chapter 1A: supplemental

(1) Regulations under section 75A or 75B may – …

(2) In sections 75A and 75B 'prescribed' means prescribed by regulations made by the Secretary of State.

CHAPTER II

PARENTAL LEAVE

76   Entitlement to parental leave

(1) The Secretary of State shall make regulations entitling an employee who satisfies specified conditions –

    (a) as to duration of employment, and

    (b) as to having, or expecting to have, responsibility for a child,

to be absent from work on parental leave for the purpose of caring for a child.

(2) The regulations shall include provision for determining –

    (a) the extent of an employee's entitlement to parental leave in respect of a child;

    (b) when parental leave may be taken.

(3) Provision under subsection (2)(a) shall secure that where an employee is entitled to parental leave in respect of a child he is entitled to a period or total period of leave of at least three months; but this subsection is without prejudice to any provision which may be made by the regulations for cases in which –

    (a) a person ceases to satisfy conditions under subsection (1);

    (b) an entitlement to parental leave is transferred.

(4) Provision under subsection (2)(b) may, in particular, refer to –

    (a) a child's age, or

    (b) a specified period of time starting from a specified event.

(5) Regulations under subsection (1) may –

    (a) specify things which are, or are not, to be taken as done for the purpose of caring for a child;

(b) require parental leave to be taken as a single period of absence in all cases or in specified cases;

(c) require parental leave to be taken as a series of periods of absence in all cases or in specified cases;

(d) require all or specified parts of a period of parental leave to be taken at or by specified times;

(e) make provision about the postponement by an employer of a period of parental leave which an employee wishes to take;

(f) specify a minimum or maximum period of absence which may be taken as part of a period of parental leave.

(g) specify a maximum aggregate of periods of parental leave which may be taken during a specified period of time.

77 Rights during and after parental leave

(1) Regulations under section 76 shall provide –

(a) that an employee who is absent on parental leave is entitled, for such purposes and to such extent as may be prescribed, to the benefit of the terms and conditions of employment which would have applied if he had not been absent,

(b) that an employee who is absent on parental leave is bound, for such purposes and to such extent as may be prescribed, by any obligations arising under those terms and conditions (except in so far as they are inconsistent with section 76(1)), and

(c) that an employee who is absent on parental leave is entitled, subject to section 78(1), to return from leave to a job of such kind as the regulations may specify.

(2) In subsection (1)(a) 'terms and conditions of employment' –

(a) includes matters connected with an employee's employment whether or not they arise under a contract of employment, but

(b) does not include terms and conditions about remuneration.

(3) Regulations under section 76 may specify matters which are, or are not, to be treated as remuneration for the purposes of subsection (2)(b) above.

(4) The regulations may make provision, in relation to the right to return mentioned in subsection (1)(c), about –

(a) seniority, pension rights and similar rights;

(b) terms and conditions of employment on return.

78 Special cases

(1) Regulations under section 76 may make provision –

(a) about redundancy during a period of parental leave;

(b) about dismissal (other than by reason of redundancy) during a period of parental leave.

(2) Provision by virtue of subsection (1) may include –

(a) provision requiring an employer to offer alternative employment;

(b) provision for the consequences of failure to comply with the regulations (which may include provision for a dismissal to be treated as unfair for the purposes of Part X).

(3) Regulations under section 76 may provide for an employee to be entitled to choose to exercise all or part of his entitlement to parental leave –

(a) by varying the terms of his contract of employment as to hours of work, or

(b) by varying his normal working practice as to hours of work,

in a way specified in or permitted by the regulations for a period specified in the regulations.

(4) Provision by virtue of subsection (3) –

(a) may restrict an entitlement to specified circumstances;

(b) may make an entitlement subject to specified conditions (which may include conditions relating to obtaining the employer's consent);

(c) may include consequential and incidental provision.

(5) Regulations under section 76 may make provision permitting all or part of an employee's entitlement to parental leave in respect of a child to be transferred to another employee in specified circumstances.

(6) The reference in section 77(1)(c) to absence on parental leave includes, where appropriate, a reference to a continuous period of absence attributable partly to parental leave and partly to –

(a) maternity leave, or

(b) adoption leave,

or to both.

(7) Regulations under section 76 may provide for specified provisions of the regulations not to apply in relation to an employee if any provision of his contract of employment –

(a) confers an entitlement to absence from work for the purpose of caring for a child, and

(b) incorporates or operates by reference to all or part of a collective agreement, or workforce agreement, of a kind specified in the regulations.

79   Supplemental

(1) Regulations under section 76 may, in particular –

(a) make provision about notices to be given and evidence to be produced by employees to employers, by employers to employees, and by employers to other employers;

(b) make provision requiring employers or employees to keep records;

(c) make provision about other procedures to be followed by employees and employers;

(d) make provision (including provision creating criminal offences) specifying the consequences of failure to give notices, to produce evidence, to keep records or to comply with other procedural requirements;

(e) make provision specifying the consequences of failure to act in accordance with a notice given by virtue of paragraph (a);

(f) make special provision for cases where an employee has a right which corresponds to a right conferred by the regulations and which arises under his contract of employment or otherwise;

(g) make provision applying, modifying or excluding an enactment, in such circumstances as may be specified and subject to any conditions specified, in relation to a person entitled to parental leave;

(h) make different provision for different cases or circumstances.

(2) The regulations may make provision modifying the effect of Chapter II of Part XIV (calculation of a week's pay) in relation to an employee who is or has been absent from work on parental leave.

(3) Without prejudice to the generality of section 76, the regulations may make any provision which appears to the Secretary of State to be necessary or expedient –

(a) for the purpose of implementing Council Directive 96/34/EC on the framework agreement on parental leave, or

(b) for the purpose of dealing with any matter arising out of or related to the United Kingdom's obligations under that Directive.

80   Complaint to employment tribunal

(1) An employee may present a complaint to an employment tribunal that his employer –

(a) has unreasonably postponed a period of parental leave requested by the employee, or

(b) has prevented or attempted to prevent the employee from taking parental leave.

(2) An employment tribunal shall not consider a complaint under this section unless it is presented –

(a) before the end of the period of three months beginning with the date (or last date) of the matters complained of, or

(b) within such further period as the tribunal considers reasonable in a case where it is satisfied that it was not reasonably practicable for the complaint to be presented before the end of that period of three months.

(3) Where an employment tribunal finds a complaint under this section well-founded it –

(a) shall make a declaration to that effect, and

(b) may make an award of compensation to be paid by the employer to the employee.

(4) The amount of compensation shall be such as the tribunal considers just and equitable in all the circumstances having regard to –

(a) the employer's behaviour, and

(b) any loss sustained by the employee which is attributable to the matters complained of.

CHAPTER 3

PATERNITY LEAVE

80A   Entitlement to paternity leave: birth

(1) The Secretary of State shall make regulations entitling an employee who satisfies specified conditions –

(a) as to duration of employment,

(b) as to relationship with a newborn, or expected, child, and

(c) as to relationship with the child's mother,

to be absent from work on leave under this section for the purpose of caring for the child or supporting the mother.

(2) The regulations shall include provision for determining –

(a) the extent of an employee's entitlement to leave under this section in respect of a child;

(b) when leave under this section may be taken.

(3) Provision under subsection (2)(a) shall secure that where an employee is entitled to leave under this section in respect of a child he is entitled to at least two weeks' leave.

(4) Provision under subsection (2)(b) shall secure that leave under this section must be taken before the end of a period of at least 56 days beginning with the date of the child's birth.

(5) Regulations under subsection (1) may –

(a) specify things which are, or are not, to be taken as done for the purpose of caring for a child or supporting the child's mother;

(b) make provision excluding the right to be absent on leave under this section in respect of a child where more than one child is born as a result of the same pregnancy;

(c) make provision about how leave under this section may be taken.

(6) Where more than one child is born as a result of the same pregnancy, the reference in subsection (4) to the date of the child's birth shall be read as a reference to the date of birth of the first child born as a result of the pregnancy.

(7) In this section –

'newborn child' includes a child stillborn after twenty-four weeks of pregnancy;

'week' means any period of seven days.

80B Entitlement to paternity leave: adoption

(1) The Secretary of State shall make regulations entitling an employee who satisfies specified conditions –

(a) as to duration of employment,

(b) as to relationship with a child placed, or expected to be placed, for adoption under the law of any part of the United Kingdom, and

(c) as to relationship with a person with whom the child is, or is expected to be, so placed for adoption,

to be absent from work on leave under this section for the purpose of caring for the child or supporting the person by reference to whom he satisfies the condition under paragraph (c).

(2) The regulations shall include provision for determining –

(a) the extent of an employee's entitlement to leave under this section in respect of a child;

(b) when leave under this section may be taken.

(3) Provision under subsection (2)(a) shall secure that where an employee is entitled to leave under this section in respect of a child he is entitled to at least two weeks' leave.

(4) Provision under subsection (2)(b) shall secure that leave under this section must be taken before the end of a period of at least 56 days beginning with the date of the child's placement for adoption.

(6) Where more than one child is placed for adoption as part of the same arrangement, the reference in subsection (4) to the date of the child's placement shall be read as a reference to the date of placement of the first child to be placed as part of the arrangement.

(7) In this section, 'week' means any period of seven days.

(8) The Secretary of State may by regulations provide for this section to have effect in relation to cases which involve adoption, but not the placement of a child for adoption under the law of any part of the United Kingdom, with such modifications as the regulations may prescribe.

80C Rights during and after paternity leave

(1) Regulations under section 80A shall provide –

(a) that an employee who is absent on leave under that section is entitled, for such purposes and to such extent as the regulations may prescribe, to the benefit of the terms and conditions of employment which would have applied if he had not been absent;

(b) that an employee who is absent on leave under that section is bound, for such purposes and to such extent as the regulations may prescribe, by obligations arising under those terms and conditions (except in so far as they are inconsistent with subsection (1) of that section), and

(c) that an employee who is absent on leave under that section is entitled to return from leave to a job of a kind prescribed by regulations, subject to section 80D(1).

(2) The reference in subsection (1)(c) to absence on leave under section 80A includes, where appropriate, a reference to a continuous period of absence attributable partly to leave under that section and partly to any one or more of the following –

(a) maternity leave,

(b) adoption leave, and

(c) parental leave.

(3) Subsection (1) shall apply to regulations under section 80B as it applies to regulations under section 80A.

(4) In the application of subsection (1)(c) to regulations under section 80B, the reference to absence on leave under that section includes, where appropriate, a reference to a continuous period of absence attributable partly to leave under that section and partly to any one or more of the following –

(a) maternity leave,

(b) adoption leave,

(c) parental leave, and

(d) leave under section 80A.

(5) In subsection (1)(a), 'terms and conditions of employment' –

(a) includes matters connected with an employee's employment whether or not they arise under his contract of employment, but

(b) does not include terms and conditions about remuneration.

(6) Regulations under section 80A or 80B may specify matters which are, or are not, to be treated as remuneration for the purposes of this section.

(7) Regulations under section 80A or 80B may make provision, in relation to the right to return mentioned in subsection (1)(c), about –

(a) seniority, pension rights and similar rights;

(b) terms and conditions of employment on return.

80D   Special cases

(1) Regulations under section 80A or 80B may make provision about –

(a) redundancy, or

(b) dismissal (other than by reason of redundancy),

during a period of leave under that section. ...

PART 8A

FLEXIBLE WORKING

80F   Statutory right to request contract variation

(1) A qualifying employee may apply to his employer for a change in his terms and conditions of employment if –

(a) the change relates to –

(i) the hours he is required to work,

(ii) the times when he is required to work,

(iii) where, as between his home and a place of business of his employer, he is required to work, or

(iv) such other aspect of his terms and conditions of employment as the Secretary of State may specify by regulations, and

(b) his purpose in applying for the change is to enable him to care for someone who, at the time of application, is a child in respect of whom he satisfies such conditions as to relationship as the Secretary of State may specify by regulations.

(2) An application under this section must –

(a) state that it is such an application,

(b) specify the change applied for and the date on which it is proposed the change should become effective,

(c) explain what effect, if any, the employee thinks making the change applied for would have on his employer and how, in his opinion, any such effect might be dealt with, and

(d) explain how the employee meets, in respect of the child concerned, the conditions as to relationship mentioned in subsection (1)(b).

(3) An application under this section must be made before the fourteenth day before the day on which the child concerned reaches the age of six or, if disabled, eighteen.

(4) If an employee has made an application under this section, he may not make a further application under this section to the same employer before the end of the period of twelve months beginning with the date on which the previous application was made.

(5) The Secretary of State may by regulations make provision about –

(a) the form of applications under this section, and

(b) when such an application is to be taken as made.

(6) The Secretary of State may by order substitute a different age for the first of the ages specified in subsection (3).

(7) In subsection (3), the reference to a disabled child is to a child who is entitled to a disability living allowance within the meaning of section 71 of the Social Security Contributions and Benefits Act 1992 (c 4).

(8) For the purposes of this section, an employee is –

(a) a qualifying employee if he –

(i) satisfies such conditions as to duration of employment as the Secretary of State may specify by regulations, and

(ii) is not an agency worker;

(b) an agency worker if he is supplied by a person ('the agent') to do work for another ('the principal') under a contract or other arrangement made between the agent and the principal.

80G Employer's duties in relation to application under section 80F

(1) An employer to whom an application under section 80F is made –

(a) shall deal with the application in accordance with regulations made by the Secretary of State, and

(b) shall only refuse the application because he considers that one or more of the following grounds applies –

(i) the burden of additional costs,

(ii) detrimental effect on ability to meet customer demand,

(iii) inability to re-organise work among existing staff,

(iv) inability to recruit additional staff,

(v) detrimental impact on quality,

(vi) detrimental impact on performance,

(vii) insufficiency of work during the periods the employee proposes to work,

(viii) planned structural changes, and

(ix) such other grounds as the Secretary of State may specify by regulations.
...

80H Complaints to employment tribunals

(1) An employee who makes an application under section 80F may present a complaint to an employment tribunal –

(a) that his employer has failed in relation to the application to comply with section 80G(1), or

(b) that a decision by his employer to reject the application was based on incorrect facts.

(2) No complaint under this section may be made in respect of an application which has been disposed of by agreement or withdrawn.

(3) In the case of an application which has not been disposed of by agreement or withdrawn, no complaint under this section may be made until the employer –

(a) notifies the employee of a decision to reject the application on appeal, or

(b) commits a breach of regulations under section 80G(1)(a) of such description as the Secretary of State may specify by regulations.

(4) No complaint under this section may be made in respect of failure to comply with provision included in regulations under subsection (1)(a) of section 80G because of subsection (2)(k), (l) or (m) of that section.

(5) An employment tribunal shall not consider a complaint under this section unless it is presented –

(a) before the end of the period of three months beginning with the relevant date, or

(b) within such further period as the tribunal considers reasonable in a case where it is satisfied that it was not reasonably practicable for the complaint to be presented before the end of that period of three months.

(6) In subsection (5)(a), the reference to the relevant date is –

(a) in the case of a complaint permitted by subsection (3)(a), the date on which the employee is notified of the decision on the appeal, and

(b) in the case of a complaint permitted by subsection (3)(b), the date on which the breach concerned was committed.

80I Remedies

(1) Where an employment tribunal finds a complaint under section 80H well-founded it shall make a declaration to that effect and may –

(a) make an order for reconsideration of the application, and

(b) make an award of compensation to be paid by the employer to the employee.

(2) The amount of compensation shall be such amount, not exceeding the permitted maximum, as the tribunal considers just and equitable in all the circumstances.

(3) For the purposes of subsection (2), the permitted maximum is such number of weeks' pay as the Secretary of State may specify by regulations.

(4) Where an employment tribunal makes an order under subsection (1)(a), section 80G, and the regulations under that section, shall apply as if the application had been made on the date of the order.

PART IX

TERMINATION OF EMPLOYMENT

86   Rights of employer and employee to minimum notice

(1) The notice required to be given by an employer to terminate the contract of employment of a person who has been continuously employed for one month or more –

(a) is not less than one week's notice if his period of continuous employment is less than two years,

(b) is not less than one week's notice for each year of continuous employment if his period of continuous employment is two years or more but less than twelve years, and

(c) is not less than twelve weeks' notice if his period of continuous employment is twelve years or more.

(2) The notice required to be given by an employee who has been continuously employed for one month or more to terminate his contract of employment is not less than one week.

(3) Any provision for shorter notice in any contract of employment with a person who has been continuously employed for one month or more has effect subject to subsections (1) and (2); but this section does not prevent either party from waiving his right to notice on any occasion or from accepting a payment in lieu of notice.

(4) Any contract of employment of a person who has been continuously employed for three months or more which is a contract for a term certain of one month or less shall have effect as if it were for an indefinite period; and, accordingly, subsections (1) and (2) apply to the contract.

(6) This section does not affect any right of either party to a contract of employment to treat the contract as terminable without notice by reason of the conduct of the other party.

87   Rights of employee in period of notice

(1) If an employer gives notice to terminate the contract of employment of a person who has been continuously employed for one month or more, the provisions of sections 88 to 91 have effect as respects the liability of the employer for the period of notice required by section 86(1).

(2) If an employee who has been continuously employed for one month or more gives notice to terminate his contract of employment, the provisions of sections 88 to 91 have effect as respects the liability of the employer for the period of notice required by section 86(2).

(3) In sections 88 to 91 'period of notice' means –

(a) where notice is given by an employer, the period of notice required by section 86(1), and

(b) where notice is given by an employee, the period of notice required by section 86(2).

(4) This section does not apply in relation to a notice given by the employer or the employee if the notice to be given by the employer to terminate the contract must be at least one week more than the notice required by section 86(1).

88 Employments with normal working hours

(1) If an employee has normal working hours under the contract of employment in force during the period of notice and during any part of those normal working hours –

(a) the employee is ready and willing to work but no work is provided for him by his employer,

(b) the employee is incapable of work because of sickness or injury,

(c) the employee is absent from work wholly or partly because of pregnancy or childbirth or on adoption leave, parental leave or paternity leave, or

(d) the employee is absent from work in accordance with the terms of his employment relating to holidays,

the employer is liable to pay the employee for the part of normal working hours covered by any of paragraphs (a), (b), (c) and (d) a sum not less than the amount of remuneration for that part of normal working hours calculated at the average hourly rate of remuneration produced by dividing a week's pay by the number of normal working hours.

(2) Any payments made to the employee by his employer in respect of the relevant part of the period of notice (whether by way of sick pay, statutory sick pay, maternity pay, statutory maternity pay, paternity pay, statutory paternity pay, adoption pay, statutory adoption pay, holiday pay or otherwise) go towards meeting the employer's liability under this section.

(3) Where notice was given by the employee, the employer's liability under this section does not arise unless and until the employee leaves the service of the employer in pursuance of the notice.

89 Employments without normal working hours

(1) If an employee does not have normal working hours under the contract of employment in force in the period of notice, the employer is liable to pay the employee for each week of the period of notice a sum not less than a week's pay.

(2) The employer's liability under this section is conditional on the employee being ready and willing to do work of a reasonable nature and amount to earn a week's pay.

(3) Subsection (2) does not apply –

(a) in respect of any period during which the employee is incapable of work because of sickness or injury,

(b) in respect of any period during which the employee is absent from work wholly or partly because of pregnancy or childbirth or on adoption leave, parental leave or paternity leave, or

(c) in respect of any period during which the employee is absent from work in accordance with the terms of his employment relating to holidays.

(4) Any payment made to an employee by his employer in respect of a period within subsection (3) (whether by way of sick pay, statutory sick pay, maternity pay, statutory maternity pay, paternity pay, statutory paternity pay, adoption pay, statutory adoption pay, holiday pay or otherwise) shall be taken into account for the purposes of this section as if it were remuneration paid by the employer in respect of that period.

(5) Where notice was given by the employee, the employer's liability under this section does not arise unless and until the employee leaves the service of the employer in pursuance of the notice.

90   Short-term incapacity benefit and industrial injury benefit

(1) This section has effect where the arrangements in force relating to the employment are such that –

(a) payments by way of sick pay are made by the employer to employees to whom the arrangements apply, in cases where any such employees are incapable of work because of sickness or injury, and

(b) in calculating any payment so made to any such employee an amount representing, or treated as representing, short-term incapacity benefit or industrial injury benefit is taken into account, whether by way of deduction or by way of calculating the payment as a supplement to that amount.

(2) If –

(a) during any part of the period of notice the employee is incapable of work because of sickness or injury,

(b) one or more payments by way of sick pay are made to him by the employer in respect of that part of the period of notice, and

(c) in calculating any such payment such an amount as is referred to in paragraph (b) of subsection (1) is taken into account as mentioned in that paragraph,

for the purposes of section 88 or 89 the amount so taken into account shall be treated as having been paid by the employer to the employee by way of sick pay in respect of that part of that period, and shall go towards meeting the liability of the employer under that section accordingly.

91   Supplementary

(1) An employer is not liable under section 88 or 89 to make any payment in respect of a period during which an employee is absent from work with the leave of the

employer granted at the request of the employee, including any period of time off taken in accordance with –

(a) Part VI of this Act, or

(b) section 168 or 170 of the Trade Union and Labour Relations (Consolidation) Act 1992 (trade union duties and activities).

(2) No payment is due under section 88 or 89 in consequence of a notice to terminate a contract given by an employee if, after the notice is given and on or before the termination of the contract, the employee takes part in a strike of employees of the employer.

(3) If, during the period of notice, the employer breaks the contract of employment, payments received under section 88 or 89 in respect of the part of the period after the breach go towards mitigating the damages recoverable by the employee for loss of earnings in that part of the period of notice.

(4) If, during the period of notice, the employee breaks the contract and the employer rightfully treats the breach as terminating the contract, no payment is due to the employee under section 88 or 89 in respect of the part of the period falling after the termination of the contract.

(5) If an employer fails to give the notice required by section 86, the rights conferred by sections 87 to 90 and this section shall be taken into account in assessing his liability for breach of the contract.

(6) Sections 86 to 90 and this section apply in relation to a contract all or any of the terms of which are terms which take effect by virtue of any provision contained in or having effect under an Act (whether public or local) as in relation to any other contract; and the reference in this subsection to an Act includes, subject to any express provision to the contrary, an Act passed after this Act.

92   Right to written statement of reasons for dismissal

(1) An employee is entitled to be provided by his employer with a written statement giving particulars of the reasons for the employee's dismissal –

(a) if the employee is given by the employer notice of termination of his contract of employment,

(b) if the employee's contract of employment is terminated by the employer without notice, or

(c) if the employee is employed under a limited-term contract and the contract terminates by virtue of the limiting event without being renewed under the same contract.

(2) Subject to subsections (4) and (4A), an employee is entitled to a written statement under this section only if he makes a request for one; and a statement shall be provided within fourteen days of such a request.

(3) Subject to subsections (4) and (4A), an employee is not entitled to a written statement under this section unless on the effective date of termination he has

been, or will have been, continuously employed for a period of not less than one year ending with that date.

(4) An employee is entitled to a written statement under this section without having to request it and irrespective of whether she has been continuously employed for any period if she is dismissed –

(a) at any time while she is pregnant, or

(b) after childbirth in circumstances in which her ordinary or additional maternity leave period ends by reason of the dismissal.

(4A) An employee who is dismissed while absent from work during an ordinary or additional adoption leave period is entitled to a written statement under this section without having to request it and irrespective of whether he has been continuously employed for any period if he is dismissed in circumstances in which that period ends by reason of the dismissal.

(5) A written statement under this section is admissible in evidence in any proceedings.

(6) Subject to subsection (7), in this section 'the effective date of termination' –

(a) in relation to an employee whose contract of employment is terminated by notice, means the date on which the notice expires,

(b) in relation to an employee whose contract of employment is terminated without notice, means the date on which the termination takes effect, and

(c) in relation to an employee who is employed under a limited-term contract which terminates by virtue of the limiting event without being renewed under the same contract, means the date on which the termination takes effect.

(7) Where –

(a) the contract of employment is terminated by the employer, and

(b) the notice required by section 86 to be given by an employer would, if duly given on the material date, expire on a date later than the effective date of termination (as defined by subsection (6)),

the later date is the effective date of termination.

(8) In subsection (7)(b) 'the material date' means –

(a) the date when notice of termination was given by the employer, or

(b) where no notice was given, the date when the contract of employment was terminated by the employer.

93   Complaints to employment tribunal

(1) A complaint may be presented to an employment tribunal by an employee on the ground that –

(a) the employer unreasonably failed to provide a written statement under section 92, or

(b) the particulars of reasons given in purported compliance with that section are inadequate or untrue.

(2) Where an employment tribunal finds a complaint under this section well-founded, the tribunal –

(a) may make a declaration as to what it finds the employer's reasons were for dismissing the employee, and

(b) shall make an award that the employer pay to the employee a sum equal to the amount of two weeks' pay.

(3) An employment tribunal shall not consider a complaint under this section relating to the reasons for a dismissal unless it is presented to the tribunal at such a time that the tribunal would, in accordance with section 111, consider a complaint of unfair dismissal in respect of that dismissal presented at the same time.

PART X

UNFAIR DISMISSAL

CHAPTER I

RIGHT NOT TO BE UNFAIRLY DISMISSED

94   The right

(1) An employee has the right not to be unfairly dismissed by his employer.

(2) Subsection (1) has effect subject to the following provisions of this Part (in particular sections 108 to 110) and to the provisions of the Trade Union and Labour Relations (Consolidation) Act 1992 (in particular sections 237 to 239).

95   Circumstances in which an employee is dismissed

(1) For the purposes of this Part an employee is dismissed by his employer if (and, subject to subsection (2), only if) –

(a) the contract under which he is employed is terminated by the employer (whether with or without notice),

(b) he is employed under a limited-term contract and that contract terminates by virtue of the limiting event without being renewed under the same contract, or

(c) the employee terminates the contract under which he is employed (with or without notice) in circumstances in which he is entitled to terminate it without notice by reason of the employer's conduct.

(2) An employee shall be taken to be dismissed by his employer for the purposes of this Part if –

(a) the employer gives notice to the employee to terminate his contract of employment, and

(b) at a time within the period of that notice the employee gives notice to the employer to terminate the contract of employment on a date earlier than the date on which the employer's notice is due to expire;

and the reason for the dismissal is to be taken to be the reason for which the employer's notice is given.

97 Effective date of termination

(1) Subject to the following provisions of this section, in this Part 'the effective date of termination' –

(a) in relation to an employee whose contract of employment is terminated by notice, whether given by his employer or by the employee, means the date on which the notice expires,

(b) in relation to an employee whose contract of employment is terminated without notice, means the date on which the termination takes effect, and

(c) in relation to an employee who is employed under a limited-term contract which terminates by virtue of the limiting event without being renewed under the same contract, means the date on which the termination takes effect.

(2) Where –

(a) the contract of employment is terminated by the employer, and

(b) the notice required by section 86 to be given by an employer would, if duly given on the material date, expire on a date later than the effective date of termination (as defined by subsection (1)),

for the purposes of sections 108(1), 119(1) and 227(3) the later date is the effective date of termination.

(3) In subsection (2)(b) 'the material date' means –

(a) the date when notice of termination was given by the employer, or

(b) where no notice was given, the date when the contract of employment was terminated by the employer.

(4) Where –

(a) the contract of employment is terminated by the employee,

(b) the material date does not fall during a period of notice given by the employer to terminate that contract, and

(c) had the contract been terminated not by the employee but by notice given on the material date by the employer, that notice would have been required by section 86 to expire on a date later than the effective date of termination (as defined by subsection (1)),

for the purposes of sections 108(1), 119(1) and 227(3) the later date is the effective date of termination.

(5) In subsection (4) 'the material date' means –

(a) the date when notice of termination was given by the employee, or

(b) where no notice was given, the date when the contract of employment was terminated by the employee.

98 General

(1) In determining for the purposes of this Part whether the dismissal of an employee is fair or unfair, it is for the employer to show –

(a) the reason (or, if more than one, the principal reason) for the dismissal, and

(b) that it is either a reason falling within subsection (2) or some other substantial reason of a kind such as to justify the dismissal of an employee holding the position which the employee held.

(2) A reason falls within this subsection if it –

(a) relates to the capability or qualifications of the employee for performing work of the kind which he was employed by the employer to do,

(b) relates to the conduct of the employee,

(c) is that the employee was redundant, or

(d) is that the employee could not continue to work in the position which he held without contravention (either on his part or on that of his employer) of a duty or restriction imposed by or under an enactment.

(3) In subsection (2)(a) –

(a) 'capability', in relation to an employee, means his capability assessed by reference to skill, aptitude, health or any other physical or mental quality, and

(b) 'qualifications', in relation to an employee, means any degree, diploma or other academic, technical or professional qualification relevant to the position which he held.

(4) Where the employer has fulfilled the requirements of subsection (1), the determination of the question whether the dismissal is fair or unfair (having regard to the reason shown by the employer) –

(a) depends on whether in the circumstances (including the size and administrative resources of the employer's undertaking) the employer acted reasonably or unreasonably in treating it as a sufficient reason for dismissing the employee, and

(b) shall be determined in accordance with equity and the substantial merits of the case.

(6) Subsection (4) is subject to –

(a) sections 98A to 107 of this Act, and

(b) sections 152, 153, 238 and 238A of the Trade Union and Labour Relations (Consolidation) Act 1992 (dismissal on ground of trade union membership or activities or in connection with industrial action).

98A Procedural fairness

(1) An employee who is dismissed shall be regarded for the purposes of this Part as unfairly dismissed if –

(a) one of the procedures set out in Part 1 of Schedule 2 to the Employment Act 2002 (dismissal and disciplinary procedures) applies in relation to the dismissal,

(b) the procedure has not been completed, and

(c) the non-completion of the procedure is wholly or mainly attributable to failure by the employer to comply with its requirements.

(2) Subject to subsection (1), failure by an employer to follow a procedure in relation to the dismissal of an employee shall not be regarded for the purposes of section 98(4)(a) as by itself making the employer's action unreasonable if he shows that he would have decided to dismiss the employee if he had followed the procedure.

(3) For the purposes of this section, any question as to the application of a procedure set out in Part 1 of Schedule 2 to the Employment Act 2002, completion of such a procedure or failure to comply with the requirements of such a procedure shall be determined by reference to regulations under section 31 of that Act.

98B Jury service

(1) An employee who is dismissed shall be regarded for the purposes of this Part as unfairly dismissed if the reason (or, if more than one, the principal reason) for the dismissal is that the employee –

(a) has been summoned under the Juries Act 1974, the Coroners Act 1988 ... to attend for service as a juror, or

(b) has been absent from work because he attended at any place in pursuance of being so summoned.

(2) Subsection (1) does not apply in relation to an employee who is dismissed if the employer shows –

(a) that the circumstances were such that the employee's absence in pursuance of being so summoned was likely to cause substantial injury to the employer's undertaking,

(b) that the employer brought those circumstances to the attention of the employee,

(c) that the employee refused or failed to apply to the appropriate officer for excusal from or a deferral of the obligation to attend in pursuance of being so summoned, and

(d) that the refusal or failure was not reasonable.

(3) In paragraph (c) of subsection (2) 'the appropriate officer' means –

(a) in the case of a person who has been summoned under the Juries Act 1974, the officer designated for the purposes of section 8, 9 or, as the case may be, 9A of that Act;

(b) in the case of a person who has been summoned under the Coroners Act 1988, a person who is the appropriate officer for the purposes of any rules made under subsection (1) of section 32 of that Act by virtue of subsection (2) of that section; ...

99   Leave for family reasons

(1) An employee who is dismissed shall be regarded for the purposes of this Part as unfairly dismissed if –

(a) the reason or principal reason for the dismissal is of a prescribed kind, or

(b) the dismissal takes place in prescribed circumstances.

(2) In this section 'prescribed' means prescribed by regulations made by the Secretary of State.

(3) A reason or set of circumstances prescribed under this section must relate to –

(a) pregnancy, childbirth or maternity,

(b) ordinary, compulsory or additional maternity leave,

(ba) ordinary or additional adoption leave,

(c) parental leave,

(ca) paternity leave, or

(d) time off under section 57A;

and it may also relate to redundancy or other factors.

(4) A reason or set of circumstances prescribed under subsection (1) satisfies subsection (3)(c) or (d) if it relates to action which an employee –

(a) takes,

(b) agrees to take, or

(c) refuses to take,

under or in respect of a collective or workforce agreement which deals with parental leave.

(5) Regulations under this section may –

(a) make different provision for different cases or circumstances,

(b) apply any enactment, in such circumstances as may be specified and subject to any conditions specified, in relation to persons regarded as unfairly dismissed by reason of this section.

100   Health and safety cases

(1) An employee who is dismissed shall be regarded for the purposes of this Part as unfairly dismissed if the reason (or, if more than one, the principal reason) for the dismissal is that –

(a) having been designated by the employer to carry out activities in connection

—— 402 ——

with preventing or reducing risks to health and safety at work, the employee carried out (or proposed to carry out) any such activities,

(b) being a representative of workers on matters of health and safety at work or member of a safety committee –

(i) in accordance with arrangements established under or by virtue of any enactment, or

(ii) by reason of being acknowledged as such by the employer,

the employee performed (or proposed to perform) any functions as such a representative or a member of such a committee,

(ba) the employee took part (or proposed to take part) in consultation with the employer pursuant to the Health and Safety (Consultation with Employees) Regulations 1996 or in an election of representatives of employee safety within the meaning of those Regulations (whether as a candidate or otherwise),

(c) being an employee at a place where –

(i) there was no such representative or safety committee, or

(ii) there was such a representative or safety committee but it was not reasonably practicable for the employee to raise the matter by those means,

he brought to his employer's attention, by reasonable means, circumstances connected with his work which he reasonably believed were harmful or potentially harmful to health or safety,

(d) in circumstances of danger which the employee reasonably believed to be serious and imminent and which he could not reasonably have been expected to avert, he left (or proposed to leave) or (while the danger persisted) refused to return to his place of work or any dangerous part of his place of work, or

(e) in circumstances of danger which the employee reasonably believed to be serious and imminent, he took (or proposed to take) appropriate steps to protect himself or other persons from the danger.

(2) For the purposes of subsection (1)(e) whether steps which an employee took (or proposed to take) were appropriate is to be judged by reference to all the circumstances including, in particular, his knowledge and the facilities and advice available to him at the time.

(3) Where the reason (or, if more than one, the principal reason) for the dismissal of an employee is that specified in subsection (1)(e), he shall not be regarded as unfairly dismissed if the employer shows that it was (or would have been) so negligent for the employee to take the steps which he took (or proposed to take) that a reasonable employer might have dismissed him for taking (or proposing to take) them.

101 Shop workers and betting workers who refuse Sunday work

(1) Where an employee who is –

(a) a protected shop worker or an opted-out shop worker, or

(b) a protected betting worker or an opted-out betting worker,

is dismissed, he shall be regarded for the purposes of this Part as unfairly dismissed if the reason (or, if more than one, the principal reason) for the dismissal is that he refused (or proposed to refuse) to do shop work, or betting work, on Sunday or on a particular Sunday.

(2) Subsection (1) does not apply in relation to an opted-out shop worker or an opted-out betting worker where the reason (or principal reason) for the dismissal is that he refused (or proposed to refuse) to do shop work, or betting work, on any Sunday or Sundays falling before the end of the notice period.

(3) A shop worker or betting worker who is dismissed shall be regarded for the purposes of this Part as unfairly dismissed if the reason (or, if more than one, the principal reason) for the dismissal is that the shop worker or betting worker gave (or proposed to give) an opting-out notice to the employer.

(4) For the purposes of section 36(2)(b) or 41(1)(b), the appropriate date in relation to this section is the effective date of termination.

101A Working time cases

(1) An employee who is dismissed shall be regarded for the purposes of this Part as unfairly dismissed if the reason (or, if more than one, the principal reason) for the dismissal is that the employee –

(a) refused (or proposed to refuse) to comply with a requirement which the employer imposed (or proposed to impose) in contravention of the Working Time Regulations 1998,

(b) refused (or proposed to refuse) to forgo a right conferred on him by those Regulations,

(c) failed to sign a workforce agreement for the purposes of those Regulations, or to enter into, or agree to vary or extend, any other agreement with his employer which is provided for in those Regulations, or

(d) being –

(i) a representative of members of the workforce for the purposes of Schedule 1 to those Regulations, or

(ii) a candidate in an election in which any person elected will, on being elected, be such a representative,

performed (or proposed to perform) any functions or activities as such a representative or candidate. ...

102 Trustees of occupational pension schemes

(1) An employee who is dismissed shall be regarded for the purposes of this Part as unfairly dismissed if the reason (or, if more than one, the principal reason) for the dismissal is that, being a trustee of a relevant occupational pension scheme

which relates to his employment, the employee performed (or proposed to perform) any functions as such a trustee.

(1A) This section applies to an employee who is a director of a company which is a trustee of a relevant occupational pension scheme as it applies to an employee who is a trustee of such a scheme (references to such a trustee being read for this purpose as references to such a director).

(2) In this section 'relevant occupational pension scheme' means an occupational pension scheme (as defined in section 1 of the Pension Schemes Act 1993) established under a trust.

103   Employee representatives

(1) An employee who is dismissed shall be regarded for the purposes of this Part as unfairly dismissed if the reason (or, if more than one, the principal reason) for the dismissal is that the employee, being –

   (a) an employee representative for the purposes of Chapter II of Part IV of the Trade Union and Labour Relations (Consolidation) Act 1992 (redundancies) or Regulations 10 and 11 of the Transfer of Undertakings (Protection of Employment) Regulations 1981, or

   (b) a candidate in an election in which any person elected will, on being elected, be such an employee representative,

performed (or proposed to perform) any functions or activities as such an employee representative or candidate.

(2) An employee who is dismissed shall be regarded for the purposes of this Part as unfairly dismissed if the reason (or, if more than one, the principal reason) for the dismissal is that the employee took part in an election of employee representatives for the purposes of Chapter II of Part IV of the Trade Union and Labour Relations (Consolidation) Act 1992 (redundancies) or Regulations 10 and 11 of the Transfer of Undertakings (Protection of Employment) Regulations 1981.

103A   Protected disclosure

An employee who is dismissed shall be regarded for the purposes of this Part as unfairly dismissed if the reason (or, if more than one, the principal reason) for the dismissal is that the employee made a protected disclosure.

104   Assertion of statutory right

(1) An employee who is dismissed shall be regarded for the purposes of this Part as unfairly dismissed if the reason (or, if more than one, the principal reason) for the dismissal is that the employee –

   (a) brought proceedings against the employer to enforce a right of his which is a relevant statutory right, or

   (b) alleged that the employer had infringed a right of his which is a relevant statutory right.

(2) It is immaterial for the purposes of subsection (1) –

(a) whether or not the employee has the right, or

(b) whether or not the right has been infringed;

but, for that subsection to apply, the claim to the right and that it has been infringed must be made in good faith.

(3) It is sufficient for subsection (1) to apply that the employee, without specifying the right, made it reasonably clear to the employer what the right claimed to have been infringed was.

(4) The following are relevant statutory rights for the purposes of this section –

(a) any right conferred by this Act for which the remedy for its infringement is by way of a complaint or reference to an employment tribunal,

(b) the right conferred by section 86 of this Act,

(c) the rights conferred by sections 68, 86, 145A, 145B, 146, 168, 168A, 169 and 170 of the Trade Union and Labour Relations (Consolidation) Act 1992 (deductions from pay, union activities and time off), and

(d) the rights conferred by the Working Time Regulations 1998 ...

(5) In this section any reference to an employer includes, where the right in question is conferred by section 63A, the principal (within the meaning of section 63A(3)).

104A   The national minimum wage

(1) An employee who is dismissed shall be regarded for the purposes of this Part as unfairly dismissed if the reason (or, if more than one, the principal reason) for this dismissal is that –

(a) any action was taken, or was proposed to be taken, by or on behalf of the employee with a view to enforcing, or otherwise securing the benefit of, a right of the employee's to which this section applies; or

(b) the employer was prosecuted for an offence under section 31 of the National Minimum Wage Act 1998 as a result of action taken by or on behalf of the employee for the purpose of enforcing, or otherwise securing the benefit of, a right of the employee's to which this section applies; or

(c) the employee qualifies, or will or might qualify, for the national minimum wage or for a particular rate of national minimum wage.

(2) It is immaterial for the purposes of paragraph (a) or (b) of subsection (1) above –

(a) whether or not the employee has the right, or

(b) whether or not the right has been infringed,

but, for that subsection to apply, the claim to the right and, if applicable, the claim that it has been infringed must be made in good faith.

(3) The following are the rights to which this section applies –

(a) any right conferred by, or by virtue of, any provision of the National Minimum Wage Act 1998 for which the remedy for its infringement is by way of a complaint to an employment tribunal; and

(b) any right conferred by section 17 of the National Minimum Wage Act 1998 (worker receiving less than national minimum wage entitled to additional remuneration).

104B Tax credit

(1) An employee who is dismissed shall be regarded for the purposes of this Part as unfairly dismissed if the reason (or, if more than one, the principal reason) for the dismissal is that –

(a) any action was taken, or was proposed to be taken, by or on behalf of the employee with a view to enforcing, or otherwise securing the benefit of, a right conferred on the employee by regulations under section 6(2)(a) or (c) of the Tax Credits Act 1999;

(b) a penalty was imposed on the employer, or proceedings for a penalty were brought against him, under section 9 of that Act, as a result of action taken by or on behalf of the employee for the purpose of enforcing, or otherwise securing the benefit of, such a right; or

(c) the employee is entitled, or will or may be entitled, to working families' tax credit or disabled person's tax credit.

(2) It is immaterial for the purposes of paragraph (a) or (b) of subsection (1) above –

(a) whether or not the employee has the right, or

(b) whether or not the right has been infringed,

but, for that subsection to apply, the claim to the right and, if applicable, the claim that it has been infringed must be made in good faith.

104C Flexible working

An employee who is dismissed shall be regarded for the purposes of this Part as unfairly dismissed if the reason (or, if more than one, the principal reason) for the dismissal is that the employee –

(a) made (or proposed to make) an application under section 80F,

(b) exercised (or proposed to exercise) a right conferred on him under section 80G,

(c) brought proceedings against the employer under section 80H, or

(d) alleged the existence of any circumstance which would constitute a ground for bringing such proceedings.

105 Redundancy

(1) An employee who is dismissed shall be regarded for the purposes of this Part as unfairly dismissed if –

(a) the reason (or, if more than one, the principal reason) for the dismissal is that the employee was redundant,

(b) it is shown that the circumstances constituting the redundancy applied equally to one or more other employees in the same undertaking who held positions similar to that held by the employee and who have not been dismissed by the employer, and

(c) it is shown that any of subsections (2A) to (7F). (7G) or (7H) applies.

(2A) This subsection applies if the reason (or, if more than one, the principal reason) for which the employee was selected for dismisal was one of those specified in subsection (1) of section 98B (unless the case is one to which subsection (2) of that section applies).

(3) This subsection applies if the reason (or, if more than one, the principal reason) for which the employee was selected for dismissal was one of those specified in subsection (1) of section 100 (read with subsections (2) and (3) of that section).

(4) This subsection applies if either –

(a) the employee was a protected shop worker or an opted-out shop worker, or a protected betting worker or an opted-out betting worker, and the reason (or, if more than one, the principal reason) for which the employee was selected for dismissal was that specified in subsection (1) of section 101 (read with subsection (2) of that section), or

(b) the employee was a shop worker or a betting worker and the reason (or, if more than one, the principal reason) for which the employee was selected for dismissal was that specified in subsection (3) of that section.

(4A) This subsection applies if the reason (of, if more than one, the principal reason) for which the employee was selected for dismissal was one of those specified in section 101A.

(5) This subsection applies if the reason (or, if more than one, the principal reason) for which the employee was selected for dismissal was that specified in section 102(1).

(6) This subsection applies if the reason (or, if more than one, the principal reason) for which the employee was selected for dismissal was that specified in section 103.

(6A) This subsection applies if the reason (or, if more than one, the principal reason) for which the employee was selected for dismissal was that specified in section 103A.

(7) This subsection applies if the reason (or, if more than one, the principal reason) for which the employee was selected for dismissal was one of those specified in subsection (1) of section 104 (read with subsections (2) and (3) of that section).

(7A) This subsection applies if the reason (or, if more than one, the principal reason) for which the employee was selected for dismissal was one of those specified in subsection (1) of section 104A (read with subsection (2) of that section).

(7B) This subsection applies if the reason (or, if more than one, the principal reason) for which the employee was selected for dismissal was one of those specified in subsection (1) of section 104B (read with subsection (2) of that section).

(7BA) This subsection applies if the reason (or, if more than one, the principal reason) for which the employee was selected for dismissal was one of those specified in section 104C.

(7C) This subsection applies if –

(a) the reason (or, if more than one, the principal reason) for which the employee was selected for dismissal was the reason mentioned in section 238A(2) of the Trade Union and Labour Relations (Consolidation) Act 1992 (participation in official industrial action), and

(b) subsection (3), (4) or (5) of that section applies to the dismissal.

(7D) This subsection applies if the reason (or, if more than one, the principal reason) for which the employee was selected for dismissal was one specified in paragraph (3) or (6) or regulation 28 of the Transnational Information and Consultation of Employees Regulations 1999 (read with paragraphs (4) and (7) of that regulation).

(7E) This subsection applies if the reason (or, if more than one, the principal reason) for which the employee was selected for dismissal was one specified in paragraph (3) of regulation 7 of the Part-time Workers (Prevention of Less Favourable Treatment) Regulations 2000 (unless the case is one to which paragraph (4) of that regulation applies).

(7F) This subsection applies if the reason (or, if more than one, the principal reason) for which the employee was selected for dismissal was one specified in paragraph (3) of regulation 6 of the Fixed-term Employees (Prevention of Less Favourable Treatment) Regulations 2002 (unless the case is one to which paragraph (4) of that regulation applies).

(7G) This subsection applies if the reason (or, if more than one, the principal reason) for which the employee was selected for dismissal was one specified in paragraph (3) or (6) of regulation 42 of the European Public Limited-Liability Company Regulations 2004 (read with paragraphs (4) and (7) of that regulation).

(7H) This subsection applies if the reason (or, if more than one, the principal reason) for which the employee was selected for dismissal was one specified in paragraph (3) or (6) of regulation 30 of the Information and Consultation of Employees Regulations 2004 (read with paragraphs (4) and (7) of that regulation).

(8) For the purposes of section 36(2)(b) or 41(1)(b), the appropriate date in relation to this section is the effective date of termination.

(9) In this Part 'redundancy case' means a case where paragraphs (a) and (b) of subsection (1) of this section are satisfied.

106 Replacements

(1) Where this section applies to an employee he shall be regarded for the purposes

of section 98(1)(b) as having been dismissed for a substantial reason of a kind such as to justify the dismissal of an employee holding the position which the employee held.

(2) This section applies to an employee where –

(a) on engaging him the employer informs him in writing that his employment will be terminated on the resumption of work by another employee who is, or will be, absent wholly or partly because of pregnancy or childbirth or on adoption leave, and

(b) the employer dismisses him in order to make it possible to give work to the other employee.

(3) This section also applies to an employee where –

(a) on engaging him the employer informs him in writing that his employment will be terminated on the end of a suspension of another employee from work on medical grounds or maternity grounds (within the meaning of Part VII), and

(b) the employer dismisses him in order to make it possible to allow the resumption of work by the other employee.

(4) Subsection (1) does not affect the operation of section 98(4) in a case to which this section applies.

107 Pressure on employer to dismiss unfairly

(1) This section applies where there falls to be determined for the purposes of this Part a question –

(a) as to the reason, or principal reason, for which an employee was dismissed,

(b) whether the reason or principal reason for which an employee was dismissed was a reason fulfilling the requirement of section 98(1)(b), or

(c) whether an employer acted reasonably in treating the reason or principal reason for which an employee was dismissed as a sufficient reason for dismissing him.

(2) In determining the question no account shall be taken of any pressure which by calling, organising, procuring or financing a strike or other industrial action, or threatening to do so, was exercised on the employer to dismiss the employee; and the question shall be determined as if no such pressure had been exercised.

108 Qualifying period of employment

(1) Section 94 does not apply to the dismissal of an employee unless he has been continuously employed for a period of not less than one year ending with the effective date of termination.

(2) If an employee is dismissed by reason of any such requirement or recommendation as is referred to in section 64(2), subsection (1) has effect in relation to that dismissal as if for the words 'one year' there were substituted the words 'one month'.

(3) Subsection (1) does not apply if –

(aa) subsection (1) of section 98B (read with subsection (2) of that section) applies,

(b) subsection (1) of section 99 (read with subsection (2) of that section) or subsection (3) of that section applies,

(c) subsection (1) of section 100 (read with subsections (2) and (3) of that section) applies,

(d) subsection (1) of section 101 (read with subsection (2) of that section) or subsection (3) of that section applies,

(dd) section 101A applies,

(e) section 102 applies,

(f) section 103 applies,

(ff) section 103A applies,

(g) subsection (1) of section 104 (read with subsections (2) and (3) of that section) applies,

(gg) subsection (1) of section 104A (read with subsection (2) of that section) applies,

(gh) subsection (1) of section 104B (read with subsection (2) of that section) applies,

(gi) section 104C applies,

(h) section 105 applies,

(hh) paragraph (3) or (6) of regulation 28 of the Transnational Information and Consultation of Employees Regulations 1999 (read with paragraphs (4) and (7) of that regulation) applies,

(i) paragraph (1) of regulation 7 of the Part-time Workers (Prevention of Less Favourable Treatment) Regulations 2000 applies,

(j) paragraph (1) of regulation 6 of the Fixed-term Employees (Prevention of Less Favourable Treatment) Regulations 2002 applies,

(k) paragraph (3) or (6) of regulation 42 of the European Public Limited-Liability Company Regulations 2004 applies, or

(l) paragraph (3) or (6) of regulation 30 of the Information and Consultation of Employees Regulations 2004 (read with paragraphs (4) and (7) of that regulation) applies.

109 Upper age limit

(1) Section 94 does not apply to the dismissal of an employee if on or before the effective date of termination he has attained –

(a) in a case where –

(i) in the undertaking in which the employee was employed there was a normal retiring age for an employee holding the position held by the employee, and

(ii) the age was the same whether the employee holding that position was a man or a woman,

that normal retiring age, and

(b) in any other case, the age of sixty-five.

(2) Subsection (1) does not apply if –

(aa) subsection (1) of section 96B (read with subsection (2) of that section) applies,

(b) subsection (1) of section 99 (read with subsection (2) of that section) or subsection (3) of that section applies,

(c) subsection (1) of section 100 (read with subsections (2) and (3) of that section) applies,

(d) subsection (1) of section 101 (read with subsection (2) of that section) or subsection (3) of that section applies,

(dd) section 101A applies,

(e) section 102 applies,

(f) section 103 applies,

(ff) section 103A applies,

(g) subsection (1) of section 104 (read with subsections (2) and (3) of that section) applies,

(gg) subsection (1) of section 104A (read with subsection (2) of that section) applies,

(gh) subsection (1) of section 104B (read with subsection (2) of that section) applies,

(gi) section 104C applies,

(h) section 105 applies,

(hh) paragraph (3) or (6) or regulation 28 of the Transnational Information and Consultation of Employees Regulations 1999 (read with paragraphs (4) and (7) of that regulation) applies,

(i) paragraph (1) of regulation 7 of the Part-time Workers (Prevention of Less Favourable Treatment) Regulations 2000 applies,

(j) paragraph (1) of regulation 6 of the Fixed-term Employees (Prevention of Less Favourable Treatment) Regulations 2002 applies,

(k) paragraph (3) or (6) of regulation 42 of the European Public Limited-Liability Company Regulations 2004 applies, or

(l) paragraph (3) or (6) of regulation 30 of the Information and Consultation of Employees Regulations 2004 (read with paragraphs (4) and (7) of that regulation) applies.

110 Dismissal procedures agreements

(1) Where a dismissal procedures agreement is designated by an order under subsection (3) which is for the time being in force –

(a) the provisions of that agreement relating to dismissal shall have effect in substitution for any rights under section 94, and

(b) accordingly, section 94 does not apply to the dismissal of an employee from any employment if it is employment to which, and he is an employee to whom, those provisions of the agreement apply.

(2) But if the agreement includes provision that it does not apply to dismissals of particular descriptions, subsection (1) does not apply in relation to a dismissal of any such description.

(3) An order designating a dismissal procedures agreement may be made by the Secretary of State, on an application being made to him jointly by all the parties to the agreement, if he is satisfied that –

(a) every trade union which is a party to the agreement is an independent trade union,

(b) the agreement provides for procedures to be followed in cases where an employee claims that he has been, or is in the course of being, unfairly dismissed,

(c) those procedures are available without discrimination to all employees falling within any description to which the agreement applies,

(d) the remedies provided by the agreement in respect of unfair dismissal are on the whole as beneficial as (but not necessarily identical with) those provided in respect of unfair dismissal by this Part,

(e) the agreement includes provision either for arbitration in every case or for –

(i) arbitration where (by reason of equality of votes or for any other reason) a decision under the agreement cannot otherwise be reached, and

(ii) a right to submit to arbitration any question of law arising out of such a decision, and

(f) the provisions of the agreement are such that it can be determined with reasonable certainty whether or not a particular employee is one to whom the agreement applies.

(4) If at any time when an order under subsection (3) is in force in relation to a dismissal procedures agreement the Secretary of State is satisfied, whether on an application made to him by any of the parties to the agreement or otherwise, either –

(a) that it is the desire of all the parties to the agreement that the order should be revoked, or

(b) that the agreement no longer satisfies all the conditions specified in subsection (3),

the Secretary of State shall revoke the order by an order under this subsection.

(5) The transitional provisions which may be made in an order under subsection (4) include, in particular, provisions directing –

(a) that an employee –

(i) shall not be excluded from his right under section 94 where the effective date of termination falls within a transitional period which ends with the date on which the order takes effect and which is specified in the order, and

(ii) shall have an extended time for presenting a complaint under section 111 in respect of a dismissal where the effective date of termination falls within that period, and

(b) that, where the effective date of termination falls within such a transitional period, an industrial tribunal shall, in determining any complaint of unfair dismissal presented by an employee to whom the dismissal procedures agreement applies, have regard to such considerations as are specified in the order (in addition to those specified in this Part and section 10(4) and (5) of the Employment Tribunals Act 1996).

(6) Where an award is made under a designated dismissal procedures agreement –

(a) in England and Wales it may be enforced, by leave of a county court, in the same manner as a judgment of the court to the same effect and, where leave is given, judgment may be entered in terms of the award …

[*See Appendix, Employment Act 2002, s44.*]

CHAPTER II

REMEDIES FOR UNFAIR DISMISSAL

111   Complaints to employment tribunal

(1) A complaint may be presented to an employment industrial tribunal against an employer by any person that he was unfairly dismissed by the employer.

(2) Subject to subsection (3), an employment tribunal shall not consider a complaint under this section unless it is presented to the tribunal –

(a) before the end of the period of three months beginning with the effective date of termination, or

(b) within such further period as the tribunal considers reasonable in a case where it is satisfied that it was not reasonably practicable for the complaint to be presented before the end of that period of three months.

(3) Where a dismissal is with notice, an employment tribunal shall consider a complaint under this section if it is presented after the notice is given but before the effective date of termination.

(4) In relation to a complaint which is presented as mentioned in subsection (3), the provisions of this Act, so far as they relate to unfair dismissal, have effect as if –

(a) references to a complaint by a person that he was unfairly dismissed by his employer included references to a complaint by a person that his employer has given him notice in such circumstances that he will be unfairly dismissed when the notice expires,

(b) references to reinstatement included references to the withdrawal of the notice by the employer,

(c) references to the effective date of termination included references to the date which would be the effective date of termination on the expiry of the notice, and

(d) references to an employee ceasing to be employed included references to an employee having been given notice of dismissal.

112   The remedies: orders and compensation

(1) This section applies where, on a complaint under section 111, an employment tribunal finds that the grounds of the complaint are well-founded.

(2) The tribunal shall –

(a) explain to the complainant what orders may be made under section 113 and in what circumstances they may be made, and

(b) ask him whether he wishes the tribunal to make such an order.

(3) If the complainant expresses such a wish, the tribunal may make an order under section 113.

(4) If no order is made under section 113, the tribunal shall make an award of compensation for unfair dismissal (calculated in accordance with sections 118 to 126) to be paid by the employer to the employee.

(5) Where –

(a) an employee is regarded as unfairly dismissed by virtue of section 98A(1) (whether or not his dismissal is unfair or regarded as unfair for any other reason), and

(b) an order is made in respect of the employee under section 113,

the employment tribunal shall, subject to subsection (6), also make an award of four weeks' pay to be paid by the employer to the employee.

(6) An employment tribunal shall not be required to make an award under subsection (5) if it considers that such an award would result in injustice to the employer.

113   The orders

An order under this section may be –

(a) an order for reinstatement (in accordance with section 114), or

(b) an order for re-engagement (in accordance with section 115),

as the tribunal may decide.

114 Order for reinstatement

(1) An order for reinstatement is an order that the employer shall treat the complainant in all respects as if he had not been dismissed.

(2) On making an order for reinstatement the tribunal shall specify –

(a) any amount payable by the employer in respect of any benefit which the complainant might reasonably be expected to have had but for the dismissal (including arrears of pay) for the period between the date of termination of employment and the date of reinstatement,

(b) any rights and privileges (including seniority and pension rights) which must be restored to the employee, and

(c) the date by which the order must be complied with.

(3) If the complainant would have benefited from an improvement in his terms and conditions of employment had he not been dismissed, an order for reinstatement shall require him to be treated as if he had benefited from that improvement from the date on which he would have done so but for being dismissed.

(4) In calculating for the purposes of subsection (2)(a) any amount payable by the employer, the tribunal shall take into account, so as to reduce the employer's liability, any sums received by the complainant in respect of the period between the date of termination of employment and the date of reinstatement by way of –

(a) wages in lieu of notice or ex gratia payments paid by the employer, or

(b) remuneration paid in respect of employment with another employer,

and such other benefits as the tribunal thinks appropriate in the circumstances.

115 Order for re-engagement

(1) An order for re-engagement is an order, on such terms as the tribunal may decide, that the complainant be engaged by the employer, or by a successor of the employer or by an associated employer, in employment comparable to that from which he was dismissed or other suitable employment.

(2) On making an order for re-engagement the tribunal shall specify the terms on which re-engagement is to take place, including –

(a) the identity of the employer,

(b) the nature of the employment,

(c) the remuneration for the employment,

(d) any amount payable by the employer in respect of any benefit which the complainant might reasonably be expected to have had but for the dismissal (including arrears of pay) for the period between the date of termination of employment and the date of re-engagement,

(e) any rights and privileges (including seniority and pension rights) which must be restored to the employee, and

(f) the date by which the order must be complied with.

(3) In calculating for the purposes of subsection (2)(d) any amount payable by the employer, the tribunal shall take into account, so as to reduce the employer's liability, any sums received by the complainant in respect of the period between the date of termination of employment and the date of re-engagement by way of –

(a) wages in lieu of notice or ex gratia payments paid by the employer, or

(b) remuneration paid in respect of employment with another employer,

and such other benefits as the tribunal thinks appropriate in the circumstances.

116 Choice of order and its terms

(1) In exercising its discretion under section 113 the tribunal shall first consider whether to make an order for reinstatement and in so doing shall take into account –

(a) whether the complainant wishes to be reinstated,

(b) whether it is practicable for the employer to comply with an order for reinstatement, and

(c) where the complainant caused or contributed to some extent to the dismissal, whether it would be just to order his reinstatement.

(2) If the tribunal decides not to make an order for reinstatement it shall then consider whether to make an order for re-engagement and, if so, on what terms.

(3) In so doing the tribunal shall take into account –

(a) any wish expressed by the complainant as to the nature of the order to be made,

(b) whether it is practicable for the employer (or a successor or an associated employer) to comply with an order for re-engagement, and

(c) where the complainant caused or contributed to some extent to the dismissal, whether it would be just to order his re-engagement and (if so) on what terms.

(4) Except in a case where the tribunal takes into account contributory fault under subsection (3)(c) it shall, if it orders re-engagement, do so on terms which are, so far as is reasonably practicable, as favourable as an order for reinstatement.

(5) Where in any case an employer has engaged a permanent replacement for a dismissed employee, the tribunal shall not take that fact into account in determining, for the purposes of subsection (1)(b) or (3)(b), whether it is practicable to comply with an order for reinstatement or re-engagement.

(6) Subsection (5) does not apply where the employer shows –

(a) that it was not practicable for him to arrange for the dismissed employee's work to be done without engaging a permanent replacement, or

(b) that –

(i) he engaged the replacement after the lapse of a reasonable period, without having heard from the dismissed employee that he wished to be reinstated or re-engaged, and

(ii) when the employer engaged the replacement it was no longer reasonable for him to arrange for the dismissed employee's work to be done except by a permanent replacement.

117 Enforcement of order and compensation

(1) An employment tribunal shall make an award of compensation, to be paid by the employer to the employee, if –

(a) an order under section 113 is made and the complainant is reinstated or re-engaged, but

(b) the terms of the order are not fully complied with.

(2) Subject to section 124, the amount of the compensation shall be such as the tribunal thinks fit having regard to the loss sustained by the complainant in consequence of the failure to comply fully with the terms of the order.

(2A) There shall be deducted from any award under subsection (1) the amount of any award made under section 112(5) at the time of the order under section 113.

(3) Subject to subsections (1) and (2), if an order under section 113 is made but the complainant is not reinstated or re-engaged in accordance with the order, the tribunal shall make –

(a) an award of compensation for unfair dismissal (calculated in accordance with sections 118 to 126), and

(b) except where this paragraph does not apply, an additional award of compensation of an amount not less than twenty-six nor more than fifty-two weeks' pay,

to be paid by the employer to the employee.

(4) Subsection (3)(b) does not apply where –

(a) the employer satisfies the tribunal that it was not practicable to comply with the order.

(7) Where in any case an employer has engaged a permanent replacement for a dismissed employee, the tribunal shall not take that fact into account in determining for the purposes of subsection (4)(a) whether it was practicable to comply with the order for reinstatement or re-engagement unless the employer shows that it was not practicable for him to arrange for the dismissed employee's work to be done without engaging a permanent replacement.

(8) Where in any case an employment tribunal finds that the complainant has unreasonably prevented an order under section 113 from being complied with, in making an award of compensation for unfair dismissal it shall take that conduct into account as a failure on the part of the complainant to mitigate his loss.

118   General

(1) Where a tribunal makes an award of compensation for unfair dismissal under section 112(4) or 117(3)(a) the award shall consist of –

(a) a basic award (calculated in accordance with sections 119 to 122 and 126), and

(b) a compensatory award (calculated in accordance with sections 123, 124, 124A and 126).

119   Basic award

(1) Subject to the provisions of this section, sections 120 to 122 and section 126, the amount of the basic award shall be calculated by –

(a) determining the period, ending with the effective date of termination, during which the employee has been continuously employed,

(b) reckoning backwards from the end of that period the number of years of employment falling within that period, and

(c) allowing the appropriate amount for each of those years of employment.

(2) In subsection (1)(c) 'the appropriate amount' means –

(a) one and a half weeks' pay for a year of employment in which the employee was not below the age of forty-one,

(b) one week's pay for a year of employment (not within paragraph (a)) in which he was not below the age of twenty-two, and

(c) half a week's pay for a year of employment not within paragraph (a) or (b).

(3) Where twenty years of employment have been reckoned under subsection (1), no account shall be taken under that subsection of any year of employment earlier than those twenty years.

(4) Where the effective date of termination is after the sixty-fourth anniversary of the day of the employee's birth, the amount arrived at under subsections (1) to (3) shall be reduced by the appropriate fraction.

(5) In subsection (4) 'the appropriate fraction' means the fraction of which –

(a) the numerator is the number of whole months reckoned from the sixty-fourth anniversary of the day of the employee's birth in the period beginning with that anniversary and ending with the effective date of termination, and

(b) the denominator is twelve.

120   Basic award: minimum in certain cases

(1) The amount of the basic award (before any reduction under section 122) shall not be less than £3,800 where the reason (or, if more than one, the principal reason) –

(a) in a redundancy case, for selecting the employee for dismissal, or

(b) otherwise, for the dismissal,

is one of those specified in section 100(1)(a) and (b), 101A(d), 102(1) or 103.

(1A) Where –

(a) an employee is regarded as unfairly dismissed by virtue of section 98A(1) (whether or not his dismissal is unfair or regarded as unfair for any other reason),

(b) an award of compensation falls to be made under section 112(4), and

(c) the amount of the award under section 118(1)(a), before any reduction under section 122(3A) or (4), is less than the amount of four weeks' pay,

the employment tribunal shall, subject to subsection (1B), increase the award under section 118(1)(a) to the amount of four weeks' pay.

(1B) An employment tribunal shall not be required by subsection (1A) to increase the amount of an award if it considers that the increase would result in injustice to the employer.

121 Basic award of two weeks' pay in certain cases

The amount of the basic award shall be two weeks' pay where the tribunal finds that the reason (or, where there is more than one, the principal reason) for the dismissal of the employee is that he was redundant and the employee –

(a) by virtue of section 138 is not regarded as dismissed for the purposes of Part XI, or

(b) by virtue of section 141 is not, or (if he were otherwise entitled) would not be, entitled to a redundancy payment.

122 Basic award: reductions

(1) Where the tribunal finds that the complainant has unreasonably refused an offer by the employer which (if accepted) would have the effect of reinstating the complainant in his employment in all respects as if he had not been dismissed, the tribunal shall reduce or further reduce the amount of the basic award to such extent as it considers just and equitable having regard to that finding.

(2) Where the tribunal considers that any conduct of the complainant before the dismissal (or, where the dismissal was with notice, before the notice was given) was such that it would be just and equitable to reduce or further reduce the amount of the basic award to any extent, the tribunal shall reduce or further reduce that amount accordingly.

(3) Subsection (2) does not apply in a redundancy case unless the reason for selecting the employee for dismissal was one of those specified in section 100(1)(a) and (b), 101A(d), 102(1) or 103; and in such a case subsection (2) applies only to so much of the basic award as is payable because of section 120.

(3A) Where the complainant has been awarded any amount in respect of the dismissal under a designated dismissal procedures agreement, the tribunal shall reduce or further reduce the amount of the basic award to such extent as it considers just and equitable having regard to that award.

(4) The amount of the basic award shall be reduced or further reduced by the amount of –

(a) any redundancy payment awarded by the tribunal under Part XI in respect of the same dismissal, or

(b) any payment made by the employer to the employee on the ground that the dismissal was by reason of redundancy (whether in pursuance of Part XI or otherwise).

123   Compensatory award

(1) Subject to the provisions of this section and sections 124, 124A and 126 and 127A(1), (3) and (4), the amount of the compensatory award shall be such amount as the tribunal considers just and equitable in all the circumstances having regard to the loss sustained by the complainant in consequence of the dismissal in so far as that loss is attributable to action taken by the employer.

(2) The loss referred to in subsection (1) shall be taken to include –

(a) any expenses reasonably incurred by the complainant in consequence of the dismissal, and

(b) subject to subsection (3), loss of any benefit which he might reasonably be expected to have had but for the dismissal.

(3) The loss referred to in subsection (1) shall be taken to include in respect of any loss of –

(a) any entitlement or potential entitlement to a payment on account of dismissal by reason of redundancy (whether in pursuance of Part XI or otherwise), or

(b) any expectation of such a payment,

only the loss referable to the amount (if any) by which the amount of that payment would have exceeded the amount of a basic award (apart from any reduction under section 122) in respect of the same dismissal.

(4) In ascertaining the loss referred to in subsection (1) the tribunal shall apply the same rule concerning the duty of a person to mitigate his loss as applies to damages recoverable under the common law of England and Wales ...

(5) In determining, for the purposes of subsection (1), how far any loss sustained by the complainant was attributable to action taken by the employer, no account shall be taken of any pressure which by –

(a) calling, organising, procuring or financing a strike or other industrial action, or

(b) threatening to do so,

was exercised on the employer to dismiss the employee; and that question shall be determined as if no such pressure had been exercised.

(6) Where the tribunal finds that the dismissal was to any extent caused or

contributed to by any action of the complainant, it shall reduce the amount of the compensatory award by such proportion as it considers just and equitable having regard to that finding.

(7) If the amount of any payment made by the employer to the employee on the ground that the dismissal was by reason of redundancy (whether in pursuance of Part XI or otherwise) exceeds the amount of the basic award which would be payable but for section 122(4), that excess goes to reduce the amount of the compensatory award.

(8) Where the amount of the compensatory award falls to be calculated for the purposes of an award under section 117(3)(a), there shall be deducted from the compensatory award any award made under section 112(5) at the time of the order under section 113.

124 Limit of compensatory award, etc

(1) The amount of –

    (a) any compensation awarded to a person under section 117(1) and (2), or

    (b) a compensatory award to a person calculated in accordance with section 123,

shall not exceed £56,800.

(1A) Subsection (1) shall not apply to compensation awarded, or a compensatory award made, to a person in a case where he is regarded as unfairly dismissed by virtue of section 100, 103A, 105(3) or 105(6A).

(3) In the case of compensation awarded to a person under section 117(1) and (2), the limit imposed by this section may be exceeded to the extent necessary to enable the award fully to reflect the amount specified as payable under section 114(2)(a) or section 115(2)(d).

(4) Where –

    (a) a compensatory award is an award under paragraph (a) of subsection (3) of section 117, and

    (b) an additional award falls to be made under paragraph (b) of that subsection,

the limit imposed by this section on the compensatory award may be exceeded to the extent necessary to enable the aggregate of the compensatory and additional awards fully to reflect the amount specified as payable under section 114(2)(a) or section 115(2)(d).

(5) The limit imposed by this section applies to the amount which the employment tribunal would, apart from this section, award in respect of the subject matter of the complaint after taking into account –

    (a) any payment made by the respondent to the complainant in respect of that matter, and

    (b) any reduction in the amount of the award required by any enactment or rule of law.

124A Adjustments under the Employment Act 2002

Where an award of compensation for unfair dismissal falls to be –

(a) reduced or increased under section 31 of the Employment Act 2002 (non-completion of statutory procedures), or

(b) increased under section 38 of that Act (failure to give statement of employment particulars),

the adjustment shall be in the amount awarded under section 118(1)(b) and shall be applied immediately before any reduction under section 123(6) or (7).

126 Acts which are both unfair dismissal and discrimination

(1) This section applies where compensation falls to be awarded in respect of any act both under –

(a) the provisions of this Act relating to unfair dismissal, and

(b) any one or more of the Sex Discrimination Act 1975, the Race Relations Act 1976, the Disability Discrimination Act 1995, the Employment Equality (Sexual Orientation) Regulations 2003 and the Employment Equality (Religion or Belief) Regulations 2003.

(2) An employment tribunal shall not award compensation under any one of those Acts or Regulations in respect of any loss or other matter which is or has been taken into account under any other of them by the tribunal (or another employment tribunal) in awarding compensation on the same or another complaint in respect of that act.

128 Interim relief pending determination of complaint

(1) An employee who presents a complaint to an employment tribunal –

(a) that he has been unfairly dismissed by his employer, and

(b) that the reason (or, if more than one, the principal reason) for the dismissal is one of those specified in section 100(1)(a) and (b), 101A(d), 102(1), 103 or in paragraph 161(2) of Schedule A1 to the Trade Union and Labour Relations (Consolidation) Act 1992 or 103A,

may apply to the tribunal for interim relief.

(2) The tribunal shall not entertain an application for interim relief unless it is presented to the tribunal before the end of the period of seven days immediately following the effective date of termination (whether before, on or after that date).

(3) The tribunal shall determine the application for interim relief as soon as practicable after receiving the application.

(4) The tribunal shall give to the employer not later than seven days before the date of the hearing a copy of the application together with notice of the date, time and place of the hearing.

(5) The tribunal shall not exercise any power it has of postponing the hearing of an application for interim relief except where it is satisfied that special circumstances exist which justify it in doing so.

129 Procedure on hearing of application and making of order

(1) This section applies where, on hearing an employee's application for interim relief, it appears to the tribunal that it is likely that on determining the complaint to which the application relates the tribunal will find that the reason (or, if more than one, the principal reason) for his dismissal is one of those specified in section 100(1)(a) and (b), 101A(d), 102(1), 103 or in paragraph 161(2) of Schedule A1 to the Trade Union and Labour Relations (Consolidation) Act 1992 or 103A.

(2) The tribunal shall announce its findings and explain to both parties (if present) –

(a) what powers the tribunal may exercise on the application, and

(b) in what circumstances it will exercise them.

(3) The tribunal shall ask the employer (if present) whether he is willing, pending the determination or settlement of the complaint –

(a) to reinstate the employee (that is, to treat him in all respects as if he had not been dismissed), or

(b) if not, to re-engage him in another job on terms and conditions not less favourable than those which would have been applicable to him if he had not been dismissed.

(4) For the purposes of subsection (3)(b) 'terms and conditions not less favourable than those which would have been applicable to him if he had not been dismissed' means, as regards seniority, pension rights and other similar rights, that the period prior to the dismissal should be regarded as continuous with his employment following the dismissal.

(5) If the employer states that he is willing to reinstate the employee, the tribunal shall make an order to that effect.

(6) If the employer –

(a) states that he is willing to re-engage the employee in another job, and

(b) specifies the terms and conditions on which he is willing to do so,

the tribunal shall ask the employee whether he is willing to accept the job on those terms and conditions.

(7) If the employee is willing to accept the job on those terms and conditions, the tribunal shall make an order to that effect.

(8) If the employee is not willing to accept the job on those terms and conditions –

(a) where the tribunal is of the opinion that the refusal is reasonable, the tribunal shall make an order for the continuation of his contract of employment, and

(b) otherwise, the tribunal shall make no order.

(9) If on the hearing of an application for interim relief the employer –

(a) fails to attend before the tribunal, or

(b) states that he is unwilling either to reinstate or re-engage the employee as mentioned in subsection (3),

the tribunal shall make an order for the continuation of the employee's contract of employment.

130   Order for continuation of contract of employment

(1) An order under section 129 for the continuation of a contract of employment is an order that the contract of employment continue in force –

(a) for the purposes of pay or any other benefit derived from the employment, seniority, pension rights and other similar matters, and

(b) for the purposes of determining for any purpose the period for which the employee has been continuously employed,

from the date of its termination (whether before or after the making of the order) until the determination or settlement of the complaint.

(2) Where the tribunal makes such an order it shall specify in the order the amount which is to be paid by the employer to the employee by way of pay in respect of each normal pay period, or part of any such period, falling between the date of dismissal and the determination or settlement of the complaint.

(3) Subject to the following provisions, the amount so specified shall be that which the employee could reasonably have been expected to earn during that period, or part, and shall be paid –

(a) in the case of a payment for any such period falling wholly or partly after the making of the order, on the normal pay day for that period, and

(b) in the case of a payment for any past period, within such time as may be specified in the order.

(4) If an amount is payable in respect only of part of a normal pay period, the amount shall be calculated by reference to the whole period and reduced proportionately.

(5) Any payment made to an employee by an employer under his contract of employment, or by way of damages for breach of that contract, in respect of a normal pay period, or part of any such period, goes towards discharging the employer's liability in respect of that period under subsection (2); and, conversely, any payment under that subsection in respect of a period goes towards discharging any liability of the employer under, or in respect of breach of, the contract of employment in respect of that period.

(6) If an employee, on or after being dismissed by his employer, receives a lump sum which, or part of which, is in lieu of wages but is not referable to any normal pay period, the tribunal shall take the payment into account in determining the amount of pay to be payable in pursuance of any such order.

(7) For the purposes of this section, the amount which an employee could reasonably have been expected to earn, his normal pay period and the normal pay day for each such period shall be determined as if he had not been dismissed.

131 Application for variation or revocation of order

(1) At any time between –

(a) the making of an order under section 129, and

(b) the determination or settlement of the complaint,

the employer or the employee may apply to an employment tribunal for the revocation or variation of the order on the ground of a relevant change of circumstances since the making of the order.

(2) Sections 128 and 129 apply in relation to such an application as in relation to an original application for interim relief except that, in the case of an application by the employer, section 128(4) has effect with the substitution of a reference to the employee for the reference to the employer.

132 Consequence of failure to comply with order

(1) If, on the application of an employee, an employment tribunal is satisfied that the employer has not complied with the terms of an order for the reinstatement or re-engagement of the employee under section 129(5) or (7), the tribunal shall –

(a) make an order for the continuation of the employee's contract of employment, and

(b) order the employer to pay compensation to the employee.

(2) Compensation under subsection (1)(b) shall be of such amount as the tribunal considers just and equitable in all the circumstances having regard –

(a) to the infringement of the employee's right to be reinstated or re-engaged in pursuance of the order, and

(b) to any loss suffered by the employee in consequence of the non-compliance.

(3) Section 130 applies to an order under subsection (1)(a) as in relation to an order under section 129.

(4) If on the application of an employee an employment tribunal is satisfied that the employer has not complied with the terms of an order for the continuation of a contract of employment subsection (5) or (6) applies.

(5) Where the non-compliance consists of a failure to pay an amount by way of pay specified in the order –

(a) the tribunal shall determine the amount owed by the employer on the date of the determination, and

(b) if on that date the tribunal also determines the employee's complaint that he has been unfairly dismissed, it shall specify that amount separately from any other sum awarded to the employee.

(6) In any other case, the tribunal shall order the employer to pay the employee such compensation as the tribunal considers just and equitable in all the circumstances having regard to any loss suffered by the employee in consequence of the non-compliance.

CHAPTER III

SUPPLEMENTARY

133 Death of employer or employee

(1) Where –

(a) an employer has given notice to an employee to terminate his contract of employment, and

(b) before that termination the employee or the employer dies,

this Part applies as if the contract had been duly terminated by the employer by notice expiring on the date of the death.

(2) Where –

(a) an employee's contract of employment has been terminated,

(b) by virtue of subsection (2) or (4) of section 97 a date later than the effective date of termination as defined in subsection (1) of that section is to be treated for certain purposes as the effective date of termination, and

(c) the employer or the employee dies before that date,

subsection (2) or (4) of section 97 applies as if the notice referred to in that subsection as required by section 86 expired on the date of the death.

(3) Where an employee has died, sections 113 to 116 do not apply; and, accordingly, if the employment tribunal finds that the grounds of the complaint are well-founded, the case shall be treated as falling within section 112(4) as a case in which no order is made under section 113.

(4) Subsection (3) does not prejudice an order for reinstatement or re-engagement made before the employee's death.

(5) Where an order for reinstatement or re-engagement has been made and the employee dies before the order is complied with –

(a) if the employer has before the death refused to reinstate or re-engage the employee in accordance with the order, subsections (3) to (6) of section 117 apply, and an award shall be made under subsection (3)(b) of that section, unless the employer satisfies the tribunal that it was not practicable at the time of the refusal to comply with the order, and

(b) if there has been no such refusal, subsections (1) and (2) of that section apply if the employer fails to comply with any ancillary terms of the order which remain capable of fulfilment after the employee's death as they would apply to such a failure to comply fully with the terms of an order where the employee had been reinstated or re-engaged.

PART XI

REDUNDANCY PAYMENTS, ETC.

CHAPTER I

RIGHT TO REDUNDANCY PAYMENT

135 The right

(1) An employer shall pay a redundancy payment to any employee of his if the employee –

(a) is dismissed by the employer by reason of redundancy, or

(b) is eligible for a redundancy payment by reason of being laid off or kept on short-time.

(2) Subsection (1) has effect subject to following provisions of this Part (including, in particular, sections 140 to 144, 149 to 152, 155 to 161 and 164).

CHAPTER II

RIGHT ON DISMISSAL BY REASON OF REDUNDANCY

136 Circumstances in which an employee is dismissed

(1) Subject to the provisions of this section and sections 137 and 138, for the purposes of this Part an employee is dismissed by his employer if (and only if) –

(a) the contract under which he is employed by the employer is terminated by the employer (whether with or without notice),

(b) he is employed under a limited term contract and that contract terminates by virtue of the limiting event without being renewed under the same contract, or

(c) the employee terminates the contract under which he is employed (with or without notice) in circumstances in which he is entitled to terminate it without notice by reason of the employer's conduct.

(2) Subsection (1)(c) does not apply if the employee terminates the contract without notice in circumstances in which he is entitled to do so by reason of a lock-out by the employer.

(3) An employee shall be taken to be dismissed by his employer for the purposes of this Part if –

(a) the employer gives notice to the employee to terminate his contract of employment, and

(b) at a time within the obligatory period of notice the employee gives notice in writing to the employer to terminate the contract of employment on a date earlier than the date on which the employer's notice is due to expire.

(4) In this Part the 'obligatory period of notice', in relation to notice given by an employer to terminate an employee's contract of employment, means –

(a) the actual period of the notice in a case where the period beginning at the time when the notice is given and ending at the time when it expires is equal to the minimum period which (by virtue of any enactment or otherwise) is required to be given by the employer to terminate the contract of employment, and

(b) the period which –

(i) is equal to the minimum period referred to in paragraph (a), and

(ii) ends at the time when the notice expires,

in any other case.

(5) Where in accordance with any enactment or rule of law –

(a) an act on the part of an employer, or

(b) an event affecting an employer (including, in the case of an individual, his death),

operates to terminate a contract under which an employee is employed by him, the act or event shall be taken for the purposes of this Part to be a termination of the contract by the employer.

138 No dismissal in cases of renewal of contract or re-engagement

(1) Where –

(a) an employee's contract of employment is renewed, or he is re-engaged under a new contract of employment in pursuance of an offer (whether in writing or not) made before the end of his employment under the previous contract, and

(b) the renewal or re-engagement takes effect either immediately on, or after an interval of not more than four weeks after, the end of that employment,

the employee shall not be regarded for the purposes of this Part as dismissed by his employer by reason of the ending of his employment under the previous contract.

(2) Subsection (1) does not apply if –

(a) the provisions of the contract as renewed, or of the new contract, as to –

(i) the capacity and place in which the employee is employed, and

(ii) the other terms and conditions of his employment,

differ (wholly or in part) from the corresponding provisions of the previous contract, and

(b) during the period specified in subsection (3) –

(i) the employee (for whatever reason) terminates the renewed or new contract, or gives notice to terminate it and it is in consequence terminated, or

(ii) the employer, for a reason connected with or arising out of any difference between the renewed or new contract and the previous contract, terminates the renewed or new contract, or gives notice to terminate it and it is in consequence terminated.

(3) The period referred to in subsection (2)(b) is the period –

(a) beginning at the end of the employee's employment under the previous contract, and

(b) ending with –

(i) the period of four weeks beginning with the date on which the employee starts work under the renewed or new contract, or

(ii) such longer period as may be agreed in accordance with subsection (6) for the purpose of retraining the employee for employment under that contract;

and is in this Part referred to as the 'trial period'.

(4) Where subsection (2) applies, for the purposes of this Part –

(a) the employee shall be regarded as dismissed on the date on which his employment under the previous contract (or, if there has been more than one trial period, the original contract) ended, and

(b) the reason for the dismissal shall be taken to be the reason for which the employee was then dismissed, or would have been dismissed had the offer (or original offer) of renewed or new employment not been made, or the reason which resulted in that offer being made.

(5) Subsection (2) does not apply if the employee's contract of employment is again renewed, or he is again re-engaged under a new contract of employment, in circumstances such that subsection (1) again applies.

(6) For the purposes of subsection (3)(b)(ii) a period of retraining is agreed in accordance with this subsection only if the agreement –

(a) is made between the employer and the employee or his representative before the employee starts work under the contract as renewed, or the new contract,

(b) is in writing,

(c) specifies the date on which the period of retraining ends, and

(d) specifies the terms and conditions of employment which will apply in the employee's case after the end of that period.

139 Redundancy

(1) For the purposes of this Act an employee who is dismissed shall be taken to be dismissed by reason of redundancy if the dismissal is wholly or mainly attributable to –

(a) the fact that his employer has ceased or intends to cease –

(i) to carry on the business for the purposes of which the employee was employed by him, or

(ii) to carry on that business in the place where the employee was so employed, or

(b) the fact that the requirements of that business –

(i) for employees to carry out work of a particular kind, or

(ii) for employees to carry out work of a particular kind in the place where the employee was employed by the employer,

have ceased or diminished or are expected to cease or diminish.

(2) For the purposes of subsection (1) the business of the employer together with the business or businesses of his associated employers shall be treated as one (unless either of the conditions specified in paragraphs (a) and (b) of that subsection would be satisfied without so treating them).

(3) For the purposes of subsection (1) the activities carried on by a local education authority with respect to the schools maintained by it, and the activities carried on by the governing bodies of those schools, shall be treated as one business (unless either of the conditions specified in paragraphs (a) and (b) of that subsection would be satisfied without so treating them).

(4) Where –

(a) the contract under which a person is employed is treated by section 136(5) as terminated by his employer by reason of an act or event, and

(b) the employee's contract is not renewed and he is not re-engaged under a new contract of employment,

he shall be taken for the purposes of this Act to be dismissed by reason of redundancy if the circumstances in which his contract is not renewed, and he is not re-engaged, are wholly or mainly attributable to either of the facts stated in paragraphs (a) and (b) of subsection (1).

(5) In its application to a case within subsection (4), paragraph (a)(i) of subsection (1) has effect as if the reference in that subsection to the employer included a reference to any person to whom, in consequence of the act or event, power to dispose of the business has passed.

(6) In subsection (1) 'cease' and 'diminish' mean cease and diminish either permanently or temporarily and for whatever reason.

140 Summary dismissal

(1) Subject to subsections (2) and (3), an employee is not entitled to a redundancy payment by reason of dismissal where his employer, being entitled to terminate his contract of employment without notice by reason of the employee's conduct, terminates it either –

(a) without notice,

(b) by giving shorter notice than that which, in the absence of conduct entitling the employer to terminate the contract without notice, the employer would be required to give to terminate the contract, or

(c) by giving notice which includes, or is accompanied by, a statement in writing that the employer would, by reason of the employee's conduct, be entitled to terminate the contract without notice.

(2) Where an employee who –

(a) has been given notice by his employer to terminate his contract of employment, or

(b) has given notice to his employer under section 148(1) indicating his intention to claim a redundancy payment in respect of lay-off or short-time,

takes part in a strike at any relevant time in circumstances which entitle the employer to treat the contract of employment as terminable without notice, subsection (1) does not apply if the employer terminates the contract by reason of his taking part in the strike.

(3) Where the contract of employment of an employee who –

(a) has been given notice by his employer to terminate his contract of employment, or

(b) has given notice to his employer under section 148(1) indicating his intention to claim a redundancy payment in respect of lay-off or short-time,

is terminated as mentioned in subsection (1) at any relevant time otherwise than by reason of his taking part in a strike, an employment tribunal may determine that the employer is liable to make an appropriate payment to the employee if on a reference to the tribunal it appears to the tribunal, in the circumstances of the case, to be just and equitable that the employee should receive it.

(4) In subsection (3) 'appropriate payment' means –

(a) the whole of the redundancy payment to which the employee would have been entitled apart from subsection (1), or

(b) such part of that redundancy payment as the tribunal thinks fit.

(5) In this section 'relevant time' –

(a) in the case of an employee who has been given notice by his employer to terminate his contract of employment, means any time within the obligatory period of notice, and

(b) in the case of an employee who has given notice to his employer under section 148(1), means any time after the service of the notice.

141 Renewal of contract or re-engagement

(1) This section applies where an offer (whether in writing or not) is made to an employee before the end of his employment –

(a) to renew his contract of employment, or

(b) to re-engage him under a new contract of employment,

with renewal or re-engagement to take effect either immediately on, or after an interval of not more than four weeks after, the end of his employment.

(2) Where subsection (3) is satisfied, the employee is not entitled to a redundancy payment if he unreasonably refuses the offer.

(3) This subsection is satisfied where –

(a) the provisions of the contract as renewed, or of the new contract, as to –

(i) the capacity and place in which the employee would be employed, and

(ii) the other terms and conditions of his employment,

would not differ from the corresponding provisions of the previous contract, or

(b) those provisions of the contract as renewed, or of the new contract, would differ from the corresponding provisions of the previous contract but the offer constitutes an offer of suitable employment in relation to the employee.

(4) The employee is not entitled to a redundancy payment if –

(a) his contract of employment is renewed, or he is re-engaged under a new contract of employment, in pursuance of the offer,

(b) the provisions of the contract as renewed or new contract as to the capacity or place in which he is employed or the other terms and conditions of his employment differ (wholly or in part) from the corresponding provisions of the previous contract,

(c) the employment is suitable in relation to him, and

(d) during the trial period he unreasonably terminates the contract, or unreasonably gives notice to terminate it and it is in consequence terminated.

142 Employee anticipating expiry of employer's notice

(1) Subject to subsection (3), an employee is not entitled to a redundancy payment where –

(a) he is taken to be dismissed by virtue of section 136(3) by reason of giving to his employer notice terminating his contract of employment on a date earlier than the date on which notice by the employer terminating the contract is due to expire,

(b) before the employee's notice is due to expire, the employer gives him a notice such as is specified in subsection (2), and

(c) the employee does not comply with the requirements of that notice.

(2) The employer's notice referred to in subsection (1)(b) is a notice in writing –

(a) requiring the employee to withdraw his notice terminating the contract of employment and to continue in employment until the date on which the employer's notice terminating the contract expires, and

(b) stating that, unless he does so, the employer will contest any liability to pay to him a redundancy payment in respect of the termination of his contract of employment.

(3) An employment tribunal may determine that the employer is liable to make an appropriate payment to the employee if on a reference to the tribunal it appears to the tribunal, having regard to –

(a) the reasons for which the employee seeks to leave the employment, and

(b) the reasons for which the employer requires him to continue in it,

to be just and equitable that the employee should receive the payment.

(4) In subsection (3) 'appropriate payment' means –

(a) the whole of the redundancy payment to which the employee would have been entitled apart from subsection (1), or

(b) such part of that redundancy payment as the tribunal thinks fit.

143 Strike during currency of employer's notice

(1) This section applies where –

(a) an employer has given notice to an employee to terminate his contract of employment ('notice of termination'),

(b) after the notice is given the employee begins to take part in a strike of employees of the employer, and

(c) the employer serves on the employee a notice of extension.

(2) A notice of extension is a notice in writing which –

(a) requests the employee to agree to extend the contract of employment beyond the time of expiry by a period comprising as many available days as the number of working days lost by striking ('the proposed period of extension'),

(b) indicates the reasons for which the employer makes that request, and

(c) states that the employer will contest any liability to pay the employee a redundancy payment in respect of the dismissal effected by the notice of termination unless either –

(i) the employee complies with the request, or

(ii) the employer is satisfied that, in consequence of sickness or injury or otherwise, the employee is unable to comply with it or that (even though he is able to comply with it) it is reasonable in the circumstances for him not to do so.

(3) Subject to subsections (4) and (5), if the employee does not comply with the request contained in the notice of extension, he is not entitled to a redundancy payment by reason of the dismissal effected by the notice of termination.

(4) Subsection (3) does not apply if the employer agrees to pay a redundancy payment to the employee in respect of the dismissal effected by the notice of termination even though he has not complied with the request contained in the notice of extension.

(5) An employment tribunal may determine that the employer is liable to make an appropriate payment to the employee if on a reference to the tribunal it appears to the tribunal that –

(a) the employee has not complied with the request contained in the notice of extension and the employer has not agreed to pay a redundancy payment in respect of the dismissal effected by the notice of termination, but

(b) either the employee was unable to comply with the request or it was reasonable in the circumstances for him not to comply with it.

(6) In subsection (5) 'appropriate payment' means –

(a) the whole of the redundancy payment to which the employee would have been entitled apart from subsection (3), or

(b) such part of that redundancy payment as the tribunal thinks fit.

(7) If the employee –

(a) complies with the request contained in the notice of extension, or

(b) does not comply with it but attends at his proper or usual place of work and is ready and willing to work on one or more (but not all) of the available days within the proposed period of extension,

the notice of termination has effect, and shall be deemed at all material times to have had effect, as if the period specified in it had been appropriately extended; and sections 87 to 91 accordingly apply as if the period of notice required by section 86 were extended to a corresponding extent.

(8) In subsection (7) 'appropriately extended' means –

(a) in a case within paragraph (a) of that subsection, extended beyond the time of expiry by an additional period equal to the proposed period of extension, and

(b) in a case within paragraph (b) of that subsection, extended beyond the time of expiry up to the end of the day (or last of the days) on which he attends at his proper or usual place of work and is ready and willing to work.

144 Provisions supplementary to section 143

(1) For the purposes of section 143 an employee complies with the request contained in a notice of extension if, but only if, on each available day within the proposed period of extension, he –

(a) attends at his proper or usual place of work, and

(b) is ready and willing to work,

whether or not he has signified his agreement to the request in any other way.

(2) The reference in section 143(2) to the number of working days lost by striking is a reference to the number of working days in the period –

(a) beginning with the date of service of the notice of termination, and

(b) ending with the time of expiry,

which are days on which the employee in question takes part in a strike of employees of his employer.

(3) In section 143 and this section –

'available day', in relation to an employee, means a working day beginning at or after the time of expiry which is a day on which he is not taking part in a strike of employees of the employer,

'available day within the proposed period of extension' means an available day which begins before the end of the proposed period of extension,

'time of expiry', in relation to a notice of termination, means the time at which the notice would expire apart from section 143, and

'working day', in relation to an employee, means a day on which, in accordance with his contract of employment, he is normally required to work.

(4) Neither the service of a notice of extension nor any extension by virtue of section 143(7) of the period specified in a notice of termination affects –

(a) any right either of the employer or of the employee to terminate the contract of employment (whether before, at or after the time of expiry) by a further notice or without notice, or

(b) the operation of this Part in relation to any such termination of the contract of employment.

145 The relevant date

(1) For the purposes of the provisions of this Act relating to redundancy payments 'the relevant date' in relation to the dismissal of an employee has the meaning given by this section.

(2) Subject to the following provisions of this section, 'the relevant date' –

(a) in relation to an employee whose contract of employment is terminated by notice, whether given by his employer or by the employee, means the date on which the notice expires,

(b) in relation to an employee whose contract of employment is terminated without notice, means the date on which the termination takes effect, and

(c) in relation to an employee who is employed under a limited-term contract which terminates by virtue of the limiting event without being renewed under the same contract, means the date on which the termination takes effect.

(3) Where the employee is taken to be dismissed by virtue of section 136(3) the 'relevant date' means the date on which the employee's notice to terminate his contract of employment expires.

(4) Where the employee is regarded by virtue of section 138(4) as having been dismissed on the date on which his employment under an earlier contract ended, 'the relevant date' means –

(a) for the purposes of section 164(1), the date which is the relevant date as defined by subsection (2) in relation to the renewed or new contract or, where there has been more than one trial period, the last such contract, and

(b) for the purposes of any other provision, the date which is the relevant date as defined by subsection (2) in relation to the previous contract or, where there has been more than one such trial period, the original contract.

(5) Where –

(a) the contract of employment is terminated by the employer, and

(b) the notice required by section 86 to be given by an employer would, if duly given on the material date, expire on a date later than the relevant date (as defined by the previous provisions of this section),

for the purposes of sections 155, 162(1) and 227(3) the later date is the relevant date.

(6) In subsection (5)(b) 'the material date' means –

(a) the date when notice of termination was given by the employer, or

(b) where no notice was given, the date when the contract of employment was terminated by the employer.

146 Provisions supplementing sections 138 and 141

(1) In sections 138 and 141 –

(a) references to re-engagement are to re-engagement by the employer or an associated employer, and

(b) references to an offer are to an offer made by the employer or an associated employer.

(2) For the purposes of the application of section 138(1) or 141(1) to a contract under which the employment ends on a Friday, Saturday or Sunday –

(a) the renewal or re-engagement shall be treated as taking effect immediately on the ending of the employment under the previous contract if it takes effect on or before the next Monday after that Friday, Saturday or Sunday, and

(b) the interval of four weeks to which those provisions refer shall be calculated as if the employment had ended on that next Monday.

CHAPTER III

RIGHT BY REASON OF LAY-OFF OR SHORT-TIME

147 Meaning of 'lay-off' and 'short-time'

(1) For the purposes of this Part an employee shall be taken to be laid off for a week if –

(a) he is employed under a contract on terms and conditions such that his remuneration under the contract depends on his being provided by the employer with work of the kind which he is employed to do, but

(b) he is not entitled to any remuneration under the contract in respect of the week because the employer does not provide such work for him.

(2) For the purposes of this Part an employee shall be taken to be kept on short-time for a week if by reason of a diminution in the work provided for the employee by his employer (being work of a kind which under his contract the employee is employed to do) the employee's remuneration for the week is less than half a week's pay.

148 Eligibility by reason of lay-off or short-time

(1) Subject to the following provisions of this Part, for the purposes of this Part an employee is eligible for a redundancy payment by reason of being laid off or kept on short-time if –

(a) he gives notice in writing to his employer indicating (in whatever terms) his intention to claim a redundancy payment in respect of lay-off or short-time (referred to in this Part as 'notice of intention to claim'), and

(b) before the service of the notice he has been laid off or kept on short-time in circumstances in which subsection (2) applies.

(2) This subsection applies if the employee has been laid off or kept on short-time –

(a) for four or more consecutive weeks of which the last before the service of the notice ended on, or not more than four weeks before, the date of service of the notice, or

(b) for a series of six or more weeks (of which not more than three were consecutive) within a period of thirteen weeks, where the last week of the series before the service of the notice ended on, or not more than four weeks before, the date of service of the notice.

149 Counter-notices

Where an employee gives to his employer notice of intention to claim but –

(a) the employer gives to the employee, within seven days after the service of that notice, notice in writing (referred to in this Part as a 'counter-notice') that he will contest any liability to pay to the employee a redundancy payment in pursuance of the employee's notice, and

(b) the employer does not withdraw the counter-notice by a subsequent notice in writing,

the employee is not entitled to a redundancy payment in pursuance of his notice of intention to claim except in accordance with a decision of an employment tribunal.

150 Resignation

(1) An employee is not entitled to a redundancy payment by reason of being laid off or kept on short-time unless he terminates his contract of employment by giving

such period of notice as is required for the purposes of this section before the end of the relevant period.

(2) The period of notice required for the purposes of this section –

(a) where the employee is required by his contract of employment to give more than one week's notice to terminate the contract, is the minimum period which he is required to give, and

(b) otherwise, is one week.

(3) In subsection (1) 'the relevant period' –

(a) if the employer does not give a counter-notice within seven days after the service of the notice of intention to claim, is three weeks after the end of those seven days,

(b) if the employer gives a counter-notice within that period of seven days but withdraws it by a subsequent notice in writing, is three weeks after the service of the notice of withdrawal, and

(c) if –

(i) the employer gives a counter-notice within that period of seven days, and does not so withdraw it, and

(ii) a question as to the right of the employee to a redundancy payment in pursuance of the notice of intention to claim is referred to an employment tribunal,

is three weeks after the tribunal has notified to the employee its decision on that reference.

(4) For the purposes of subsection (3)(c) no account shall be taken of –

(a) any appeal against the decision of the tribunal, or

(b) any proceedings or decision in consequence of any such appeal.

151 Dismissal

(1) An employee is not entitled to a redundancy payment by reason of being laid off or kept on short-time if he is dismissed by his employer.

(2) Subsection (1) does not prejudice any right of the employee to a redundancy payment in respect of the dismissal.

152 Likelihood of full employment

(1) An employee is not entitled to a redundancy payment in pursuance of a notice of intention to claim if –

(a) on the date of service of the notice it was reasonably to be expected that the employee (if he continued to be employed by the same employer) would, not later than four weeks after that date, enter on a period of employment of not less than thirteen weeks during which he would not be laid off or kept on short-time for any week, and

(b) the employer gives a counter-notice to the employee within seven days after the service of the notice of intention to claim.

(2) Subsection (1) does not apply where the employee –

(a) continues or has continued, during the next four weeks after the date of service of the notice of intention to claim, to be employed by the same employer, and

(b) is or has been laid off or kept on short-time for each of those weeks.

153 The relevant date

For the purposes of the provisions of this Act relating to redundancy payments 'the relevant date' in relation to a notice of intention to claim or a right to a redundancy payment in pursuance of such a notice –

(a) in a case falling within paragraph (a) of subsection (2) of section 148, means the date on which the last of the four or more consecutive weeks before the service of the notice came to an end, and

(b) in a case falling within paragraph (b) of that subsection, means the date on which the last of the series of six or more weeks before the service of the notice came to an end.

154 Provisions supplementing sections 148 and 152

For the purposes of sections 148(2) and152(2) –

(a) it is immaterial whether a series of weeks consists wholly of weeks for which the employee is laid off or wholly of weeks for which he is kept on short-time or partly of the one and partly of the other, and

(b) no account shall be taken of any week for which an employee is laid off or kept on short-time where the lay-off or short-time is wholly or mainly attributable to a strike or a lock-out (whether or not in the trade or industry in which the employee is employed and whether in Great Britain or elsewhere).

CHAPTER IV

GENERAL EXCLUSIONS FROM RIGHT

155 Qualifying period of employment

An employee does not have any right to a redundancy payment unless he has been continuously employed for a period of not less than two years ending with the relevant date.

156 Upper age limit

(1) An employee does not have any right to a redundancy payment if before the relevant date he has attained –

(a) in a case where –

(i) in the business for the purposes of which the employee was employed there was a normal retiring age of less than sixty-five for an employee holding the position held by the employee, and

(ii) the age was the same whether the employee holding that position was a man or woman,

that normal retiring age, and

(b) in any other case, the age of sixty-five.

157 Exemption orders

(1) Where an order under this section is in force in respect of an agreement covered by this section, an employee who, immediately before the relevant date, is an employee to whom the agreement applies does not have any right to a redundancy payment.

(2) An agreement is covered by this section if it is an agreement between –

(a) one or more employers or organisations of employers, and

(b) one or more trade unions representing employees,

under which employees to whom the agreement applies have a right in certain circumstances to payments on the termination of their contracts of employment.

(3) Where, on the application of all the parties to an agreement covered by this section, the Secretary of State is satisfied, having regard to the provisions of the agreement, that the employees to whom the agreement applies should not have any right to a redundancy payment, he may make an order under this section in respect of the agreement.

(4) The Secretary of State shall not make an order under this section in respect of an agreement unless the agreement indicates (in whatever terms) the willingness of the parties to it to submit to an employment tribunal any question arising under the agreement as to –

(a) the right of an employee to a payment on the termination of his employment, or

(b) the amount of such a payment.

(5) An order revoking an earlier order under this section may be made in pursuance of an application by all or any of the parties to the agreement in question or in the absence of such an application.

158 Pension rights

(1) The Secretary of State shall by regulations make provision for excluding the right to a redundancy payment, or reducing the amount of any redundancy payment, in such cases to which subsection (2) applies as are prescribed by the regulations.

(2) This subsection applies to cases in which an employee has (whether by virtue of any statutory provision or otherwise) a right or claim (whether or not legally enforceable) to a periodical payment or lump sum by way of pension, gratuity or superannuation allowance which –

(a) is to be paid by reference to his employment by a particular employer, and

(b) is to be paid, or to begin to be paid, at the time when he leaves the employment or within such period after he leaves the employment as may be prescribed by the regulations.

(3) The regulations shall secure that the right to a redundancy payment shall not be excluded, and that the amount of a redundancy payment shall not be reduced, by reason of any right or claim to a periodical payment or lump sum, in so far as the payment or lump sum –

(a) represents compensation for loss of employment or for loss or diminution of emoluments or of pension rights, and

(b) is payable under a statutory provision (whether passed or made before or after the passing of this Act).

(4) In relation to any case where (in accordance with any provision of this Part) an employment tribunal determines that an employer is liable to pay part (but not the whole) of a redundancy payment the references in this section to a redundancy payment, or to the amount of a redundancy payment, are to the part of the redundancy payment, or to the amount of the part.

159 Public offices, etc

A person does not have any right to a redundancy payment in respect of any employment which –

(a) is employment in a public office within the meaning of section 39 of the Superannuation Act 1965, or

(b) is for the purposes of pensions and other superannuation benefits treated (whether by virtue of that Act or otherwise) as service in the civil service of the State.

160 Overseas government employment

(1) A person does not have any right to a redundancy payment in respect of employment in any capacity under the Government of an overseas territory.

(2) The reference in subsection (1) to the Government of an overseas territory includes a reference to –

(a) a Government constituted for two or more overseas territories, and

(b) any authority established for the purpose of providing or administering services which are common to, or relate to matters of common interest to, two or more overseas territories.

(3) In this section references to an overseas territory are to any territory or country outside the United Kingdom.

161 Domestic servants

(1) A person does not have any right to a redundancy payment in respect of employment as a domestic servant in a private household where the employer is the parent (or step-parent), grandparent, child (or step-child), grandchild or brother or sister (or half-brother or half-sister) of the employee.

(2) Subject to that, the provisions of this Part apply to an employee who is employed as a domestic servant in a private household as if –

(a) the household were a business, and

(b) the maintenance of the household were the carrying on of that business by the employer.

CHAPTER V

OTHER PROVISIONS ABOUT REDUNDANCY PAYMENTS

162 Amount of a redundancy payment

(1) The amount of a redundancy payment shall be calculated by –

(a) determining the period, ending with the relevant date, during which the employee has been continuously employed,

(b) reckoning backwards from the end of that period the number of years of employment falling within that period, and

(c) allowing the appropriate amount for each of those years of employment.

(2) In subsection (1)(c) 'the appropriate amount' means –

(a) one and a half weeks' pay for a year of employment in which the employee was not below the age of forty-one,

(b) one week's pay for a year of employment (not within paragraph (a)) in which he was not below the age of twenty-two, and

(c) half a week's pay for each year of employment not within paragraph (a) or (b).

(3) Where twenty years of employment have been reckoned under subsection (1), no account shall be taken under that subsection of any year of employment earlier than those twenty years.

(4) Where the relevant date is after the sixty-fourth anniversary of the day of the employee's birth, the amount arrived at under subsections (1) to (3) shall be reduced by the appropriate fraction.

(5) In subsection (4) 'the appropriate fraction' means the fraction of which –

(a) the numerator is the number of whole months reckoned from the sixty-fourth anniversary of the day of the employee's birth in the period beginning with that anniversary and ending with the relevant date, and

(b) the denominator is twelve.

(6) Subsections (1) to (5) apply for the purposes of any provision of this Part by virtue of which an employment tribunal may determine that an employer is liable to pay to an employee –

(a) the whole of the redundancy payment to which the employee would have had a right apart from some other provision, or

(b) such part of the redundancy payment to which the employee would have had a right apart from some other provision as the tribunal thinks fit,

as if any reference to the amount of a redundancy payment were to the amount of the redundancy payment to which the employee would have been entitled apart from that other provision.

(8) This section has effect subject to any regulations under section 158 by virtue of which the amount of a redundancy payment, or part of a redundancy payment, may be reduced.

163 References to employment tribunals

(1) Any question arising under this Part as to –

(a) the right of an employee to a redundancy payment, or

(b) the amount of a redundancy payment,

shall be referred to and determined by an employment tribunal.

(2) For the purposes of any such reference, an employee who has been dismissed by his employer shall, unless the contrary is proved, be presumed to have been so dismissed by reason of redundancy.

(3) Any question whether an employee will become entitled to a redundancy payment if he is not dismissed by his employer and he terminates his contract of employment as mentioned in section 150(1) shall for the purposes of this Part be taken to be a question as to the right of the employee to a redundancy payment.

(4) Where an order under section 157 is in force in respect of an agreement, this section has effect in relation to any question arising under the agreement as to the right of an employee to a payment on the termination of his employment, or as to the amount of such a payment, as if the payment were a redundancy payment and the question arose under this Part.

164 Claims for redundancy payment

(1) An employee does not have any right to a redundancy payment unless, before the end of the period of six months beginning with the relevant date –

(a) the payment has been agreed and paid,

(b) the employee has made a claim for the payment by notice in writing given to the employer,

(c) a question as to the employee's right to, or the amount of, the payment has been referred to an employment tribunal, or

(d) a complaint relating to his dismissal has been presented by the employee under section 111.

(2) An employee is not deprived of his right to a redundancy payment by subsection (1) if, during the period of six months immediately following the period mentioned in that subsection, the employee –

(a) makes a claim for the payment by notice in writing given to the employer,

(b) refers to an employment tribunal a question as to his right to, or the amount of, the payment, or

(c) presents a complaint relating to his dismissal under section 111,

and it appears to the tribunal to be just and equitable that the employee should receive a redundancy payment.

(3) In determining under subsection (2) whether it is just and equitable that an employee should receive a redundancy payment an employment tribunal shall have regard to –

(a) the reason shown by the employee for his failure to take any such step as is referred to in subsection (2) within the period mentioned in subsection (1), and

(b) all the other relevant circumstances.

165 Written particulars of redundancy payment

(1) On making any redundancy payment, otherwise than in pursuance of a decision of a tribunal which specifies the amount of the payment to be made, the employer shall give to the employee a written statement indicating how the amount of the payment has been calculated.

(2) An employer who without reasonable excuse fails to comply with subsection (1) is guilty of an offence and liable on summary conviction to a fine not exceeding level 1 on the standard scale.

(3) If an employer fails to comply with the requirements of subsection (1), the employee may by notice in writing to the employer require him to give to the employee a written statement complying with those requirements within such period (not being less than one week beginning with the day on which the notice is given) as may be specified in the notice.

(4) An employer who without reasonable excuse fails to comply with a notice under subsection (3) is guilty of an offence and liable on summary conviction to a fine not exceeding level 3 on the standard scale.

CHAPTER VI

PAYMENTS BY SECRETARY OF STATE

166 Applications for payments

(1) Where an employee claims that his employer is liable to pay to him an employer's payment and either –

(a) that the employee has taken all reasonable steps, other than legal proceedings, to recover the payment from the employer and the employer has refused or failed to pay it, or has paid part of it and has refused or failed to pay the balance, or

(b) that the employer is insolvent and the whole or part of the payment remains unpaid,

the employee may apply to the Secretary of State for a payment under this section.

(2) In this Part 'employer's payment', in relation to an employee, means –

(a) a redundancy payment which his employer is liable to pay to him under this Part,

(aa) a payment which his employer is liable to make to him under an agreement to refrain from instituting or continuing proceedings for a contravention or alleged contravention of section 135 which has effect by virtue of section 203(2)(e) or (f), or

(b) a payment which his employer is, under an agreement in respect of which an order is in force under section 157, liable to make to him on the termination of his contract of employment.

(3) In relation to any case where (in accordance with any provision of this Part) an employment tribunal determines that an employer is liable to pay part (but not the whole) of a redundancy payment the reference in subsection (2)(a) to a redundancy payment is to the part of the redundancy payment.

(4) In subsection (1)(a) 'legal proceedings' –

(a) does not include any proceedings before an employment tribunal, but

(b) includes any proceedings to enforce a decision or award of an employment tribunal.

(5) An employer is insolvent for the purposes of subsection (1)(b) –

(a) where the employer is an individual, if (but only if) subsection (6) is satisfied,

(b) where the employer is a company, if (but only if) subsection (7) is satisfied, and

(c) where the employer is a limited liability partnership, if (but only if) subsection (8) is satisfied.

(6) This subsection is satisfied in the case of an employer who is an individual –

(a) in England and Wales if –

(i) he has been adjudged bankrupt or has made a composition or arrangement with his creditors, or

(ii) he has died and his estate falls to be administered in accordance with an order under section 421 of the Insolvency Act 1986, and

(b) in Scotland if –

(i) sequestration of his estate has been awarded or he has executed a trust deed for his creditors or has entered into a composition contract, ...

(7) This subsection is satisfied in the case of an employer which is a company –

(a) if a winding up order has been made, or a resolution for voluntary winding up has been passed, with respect to the company,

(aa) if the company is in administration for the purposes of the Insolvency Act 1986,

(b) if a receiver or ... a manager of the company's undertaking has been duly appointed, or ... possession has been taken, by or on behalf of the holders of any debentures secured by a floating charge, of any property of the company comprised in or subject to the charge, or

(c) if a voluntary arrangement proposed in the case of the company for the purposes of Part I of the Insolvency Act 1986 has been approved under that Part of that Act.

(8) This subsection is satisfied in the case of an employer which is a limited liability partnership –

(a) if a winding-up order, an administration order or a determination for a voluntary winding-up has been made with respect to the limited liability partnership,

(b) if a receiver or (in England and Wales only) a manager of the undertaking of the limited liability partnership has been duly appointed, or (in England and Wales only) possession has been taken, by or on behalf of the holders of any debentures secured by a floating charge, of any property of the limited liability partnership comprised in or subject to the charge, or

(c) if a voluntary arrangement proposed in the case of the limited liability partnership for the purpose of Part I of the Insolvency Act 1986 has been approved under that Part of that Act.

167 Making of payments

(1) Where, on an application under section 166 by an employee in relation to an employer's payment, the Secretary of State is satisfied that the requirements specified in subsection (2) are met, he shall pay to the employee out of the National Insurance Fund a sum calculated in accordance with section 168 but reduced by so much (if any) of the employer's payment as has already been paid.

(2) The requirements referred to in subsection (1) are –

(a) that the employee is entitled to the employer's payment, and

(b) that one of the conditions specified in paragraphs (a) and (b) of subsection (1) of section 166 is fulfilled,

and, in a case where the employer's payment is a payment such as is mentioned in subsection (2)(b) of that section, that the employee's right to the payment arises by virtue of a period of continuous employment (computed in accordance with the provisions of the agreement in question) which is not less than two years.

(3) Where under this section the Secretary of State pays a sum to an employee in respect of an employer's payment –

(a) all rights and remedies of the employee with respect to the employer's payment, or (if the Secretary of State has paid only part of it) all the rights and remedies of the employee with respect to that part of the employer's payment, are transferred to and vest in the Secretary of State, and

(b) any decision of an employment tribunal requiring the employer's payment to be paid to the employee has effect as if it required that payment, or that part of it which the Secretary of State has paid, to be paid to the Secretary of State.

(4) Any money recovered by the Secretary of State by virtue of subsection (3) shall be paid into the National Insurance Fund.

168 Amount of payments

(1) The sum payable to an employee by the Secretary of State under section 167 –

(a) where the employer's payment to which the employee's application under section 166 relates is a redundancy payment or a part of a redundancy payment, is a sum equal to the amount of the redundancy payment or part,

(aa) where the employer's payment to which the employee's application under section 166 relates is a payment which his employer is liable to make to him under an agreement having effect by virtue of section 203(2)(e) or (f), is a sum equal to the amount of the employer's payment or of any redundancy payment which the employer would have been liable to pay to the employee but for the agreement, whichever is less, and

(b) where the employer's payment to which the employee's application under section 166 relates is a payment which the employer is liable to make under an agreement in respect of which an order is in force under section 157, is a sum equal to the amount of the employer's payment or of the relevant redundancy payment, whichever is less.

(2) The reference in subsection (1)(b) to the amount of the relevant redundancy payment is to the amount of the redundancy payment which the employer would have been liable to pay to the employee on the assumptions specified in subsection (3).

(3) The assumptions referred to in subsection (2) are that –

(a) the order in force in respect of the agreement had not been made,

(b) the circumstances in which the employer's payment is payable had been such that the employer was liable to pay a redundancy payment to the employee in those circumstances,

(c) the relevant date, in relation to any such redundancy payment, had been the date on which the termination of the employee's contract of employment is treated as having taken effect for the purposes of the agreement, and

(d) in so far as the provisions of the agreement relating to the circumstances in which the continuity of an employee's period of employment is to be treated as broken, and the weeks which are to count in computing a period of employment, are inconsistent with the provisions of Chapter I of Part XIV, the provisions of the agreement were substituted for those provisions.

169 Information relating to applications for payments

(1) Where an employee makes an application to the Secretary of State under section 166, the Secretary of State may, by notice in writing given to the employer, require the employer –

(a) to provide the Secretary of State with such information, and

(b) to produce for examination on behalf of the Secretary of State documents in his custody or under his control of such description,

as the Secretary of State may reasonably require for the purpose of determining whether the application is well-founded.

(2) Where a person on whom a notice is served under subsection (1) fails without reasonable excuse to comply with a requirement imposed by the notice, he is guilty of an offence and liable on summary conviction to a fine not exceeding level 3 on the standard scale.

(3) A person is guilty of an offence if –

(a) in providing any information required by a notice under subsection (1), he makes a statement which he knows to be false in a material particular or recklessly makes a statement which is false in a material particular, or

(b) he produces for examination in accordance with a notice under subsection (1) a document which to his knowledge has been wilfully falsified.

(4) A person guilty of an offence under subsection (3) is liable –

(a) on summary conviction, to a fine not exceeding the statutory maximum or to imprisonment for a term not exceeding three months, or to both, or

(b) on conviction on indictment, to a fine or to imprisonment for a term not exceeding two years, or to both.

170 References to employment tribunals

(1) Where on an application made to the Secretary of State for a payment under section 166 it is claimed that an employer is liable to pay an employer's payment, there shall be referred to an employment tribunal –

(a) any question as to the liability of the employer to pay the employer's payment, and

(b) any question as to the amount of the sum payable in accordance with section 168.

(2) For the purposes of any reference under this section an employee who has been dismissed by his employer shall, unless the contrary is proved, be presumed to have been so dismissed by reason of redundancy.

CHAPTER VII

SUPPLEMENTARY

174 Death of employer: dismissal

(1) Where the contract of employment of an employee is taken for the purposes of this Part to be terminated by his employer by reason of the employer's death, this Part has effect in accordance with the following provisions of this section.

(2) Section 138 applies as if –

(a) in subsection (1)(a), for the words 'in pursuance' onwards there were substituted 'by a personal representative of the deceased employer',

(b) in subsection (1)(b), for the words 'either immediately' onwards there were substituted 'not later than eight weeks after the death of the deceased employer', and

(c) in subsections (2)(b) and (6)(a), for the word 'employer' there were substituted 'personal representative of the deceased employer'.

(3) Section 141(1) applies as if –

(a) for the words 'before the end of his employment' there were substituted 'by a personal representative of the deceased employer', and

(b) for the words 'either immediately' onwards there were substituted 'not later than eight weeks after the death of the deceased employer.'

(4) For the purposes of section 141 –

(a) provisions of the contract as renewed, or of the new contract, do not differ from the corresponding provisions of the contract in force immediately before the death of the deceased employer by reason only that the personal representative would be substituted for the deceased employer as the employer, and

(b) no account shall be taken of that substitution in determining whether refusal of the offer was unreasonable or whether the employee acted reasonably in terminating or giving notice to terminate the new or renewed employment.

(5) Section 146 has effect as if –

(a) subsection (1) were omitted, and

(b) in subsection (2), paragraph (a) were omitted and, in paragraph (b), for the word 'four' there were substituted 'eight'.

(6) For the purposes of the application of this Part (in accordance with section 161(2)) in relation to an employee who was employed as a domestic servant in a private household, references in this section and sections 175 and 218(4) and (5) to a personal representative include a person to whom the management of the household has passed, otherwise than in pursuance of a sale or other disposition for valuable consideration, in consequence of the death of the employer.

175 Death of employer: lay-off and short-time

(1) Where an employee is laid off or kept on short-time and his employer dies, this Part has effect in accordance with the following provisions of this section.

(2) Where the employee –

(a) has been laid off or kept on short-time for one or more weeks before the death of the employer,

(b) has not given the deceased employer notice of intention to claim before the employer's death,

(c) after the employer's death has his contract of employment renewed, or is re-engaged under a new contract, by a personal representative of the deceased employer, and

(d) after renewal or re-engagement is laid off or kept on short-time for one or more weeks by the personal representative,

the week in which the employer died and the first week of the employee's employment by the personal representative shall be treated for the purposes of Chapter III as consecutive weeks (and references to four weeks or thirteen weeks shall be construed accordingly).

(3) The following provisions of this section apply where –

(a) the employee has given the deceased employer notice of intention to claim before the employer's death,

(b) the employer's death occurred before the end of the period of four weeks after the service of the notice, and

(c) the employee has not terminated his contract of employment by notice expiring before the employer's death.

(4) If the contract of employment is not renewed, and the employee is not re-engaged under a new contract, by a personal representative of the deceased employer before the end of the period of four weeks after the service of the notice of intention to claim –

(a) sections 149 and 152 do not apply, but

(b) (subject to that) Chapter III applies as if the employer had not died and the employee had terminated the contract of employment by a week's notice, or by the minimum notice which he is required to give to terminate the contract (if longer than a week), expiring at the end of that period.

(5) If –

(a) the contract of employment is renewed, or the employee is re-engaged under a new contract, by a personal representative of the deceased employer before the end of the period of four weeks after the service of the notice of intention to claim, and

(b) the employee was laid off or kept on short-time by the deceased employer for one or more of those weeks and is laid off or kept on short-time by the personal representative for the week, or for the next two or more weeks, following the renewal or re-engagement,

subsection (6) has effect.

(6) Where this subsection has effect Chapter III applies as if –

(a) all the weeks mentioned in subsection (5) were consecutive weeks during which the employee was employed (but laid off or kept on short-time) by the same employer, and

(b) the periods specified by section 150(3)(a) and (b) as the relevant period were extended by any week or weeks any part of which was after the death of the employer and before the date on which the renewal or re-engagement took effect.

176 Death of employee

(1) Where an employee whose employer has given him notice to terminate his contract of employment dies before the notice expires, this Part applies as if the contract had been duly terminated by the employer by notice expiring on the date of the employee's death.

(2) Where –

(a) an employee's contract of employment has been terminated by the employer,

(b) (by virtue of subsection (5) of section 145) a date later than the relevant date as defined by the previous provisions of that section is the relevant date for the purposes of certain provisions of this Act, and

(c) the employee dies before that date,

that subsection applies as if the notice to which it refers would have expired on the employee's death.

(3) Where –

(a) an employer has given notice to an employee to terminate his contract of employment and has offered to renew his contract of employment or to re-engage him under a new contract, and

(b) the employee dies without having accepted or refused the offer and without the offer having been withdrawn, section 141(2) applies as if for the words 'he unreasonably refuses' there were substituted 'it would have been unreasonable on his part to refuse'.

(4) Where an employee's contract of employment has been renewed or he has been re-engaged under a new contract –

(a) if he dies during the trial period without having terminated, or given notice to terminate, the contract, section 141(4) applies as if for paragraph (d) there were substituted –

'(d) it would have been unreasonable for the employee during the trial period to terminate or give notice to terminate the contract.', and

(b) if during that trial period he gives notice to terminate the contract but dies before the notice expires, sections 138(2) and 141(4) apply as if the notice had expired (and the contract had been terminated by its expiry) on the date of the employee's death.

(5) Where in the circumstances specified in paragraphs (a) and (b) of subsection (3) of section 136 the employee dies before the notice given by him under paragraph (b) of that subsection expires –

(a) if he dies before his employer has given him a notice such as is specified in subsection (2) of section 142, subsections (3) and (4) of that section apply as if the employer had given him such a notice and he had not complied with it, and

(b) if he dies after his employer has given him such a notice, that section applies as if the employee had not died but did not comply with the notice.

(6) Where an employee has given notice of intention to claim –

(a) if he dies before he has given notice to terminate his contract of employment and before the relevant period (as defined in subsection (3) of section 150) has expired, that section does not apply, and

(b) if he dies within the period of seven days after the service of the notice of intention to claim, and before the employer has given a counter-notice, Chapter III applies as if the employer had given a counter-notice within that period of seven days.

(7) Where a claim for a redundancy payment is made by a personal representative of a deceased employee –

(a) if the employee died before the end of the period of six months beginning with the relevant date, subsection (1) of section 164, and

(b) if the employee died after the end of the period of six months beginning with the relevant date but before the end of the following period of six months, subsection (2) of that section,

applies as if for the words 'six months' there were substituted 'one year'.

178 Old statutory compensation schemes

(1) The Secretary of State may make provision by regulations for securing that where –

(a) (apart from this section) a person is entitled to compensation under a statutory provision to which this section applies, and

(b) the circumstances are such that he is also entitled to a redundancy payment,

the amount of the redundancy payment shall be set off against the compensation to which he would be entitled apart from this section; and any statutory provision to which any such regulations apply shall have effect subject to the regulations.

(2) This section applies to any statutory provision –

(a) which was in force immediately before 6th December 1965, and

(b) under which the holders of such situations, places or employments as are specified in that provision are, or may become, entitled to compensation for loss of employment, or for loss or diminution of emoluments or of pension rights, in consequence of the operation of any other statutory provision referred to in that provision.

179 Notices

(1) Any notice which under this Part is required or authorised to be given by an employer to an employee may be given by being delivered to the employee, or left for him at his usual or last-known place of residence, or sent by post addressed to him at that place.

(2) Any notice which under this Part is required or authorised to be given by an employee to an employer may be given either by the employee himself or by a person authorised by him to act on his behalf, and (whether given by or on behalf of the employee) –

(a) may be given by being delivered to the employer, or sent by post addressed to him at the place where the employee is or was employed by him, or

(b) if arrangements have been made by the employer, may be given by being delivered to a person designated by the employer in pursuance of the arrangements, left for such a person at a place so designated or sent by post to such a person at an address so designated.

(3) In this section any reference to the delivery of a notice includes, in relation to a notice which is not required by this Part to be in writing, a reference to the oral communication of the notice.

(4) Any notice which, in accordance with any provision of this section, is left for a person at a place referred to in that provision shall, unless the contrary is proved, be presumed to have been received by him on the day on which it was left there.

(5) Nothing in subsection (1) or (2) affects the capacity of an employer to act by a servant or agent for the purposes of any provision of this Part (including either of those subsections).

(6) In relation to an employee to whom section 173 applies, this section has effect as if –

(a) any reference in subsection (1) or (2) to a notice required or authorised to be given by or to an employer included a reference to a notice which, by virtue of that section, is required or authorised to be given by or to the person by whom the remuneration is payable,

(b) in relation to a notice required or authorised to be given to that person, any reference to the employer in paragraph (a) or (b) of subsection (2) were a reference to that person, and

(c) the reference to an employer in subsection (5) included a reference to that person.

180 Offences

(1) Where an offence under this Part committed by a body corporate is proved –

(a) to have been committed with the consent or connivance of, or

(b) to be attributable to any neglect on the part of,

any director, manager, secretary or other similar officer of the body corporate, or any person who was purporting to act in any such capacity, he (as well as the body corporate) is guilty of the offence and liable to be proceeded against and punished accordingly.

(2) In this section 'director', in relation to a body corporate established by or under any enactment for the purpose of carrying on under national ownership any industry or part of an industry or undertaking, being a body corporate whose affairs are managed by its members, means a member of that body corporate.

181 Interpretation

(1) In this Part –

'counter-notice' shall be construed in accordance with section 149(a),

'dismissal' and 'dismissed' shall be construed in accordance with sections 136 to 138,

'employer's payment' has the meaning given by section 166,

'notice of intention to claim' shall be construed in accordance with section 148(1),

'obligatory period of notice' has the meaning given by section 136(4), and

'trial period' shall be construed in accordance with section 138(3).

(2) In this Part –

(a) references to an employee being laid off or being eligible for a redundancy payment by reason of being laid off, and

(b) references to an employee being kept on short-time or being eligible for a redundancy payment by reason of being kept on short-time,

shall be construed in accordance with sections 147 and 148.

PART XII

INSOLVENCY OF EMPLOYERS

182 Employee's rights on insolvency of employer

If, on an application made to him in writing by an employee, the Secretary of State is satisfied that –

(a) the employee's employer has become insolvent,

(b) the employee's employment has been terminated, and

(c) on the appropriate date the employee was entitled to be paid the whole or part of any debt to which this Part applies,

the Secretary of State shall, subject to section 186, pay the employee out of the National Insurance Fund the amount to which, in the opinion of the Secretary of State, the employee is entitled in respect of the debt.

183 Insolvency

(1) An employer has become insolvent for the purposes of this Part –

(a) where the employer is an individual, if (but only if) subsection (2) is satisfied,

(b) where the employer is a company, if (but only if) subsection (3) is satisfied, and

(c) where the employer is a limited liability partnership, if (but only if) subsection (4) is satisfied.

(2) This subsection is satisfied in the case of an employer who is an individual –

(a) in England and Wales if –

(i) he has been adjudged bankrupt or has made a composition or arrangement with his creditors, or

(ii) he has died and his estate falls to be administered in accordance with an order under section 421 of the Insolvency Act 1986, ...

(3) This subsection is satisfied in the case of an employer which is a company –

(a) if a winding up order has been made, or a resolution for voluntary winding up has been passed, with respect to the company,

(aa) if the company is in administration for the purposes of the Insolvency Act 1986,

(b) if a receiver or ... a manager of the company's undertaking has been duly appointed, or ... possession has been taken, by or on behalf of the holders of any debentures secured by a floating charge, of any property of the company comprised in or subject to the charge, or

(c) if a voluntary arrangement proposed in the case of the company for the purposes of Part I of the Insolvency Act 1986 has been approved under that Part of that Act.

(4) This subsection is satisfied in the case of an employer which is a limited liability partnership –

(a) if a winding-up order, an administration order or a determination for a voluntary winding-up has been made with respect to the limited liability partnership,

(b) if a receiver or (in England and Wales only) a manager of the undertaking of the limited liability partnership has been duly appointed, or (in England and Wales only) possession has been taken, by or on behalf of the holders of any debentures secured by a floating charge, of any property of the limited liability partnership comprised in or subject to the charge, or

(c) if a voluntary arrangement proposed in the case of the limited liability partnership for the purposes of Part I of the Insolvency Act 1986 has been approved under that Part of that Act.

184 Debts to which Part applies

(1) This Part applies to the following debts –

(a) any arrears of pay in respect of one or more (but not more than eight) weeks,

(b) any amount which the employer is liable to pay the employee for the period of notice required by section 86(1) or (2) or for any failure of the employer to give the period of notice required by section 86(1),

(c) any holiday pay –

(i) in respect of a period or periods of holiday not exceeding six weeks in all, and

(ii) to which the employee became entitled during the twelve months ending with the appropriate date,

(d) any basic award of compensation for unfair dismissal or so much of an award under a designated dismissal procedures agreement as does not exceed any basic award of compensation for unfair dismissal to which the employee would be entitled but for the agreement, and

(e) any reasonable sum by way of reimbursement of the whole or part of any fee or premium paid by an apprentice or articled clerk.

(2) For the purposes of subsection (1)(a) the following amounts shall be treated as arrears of pay –

(a) a guarantee payment,

(b) any payment for time off under Part VI of this Act or section 169 of the Trade Union and Labour Relations (Consolidation) Act 1992 (payment for time off for carrying out trade union duties etc.),

(c) remuneration on suspension on medical grounds under section 64 of this Act and remuneration on suspension on maternity grounds under section 68 of this Act, and

(d) remuneration under a protective award under section 189 of the Trade Union and Labour Relations (Consolidation) Act 1992.

(3) In subsection (1)(c) 'holiday pay', in relation to an employee, means –

(a) pay in respect of a holiday actually taken by the employee, or

(b) any accrued holiday pay which, under the employee's contract of employment, would in the ordinary course have become payable to him in respect of the period of a holiday if his employment with the employer had continued until he became entitled to a holiday.

(4) A sum shall be taken to be reasonable for the purposes of subsection (1)(e) in a case where a trustee in bankruptcy ... or liquidator has been or is required to be appointed –

(a) as respects England and Wales, if it is admitted to be reasonable by the trustee in bankruptcy or liquidator under section 348 of the Insolvency Act 1986 (effect of bankruptcy on apprenticeships etc.), whether as originally enacted or as applied to the winding up of a company by rules under section 411 of that Act ...

185 The appropriate date

In this Part 'the appropriate date' –

(a) in relation to arrears of pay (not being remuneration under a protective award made under section 189 of the Trade Union and Labour Relations (Consolidation) Act 1992) and to holiday pay, means the date on which the employer became insolvent,

(b) in relation to a basic award of compensation for unfair dismissal and to remuneration under a protective award so made, means whichever is the latest of –

(i) the date on which the employer became insolvent,

(ii) the date of the termination of the employee's employment, and

(iii) the date on which the award was made, and

(c) in relation to any other debt to which this Part applies, means whichever is the later of –

(i) the date on which the employer became insolvent, and

(ii) the date of the termination of the employee's employment.

186 Limit on amount payable under section 182

(1) The total amount payable to an employee in respect of any debt to which this Part applies, where the amount of the debt is referable to a period of time, shall not exceed –

(a) £280 in respect of any one week, or

(b) in respect of a shorter period, an amount bearing the same proportion to £280 as that shorter period bears to a week.

187 Role of relevant officer

(1) Where a relevant officer has been, or is required to be, appointed in connection with an employer's insolvency, the Secretary of State shall not make a payment under section 182 in respect of a debt until he has received a statement from the relevant officer of the amount of that debt which appears to have been owed to the employee on the appropriate date and to remain unpaid.

(2) If the Secretary of State is satisfied that he does not require a statement under subsection (1) in order to determine the amount of a debt which was owed to the employee on the appropriate date and remains unpaid, he may make a payment under section 182 in respect of the debt without having received such a statement.

(3) A relevant officer shall, on request by the Secretary of State, provide him with a statement for the purposes of subsection (1) as soon as is reasonably practicable.

(4) The following are relevant officers for the purposes of this section –

(a) a trustee in bankruptcy ...

(b) a liquidator,

(c) an administrator,

(d) a receiver or manager,

(e) a trustee under a composition or arrangement between the employer and his creditors, and

(f) a trustee under a trust deed for his creditors executed by the employer.

(5) In subsection (4)(e) 'trustee' includes the supervisor of a voluntary arrangement proposed for the purposes of, and approved under, Part I or VIII of the Insolvency Act 1986.

188 Complaints to employment tribunals

(1) A person who has applied for a payment under section 182 may present a complaint to an employment tribunal –

(a) that the Secretary of State has failed to make any such payment, or

(b) that any such payment made by him is less than the amount which should have been paid.

(2) An employment tribunal shall not consider a complaint under subsection (1) unless it is presented –

(a) before the end of the period of three months beginning with the date on which the decision of the Secretary of State on the application was communicated to the applicant, or

(b) within such further period as the tribunal considers reasonable in a case where it is not reasonably practicable for the complaint to be presented before the end of that period of three months.

(3) Where an employment tribunal finds that the Secretary of State ought to make a payment under section 182, the tribunal shall –

(a) make a declaration to that effect, and

(b) declare the amount of any such payment which it finds the Secretary of State ought to make.

189 Transfer to Secretary of State of rights and remedies

(1) Where, in pursuance of section 182, the Secretary of State makes a payment to an employee in respect of a debt to which this Part applies –

(a) on the making of the payment any rights and remedies of the employee in respect of the debt (or, if the Secretary of State has paid only part of it, in respect of that part) become rights and remedies of the Secretary of State, and

(b) any decision of an employment tribunal requiring an employer to pay that debt to the employee has the effect that the debt (or the part of it which the Secretary of State has paid) is to be paid to the Secretary of State.

(2) Where a debt (or any part of a debt) in respect of which the Secretary of State has made a payment in pursuance of section 182 constitutes –

(a) a preferential debt within the meaning of the Insolvency Act 1986 for the purposes of any provision of that Act (including any such provision as applied by any order made under that Act) or any provision of the Companies Act 1985 ...

the rights which become rights of the Secretary of State in accordance with subsection (1) include any right arising under any such provision by reason of the status of the debt (or that part of it) as a preferential ... debt.

(3) In computing for the purposes of any provision mentioned in subsection (2)(a) or (b) the aggregate amount payable in priority to other creditors of the employer in respect of –

(a) any claim of the Secretary of State to be paid in priority to other creditors of the employer by virtue of subsection (2), and

(b) any claim by the employee to be so paid made in his own right,

any claim of the Secretary of State to be so paid by virtue of subsection (2) shall be treated as if it were a claim of the employee.

(5) Any sum recovered by the Secretary of State in exercising any right, or pursuing any remedy, which is his by virtue of this section shall be paid into the National Insurance Fund.

190 Power to obtain information

(1) Where an application is made to the Secretary of State under section 182 in respect of a debt owed by an employer, the Secretary of State may require –

(a) the employer to provide him with such information as he may reasonably require for the purpose of determining whether the application is well-founded, and

(b) any person having the custody or control of any relevant records or other documents to produce for examination on behalf of the Secretary of State any such document in that person's custody or under his control which is of such a description as the Secretary of State may require.

(2) Any such requirement –

(a) shall be made by notice in writing given to the person on whom the requirement is imposed, and

(b) may be varied or revoked by a subsequent notice so given.

(3) If a person refuses or wilfully neglects to furnish any information or produce any document which he has been required to furnish or produce by a notice under this section he is guilty of an offence and liable on summary conviction to a fine not exceeding level 3 on the standard scale.

(4) If a person, in purporting to comply with a requirement of a notice under this section, knowingly or recklessly makes any false statement he is guilty of an offence and liable on summary conviction to a fine not exceeding level 5 on the standard scale.

(5) Where an offence under this section committed by a body corporate is proved –

(a) to have been committed with the consent or connivance of, or

(b) to be attributable to any neglect on the part of,

any director, manager, secretary or other similar officer of the body corporate, or any person who was purporting to act in any such capacity, he (as well as the body corporate) is guilty of the offence and liable to be proceeded against and punished accordingly.

(6) Where the affairs of a body corporate are managed by its members, subsection (5) applies in relation to the acts and defaults of a member in connection with his functions of management as if he were a director of the body corporate.

PART XIII

MISCELLANEOUS

CHAPTER I

PARTICULAR TYPES OF EMPLOYMENT

191 Crown employment

(1) Subject to sections 192 [Armed forces] and 193, provisions of this Act to which this section applies have effect in relation to Crown employment and persons in Crown employment as they have effect in relation to other employment and other employees or workers.

(2) This section applies to –

(a) Parts I to III,

(aa) Part IVA,

(b) Part V, apart from section 45,

(c) Parts 6 to 8A,

(d) in Part IX, sections 92 and 93,

(e) Part X, apart from section 101, and

(f) this Part and Parts XIV and XV.

(3) In this Act 'Crown employment' means employment under or for the purposes of a government department or any officer or body exercising on behalf of the Crown functions conferred by a statutory provision.

(4) For the purposes of the application of provisions of this Act in relation to Crown employment in accordance with subsection (1) –

(a) references to an employee or a worker shall be construed as references to a person in Crown employment,

(b) references to a contract of employment, or a worker's contract, shall be construed as references to the terms of employment of a person in Crown employment,

(c) references to dismissal, or to the termination of a worker's contract, shall be construed as references to the termination of Crown employment,

(d) references to redundancy shall be construed as references to the existence of such circumstances as are treated, in accordance with any arrangements falling within section 177(3) for the time being in force, as equivalent to redundancy in relation to Crown employment,

(da) the reference in section 98B(2)(a) to the employer's undertaking shall be construed as a reference to the national interest, and

(e) any other reference to an undertaking shall be construed –

(i) in relation to a Minister of the Crown, as references to his functions or (as the context may require) to the department of which he is in charge, and

(ii) in relation to a government department, officer or body, as references to the functions of the department, officer or body or (as the context may require) to the department, officer or body.

(5) Where the terms of employment of a person in Crown employment restrict his right to take part in –

(a) certain political activities, or

(b) activities which may conflict with his official functions,

nothing in section 50 requires him to be allowed time off work for public duties connected with any such activities.

(6) Sections 159 and 160 are without prejudice to any exemption or immunity of the Crown.

193 National security

Part IVA and section 47B of this Act do not apply in relation to employment for the purposes of –

(a) the Security Service,

(b) the Secret Intelligence Service, or

(c) the Government Communications Headquarters

198 Short-term employment

Sections 1 to 7 do not apply to an employee if his employment continues for less than one month.

CHAPTER II

OTHER MISCELLANEOUS MATTERS

202 National security

(1) Where in the opinion of any Minister of the Crown the disclosure of any information would be contrary to the interests of national security –

(a) nothing in any of the provisions to which this section applies requires any person to disclose the information, and

(b) no person shall disclose the information in any proceedings in any court or tribunal relating to any of those provisions.

(2) This section applies to –

(a) Part I, so far as it relates to employment particulars,

(b) in Part V, sections 43M, 44, 45A, 47 and 47C, and sections 48 and 49 so far as relating to those sections,

(c) in Part VI, sections 55 to 57B and 61 to 63,

(d) in Part VII, sections 66 to 68, and sections 69 and 70 so far as relating to those sections,

(e) Part VIII,

(f) in Part IX, sections 92 and 93 where they apply by virtue of section 92(4),

(g) Part X so far as relating to a dismissal which is treated as unfair –

(i) by section 98B, 99, 100, 101A(d) or 103, or by section 104 in its application in relation to time off under section 57A,

(ii) by subsection (1) of section 105 by reason of the application of subsection (2A), (3) or (6) of that section, or by reason of the application of subsection (4A) in so far as it applies where the reason (or, if more than one, the principal reason) for which an employee was selected for dismissal was that specified in section 101A(d), and

(h) this Part and Parts XIV and XV (so far as relating to any of the provisions in paragraphs (a) to (g)).

203 Restrictions on contracting out

(1) Any provision in an agreement (whether a contract of employment or not) is void in so far as it purports –

(a) to exclude or limit the operation of any provision of this Act, or

(b) to preclude a person from bringing any proceedings under this Act before an employment tribunal.

(2) Subsection (1) –

(a) does not apply to any provision in a collective agreement excluding rights under section 28 if an order under section 35 is for the time being in force in respect of it,

(b) does not apply to any provision in a dismissal procedures agreement excluding the right under section 94 if that provision is not to have effect unless an order under section 110 is for the time being in force in respect of it,

(c) does not apply to any provision in an agreement if an order under section 157 is for the time being in force in respect of it,

(e) does not apply to any agreement to refrain from instituting or continuing proceedings where a conciliation officer has taken action under section 18 of the Employment Tribunals Act 1996, and

(f) does not apply to any agreement to refrain from instituting or continuing any proceedings within the following provisions of section 18(1) of the Employment Tribunals Act 1996 (cases where conciliation available) –

(i) paragraph (d) (proceedings under this Act),

(ii) paragraph (h) (proceedings arising out of the Part-time Workers (Prevention of Less Favourable Treatment) Regulations 2000),

(iii) paragraph (i) (proceedings arising out of the Fixed-term Employees (Prevention of Less Favourable Treatment) Regulations 2002),

(iv) paragraph (j) (proceedings under those Regulations),

if the conditions regulating compromise agreements under this Act are satisfied in relation to the agreement.

(3) For the purposes of subsection (2)(f) the conditions regulating compromise agreements under this Act are that –

(a) the agreement must be in writing,

(b) the agreement must relate to the particular proceedings,

(c) the employee or worker must have received advice from a relevant independent adviser as to the terms and effect of the proposed agreement and, in particular, its effect on his ability to pursue his rights before an employment tribunal,

(d) there must be in force, when the adviser gives the advice, a contract of insurance, or an indemnity provided for members of a profession or professional body, covering the risk of a claim by the employee or worker in respect of loss arising in consequence of the advice,

(e) the agreement must identify the adviser, and

(f) the agreement must state that the conditions regulating compromise agreements under this Act are satisfied.

(3A) A person is a relevant independent adviser for the purposes of subsection (3)(c) –

(a) if he is a qualified lawyer,

(b) if he is an officer, official, employee or member of an independent trade union who has been certified in writing by the trade union as competent to give advice and as authorised to do so on behalf of the trade union,

(c) if he works at an advice centre (whether as an employee or a volunteer) and has been certified in writing by the centre as competent to give advice and as authorised to do so on behalf of the centre, or

(d) if he is a person of a description specified in an order made by the Secretary of State.

(3B) But a person is not a relevant independent adviser for the purposes of subsection (3)(c) in relation to the employee or worker –

(a) if he is, is employed by or is acting in the matter for the employer or an associated employer,

(b) in the case of a person within subsection (3A)(b) or (c), if the trade union or advice centre is the employer or an associated employer,

(c) in the case of a person within subsection (3A)(c), if the employee or worker makes a payment for the advice received from him, or

(d) in the case of a person of a description specified in an order under subsection (3A)(d), if any condition specified in the order in relation to the giving of advice by persons of that description is not satisfied.

(4) In subsection (3A)(a) 'qualified lawyer' means –

(as respects England and Wales, a barrister (whether in practice as such or employed to give legal advice), a solicitor who holds a practising certificate, or a person other than a barrister or solicitor who is an authorised advocate or authorised litigator (within the meaning of the Courts and Legal Services Act 1990) ...

(5) An agreement under which the parties agree to submit a dispute to arbitration –

(a) shall be regarded for the purposes of subsection (2)(e) and (f) as being an agreement to refrain from instituting or continuing proceedings if –

(i) the dispute is covered by a scheme having effect by virtue of an order under section 212A of the Trade Union and Labour Relations (Consolidation) Act 1992, and

(ii) the agreement is to submit it to arbitration in accordance with the scheme, but

(b) shall be regarded as neither being nor including such an agreement in any other case.

204 Law governing employment

(1) For the purposes of this Act it is immaterial whether the law which (apart from this Act) governs any person's employment is the law of the United Kingdom, or of a part of the United Kingdom, or not.

205 Remedy for infringement of certain rights

(1) The remedy of an employee for infringement of any of the rights conferred by section 8, Part III, Parts V to VIII, section 92, Part X and Part XII is, where provision is made for a complaint or the reference of a question to an employment tribunal, by way of such a complaint or reference and not otherwise.

(1ZA) In relation to the right conferred by section 45A, the reference in subsection (1) to an employee has effect as a reference to a worker.

(1A) In relation to the right conferred by section 47B, the reference in subsection (1) to an employee has effect as a reference to a worker.

(2) The remedy of a worker in respect of any contravention of section 13, 15, 18(1) or 21(1) is by way of a complaint under section 23 and not otherwise.

206 Institution or continuance of tribunal proceedings

(1) Where an employer has died, any tribunal proceedings arising under any of the provisions of this Act to which this section applies may be defended by a personal representative of the deceased employer.

(2) This section and section 207 apply to –

    (a) Part I, so far as it relates to itemised pay statements,

    (b) Part III,

    (c) Part V,

    (d) Part VI, apart from sections 58 to 60,

    (e) Parts VII and VIII,

    (f) in Part IX, sections 92 and 93, and

    (g) Parts X to XII.

(3) Where an employee has died, any tribunal proceedings arising under any of the provisions of this Act to which this section applies may be instituted or continued by a personal representative of the deceased employee.

(4) If there is no personal representative of a deceased employee, any tribunal proceedings arising under any of the provisions of this Act to which this section applies may be instituted or continued on behalf of the estate of the deceased employee by any appropriate person appointed by the employment tribunal.

(5) In subsection (4) 'appropriate person' means a person who is –

    (a) authorised by the employee before his death to act in connection with the proceedings, or

(b) the widow or widower, child, parent or brother or sister of the deceased employee;

and in Part XI and the following provisions of this section and section 207 references to a personal representative include a person appointed under subsection (4).

(6) In a case where proceedings are instituted or continued by virtue of subsection (4), any award made by the employment tribunal shall be –

(a) made in such terms, and

(b) enforceable in such manner,

as the Secretary of State may by regulations provide.

(7) Any reference in the provisions of this Act to which this section applies to the doing of anything by or in relation to an employer or employee includes a reference to the doing of the thing by or in relation to a personal representative of the deceased employer or employee.

(8) Any reference in the provisions of this Act to which this section applies to a thing required or authorised to be done by or in relation to an employer or employee includes a reference to a thing required or authorised to be done by or in relation to a personal representative of the deceased employer or employee.

(9) Subsections (7) and (8) do not prevent a reference to a successor of an employer including a personal representative of a deceased employer.

207 Rights and liabilities accruing after death

(1) Any right arising under any of the provisions of this Act to which this section applies which accrues after the death of an employee devolves as if it had accrued before his death.

(2) Where an employment tribunal determines under any provision of Part XI that an employer is liable to pay to a personal representative of a deceased employee –

(a) the whole of a redundancy payment to which he would have been entitled but for some provision of Part XI or section 206, or

(b) such part of such a redundancy payment as the tribunal thinks fit,

the reference in subsection (1) to a right includes any right to receive it.

(3) Where –

(a) by virtue of any of the provisions to which this section applies a personal representative is liable to pay any amount, and

(b) the liability has not accrued before the death of the employer,

it shall be treated as a liability of the deceased employer which had accrued immediately before his death.

209 Powers to amend Act

(1) The Secretary of State may by order –

(a) provide that any provision of this Act, other than any to which this paragraph does not apply, which is specified in the order shall not apply to persons, or to employments, of such classes as may be prescribed in the order,

(b) provide that any provision of this Act, other than any to which this paragraph does not apply, shall apply to persons or employments of such classes as may be prescribed in the order subject to such exceptions and modifications as may be so prescribed, or

(c) vary, or exclude the operation of, any of the provisions to which this paragraph applies. ...

(8) The provisions of this section are without prejudice to any other power of the Secretary of State to amend, vary or repeal any provision of this Act or to extend or restrict its operation in relation to any person or employment.

PART XIV

INTERPRETATION

CHAPTER I

CONTINUOUS EMPLOYMENT

210 Introductory

(1) References in any provision of this Act to a period of continuous employment are (unless provision is expressly made to the contrary) to a period computed in accordance with this Chapter.

(2) In any provision of this Act which refers to a period of continuous employment expressed in months or years –

(a) a month means a calendar month, and

(b) a year means a year of twelve calendar months.

(3) In computing an employee's period of continuous employment for the purposes of any provision of this Act, any question –

(a) whether the employee's employment is of a kind counting towards a period of continuous employment, or

(b) whether periods (consecutive or otherwise) are to be treated as forming a single period of continuous employment,

shall be determined week by week; but where it is necessary to compute the length of an employee's period of employment it shall be computed in months and years of twelve months in accordance with section 211.

(4) Subject to sections 215 to 217 [Reinstatement after military service], a week

which does not count in computing the length of a period of continuous employment breaks continuity of employment.

(5) A person's employment during any period shall, unless the contrary is shown, be presumed to have been continuous.

211 Period of continuous employment

(1) An employee's period of continuous employment for the purposes of any provision of this Act –

(a) (subject to subsections (2) and (3)) begins with the day on which the employee starts work, and

(b) ends with the day by reference to which the length of the employee's period of continuous employment is to be ascertained for the purposes of the provision.

(2) For the purposes of sections 155 and 162(1), an employee's period of continuous employment shall be treated as beginning on the employee's eighteenth birthday if that is later than the day on which the employee starts work.

(3) If an employee's period of continuous employment includes one or more periods which (by virtue of section 215, 216 or 217) while not counting in computing the length of the period do not break continuity of employment, the beginning of the period shall be treated as postponed by the number of days falling within that intervening period, or the aggregate number of days falling within those periods, calculated in accordance with the section in question.

212 Weeks counting in computing period

(1) Any week during the whole or part of which an employee's relations with his employer are governed by a contract of employment counts in computing the employee's period of employment.

(3) Subject to subsection (4), any week (not within subsection (1)) during the whole or part of which an employee is –

(a) incapable of work in consequence of sickness or injury,

(b) absent from work on account of a temporary cessation of work, or

(c) absent from work in circumstances such that, by arrangement or custom, he is regarded as continuing in the employment of his employer for any purpose,

counts in computing the employee's period of employment.

(4) Not more than twenty-six weeks count under subsection (3)(a) between any periods falling under subsection (1).

213 Intervals in employment

(1) Where in the case of an employee a date later than the date which would be the effective date of termination by virtue of subsection (1) of section 97 is treated for certain purposes as the effective date of termination by virtue of subsection (2) or (4)

of that section, the period of the interval between the two dates counts as a period of employment in ascertaining for the purposes of section 108(1) or 119(1) the period for which the employee has been continuously employed.

(2) Where an employee is by virtue of section 138(1) regarded for the purposes of Part XI as not having been dismissed by reason of a renewal or re-engagement taking effect after an interval, the period of the interval counts as a period of employment in ascertaining for the purposes of section 155 or 162(1) the period for which the employee has been continuously employed (except so far as it is to be disregarded under section 214 or 215).

(3) Where in the case of an employee a date later than the date which would be the relevant date by virtue of subsections (2) to (4) of section 145 is treated for certain purposes as the relevant date by virtue of subsection (5) of that section, the period of the interval between the two dates counts as a period of employment in ascertaining for the purposes of section 155 or 162(1) the period for which the employee has been continuously employed (except so far as it is to be disregarded under section 214 or 215).

214 Special provisions for redundancy payments

(1) This section applies where a period of continuous employment has to be determined in relation to an employee for the purposes of the application of section 155 or 162(1).

(2) The continuity of a period of employment is broken where –

(a) a redundancy payment has previously been paid to the employee (whether in respect of dismissal or in respect of lay-off or short-time), and

(b) the contract of employment under which the employee was employed was renewed (whether by the same or another employer) or the employee was re-engaged under a new contract of employment (whether by the same or another employer).

(3) The continuity of a period of employment is also broken where –

(a) a payment has been made to the employee (whether in respect of the termination of his employment or lay-off or short-time) in accordance with a scheme under section 1 of the Superannuation Act 1972 or arrangements falling within section 177(3), and

(b) he commenced new, or renewed, employment.

(4) The date on which the person's continuity of employment is broken by virtue of this section –

(a) if the employment was under a contract of employment, is the date which was the relevant date in relation to the payment mentioned in subsection (2)(a) or (3)(a), and

(b) if the employment was otherwise than under a contract of employment, is the date which would have been the relevant date in relation to the payment mentioned in subsection (2)(a) or (3)(a) had the employment been under a contract of employment.

(5) For the purposes of this section a redundancy payment shall be treated as having been paid if –

(a) the whole of the payment has been paid to the employee by the employer,

(b) a tribunal has determined liability and found that the employer must pay part (but not all) of the redundancy payment and the employer has paid that part, or

(c) the Secretary of State has paid a sum to the employee in respect of the redundancy payment under section 167.

215 Employment abroad, etc

(1) This Chapter applies to a period of employment –

(a) (subject to the following provisions of this section) even where during the period the employee was engaged in work wholly or mainly outside Great Britain, and

(b) even where the employee was excluded by or under this Act from any right conferred by this Act.

(2) For the purposes of sections 155 and 162(1) a week of employment does not count in computing a period of employment if the employee –

(a) was employed outside Great Britain during the whole or part of the week, and

(b) was not during that week an employed earner for the purposes of the Social Security Contributions and Benefits Act 1992 in respect of whom a secondary Class 1 contribution was payable under that Act (whether or not the contribution was in fact paid).

(3) Where by virtue of subsection (2) a week of employment does not count in computing a period of employment, the continuity of the period is not broken by reason only that the week does not count in computing the period; and the number of days which, for the purposes of section 211(3), fall within the intervening period is seven for each week within this subsection.

(4) Any question arising under subsection (2) whether –

(a) a person was an employed earner for the purposes of the Social Security Contributions and Benefits Act 1992, or

(b) if so, whether a secondary Class 1 contribution was payable in respect of him under that Act,

shall be determined by an officer of the Commissioners for Her Majesty's Revenue and Customs.

(5) Part II of the Social Security Contributions (Transfer of Functions, etc) Act 1999 (decisions and appeals) shall apply in relation to the determination of any

issue by the Inland Revenue under subsection (4) as if it were a decision falling within section 8(1) of that Act.

(6) Subsection (2) does not apply in relation to a person who is –

(a) employed as a master or seaman in a British ship, and

(b) ordinarily resident in Great Britain.

216 Industrial disputes

(1) A week does not count under section 212 if during the week, or any part of the week, the employee takes part in a strike.

(2) The continuity of an employee's period of employment is not broken by a week which does not count under this Chapter (whether or not by virtue only of subsection (1)) if during the week, or any part of the week, the employee takes part in a strike; and the number of days which, for the purposes of section 211(3), fall within the intervening period is the number of days between the last working day before the strike and the day on which work was resumed.

(3) The continuity of an employee's period of employment is not broken by a week if during the week, or any part of the week, the employee is absent from work because of a lock-out by the employer; and the number of days which, for the purposes of section 211(3), fall within the intervening period is the number of days between the last working day before the lock-out and the day on which work was resumed.

218 Change of employer

(1) Subject to the provisions of this section, this Chapter relates only to employment by the one employer.

(2) If a trade or business, or an undertaking (whether or not established by or under an Act), is transferred from one person to another –

(a) the period of employment of an employee in the trade or business or undertaking at the time of the transfer counts as a period of employment with the transferee, and

(b) the transfer does not break the continuity of the period of employment.

(3) If by or under an Act (whether public or local and whether passed before or after this Act) a contract of employment between any body corporate and an employee is modified and some other body corporate is substituted as the employer –

(a) the employee's period of employment at the time when the modification takes effect counts as a period of employment with the second body corporate, and

(b) the change of employer does not break the continuity of the period of employment.

(4) If on the death of an employer the employee is taken into the employment of the personal representatives or trustees of the deceased –

(a) the employee's period of employment at the time of the death counts as a period of employment with the employer's personal representatives or trustees, and

(b) the death does not break the continuity of the period of employment.

(5) If there is a change in the partners, personal representatives or trustees who employ any person –

(a) the employee's period of employment at the time of the change counts as a period of employment with the partners, personal representatives or trustees after the change, and

(b) the change does not break the continuity of the period of employment.

(6) If an employee of an employer is taken into the employment of another employer who, at the time when the employee enters the second employer's employment, is an associated employer of the first employer –

(a) the employee's period of employment at that time counts as a period of employment with the second employer, and

(b) the change of employer does not break the continuity of the period of employment.

(7) If an employee of the governing body of a school maintained by a local education authority is taken into the employment of the authority or an employee of a local education authority is taken into the employment of the governing body of a school maintained by the authority –

(a) his period of employment at the time of the change of employer counts as a period of employment with the second employer, and

(b) the change does not break the continuity of the period of employment.

(8) If a person employed in relevant employment by a health service employer is taken into relevant employment by another such employer, his period of employment at the time of the change of employer counts as a period of employment with the second employer and the change does not break the continuity of the period of employment.

(9) For the purposes of subsection (8) employment is relevant employment if it is employment of a description –

(a) in which persons are engaged while undergoing professional training which involves their being employed successively by a number of different health service employers, and

(b) which is specified in an order made by the Secretary of State.

(10) The following are health service employers for the purposes of subsections (8) and (9) –

(a) Strategic Health Authorities and Health Authorities established under section 8 of the National Health Service Act 1977,

(b) Special Health Authorities established under section 11 of that Act, (bb) Primary Care Trusts established under section 16A of that Act,

(c) National Health Service trusts established under Part I of the National Health Service and Community Care Act 1990,

(ca) NHS foundation trusts,

(d) the Dental Practice Board,

(dd) the Health Protection Agency

219 Reinstatement or re-engagement of dismissed employee

(1) Regulations made by the Secretary of State may make provision –

(a) for preserving the continuity of a person's period of employment for the purposes of this Chapter or for the purposes of this Chapter as applied by or under any other enactment specified in the regulations, or

(b) for modifying or excluding the operation of section 214 subject to the recovery of any such payment as is mentioned in that section,

in cases where a dismissed employee is reinstated, re-engaged or otherwise re-employed by his employer in any circumstances prescribed by the regulations.

CHAPTER II

A WEEK'S PAY

220 Introductory

The amount of a week's pay of an employee shall be calculated for the purposes of this Act in accordance with this Chapter.

221 General

(1) This section and sections 222 and 223 apply where there are normal working hours for the employee when employed under the contract of employment in force on the calculation date.

(2) Subject to section 222, if the employee's remuneration for employment in normal working hours (whether by the hour or week or other period) does not vary with the amount of work done in the period, the amount of a week's pay is the amount which is payable by the employer under the contract of employment in force on the calculation date if the employee works throughout his normal working hours in a week.

(3) Subject to section 222, if the employee's remuneration for employment in normal working hours (whether by the hour or week or other period) does vary with the amount of work done in the period, the amount of a week's pay is the amount of remuneration for the number of normal working hours in a week calculated at the average hourly rate of remuneration payable by the employer to the employee in respect of the period of twelve weeks ending –

(a) where the calculation date is the last day of a week, with that week, and

(b) otherwise, with the last complete week before the calculation date.

(4) In this section references to remuneration varying with the amount of work done includes remuneration which may include any commission or similar payment which varies in amount.

(5) This section is subject to sections 227 and 228.

222 Remuneration varying according to time of work

(1) This section applies if the employee is required under the contract of employment in force on the calculation date to work during normal working hours on days of the week, or at times of the day, which differ from week to week or over a longer period so that the remuneration payable for, or apportionable to, any week varies according to the incidence of those days or times.

(2) The amount of a week's pay is the amount of remuneration for the average number of weekly normal working hours at the average hourly rate of remuneration.

(3) For the purposes of subsection (2) –

(a) the average number of weekly hours is calculated by dividing by twelve the total number of the employee's normal working hours during the relevant period of twelve weeks, and

(b) the average hourly rate of remuneration is the average hourly rate of remuneration payable by the employer to the employee in respect of the relevant period of twelve weeks.

(4) In subsection (3) 'the relevant period of twelve weeks' means the period of twelve weeks ending –

(a) where the calculation date is the last day of a week, with that week, and

(b) otherwise, with the last complete week before the calculation date.

(5) This section is subject to sections 227 and 228.

223 Supplementary

(1) For the purposes of sections 221 and 222, in arriving at the average hourly rate of remuneration, only –

(a) the hours when the employee was working, and

(b) the remuneration payable for, or apportionable to, those hours,

shall be brought in.

(2) If for any of the twelve weeks mentioned in sections 221 and 222 no remuneration within subsection (1)(b) was payable by the employer to the employee, account shall be taken of remuneration in earlier weeks so as to bring up to twelve the number of weeks of which account is taken.

(3) Where –

(a) in arriving at the average hourly rate of remuneration, account has to be taken of remuneration payable for, or apportionable to, work done in hours other than normal working hours, and

(b) the amount of that remuneration was greater than it would have been if the work had been done in normal working hours (or, in a case within section 234(3), in normal working hours falling within the number of hours without overtime),

account shall be taken of that remuneration as if the work had been done in such hours and the amount of that remuneration had been reduced accordingly.

224 Employments with no normal working hours

(1) This section applies where there are no normal working hours for the employee when employed under the contract of employment in force on the calculation date.

(2) The amount of a week's pay is the amount of the employee's average weekly remuneration in the period of twelve weeks ending –

(a) where the calculation date is the last day of a week, with that week, and

(b) otherwise, with the last complete week before the calculation date.

(3) In arriving at the average weekly remuneration no account shall be taken of a week in which no remuneration was payable by the employer to the employee and remuneration in earlier weeks shall be brought in so as to bring up to twelve the number of weeks of which account is taken.

(4) This section is subject to sections 227 and 228.

225 Rights during employment

(1) Where the calculation is for the purposes of section 30, the calculation date is –

(a) where the employee's contract has been varied, or a new contract entered into, in connection with a period of short-time working, the last day on which the original contract was in force, and

(b) otherwise, the day in respect of which the guarantee payment is payable.

(2) Where the calculation is for the purposes of section 53 or 54, the calculation date is the day on which the employer's notice was given.

(3) Where the calculation is for the purposes of section 56, the calculation date is the day of the appointment.

(4) Where the calculation is for the purposes of section 62, the calculation date is the day on which the time off was taken or on which it is alleged the time off should have been permitted.

(4A) Where the calculation is for the purposes of section 63B, the calculation date is the day on which the time off was taken or on which it is alleged the time off should have been permitted.

(5) Where the calculation is for the purposes of section 69 –

(a) in the case of an employee suspended on medical grounds, the calculation date is the day before that on which the suspension begins, and

(b) in the case of an employee suspended on maternity grounds, the calculation date is –

(i) where the day before that on which the suspension begins falls during a period of ordinary or additional maternity leave, the day before the beginning of that period,

(ii) otherwise, the day before that on which the suspension begins.

(6) Where the calculation is for the purposes of section 80I, the calculation date is the day on which the application under section 80F was made.

226 Rights on termination

(1) Where the calculation is for the purposes of section 88 or 89, the calculation date is the day immediately preceding the first day of the period of notice required by section 86(1) or (2).

(2) Where the calculation is for the purposes of section 93, 117 or 125, the calculation date is –

(a) if the dismissal was with notice, the date on which the employer's notice was given, and

(b) otherwise, the effective date of termination.

(3) Where the calculation is for the purposes of section 112, 119, 120 or 121 the calculation date is –

(b) if by virtue of subsection (2) or (4) of section 97 a date later than the effective date of termination as defined in subsection (1) of that section is to be treated for certain purposes as the effective date of termination, the effective date of termination as so defined, and

(c) otherwise, the date specified in subsection (6).

(4) Where the calculation is for the purposes of section 147(2), the calculation date is the day immediately preceding the first of the four, or six, weeks referred to in section 148(2).

(5) Where the calculation is for the purposes of section 162, the calculation date is –

(b) if by virtue of subsection (5) of section 145 a date is to be treated for certain purposes as the relevant date which is later than the relevant date as defined by the previous provisions of that section, the relevant date as so defined, and

(c) otherwise, the date specified in subsection (6).

(6) The date referred to in subsections (3)(c) and (5)(c) is the date on which notice would have been given had –

(a) the contract been terminable by notice and been terminated by the employer giving such notice as is required by section 86 to terminate the contract, and

(b) the notice expired on the effective date of termination, or the relevant date,

(whether or not those conditions were in fact fulfilled).

227 Maximum amount

(1) For the purpose of calculating –

(za) an award of compensation under section 80I(1)(b),

(a) a basic award of compensation for unfair dismissal,

(b) an additional award of compensation for unfair dismissal,

(ba) an award under section 112(5), or

(c) a redundancy payment,

the amount of a week's pay shall not exceed £280.

228 New employments and other special cases

(1) In any case in which the employee has not been employed for a sufficient period to enable a calculation to be made under the preceding provisions of this Chapter, the amount of a week's pay is the amount which fairly represents a week's pay.

(2) In determining that amount the employment tribunal –

(a) shall apply as nearly as may be such of the preceding provisions of this Chapter as it considers appropriate, and

(b) may have regard to such of the considerations specified in subsection (3) as it thinks fit.

(3) The considerations referred to in subsection (2)(b) are –

(a) any remuneration received by the employee in respect of the employment in question,

(b) the amount offered to the employee as remuneration in respect of the employment in question,

(c) the remuneration received by other persons engaged in relevant comparable employment with the same employer, and

(d) the remuneration received by other persons engaged in relevant comparable employment with other employers.

(4) The Secretary of State may by regulations provide that in cases prescribed by the regulations the amount of a week's pay shall be calculated in such manner as may be so prescribed.

229 Supplementary

(1) In arriving at –

(a) an average hourly rate of remuneration, or

(b) average weekly remuneration,

under this Chapter, account shall be taken of work for a former employer within the period for which the average is to be taken if, by virtue of Chapter I of this Part, a period of employment with the former employer counts as part of the employee's continuous period of employment.

(2) Where under this Chapter account is to be taken of remuneration or other payments for a period which does not coincide with the periods for which the remuneration or other payments are calculated, the remuneration or other payments shall be apportioned in such manner as may be just.

CHAPTER III

OTHER INTERPRETATION PROVISIONS

230 Employees, workers, etc

(1) In this Act 'employee' means an individual who has entered into or works under (or, where the employment has ceased, worked under) a contract of employment.

(2) In this Act 'contract of employment' means a contract of service or apprenticeship, whether express or implied, and (if it is express) whether oral or in writing.

(3) In this Act 'worker' (except in the phrases 'shop worker' and 'betting worker') means an individual who has entered into or works under (or, where the employment has ceased, worked under) –

(a) a contract of employment, or

(b) any other contract, whether express or implied and (if it is express) whether oral or in writing, whereby the individual undertakes to do or perform personally any work or services for another party to the contract whose status is not by virtue of the contract that of a client or customer of any profession or business undertaking carried on by the individual;

and any reference to a worker's contract shall be construed accordingly.

(4) In this Act 'employer', in relation to an employee or a worker, means the person by whom the employee or worker is (or, where the employment has ceased, was) employed.

(5) In this Act 'employment' –

(a) in relation to an employee, means (except for the purposes of section 171) employment under a contract of employment, and

(b) in relation to a worker, means employment under his contract;

and 'employed' shall be construed accordingly.

(6) This section has effect subject to sections 43K and 47B(3); and for the purposes of Part XIII so far as relating to Part IVA or section 47B, 'worker', 'worker's contract'

and, in relation to a worker, 'employer', 'employment' and 'employed' have the extended meaning given by section 43K.

231 Associated employers

For the purposes of this Act any two employers shall be treated as associated if –

(a) one is a company of which the other (directly or indirectly) has control, or

(b) both are companies of which a third person (directly or indirectly) has control;

and 'associated employer' shall be construed accordingly.

232 Shop workers

(1) In this Act 'shop worker' means an employee who, under his contract of employment, is or may be required to do shop work.

(2) In this Act 'shop work' means work in or about a shop on a day on which the shop is open for the serving of customers.

(3) Subject to subsection (4), in this Act 'shop' includes any premises where any retail trade or business is carried on.

(4) Where premises are used mainly for purposes other than those of retail trade or business and would not (apart from subsection (3)) be regarded as a shop, only such part of the premises as –

(a) is used wholly or mainly for the purposes of retail trade or business, or

(b) is used both for the purposes of retail trade or business and for the purposes of wholesale trade and is used wholly or mainly for those two purposes considered together,

is to be regarded as a shop for the purposes of this Act.

(5) In subsection (4)(b) 'wholesale trade' means the sale of goods for use or resale in the course of a business or the hire of goods for use in the course of a business.

(6) In this section 'retail trade or business' includes –

(a) the business of a barber or hairdresser,

(b) the business of hiring goods otherwise than for use in the course of a trade or business, and

(c) retail sales by auction,

but does not include catering business or the sale at theatres and places of amusement of programmes, catalogues and similar items.

(7) In subsection (6) 'catering business' means –

(a) the sale of meals, refreshments or alcohol ... for consumption on the premises on which they are sold, or

(b) the sale of meals or refreshments prepared to order for immediate consumption off the premises;

and in paragraph (a) 'alcohol' has the same meaning as in the Licensing Act 2003.
...

(8) In this Act –

'notice period', in relation to an opted-out shop worker, has the meaning given by section 41(3),

'opted-out', in relation to a shop worker, shall be construed in accordance with section 41(1) and (2),

'opting-in notice', in relation to a shop worker, has the meaning given by section 36(6),

'opting-out notice', in relation to a shop worker, has the meaning given by section 40(2), and

'protected', in relation to a shop worker, shall be construed in accordance with section 36(1) to (5).

233 Betting workers

(1) In this Act 'betting worker' means an employee who, under his contract of employment, is or may be required to do betting work.

(2) In this Act 'betting work' means –

(a) work at a track for a bookmaker on a day on which the bookmaker acts as such at the track, being work which consists of or includes dealing with betting transactions, and

(b) work in a licensed betting office in England or Wales on a day on which the office is open for use for the effecting of betting transactions.

(3) In subsection (2) 'betting transactions' includes the collection or payment of winnings on a bet and any transaction in which one or more of the parties is acting as a bookmaker.

(4) In this section 'bookmaker' means any person who –

(a) whether on his own account or as servant or agent to any other person, carries on (whether occasionally or regularly) the business of receiving or negotiating bets or conducting pool betting operations, or

(b) by way of business in any manner holds himself out, or permits himself to be held out, as a person who receives or negotiates bets or conducts such operations.

(5) Expressions used in this section and in the Betting, Gaming and Lotteries Act 1963 have the same meaning in this section as in that Act.

(6) In this Act –

'notice period', in relation to an opted-out betting worker, has the meaning given by section 41(3), 'opted-out', in relation to a betting worker, shall be construed in accordance with section 41(1) and (2),

'opting-in notice', in relation to a betting worker, has the meaning given by section 36(6),

'opting-out notice', in relation to a betting worker, has the meaning given by section 40(2), and

'protected', in relation to a betting worker, shall be construed in accordance with section 36(1) to (5).

234 Normal working hours

(1) Where an employee is entitled to overtime pay when employed for more than a fixed number of hours in a week or other period, there are for the purposes of this Act normal working hours in his case.

(2) Subject to subsection (3), the normal working hours in such a case are the fixed number of hours.

(3) Where in such a case –

(a) the contract of employment fixes the number, or minimum number, of hours of employment in a week or other period (whether or not it also provides for the reduction of that number or minimum in certain circumstances), and

(b) that number or minimum number of hours exceeds the number of hours without overtime,

the normal working hours are that number or minimum number of hours (and not the number of hours without overtime).

235 Other definitions

(1) In this Act, except in so far as the context otherwise requires –

'act' and 'action' each includes omission and references to doing an act or taking action shall be construed accordingly,

'basic award of compensation for unfair dismissal' shall be construed in accordance with section 118,

'business' includes a trade or profession and includes any activity carried on by a body of persons (whether corporate or unincorporated),

'childbirth' means the birth of a living child or the birth of a child whether living or dead after twenty-four weeks of pregnancy,

'collective agreement' has the meaning given by section 178(1) and (2) of the Trade Union and Labour Relations (Consolidation) Act 1992,

'conciliation officer' means an officer designated by the Advisory, Conciliation and Arbitration Service under section 211 of that Act,

'dismissal procedures agreement' means an agreement in writing with respect to procedures relating to dismissal made by or on behalf of one or more independent trade unions and one or more employers or employers' associations,

'employers' association' has the same meaning as in the Trade Union and Labour Relations (Consolidation) Act 1992,

'expected week of childbirth' means the week, beginning with midnight between Saturday and Sunday, in which it is expected that childbirth will occur,

'guarantee payment' has the meaning given by section 28,

'independent trade union' means a trade union which –

(a) is not under the domination or control of an employer or a group of employers or of one or more employers' associations, and

(b) is not liable to interference by an employer or any such group or association (arising out of the provision of financial or material support or by any other means whatever) tending towards such control,

'job', in relation to an employee, means the nature of the work which he is employed to do in accordance with his contract and the capacity and place in which he is so employed,

'paternity leave' means leave under section 80A or 80B,

'position', in relation to an employee, means the following matters taken as a whole –

(a) his status as an employee,

(b) the nature of his work, and

(c) his terms and conditions of employment,

'protected disclosure' has the meaning given by section 43A,

'redundancy payment' has the meaning given by Part XI,

'relevant date' has the meaning given by sections 145 and 153,

'renewal' includes extension, and any reference to renewing a contract or a fixed term shall be construed accordingly,

'statutory provision' means a provision, whether of a general or a special nature, contained in, or in any document made or issued under, any Act, whether of a general or special nature,

'successor', in relation to the employer of an employee, means (subject to subsection (2)) a person who in consequence of a change occurring (whether by virtue of a sale or other disposition or by operation of law) in the ownership of the undertaking, or of the part of the undertaking, for the purposes of which the employee was employed, has become the owner of the undertaking or part,

'trade union' has the meaning given by section 1 of the Trade Union and Labour Relations (Consolidation) Act 1992,

'week' –

(a) in Chapter I of this Part means a week ending with Saturday, and

(b) otherwise, except in sections 80A, 80B and 86 means, in relation to an employee whose remuneration is calculated weekly by a week ending with a day other than Saturday, a week ending with that other day and, in relation to any other employee, a week ending with Saturday.

(2) The definition of 'successor' in subsection (1) has effect (subject to the necessary modifications) in relation to a case where –

(a) the person by whom an undertaking or part of an undertaking is owned immediately before a change is one of the persons by whom (whether as partners, trustees or otherwise) it is owned immediately after the change, or

(b) the persons by whom an undertaking or part of an undertaking is owned immediately before a change (whether as partners, trustees or otherwise) include the persons by whom, or include one or more of the persons by whom, it is owned immediately after the change,

as it has effect where the previous owner and the new owner are wholly different persons.

(2A) For the purposes of this Act a contract of employment is a 'limited-term contract' if –

(a) the employment under the contract is not intended to be permanent, and

(b) provision is accordingly made in the contract for it to terminate by virtue of a limiting event.

(2B) In this Act, 'limiting event', in relation to a contract of employment means –

(a) in the case of a contract for a fixed-term, the expiry of the term,

(b) in the case of a contract made in contemplation of the performance of a specific task, the performance of the task, and

(c) in the case of a contract which provides for its termination on the occurrence of an event (or the failure of an event to occur), the occurrence of the event (or the failure of the event to occur).

(3) References in this Act to redundancy, dismissal by reason of redundancy and similar expressions shall be construed in accordance with section 139.

(4) In sections 136(2), 154 and 216(3) and paragraph 14 of Schedule 2 'lock-out' means –

(a) the closing of a place of employment,

(b) the suspension of work, or

(c) the refusal by an employer to continue to employ any number of persons employed by him in consequence of a dispute,

done with a view to compelling persons employed by the employer, or to aid another employer in compelling persons employed by him, to accept terms or conditions of or affecting employment.

(5) In sections 91(2), 140(2) and (3), 143(1), 144(2) and (3), 154 and 216(1) and (2) and paragraph 14 of Schedule 2 'strike' means –

(a) the cessation of work by a body of employed persons acting in combination, or

(b) a concerted refusal, or a refusal under a common understanding, of any number of employed persons to continue to work for an employer in consequence of a dispute,

done as a means of compelling their employer or any employed person or body of employed persons, or to aid other employees in compelling their employer or any employed person or body of employed persons, to accept or not to accept terms or conditions of or affecting employment.

PART XV

GENERAL AND SUPPLEMENTARY

236 Orders and regulations

(1) Any power conferred by any provision of this Act to make any order (other than an Order in Council) or regulations is exercisable by statutory instrument. ...

As amended by the Health and Safety (Consultation with Employees) Regulations 1996, reg 8; National Minimum Wage Act 1998, ss25(1)–(4), 53, Schedule 3; School Standards and Framework Act 1998, s140(3), Schedule 31; Employment Rights (Dispute Resolution) Act 1998, ss1(2)(a)–(c), 8(5), 9(1), (2)(e), 10(1), (2)(e), 11(2), (3), 12(1)–(5), 13, 14(2)–(4), 15, Schedule 1, paras 18–26, Schedule 2; Public Interest Disclosure Act 1998, ss1–7, 9, 10, 14, 14; Working Time Regulations 1998, regs 31(1)–(3), (5), (7), 32(1)–(6); Teaching and Higher Education Act 1998, ss32, 44(1), Schedule 3, paras 10–12, 14; Employment Relations Act 1999, ss6–9, 16, 18(2), (3), 32(3), 33(1)(a), (2), 34(4), 35, 36(1)(a), 37(1), 41, 44, Schedule 4, Pts I, II and III, paras 5–12, 14–23, 26–30, 36, 38–41, Schedule 5, para 5, Schedule 8, para 1, Schedule 9(2), (3), (9)–(11); Tax Credit Act 1999, ss7, 19(4), Schedule 3, para 3, Schedule 6; Welfare Reform and Pensions Act 1999, s18, Schedule 2, para 19(1)–(3); Social Security Contributions (Transfer of Functions, etc) Act 1999, s18, Schedule7, para 21; Collective Redundancies and Transfer of Undertakings (Protection of Employment) (Amendment) Regulations 1999, regs 12, 13 15; Ionising Radiation Regulations 1999, reg 41(1), Schedule 9, para 2; Unfair Dismissal and Statement of Reasons for Dismissal (Variation of Qualifying Period) Order 1999, arts 2–4; Transnational Information and Consultation of Employees Regulations 1999, reg 29(1)–(3); Scotland Act 1998 (Consequential Modifications) Order 2000, art 2, Schedule, Pt I, para 19; Health Act 1999 (Supplementary, Consequential etc Provisions) Order 2000, arts 3(1), 30(1), (3), Schedule 1, para 30(1), (2); Part-time Workers (Prevention of Less Favourable Treatment) Regulations 2000, reg 10, Schedule, para 2(1)–(3); Time Off for Public Duties Order 2000, art 2; Learning and Skills Act 2000, s149, Schedule 9, paras 1, 50; Local Authorities (Executive and Alternative Arrangements) (Modification of Enactments and Other Provisions) (England) Order 2001, art 30(a), (b) (as to Wales, SI 2002/808, arts 2(o), 29(a), (b)); Nursing and Midwifery Order 2001, art 54(3), Schedule 5, para 13; Limited Liability Partnerships Regulations 2001, reg 9, Schedule 5, paras 18(1)–(3), 19(1), (2); Part-time Workers (Prevention of Less Favourable Treatment) Regulations 2001, reg 3; Fixed-term Employees (Prevention of Less Favourable Treatment) Regulations 2002, reg 11, Schedule 2, Pt I, para 3(1)–(15), (17), (18); Ministry of Agriculture, Fisheries and Food (Dissolution) Order 2002, art 5(1), Schedule 1, para 37; Employment Rights (Increase of Limits) Order 2002, art 3, Schedule; Educaton Act 2002, s215(1), Schedule 21, paras 31, 32; National Health Service Reform and Health Care Professions Act (Supplementary, Consequential, etc, Provisions) Regulations 2002, reg 4, Schedule 1, para 22; Enterprise Act 2002, ss248(3), 278(2), Schedule 17, para 49, Schedule 26; National Health Service Reform and Health Care Professions Act 2002, s2(5), Schedule 2, Pt 2, para 63; Employment Act 2002, ss1, 3, 17, 34–37, 39, 47(1), (3), (4), 53, 54, Schedule 7, paras 24–41, 45–48, Schedule 8(1); Tax Credits Act 2002, s27, Schedule 1, para 1; Sunday Working (Scotland) Act 2003, s1(1), (3)(a), (4); Licensing Act 2003, s198, Schedule 6, para 114; Health and Social Care (Community Health and Standards) Act 2003, ss34, 184, 190, 196, Schedule 4, paras 90–101, Schedule 11, para 65, Schedule 13, para 8, Schedule 14, Pts 4, 7; Employment Equality (Sexual Orientation) Regulations 2003, reg 39, Schedule 5, para 2; Employment Equality (Religion or Belief) Regulations 2003, reg 39(2), Schedule 5, para 2; Health Protection Agency Act 2004, s11(1), Schedule 3, para 13; Health Protection Agency Act 2004, s11(1), Schedule 3, para 13; Employment Rights (Increase of Limits) Order 2004, art 3, Schedule; Health Act 1999 (Consequential Amendments) (Nursing and Midwifery) Order 2004, art 3, Schedule, para 3; Employment Relations Act 2004, ss40(1)–(7), 41(4)–(6), 57(1), Schedule 1, paras 28–31, 34, 39, Schedule 2; European Public Limited-Liability Company Regulations 2004, reg 43; Information and Consultation of Employees Regulations 2004, reg 31; Commissioners for Revenue and Customs Act 2005, s50(1).

NATIONAL MINIMUM WAGE ACT 1998
(1998 c 39)

1   Workers to be paid at least the national minimum wage

(1) A person who qualifies for the national minimum wage shall be remunerated by his employer in respect of his work in any pay reference period at a rate which is not less than the national minimum wage.

(2) A person qualifies for the national minimum wage if he is an individual who –

(a) is a worker;

(b) is working, or ordinarily works, in the United Kingdom under his contract; and

(c) has ceased to be of compulsory school age.

(3) The national minimum wage shall be such single hourly rate as the Secretary of State may from time to time prescribe.

(4) For the purposes of this Act a 'pay reference period' is such period as the Secretary of State may prescribe for the purpose.

(5) Subsections (1) to (4) above are subject to the following provisions of this Act.

2   Determination of hourly rate of remuneration

(1) The Secretary of State may by regulations make provision for determining what is the hourly rate at which a person is to be regarded for the purposes of this Act as remunerated by his employer in respect of his work in any pay reference period.
…

(8) No provision shall be made under this section which treats the same circumstances differently in relation to –

(a) different areas;

(b) different sectors of employment;

(c) undertakings of different sizes;

(d) persons of different ages; or

(e) persons of different occupations.

3   Exclusion of, and modifications for, certain classes of person

(1) This section applies to persons who have not attained the age of 26.

(1A) This section also applies to persons who have attained the age of 26 who are –

(a) within the first six months after the commencement of their employment with an employer by whom they have not previously been employed;

(b) participating in a scheme under which shelter is provided in return for work;

(c) participating in a scheme designed to provide training, work experience or temporary work;

(d) participating in a scheme to assist in the seeking or obtaining of work; or

(e) attending a course of higher education requiring attendance for a period of work experience.

(2) The Secretary of State may by regulations make provision in relation to any of the persons to whom this section applies –

(a) preventing them being persons who qualify for the national minimum wage; or

(b) prescribing an hourly rate for the national minimum wage other than the single hourly rate for the time being prescribed under section 1(3) above.

(3) No provision shall be made under subsection (2) above which treats persons differently in relation to –

(a) different areas;

(b) different sectors of employment;

(c) undertakings of different sizes; or

(d) different occupations.

(4) If any description of persons who have attained the age of 26 is added by regulations under section 4 below to the descriptions of person to whom this section applies, no provision shall be made under subsection (2) above which treats persons of that description differently in relation to different ages over 26.

4 Power to add to the persons to whom section 3 applies

(1) The Secretary of State may by regulations amend section 3 above by adding descriptions of persons who have attained the age of 26 to the descriptions of person to whom that section applies.

(2) No amendment shall be made under subsection (1) above which treats persons differently in relation to –

(a) different areas;

(b) different sectors of employment;

(c) undertakings of different sizes;

(d) different ages over 26; or

(e) different occupations.

5 The first regulations: referral to the Low Pay Commission

(1) Before making the first regulations under section 1(3) or (4) or 2 above, the Secretary of State shall refer the matters specified in subsection (2) below to the Low Pay Commission for their consideration.

(2) Those matters are –

(a) what single hourly rate should be prescribed under section 1(3) above as the national minimum wage;

(b) what period or periods should be prescribed under section 1(4) above;

(c) what method or methods should be used for determining under section 2 above the hourly rate at which a person is to be regarded as remunerated for the purposes of this Act;

(d) whether any, and if so what, provision should be made under section 3 above; and

(e) whether any, and if so what, descriptions of person should be added to the descriptions of person to whom section 3 above applies and what provision should be made under that section in relation to persons of those descriptions.

(3) Where matters are referred to the Low Pay Commission under subsection (1) above, the Commission shall, after considering those matters, make a report to the Prime Minister and the Secretary of State which shall contain the Commission's recommendations about each of those matters. ...

6 Referral of matters to the Low Pay Commission at any time

(1) The Secretary of State may at any time refer to the Low Pay Commission such matters relating to this Act as the Secretary of State thinks fit.

(2) Where matters are referred to the Low Pay Commission under subsection (1) above, the Commission shall, after considering those matters, make a report to the Prime Minister and the Secretary of State which shall contain the Commission's recommendations about each of those matters. ...

7 Referrals to, and reports of, the Low Pay Commission: supplementary

(1) This section applies where matters are referred to the Low Pay Commission under section 5 or 6 above.

(2) The Secretary of State may by notice require the Low Pay Commission to make their report within such time as may be specified in the notice.

(3) The time allowed to the Low Pay Commission for making their report may from time to time be extended by further notice given to them by the Secretary of State.

(4) Before arriving at the recommendations to be included in their report, the Low Pay Commission shall consult –

(a) such organisations representative of employers as they think fit;

(b) such organisations representative of workers as they think fit; and

(c) if they think fit, any other body or person.

(5) In considering what recommendations to include in their report, the Low Pay Commission –

(a) shall have regard to the effect of this Act on the economy of the United Kingdom as a whole and on competitiveness; and

(b) shall take into account any additional factors which the Secretary of State specifies in referring the matters to them. ...

(8) In this section –

'recommendations' means the recommendations required to be contained in a report under section 5(3) or 6(2) above, as the case may be;

'report' means the report which the Low Pay Commission are required to make under section 5(3) or 6(2) above, as the case may be, on the matters referred to them as mentioned in subsection (1) above.

8   The Low Pay Commission

(9) The Secretary of State may at any time appoint a body, to be known as 'the Low Pay Commission', to discharge the functions conferred or imposed on the Low Pay Commission under this Act.

(10) Schedule 1 to this Act shall have effect with respect to the constitution and proceedings of the body appointed under subsection (9) above. ...

9   Duty of employers to keep records

For the purposes of this Act, the Secretary of State may by regulations make provision requiring employers –

(a) to keep, in such form and manner as may be prescribed, such records as may be prescribed; and

(b) to preserve those records for such period as may be prescribed.

10   Worker's right of access to records

(1) A worker may, in accordance with the following provisions of this section, –

(a) require his employer to produce any relevant records; and

(b) inspect and examine those records and copy any part of them.

(2) The rights conferred by subsection (1) above are exercisable only if the worker believes on reasonable grounds that he is or may be being, or has or may have been, remunerated for any pay reference period by his employer at a rate which is less than the national minimum wage.

(3) The rights conferred by subsection (1) above are exercisable only for the purpose of establishing whether or not the worker is being, or has been, remunerated for any

pay reference period by his employer at a rate which is less than the national minimum wage.

(4) The rights conferred by subsection (1) above are exercisable –

(a) by the worker alone; or

(b) by the worker accompanied by such other person as the worker may think fit.

(5) The rights conferred by subsection (1) above are exercisable only if the worker gives notice (a 'production notice') to his employer requesting the production of any relevant records relating to such period as may be described in the notice.

(6) If the worker intends to exercise the right conferred by subsection (4)(b) above, the production notice must contain a statement of that intention.

(7) Where a production notice is given, the employer shall give the worker reasonable notice of the place and time at which the relevant records will be produced.

(8) The place at which the relevant records are produced must be –

(a) the worker's place of work; or

(b) any other place at which it is reasonable, in all the circumstances, for the worker to attend to inspect the relevant records; or

(c) such other place as may be agreed between the worker and the employer.

(9) The relevant records must be produced –

(a) before the end of the period of fourteen days following the date of receipt of the production notice; or

(b) at such later time as may be agreed during that period between the worker and the employer.

(10) In this section –

'records' means records which the worker's employer is required to keep and, at the time of receipt of the production notice, preserve in accordance with section 9 above;

'relevant records' means such parts of, or such extracts from, any records as are relevant to establishing whether or not the worker has, for any pay reference period to which the records relate, been remunerated by the employer at a rate which is at least equal to the national minimum wage.

11 Failure of employer to allow access to records

(1) A complaint may be presented to an employment tribunal by a worker on the ground that the employer –

(a) failed to produce some or all of the relevant records in accordance with subsections (8) and (9) of section 10 above; or

(b) failed to allow the worker to exercise some or all of the rights conferred by subsection (1)(b) or (4)(b) of that section.

(2) Where an employment tribunal finds a complaint under this section well-founded, the tribunal shall –

(a) make a declaration to that effect; and

(b) make an award that the employer pay to the worker a sum equal to 80 times the hourly amount of the national minimum wage (as in force when the award is made).

(3) An employment tribunal shall not consider a complaint under this section unless it is presented to the tribunal before the expiry of the period of three months following –

(a) the end of the period of fourteen days mentioned in paragraph (a) of subsection (9) of section 10 above; or

(b) in a case where a later day was agreed under paragraph (b) of that subsection, that later day.

(4) Where the employment tribunal is satisfied that it was not reasonably practicable for a complaint under this section to be presented before the expiry of the period of three months mentioned in subsection (3) above, the tribunal may consider the complaint if it is presented within such further period as the tribunal considers reasonable.

(5) Expressions used in this section and in section 10 above have the same meaning in this section as they have in that section.

12 Employer to provide worker with national minimum wage statement

(1) Regulations may make provision for the purpose of conferring on a worker the right to be given by his employer, at or before the time at which any payment of remuneration is made to the worker, a written statement. ...

(3) Any statement required to be given under this section to a worker by his employer may, if the worker is an employee, be included in the written itemised pay statement required to be given to him by his employer under section 8 of the Employment Rights Act 1996 ...

13 Appointment of officers

(1) The Secretary of State –

(a) may appoint officers to act for the purposes of this Act; and

(b) may, instead of or in addition to appointing any officers under this section, arrange with any Minister of the Crown or government department, or any body performing functions on behalf of the Crown, that officers of that Minister, department or body shall act for those purposes.

(2) When acting for the purposes of this Act, an officer shall, if so required, produce some duly authenticated document showing his authority so to act.

(3) If it appears to an officer that any person with whom he is dealing while acting for the purposes of this Act does not know that he is an officer so acting, the officer shall identify himself as such to that person.

14 Powers of officers

(1) An officer acting for the purposes of this Act shall have power for the performance of his duties –

(a) to require the production by a relevant person of any records required to be kept and preserved in accordance with regulations under section 9 above and to inspect and examine those records and to copy any material part of them;

(b) to require a relevant person to furnish to him (either alone or in the presence of any other person, as the officer thinks fit) an explanation of any such records;

(c) to require a relevant person to furnish to him (either alone or in the presence of any other person, as the officer thinks fit) any additional information known to the relevant person which might reasonably be needed in order to establish whether this Act, or any enforcement notice under section 19 below, is being or has been complied with;

(d) at all reasonable times to enter any relevant premises in order to exercise any power conferred on the officer by paragraphs (a) to (c) above.

(2) No person shall be required under paragraph (b) or (c) of subsection (1) above to answer any question or furnish any information which might incriminate the person or, if married or a civil partner, the person's spouse or civil partner.

(3) The powers conferred by subsection (1) above include power, on reasonable written notice, to require a relevant person –

(a) to produce any such records as are mentioned in paragraph (a) of that subsection to an officer at such time and place as may be specified in the notice; or

(b) to attend before an officer at such time and place as may be specified in the notice to furnish any such explanation or additional information as is mentioned in paragraph (b) or (c) of that subsection.

(4) In this section 'relevant person' means any person whom an officer acting for the purposes of this Act has reasonable cause to believe to be –

(a) the employer of a worker;

(b) a person who for the purposes of section 34 below is the agent or the principal;

(c) a person who supplies work to an individual who qualifies for the national minimum wage;

(d) a worker, servant or agent of a person falling within paragraph (a), (b) or (c) above; or

(e) a person who qualifies for the national minimum wage.

(5) In this section 'relevant premises' means any premises which an officer acting for the purposes of this Act has reasonable cause to believe to be –

(a) premises at which an employer carries on business;

(b) premises which an employer uses in connection with his business (including any place used, in connection with that business, for giving out work to home workers, within the meaning of section 35 below); or

(c) premises of a person who for the purposes of section 34 below is the agent or the principal.

15 Information obtained by officers

(1) This section applies to any information obtained by an officer acting for the purposes of this Act, whether by virtue of paragraph (a) or paragraph (b) of section 13(1) above.

(2) Information to which this section applies vests in the Secretary of State.

(3) Information to which this section applies may be used for any purpose relating to this Act by –

(a) the Secretary of State; or

(b) any relevant authority whose officer obtained the information. ...

(8) In this section 'relevant authority' means any Minister of the Crown who, or government department or other body which, is party to arrangements made with the Secretary of State which are in force under section 13(1)(b) above.

17 Non-compliance: worker entitled to additional remuneration

(1) If a worker who qualifies for the national minimum wage is remunerated for any pay reference period by his employer at a rate which is less than the national minimum wage, the worker shall be taken to be entitled under his contract to be paid, as additional remuneration in respect of that period, the amount described in subsection (2) below.

(2) That amount is the difference between –

(a) the relevant remuneration received by the worker for the pay reference period; and

(b) the relevant remuneration which the worker would have received for that period had he been remunerated by the employer at a rate equal to the national minimum wage.

(3) In subsection (2) above, 'relevant remuneration' means remuneration which falls to be brought into account for the purposes of regulations under section 2 above.

18 Enforcement in the case of special classes of worker

(1) If the persons who are the worker and the employer for the purposes of section 17 above would not (apart from this section) fall to be regarded as the worker and the employer for the purposes of –

(a) Part II of the Employment Rights Act 1996 (protection of wages), ...

they shall be so regarded for the purposes of the application of that Part in relation to the entitlement conferred by that section.

(2) In the application by virtue of subsection (1) above of –

(a) Part II of the Employment Rights Act 1996, ...

in a case where there is or was, for the purposes of that Part, no worker's contract between the persons who are the worker and the employer for the purposes of section 17 above, it shall be assumed that there is or, as the case may be, was such a contract.

(3) For the purpose of enabling the amount described as additional remuneration in subsection (1) of section 17 above to be recovered in civil proceedings on a claim in contract in a case where in fact there is or was no worker's contract between the persons who are the worker and the employer for the purposes of that section, it shall be assumed for the purpose of any civil proceedings, so far as relating to that amount, that there is or, as the case may be, was such a contract.

19 Power of officer to issue enforcement notice

(1) If an officer acting for the purposes of this Act is of the opinion that a worker who qualifies for the national minimum wage has not been remunerated for any pay reference period by his employer at a rate at least equal to the national minimum wage, the officer may serve a notice (an 'enforcement notice') on the employer requiring the employer to remunerate the worker for pay reference periods ending on or after the date of the notice at a rate equal to the national minimum wage.

(2) An enforcement notice may also require the employer to pay to the worker within such time as may be specified in the notice the sum due to the worker under section 17 above in respect of the employer's previous failure to remunerate the worker at a rate at least equal to the national minimum wage.

(2A) If an officer acting for the purposes of this Act is of the opinion that a worker who has at any time qualified for the national minimum wage has not been remunerated for any pay reference period (whether ending before or after the coming into force of this subsection) by his employer at a rate at least equal to the national minimum wage, the officer may serve on the employer an enforcement notice which imposes a requirement under subsection (2) above in relation to the worker, whether or not a requirement under subsection (1) above is, or may be, imposed in relation to that worker (or any other worker to whom the notice relates).

(2B) An enforcement notice may not impose a requirement under subsection (2) above in respect of any pay reference period ending more than 6 years before the date on which the notice is served.

(2C) Where an enforcement notice imposes a requirement under subsection (2) above, the amount specified in the notice as the sum due to the worker under section 17 above need not include any sum so due to him in respect of any very recent pay reference period (although the amount so specified may include any such sum).

(2D) In subsection (2C) above a 'very recent' pay reference period means a pay reference period ending less than 3 months before the date on which the notice is served.

(3) An enforcement notice may relate to more than one worker (and, where it does so, may be so framed as to relate to workers specified in the notice or to workers of a description so specified).

(4) A person on whom an enforcement notice is served may appeal against the notice before the end of the period of four weeks following the date of service of the notice.

(5) An appeal under subsection (4) above lies to an employment tribunal.

(6) On an appeal under subsection (4) above, the employment tribunal shall dismiss the appeal unless it is established –

    (a) that, in the case of the worker or workers to whom the enforcement notice relates, the facts are such that an officer who was aware of them would have had no reason to serve any enforcement notice on the appellant; or

    (b) where the enforcement notice relates to two or more workers, that the facts are such that an officer who was aware of them would have had no reason to include some of the workers in any enforcement notice served on the appellant; or

    (c) where the enforcement notice imposes a requirement under subsection (2) above in relation to a worker, –

        (i) that no sum was due to the worker under section 17 above; or

        (ii) that the amount specified in the notice as the sum due to the worker under that section is too great; or

        (iii) that the notice contravenes subsection (2B) above;

and in this subsection any reference to a worker includes a reference to a person whom the enforcement notice purports to treat as a worker.

(7) Where an appeal is allowed by virtue of paragraph (a) of subsection (6) above, the employment tribunal shall rescind the enforcement notice.

(8) If, in a case where subsection (7) above does not apply, an appeal is allowed by virtue of paragraph (b) or (c) of subsection (6) above –

    (a) the employment tribunal shall rectify the enforcement notice; and

    (b) the enforcement notice shall have effect as if it had originally been served as so rectified.

(9) The powers of an employment tribunal in allowing an appeal in a case where subsection (8) above applies shall include power to rectify, as the tribunal may consider appropriate in consequence of its decision on the appeal, any penalty notice which has been served under section 21 below in respect of the enforcement notice.

(10) Where a penalty notice is rectified under subsection (9) above, it shall have effect as if it had originally been served as so rectified.

20   Non-compliance: power of officer to sue on behalf of worker

(1) If an enforcement notice is not complied with in whole or in part, an officer acting for the purposes of this Act may, on behalf of any worker to whom the notice relates, –

(a) present a complaint under section 23(1)(a) of the Employment Rights Act 1996 (deductions from worker's wages in contravention of section 13 of that Act) to an employment tribunal in respect of any sums due to the worker by virtue of section 17 above; ...

(c) commence other civil proceedings for the recovery, on a claim in contract, of any sums due to the worker by virtue of section 17 above.

(2) The powers conferred by subsection (1) above for the recovery of sums due from an employer to a worker shall not be in derogation of any right which the worker may have to recover such sums by civil proceedings.

21   Financial penalty for non-compliance

(1) If an officer acting for the purposes of this Act is satisfied that a person on whom an enforcement notice has been served has failed, in whole or in part, to comply with the notice, the officer may serve on that person a notice (a 'penalty notice') requiring the person to pay a financial penalty to the Secretary of State. ...

22   Appeals against penalty notices

(1) A person on whom a penalty notice is served may appeal against the notice before the end of the period of four weeks following the date of service of the notice.

(2) An appeal under subsection (1) above lies to an employment tribunal. ...

23   The right not to suffer detriment

(1) A worker has the right not to be subjected to any detriment by any act, or any deliberate failure to act, by his employer, done on the ground that –

(a) any action was taken, or was proposed to be taken, by or on behalf of the worker with a view to enforcing, or otherwise securing the benefit of, a right of the worker's to which this section applies; or

(b) the employer was prosecuted for an offence under section 31 below as a result of action taken by or on behalf of the worker for the purpose of enforcing, or otherwise securing the benefit of, a right of the worker's to which this section applies; or

(c) the worker qualifies, or will or might qualify, for the national minimum wage or for a particular rate of national minimum wage.

(2) It is immaterial for the purposes of paragraph (a) or (b) of subsection (1) above –

(a) whether or not the worker has the right, or

(b) whether or not the right has been infringed,

but, for that subsection to apply, the claim to the right and, if applicable, the claim that it has been infringed must be made in good faith.

(3) The following are the rights to which this section applies –

(a) any right conferred by, or by virtue of, any provision of this Act for which the remedy for its infringement is by way of a complaint to an employment tribunal; and

(b) any right conferred by section 17 above.

(4) This section does not apply where the detriment in question amounts to dismissal within the meaning of –

(a) Part X of the Employment Rights Act 1996 (unfair dismissal) ...

24 Enforcement of the right

(1) A worker may present a complaint to an employment tribunal that he has been subjected to a detriment in contravention of section 23 above.

(2) Subject to the following provisions of this section, the provisions of –

(a) sections 48(2) to (4) and 49 of the Employment Rights Act 1996 (complaints to employment tribunals and remedies), or ...

shall apply in relation to a complaint under this section as they apply in relation to a complaint under section 48 of that Act ..., but taking references in those provisions to the employer as references to the employer within the meaning of section 23(1) above.

(3) Where –

(a) the detriment to which the worker is subjected is the termination of his worker's contract, but

(b) that contract is not a contract of employment,

any compensation awarded under section 49 of the Employment Rights Act 1996 ... by virtue of subsection (2) above must not exceed the limit specified in subsection (4) below.

(4) The limit mentioned in subsection (3) above is the total of –

(a) the sum which would be the basic award for unfair dismissal, calculated in accordance with section 119 of the Employment Rights Act 1996 ..., if the worker had been an employee and the contract terminated had been a contract of employment; and

(b) the sum for the time being specified in section 124(1) of that Act ... which is the limit for a compensatory award to a person calculated in accordance with section 123 of that Act ...

(5) Where the worker has been working under arrangements which do not fall to be regarded as a worker's contract for the purposes of –

(a) the Employment Rights Act 1996, ...

he shall be treated for the purposes of subsections (3) and (4) above as if any arrangements under which he has been working constituted a worker's contract falling within section 230(3)(b) of that Act ...

28 Reversal of burden of proof

(1) Where in any civil proceedings any question arises as to whether an individual qualifies or qualified at any time for the national minimum wage, it shall be presumed that the individual qualifies or, as the case may be, qualified at that time for the national minimum wage unless the contrary is established.

(2) Where –

(a) a complaint is made –

(i) to an employment tribunal under section 23(1)(a) of the Employment Rights Act 1996 (unauthorised deductions from wages), or ... and

(b) the complaint relates in whole or in part to the deduction of the amount described as additional remuneration in section 17(1) above,

it shall be presumed for the purposes of the complaint, so far as relating to the deduction of that amount, that the worker in question was remunerated at a rate less than the national minimum wage unless the contrary is established.

(3) Where in any civil proceedings a person seeks to recover on a claim in contract the amount described as additional remuneration in section 17(1) above, it shall be presumed for the purposes of the proceedings, so far as relating to that amount, that the worker in question was remunerated at a rate less than the national minimum wage unless the contrary is established.

31 Offences

(1) If the employer of a worker who qualifies for the national minimum wage refuses or wilfully neglects to remunerate the worker for any pay reference period at a rate which is at least equal to the national minimum wage, that employer is guilty of an offence.

(2) If a person who is required to keep or preserve any record in accordance with regulations under section 9 above fails to do so, that person is guilty of an offence.

(3) If a person makes, or knowingly causes or allows to be made, in a record required to be kept in accordance with regulations under section 9 above any entry which he knows to be false in a material particular, that person is guilty of an offence.

(4) If a person, for purposes connected with the provisions of this Act, produces or furnishes, or knowingly causes or allows to be produced or furnished, any record or information which he knows to be false in a material particular, that person is guilty of an offence.

(5) If a person –

(a) intentionally delays or obstructs an officer acting for the purposes of this Act in the exercise of any power conferred by this Act, or

(b) refuses or neglects to answer any question, furnish any information or produce any document when required to do so under section 14(1) above,

that person is guilty of an offence.

(6) Where the commission by any person of an offence under subsection (1) or (2) above is due to the act or default of some other person, that other person is also guilty of the offence.

(7) A person may be charged with and convicted of an offence by virtue of subsection (6) above whether or not proceedings are taken against any other person.

(8) In any proceedings for an offence under subsection (1) or (2) above it shall be a defence for the person charged to prove that he exercised all due diligence and took all reasonable precautions to secure that the provisions of this Act, and of any relevant regulations made under it, were complied with by himself and by any person under his control.

(9) A person guilty of an offence under this section shall be liable on summary conviction to a fine not exceeding level 5 on the standard scale.

32 Offences by bodies corporate, etc

(1) This section applies to any offence under this Act.

(2) If an offence committed by a body corporate is proved –

(a) to have been committed with the consent or connivance of an officer of the body, or

(b) to be attributable to any neglect on the part of such an officer,

the officer as well as the body corporate is guilty of the offence and liable to be proceeded against and punished accordingly.

(3) In subsection (2) above 'officer', in relation to a body corporate, means a director, manager, secretary or other similar officer of the body, or a person purporting to act in any such capacity.

(4) If the affairs of a body corporate are managed by its members, subsection (2) above applies in relation to the acts and defaults of a member in connection with his functions of management as if he were a director of the body corporate. ...

33 Proceedings for offences

(1) The persons who may conduct proceedings for an offence under this Act –

(a) in England and Wales, before a magistrates' court, ...

shall include any person authorised for the purpose by the Secretary of State even if that person is not a barrister or solicitor.

(2) In England and Wales ..., proceedings for an offence under this Act may be begun at any time within whichever of the following periods expires the later, that is to say –

(a) the period of 6 months from the date on which evidence, sufficient in the opinion of the Secretary of State to justify a prosecution for the offence, comes to the knowledge of the Secretary of State, or

(b) the period of 12 months from the commission of the offence,

notwithstanding anything in any other enactment ... or in any instrument made under an enactment. ...

34 Agency workers who are not otherwise 'workers'

(1) This section applies in any case where an individual ('the agency worker') –

(a) is supplied by a person ('the agent') to do work for another ('the principal') under a contract or other arrangements made between the agent and the principal; but

(b) is not, as respects that work, a worker, because of the absence of a worker's contract between the individual and the agent or the principal; and

(c) is not a party to a contract under which he undertakes to do the work for another party to the contract whose status is, by virtue of the contract, that of a client or customer of any profession or business undertaking carried on by the individual.

(2) In a case where this section applies, the other provisions of this Act shall have effect as if there were a worker's contract for the doing of the work by the agency worker made between the agency worker and –

(a) whichever of the agent and the principal is responsible for paying the agency worker in respect of the work; or

(b) if neither the agent nor the principal is so responsible, whichever of them pays the agency worker in respect of the work.

35 Home workers who are not otherwise 'workers'

(1) In determining for the purposes of this Act whether a home worker is or is not a worker, section 54(3)(b) below shall have effect as if for the word 'personally' there were substituted '(whether personally or otherwise)'.

(2) In this section 'home worker' means an individual who contracts with a person, for the purposes of that person's business, for the execution of work to be done in a place not under the control or management of that person.

36 Crown employment

(1) Subject to section 37 below, the provisions of this Act have effect in relation to Crown employment and persons in Crown employment as they have effect in relation to other employment and other workers.

(2) In this Act, subject to section 37 below, 'Crown employment' means employment under or for the purposes of a government department or any officer or body exercising on behalf of the Crown functions conferred by statutory provision. ...

41 Power to apply Act to individuals who are not otherwise 'workers'

The Secretary of State may by regulations make provision for this Act to apply, with or without modifications, as if –

(a) any individual of a prescribed description who would not otherwise be a worker for the purposes of this Act were a worker for those purposes;

(b) there were in the case of any such individual a worker's contract of a prescribed description under which the individual works; and

(c) a person of a prescribed description were the employer under that contract.

42 Power to apply Act to offshore employment

(1) In this section 'offshore employment' means employment for the purposes of activities –

(a) in the territorial waters of the United Kingdom, or

(b) connected with the exploration of the sea-bed or subsoil, or the exploitation of their natural resources, in the United Kingdom sector of the continental shelf, or

(c) connected with the exploration or exploitation, in a foreign sector of the continental shelf, of a cross-boundary petroleum field.

(2) Her Majesty may by Order in Council provide that the provisions of this Act apply, to such extent and for such purposes as may be specified in the Order (with or without modification), to or in relation to a person in offshore employment. …

44 Voluntary workers

(1) A worker employed by a charity, a voluntary organisation, an associated fund-raising body or a statutory body does not qualify for the national minimum wage in respect of that employment if he receives, and under the terms of his employment (apart from this Act) is entitled to, –

(a) no monetary payments of any description, or no monetary payments except in respect of expenses –

(i) actually incurred in the performance of his duties; or

(ii) reasonably estimated as likely to be or to have been so incurred; and

(b) no benefits in kind of any description, or no benefits in kind other than the provision of some or all of his subsistence or of such accommodation as is reasonable in the circumstances of the employment.

(2) A person who would satisfy the conditions in subsection (1) above but for receiving monetary payments made solely for the purpose of providing him with means of subsistence shall be taken to satisfy those conditions if –

(a) he is employed to do the work in question as a result of arrangements made between a charity acting in pursuance of its charitable purposes and the body for which the work is done; and

(b) the work is done for a charity, a voluntary organisation, an associated fund-raising body or a statutory body.

(3) For the purposes of subsection (1)(b) above –

(a) any training (other than that which a person necessarily acquires in the course of doing his work) shall be taken to be a benefit in kind; but

(b) there shall be left out of account any training provided for the sole or main purpose of improving the worker's ability to perform the work which he has agreed to do.

(4) In this section –

'associated fund-raising body' means a body of persons the profits of which are applied wholly for the purposes of a charity or voluntary organisation;

'charity' means a body of persons, or the trustees of a trust, established for charitable purposes only;

'receive', in relation to a monetary payment or a benefit in kind, means receive in respect of, or otherwise in connection with, the employment in question (whether or not under the terms of the employment);

'statutory body' means a body established by or under an enactment (including an enactment comprised in Northern Ireland legislation);

'subsistence' means such subsistence as is reasonable in the circumstances of the employment in question, and does not include accommodation;

'voluntary organisation' means a body of persons, or the trustees of a trust, which is established only for charitable purposes (whether or not those purposes are charitable within the meaning of any rule of law), benevolent purposes or philanthropic purposes, but which is not a charity.

44A Religious and other communities: resident workers

(1) A residential member of a community to which this section applies does not qualify for the national minimum wage in respect of employment by the community.

(2) Subject to subsection (3), this section applies to a community if –

(a) it is a charity or is established by a charity,

(b) a purpose of the community is to practise or advance a belief of a religious or similar nature, and

(c) all or some of its members live together for that purpose.

(3) This section does not apply to a community which –

(a) is an independent school, or

(b) provides a course of further or higher education.

(4) The residential members of a community are those who live together as mentioned in subsection (2)(c). ...

45　Prisoners

(1) A prisoner does not qualify for the national minimum wage in respect of any work which he does in pursuance of prison rules.

(2) In this section –

'prisoner' means a person detained in, or on temporary release from, a prison ...

45A　Persons discharging fines by unpaid work

A person does not qualify for the national minimum wage in respect of any work that he does in pursuance of a work order under Schedule 6 to the Courts Act 2003 (discharge of fines by unpaid work).

48　Application of Act to superior employers

Where –

(a) the immediate employer of a worker is himself in the employment of some other person, and

(b) the worker is employed on the premises of that other person,

that other person shall be deemed for the purposes of this Act to be the employer of the worker jointly with the immediate employer.

49　Restrictions on contracting out

(1) Any provision in any agreement (whether a worker's contract or not) is void in so far as it purports –

(a) to exclude or limit the operation of any provision of this Act; or

(b) to preclude a person from bringing proceedings under this Act before an employment tribunal.

(2) Subsection (1) above does not apply to any agreement to refrain from instituting or continuing proceedings where a conciliation officer has taken action under –

(a) section 18 of the Employment Tribunals Act 1996 (conciliation) ...

(3) Subsection (1) above does not apply to any agreement to refrain from instituting or continuing before an employment tribunal any proceedings within –

(a) section 18(1)(dd) of the Employment Tribunals Act 1996 (proceedings under or by virtue of this Act where conciliation is available), ...

if the conditions regulating compromise agreements under this Act are satisfied in relation to the agreement.

(4) For the purposes of subsection (3) above the conditions regulating compromise agreements under this Act are that –

(a) the agreement must be in writing,

(b) the agreement must relate to the particular proceedings,

(c) the employee or worker must have received advice from a relevant independent adviser as to the terms and effect of the proposed agreement and, in particular, its effect on his ability to pursue his rights before an employment tribunal,

(d) there must be in force, when the adviser gives the advice, a contract of insurance, or an indemnity provided for members of a profession or a professional body, covering the risk of a claim by the employee or worker in respect of loss arising in consequence of the advice,

(e) the agreement must identify the adviser, and

(f) the agreement must state that the conditions regulating compromise agreements under this Act are satisfied.

(5) A person is a relevant independent adviser for the purposes of subsection (4)(c) above –

(a) if he is a qualified lawyer,

(b) if he is an officer, official, employee or member of an independent trade union who has been certified in writing by the trade union as competent to give advice and as authorised to do so on behalf of the trade union,

(c) if he works at an advice centre (whether as an employee or a volunteer) and has been certified in writing by the centre as competent to give advice and as authorised to do so on behalf of the centre, or

(d) if he is a person of a description specified in an order made by the Secretary of State.

(6) But a person is not a relevant independent adviser for the purposes of subsection (4)(c) above in relation to the employee or worker –

(a) if he is employed by, or is acting in the matter for, the employer or an associated employer,

(b) in the case of a person within subsection (5)(b) or (c) above, if the trade union or advice centre is the employer or an associated employer,

(c) in the case of a person within subsection (5)(c) above, if the employee or worker makes a payment for the advice received from him, or

(d) in the case of a person of a description specified in an order under subsection (5)(d) above, if any condition specified in the order in relation to the giving of advice by persons of that description is not satisfied.

(7) In this section 'qualified lawyer' means –

(a) as respects England and Wales –

(i) a barrister (whether in practice as such or employed to give legal advice);

(ii) a solicitor who holds a practising certificate; or

(iii) a person other than a barrister or solicitor who is an authorised advocate or authorised litigator (within the meaning of the Courts and Legal Services Act 1990); ...

(8) For the purposes of this section any two employers shall be treated as associated if –

(a) one is a company of which the other (directly or indirectly) has control; or

(b) both are companies of which a third person (directly or indirectly) has control;

and 'associated employer' shall be construed accordingly. ...

50   Publicity

(1) The Secretary of State shall arrange for information about this Act and regulations under it to be published by such means as appear to the Secretary of State to be most appropriate for drawing the provisions of this Act and those regulations to the attention of persons affected by them. ...

51   Regulations and orders

(1) Except to the extent that this Act makes provision to the contrary, any power conferred by this Act to make an Order in Council, regulations or an order includes power –

(a) to make different provision for different cases or for different descriptions of person; and

(b) to make incidental, consequential, supplemental or transitional provision and savings.

(2) Paragraph (a) of subsection (1) above does not have effect in relation to regulations under section 1(3) above or an order under section 49 above. ...

54   Meaning of 'worker', 'employee', etc

(1) In this Act 'employee' means an individual who has entered into or works under (or, where the employment has ceased, worked under) a contract of employment.

(2) In this Act 'contract of employment' means a contract of service or apprenticeship, whether express or implied, and (if it is express) whether oral or in writing.

(3) In this Act 'worker' (except in the phrases 'agency worker' and 'home worker') means an individual who has entered into or works under (or, where the employment has ceased, worked under) –

(a) a contract of employment; or

(b) any other contract, whether express or implied and (if it is express) whether oral or in writing, whereby the individual undertakes to do or perform personally any work or services for another party to the contract whose status is not by virtue of the contract that of a client or customer of any profession or business undertaking carried on by the individual;

and any reference to a worker's contract shall be construed accordingly.

(4) In this Act 'employer', in relation to an employee or a worker, means the person by whom the employee or worker is (or, where the employment has ceased, was) employed.

(5) In this Act 'employment' –

(a) in relation to an employee, means employment under a contract of employment; and

(b) in relation to a worker, means employment under his contract;

and 'employed' shall be construed accordingly.

55   Interpretation

(1) In this Act, unless the context otherwise requires, –

'civil proceedings' means proceedings before an employment tribunal or civil proceedings before any other court;

'enforcement notice' shall be construed in accordance with section 19 above; ...

'notice' means notice in writing;

'pay reference period' shall be construed in accordance with section 1(4) above;

'penalty notice' shall be construed in accordance with section 21 above;

'person who qualifies for the national minimum wage' shall be construed in accordance with section 1(2) above; and related expressions shall be construed accordingly;

'prescribe' means prescribe by regulations;

'regulations' means regulations made by the Secretary of State, except in the case of regulations under section 47(2) or (4) above made by the Secretary of State and the Minister of Agriculture, Fisheries and Food acting jointly ...

(2) Any reference in this Act to a person being remunerated for a pay reference period is a reference to the person being remunerated by his employer in respect of his work in that pay reference period.

(3) Any reference in this Act to doing work includes a reference to performing services; and 'work' and other related expressions shall be construed accordingly. ...

SCHEDULE 1

THE LOW PAY COMMISSION

1. – (1) The Low Pay Commission appointed under section 8(9) of this Act (in this Schedule referred to as 'the Commission') shall consist of a chairman and eight other members appointed by the Secretary of State.

(2) In appointing members, the Secretary of State shall have regard to the desirability of securing that there is such a balance as the Secretary of State considers appropriate between –

(a) members with knowledge or experience of, or interest in, trade unions or matters relating to workers generally;

(b) members with knowledge or experience of, or interest in, employers' associations or matters relating to employers generally; and

(c) members with other relevant knowledge or experience. ...

As amended by the National Minimum Wage Act 1998 (Amendment) Regulations 1999, reg 2; Employment Relations Act 1999, ss18(4), 22; National Minimum Wage (Enforcement Notices) Act 2003, s1; Courts Act 2003, s109(1), Schedule 8, para 382; Statute Law (Repeals) Act 2004, s1(1), Schedule 1, Pt 8; Civil Partnership Act 2004, s261(1), Schedule 27, para 155; Employment Relations Act 2004, ss45, 46(2).

DISABILITY RIGHTS
COMMISSION ACT 1999
(1999 c 17)

1   The Disability Rights Commission

(1) There shall be a body known as the Disability Rights Commission (referred to in this Act as 'the Commission').

(2) The Secretary of State shall pay to the Commission such sums as he thinks fit to enable it to meet its expenses.

(3) Schedule 1 (the Commission's constitution and related matters) has effect.

2   General functions

(1) The Commission shall have the following duties –

(a) to work towards the elimination of discrimination against and harassment of disabled persons;

(b) to promote the equalisation of opportunities for disabled persons;

(c) to take such steps as it considers appropriate with a view to encouraging good practice in the treatment of disabled persons; and

(d) to keep under review the working of the Disability Discrimination Act 1995 (referred to in this Act as 'the 1995 Act') and this Act.

(2) The Commission may, for any purpose connected with the performance of its functions –

(a) make proposals or give other advice to any Minister of the Crown as to any aspect of the law or a proposed change to the law;

(b) make proposals or give other advice to any Government agency or other public authority as to the practical application of any law;

(c) undertake, or arrange for or support (whether financially or otherwise), the carrying out of research or the provision of advice or information.

Nothing in this subsection is to be regarded as limiting the Commission's powers.

(3) The Commission shall make proposals or give other advice under subsection (2)(a) on any matter specified in a request from a Minister of the Crown.

(4) The Commission may make charges for facilities or services made available by it for any purpose.

(5) In this section –

'disabled persons' includes persons who have had a disability;

'discrimination' means anything which is discrimination for the purposes of any provision of Part 2, 3 or 4 of the 1995 Act;

'harassment' means anything which is harassment for the purposes of any provision of Part 2, 3 or 4 of the 1995 Act; and

'the law' includes Community law and the international obligations of the United Kingdom.

3 Formal investigations

(1) The Commission may decide to conduct a formal investigation for any purpose connected with the performance of its duties under section 2(1).

(2) The Commission shall conduct a formal investigation if directed to do so by the Secretary of State for any such purpose.

(3) The Commission may at any time decide to stop or to suspend the conduct of a formal investigation; but any such decision requires the approval of the Secretary of State if the investigation is being conducted in pursuance of a direction under subsection (2).

(4) The Commission may, as respects any formal investigation which it has decided or been directed to conduct –

(a) nominate one or more commissioners, with or without one or more additional commissioners appointed for the purposes of the investigation, to conduct the investigation on its behalf; and

(b) authorise those persons to exercise such of its functions in relation to the investigation (which may include drawing up or revising terms of reference) as it may determine. ...

4 Non-discrimination notices

(1) If in the course of a formal investigation the Commission is satisfied that a person has committed or is committing an unlawful act, it may serve on him a notice (referred to in this Act as a non-discrimination notice) which –

(a) gives details of the unlawful act which the Commission has found that he has committed or is committing; and

(b) requires him not to commit any further unlawful acts of the same kind (and, if the finding is that he is committing an unlawful act, to cease doing so).

(2) The notice may include recommendations to the person concerned as to action which the Commission considers he could reasonably be expected to take with a view to complying with the requirement mentioned in subsection (1)(b). ...

(5) In this section 'unlawful act' means an act which is unlawful for the purposes of any provision of Part 2, 3 or 4 of the 1995 Act or any other unlawful act of a description prescribed for the purposes of this section. ...

5   Agreements in lieu of enforcement action

(1) If the Commission has reason to believe that a person has committed or is committing an unlawful act, it may (subject to section 3(3)) enter into an agreement in writing under this section with that person on the assumption that that belief is well founded (whether or not that person admits that he committed or is committing the act in question).

(2) An agreement under this section is one by which –

(a) the Commission undertakes not to take any relevant enforcement action in relation to the unlawful act in question; and

(b) the person concerned undertakes –

(i) not to commit any further unlawful acts of the same kind (and, where appropriate, to cease committing the unlawful act in question); and

(ii) to take such action (which may include ceasing an activity or taking continuing action over any period) as may be specified in the agreement.

(3) Those undertakings are binding on the parties to the agreement; but undertakings under subsection (2)(b) are enforceable by the Commission only as provided by subsection (8). ...

(8) The Commission may apply to a county court or by summary application to the sheriff for an order under this subsection if –

(a) the other party to an agreement under this section has failed to comply with any undertaking under subsection (2)(b); or

(b) the Commission has reasonable cause to believe that he intends not to comply with any such undertaking.

(9) An order under subsection (8) is an order requiring the other party to comply with the undertaking or with such directions for the same purpose as are contained in the order.

(10) Nothing in this section affects the Commission's powers to settle or compromise legal proceedings of any description. ...

SCHEDULE 1

CONSTITUTION ETC

1. – (1) The Commission is a body corporate.

(2) The Commission is not the servant or agent of the Crown, it does not enjoy any status, immunity or privilege of the Crown and its property is not to be regarded as property of or as held on behalf of the Crown.

2. – (1) The Commission shall consist of not less than 10 and not more than 15 commissioners appointed by the Secretary of State. ...

(2) The Secretary of State may appoint as a commissioner a person who is not

disabled and has not had a disability only if satisfied that after the appointment more than half of the commissioners will be disabled persons or persons who have had a disability. ...

As amended by the Special Educational Needs and Disability Act 2001, s35, Schedule 7, paras 1–3; Disability Discrimination Act 1995 (Amendment) Regulations 2003, regs 3(2), 30; Statute Law (Repeals) Act 2004, s1(1), Schedule, Pt 5, Group 3; Disability Discrimination Act 2005, s19(1), Schedule 1, Pt 2, para 50(1)–(3).

EMPLOYMENT RELATIONS ACT 1999
(1999 c 26)

3   Blacklists

(1) The Secretary of State may make regulations prohibiting the compilation of lists which –

(a) contain details of members of trade unions or persons who have taken part in the activities of trade unions, and

(b) are compiled with a view to being used by employers or employment agencies for the purposes of discrimination in relation to recruitment or in relation to the treatment of workers.

(2) The Secretary of State may make regulations prohibiting –

(a) the use of lists to which subsection (1) applies;

(b) the sale or supply of lists to which subsection (1) applies. ...

(5) In this section –

'list' includes any index or other set of items whether recorded electronically or by any other means, and

'worker' has the meaning given by section 13.

(6) Subject to subsection (5), expressions used in this section and in the Trade Union and Labour Relations (Consolidation) Act 1992 have the same meaning in this section as in that Act.

10   Right to be accompanied

(1) This section applies where a worker –

(a) is required or invited by his employer to attend a disciplinary or grievance hearing, and

(b) reasonably requests to be accompanied at the hearing.

(2A) Where this section applies, the employer must permit the worker to be accompanied at the hearing by one companion who –

(a) is chosen by the worker; and

(b) is within subsection (3).

(2B) The employer must permit the worker's companion to –

(a) address the hearing in order to do any or all of the following –

(i) put the worker's case;

(ii) sum up that case;

(iii) respond on the worker's behalf to any view expressed at the hearing;

(b) confer with the worker during the hearing.

(2C) Subsection (2B) does not require the employer to permit the worker's companion to –

(a) answer questions on behalf of the worker;

(b) address the hearing if the worker indicates at it that he does not wish his companion to do so; or

(c) use the powers conferred by that subsection in a way that prevents the employer from explaining his case or prevents any other person at the hearing from making his contribution to it.

(3) A person is within this subsection if he is –

(a) employed by a trade union of which he is an official within the meaning of sections 1 and 119 of the Trade Union and Labour Relations (Consolidation) Act 1992,

(b) an official of a trade union (within that meaning) whom the union has reasonably certified in writing as having experience of, or as having received training in, acting as a worker's companion at disciplinary or grievance hearings, or

(c) another of the employer's workers.

(4) If –

(a) a worker has a right under this section to be accompanied at a hearing,

(b) his chosen companion will not be available at the time proposed for the hearing by the employer, and

(c) the worker proposes an alternative time which satisfies subsection (5),

the employer must postpone the hearing to the time proposed by the worker.

(5) An alternative time must –

(a) be reasonable, and

(b) fall before the end of the period of five working days beginning with the first working day after the day proposed by the employer.

(6) An employer shall permit a worker to take time off during working hours for the purpose of accompanying another of the employer's workers in accordance with a request under subsection (1)(b).

(7) Sections 168(3) and (4), 169 and 171 to 173 of the Trade Union and Labour Relations (Consolidation) Act 1992 (time off for carrying out trade union duties) shall apply in relation to subsection (6) above as they apply in relation to section 168(1) of that Act.

11 Complaint to employment tribunal

(1) A worker may present a complaint to an employment tribunal that his employer has failed, or threatened to fail, to comply with section 10(2A), (2B) or (4).

(2) A tribunal shall not consider a complaint under this section in relation to a failure or threat unless the complaint is presented –

(a) before the end of the period of three months beginning with the date of the failure or threat, or

(b) within such further period as the tribunal considers reasonable in a case where it is satisfied that it was not reasonably practicable for the complaint to be presented before the end of that period of three months.

(3) Where a tribunal finds that a complaint under this section is well-founded it shall order the employer to pay compensation to the worker of an amount not exceeding two weeks' pay.

(4) Chapter II of Part XIV of the Employment Rights Act 1996 (calculation of a week's pay) shall apply for the purposes of subsection (3); and in applying that Chapter the calculation date shall be taken to be –

(a) in the case of a claim which is made in the course of a claim for unfair dismissal, the date on which the employer's notice of dismissal was given or, if there was no notice, the effective date of termination, and

(b) in any other case, the date on which the relevant hearing took place (or was to have taken place).

(5) The limit in section 227(1) of the Employment Rights Act 1996 (maximum amount of week's pay) shall apply for the purposes of subsection (3) above.

12 Detriment and dismissal

(1) A worker has the right not to be subjected to any detriment by any act, or any deliberate failure to act, by his employer done on the ground that he –

(a) exercised or sought to exercise the right under section 10(2A), (2B) or (4), or

(b) accompanied or sought to accompany another worker (whether of the same employer or not) pursuant to a request under that section.

(2) Section 48 of the Employment Rights Act 1996 shall apply in relation to contraventions of subsection (1) above as it applies in relation to contraventions of certain sections of that Act.

(3) A worker who is dismissed shall be regarded for the purposes of Part X of the Employment Rights Act 1996 as unfairly dismissed if the reason (or, if more than one, the principal reason) for the dismissal is that he –

(a) exercised or sought to exercise the right under section 10(2A), (2B) or (4), or

(b) accompanied or sought to accompany another worker (whether of the same employer or not) pursuant to a request under that section.

(4) Sections 108 and 109 of that Act (qualifying period of employment and upper age limit) shall not apply in relation to subsection (3) above.

(5) Sections 128 to 132 of that Act (interim relief) shall apply in relation to dismissal for the reason specified in subsection (3)(a) or (b) above as they apply in relation to dismissal for a reason specified in section 128(1)(b) of that Act.

(6) In the application of Chapter II of Part X of that Act in relation to subsection (3) above, a reference to an employee shall be taken as a reference to a worker.

(7) References in this section to a worker having accompanied or sought to accompany another worker include references to his having exercised or sought to exercise any of the powers conferred by section 10(2A) or (2B).

13   Interpretation

(1) In sections 10 to 12 and this section 'worker' means an individual who is –

(a) a worker within the meaning of section 230(3) of the Employment Rights Act 1996,

(b) an agency worker,

(c) a home worker,

(d) a person in Crown employment within the meaning of section 191 of that Act, other than a member of the naval, military, air or reserve forces of the Crown, or

(e) employed as a relevant member of the House of Lords staff or the House of Commons staff within the meaning of section 194(6) or 195(5) of that Act.

(2) In subsection (1) 'agency worker' means an individual who –

(a) is supplied by a person ('the agent') to do work for another ('the principal') by arrangement between the agent and the principal,

(b) is not a party to a worker's contract, within the meaning of section 230(3) of that Act, relating to that work, and

(c) is not a party to a contract relating to that work under which he undertakes to do the work for another party to the contract whose status is, by virtue of the contract, that of a client or customer of any professional or business undertaking carried on by the individual;

and, for the purposes of sections 10 to 12, both the agent and the principal are employers of an agency worker.

(3) In subsection (1) 'home worker' means an individual who –

(a) contracts with a person, for the purposes of the person's business, for the execution of work to be done in a place not under the person's control or management, and

(b) is not a party to a contract relating to that work under which the work is to be executed for another party to the contract whose status is, by virtue of the contract, that of a client or customer of any professional or business undertaking carried on by the individual;

and, for the purposes of sections 10 to 12, the person mentioned in paragraph (a) is the home worker's employer.

(4) For the purposes of section 10 a disciplinary hearing is a hearing which could result in –

(a) the administration of a formal warning to a worker by his employer,

(b) the taking of some other action in respect of a worker by his employer, or

(c) the confirmation of a warning issued or some other action taken.

(5) For the purposes of section 10 a grievance hearing is a hearing which concerns the performance of a duty by an employer in relation to a worker.

(6) For the purposes of section 10(5)(b) in its application to a part of Great Britain a working day is a day other than –

(a) a Saturday or a Sunday,

(b) Christmas Day or Good Friday, or

(c) a day which is a bank holiday under the Banking and Financial Dealings Act 1971 in that part of Great Britain.

14 Contracting out and conciliation

Sections 10 to 13 of this Act shall be treated as provisions of Part V of the Employment Rights Act 1996 for the purposes of –

(a) section 203(1), (2)(e) and (f), (3) and (4) of that Act (restrictions on contracting out), and

(b) section 18(1)(d) of the Employment Tribunals Act 1996 (conciliation).

15 National security employees

Sections 10 to 13 of this Act shall not apply in relation to a person employed for the purposes of –

(a) the Security Service,

(b) the Secret Intelligence Service, or

(c) the Government Communications Headquarters.

19 Part-time work: discrimination

(1) The Secretary of State shall make regulations for the purpose of securing that persons in part-time employment are treated, for such purposes and to such extent as the regulations may specify, no less favourably than persons in full-time employment.

(2) The regulations may –

(a) specify classes of person who are to be taken to be, or not to be, in part-time employment;

(b) specify classes of person who are to be taken to be, or not to be, in full-time employment;

(c) specify circumstances in which persons in part-time employment are to be taken to be, or not to be, treated less favourably than persons in full-time employment;

(d) make provision which has effect in relation to persons in part-time employment generally or provision which has effect only in relation to specified classes of persons in part-time employment. ...

20   Part-time work: code of practice

(1) The Secretary of State may issue codes of practice containing guidance for the purpose of –

(a) eliminating discrimination in the field of employment against part-time workers;

(b) facilitating the development of opportunities for part-time work;

(c) facilitating the flexible organisation of working time taking into account the needs of workers and employers;

(d) any matter dealt with in the framework agreement on part-time work annexed to Council Directive 97/81/EC.

(2) The Secretary of State may revise a code and issue the whole or part of the revised code.

(3) A person's failure to observe a provision of a code does not make him liable to any proceedings.

(4) A code –

(a) is admissible in evidence in proceedings before an employment tribunal, and

(b) shall be taken into account by an employment tribunal in any case in which it appears to the tribunal to be relevant.

21   Code of practice: supplemental

(1) Before issuing or revising a code of practice under section 20 the Secretary of State shall consult such persons as he considers appropriate. ...

23   Power to confer rights on individuals

(1) This section applies to any right conferred on an individual against an employer (however defined) under or by virtue of any of the following –

(a) the Trade Union and Labour Relations (Consolidation) Act 1992;

(b) the Employment Rights Act 1996;

(ba) the Employment Act 2002,

(c) this Act;

(d) any instrument made under section 2(2) of the European Communities Act 1972.

(2) The Secretary of State may by order make provision which has the effect of conferring any such right on individuals who are of a specified description.

(3) The reference in subsection (2) to individuals includes a reference to individuals expressly excluded from exercising the right.

(4) An order under this section may –

(a) provide that individuals are to be treated as parties to workers' contracts or contracts of employment;

(b) make provision as to who are to be regarded as the employers of individuals;

(c) make provision which has the effect of modifying the operation of any right as conferred on individuals by the order;

(d) include such consequential, incidental or supplementary provisions as the Secretary of State thinks fit.

(5) An order under this section may make provision in such way as the Secretary of State thinks fit. ...

30 Partnerships at work

(1) The Secretary of State may spend money or provide money to other persons for the purpose of encouraging and helping employers (or their representatives) and employees (or their representatives) to improve the way they work together.

(2) Money may be provided in such way as the Secretary of State thinks fit (whether as grants or otherwise) and on such terms as he thinks fit (whether as to repayment or otherwise).

34 Indexation of amounts, etc

(1) This section applies to the sums specified in the following provisions –

(a) section 31(1) of the Employment Rights Act 1996 (guarantee payments: limits);

(b) section 120(1) of that Act (unfair dismissal: minimum amount of basic award);

(c) section 124(1) of that Act (unfair dismissal: limit of compensatory award);

(d) section 186(1)(a) and (b) of that Act (employee's rights on insolvency of employer: maximum amount payable);

(e) section 227(1) of that Act (maximum amount of a week's pay for purposes of certain calculations);

(ea) section 145E(3) of the Trade Union and Labour Relations (Consolidation) Act 1992 (unfair inducements: amount of award);

(f) section 156(1) of that Act (unfair dismissal: minimum basic award);

(g) section 176(6A) of that Act (right to membership of trade union: remedies).

(2) If the retail prices index for September of a year is higher or lower than the index for the previous September, the Secretary of State shall as soon as practicable make an order in relation to each sum mentioned in subsection (1) –

(a) increasing each sum, if the new index is higher, or

(b) decreasing each sum, if the new index is lower,

by the same percentage as the amount of the increase or decrease of the index.

(3) In making the calculation required by subsection (2) the Secretary of State shall –

(a) in the case of the sum mentioned in subsection (1)(a), round the result up to the nearest 10 pence,

(b) in the case of the sums mentioned in subsection (1)(b), (c), (ea), (f) and (g), round the result up to the nearest £100, and

(c) in the case of the sums mentioned in subsection (1)(d) and (e), round the result up to the nearest £10. ...

38   Transfer of undertakings

(1) This section applies where regulations under section 2(2) of the European Communities Act 1972 (general implementation of Treaties) make provision for the purpose of implementing, or for a purpose concerning, a Community obligation of the United Kingdom which relates to the treatment of employees on the transfer of an undertaking or business or part of an undertaking or business.

(2) The Secretary of State may by regulations make the same or similar provision in relation to the treatment of employees in circumstances other than those to which the Community obligation applies (including circumstances in which there is no transfer, or no transfer to which the Community obligation applies). ...

39   Minimum wage: information

(1) Information obtained by a revenue official in the course of carrying out a function of the Commissioners for Her Majesty's Revenue and Customs may be –

(a) supplied by the Commissioners for Her Majesty's Revenue and Customs to the Secretary of State for any purpose relating to the National Minimum Wage Act 1998;

(b) supplied by the Secretary of State with the authority of the Commissioners for Her Majesty's Revenue and Customs to any person acting under section 13(1)(b) of that Act;

(c) supplied by the Secretary of State with the authority of the Commissioners for Her Majesty's Revenue and Customs to an officer acting for the purposes of any of the agricultural wages legislation.

(2) In this section –

'revenue official' means an officer of the Commissioners for Her Majesty's

Revenue and Customs appointed under section 4 of the Inland Revenue
Regulation Act 1890 (appointment of collectors, officers and other persons), and
'the agricultural wages legislation' has the same meaning as in section 16 of the
National Minimum Wage Act 1998 (agricultural wages officers).

As amended by the Employment Act 2002, ss41, 53, 54, Schedule 7, para 54, Schedule 8(1);
Employment Relations Act 2004, ss37, 39(1), (2), 57(1), (2), Schedule 1, para 42, Schedule 2;
Commissioners for Revenue and Customs Act 2005, s50(1).

EMPLOYMENT ACT 2002
(2002 c 22)

PART 1

STATUTORY LEAVE AND PAY

CHAPTER 1

PATERNITY AND ADOPTION

7   Funding of employers' liabilities

(1) The Secretary of State shall by regulations make provision for the payment by employers of statutory paternity pay and statutory adoption pay to be funded by the Commissioners for Her Majesty's Revenue and Customs to such extent as the regulations may specify.

(2) Regulations under subsection (1) shall –

  (a) make provision for a person who has made a payment of statutory paternity pay or statutory adoption pay to be entitled, except in such circumstances as the regulations may provide, to recover an amount equal to the sum of –

   (i) the aggregate of such of those payments as qualify for small employers' relief; and

   (ii) an amount equal to 92 per cent of the aggregate of such of those payments as do not so qualify; and

  (b) include provision for a person who has made a payment of statutory paternity pay or statutory adoption pay qualifying for small employers' relief to be entitled, except in such circumstances as the regulations may provide, to recover an additional amount equal to the amount to which the person would have been entitled under section 167(2)(b) of the Social Security Contributions and Benefits Act 1992 (corresponding provision for statutory maternity pay) had the payment been a payment of statutory maternity pay.

(3) For the purposes of subsection (2), a payment of statutory paternity pay or statutory adoption pay qualifies for small employers' relief if it would have so qualified were it a payment of statutory maternity pay, treating the period for which the payment is made, in the case of statutory paternity pay, or the payee's adoption pay period, in the case of statutory adoption pay, as the maternity pay period. ...

10   Powers to require information

(1) The Secretary of State may by regulations make provision enabling an officer of the Commissioners for Her Majesty's Revenue and Customs authorised by them for the purposes of this section to require persons of a description specified in the regulations to provide, or produce for inspection, within such period as the regulations may require, such information or documents as the officer may reasonably require for the purpose of ascertaining whether statutory paternity pay or statutory adoption pay is or was payable to or in respect of any person.

(2) The descriptions of person which may be specified by regulations under subsection (1) include, in particular – ...

(3) Regulations under subsection (1) must be made with the concurrence of the Commissioners for Her Majesty's Revenue and Customs.

16   Interpretation

In sections 5 to 15 –

'the Department' means the Department for Social Development or the Department for Employment and Learning;

'employer' and 'employee' have the same meanings as in Parts 12ZA and 12ZB of the Social Security Contributions and Benefits Act 1992.

PART 3

DISPUTE RESOLUTION, ETC

29   Statutory dispute resolution procedures

(1) Schedule 2 (which sets out the statutory dispute resolution procedures) shall have effect.

(2) The Secretary of State may by order –

(a) amend Schedule 2;

(b) make provision for the Schedule to apply, with or without modifications, as if –

(i) any individual of a description specified in the order who would not otherwise be an employee for the purposes of the Schedule were an employee for those purposes; and

(ii) a person of a description specified in the order were, in the case of any such individual, the individual's employer for those purposes.

(3) Before making an order under this section, the Secretary of State must consult the Advisory, Conciliation and Arbitration Service.

30   Contracts of employment

(1) Every contract of employment shall have effect to require the employer and employee to comply, in relation to any matter to which a statutory procedure applies, with the requirements of the procedure.

(2) Subsection (1) shall have effect notwithstanding any agreement to the contrary, but does not affect so much of an agreement to follow a particular procedure as requires the employer or employee to comply with a requirement which is additional to, and not inconsistent with, the requirements of the statutory procedure.

(3) The Secretary of State may for the purpose of this section by regulations make provision about the application of the statutory procedures.

(4) In this section, 'contract of employment' has the same meaning as in the Employment Rights Act 1996 (c 18).

31   Non-completion of statutory procedure: adjustment of awards

(1) This section applies to proceedings before an employment tribunal relating to a claim under any of the jurisdictions listed in Schedule 3 by an employee.

(2) If, in the case of proceedings to which this section applies, it appears to the employment tribunal that –

(a) the claim to which the proceedings relate concerns a matter to which one of the statutory procedures applies,

(b) the statutory procedure was not completed before the proceedings were begun, and

(c) the non-completion of the statutory procedure was wholly or mainly attributable to failure by the employee –

(i) to comply with a requirement of the procedure, or

(ii) to exercise a right of appeal under it,

it must, subject to subsection (4), reduce any award which it makes to the employee by 10 per cent, and may, if it considers it just and equitable in all the circumstances to do so, reduce it by a further amount, but not so as to make a total reduction of more than 50 per cent.

(3) If, in the case of proceedings to which this section applies, it appears to the employment tribunal that –

(a) the claim to which the proceedings relate concerns a matter to which one of the statutory procedures applies,

(b) the statutory procedure was not completed before the proceedings were begun, and

(c) the non-completion of the statutory procedure was wholly or mainly attributable to failure by the employer to comply with a requirement of the procedure, it must, subject to subsection (4), increase any award which it makes to the employee by 10 per cent and may, if it considers it just and equitable in all the circumstances to do so, increase it by a further amount, but not so as to make a total increase of more than 50 per cent.

(4) The duty under subsection (2) or (3) to make a reduction or increase of 10 per cent does not apply if there are exceptional circumstances which would make a reduction or increase of that percentage unjust or inequitable, in which case the tribunal may make no reduction or increase or a reduction or increase of such lesser percentage as it considers just and equitable in all the circumstances.

(5) Where an award falls to be adjusted under this section and under section 38, the adjustment under this section shall be made before the adjustment under that section.

(6) The Secretary of State may for the purposes of this section by regulations – ...

(7) The Secretary of State may by order – ...

32 Complaints about grievances

(1) This section applies to the jurisdictions listed in Schedule 4.

(2) An employee shall not present a complaint to an employment tribunal under a jurisdiction to which this section applies if –

(a) it concerns a matter in relation to which the requirement in paragraph 6 or 9 of Schedule 2 applies, and

(b) the requirement has not been complied with.

(3) An employee shall not present a complaint to an employment tribunal under a jurisdiction to which this section applies if –

(a) it concerns a matter in relation to which the requirement in paragraph 6 or 9 of Schedule 2 has been complied with, and

(b) less than 28 days have passed since the day on which the requirement was complied with.

(4) An employee shall not present a complaint to an employment tribunal under a jurisdiction to which this section applies if –

(a) it concerns a matter in relation to which the requirement in paragraph 6 or 9 of Schedule 2 has been complied with, and

(b) the day on which the requirement was complied with was more than one month after the end of the original time limit for making the complaint.

(5) In such circumstances as the Secretary of State may specify by regulations, an employment tribunal may direct that subsection (4) shall not apply in relation to a particular matter.

(6) An employment tribunal shall be prevented from considering a complaint presented in breach of subsections (2) to (4), but only if –

(a) the breach is apparent to the tribunal from the information supplied to it by the employee in connection with the bringing of the proceedings, or

(b) the tribunal is satisfied of the breach as a result of his employer raising the issue of compliance with those provisions in accordance with regulations under section 7 of the Employment Tribunals Act 1996 (c 17) (employment tribunal procedure regulations).

(7) The Secretary of State may for the purposes of this section by regulations – ...

(8) The Secretary of State may by order – ...

(9) Before making an order under subsection (8)(a), the Secretary of State must consult the Advisory, Conciliation and Arbitration Service.

(10) In its application to orders under subsection (8)(a), section 51(1)(b) includes power to amend this section.

33   Consequential adjustment of time limits

(1) The Secretary of State may, in relation to a jurisdiction listed in Schedule 3 or 4, by regulations make provision about the time limit for beginning proceedings in respect of a claim concerning a matter to which a statutory procedure applies.

(2) Regulations under this section may, in particular – ...

38   Failure to give statement of employment particulars etc.

(1) This section applies to proceedings before an employment tribunal relating to a claim by an employee under any of the jurisdictions listed in Schedule 5.

(2) If in the case of proceedings to which this section applies –

(a) the employment tribunal finds in favour of the employee, but makes no award to him in respect of the claim to which the proceedings relate, and

(b) when the proceedings were begun the employer was in breach of his duty to the employee under section 1(1) or 4(1) of the Employment Rights Act 1996 (c 18) (duty to give a written statement of initial employment particulars or of particulars of change),

the tribunal must, subject to subsection (5), make an award of the minimum amount to be paid by the employer to the employee and may, if it considers it just and equitable in all the circumstances, award the higher amount instead.

(3) If in the case of proceedings to which this section applies –

(a) the employment tribunal makes an award to the employee in respect of the claim to which the proceedings relate, and

(b) when the proceedings were begun the employer was in breach of his duty to the employee under section 1(1) or 4(1) of the Employment Rights Act 1996,

the tribunal must, subject to subsection (5), increase the award by the minimum amount and may, if it considers it just and equitable in all the circumstances, increase the award by the higher amount instead.

(4) In subsections (2) and (3) –

(a) references to the minimum amount are to an amount equal to two weeks' pay, and

(b) references to the higher amount are to an amount equal to four weeks' pay.

(5) The duty under subsection (2) or (3) does not apply if there are exceptional circumstances which would make an award or increase under that subsection unjust or inequitable.

(6) The amount of a week's pay of an employee shall –

(a) be calculated for the purposes of this section in accordance with Chapter 2 of Part 14 of the Employment Rights Act 1996 (c 18), and

(b) not exceed the amount for the time being specified in section 227 of that Act (maximum amount of week's pay).

(7) For the purposes of Chapter 2 of Part 14 of the Employment Rights Act 1996 as applied by subsection (6), the calculation date shall be taken to be –

(a) if the employee was employed by the employer on the date the proceedings were begun, that date, and

(b) if he was not, the effective date of termination as defined by section 97 of that Act.

(8) The Secretary of State may by order – ...

40 Interpretation of Part 3

In this Part –

'employer' and 'employee' have the same meanings as in the Employment Rights Act 1996 (c 18);

'statutory procedure' means a procedure set out in Schedule 2.

PART 4

MISCELLANEOUS AND GENERAL

45 Fixed-term work

(1) The Secretary of State shall make regulations –

(a) for the purpose of securing that employees in fixed-term employment are treated, for such purposes and to such extent as the regulations may specify, no less favourably than employees in permanent employment, and

(b) for the purpose of preventing abuse arising from the use of successive periods of fixed-term employment. ...

SCHEDULE 2

STATUTORY DISPUTE RESOLUTION PROCEDURES

PART 1

DISMISSAL AND DISCIPLINARY PROCEDURES

CHAPTER 1

STANDARD PROCEDURE

Step 1: statement of grounds for action and invitation to meeting

1. – (1) The employer must set out in writing the employee's alleged conduct or characteristics, or other circumstances, which lead him to contemplate dismissing or taking disciplinary action against the employee.

(2) The employer must send the statement or a copy of it to the employee and invite the employee to attend a meeting to discuss the matter.

Step 2: meeting

2. – (1) The meeting must take place before action is taken, except in the case where the disciplinary action consists of suspension.

(2) The meeting must not take place unless –

(a) the employer has informed the employee what the basis was for including in the statement under paragraph 1(1) the ground or grounds given in it, and

(b) the employee has had a reasonable opportunity to consider his response to that information.

(3) The employee must take all reasonable steps to attend the meeting.

(4) After the meeting, the employer must inform the employee of his decision and notify him of the right to appeal against the decision if he is not satisfied with it.

Step 3: appeal

3. – (1) If the employee does wish to appeal, he must inform the employer.

(2) If the employee informs the employer of his wish to appeal, the employer must invite him to attend a further meeting.

(3) The employee must take all reasonable steps to attend the meeting.

(4) The appeal meeting need not take place before the dismissal or disciplinary action takes effect.

(5) After the appeal meeting, the employer must inform the employee of his final decision.

CHAPTER 2

MODIFIED PROCEDURE

Step 1: statement of grounds for action

4. The employer must –

(a) set out in writing –

(i) the employee's alleged misconduct which has led to the dismissal,

(ii) what the basis was for thinking at the time of the dismissal that the employee was guilty of the alleged misconduct, and

(iii) the employee's right to appeal against dismissal, and

(b) send the statement or a copy of it to the employee.

Step 2: appeal

5. – (1) If the employee does wish to appeal, he must inform the employer.

(2) If the employee informs the employer of his wish to appeal, the employer must invite him to attend a meeting.

(3) The employee must take all reasonable steps to attend the meeting.

(4) After the appeal meeting, the employer must inform the employee of his final decision.

PART 2

GRIEVANCE PROCEDURES

CHAPTER 1

STANDARD PROCEDURE

Step 1: statement of grievance

6. The employee must set out the grievance in writing and send the statement or a copy of it to the employer.

Step 2: meeting

7. – (1) The employer must invite the employee to attend a meeting to discuss the grievance.

(2) The meeting must not take place unless –

(a) the employee has informed the employer what the basis for the grievance was when he made the statement under paragraph 6, and

(b) the employer has had a reasonable opportunity to consider his response to that information.

(3) The employee must take all reasonable steps to attend the meeting.

(4) After the meeting, the employer must inform the employee of his decision as to his response to the grievance and notify him of the right to appeal against the decision if he is not satisfied with it.

Step 3: appeal

8. – (1) If the employee does wish to appeal, he must inform the employer.

(2) If the employee informs the employer of his wish to appeal, the employer must invite him to attend a further meeting.

(3) The employee must take all reasonable steps to attend the meeting.

(4) After the appeal meeting, the employer must inform the employee of his final decision.

CHAPTER 2

MODIFIED PROCEDURE

Step 1: statement of grievance

9. The employee must –

    (a) set out in writing –

        (i) the grievance, and
        (ii) the basis for it, and

    (b) send the statement or a copy of it to the employer.

Step 2: response

10. The employer must set out his response in writing and send the statement or a copy of it to the employee.

PART 3

GENERAL REQUIREMENTS

Introductory

11. The following requirements apply to each of the procedures set out above (so far as applicable).

Timetable

12. Each step and action under the procedure must be taken without unreasonable delay.

Meetings

13. – (1) Timing and location of meetings must be reasonable.

(2) Meetings must be conducted in a manner that enables both employer and employee to explain their cases.

(3) In the case of appeal meetings which are not the first meeting, the employer should, as far as is reasonably practicable, be represented by a more senior manager than attended the first meeting (unless the most senior manager attended that meeting).

PART 4

SUPPLEMENTARY

Status of meetings

14. A meeting held for the purposes of this Schedule is a hearing for the purposes of section 13(4) and (5) of the Employment Relations Act 1999 (c 26) (definition of 'disciplinary hearing' and 'grievance hearing' in relation to the right to be accompanied under section 10 of that Act).

Scope of grievance procedures

15. – (1) The procedures set out in Part 2 are only applicable to matters raised by an employee with his employer as a grievance.

(2) Accordingly, those procedures are only applicable to the kind of disclosure dealt with in Part 4A of the Employment Rights Act 1996 (c 18) (protected disclosures of information) if information is disclosed by an employee to his employer in circumstances where –

(a) the information relates to a matter which the employee could raise as a grievance with his employer, and

(b) it is the intention of the employee that the disclosure should constitute the raising of the matter with his employer as a grievance.

SCHEDULE 3

TRIBUNAL JURISDICTIONS TO WHICH SECTION 31 APPLIES

Section 2 of the Equal Pay Act 1970 (c 41) (equality clauses)

Section 63 of the Sex Discrimination Act 1975 (c 65) (discrimination in the employment field)

Section 54 of the Race Relations Act 1976 (c 74) (discrimination in the employment field)

Section 145A of the Trade Union and Labour Relations (Consolidation) Act 1992 (inducements relating to union membership or activities)

Section 145B of that Act (inducements relating to collective bargaining)

Section 146 of that Act (detriment in relation to union membership and activities)

Paragraph 156 of Schedule A1 to that Act (detriment in relation to union recognition rights)

Section 8 of the Disability Discrimination Act 1995 (c 50) (discrimination in the employment field)

Section 23 of the Employment Rights Act 1996 (c 18) (unauthorised deductions and payments)

Section 48 of that Act (detriment in employment)

Section 111 of that Act (unfair dismissal)

Section 163 of that Act (redundancy payments)

Section 24 of the National Minimum Wage Act 1998 (c 39) (detriment in relation to national minimum wage)

Schedule 3 to the Tax Credits Act 1999 (c 10) (detriment in relation to tax credits)

The Employment Tribunal Extension of Jurisdiction (England and Wales) Order 1994 (SI 1994/1623) (breach of employment contract and termination) ...

Regulation 30 of the Working Time Regulations 1998 (SI 1998/1833) (breach of regulations)

Regulation 32 of the Transnational Information and Consultation of Employees Regulations 1999 (SI 1999/3323) (detriment relating to European Works Councils)

Regulation 28 of the Employment Equality (Religion or Belief) Regulations 2003 (discrimination in the employment field)

Regulation 28 of the Employment Equality (Sexual Orientation) Regulations 2003 (discrimination in the employment field)

SCHEDULE 4

TRIBUNAL JURISDICTIONS TO WHICH SECTION 32 APPLIES

Section 2 of the Equal Pay Act 1970 (c 41) (equality clauses)

Section 63 of the Sex Discrimination Act 1975 (c 65) (discrimination in the employment field)

Section 54 of the Race Relations Act 1976 (c 74) (discrimination in the employment field)

Section 145A of the Trade Union and Labour Relations (Consolidation) Act 1992 (inducements relating to union membership or activities)

Section 145B of that Act (inducements relating to collective bargaining)

Section 146 of that Act (detriment in relation to union membership and activities)

Paragraph 156 of Schedule A1 to that Act (detriment in relation to union recognition rights)

Section 17A of the Disability Discrimination Act 1995 (c 50) (discrimination in the employment field)

Section 23 of the Employment Rights Act 1996 (c 18) (unauthorised deductions and payments)

Section 48 of that Act (detriment in employment)

Section 111 of that Act (unfair dismissal)

Section 163 of that Act (redundancy payments)

Section 24 of the National Minimum Wage Act 1998 (c 39) (detriment in relation to national minimum wage)

Regulation 30 of the Working Time Regulations 1998 (SI 1998/1833) (breach of regulations)

Regulation 32 of the Transnational Information and Consultation of Employees Regulations 1999 (SI 1999/3323) (detriment relating to European Works Councils)

Regulation 28 of the Employment Equality (Religion or Belief) Regulations 2003 (discrimination in the employment field)

Regulation 28 of the Employment Equality (Sexual Orientation) Regulations 2003 (discrimination in the employment field)

SCHEDULE 5

TRIBUNAL JURISDICTIONS TO WHICH SECTION 38 APPLIES

Section 2 of the Equal Pay Act 1970 (equality clauses)

Section 63 of the Sex Discrimination Act 1975 (c 65) (discrimination in the employment field)

Section 54 of the Race Relations Act 1976 (c 74) (discrimination in the employment field)

Section 145A of the Trade Union and Labour Relations (Consolidation) Act 1992 (inducements relating to union membership or activities)

Section 145B of that Act (inducements relating to collective bargaining)

Section 146 of that Act (detriment in relation to union membership and activities)

Paragraph 156 of Schedule A1 to that Act (detriment in relation to union recognition rights)

Section 17A of the Disability Discrimination Act 1995 (c 50) (discrimination in the employment field)

Section 23 of the Employment Rights Act 1996 (c 18) (unauthorised deductions and payments)

Section 48 of that Act (detriment in employment)

Section 111 of that Act (unfair dismissal)

Section 163 of that Act (redundancy payments)

Section 24 of the National Minimum Wage Act 1998 (c 39) (detriment in relation to national minimum wage)

The Employment Tribunal Extension of Jurisdiction (England and Wales) Order 1994 (SI 1994/1623) (breach of employment contract and termination) ...

Regulation 30 of the Working Time Regulations 1998 (SI 1998/1833) (breach of regulations)

Regulation 32 of the Transnational Information and Consultation of Employees Regulations 1999 (SI 1999/3323) (detriment relating to European Works Councils)

Regulation 28 of the Employment Equality (Religion or Belief) Regulations 2003 (discrimination in the employment field)

Regulation 28 of the Employment Equality (Sexual Orientation) Regulations 2003 (discrimination in the employment field)

NB Section 30(1), (2), (4), above was not in force on 1 October 2005.

As amended by the Tax Credits Act 2002, s60, Schedule 6; Disability Discrimination Act 1995 (Amendment) Regulations 2003, regs 3(2), 31(3); Employment Equality (Religion or Belief) Regulations 2003, reg 39(2), Schedule 5, para 4; Employment Equality (Sexual Orientation) Regulations 2003, reg 39, Schedule 5, para 4; Employment Relations Act 2004, s57(1), Schedule 1, para 43.

EMPLOYMENT RELATIONS ACT 2004
(2004 c 24)

42   Information and consultation: Great Britain

(1) The Secretary of State may make regulations for the purpose of conferring on employees of an employer to whom the regulations apply, or on representatives of those employees, rights –

(a) to be informed by the employer about prescribed matters;

(b) to be consulted by the employer about prescribed matters.

(2) Regulations made under subsection (1) must make provision as to the employers to whom the regulations apply which may include provision –

(a) applying the regulations by reference to factors including the number of employees in the United Kingdom in the employer's undertaking;

(b) as to the method by which the number of employees in an employer's undertaking is to be calculated; and

(c) applying the regulations to different descriptions of employer with effect from different dates.

(3) Regulations made under subsection (1) may make provision –

(a) as to the circumstances in which the rights mentioned in subsection (1) arise and the extent of those rights;

(b) for and about the initiation and conduct of negotiations between employers to whom the regulations apply and their employees for the purposes of reaching an agreement satisfying prescribed conditions about the provision of information to the employees, and consultation of them (whether that provision or consultation is to be direct or through representatives);

(c) about the representatives the employees may have for the purposes of the regulations and the method by which those representatives are to be selected;

(d) as to the resolution of disputes and the enforcement of obligations imposed by the regulations or by an agreement of the kind mentioned in paragraph (b).

(4) Regulations made under subsection (1) may –

(a) confer jurisdiction (including exclusive jurisdiction) on employment tribunals and on the Employment Appeal Tribunal;

(b) confer functions on the Central Arbitration Committee;

(c) require or authorise the holding of ballots;

(d) amend, apply with or without modifications, or make provision similar to any provision of the Employment Rights Act 1996 (c 18) (including, in particular, Parts 5, 10 and 13), the Employment Tribunals Act 1996 (c 17) or the 1992 Act;

(e) include supplemental, incidental, consequential and transitional provision, including provision amending any enactment;

(f) make different provision for different cases or circumstances.

(5) Regulations made under subsection (1) may make any provision which appears to the Secretary of State to be necessary or expedient –

(a) for the purpose of implementing Directive 2002/14/EC of the European Parliament and of the Council of 11 March 2002 establishing a general framework for informing and consulting employees in the European Community;

(b) for the purpose of dealing with any matter arising out of or related to the United Kingdom's obligations under that Directive.

(6) Nothing in subsections (2) to (5) prejudices the generality of this section.

(7) Regulations under this section shall be made by statutory instrument.

(8) No such regulations may be made unless a draft of the regulations has been laid before Parliament and approved by a resolution of each House of Parliament.

(9) In this section 'prescribed' means prescribed by regulations under this section.

54   Means of voting in ballots and elections

(1) The Secretary of State may by order provide, in relation to any description of ballot or election authorised or required by the 1992 Act, that any ballot or election of that description is to be conducted by such one or more permissible means as the responsible person determines.

(2) A 'permissible means' is a means of voting that the order provides is permissible for that description of ballot or election.

(3) 'The responsible person' is a person specified, or of a description specified, by the order.

(4) An order under this section may –

(a) include provision about the determinations that may be made by the responsible person, including provision requiring specified factors to be taken into account, or specified criteria to be applied, in making a determination;

(b) allow the determination of different means of voting for voters in different circumstances;

(c) allow a determination to be such that voters have a choice of means of voting.

(5) The means that an order specifies as permissible means must, in the case of any description of ballot or election, include (or consist of) postal voting.

(6) An order under this section may –

(a) include supplemental, incidental and consequential provisions;

(b) make different provision for different cases or circumstances.

(7) An order under this section may –

(a) modify the provisions of the 1992 Act;

(b) exclude or apply (with or without modifications) any provision of that Act;

(c) make provision as respects any ballot or election conducted by specified means which is similar to any provision of that Act relating to ballots or elections.

(8) The power to make an order under this section is exercisable by statutory instrument.

(9) No order may be made under this section unless a draft of the order has been laid before Parliament and approved by a resolution of each House.

(10) The Secretary of State shall not make an order under this section which provides that a means of voting is permissible for a description of ballot or election unless he considers –

(a) that a ballot or election of that description conducted by that means could, if particular conditions were satisfied, meet the required standard; and

(b) that, in relation to any ballot or election of that description held after the order comes into force, the responsible person will not be permitted to determine that that means must or may be used by any voters unless he has taken specified factors into account or applied specified criteria.

(11) In specifying in an order under this section factors to be taken into account or criteria to be applied by the responsible person, the Secretary of State must have regard to the need for ballots and elections to meet the required standard.

(12) For the purposes of subsections (10) and (11) a ballot or election meets 'the required standard' if it is such that –

(a) those entitled to vote have an opportunity to do so;

(b) votes cast are secret;

(c) the risk of any unfairness or malpractice is minimised.

(13) In this section 'specified' means specified in an order under this section.

56   Meaning of 'the 1992 Act'

In this Act 'the 1992 Act' means the Trade Union and Labour Relations (Consolidation) Act 1992 (c 52).

TRANSFER OF UNDERTAKINGS (PROTECTION OF EMPLOYMENT) REGULATIONS 1981

(SI 1981 No 1794)

1. – (1) These Regulations may be cited as the Transfer of Undertakings (Protection of Employment) Regulations 1981.

(2) These Regulations, except Regulations 4 to 9 and 14, shall come into operation on 1st February 1982 and Regulations 4 to 9 and 14 shall come into operation on 1st May 1982. ...

2. – (1) In these Regulations –

'collective agreement', 'employers' association', and 'trade union' have the same meanings respectively as in the 1974 Act ...

'collective bargaining' has the same meaning as it has in the 1975 Act ...

'contract of employment' means any agreement between an employee and his employer determining the terms and conditions of his employment;

'employee' means any individual who works for another person whether under a contract of service or apprenticeship or otherwise but does not include anyone who provides services under a contract for services and references to a person's employer shall be construed accordingly;

'the 1974 Act', 'the 1975 Act', 'the 1978 Act' ... mean, respectively, the Trade Union and Labour Relations Act 1974, the Employment Protection Act 1975, the Employment Protection (Consolidation) Act 1978 ...;

'recognised', in relation to a trade union, means recognised to any extent by an employer, or two or more associated employers, (within the meaning of the 1978 Act ... for the purpose of collective bargaining;

'relevant transfer' means a transfer to which these Regulations apply and 'transferor' and 'transferee' shall be construed accordingly; and

'undertaking' includes any trade or business.

(2) References in these Regulations to the transfer of part of an undertaking are references to a transfer of a part which is being transferred as a business and, accordingly, do not include references to a transfer of a ship without more.

(3) For the purposes of these Regulations the representative of a trade union recognised by an employer is an official or other person authorised to carry on collective bargaining with that employer by that union.

3. – (1) Subject to the provisions of these Regulations, these Regulations apply to a transfer from one person to another of an undertaking situated immediately before the transfer in the United Kingdom or a part of one which is so situated.

(2) Subject as aforesaid, these Regulations so apply whether the transfer is effected by sale or by some other disposition or by operation of law.

(3) Subject as aforesaid, these Regulations so apply notwithstanding –

(a) that the transfer is governed or effected by the law of a country or territory outside the United Kingdom;

(b) that persons employed in the undertaking or part transferred ordinarily work outside the United Kingdom;

(c) that the employment of any of those persons is governed by any such law.

(4) It is hereby declared that a transfer of an undertaking or part of one –

(a) may be effected by a series of two or more transactions; and

(b) may take place whether or not any property is transferred to the transferee by the transferor. ...

4. – (1) Where the receiver of the property or part of the property of a company or the administrator of a company appointed under Part II of the Insolvency Act 1986 or, in the case of a creditors' voluntary winding up, the liquidator of a company transfers the company's undertaking, or part of the company's undertaking (the 'relevant undertaking') to a wholly owned subsidiary of the company, the transfer shall for the purposes of these Regulations be deemed not to have been effected until immediately before –

(a) the transferee company ceases (otherwise than by reason of its being wound up) to be a wholly owned subsidiary of the transferor company; or

(b) the relevant undertaking is transferred by the transferee company to another person;

whichever first occurs, and, for the purposes of these Regulations, the transfer of the relevant undertaking shall be taken to have been effected immediately before that date by one transaction only.

(2) In this Regulation –

'creditors' voluntary winding up' has the same meaning as in the Companies Act 1948 ... and

'wholly owned subsidiary' has the same meaning as it has for the purposes of section 150 of the Companies Act 1948 ...

5. – (1) Except where objection is made under paragraph (4A) below, a relevant transfer shall not operate so as to terminate the contract of employment of any person employed by the transferor in the undertaking or part transferred but any such contract which would otherwise have been terminated by the transfer shall have effect after the transfer as if originally made between the person so employed and the transferee.

(2) Without prejudice to paragraph (1) above but subject to paragraph (4A) below, on the completion of a relevant transfer –

(a) all the transferor's rights, powers, duties and liabilities under or in connection with any such contract, shall be transferred by virtue of this Regulation to the transferee; and

(b) anything done before the transfer is completed by or in relation to the transferor in respect of that contract or a person employed in that undertaking or part shall be deemed to have been done by or in relation to the transferee.

(3) Any reference in paragraph (1) or (2) above to a person employed in an undertaking or part of one transferred by a relevant transfer is a reference to a person so employed immediately before the transfer, including, where the transfer is effected by a series of two or more transactions, a person so employed immediately before any of those transactions.

(4) Paragraph (2) above shall not transfer or otherwise affect the liability of any person to be prosecuted for, convicted of and sentenced for any offence.

(4A) Paragraphs (1) and (2) above shall not operate to transfer his contract of employment and the rights, powers, duties and liabilities under or in connection with it if the employee informs the transferor or the transferee that he objects to becoming employed by the transferee.

(4B) Where an employee so objects the transfer of the undertaking or part in which he is employed shall operate so as to terminate his contract of employment with the transferor but he shall not be treated, for any purpose, as having been dismissed by the transferor.

(5) Paragraphs (1) and (4A) above are without prejudice to any right of an employee arising apart from these Regulations to terminate his contract of employment without notice if a substantial change is made in his working conditions to his detriment; but no such right shall arise by reason only that, under that paragraph, the identity of his employer changes unless the employee shows that, in all the circumstances, the change is a significant change and is to his detriment.

6. Where at the time of a relevant transfer there exists a collective agreement made by or on behalf of the transferor with a trade union recognised by the transferor in respect of any employee whose contract of employment is preserved by Regulation 5(1) above, then, –

(a) without prejudice to section 18 of the 1974 Act ... (collective agreements presumed to be unenforceable in specified circumstances) that agreement, in its application in relation to the employee, shall, after the transfer, have effect as if made by or on behalf of the transferee with that trade union, and accordingly anything done under or in connection with it, in its application as aforesaid, by or in relation to the transferor before the transfer, shall, after the transfer, be deemed to have been done by or in relation to the transferee; and

(b) any order made in respect of that agreement, in its application in relation to the employee, shall, after the transfer, have effect as if the transferee were a party to the agreement.

7. – (1) Regulations 5 and 6 above shall not apply –

(a) to so much of a contract of employment or collective agreement as relates to an occupational pension scheme within the meaning of the Social Security Pensions Act 1975 ... or

(b) to any rights, powers, duties or liabilities under or in connection with any such contract or subsisting by virtue of any such agreement and relating to such a scheme or otherwise arising in connection with that person's employment and relating to such a scheme.

(2) For the purposes of paragraph (1) above any provisions of an occupational pension scheme which do not relate to benefits for old age, invalidity or survivors shall be treated as not being part of the scheme.

8. – (1) Where either before or after a relevant transfer, any employee of the transferor or transferee is dismissed, that employee shall be treated for the purposes of Part V of the 1978 Act ... (unfair dismissal) as unfairly dismissed if the transfer or a reason connected with it is the reason or principal reason for his dismissal.

(2) Where an economic, technical or organisational reason entailing changes in the workforce of either the transferor or the transferee before or after relevant transfer is the reason or principal reason for dismissing an employee –

(a) paragraph (1) above shall not apply to his dismissal; but

(b) with prejudice to the application of section 57(3) of the 1978 ... (test of fair dismissal), the dismissal shall for the purposes of section 57(1)(b) of that ... (substantial reason for dismissal) be regarded as having been for a substantial reason of a kind such as to justify the dismissal of an employee holding the position which that employee held.

(3) The provisions of this Regulation apply whether or not the employee in question is employed in the undertaking or part of the undertaking transferred or to be transferred.

(4) Paragraph (1) above shall not apply in relation to the dismissal of any employee which was required by reason of the application of section 5 of the Aliens Restriction (Amendment) Act 1919 to his employment.

(5) Paragraph (1) above shall not apply in relation to a dismissal of an employee if –

(a) the application of section 54 of the 1978 Act to the dismissal of the employee is excluded by or under any provision of Part V or sections 141 to 149 of the 1978 Act or of section 237 or 238 of the Trade Union and Labour Relations (Consolidation) Act 1992; ...

9. – (1) This Regulation applies where after a relevant transfer the undertaking or part of the undertaking transferred maintains an identity distinct from the remainder of the transferee's undertaking.

(2) Where before such a transfer an independent trade union is recognised to any

extent by the transferor in respect of employees of any description who in consequence of the transfer become employees of the transferee, then, after the transfer –

(a) the union shall be deemed to have been recognised by the transferee to the same extent in respect of employees of that description so employed; and

(b) any agreement for recognition may be varied or rescinded accordingly.

10. – (1) In this Regulation and Regulation 11 references to affected employees, in relation to a relevant transfer, are to any employees of the transferor or the transferee (whether or not employed in the undertaking or the part of the undertaking to be transferred) who may be affected by the transfer or may be affected by measures taken in connection with it; and references to the employer shall be construed accordingly.

(2) Long enough before a relevant transfer to enable the employer of any affected employees to consult all the persons who are appropriate representatives of any of those affected employees, the employer shall inform those representatives of –

(a) the fact that the relevant transfer is to take place, when, approximately, it is to take place and the reasons for it; and

(b) the legal, economic and social implications of the transfer for the affected employees; and

(c) the measures which he envisages he will, in connection with the transfer, take in relation to those employees or, if he envisages that no measures will be so taken, that fact; and

(d) if the employer is the transferor, the measures which the transferee envisages he will, in connection with the transfer, take in relation to such of those employees as, by virtue of Regulation 5 above, become employees of the transferee after the transfer or, if he envisages that no measures will be so taken, that fact.

(2A) For the purposes of this Regulation the appropriate representatives of any employees are –

(a) if the employees are of a description in respect of which an independent trade union is recognised by their employer, representatives of the trade union, or

(b) in any other case, whichever of the following employee representatives the employer chooses –

(i) employee representatives appointed or elected by the affected employees otherwise than for the purposes of this Regulation, who (having regard to the purposes for and the method by which they were appointed or elected) have authority from those employees to receive information and to be consulted about the transfer on their behalf;

(ii) employee representatives elected by them, for the purposes of this Regulation, in an election satisfying the requirements of Regulation 10A(1).

(3) The transferee shall give the transferor such information at such a time as will

enable the transferor to perform the duty imposed on him by virtue of paragraph (2)(d) above.

(4) The information which is to be given to the appropriate representatives shall be given to each of them by being delivered to them, or sent by post to an address notified by them to the employer, or (in the case of representatives of a trade union) sent by post to the union at the address of its head or main office.

(5) Where an employer of any affected employees envisages that he will, in connection with the transfer, be taking measures in relation to any such employees he shall consult all the persons who are appropriate representatives of any of the affected employees in relation to whom he envisages taking measures with a view to seeking their agreement to measures to be taken.

(6) In the course of those consultations the employer shall –

(a) consider any representations made by the appropriate representatives; and

(b) reply to those representations and, if he rejects any of those representations, state his reasons.

(6A) The employer shall allow the appropriate representatives access to the affected employees and shall afford to those representatives such accommodation and other facilities as may be appropriate.

(7) If in any case there are special circumstances which render it not reasonably practicable for an employer to perform a duty imposed on him by any of paragraphs (2) to (6), he shall take all such steps towards performing that duty as are reasonably practicable in the circumstances.

(8) Where –

(a) the employer has invited any of the affected employees to elect employee representatives, and

(b) the invitation was issued long enough before the time when the employer is required to give information under paragraph (2) above to allow them to elect representatives by that time,

the employer shall be treated as complying with the requirements of this Regulation in relation to those employees if he complies with those requirements as soon as is reasonably practicable after the election of the representatives.

(8A) If, after the employer has invited affected employees to elect representatives, they fail to do so within a reasonable time, he shall give to each affected employee the information set out in paragraph (2).

10A. – (1) The requirements for the election of employee representatives under Regulation 10(2A) are that –

(a) the employer shall make such arrangements as are reasonably practical to ensure that the election is fair;

(b) the employer shall determine the number of representatives to be elected so that there are sufficient representatives to represent the interests of all the affected employees having regard to the number and classes of those employees;

(c) the employer shall determine whether the affected employees should be represented either by representatives of all the affected employees or by representatives of particular classes of those employees;

(d) before the election the employer shall determine the term of office as employee representatives so that it is of sufficient length to enable information to be given and consultations under Regulation 10 to be completed;

(e) the candidates for election as employee representatives are affected employees on the date of the election;

(f) no affected employee is unreasonably excluded from standing for election;

(g) all affected employees on the date of the election are entitled to vote for employee representatives;

(h) the employees entitled to vote may vote for as many candidates as there are representatives to be elected to represent them or, if there are to be representatives for particular classes of employees, may vote for as many candidates as there are representatives to be elected to represent their particular class of employee;

(i) the election is conducted so as to secure that –

(i) so far as is reasonable practicable, those voting do so in secret, and

(ii) the votes given at the election are accurately counted.

(2) Where, after an election of employee representatives satisfying the requirements of paragraph (1) has been held, one of those elected ceases to act as an employee representative and any of those employees are no longer represented, those employees shall elect another representative by an election satisfying the requirements of paragraph 1(a), (e), (f) and (i).

11. – (1) Where an employer has failed to comply with a requirement of Regulation 10 or Regulation 10A, a complaint may be presented to an employment tribunal on that ground –

(a) in the case of a failure relating to the election of employee representatives, by any of his employees who are affected employees;

(b) in the case of any other failure relating to employee representatives, by any of the employee representatives to whom the failure related;,

(c) in the case of failure relating to representatives of a trade union, by the trade union, and

(d) in any other case, by any of his employees who are affected employees.

(2) If on a complaint under paragraph (1) above a question arises whether or not it was reasonably practicable for an employer to perform a particular duty or what steps he took towards performing it, it shall be for him to show –

(a) that there were special circumstances which rendered it not reasonably practicable for him to perform the duty; and

(b) that he took all such steps towards its performance as were reasonably practicable in those circumstances.

(2A) If on a complaint under paragraph (1) a question arises as to whether or not any employee representative was an appropriate representative for the purposes of Regulation 10, it shall be for the employer to show that the employee representative had the necessary authority to represent the affected employees.

(2B) On a complaint under sub-paragraph (1)(a) it shall be for the employer to show that the requirements in Regulation 10A have been satisfied.

(3) On any such complaint against a transferor that he had failed to perform the duty imposed upon him by virtue of paragraph (2)(d) or, so far as relating thereto, paragraph (7) of Regulation 10 above, he may not show that it was not reasonably practicable for him to perform the duty in question for the reason that the transferee had failed to give him the requisite information at the requisite time in accordance with Regulation 10(3) above unless he gives the transferee notice of his intention to show that fact; and the giving of the notice shall make the transferee a party to the proceedings.

(4) Where the tribunal finds a complaint under paragraph (1) above well-founded it shall make a declaration to that effect and may –

(a) order the employer to pay appropriate compensation to such descriptions of affected employees as may be specified in the award; or

(b) if the complaint is that the transferor did not perform the duty mentioned in paragraph (3) above and the transferor (after giving due notice) shows the facts so mentioned, order the transferee to pay appropriate compensation to such descriptions of affected employees as may be specified in the award.

(5) An employee may present a complaint to an employment tribunal on the ground that he is an employee of a description to which an order under paragraph (4) above relates and that the transferor or the transferee has failed, wholly or in part, to pay him compensation in pursuance of the order.

(6) Where the tribunal finds a complaint under paragraph (5) above well-founded it shall order the employer to pay the complainant the amount of compensation which it finds is due to him.

(8) An employment tribunal shall not consider a complaint under paragraph (1) or (5) above unless it is presented to the tribunal before the end of the period of three months beginning with –

(a) the date on which the relevant transfer is completed, in the case of a complaint under paragraph (1);

(b) the date of the tribunal's order under paragraph (4) above, in the case of a complaint under paragraph (5);

or within such further period as the tribunal considers reasonable in a case where it is satisfied that it was not reasonably practicable for the complaint to be presented before the end of the period of three months.

(9) Section 129 of the 1978 Act (complaint to be sole remedy for breach of relevant rights) and section 133 of that Act (functions of conciliation officer ... shall apply to the rights conferred by this Regulation and to proceedings under this Regulation

as they apply to the rights conferred by that Act ... and the industrial tribunal proceedings mentioned therein.

(10) An appeal shall lie and shall lie only to the Employment Appeal Tribunal on a question of law arising from any decision of, or arising in any proceedings before, an employment tribunal under or by virtue of these Regulations; and section 13(1) of the Tribunals and Inquiries Act 1971 (appeal from certain tribunals to the High Court) shall not apply in relation to any such proceedings.

(11) In this Regulation 'appropriate compensation' means such sum not exceeding thirteen weeks' pay for the employee in question as the tribunal considers just and equitable having regard to the seriousness of the failure of the employer to comply with his duty.

(12) Schedule 14 to the 1978 ... shall apply for calculating the amount of a week's pay for any employee for the purposes of paragraph (11) above; and, for the purposes of that calculation, the calculation date shall be –

   (a) in the case of an employee who is dismissed by reason of redundancy (within the meaning of section 81 of the 1978 Act ...) the date which is the calculation date for the purposes of any entitlement of his to a redundancy payment (within the meaning of that section) or which would be that calculation date if he were so entitled;

   (b) in the case of an employee who is dismissed for any other reason, the effective date of termination (within the meaning of section 55 of the 1978 Act ...) of his contract of employment;

   (c) in any other case, the date of the transfer in question.

11A. For the purposes of Regulations 10 and 11 above persons are employee representatives if –

   (a) they have been elected by employees for the specific purpose of being given information and consulted by their employer under Regulation 10 above; or

   (b) having been elected or appointed by employees otherwise than for that specific purpose, it is appropriate (having regard to the purposes for which they were elected) for their employer to inform and consult them under that Regulation,

and (in either case) they are employed by the employer at the time when they are elected or appointed.

12. Any provision of any agreement (whether a contract of employment or not) shall be void in so far as it purports to exclude or limit the operation of Regulation 5, 8 or 10 above or to preclude any person from presenting a complaint to an employment tribunal under Regulation 11 above.

13. – (1) Regulations 8, 10 and 11 of these Regulations do not apply to employment where under his contract of employment the employee ordinarily works outside the United Kingdom. ...

14. – (1) In section 4(4) of the 1978 Act (written statement to be given to employee

on change of his employer), in paragraph (b), the reference to paragraph 17 of Schedule 13 to that Act (continuity of employment where change of employer) shall include a reference to these Regulations. ...

NB The relevant provisions of the 1974 Act, the 1975 Act, the 1978 Act and the Companies Act 1948 have been repealed. By virtue of s17(2)(a) of the Interpretation Act 1978, the relevant definitions are now to be found in the Acts by which they were repealed and re-enacted.

As amended by the Transfer of Undertakings (Protection of Employment) (Amendment) Regulations 1987, reg 2; Trade Union Reform and Employment Rights Act 1993, ss33, 51, Schedule 10; Collective Redundancies and Transfer of Undertakings (Protection of Employment) (Amendment) Regulations 1995, regs 8–11; Employment Rights (Dispute Resolution) Act 1998, s1(2)(a); Collective Redundancies and Transfer of Undertakings (Protectionof Employment) (Amendment) Regulations 1999, regs 8–11; Transfer of Undertakings (Protection of Employment) (Amendment) Regulations 1999, reg 3.

DISABILITY DISCRIMINATION (MEANING OF DISABILITY) REGULATIONS 1996

(SI 1996 No 1455)

1. – (1) These Regulations may be cited as the Disability Discrimination (Meaning of Disability) Regulations 1996 and shall come into force on 30th July 1996.

2. In these Regulations –

'the Act' means the Disability Discrimination Act 1995; and

'addiction' includes a dependency.

(1) Subject to paragraph (2) below, addiction to alcohol, nicotine or any other substance is to be treated as not amounting to an impairment for the purposes of the Act.

(2) Paragraph (1) above does not apply to addiction which was originally the result of administration of medically prescribed drugs or other medical treatment.

4. – (1) For the purposes of the Act the following conditions are to be treated as not amounting to impairments: –

   (a) a tendency to set fires,
   (b) a tendency to steal,
   (c) a tendency to physical or sexual abuse of other persons,
   (d) exhibitionism, and
   (e) voyeurism.

(2) Subject to paragraph (3) below for the purposes of the Act the condition known as seasonal allergic rhinitis shall be treated as not amounting to an impairment.

(3) Paragraph (2) above shall not prevent that condition from being taken into account for the purposes of the Act where it aggravates the effect of another condition.

5. For the purposes of paragraph 3 of Schedule 1 to the Act a severe disfigurement is not to be treated as having a substantial adverse effect on the ability of the person concerned to carry out normal day-to-day activities if it consists of –

   (a) a tattoo (which has not been removed), or
   (b) a piercing of the body for decorative or other non-medical purposes, including any object attached through the piercing for such purposes.

6. For the purposes of the Act where a child under six years of age has an impairment which does not have an effect falling within paragraph 4(1) of Schedule 1 to the Act that impairment is to be taken to have a substantial and long-term adverse effect on the ability of that child to carry out normal day-to-day activities where it would normally have a substantial and long-term adverse effect on the ability of a person aged 6 years or over to carry out normal day-to-day activities.

EMPLOYMENT PROTECTION (CONTINUITY OF EMPLOYMENT) REGULATIONS 1996
(SI 1996 No 3147)

1. – (1) These Regulations may be cited as the Employment Protection (Continuity of Employment) Regulations 1996 and shall come into force on 13th January 1997.

(2) The Employment Protection (Continuity of Employment) Regulations 1993 are revoked.

2. These Regulations apply to any action taken in relation to the dismissal of an employee which consists of –

(a) his making a claim in accordance with a dismissal procedures agreement designated by an order under section 110 of the Employment Rights Act 1996,

(b) the presentation by him of a relevant complaint of dismissal,

(c) any action taken by a conciliation officer under section 18 of the Employment Tribunals Act 1996,

(d) the making of a relevant compromise contract,

(e) the making of an agreement to submit a dispute to arbitration in accordance with a scheme having effect by virtue of an order under section 212A of the Trade Union and Labour Relations (Consolidation) Act 1992, or

(f) a decision taken arising out of the use of a statutory dispute resolution procedure contained in Schedule 2 to the Employment Act 2002 in a case where, in accordance with the Employment Act 2002 (Dispute Resolution) Regulations 2004, such a procedure applies.

3. – (1) The provisions of this regulation shall have effect to preserve the continuity of a person's period of employment for the purposes of –

(a) Chapter I of Part XIV of the Employment Rights Act 1996 (continuous employment), and

(b) that Chapter as applied by subsection (2) of section 282 of the Trade Union and Labour Relations (Consolidation) Act 1992 for the purposes of that section.

(2) If in consequence of any action to which these Regulations apply a dismissed employee is reinstated or re-employed by his employer or by a successor or associated employer of the employer –

(a) the continuity of that employee's period of employment shall be preserved, and

(b) the period beginning with the date on which the dismissal takes effect and ending with the date of reinstatement or re-engagement shall count in the computation of the employee's period of continuous employment.

4. – (1) Section 214 of the Employment Rights Act 1996 (continuity broken where employee re-employed after the making of a redundancy payment or equivalent payment) shall not apply where –

(a) in consequence of any action to which these Regulations apply a dismissed employee is reinstated or re-employed by his employer or by a successor or associated employer of the employer,

(b) the terms upon which he is so reinstated or re-engaged include provision for him to repay the amount of a redundancy payment or an equivalent payment paid in respect of the relevant dismissal, and

(c) that provision is complied with.

(2) For the purposes of this regulation the cases in which a redundancy payment shall be treated as having been paid are the cases mentioned in section 214(5) of the Employment Rights Act 1996.

As amended by the Employment Rights (Dispute Resolution) Act 1998, s1(2)(c); Employment Protection (Continuity of Employment) (Amendment) Regulations 2001, reg 2(1), (2)(a)–(c); Employment Act 2002 (Dispute Resolution) Regulations 2004, reg 17(e).

PART-TIME WORKERS (PREVENTION OF LESS FAVOURABLE TREATMENT) REGULATIONS 2000
(SI 2000 No 1551)

GENERAL AND INTERPRETATION

1. – (1) These Regulations may be cited as the Part-time Workers (Prevention of Less Favourable Treatment) Regulations 2000 and shall come into force on 1st July 2000.

(2) In these Regulations –

'the 1996 Act' means the Employment Rights Act 1996;

'contract of employment' means a contract of service or of apprenticeship, whether express or implied, and (if it is express) whether oral or in writing;

'employee' means an individual who has entered into or works under or (except where a provision of these Regulations otherwise requires) where the employment has ceased, worked under a contract of employment;

'employer', in relation to any employee or worker, means the person by whom the employee or worker is or (except where a provision of these Regulations otherwise requires) where the employment has ceased, was employed;

'pro rata principle' means that where a comparable full-time worker receives or is entitled to receive pay or any other benefit, a part-time worker is to receive or be entitled to receive not less than the proportion of that pay or other benefit that the number of his weekly hours bears to the number of weekly hours of the comparable full-time worker;

'worker' means an individual who has entered into or works under or (except where a provision of these Regulations otherwise requires) where the employment has ceased, worked under –

(a) a contract of employment; or

(b) any other contract, whether express or implied and (if it is express) whether oral or in writing, whereby the individual undertakes to do or perform personally any work or services for another party to the contract whose status is not by virtue of the contract that of a client or customer of any profession or business undertaking carried on by the individual.

(3) In the definition of the pro rata principle and in regulations 3 and 4 'weekly

hours' means the number of hours a worker is required to work under his contract of employment in a week in which he has no absences from work and does not work any overtime or, where the number of such hours varies according to a cycle, the average number of such hours.

2. – (1) A worker is a full-time worker for the purpose of these Regulations if he is paid wholly or in part by reference to the time he works and, having regard to the custom and practice of the employer in relation to workers employed by the worker's employer under the same type of contract, is identifiable as a full-time worker.

(2) A worker is a part-time worker for the purpose of these Regulations if he is paid wholly or in part by reference to the time he works and, having regard to the custom and practice of the employer in relation to workers employed by the worker's employer under the same type of contract, is not identifiable as a full-time worker.

(3) For the purposes of paragraphs (1), (2) and (4), the following shall be regarded as being employed under different types of contract –

(a) employees employed under a contract that is not a contract of apprenticeship;

(b) employees employed under a contract of apprenticeship;

(c) workers who are not employees;

(d) any other description of worker that it is reasonable for the employer to treat differently from other workers on the ground that workers of that description have a different type of contract.

(4) A full-time worker is a comparable full-time worker in relation to a part-time worker if, at the time when the treatment that is alleged to be less favourable to the part-time worker takes place –

(a) both workers are –

(i) employed by the same employer under the same type of contract, and

(ii) engaged in the same or broadly similar work having regard, where relevant, to whether they have a similar level of qualification, skills and experience; and

(b) the full-time worker works or is based at the same establishment as the part-time worker or, where there is no full-time worker working or based at that establishment who satisfies the requirements of sub-paragraph (a), works or is based at a different establishment and satisfies those requirements.

3. – (1) This regulation applies to a worker who –

(a) was identifiable as a full-time worker in accordance with regulation 2(1); and

(b) following a termination or variation of his contract, continues to work under a new or varied contract, whether of the same type or not, that requires him to work for a number of weekly hours that is lower than the number he was required to work immediately before the termination or variation.

(2) Notwithstanding regulation 2(4), regulation 5 shall apply to a worker to whom this regulation applies as if he were a part-time worker and as if there were a

comparable full-time worker employed under the terms that applied to him immediately before the variation or termination.

(3) The fact that this regulation applies to a worker does not affect any right he may have under these Regulations by virtue of regulation 2(4).

4. – (1) This regulation applies to a worker who –

(a) was identifiable as a full-time worker in accordance with regulation 2(1) immediately before a period of absence (whether the absence followed a termination of the worker's contract or not);

(b) returns to work for the same employer within a period of less than twelve months beginning with the day on which the period of absence started;

(c) returns to the same job or to a job at the same level under a contract, whether it is a different contract or a varied contract and regardless of whether it is of the same type, under which he is required to work for a number of weekly hours that is lower than the number he was required to work immediately before the period of absence.

(2) Notwithstanding regulation 2(4), regulation 5 shall apply to a worker to whom this regulation applies ('the returning worker') as if he were a part-time worker and as if there were a comparable full-time worker employed under –

(a) the contract under which the returning worker was employed immediately before the period of absence; or

(b) where it is shown that, had the returning worker continued to work under the contract mentioned in sub-paragraph (a) a variation would have been made to its term during the period of absence, the contract mentioned in that sub-paragraph including that variation.

(3) The fact that this regulation applies to a worker does not affect any right he may have under these Regulations by virtue of regulation 2(4).

PART II

RIGHTS AND REMEDIES

5. – (1) A part-time worker has the right not to be treated by his employer less favourably than the employer treats a comparable full-time worker –

(a) as regards the terms of his contract; or

(b) by being subjected to any other detriment by any act, or deliberate failure to act, of his employer.

(2) The right conferred by paragraph (1) applies only if –

(a) the treatment is on the ground that the worker is a part-time worker, and

(b) the treatment is not justified on objective grounds.

(3) In determining whether a part-time worker has been treated less favourably

than a comparable full-time worker the pro rata principle shall be applied unless it is inappropriate.

(4) A part-time worker paid at a lower rate for overtime worked by him in a period than a comparable full-time worker is or would be paid for overtime worked by him in the same period shall not, for that reason, be regarded as treated less favourably than the comparable full-time worker where, or to the extent that, the total number of hours worked by the part-time worker in the period, including overtime, does not exceed the number of hours the comparable full-time worker is required to work in the period, disregarding absences from work and overtime.

6. – (1) If a worker who considers that his employer may have treated him in a manner which infringes a right conferred on him by regulation 5 requests in writing from his employer a written statement giving particulars of the reasons for the treatment, the worker is entitled to be provided with such a statement within twenty-one days of his request.

(2) A written statement under this regulation is admissable as evidence in any proceedings under these Regulations.

(3) If it appears to the tribunal in any proceedings under these Regulations –

(a) that the employer deliberately, and without reasonable excuse, omitted to provide a written statement, or

(b) that the written statement is evasive or equivocal,

it may draw any inference which it considers it just and equitable to draw, including an inference that the employer has infringed the right in question.

(4) This regulation does not apply where the treatment in question consists of the dismissal of an employee, and the employee is entitled to a written statement of reasons for his dismissal under section 92 of the 1996 Act.

7. – (1) An employee who is dismissed shall be regarded as unfairly dismissed for the purposes of Part X of the 1996 Act if the reason (or, if more than one, the principal reason) for the dismissal is a reason specified in paragraph (3).

(2) A worker has the right not to be subjected to any detriment by any act, or any deliberate failure to act, by his employer done on a ground specified in paragraph (3).

(3) The reasons or, as the case may be, grounds are –

(a) that the worker has –

(i) brought proceedings against the employer under these Regulations;

(ii) requested from his employer a written statement of reasons under regulation 6;

(iii) given evidence or information in connection with such proceedings brought by any worker;

(iv) otherwise done anything under these Regulations in relation to the employer or any other person;

(v) alleged that the employer had infringed these Regulations; or

(vi) refused (or proposed to refuse) to forgo a right conferred on him by these Regulations, or

(b) that the employer believes or suspects that the worker has done or intends to do any of the things mentioned in sub-paragraph (a).

(4) Where the reason or principal reason for dismissal or, as the case may be, ground for subjection to any act or deliberate failure to act, is that mentioned in paragraph (3)(a)(v), or (b) so far as it relates thereto, neither paragraph (1) nor paragraph (2) applies if the allegation made by the worker is false and not made in good faith.

(5) Paragraph (2) does not apply where the detriment in question amounts to the dismissal of an employee within the meaning of Part X of the 1996 Act.

8. – (1) Subject to regulation 7(5), a worker may present a complaint to an employment tribunal that his employer has infringed a right conferred on him by regulation 5 or 7(2).

(2) Subject to paragraph (3), an employment tribunal shall not consider a complaint under this regulation unless it is presented before the end of the period of three months (or, in a case to which regulation 13 applies, six months) beginning with the date of the less favourable treatment or detriment to which the complaint relates or, where an act or failure to act is part of a series of similar acts or failures comprising the less favourable treatment or detriment, the last of them.

(3) A tribunal may consider any such complaint which is out of time if, in all the circumstances of the case, it considers that it is just and equitable to do so.

(4) For the purposes of calculating the date of the less favourable treatment or detriment under paragraph (2) –

(a) where a term in a contract is less favourable, that treatment shall be treated, subject to paragraph (b), as taking place on each day of the period during which the term is less favourable;

(b) where an application relies on regulation 3 or 4 the less favourable treatment shall be treated as occurring on, and only on, in the case of regulation 3, the first day on which the applicant worked under the new or varied contract and, in the case of regulation 4, the day on which the applicant returned; and

(c) a deliberate failure to act contrary to regulation 5 or 7(2) shall be treated as done when it was decided on.

(5) In the absence of evidence establishing the contrary, a person shall be taken for the purposes of paragraph (4)(c) to decide not to act –

(a) when he does an act inconsistent with doing the failed act; or

(b) if he has done no such inconsistent act, when the period expires within which he might reasonably have been expected to have done the failed act if it was to be done.

(6) Where a worker presents a complaint under this regulation it is for the employer to identify the ground for the less favourable treatment or detriment.

(7) Where an employment tribunal finds that a complaint presented to it under this regulation is well founded, it shall take such of the following steps as it considers just and equitable –

(a) making a declaration as to the rights of the complainant and the employer in relation to the matters to which the complaint relates;

(b) ordering the employer to pay compensation to the complainant;

(c) recommending that the employer take, within a specified period, action appearing to the tribunal to be reasonable, in all the circumstances of the case, for the purpose of obviating or reducing the adverse effect on the complainant of any matter to which the complaint relates.

(9) Where a tribunal orders compensation under paragraph (7)(b), the amount of the compensation awarded shall be such as the tribunal considers just and equitable in all the circumstances having regard to –

(a) the infringement to which the complaint relates, and

(b) any loss which is attributable to the infringement having regard, in the case of an infringement of the right conferred by regulation 5, to the pro rata principle except where it is inappropriate to do so.

(10) The loss shall be taken to include –

(a) any expenses reasonably incurred by the complainant in consequence of the infringement, and

(b) loss of any benefit which he might reasonably be expected to have had but for the infringement.

(11) Compensation in respect of treating a worker in a manner which infringes the right conferred on him by regulation 5 shall not include compensation for injury to feelings.

(12) In ascertaining the loss the tribunal shall apply the same rule concerning the duty of a person to mitigate his loss as applies to damages recoverable under the common law of England and Wales …

(13) Where the tribunal finds that the act, or failure to act, to which the complaint relates was to any extent caused or contributed to by action of the complainant, it shall reduce the amount of the compensation by such proportion as it considers just and equitable having regard to that finding.

(14) If the employer fails, without reasonable justification, to comply with a recommendation made by an employment tribunal under paragraph (7)(c) the tribunal may, if it thinks it just and equitable to do so –

(a) increase the amount of compensation required to be paid to the complainant in respect of the complaint, where an order was made under paragraph (7)(b); or

(b) make an order under paragraph (7)(b).

9. Section 203 of the 1996 Act (restrictions on contracting out) shall apply in relation to these Regulations as if they were contained in that Act.

PART III

MISCELLANEOUS

11. – (1) Anything done by a person in the course of his employment shall be treated for the purposes of these Regulations as also done by his employer, whether or not it was done with the employer's knowledge or approval.

(2) Anything done by a person as agent for the employer with the authority of the employer shall be treated for the purposes of these Regulations as also done by the employer.

(3) In proceedings under these Regulations against any person in respect of an act alleged to have been done by a worker of his, it shall be a defence for that person to prove that he took such steps as were reasonably practicable to prevent the worker from –

    (a) doing that act; or

    (b) doing, in the course of his employment, acts of that discription.

PART IV

SPECIAL CLASSES OF PERSON

12. – (1) Subject to regulation 13, these Regulations have effect in relation to Crown employment and persons in Crown employment as they have effect in relation to other employment and other employees and workers.

(2) In paragraph (1) 'Crown employment' means employment under or for the purposes of a government department or any officer or body exercising on behalf of the Crown functions conferred by a statutory provision.

(3) For the purposes of the application of the provisions of these Regulations in relation to Crown employment in accordance with paragraph (1) –

    (a) references to an employee and references to a worker shall be construed as references to a person in Crown employment to whom the definition of employee or, as the case may be, worker is appropriate; and

    (b) references to a contract in relation to an employee and references to a contract in relation to a worker shall be construed as references to the terms of employment of a person in Crown employment to whom the definition of employee or, as the case may be, worker is appropriate. ...

17. These Regulations do not apply to any individual in his capacity as the holder of a judicial office if he is remunerated on a daily fee-paid basis.

As amended by the Part-time Workers (Prevention of Less Favourable Treatment) Regulations 2000 (Amendment) Regulations 2002, regs 1, 2.

FIXED-TERM EMPLOYEES (PREVENTION OF LESS FAVOURABLE TREATMENT) REGULATIONS 2002

(SI 2002 No 2034)

PART 1

GENERAL AND INTERPRETATION

1. – (1) These Regulations may be cited as the Fixed-term Employees (Prevention of Less Favourable Treatment) Regulations 2002 and shall come into force on 1st October 2002.

(2) In these Regulations –

'the 1996 Act' means the Employment Rights Act 1996;

'collective agreement' means a collective agreement within the meaning of section 178 of the Trade Union and Labour Relations (Consolidation) Act 1992; the trade union parties to which are independent trade unions within the meaning of section 5 of that Act;

'employer', in relation to any employee, means the person by whom the employee is (or, where the employment has ceased, was) employed;

'fixed-term contract' means a contract of employment that, under its provisions determining how it will terminate in the normal course, will terminate –

    (a) on the expiry of a specific term,

    (b) on the completion of a particular task, or

    (c) on the occurrence or non-occurrence of any other specific event other than the attainment by the employee of any normal and bona fide retiring age in the establishment for an employee holding the position held by him,

and any reference to 'fixed-term' shall be construed accordingly;

'fixed-term employee' means an employee who is employed under a fixed-term contract;

'permanent employee' means an employee who is not employed under a fixed-term contract, and any reference to 'permanent employment' shall be construed accordingly;

'pro rata principle' means that where a comparable permanent employee receives or is entitled to pay or any other benefit, a fixed-term employee is to receive or be entitled to such proportion of that pay or other benefit as is reasonable in the circumstances having regard to the length of his contract of employment and to the terms on which the pay or other benefit is offered;

'renewal' includes extension and references to renewing a contract shall be construed accordingly;

'workforce agreement' means an agreement between an employer and his employees or their representatives in respect of which the conditions set out in Schedule 1 to these Regulations are satisfied.

2. – (1) For the purposes of these Regulations, an employee is a comparable permanent employee in relation to a fixed-term employee if, at the time when the treatment that is alleged to be less favourable to the fixed-term employee takes place,

(a) both employees are –

(i) employed by the same employer, and

(ii) engaged in the same or broadly similar work having regard, where relevant, to whether they have a similar level of qualification and skills; and

(b) the permanent employee works or is based at the same establishment as the fixed-term employee or, where there is no comparable permanent employee working or based at that establishment who satisfies the requirements of sub-paragraph (a), works or is based at a different establishment and satisfies those requirements.

(2) For the purposes of paragraph (1), an employee is not a comparable permanent employee if his employment has ceased.

PART 2

RIGHTS AND REMEDIES

3. – (1) A fixed-term employee has the right not to be treated by his employer less favourably than the employer treats a comparable permanent employee –

(a) as regards the terms of his contract; or

(b) by being subjected to any other detriment by any act, or deliberate failure to act, of his employer.

(2) Subject to paragraphs (3) and (4), the right conferred by paragraph (1) includes in particular the right of the fixed-term employee in question not to be treated less favourably than the employer treats a comparable permanent employee in relation to –

(a) any period of service qualification relating to any particular condition of service,

(b) the opportunity to receive training, or

(c) the opportunity to secure any permanent position in the establishment.

(3) The right conferred by paragraph (1) applies only if –

(a) the treatment is on the ground that the employee is a fixed-term employee, and

(b) the treatment is not justified on objective grounds.

(4) Paragraph (3)(b) is subject to regulation 4.

(5) In determining whether a fixed-term employee has been treated less favourably than a comparable permanent employee, the pro rata principle shall be applied unless it is inappropriate.

(6) In order to ensure that an employee is able to exercise the right conferred by paragraph (1) as described in paragraph (2)(c) the employee has the right to be informed by his employer of available vacancies in the establishment.

(7) For the purposes of paragraph (6) an employee is 'informed by his employer' only if the vacancy is contained in an advertisement which the employee has a reasonable opportunity of reading in the course of his employment or the employee is given reasonable notification of the vacancy in some other way.

4. – (1) Where a fixed-term employee is treated by his employer less favourably than the employer treats a comparable permanent employee as regards any term of his contract, the treatment in question shall be regarded for the purposes of regulation 3(3)(b) as justified on objective grounds if the terms of the fixed-term employee's contract of employment, taken as a whole, are at least as favourable as the terms of the comparable permanent employee's contract of employment.

(2) Paragraph (1) is without prejudice to the generality of regulation 3(3)(b).

5. – (1) If an employee who considers that his employer may have treated him in a manner which infringes a right conferred on him by regulation 3 requests in writing from his employer a written statement giving particulars of the reasons for the treatment, the employee is entitled to be provided with such a statement within twenty-one days of his request.

(2) A written statement under this regulation is admissible as evidence in any proceedings under these Regulations.

(3) If it appears to the tribunal in any proceedings under these Regulations –

(a) that the employer deliberately, and without reasonable excuse, omitted to provide a written statement, or

(b) that the written statement is evasive or equivocal,

it may draw any inference which it considers it just and equitable to draw, including an inference that the employer has infringed the right in question.

(4) This regulation does not apply where the treatment in question consists of the dismissal of an employee, and the employee is entitled to a written statement of reasons for his dismissal under section 92 of the 1996 Act.

6. – (1) An employee who is dismissed shall be regarded as unfairly dismissed for

the purposes of Part 10 of the 1996 Act if the reason (or, if more than one, the principal reason) for the dismissal is a reason specified in paragraph (3).

(2) An employee has the right not to be subjected to any detriment by any act, or any deliberate failure to act, of his employer done on a ground specified in paragraph (3).

(3) The reasons or, as the case may be, grounds are –

(a) that the employee –

(i) brought proceedings against the employer under these Regulations;

(ii) requested from his employer a written statement under regulation 5 or regulation 9;

(iii) gave evidence or information in connection with such proceedings brought by any employee;

(iv) otherwise did anything under these Regulations in relation to the employer or any other person;

(v) alleged that the employer had infringed these Regulations;

(vi) refused (or proposed to refuse) to forgo a right conferred on him by these Regulations;

(vii) declined to sign a workforce agreement for the purposes of these Regulations, or

(viii) being –

(aa) a representative of members of the workforce for the purposes of Schedule 1, or

(bb) a candidate in an election in which any person elected will, on being elected,

become such a representative,

performed (or proposed to perform) any functions or activities as such a representative or candidate, or

(b) that the employer believes or suspects that the employee has done or intends to do any of the things mentioned in sub-paragraph (a).

(4) Where the reason or principal reason for dismissal or, as the case may be, ground for subjection to any act or deliberate failure to act, is that mentioned in paragraph (3)(a)(v), or (b) so far as it relates thereto, neither paragraph (1) nor paragraph (2) applies if the allegation made by the employee is false and not made in good faith.

(5) Paragraph (2) does not apply where the detriment in question amounts to dismissal within the meaning of Part 10 of the 1996 Act.

7. – (1) An employee may present a complaint to an employment tribunal that his employer has infringed a right conferred on him by regulation 3, or (subject to regulation 6(5)), regulation 6(2).

(2) Subject to paragraph (3), an employment tribunal shall not consider a complaint

under this regulation unless it is presented before the end of the period of three months beginning –

(a) in the case of an alleged infringement of a right conferred by regulation 3(1) or 6(2), with the date of the less favourable treatment or detriment to which the complaint relates or, where an act or failure to act is part of a series of similar acts or failures comprising the less favourable treatment or detriment, the last of them;

(b) in the case of an alleged infringement of the right conferred by regulation 3(6), with the date, or if more than one the last date, on which other individuals, whether or not employees of the employer, were informed of the vacancy.

(3) A tribunal may consider any such complaint which is out of time if, in all the circumstances of the case, it considers that it is just and equitable to do so.

(4) For the purposes of calculating the date of the less favourable treatment or detriment under paragraph (2)(a) –

(a) where a term in a contract is less favourable, that treatment shall be treated, subject to paragraph (b), as taking place on each day of the period during which the term is less favourable;

(b) a deliberate failure to act contrary to regulation 3 or 6(2) shall be treated as done when it was decided on.

(5) In the absence of evidence establishing the contrary, a person shall be taken for the purposes of paragraph (4)(b) to decide not to act –

(a) when he does an act inconsistent with doing the failed act; or

(b) if he has done no such inconsistent act, when the period expires within which he might reasonably have been expected to have done the failed act if it was to be done.

(6) Where an employee presents a complaint under this regulation in relation to a right conferred on him by regulation 3 or 6(2) it is for the employer to identify the ground for the less favourable treatment or detriment.

(7) Where an employment tribunal finds that a complaint presented to it under this regulation is well founded, it shall take such of the following steps as it considers just and equitable –

(a) making a declaration as to the rights of the complainant and the employer in relation to the matters to which the complaint relates;

(b) ordering the employer to pay compensation to the complainant;

(c) recommending that the employer take, within a specified period, action appearing to the tribunal to be reasonable, in all the circumstances of the case, for the purpose of obviating or reducing the adverse effect on the complainant of any matter to which the complaint relates.

(8) Where a tribunal orders compensation under paragraph (7)(b), the amount of the compensation awarded shall be such as the tribunal considers just and equitable in all the circumstances having regard to –

(a) the infringement to which the complaint relates, and

(b) any loss which is attributable to the infringement.

(9) The loss shall be taken to include –

(a) any expenses reasonably incurred by the complainant in consequence of the infringement, and

(b) loss of any benefit which he might reasonably be expected to have had but for the infringement.

(10) Compensation in respect of treating an employee in a manner which infringes the right conferred on him by regulation 3 shall not include compensation for injury to feelings.

(11) In ascertaining the loss the tribunal shall apply the same rule concerning the duty of a person to mitigate his loss as applies to damages recoverable under the common law of England and Wales ...

(12) Where the tribunal finds that the act, or failure to act, to which the complaint relates was to any extent caused or contributed to by action of the complainant, it shall reduce the amount of the compensation by such proportion as it considers just and equitable having regard to that finding.

(13) If the employer fails, without reasonable justification, to comply with a recommendation made by an employment tribunal under paragraph (7)(c) the tribunal may, if it thinks it just and equitable to do so –

(a) increase the amount of compensation required to be paid to the complainant in respect of the complaint, where an order was made under paragraph (7)(b); or

(b) make an order under paragraph (7)(b).

8. – (1) This regulation applies where –

(a) an employee is employed under a contract purporting to be a fixed-term contract, and

(b) the contract mentioned in sub-paragraph (a) has previously been renewed, or the employee has previously been employed on a fixed-term contract before the start of the contract mentioned in sub-paragraph (a).

(2) Where this regulation applies then, with effect from the date specified in paragraph (3), the provision of the contract mentioned in paragraph (1)(a) that restricts the duration of the contract shall be of no effect, and the employee shall be a permanent employee, if –

(a) the employee has been continuously employed under the contract mentioned in paragraph 1(a), or under that contract taken with a previous fixed-term contract, for a period of four years or more, and

(b) the employment of the employee under a fixed-term contract was not justified on objective grounds –

(i) where the contract mentioned in paragraph (1)(a) has been renewed, at the time when it was last renewed;

(ii) where that contract has not been renewed, at the time when it was entered into.

(3) The date referred to in paragraph (2) is whichever is the later of –

(a) the date on which the contract mentioned in paragraph (1)(a) was entered into or last renewed, and

(b) the date on which the employee acquired four years' continuous employment.

(4) For the purposes of this regulation Chapter 1 of Part 14 of the 1996 Act shall apply in determining whether an employee has been continuously employed, and any period of continuous employment falling before the 10th July 2002 shall be disregarded.

(5) A collective agreement or a workforce agreement may modify the application of paragraphs (1) to (3) of this regulation in relation to any employee or specified description of employees, by substituting for the provisions of paragraph (2) or paragraph (3), or for the provisions of both of those paragraphs, one or more different provisions which, in order to prevent abuse arising from the use of successive fixed-term contracts, specify one or more of the following –

(a) the maximum total period for which the employee or employees of that description may be continuously employed on a fixed-term contract or on successive fixed-term contracts;

(b) the maximum number of successive fixed-term contracts and renewals of such contracts under which the employee or employees of that description may be employed; or

(c) objective grounds justifying the renewal of fixed-term contracts, or the engagement of the employee or employees of that description under successive fixed-term contracts,

and those provisions shall have effect in relation to that employee or an employee of that description as if they were contained in paragraphs (2) and (3).

9. – (1) If an employee who considers that, by virtue of regulation 8, he is a permanent employee requests in writing from his employer a written statement confirming that his contract is no longer fixed-term or that he is now a permanent employee, he is entitled to be provided, within twenty-one days of his request, with either –

(a) such a statement, or

(b) a statement giving reasons why his contract remains fixed-term.

(2) If the reasons stated under paragraph (1)(b) include an assertion that there were objective grounds for the engagement of the employee under a fixed-term contract, or the renewal of such a contract, the statement shall include a statement of those grounds.

(3) A written statement under this regulation is admissible as evidence in any

proceedings before a court, an employment tribunal and the Commissioners of the Inland Revenue.

(4) If it appears to the court or tribunal in any proceedings –

(a) that the employer deliberately, and without reasonable excuse, omitted to provide a written statement, or

(b) that the written statement is evasive or equivocal,

it may draw any inference which it considers it just and equitable to draw.

(5) An employee who considers that, by virtue of regulation 8, he is a permanent employee may present an application to an employment tribunal for a declaration to that effect.

(6) No application may be made under paragraph (5) unless –

(a) the employee in question has previously requested a statement under paragraph (1) and the employer has either failed to provide a statement or given a statement of reasons under paragraph (1)(b), and

(b) the employee is at the time the application is made employed by the employer.

PART 3

MISCELLANEOUS

10. Section 203 of the 1996 Act (restrictions on contracting out) shall apply in relation to these Regulations as if they were contained in that Act.

12. – (1) Anything done by a person in the course of his employment shall be treated for the purposes of these Regulations as also done by his employer, whether or not it was done with the employer's knowledge or approval.

(2) Anything done by a person as agent for the employer with the authority of the employer shall be treated for the purposes of these Regulations as also done by the employer.

(3) In proceedings under these Regulations against any person in respect of an act alleged to have been done by an employee of his, it shall be a defence for that person to prove that he took such steps as were reasonably practicable to prevent the employee from –

(a) doing that act, or

(b) doing, in the course of his employment, acts of that description.

PART 4

SPECIAL CLASSES OF PERSON

13. – (1) Subject to regulation 14, these Regulations have effect in relation to Crown

employment and persons in Crown employment as they have effect in relation to other employment and other employees.

(2) For the purposes of paragraphs (1) and (3) a person is to be regarded as being in Crown employment only if –

(a) he is in employment under or for the purposes of a government department or any officer or body exercising on behalf of the Crown functions conferred by a statutory provision, and

(b) having regard to the terms and conditions under which he works, he would be an employee if he was not in Crown employment.

(3) For the purposes of the application of the provisions of these Regulations in relation to Crown employment and persons in Crown employment in accordance with paragraph (1) –

(a) references to an employee shall be construed as references to a person in Crown employment;

(b) references to a contract of employment shall be construed, in relation to a person in Crown employment, as references to the terms and conditions mentioned in paragraph (2)(b); and

(c) references to dismissal shall be construed as references to the termination of Crown employment.

PART 5

EXCLUSIONS

18. – (1) These Regulations shall not have effect in relation to a fixed-term employee who is employed on a scheme, designed to provide him with training or work experience for the purpose of assisting him to seek or obtain work, which is either –

(a) provided to him under arrangements made by the Government, or

(b) funded in whole or part by an Institution of the European Community.

(2) These Regulations shall not have effect in relation to a fixed-term employee whose employment consists in attending a period of work experience not exceeding one year that he is required to attend as part of a higher education course.

(3) For the purpose of paragraph (2) 'a higher education course' means –

(a) in England and Wales, a course of a description referred to in Schedule 6 to the Education Reform Act 1988; ...

19. – (1) These Regulations shall not have effect in relation to employment under a fixed-term contract where the employee is an agency worker.

(2) In this regulation 'agency worker' means any person who is supplied by an employment business to do work for another person under a contract or other arrangements made between the employment business and the other person.

(3) In this regulation 'employment business' means the business (whether or not

carried on with a view to profit and whether or not carried on in conjunction with any other business) of supplying persons in the employment of the person carrying on the business, to act for, and under the control of, other persons in any capacity.

20. These Regulations shall not have effect in relation to employment under a fixed-term contract where the contract is a contract of apprenticeship.

SCHEDULE 1

WORKFORCE AGREEMENTS

1. An agreement is a workforce agreement for the purposes of these Regulations if the following conditions are satisfied –

(a) the agreement is in writing;

(b) it has effect for a specified period not exceeding five years;

(c) it applies either –

(i) to all of the relevant members of the workforce, or

(ii) to all of the relevant members of the workforce who belong to a particular group;

(d) the agreement is signed –

(i) in the case of an agreement of the kind referred to in sub-paragraph (c)(i), by the representatives of the workforce, and in the case of an agreement of the kind referred to in sub-paragraph (c)(ii) by the representatives of the group to which the agreement applies (excluding, in either case, any representative not a relevant member of the workforce on the date on which the agreement was first made available for signature), or

(ii) if the employer employed 20 or fewer employees on the date referred to in sub-paragraph (d)(i), either by the appropriate representatives in accordance with that sub-paragraph or by the majority of the employees employed by him;

(e) before the agreement was made available for signature, the employer provided all the employees to whom it was intended to apply on the date on which it came into effect with copies of the text of the agreement and such guidance as those employees might reasonably require in order to understand it fully.

2. For the purposes of this Schedule –

'a particular group' is a group of the relevant members of a workforce who undertake a particular function, work at a particular workplace or belong to a particular department or unit within their employer's business;

'relevant members of the workforce' are all of the employees employed by a particular employer, excluding any employee whose terms and conditions of employment are provided for, wholly or in part, in a collective agreement;

'representatives of the workforce' are employees duly elected to represent the relevant members of the workforce, 'representatives of the group' are employees duly elected to represent the members of a particular group, and representatives are 'duly elected' if the election at which they were elected satisfied the requirements of paragraph 3 of this Schedule.

3. The requirements concerning elections referred to in paragraph 2 are that –

(a) the number of representatives to be elected is determined by the employer;

(b) the candidates for election as representatives of the workforce are relevant members of the workforce, and the candidates for election as representatives of a group are members of that group;

(c) no employee who is eligible to be a candidate is unreasonably excluded from standing for election;

(d) all the relevant members of the workforce are entitled to vote for representatives of the workforce, and all the members of a particular group are entitled to vote for representatives of the group;

(e) the employees entitled to vote may vote for as many candidates as there are representatives to be elected;

(f) the election is conducted so as to secure that –

(i) so far as is reasonably practicable, those voting do so in secret, and

(ii) the votes given at the election are fairly and accurately counted.

APPENDIX

APPENDIX

EMPLOYMENT ACT 2002
(2002 c 22)

28 Pre-hearing reviews

(1) Section 9 of the Employment Tribunals Act 1996 (pre-hearing reviews) is amended as follows.

(2) In subsection (1) (power to make provision for pre-hearing reviews), for paragraph (a) there is substituted –

'(a) for authorising an employment tribunal to carry out a review of any proceedings before it at any time before a hearing held for the purpose of determining them (a 'pre-hearing review'),'.

44 Dismissal procedures agreements

In section 110 of the Employment Rights Act 1996 (c 18) (dismissal procedures agreements) after subsection (3) there is inserted –

'(3A) The Secretary of State may by order amend subsection (3) so as to add to the conditions specified in that subsection such conditions as he may specify in the order.'

CONSTITUTIONAL REFORM ACT 2005
(2005 c 4)

15 Other functions of the Lord Chancellor and organisation of the courts

(1) Schedule 4 provides for –

(a) the transfer of functions to or from the Lord Chancellor,

(b) the modification of other functions of the Lord Chancellor,

(c) the modification of enactments relating to those functions, and

(d) the modification of enactments relating to the organisation of the courts.

59 Renaming of Supreme Courts of England and Wales and Northern Ireland

(1) The Supreme Court of England and Wales is renamed the Senior Courts of England and Wales. ...

SCHEDULE 4

OTHER FUNCTIONS OF THE LORD CHANCELLOR AND ORGANISATION OF THE COURTS

PART 1

AMENDMENTS ...

Employment Tribunals Act 1996 (c 17)

245. The Employment Tribunals Act 1996 is amended as follows.

246. – (1) Section 22 (membership of appeal tribunal) is amended as follows.

(2) In subsection (1)(a) –

(a) for 'by the Lord Chancellor' substitute 'by the Lord Chief Justice, after consulting the Lord Chancellor,';

(b) omit '(other than the Lord Chancellor)'.

(3) In subsection (3) for 'Lord Chancellor shall, after consultation with the Lord President of the Court of Session,' substitute 'Lord Chief Justice shall'.

(4) After subsection (3) insert –

'(3A) The Lord Chief Justice must not make an appointment under subsection (3) unless –

(a) he has consulted the Lord Chancellor, and

(b) the Lord President of the Court of Session agrees.'

(5) After subsection (4) insert –

'(5) The Lord Chief Justice may nominate a judicial office holder (as defined in section 109(4) of the Constitutional Reform Act 2005) to exercise his functions under this section.

(6) The Lord President of the Court of Session may nominate a judge of the Court of Session who is a member of the First or Second Division of the Inner House of that Court to exercise his functions under subsection (3A)(b).'

247. – (1) Section 23 (temporary membership) is amended as follows.

(2) In subsection (1) for 'Lord Chancellor' substitute 'Lord Chief Justice'.

(3) In subsection (2)(a) for 'Lord Chancellor' substitute 'Lord Chief Justice'.

(4) After subsection (5) insert –

'(6) The functions conferred on the Lord Chief Justice by the preceding provisions of this section may be exercised only after consulting the Lord Chancellor.

(7) The functions conferred on the Lord Chancellor by subsection (3) may be exercised only after consultation with the Lord Chief Justice.

(8) The Lord Chief Justice may nominate a judicial office holder (as defined in section 109(4) of the Constitutional Reform Act 2005) to exercise his functions under this section.'

248. – (1) Section 24 (temporary additional judicial membership) is amended as follows.

(2) For subsection (1) substitute –

'(1) This section applies if both of the following conditions are met –

(a) the Lord Chancellor thinks that it is expedient, after consulting the Lord Chief Justice, for a qualified person to be appointed to be a temporary additional judge of the Appeal Tribunal in order to facilitate in England and Wales the disposal of business in the Appeal Tribunal;

(b) the Lord Chancellor requests the Lord Chief Justice to make such an appointment.

(1A) The Lord Chief Justice may, after consulting the Lord Chancellor, appoint a qualified person as mentioned in subsection (1)(a).

(1B) An appointment under this section is –

(a) for such period, or

(b) on such occasions,

as the Lord Chief Justice determines, after consulting the Lord Chancellor.'

(3) In subsection (2) for 'subsection (1)' substitute 'this section'.

(4) After subsection (3) insert –

'(4) The Lord Chief Justice may nominate a judicial office holder (as defined in section 109(4) of the Constitutional Reform Act 2005) to exercise his functions under this section.'

249. In section 25 (tenure of appointed members) after subsection (4) insert –

'(5) The Lord Chancellor may declare an appointed member's office vacant under subsection (4) only with the concurrence of the appropriate senior judge.

(6) The appropriate senior judge is the Lord Chief Justice of England and Wales, unless the member whose office is to be declared vacant exercises functions wholly or mainly in Scotland, in which case it is the Lord President of the Court of Session.'

SCHEDULE 11

RENAMING OF THE SUPREME [COURT] OF ENGLAND AND WALES ...

PART 1

CITATION OF ACTS AND RULES

1. – (1) The Supreme Court Act 1981 (c 54) may be cited as the Senior Courts Act 1981.

(2) For the words 'Supreme Court Act 1981' wherever they occur in any enactment substitute 'Senior Courts Act 1981'. ...

SCHEDULE 18

REPEALS AND REVOCATIONS ...

Employment Tribunals Act 1996 (c 17)	In section 22(1)(a) '(other than the Lord Chancellor)'. ...

INDEX